DATA RE[...] with and Without PROGRAMMING

By
Tarun Tyagi

BPB PUBLICATIONS
B-14, CONNAUGHT PLACE, NEW DELHI-1

FIRST EDITION 2004

Distributors:

MICRO BOOK CENTRE
2, City Centre, CG Road,
Near Swastic Char Rasta,
AHMEDABAD-380009 Phone: 26421611

COMPUTER BOOK CENTRE
12, Shrungar Shopping Centre, M.G. Road,
BANGALORE-560001 Phone: 5587923, 5584641

MICRO BOOKS
Shanti Niketan Building, 8, Camac Street,
KOLKATTA-700017 Phone: 2826518, 2826519

BUSINESS PROMOTION BUREAU
8/1, Ritchie Street, Mount Road,
CHENNAI-600002 Phone: 28534796, 28550491

DECCAN AGENCIES
4-3-329, Bank Street,
HYDERABAD-500195 Phone: 24756400, 24756967

MICRO MEDIA
Shop No. 5, Mahendra Chambers, 150 D.N. Road,
Next to Capital Cinema V.T. (C.S.T.) Station,
MUMBAI-400001
Ph.: 22078296, 22078297, 22002732

BPB PUBLICATIONS
B-14, Connaught Place, **NEW DELHI-110001**
Phone: 23325760, 23723393, 23737742

INFOTECH
G-2, Sidhartha Building, 96 Nehru Place,
NEW DELHI-110019
Phone: 26438245, 26415092, 26234208

INFOTECH
Shop No. 2, F-38, South Extension Part-1
NEW DELHI-110049
Phone: 24691288, 24641941

BPB BOOK CENTRE
376, Old Lajpat Rai Market,
DELHI-110006 PHONE: 23861747

Copyright © BPB PUBLICATIONS

All Rights Reserved. No part of this publication can be stored in any retrieval system or reproduced in any form or by any means without the prior written permission of the publishers.

LIMITS OF LIABILITY AND DISCLAIMER OF WARRANTY

The Author and Publisher of this book have tried their best to ensure that the programmes, procedures and functions described in the book are correct. However, the author and the publishers make no warranty of any kind, expressed or implied, with regard to these programmes or the documentation contained in the book. The author and publishers shall not be liable in any event of any damages, incidental or consequential, in connection with, or arising out of the furnishing, performance or use of these programmes, procedures and functions. Product name mentioned are used for identification purposes only and may be trademarks of their respective companies.

All trademarks referred to in the book are acknowledged as properties of their respective owners.

Price : Rs. 240/-

ISBN 81-7656-922-4

Published by Manish Jain for BPB Publications, B-14, Connaught Place, New Delhi-110 001 and Printed by him at Pressworks, New Delhi.

Dedicated to my Babuji Ch. Dharamveer Singh Tyagi,
My Papa Sh. Subhash Tyagi &
My Brother Sh. Sachin Tyagi.........

Disclaimer

The book and the data given in/with this book are only for educational purpose. Author and Publisher of this book are not responsible for any crashes, data loss, unhappiness or hardware damage.

The book is provided "as is" without any kind of warranty. The entire risk arising out of the information given in the book or use of the programs given in/with this book remains with you.

In no event shall the author or Publishers of this book or anyone else be liable for any damages whatsoever including, damages for loss of business profits, business interruption, loss of business information, or other pecuniary loss arising out of the use of or inability to use the programs or information given in/with this book, even the Author has been advised of the possibility of such damages.

You are using any/all the information or program given in/with this book only at your own risk. The Author and publishers are not responsible for any type of damages and can not provide any type of warranty.

Acknowledgement

For me, it is a big reason to be happy that I have so many people around me to encourage me. Without their help and encouragement, it was difficult to complete the work successfully.

I am grateful to my friend, Ms. Preeti Roy for helping me throughout the work and for reviewing and compiling each and every line of the manuscript with painstaking attention. Her encouragement helped me even in constraint environment.

I am also thankful to Mr. Alok Gupta for guiding me about professional and Technical requirements of the manuscript.

Last but not least, I thank to my family to be so helping throughout.

Preface

This book has been written to provide the knowledge of the Professional Data Recovery and its Programming to the Computer Science students and IT Professionals. Specially to help those Engineering students who want to learn professional system programming using the latest Interrupt 13H Extensions approach to access the large capacity disks.

The book is basically describing the FAT file-systems and supporting the MSDOS, Windows 9x/ME operating systems. The Programs given in/with this book for accessing the disk's data surface can not be run under Windows NT/2000/XP operating systems due to security of these operating system of not allowing the programs to access the disk surface directly. However Data Recovery (like "Raw-File" Recovery) can be done from such hard disks by connecting them under the hard disks having the supported operating systems.

It is strictly recommended that the programs or information given in this book should not be applied on such computer or disks which are having any type of important data in it. The students and the readers of this book should be prepared to suffer the data loss while learning such type of programming. Be careful before doing anything on your disks and computer by the information or the programs given in this book.

I've tried to cover all the necessary topics and required study in this book, like Description of,

- **Data Recovery Concepts**, to explain why and where Data Recovery is important and why we need to pay importance to protect the Data.
- **Hard Disks' Geometry Concepts**, to explain the physical internal geometry of the hard disk and its parts as well as description of the common terms, used about the hard disk handling.
- **Logical Structure of Disks and Operating System Internals**, to provide a wide knowledge of file system internals to find out the causes of logical crashes and to understand the data storage at a higher level.
- **Necessary Number Systems**, which will be helpful when dealing with the description of bits and bytes when calculating the logical factors of the disk and file system.
- **C Programming Techniques**, starting from basics of computer programming to advanced level programming to help those readers who are either non-programmers or have lack of programming knowledge.
- **Computer Basics (Architecture and Organization)**, to provide the help to better understand the machine codes and assembly language based C programming operations e.g. use of Interrupts etc.
- **Necessary DOS Commands**, Which may be useful during the Data Recovery operations
- **Interrupt handling and defined Disk-BIOS Functions**, to provide the knowledge of Old traditional Disk-BIOS Programming and functions as well as to teach in the easiest way, how to use interrupts in the C Programming.

- **Large Hard Disks Support,** by the use of 13H Interrupts' Extensions, even up to 9.4×10^{12} Giga Bytes capacity of hard disk can be accessed.
- **Different Cases and Operations of Data Recovery and its Programming Techniques**, starting from the smallest data loss cases to serious data damages such as Deletion, Partition Deletion, File System Problems, Format of Disk/Partition or All of them.
- **"Raw File" Recovery,** to Recover the specific files/types from the hard disk even after any type of logical crash and having any operating systems in it.
- **Programming for Data Wipers,** as we are saying that Data Recovery is possible almost from all type of logical crashes of the disk e.g. even after Format of the disk. This is for those, who want to erase their confidential data completely so that it may not be recovered and used by anyone else.
- **Developing Utilities,** to provide the knowledge that how we can develop many useful utilities using the information given in the chapters of this book.

This book is just to tell the secrets of Professional Data Recovery Programming to the students who are ready to sacrifice their data and Operating system to achieve the knowledge. I hope you have read the Disclaimer given before.

Tarun Tyagi
E-mail: taruntyagiji@yahoo.com

Quick Reference Study

Recovery Type of Data loss or Problem	Necessary and Recommended Study
Data Protection and Backups	Chapter–1, Chapter–3, Chapter–7, Chapter–11
Manually Disk Analyzing	Chapter–3, Chapter–4, Chapter–7
Hard Disk Hardware and Capacity Problems	Chapter–2, Chapter–3
Recovery of Deleted file(s)	Chapter–3, Chapter–10
Data Recovery of/from disk Format	Chapter–3, Chapter–11, Chapter–14
Data Recovery of/from Crashed Operating System	Chapter–3, Chapter–11, Chapter–12, Chapter–13, Chapter–14,
Data Recovery of/from lost Partitions	Chapter–3, Chapter–12, Chapter–14
Data Recovery of/from Unreadable Floppy	Chapter–3, Chapter–10
Data Recovery from Partial zero filling in the disk or Partial use of data wipers	Chapter–3, Chapter–14
Data Wiping or Secure (Non-Recoverable) Data Erasure	Chapter–3, Chapter–15

Contents

Preface

1. An Overview of Data Recovery 1
   Introduction to Data Recovery 1
   Understanding Data loss 1
      System Crash 1
         Human Error 2
         Software Corruption 3
         Software Malfunction 4
         Hardware Error 4
         Virus Crash 4
         Sabotage 4
         Natural Disaster 4
      Other types of data loss 5
         Loss of one or more partitions 5
         Floppy Read Error 5
         Deletion of important data 5
         Password loss 6
   Types and areas of Data Recovery 6
   Analyzing a computer before data recovery 7
      Acceptable recovery period 7
      Understanding various costs 7
         Downtime Costs 7
         Data Recovery Costs 8
      User description 8
      Defining the requirements 8
      Making objectives 8
   Some Advices before beginning the Disk troubleshooting or Data recovery procedure 8
   Some tips to Protect your Data 9
      Make the Backups 9
      Perform surface scanning monthly 9
      De-fragment of data weekly 9
      Use good antivirus program 10
      Get into the habit of keeping your floppy write-protected 10
      Do not use pirated games and software 10

2. Introduction of Hard Disks 11
   Introduction 11
   Components of hard disk 12

	Disk Platters and Media	13
	Read/Write Heads	15
	Head Crash	17
	Head Parking	17
	Head Sliders, Arms and Actuator	18
	Head Sliders	18
	Head Arms	18
	Head Actuator	18
	Spindle Motor	19
	Connectors and Jumpers	20
	Logic Board	23
	Cache and Cache Circuitry	24
Low-level hard disk geometry		26
Formatting		30
	Low-Level Formatting	30
	Partitioning	31
	High-Level Formatting	31
Formatted and Unformatted Storage Capacity		31

3. Logical Approach to Disks and OS — 33

BIOS		33
The INT 13H Interface and INT 13H Extensions		33
	Int13H Extensions	34
	The 2.1 GB limit	35
	The 33.8 GB limit	35
	ATA Specification for IDE Disks - The 137 GB limit	35
Two and Four Disk BIOS IDE Support		35
Limitations in File Systems		36
	FAT12	36
	FAT16	37
	FAT32	37
	NTFS	37
Cluster		38
Cluster Size		39
Logical Structure of a Hard Disk		42
Master Boot Record(MBR) or Master Partition Table(MPT)		42
Master Boot Record Format		43
Partition Table Entry Format		44
	Boot Type Indicator Byte	44
	Starting Cylinder – Head – Sector Number of the Partition	44
	File System Indicator Byte	46
	Ending Cylinder – Head – Sector Number of the Partition	46
	Relative Sector number of Beginning of the Partition	46
	Number of Sectors of the Partition	46
DOS Boot Record (DBR) / DOS Boot Sector		61
	Number of Root Directories	65
	Total number of Sectors	66
	Media Descriptor	66

Number of Sectors of FAT	66
Sectors Per Track (or Sectors Per Head)	66
Hidden Sectors	66
File Allocation Table (FAT)	68
How Windows detects the Improper – Shutdown	70
Root Directory	72
Long File Name (LFN)	77
Data Area (or Files Area)	79
Fragmented and Defragmented Data	79
Identifying the cause of data corruption	81
Boot the system with bootable floppy	81
Verify the MBR Information	81
If MBR is okay, Verify DBR	82

4. Number Systems — 84

Introduction	84
Decimal Number System	84
Binary Number System	85
Binary to Decimal number Conversion	86
Decimal to Binary number Conversion	86
Binary Number Formats	88
The Bit	88
The Nibble	88
The Byte	89
The Word	89
The Double Word	90
Octal Number System	90
Binary to Octal Conversion	91
Octal to Binary Conversion	91
Octal to Decimal Conversion	91
Decimal to Octal Conversion	91
Hexadecimal Number System	92
Binary to Hexadecimal Conversion	93
Hexadecimal to Binary Conversion	94
Hexadecimal to Decimal Conversion	94
Decimal to Hexadecimal Conversion	94
ASCII Code	96
Some important number system terms, often used for Data and Data Storage representation	103
Byte	104
Kilobyte	104
Megabyte	104
Gigabyte	104
Terabyte	104
Petabyte	105
Exabyte	105
Zettabyte	105
Yottabyte	105
Common Data Storage Terms	105

5. Introduction of C Programming — 106

- Introduction — 106
- Why use C in Data Recovery Programming — 106
- Let me assume that you know nothing in C — 107
- Let us start — 107
- Keywords — 108
- Compiling the program — 109
- Printing Numbers — 110
- Using Variables — 111
- Numeric Variable Types — 113
    - Initializing Numeric Variables — 118
- Operators — 119
    - Assignment Operator — 119
    - Mathematical Operators — 119
    - Relational Operators — 120
    - Logical Operators — 120
    - The Comma Operator — 121
- Something more about printf() and Scanf() — 123
- Control Statements — 124
    - The if else Statement — 124
    - The switch Statement — 126
    - The break Statement — 128
    - The continue Statement — 128
- Loops — 129
    - The while Loop — 130
    - The do while Loop — 131
    - The for Loop — 131
    - The goto Statement — 133
- Pointers — 134
- Array — 137
    - Character Arrays — 139
    - Accessing the Elements — 140
    - Initializing Array Elements — 140
    - Looping through an Array — 140
    - Multidimensional Arrays — 141
- Strings — 142
- Some Common String Functions — 143
    - The strlen Function — 143
    - The strcpy Function — 143
    - The strcmp Function — 144
    - The strcat Function — 145
    - The strtok Function — 145
- Functions — 147
    - Pass By Value Functions — 149
    - Call-by-reference — 154
    - Dereferencing — 154
- Memory Allocation in C — 155

Reallocating Memory	156
Releasing Memory	157
Structures	157
Structures with Pointer Members in C	159
Structure Initialisers in C	160
Passing Structures to Functions in C	161
Union	164
The union Keyword	165
A practical use of a union in data recovery	167
File Handling in C	169
The File Modes of fopen Function	169
Closing Files	170
Reading Files	170
Writing to Files	171
Command Line Arguments with C	172
Bitwise Manipulators	173
Bitwise AND	174
Bitwise OR	175
Bitwise Exclusive OR	175
Bitwise Compliment	176
Bitwise Shift Left	176
Bitwise Shift Right	176
Functions for Binary – Decimal Conversions	177
Function for Decimal to Binary conversion	177
Function for Decimal to Binary conversion	178
Debugging and Testing	178
Syntax Errors	178
Logic Errors	179
Testing	179
Some testing principles	179
White Box Testing	179
Black Box Testing	180
Equivalence Classes	180
Boundary Value Analysis	180
Devising a Test Plan	181

6. Introduction to Computer Basics — 182

Introduction	182
Basic concepts	183
Central Processor	183
Central Memory	183
CPU Registers	183
Assembler structure	185
Advantages of the Assembler	187
Let me keep my promise	187
Storing and loading the programs	188
Segments	190
Data movement	190

Interruptions	192
Internal Hardware Interruptions	192
External Hardware Interruptions	193
Software Interruptions	193
Int 20H, Terminate process	193
Int 21H, MS-DOS System functions	194

7. Necessary DOS Commands — 242

Introduction	242
Brief History	242
Microsoft Disk Operating System (MS-DOS) Version 1.0	242
MS-DOS Version 2.0	242
MS-DOS Version 3.0 to 5.0	243
MS-DOS Version 6.0	243
MS-DOS Version 7.0 (Windows 95)	243
Necessary commands	244
ATTRIB	244
CD (or CHDIR)	246
CHKDSK	246
CLS	247
COMMAND	247
COPY	248
DEBUG	249
COM Extension	250
EXE Extension	251
DEL (or ERASE)	252
DELTREE	253
DOSKEY	254
DIR	256
DISKCOPY	257
EDIT	258
EXIT	258
FC	258
FDISK	259
FIND	260
FORMAT	260
LABEL	261
MD (or MKDIR)	262
MORE	262
MOVE	262
RD (or RMDIR)	262
SCANDISK	263
TYPE	263
XCOPY	263
Specification shortcuts, Wildcards and Redirection	265
Shortcuts	265
Wildcards	266

Redirection	267
>	267
>>	268
<	268
|	269

8. Disk-BIOS Functions and Interrupts Handling With C — 270

- Introduction — 270
- biosdisk and _bios_disk Functions — 270
- diskinfo_t Structure — 273
- absread and abswrite Functions — 277
- Interrupt Handling with C — 278
  - SREGS Structure — 278
  - REGS Union — 279
  - BYTEREGS and WORDREGS Structures — 279
  - int86 and int86x Functions — 279
  - segread Function — 284
  - intdos and intdosx Functions — 285
- How to know the Physical Hard Drive Number — 286
- Interrupt 13H (INT 13H), ROM BIOS Disk Driver Functions — 289

9. Handling Large Hard Disks — 306

- First of all, let me tell you a Story — 306
- INT 13H Extensions — 307
- How to use INT 13H Extensions in C Programming — 341
  - Comments on Coding of the program — 344

10. Data Recovery From Corrupted Floppy — 347

- Why the floppy is not readable — 347
- How to recover — 349
  - Method – 1 — 349
    - Store the boot image of any fresh floppy — 349
      - Making the image of DOS Boot Record of a good floppy — 349
      - Comments on Program coding — 353
    - Pasting the boot image to the first sector of Unreadablefloppy — 354
      - Comments on Program coding — 357
    - Let us do it with single program — 358
      - Comments on Program coding — 362
      - Storing the boot Image in HEXADECIMAL — 363
      - Characters to use in our previous Program
      - Comments on coding of the program — 364
  - Method – 2 — 365
    - What to do if Method – 1 doesn't work — 365
    - Copy all the data of media surface to a single file — 365
      - Comments on Program coding — 367
    - Thinking for the solution of sector(s) reading error.. — 368
      - Comments on Program coding — 370
    - Paste the Data from the file to the

physical surface of fresh floppy	370
Comments on Program coding	372
Thinking for Logical Recovery for Deleted or lost Data	373
Comments on coding	379
Comments on coding	380
Comments on coding	381
Comments on coding	384
Comments on Coding	384

11. Making Backups — 386

Why Backups	386
When and what to Back up	386
Backup of MBR (Master Boot Record) and its use	387
Why Backup MBR	387
What Can Be Recovered with the Backup of MBR	387
Writing the Program to make Backup of MBR	387
Comments on Program coding	388
Program to Restore the MBR from Backup	389
Comments on Program coding	390
Backup of DBR (DOS Boot Record) and its use	391
Why Backup DBR	391
What can be recovered with the Backup of DBR	392
Programs for Making and Restoring Backups of DBR	392
Complete Disk Imaging	393
Writing the program for complete disk imaging	393
Comments on Coding	396
Comments on Coding	399

12. Reading and Modifying MBR with Programming — 401

Master Boot Record (MBR) or Master Partition Table (MPT)	401
Master boot record format	401
Partition Table Entry Format	402
Writing program to read the partition table of MBR	403
Comments on coding	406
Program to find all logical partitions and their information	407
Comments on coding	408
Comments on coding	412
Modify MBR by Programming	413
Comments on coding	414

13. Reading and Modifying DBR with Programming — 415

DOS Boot Record (DBR) / DOS Boot Sector	415
Reading DBR of Floppy and Small Volumes	415
Reading the DBR of Large Volumes	418
How to Recover DBR with Programming	424
Comments on coding	427

14. Programming for "Raw File" Recovery — 429

Raw File Recovery	429
Headers and footers of some important file types	430
Writing a program for Raw File Recovery	431

Comments on coding	435
INT 10H, function 01H – Set Cursor Type	437

15. Programming for Data Wipers — 439

Introduction	439
When the data becomes completely unrecoverable	439
Why data wiping is so important	440
Writing program for Non–Destructive data wiper	440
Comments on logic and the coding of the program	442
Writing program for Destructive Data Wiper	443
Comments on coding	446
Wiping Data Area of specific file	447
Comments on logic and coding of program	450

16. Developing more Utilities for Disks — 453

Introduction	453
Hiding Partitions	453
How the partition becomes hidden	453
Writing program to hide partition	455
Comments on coding	457
Writing program to Unhide the Partition	458
Comments on Program	460
Writing program to delete Partition	460
Comments on program	462
Formatting "Track 0 Bad" floppy	464
Writing the Disk Editing Tool	466

Appendix – I: Important C functions and Header Files	**467**
Appendix – II: Glossary of Data Recovery Terms	**484**
Appendix – III: Data Recovery Software and Data Recovery Centers	**494**
Index	**505**

Chapter – 1
An Overview of Data Recovery

Introduction to Data Recovery

A fundamental role of an organization's IT department is to protect its data. Most IT departments invest significant resources to develop, implement and maintain a process for backing up important data on their machines.

In case of computer world Data Recovery is, retrieving data, lost from a computer's storage device, due to any possible reason caused data loss. As it is clear from its name data recovery leads recovery from data lost due to mishandling of storage device, hardware failure, lack of knowledge of the user, virus attack are or any other reason.

In today's computer world, where data of any organization is the most important part in most of the cases and by any type of disaster in data may cause a lots of financial and business loss and the organization may ruin its reputation too.

It is very commonly heard problem in computer or IT world, that the employee of any company or any general computer user was having the very valuable data in his computer's hard disk, floppy or in any other storage device and he is not able to access that information or he has lost that information due to any accident, Viral attack, mishandling of storage device or any other type of mistake while handling the data. It may be due to lack of knowledge of saving or protecting the data.

Not only in organizations, but also home users may suffer the same problem. Thus we can imagine a number of possible cases and reasons of data loss. So "Where there is loss of data, there is need of data recovery."

Understanding Data loss

The IT departments of most of the organizations invest significant resources to develop, implement and maintain a process for backing up important data on their machines. Well managed environments also regularly test backups to ensure that restore operations can be performed quickly and accurately.

It is difficult to categorize the Data loss in case of computers. There may be lots of reasons that may cause the data loss. The loss of data in computers can be seen as, "The data lost last time was a bad case, but worst is yet to come."

The data loss may be due to lots of reasons some of important reasons may be as follows:

System Crash

If the computer is unable to run the boot process and operating system fails to read the stored data and instructions from the disk, due to any software or hardware problem, the disk is said to have crash. It is difficult to recover the data completely from the disk crashed by hardware problem, only by the programming however. In case of a disk crash, following messages are displayed:

"0 hard disks found"
"Drive failure"
"Hard disk failure"
"Sector not found..."
"Data error reading drive X:"
"No boot device available"
"Error loading operating system"
"OS missing or Operating system missing"
"Non-System or Disk error,
   Replace disk and press any key when ready"
"Invalid partition table"
"Track 0 bad..."

The above messages indicate a serious disk problem. The cause that leads these error messages may be logical or a physical problem. The logical problems can be because either the boot sector/partition table, FAT area or the directory area has gone bad. A detailed introduction of boot sector, partition table FAT area, root directories and data area has been given in the next chapters of this book.

A head crash is caused when the read/write heads of a hard disk come into physical contact with the disk surface that stores the information. Head crashes vary in severity but at their worst, the data on the hard disk can be rendered unrecoverable.

Every time if there is data loss in computer it has any reason of this disaster that leads the crash or even minor loss. There may be a number of possibilities but some most important factors are as follows:

Human Error

Human Error is the single largest contributor of Data loss instances. Generally, most of the cases have been noticed of Data loss are due the mistakes made by the user or employees of the organization in protecting the data or while handling the data. This includes accidental file deletion, incorrect usage or sometimes as serious as a Hard Disk Format.

For example it is possible that the employee who is not having the proper knowledge of handling the sensitive data or the software that is if used in lack of knowledge may harm the data and lead to data loss. Also some personal computer users have a tendency to execute any unknown software to know what it does without studying or without getting the information about its application and if the software has been developed for any task such that if illegally used may destroy the data partially or completely. It is also true for the executable files of virus like programs. Common human errors include:

Causes of Disk Crash

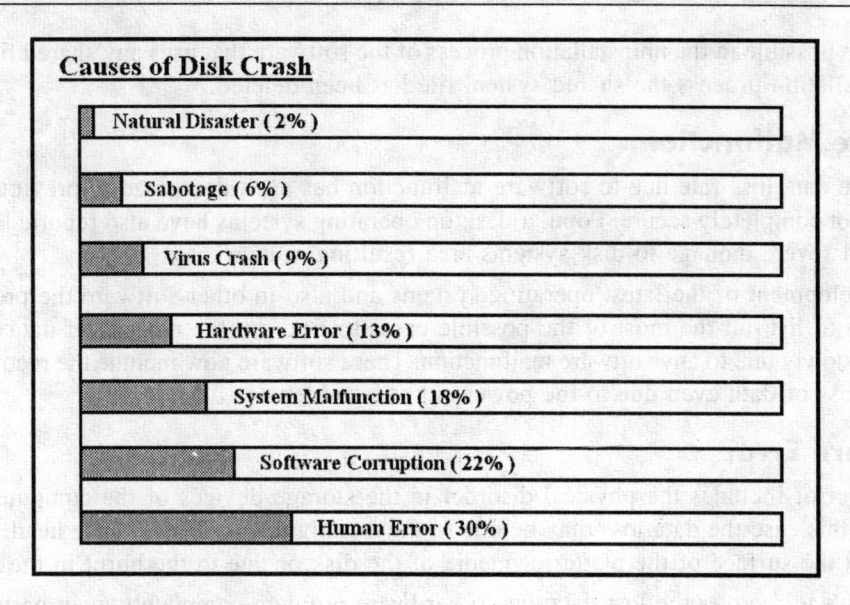

- Natural Disaster (2%)
- Sabotage (6%)
- Virus Crash (9%)
- Hardware Error (13%)
- System Malfunction (18%)
- Software Corruption (22%)
- Human Error (30%)

- Accidental drive format
- Erroneous file or folder deletion
- Administrator mistakes
- Mishandling of storage devices
- Trauma caused by drop or fall
- Lack of knowledge while using disk partitioning or troubleshooting software etc.
- Illogical operating system installation/upgrading
- Illegal power management or temperature settings in the setup system of the computer.

Software Corruption

Software corruption is also a big cause of data disaster and leads the loss of data. Most of the software development companies today give a big slice of time of the total development time of their software for adding the debugging codes to the programming of the software and try to make their program bug free. By doing so, the software may show compatibility with most of the hardware configurations and also may not get any corruption with or by any other software application or even by its own application.

Though the software is developed with proper care even then in today's IT world software corruption is the second big cause of data loss after Human error.

Let's take an example of software corruption case. Suppose you were having any software 'A' in your system that created a system files suppose named 'yyyyyy.xxx' during its installation in the system files' folder of your computer. After some time you installed any other software 'B' and it also creates the file with the same file name and in the same directory. But the newly created file may have completely different application than the previous one.

In such case if we execute the software 'A' it may call the application of the file 'yyyyyy.xxx' but this file is now replaced and will not work as described in software 'A' and in this way it may corrupt the software and may harm the data depending upon the corruption occurred in the software.

This is also possible in the uninstallation process of the software that uses any shared file and during the uninstallation process the shared system file has been deleted.

Software Malfunction

Though the data loss rate due to software malfunction has been decreased in previous years even then it is not completely secure. Popular desktop operating systems have also reported to have hung and caused severe damage to disk systems area resulting in data loss.

In the development of the latest operating systems and also in other software the proper care has been taken to list out the most of the possible cases to find out the reasons of data disaster by a sudden or slowly due to any software malfunction. These software now include the recovery program from the loss of data even due to the power cut at a sudden.

Hardware Error

Hardware error includes the physical disorder in the storage devices of the computer due to any reason. In this case the data loss may be due to the misalignment of read/write head, any possible problem in the surface of the platter or media of the disk or due to the burnt in the disk.

It is difficult to recover the lost data due to hardware problem completely even partially in some cases, only by the programming. It takes extra efforts and resources to recover data in such cases.

Virus Crash

Even today the virus is the first biggest fear that comes in one's mind when data loss takes place in any computer system. Though the antivirus technology in today's software industry has showed the appreciable results yet widespread instances of severe data loss have been reported when anti-virus software could not stop a virus from causing sever damage or when anti-virus software was not well updated.

Win-CIH (Chernobyl), Marijuana (March 6), Monkey, One-Half, Frodo, Spirit, Wyx, Nimda, Sircam, Klez are some virus that have caused major devastation and losses have been astronomical. Virus menace is still unabated and is continuing to cause data losses.

Sabotage

Cases of sabotage are being reported regularly and are increasing at an alarming rate. A majority of organizations still do not have a security policy. Unauthorized intrusions and damages caused by disgruntled employees and business competitors have resulted in major data loss. Dissatisfied employees have found crashing disks as a ploy to square up against employees.

Not only this, the jealousy of one employee from another is also responsible for the loss of data in this case. The employee who is not satisfied with the working manner or policies of another employee may try to harm the important data of the organization for which the target employee is responsible to protect.

Natural Disaster

This type of data loss is rare and reported the minimum frequency of loss of data. Flood, Fire, Lighting and Earthquake are some unavoidable causes of data loss. These causes can not be avoided by the human yet the manufacturer may have a plan while developing the storage device, to protect data in such condition.

Other types of data loss

Programming for data recovery and disk trouble shooting is not waiting the system of any organization or any user to be crashed only. There are also lots of cases that may make a user or organization feel to be in any type of data loss and it is not necessary for the system to be crashed to lead such type of data loss.

This type of data loss may also take place when system is suffering the partial crash of operating system or even in the case when your operating system is completely innocent and working properly and data is lost due to any other reason somehow. Let us try to find out some other main possible cases of data loss.

Loss of one or more partitions

The term *partial crash* of operating system may take place in such cases where we see that our operating system is working in a proper way. In such type of cases we do not feel any problem during the booting process and other operations of the operating system.

The only mystery that make the user unhappy is that he is not able to access all the logical partitions that he had earlier in his disk.

In such cases, the user may feel one or more partitions hidden of his disk and the operating system does not provide any information about these partitions. It is also a commonly possible case that you lose all the logical partitions except the boot partition of your disk in which you were having your operating system installed.

This type of loss takes place when the partitions information in the master boot sector is partially lost. It may be due to the misuse of FDISK like partitioning program in lack of knowledge or any Virus like attack in partition table entry.

Floppy Read Error

As I think, this is also one of the main reasons of data loss in any organization or for any personal computer user that causes the data loss frequently.

The floppy is one of the most unreliable sources of storage. It is a very common problem that the user was having some important data in a floppy and now the computer is displaying the message indicating floppy read error.

Though the loss of data in such cases is not major and also most of the time another backup of that data is available but in the cases when the backup were not saved or available, the loss of data takes place. The serious problem with the floppy is it frequency to display read error.

Floppy read error may also be very serious thing in some cases. For example, when you install antivirus or any other software in your computer that provides you the facility to make a backup or recovery disk which may help you to recover the system in case of some serious virus attack or due to some corruption of software, usually the backup is made in floppy disks.

In such cases it becomes very important for the floppy not to give any error when used to recover the system. The floppy read error in such case may make you to face a big trouble of data.

Deletion of important data

It is possible for any user to delete any important file by mistake under any confusion or misunderstanding. This type of data loss may be the loss of a single file or multiple files.

Password loss

The loss of password should also be included in the loss of data as it shows all the characteristics of data loss. Data loss takes place if user forgets his password and also like any other type of data loss, password is also needed to be recovered, if lost. However in this book we are not going to discuss any type password recovery.

Types and Areas of Data Recovery

Almost in every software related problem it is possible to recover the data completely or partially however accuracy of data may lie in between the range from 100% to as low as 1%.

It depends on the cause of data loss and also the procedure of the cause to take place. The following table gives an idea of areas of data recovery in different types and cases of data loss created by **software** related problems:

Type or Cause of Data loss	Comments on possible data recovery by software and programming
Recovery of Deleted file(s)	Possible recovery is 100%, if it is tried to recover just after deletion. In case some other information has been written in the disk, the new data may overwrite the information of deleted file. In such cases it decreases the accuracy of recovery of deleted file and it may be as low as 0% depending upon the overwritten file area and deleted file type of course.
Recovery of disk Format	Data may be recovered up to 100% with special efforts, but you will have to suffer the loss of original names of files and folders especially which were in root directory. I still have not come to know about even a single software or programmer which can recover all the data after format of the disk with its original File names. Also, Provided that the disk should not be overwritten new data on it.
Recovery of Crashed OS	If the problem is software related and caused by corruption of MBR, it is possible to recover data 100% in most of the cases. However complications go on increasing with the factors DBR, FAT and root directories. As it starts to affect data area, complication goes on increasing rapidly.
Recovery of lost partitions	Possible to recover up to 100%, if caused only by partition table corruption.
Recovery from unreadable floppy	Recovery of data gives accuracy range from 100% to as low as 1 or 0%, depending on the surface of the media of floppy.
After zero filling in the disk or after use of data wipers	Recoveries by software 0%. Only by using the recovery software there is no hope of recovery even partially in such cases. However, magnetic sophisticated technologies are available today that can do recovery, even in such cases, where you have run the zero filling programs in your disk, even six times.

It does not mean that you can not recover data if the problem is hardware related. But it is not possible to recover data only by programming in such cases. It is recommended that you should go to a data recovery lab/canter in such cases.

Analyzing a Computer before Data Recovery

When you are planning to recover the data on a large scale or from a complicated case of disaster, you need to analyze the problem and to finalize many important objectives to increase the accuracy of recovery and get the ease of task. This takes your attention towards the problem from many important angles.

In case of complicated disaster of the disk in which recovery of all the files including system files and OS is not possible, if you ask a user whose data has been lost, to tell you which of the file of his disk he want to recover, you just get the reply *all of them*. It is Ideal too to do so but you can not waste time and efforts on such system files and other files which are the part of OS or any other software that can be installed again later and have no importance for the user.

In this way you need to think according to following steps to prepare for data recovery:
- Acceptable recovery period
- Understanding various costs
- User description
- Defining the requirements
- Making objectives

Acceptable Recovery Period

The acceptable period for recovery may be different for different type of systems and users. For example, when we have to recover the data of an engineering workstation it has many software development tools and several source codes in their disk.

In such cases, we can not take more than 4 business hours to recover such data as delay in recovery of tools and source codes may cause delay in the project works and loss of source codes may cause significant rework and project delays.

In case of marketing department workstation which has marketing tools and related data stored in it, we can not take more than one business day to recover data. However in case of personal computer users we can take some more time to complete the data recovery operations.

Understanding Various Costs

When dealing with data recovery, it is important to understand the true costs related to these mission-critical operations. Let us take a brief idea of these costs:

Downtime Costs

You can use downtime cost estimates to make better decisions about exactly what level of data recovery is required for different type of data loss. For example the data of any accounting server is critical and need to be recovered as it is.

The delay of even a single day may cause the loss of big amount. Other important costs to be considered are hardware costs, planning costs and other additional costs.

Data Recovery Costs

The data recovery costs are the amount of money required for data recovery process for different type of data loss. This is so important because it is commonly seen behavior of the customers of any data recovery center that the user compares the cost of recovery with the importance of the data.

The user will be interested in data recovery only if the cost of recovery is not so high for him as the importance of his valuable data.

User Description

User description may be very important factor to prepare the road map of data recovery procedure. With the help of this, you can easily find the way in which preferences are to be given to the different data in case of a complicated data recovery process.

It is done so, because in such cases, you can not waste the time and efforts to recover all the files including such unnecessary files and system files etc. that can be created again easily.

Defining the requirements

It is necessary to estimate the requirements before starting the data recovery. Definition of these requirements starts with some general statement of the problem. The basic objective of this step is to understand the problem thoroughly. During the requirement specification, the focus is on clearly specifying capabilities and facilities the system should provide when the entire process is going to take place.

Making objectives

After completing all the steps described earlier, you have to make your objectives depending upon the preferences found by user description, you have to finalize your objectives for which you have to work for recovering the data. These objectives provide a step by step path to recover the lost data or to make programs for special type of problems. By following all these steps you may avoid complexity in procedure as well as you may work with better accuracy in less time consumption.

Some Advices before beginning the Disk Troubleshooting or Data recovery procedure

- **Think Positively and be confident:** However it is a little bit difficult to keep you mind cool in such a condition when your important data has become inaccessible, yet you should start any recovery procedure with the positive attitude. You should be confident and should be completely sure of what you have done and what you should do.
- **Note-down the every step, you perform:** It is a batter idea to write down the every step and procedure that you follow to recover the data or for disk troubleshooting. By doing this you can get help to know if you have skipped any step or there is any mistake in procedure you used.

    Not only this, if unfortunately you are not capable of recovering you data, the information of the steps that you have followed to recover the data, may help a lot to the data recovery center people. By this information they can easily find out the type of data loss and its cure procedure.

- **Be sure before rebooting the system:** There are many problems of computer and operating system which are resolved by a simple reboot. However, although a reboot may solve your disk problem, it can also make things worse. So do not reboot the system carelessly without knowing the status of system and data of the disk.

  If any TSR program is causing a system lockup, the simplex fix for the problem is a reboot. Even for other cases, if you have to reboot the system to cure some error, choose safe mode for rebooting.

- **Prepare a best suitable plan and stick with it:** There may be many different recovery and troubleshooting procedures for different problems. But you have to choose such a procedure that is most easy, suitable to your system configuration, performs most stable and appropriate recovery and consumes lesser time.

There are some important steps given below that may be the strong part of you recovery plan:

1. Double-check that you are not doing something wrong.
2. Check the connection of hardware.
3. Check the software.
4. Back up whatever you can before going any further.
5. Before running any diagnostic program, you must be sure that it is nondestructive diagnostics program.
6. Remove the drive and controller, clean all their connectors, push any socketed chips back in their sockets, and reassemble the system.

Some Tips to Protect your Data

"The prevention is always better than the cure". Some important tips have been listed here to protect your data. By following these tips, we can avoid the loss of data and a difficult data recovery procedure.

Make the Backups

Backing up the boot sectors and other Directory information is always a wise procedure of secure your data. The different areas on your disk should be backed up at different intervals. A complete back up program consists of the following measures:

- Make an emergency boot floppy for each system.
- Make the back of MBR once, after FDISK command of DOS.
- Make the back up of DBRs for each logical drive once, after FORMAT command of DOS.
- Make the back up of the FAT and root directories regularly.
- Make the back up of important user data regularly.

Perform surface scanning monthly

Perform the surface scan monthly to test the media of your device. By doing this you can fix the error in the very initial stage. Even if the scanning program is not capable to fix the disk, it may at least provide the information about the physical and logical status of your storage media. With this information you can get the help to back up your data and to find the solutions for the problem.

De-fragment of data weekly

With the creation of new files and deletion of older files the data of the disk becomes more and more fragmented. The fragmentation makes the accessibility of data slow and complicated. We shall discuss the disk fragmentation and defragmentation in detail, in the next chapters of this book.

The utilities for defragmentation of the data are available in the operating system. By maintaining the defragmented data, you can make the performance of the system better as well as comparatively **Defragmented data is easy to recover if there is any disk crash.**

Use good antivirus program

The viruses are the very big cause for data loss now days. To avoid the virus infection in your data and to protect your data, you must use a good antivirus program.

If you use the floppy disks and CDs in your computer, perform the scanning by antivirus before opening the disks in your computer or before copying anything from it. If you are using internet, always enable your email protection and internet security from the options of your antivirus settings.

Get into the habit of keeping your floppy write-protected

There are many viruses that have the tendency to spread their self to other computers, with the help of floppy disks by just copying their executable program to the floppy in the hidden mode.

A big proportion of viruses are boot record viruses and they cannot get at your hard disk until you boot your system from an infected floppy. You can read and write data on a floppy with an infected boot record for years and never become infected. But booting from such the floppy, even if it is not a bootable disk, will make your system infected with boot sector virus.

Do not use pirated games and software

The pirated games and software are usually prepared by some cracking or by following any other illegal procedures to run even after pirated. These procedures may not be compatible and suitable for the software and hardware configuration of every computer and may destroy you data.

Also, there is a significant number of such software, especially games which have been used as a medium to spread the viruses. Therefore using the pirated software may infect your system with some serious system virus and may cause a big data loss.

Chapter – 2

Introduction of Hard Disks

Introduction

In today's computer world hard disks have proved themselves as the most important part of a computer. Today hard disk is the main storage device that is most commonly used to store all type of data as well as one of the most interesting components of computer.

It will be very difficult for modern computer users to even consider what computer life would be without hard disk drives, as most of us today store billions of bytes of information in our computers.

In the very earliest computers there was no storage at all. Each time you wanted to run a program you would have to enter the program manually. Even more than that, it made most of what we consider today to be computing impossible, since there was no easy way to have a computer work with the same data over and over again. It was quickly realized that some sort of permanent storage was necessary if computers were to become truly useful tools.

The first storage medium used on computers was actually paper. Programs and data were recorded using holes punched into paper tape or punch cards. A special reader used a beam of light to scan the cards or tape. Where a hole was found it read a "1", and where the paper blocked the sensor, a "0" or vice-versa.

Though it was a great improvement over *nothing but* these cards were still very inconvenient to use. You basically had to write the entire program from scratch on paper, and get it working in your mind before you started trying to put it onto cards, because if you made a mistake you had to re-punch many of the cards. It was very hard to visualize what you were working with.

The next big advance over paper was the creation of magnetic tape. Recording information in a similar to way to how audio is recorded on a tape, these magnetic tapes were much more flexible, durable and faster than paper tape or punch cards.

Of course, tape is still used today on modern computers, but as a form of offline or secondary storage. Before hard disks, they were the primary storage for some computers. Their primary disadvantage is that they must be read linearly; it can take minutes to move from one end of the tape to the other, making *random access* impractical.

Well coming back to our topic. IBM introduced the very first hard disk that would be feasible for commercial development. It was not like disk drives that are used now days. They used rotating cylindrical drums, upon which the magnetic patterns of data were stored. The drums were large and hard to work with. The first true hard disks had the heads of the hard disk in contact with the surface of the disk. This was done to allow the low-sensitivity electronics of the day to be able to better read the magnetic fields on the surface of the disk but manufacturing techniques at that stage of time were not nearly as sophisticated as they are now, and it was not possible to get the disk's surface as smooth as it was necessary to allow the head to slide smoothly over the surface of the disk at high speed while it was in contact with it. Over time the heads would wear out, or wear out the magnetic coating on the surface of the disk.

As a critical discovery of new technology of IBM in which, contact with the surface of the disk was not necessary, took place it became the basis of the modern hard disks. The very first hard disk of this type was the IBM 305 RAMAC (Random Access Method of Accounting and Control) introduced in September 13, 1956. This hard disk could store five million characters that were approximately five megabytes with the data transfer rate of 8,800 bytes per second.

In 1962, IBM introduced the model 1301 Advanced Disk File. The key advance of this disk drive was the creation of heads that floated, or flew, above the surface of the disk on an air bearing with reducing the distance from the heads to the surface of the disks from 800 to 250 micro inches.

In 1973, IBM introduced the model 3340 disk drive, which is commonly considered to be the father of the modern hard disk which had two separate spindles, one permanent and the other removable, each with a capacity of 30 MB. IBM's model 3370 introduced in 1979 was the first disk with thin film heads. In the same year IBM introduced model 3310 which is the first disk drive with 8" platters, greatly reduced in size from the 14" that had been the standard for over a decade.

The first hard disk drive designed in the 5.25" form factor used in the first PCs was the Seagate ST-506. It featured four heads and a 5 MB capacity. IBM bypassed the ST-506 and chose the ST-412—a 10 MB disk in the same form factor—for the IBM PC/XT, making it the first hard disk drive widely used in the PC and PC-compatible world.

In the year 1983, Rodime introduced RO352, the first disk drive to use the 3.5" form factor, which became one of the most important industry standards. In 1985 Quantum introduced the Hardcard, a 10.5 MB hard disk mounted on an ISA expansion card for PCs that were originally built without a hard disk.

In 1986 Conner Peripherals introduced the CP340. It was the first disk drive to use a voice coil actuator. In the year 1988 Conner Peripherals introduced the CP3022, which was the first 3.5" drive to use the reduced 1" height now called "low profile" and the standard for modern 3.5" drives. In the same year PrairieTek introduced a drive using 2.5" platters. In 1990 IBM introduced the model 681 (Redwing), an 857 MB drive. It was the first to use MR heads and PRML.

IBM's "Pacifica" mainframe drive introduced in 1991 is the first to replace oxide media with thin film media on the platter surface. In the same year Integral Peripherals' 1820 is the first hard disk with 1.8" platters, later used for PC-Card disk drives. In the year **1992** Hewlett Packard introduced C3013A which is the first 1.3" drive.

There are a number of developments that took place in the history of hard disks to give the current design, shape performance and capacities to the today's disks. These are difficult to count in detail within this book.

Components of hard disk

A hard has following main components in it:
- Disk Platters and Media
- Read/Write Heads

Introduction of Hard Disks

- Head Sliders, Arms and Actuator
- Hard Disk Spindle Motor
- Connectors and Jumpers
- Logic Board
- Cache and Cache Circuitry

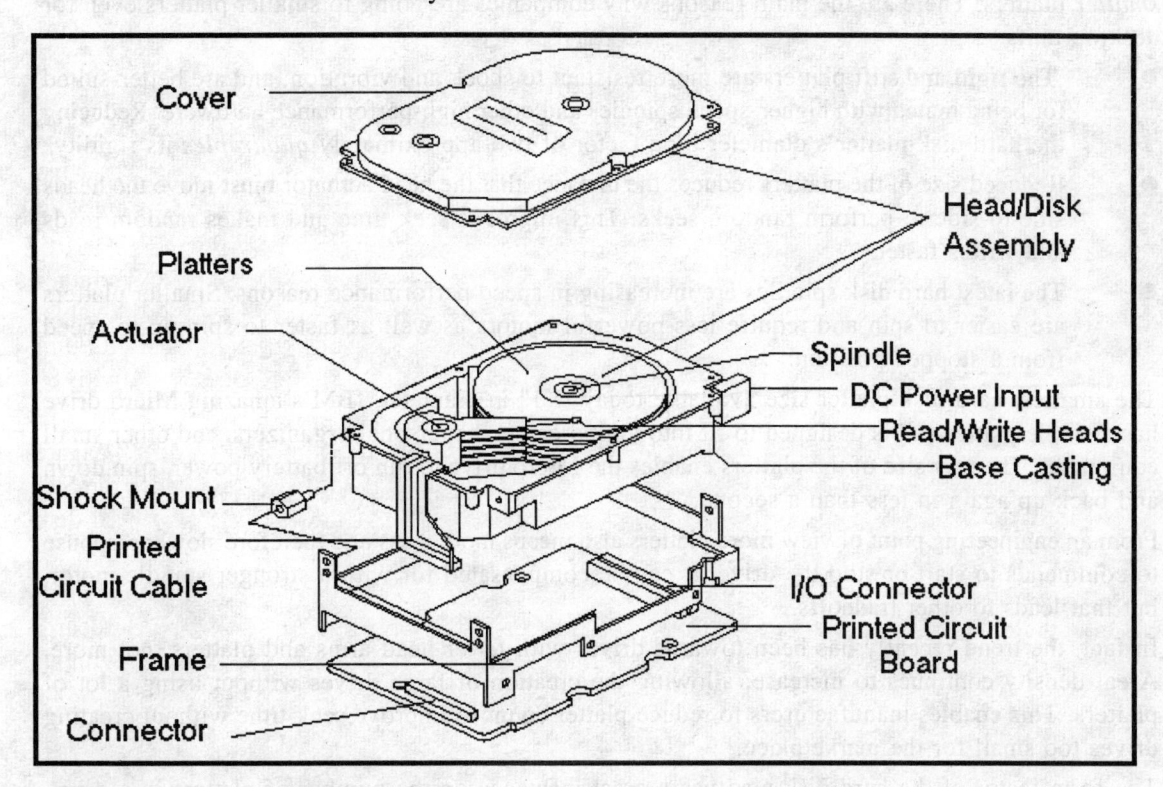

(Diagram: Exploded view of hard disk showing Cover, Platters, Actuator, Shock Mount, Printed Circuit Cable, Frame, Connector, Head/Disk Assembly, Spindle, DC Power Input, Read/Write Heads, Base Casting, I/O Connector, Printed Circuit Board)

Disk Platters and Media

Every hard disk uses one or more (generally more than one) round, flat disks called platters, coated on both sides with a special *media* material designed to store information in the form of magnetic patterns. Each *surface* of each platter on the disk can hold billions of bits of data.

Platters are composed of two main substances, a substrate material that forms the bulk of the platter and gives it structure and rigidity, and a magnetic media coating which actually holds the magnetic impulses that represent the data.

The quality of the platters and particularly, their media coating is critical. The size of the platters in the hard disk is the primary determinant of its overall physical dimensions, also generally called the drive's form factor; most drives are produced in one of the various standard hard disk form factors.

Sometimes hard disks are referred to by a size specification. If someone is having a 3.5-inch hard disk it means it usually refers to the disk's form factor, and normally, the form factor is named based on the platter size. The earlier hard disks had a *nominal* size of 5.25" but now days the most common hard disk platter size is 3.5".

Laptop drives are usually smaller, due to the expected small size and less weight of it. The platters on these drives are usually 2.5" in diameter or less; 2.5" is the standard form factor, but drives with 1.8" and even 1.0" platters are becoming more common in mobile equipment.

Though drives extend the platters to as much of the width of the physical drive package as possible, to maximize the amount of storage they can pack into the drive yet the trend overall is towards *smaller* platters. There are the main reasons why companies are going to smaller platters even for desktop units:

- The rigid and stiff platters are more resistant to shock and vibration, and are better-suited for being mated with higher-speed spindles and other high-performance hardware. Reducing the hard disk platter's diameter by a factor of two approximately *quadruples* its rigidity.
- Reduced size of the platters reduces the distance that the head actuator must move the heads side-to-side to perform random seeks. This improves seek time and makes random reads and writes faster.
- The latest hard disk spindles are increasing in speed performance reasons. Smaller platters are easier to spin and require less-powerful motors as well as faster to spin up to speed from a stopped position.

The smallest hard disk platter size available today is 1" in diameter. IBM's amazing Micro drive has a single platter and is designed to fit into digital cameras, personal organizers, and other small equipment. The tiny size of the platters enables the Micro drive to run off battery power, spin down and back up again in less than a second.

From an engineering point of view more platters also means more mass and therefore slower response to commands to start or stop the drive. It can be compensated for with a stronger spindle motor, but that leads to other tradeoffs.

In fact, the trend recently has been towards drives with *fewer* head arms and platters, not more. Areal density continues to increase, allowing the creation of large drives without using a lot of platters. This enables manufacturers to reduce platter count to improve seek time without creating drives too small for the marketplace.

The form factor of the hard disk also has a great influence on the number of platters in a drive. There are several factors that are related to the number of platters used in the disk. Drives with many platters are more difficult to engineer due to the increased mass of the spindle unit, the need to perfectly align all the drives, and the greater difficulty in keeping noise and vibration under control.

Even then, though hard disk engineers wanted to put lots of platters in a particular model, the standard "slimline" hard disk form factor is limited to 1 inch in height, which limits the number of platters that can be put in a single unit. Of course, engineers are constantly working to reduce the amount of clearance required between platters, so they can increase the number of platters in drives of a given height.

The magnetic patterns that comprise your data are recorded in a very thin media layer on the surfaces of the hard disk's platters; the bulk of the material of the platter is called the substrate and does nothing but support the media layer. To be suitable, a substrate material must be rigid, easy to work with, lightweight, stable, magnetically inert, inexpensive and readily available. The most commonly used material for making platters has traditionally been an aluminum alloy, which meets all of these criteria.

Due to the way the platters spin with the read/write heads floating just above them, the platters must be extremely smooth and flat therefore alternatives to aluminum, such as glass, glass composites, and magnesium alloys have been proposed. It now is looking increasingly likely that glass and composites made with glass will be the next standard for the platter substrate. Compared to aluminum platters, glass platters have several advantages:

- Better Quality:
- Improved Rigidity:
- Thinner Platters:
- Thermal Stability:

One *disadvantage* of glass compared to aluminum is fragility, particularly when made very thin.

The substrate material of which the platters are made forms the base upon which the actual recording media is deposited. The media layer is a very thin coating of magnetic material which is where the actual data is stored. It is typically only a few millionths of an inch in thickness.

Older hard disks used oxide media. Oxide media is inexpensive to use, but also has several important shortcomings. The first is that it is a soft material, and easily damaged from contact by a read/write head. The second is that it is only useful for relatively low-density storage. It worked fine for older hard disks with relatively low data density, but as manufacturers sought to pack more and more data into the same space, oxide was not up to the task: the oxide particles became too large for the small magnetic fields of newer designs.

Today's hard disks use thin film media. Thin film media consists of a very thin layer of magnetic material applied to the surface of the platters. Special manufacturing techniques are employed to deposit the media material on the platters.

Compared to oxide media, thin film media is much more uniform and smooth. It also has greatly superior magnetic properties, allowing it to hold much more data in the same amount of space. After applying the magnetic media, the surface of each platter is usually covered with a thin, protective, layer made of carbon. On top of this is added a super-thin lubricating layer. These materials are used to protect the disk from damage caused by accidental contact from the heads or other foreign matter that might get into the drive.

Read/Write Heads

The heads are the read/write interface to the magnetic physical media on which the data is stored in a hard disk. The heads do the work of converting bits to magnetic pulses and storing them on the platters, and then reversing the process when the data needs to be read back. Heads are one of the more expensive parts of the hard disk to enable areal densities and disk spin speeds to increase.

However GMR heads is most popular in the today's hard disk, there have several technologies been proposed at several times for read/write heads:

- Ferrite Heads
- Metal-In-Gap (MIG) Heads
- Thin Film (TF) Heads
- Anisotropic Magneto resistive (AMR/MR) Heads
- Giant Magneto resistive (GMR) Heads
- Colossal Magneto resistive (CMR) Heads

Read/write heads are an extremely critical component in determining the overall performance of the hard disk, since they play such an important role in the storage and retrieval of data. New head technologies are often the triggering point to increasing the speed and size of modern hard disks therefore read/write heads are the most sophisticated part of the hard disk, which is itself a technological marvel.

Each bit of data to be stored is recorded onto the hard disk using a special encoding method that translates zeros and ones into patterns of magnetic flux reversals. Each hard disk platter has two surfaces used to store the data generally and there is normally one head for each surface used on the drive. Since most hard disks have one to four platters, most hard disks have between two and eight heads. Some larger drives can have 20 heads or more. Only one head can read from or write to the hard disk at a given time. Special circuitry is used to control which head is active at any given time.

The head floats over the surface of the disk and do all of their work without ever physically touching the platters. The amount of space between the heads and the platters is called the floating height or flying height or head gap. The read/write head assemblies are spring-loaded using the spring steel of the head arms which causes the sliders to press against the platters when the disk is stationary.

This is done to ensure that the heads don't drift away from the platters therefore maintaining an exact floating height is essential for correct operation. When the disk spins up to operating speed, the high speed causes air to flow under the sliders and lift them off the surface of the disk. The distance from the platters to the heads is a specific design parameter that is tightly controlled by the manufacturers.

A modern hard disk has a floating height of 0.5 micro inches and even human hair has a thickness of over 2,000 micro inches that's why keeping dirt out of the hard disk is so important. It is actually quite amazing how close to the surface of the disks the heads fly without touching. Dust Particle, Finger Print even a smoke particle is a big problem for the head of a hard disk.

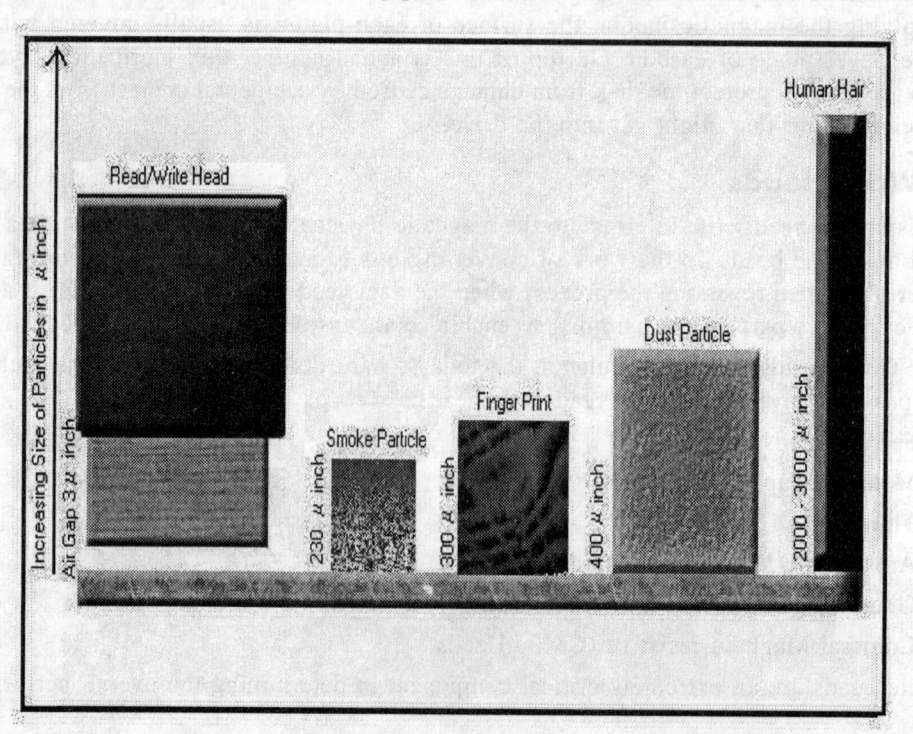

When the areal density of a drive is increased to improve capacity and performance, the magnetic fields are made smaller and weaker. To compensate, either the heads must be made more sensitive, or the floating height must be decreased.

Each time the floating height is decreased, the mechanical aspects of the disk must be adjusted to make sure that the platters are flatter, the alignment of the platter assembly and the read/write heads is perfect, and there is no dust or dirt on the surface of the platters. Vibration and shock also become more of a concern, and must be compensated for.

This is one reason why manufacturers are turning to smaller platters, as well as the use of glass platter substrates. Newer heads such as GMR are preferred because they allow a higher flying height than older, less sensitive heads, all else being equal.

Head Crash

Since the read/write heads of a hard disk are floating on a microscopic layer of air above the disk platters themselves, it is possible that the heads can make contact with the media on the hard disk under certain circumstances. Normally, the heads only contact the surface when the drive is either starting up or stopping.

A modern hard disk is turning over 100 times a second. If the heads contact the surface of the disk while it is at operational speed, the result can be loss of data, damage to the heads, damage to the surface of the disk, or all three. This is usually called a *head crash*, two of the most frightening words to any computer user. The most common causes of head crashes are contamination getting stuck in the thin gap between the head and the disk, and shock applied to the hard disk while it is in operation.

Head Parking

When the platters are not spinning, the heads rest on the surface of the disk. When the platters spin up, the heads rub along the surface of the platters until sufficient speed is gained for them to lift off and float on their cushion of air. When the drive is spun down, the process is repeated in reverse. In both of the cases, for a period of time the heads make contact with the surface of the disk while in motion.

While the platters and heads are designed with the knowledge in mind that this contact will occur, it still makes sense to avoid having this happen over an area of disk where there is data.

For this reason, most disks set aside a special track that is designated to be where the heads will be placed for takeoffs and landings. This area is called the *landing zone*, and no data is placed there. The process of moving the heads to this designated area is called *head parking*.

Almost all new operating systems have inbuilt facility to park the head automatically when it is necessary. Most early hard drives that used stepper motors did not automatically park the heads of the drive therefore as a safety precaution many small utilities were written that the user would run before shutting down the PC of those days. The utility would instruct the disk to move the heads to the landing zone, and then the PC could be shut off safely.

A parameter in the BIOS setup for the hard disk tells the system which track was the landing zone for the particular model of hard disk. Usually, it was the next consecutive-numbered track above the largest-numbered one actually used for data. Modern voice-coil actuated hard disk drives are all auto-parking. It is not necessary now to manually park the heads of modern hard disks.

Head Sliders, Arms and Actuator

When the hard disk platters are accessed for read and write operations using the read/write heads mounted on the top and bottom surfaces of each platter it is obviously, the read/write heads do not just float in space. They must be held in an exact position relative to the surfaces they are reading and also, they must be moved from track to track to allow access to the entire surface of the disk.

The heads are mounted onto a structure that facilitates this process which is often called the head assembly or actuator assembly or the head-actuator assembly. It is comprised of several different parts. The heads themselves are mounted on head sliders. The sliders are suspended over the surface of the disk at the ends of the head arms. The head arms are all mechanically fused into a single structure that is moved around the surface of the disk by the actuator.

Head Sliders

Each hard disk head is mounted to a special device called a head slider or just slider for short. The function of the slider is to physically support the head and hold it in the correct position relative to the platter as the head floats over its surface. Hard disk read/write heads are too small to be used without attaching them to a larger unit.

Sliders are given a special shape to allow them to ride precisely over the platter. As hard disk read/write heads have been shrinking in size, so have the sliders that carry them. The main advantage of using small sliders is that it reduces the weight that must be yanked around the surface of the platters, improving both positioning speed and accuracy. Smaller sliders also have less surface area to potentially contact the surface of the disk. Each slider is mounted onto a head arm to allow it to be moved over the surface of the platter to which it is mated.

Head Arms

The head arms are thin pieces of metal, usually triangular in shape onto which the head sliders carrying the read/write heads are mounted. There is one arm per read/write head, and all of them are lined up and mounted to the head actuator to form a single unit.

This means that when the actuator moves, all of the heads move together in a synchronized fashion. The arms themselves are made of a lightweight, thin material, to allow them to be moved rapidly from the inner to outer parts of the drive. Newer designs have replaced solid arms with structural shapes in order to reduce weight and improve performance.

Newer drives achieve faster seek times in part by using faster and smarter actuators and lighter, more rigid head arms, allowing the time to switch between tracks to be reduced. A recent trend in the hard disk industry has been the reduction in the number of platters in various drive families. Even some flagship drives in various families now only have three or even two platters, where four or five was commonplace a year or so ago.

One reason for this trend is that having a large number of head arms makes it difficult to make the drive with high enough precision to permit very fast positioning on random seeks. This is due to increased weight in the actuator assembly from the extra arms, and also problems aligning all the heads.

Head Actuator

The actuator is a very important part of the hard disk, because changing from track to track is the only operation on the hard disk that requires active movement. Changing heads is an electronic function, and changing sectors involves waiting for the right sector number to spin around and

Introduction of Hard Disks

come under the head. Changing tracks means the heads must be shifted, and so making sure this movement can be done quickly and accurately is of paramount importance.

The actuator is the device used to position the head arms to different tracks on the surface of the platter to different cylinders, since all head arms are moved as a synchronous unit, so each arm moves to the same track number of its respective surface. Head actuators come in two general varieties:

- Stepper Motors
- Voice Coils

The main difference between the two designs is that the stepper motor is an absolute positioning system, while the voice coil is a relative positioning system.

All modern hard disks use voice coil actuators. The voice coil actuator is not only far more adaptable and insensitive to thermal issues. It is much faster and more reliable than a stepper motor. The positioning of actuator is dynamic and is based on feedback from examining the actual position of the tracks. This closed-loop feedback system is also sometimes called a servo motor or servo positioning system and is commonly used in thousands of different applications where precise positioning is important.

Spindle Motor

The spindle motor or the spindle shaft is responsible for turning the hard disk platters, allowing the hard drive to operate. A spindle motor must provide stable, reliable and consistent turning power for thousands of hours of often continuous use, to allow the hard disk to function properly because many drive failures are actually failures with the spindle motor, not the data storage systems.

The spindle motor of a hard disk must have the following quality to live long and to keep your data, secure for a long time:

1. It must be of high quality, so it can run for thousands of hours, and tolerate thousands of start and stop cycles, without failing.
2. It must be run smoothly and with a minimum of vibration, due to the tight tolerances of the platters and heads inside the drive.
3. It must not generate excessive amounts of heat or noise.
4. It should not draw too much power.
5. It must have its speed managed so that it turns at the proper speed.

To meet these demands, all PC hard disks use servo-controlled DC spindle motors. Hard disk spindle motors are configured for *direct connection*. There are no belts or gears that are used to connect them to the hard disk platter spindle. The spindle onto which the platters are mounted is attached directly to the shaft of the motor.

The platters are machined with a hole of the exact size of the spindle, and are placed onto the spindle with separator rings between them to maintain the correct distance and provide room for the head arms. The amount of work that the spindle motor has to do is dependent on following factors:

- **The size and number of platters:** Larger platters and more platters in a drive mean more mass for the motor to turn, so more powerful motors are required. The same is true of higher-speed drives.
- **Power management:** Today, users increasingly want hard disks that will spin up from a

stopped position to operating speed quickly, which also requires faster or more powerful motors.

As in newer hard disks the spindle speed is supposed to be an important issue it has also become an important point in the hard disks to control the amount of noise, heat and vibration generated by the hard disks due to high spindle speed.

Some newer drives, especially 7200 and 10,000 RPM models can make a lot of noise when they are running. If possible, it is a good idea to check out a hard disk in operation before you buy it, to assess its noise level and see if it bothers you; this varies greatly from individual to individual. The noise produced also varies to some extent depending on the individual drive even in the same family. Heat created by the spindle motor can eventually cause damage to the hard disk, which is why newer drives newer hard disks are giving more attention to their cooling.

Connectors and Jumpers

There are several different connectors and jumpers in a hard disk which are used to configure the hard disk and connect it to the rest of the system. The number and types of connectors on the hard disk depend on the data interface it uses to connect to the system, the manufacturer of the drive, and any special features that the drive may possess.

Instructions for setting common jumpers are usually printed right on the drive. Hard disk drives use a standard, 4-pin male connector plug that takes one of the power connectors coming from the power supply. This leads 4-wire plastic connector provides +5 and +12 voltage to the hard disk.

There are two type of interfaces form which usually modern hard disk drives use one of them:

- **IDE/ATA:** It has a 40-pin rectangular connector.

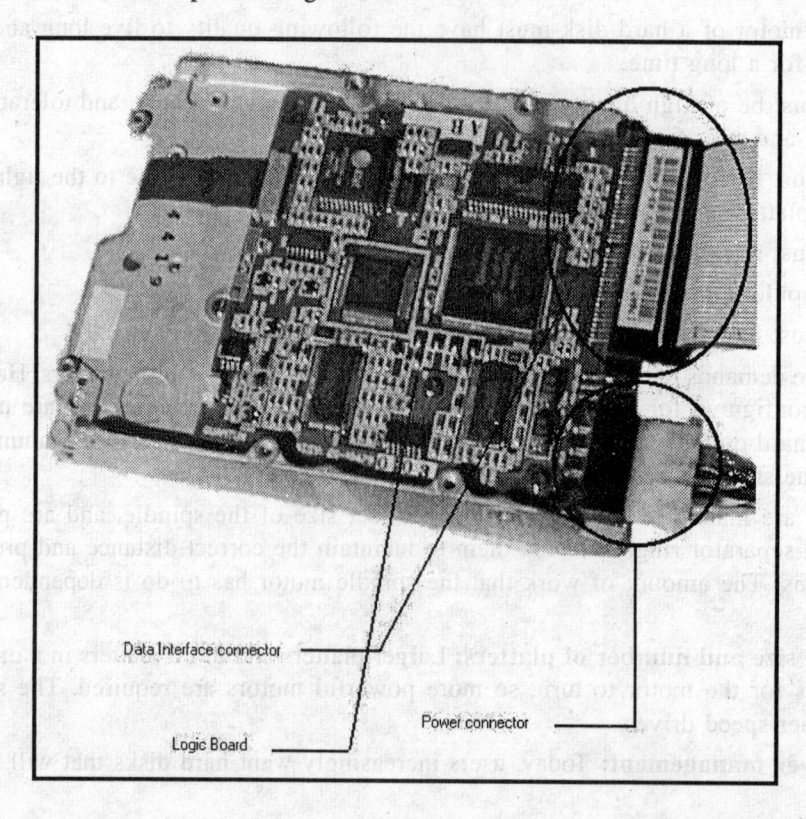

Introduction of Hard Disks

- **SCSI:** A 50-pin, 68-pin, or 80-pin D-shaped connector. All these three pin number represent a different type of SCSI disk such as:
  - A 50-pin connector means the device is narrow SCSI.
  - 68 pins means wide SCSI;
  - 80 pins mean wide SCSI using single connector attachment (SCA).

The connectors on hard disk drives are generally in the form of a 2xN rectangular grid of pins (where N is 20, 25, 34 or 40 depending on the interface). Most of the current SCSI interface connectors are keyed to prevent incorrect insertion because they are D-shaped, this is not always the case for other interfaces.

For this reason, it is important to make sure that the cable is oriented the correct way before plugging it in. The cable has a red stripe to indicate wire 1 and the hard disk uses markers of one form or another to indicate the matching pin 1.

IDE/ATA hard disks are fairly standard in terms of jumpers. There are usually only a few jumper settings and they do not vary greatly from drive to drive. Here are the jumper's settings you will normally find in a hard disk:

- **Drive Select:** There may be two drives, master and slave on the same IDE channel. A jumper is normally used to tell each drive if it should function as a master or slave on the IDE channel.

  For a single drive on a channel, most manufacturers instruct that the drive be jumpered as master, while some manufacturers notably Western Digital have a separate setting for a single drive as opposed to a master on a channel with a slave. The terms master and slave are misleading since the drives really have no operational relationship.

- **Slave Present:** Some drives have an additional jumper that is used to tell a drive configured as master that there is also a slave drive on the ATA channel. This is only required for some older drives that don't support standard master/slave IDE channel signaling.

- **Cable Select:** Some configurations use a special cable to determine which drive is master and which is slave, and when this system is used a cable select jumper is normally enabled.

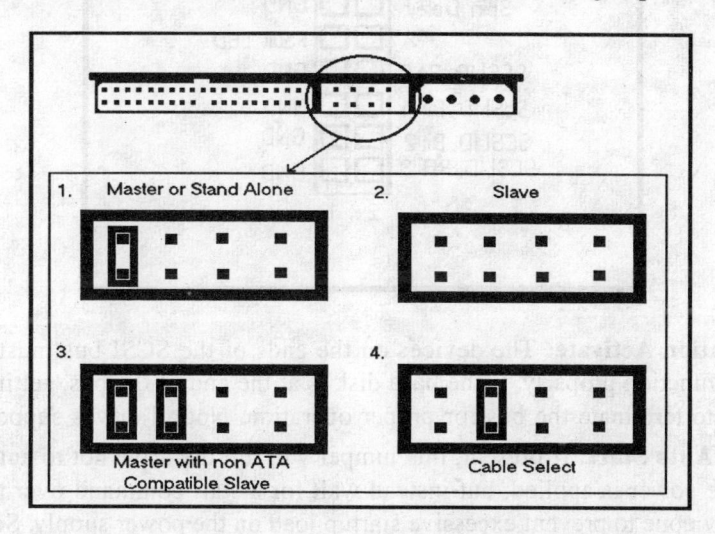

Example of jumper setting of a Seagate Technology hard Disk model

- **Size Restriction Jumper:** Some larger hard disk drives do not work properly in older computers that do not have a BIOS program or large hard disk support recognize them. To get around this, some drives have special jumpers that when set, will cause them to appear as a smaller size than they really are to the BIOS for compatibility.

    For example, some 2.5 GB hard disks have a jumper that will cause them to appear as a 2.1 GB hard disk to a system that won't support anything over 2.1 GB. These are also sometimes called capacity limitation jumpers and vary from manufacturer to manufacturer.

SCSI hard disks have more sophisticated controllers than that of IDE/ATA hard disks therefore SCSI typically have many more jumpers that can be set to control their operation. They also tend to vary much more from manufacturer to manufacturer and from model to model in the number and types of jumpers they have.

Typically the following are the most common and important SCSI drives jumpers:

- **SCSI Device ID:** Every device on a SCSI bus must be uniquely identified for addressing purposes. Narrows SCSI drives will have a set of three jumpers that can be used to assign the disk an ID number from 0 to 7. Wide SCSI drives will have four jumpers to enable ID numbers from 0 to 15. Some systems don't use jumpers to configure SCSI device IDs.

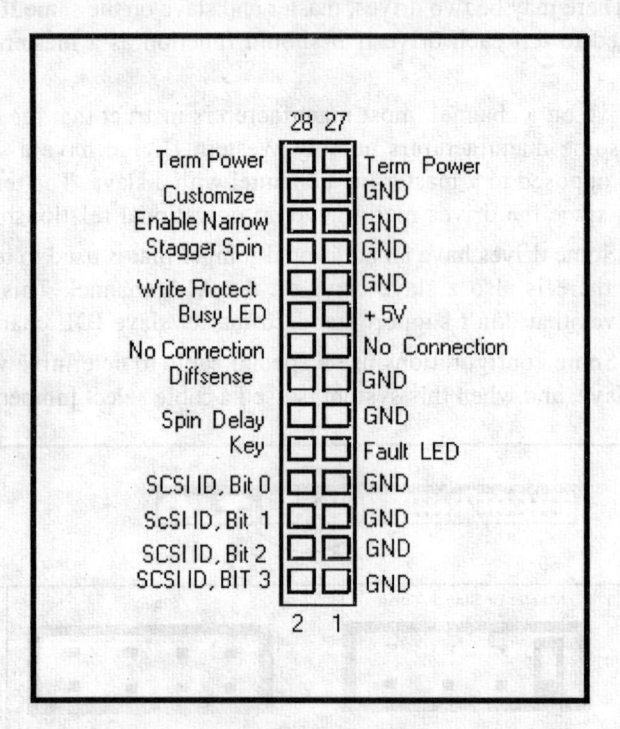

```
                       28 27
        Term Power   [] []   Term Power
          Customize  [] []   GND
       Enable Narrow [] []   GND
        Stagger Spin [] []   GND
       Write Protect [] []   GND
           Busy LED  [] []   +5V
       No Connection [] []   No Connection
           Diffsense [] []   GND
          Spin Delay [] []   GND
                Key  [] []   Fault LED
        SCSI ID, Bit 0 [] []   GND
        ScSI ID, Bit 1 [] []   GND
        SCSI ID, Bit 2 [] []   GND
        SCSI ID, BIT 3 [] []   GND
                        2  1
```

- **Termination Activate:** The devices on the ends of the SCSI bus must terminate the bus for it to function properly. If the hard disk is at the end of the bus, setting this jumper will cause it to terminate the bus for proper operation. Not all drives support termination.
- **Disable Auto Start:** If present, this jumper will tell the drive not to automatically spin up when the power is applied, but instead wait for a start command over the SCSI bus. This is usually done to prevent excessive startup load on the power supply. Some manufacturers invert the sense of this jumper; they disable startup by default and provide an *Enable Auto*

Start jumper.
- **Delay Auto Start:** This jumper tells the drive to start automatically, but wait a predefined number of seconds from when power is applied. It is also used to offset motor startup load on systems with many drives.
- **Stagger Spin:** When a system with many hard drives has this option set for each unit, the drives stagger their startup time by multiplying a user defined constant times their SCSI device ID. This ensures no two drives on the same SCSI channel will start up simultaneously.
- Narrow or Wide: Some drives have a jumper to control whether they will function in narrow or wide mode.
- Force SE: It allows Ultra2, Wide Ultra2, Ultra160, Ultra160+ or other LVD SCSI drives to be forced to use single-ended (SE) operation instead of LVD(low voltage differential).
- Disable Parity: Turns off parity checking on the SCSI bus, for compatibility with host adapters that do not support the features.

This is not all of all. Many SCSI drives have some additional special features that are enabled through more jumpers. Some drives have replaced some of their jumpers with software commands sent over the SCSI interface.

Logic Board

The newer hard disks drives have been introduced with a lot of features and faster speed in it and development is still on progress. To control all these functions and provide the disk's high performance features in advanced way in which they are expected to be, all modern hard disks are made with an intelligent circuit board integrated into the hard disk unit. This circuit board is called Hard Disk Logic Board. A logic board uses its following important components to provide a variety of functions and features to a hard disk:
- Control Circuitry
- Sense, Amplification and Conversion Circuits
- Interface Hardware
- Firmware
- Multiple Command Control and Reordering

Both of The two most common interfaces popular today for PC hard disks IDE (Integrated Drive Electronics) and SCSI (Small Computer Systems Interface) use integrated controllers. The more correct name for the IDE interface is AT Attachment or ATA (Advanced Technology Attachment). The modern hard disks have a very sophisticated logic board which contains more memory and faster internal processors than an entire PC of even the mid-1980s.

The logic board performs several important functions then before. Therefore the logic circuits needs to be more powerful, to handle changes like geometry translation, advanced reliability features, more complicated head technologies, faster interfaces, and higher bandwidth data streaming from the disk itself.

The internal logic board of a hard disk contains a microprocessor and internal memory, and other structures and circuits that control what happens inside the drive. Some of the most important functions of the control circuitry of the drive are as follows:
- Controlling the spindle motor, including making sure the spindle runs at the correct speed.
- Controlling the movement of actuator to various tracks.

- Managing all read and write operations.
- Implementing power management features.
- Handling geometry translation.
- Managing the internal cache and optimization features such as pre-fetch.
- Coordinating and integrating the other functions mentioned in this section, such as the flow of information over the hard disk interface, optimizing multiple requests, converting data to and from the form the read/write heads require it, etc.
- Implementing all advanced performance and reliability features.

The modern hard disks have internal microprocessors and most of them also have internal software that runs them. These routines run the control logic and make the drive work. In fact this is not really software in the conventional sense, because these instructions are embedded into read-only memory. This code is analogous to the system BIOS, low-level, hardware-based control routines, embedded in ROM. It is usually called *firmware*.

This is the reason why sometimes Firmware is called the middle link of hardware and software. In many drives the firmware can be updated under software control.

Cache and Cache Circuitry

The function of integrated cache (also often called a buffer) of a hard disk is to act as a buffer between a relatively fast device and a relatively slow one. For hard disks, the cache is used to hold the results of recent reads from the disk, and also to pre-fetch information that is likely to be requested in the near future, for example, the sector or sectors immediately after the one just requested.

Thus the purpose of this cache is not dissimilar to other caches used in the PC, even though it is not normally thought of as part of the regular PC cache hierarchy. You should always keep it in mind that when someone speaks generically about a disk cache, they are usually *not* referring to this small memory area inside the hard disk, but rather to a cache of system memory set aside to buffer accesses to the disk system.

The use of cache improves performance of any hard disk, by reducing the number of physical accesses to the disk on repeated reads and allowing data to stream from the disk uninterrupted when the bus is busy. Most modern hard disks have between 512 KB and 2 MB of internal cache memory even some high-performance SCSI drives have as much as 16 MB too.

The cache of a hard disk is important due to the sheer difference in the speeds of the hard disk and the hard disk interface. Finding a piece of data on the hard disk involves random positioning and incurs a penalty of *milliseconds* as the hard disk actuator is moved and the disk rotates around on the spindle. *That* is why hard disks have internal buffers.

The basic principle behind the operation of a simple cache is straightforward. Reading data from the hard disk is generally done in blocks of various sizes not just one 512-byte sector at a time. The cache is broken into segments or pieces each of which can contain one block of data.

When a request is made for data from the hard disk, the cache circuitry is first queried to see if the data is present in any of the segments of the cache. If it is present, it is supplied to the logic board without access to the hard disk platters being necessary. If the data is not in the cache, it is read from the hard disk, supplied to the controller and then placed into the cache in the event that it gets asked for again.

Since the cache is limited in size, there are only so many pieces of data that can be held before the segments must be recycled. Typically the oldest piece of data is replaced with the newest one. This is called *circular, first-in, first-out (FIFO)* or *wrap-around* caching.

In an effort to improve performance, most hard disk manufacturers today have implemented enhancements to their cache management circuitry, particularly on high-end SCSI drives:

- **Adaptive Segmentation:** Conventional caches are chopped into a number of equal sized segments. Since requests can be made for data blocks of different sizes, this can lead to some of the storage of the cache in some segments being left over and hence wasted. Many newer drives dynamically resize the segments based on how much space is required for each access, to ensure greater utilization. It can also change the number of segments. This is more complex to handle than fixed-size segments, and it can result in waste itself if the space is not managed properly.

- **Pre-Fetch:** The cache logic of a drive, based on analyzing access and usage patterns of the drive, attempts to load into part of the cache data that has not been requested yet but that it *anticipates* will be requested soon. Usually, this means loading additional data beyond that which was just read from the disk, since it is statistically more likely to be requested next. When done correctly, this will improve performance to some degree.

- **User Control:** High-end drives have implemented a set of commands that allows the user detailed control of the drive cache's operation. This includes letting the user enable or disable caching, set the size of segments, turn on or off adaptive segmentation and pre-fetch etc.

Though internal buffer is obviously improving performance yet it also has the limitations. It helps very little if.you are doing a lot of random accesses to data in different parts of the disk, because if the disk has not loaded a piece of data recently in the past, it will not be in the cache.

The buffer is also of little help if you are reading a large amount of data from the disk because normally it will be very small if you are copying a 50 MB file. For example, on a typical disk with a 512 Bytes buffer a very small part of the file could be in the buffer and the rest must be read from the disk itself.

Due to these limitations, the cache does not have as much of an impact on overall system performance as you might think. How much it helps depends on its size to some extent, but at least as much on the intelligence of its circuitry; just like the hard disk's logic overall. And just like the logic overall, it's hard to determine in many cases exactly what the cache logic on a given drive is like. However the size of the cache of the disk *is* important to its overall impact in improving the performance of the system.

Caching reads from the hard disk and caching writes to the hard disk are similar in some ways, but very different in others. They are the same in their overall objective that is to decouple the fast computer from the slow mechanics of the hard disk. The key difference is that a write involves a *change* to the hard disk while a read does not.

With no write caching, every write to the hard disk involves a performance hit while the system waits for the hard disk to access the correct location on the hard disk and write the data. This takes at least 10 milliseconds on most drives, which is a long time in the computer world and really slows down performance as the system waits for the hard disk. This mode of operation is called *write-through* caching.

When write caching is enabled and the system sends a write to the hard disk, the logic circuit records the write in its much faster cache and then immediately sends back an acknowledgement to the operating system for completion of process. The rest of the system can then proceed on its way without having to sit around waiting for the actuator to position and the disk to spin, and so on. This is called *write-back* caching, because the data is stored in the cache and only written back to the platters later on. Write-back functionality of course improves performance.

Since cache memory is volatile, if the power goes out, its contents are lost. If there were any pending writes in the cache that were not written to the disk yet, they are gone forever and the rest of the system has no way to know this because when it is told by the hard disk as the completion. Therefore not only is some data lost but also the system does not even know which data, or even that it happened. The end result can be file consistency problems, operating system corruption, and so on. Due to this risk, in some situations write caching is not used at all.

This is especially true for applications where high data integrity is critical. Due to the improvement in performance that write caching offers, however, it is increasingly being used despite the risk, and the risk is being mitigated through the use of additional technology.

The most common technique is simply ensuring that the power does not go off. For added peace of mind, better drives that employ write caching have a write flush feature that tells the drive to immediately write to disk any pending writes in its cache. This is a command that would commonly be sent before the UPS batteries ran out if a power interruption was detected by the system or just before the system was to be shut down for any other reason.

Low-level hard disk geometry

When we say low level hard disk geometry, we have not very much concerned to know the physical circuitry of the disk. Here we are going to discuss the terms with which we are going to deal now to understand the disk troubleshooting and data recovery programming above after.

The low level hard disk geometry is usually concerned with the following terms:
- Track
- Cylinder
- Sector
- Head or Side

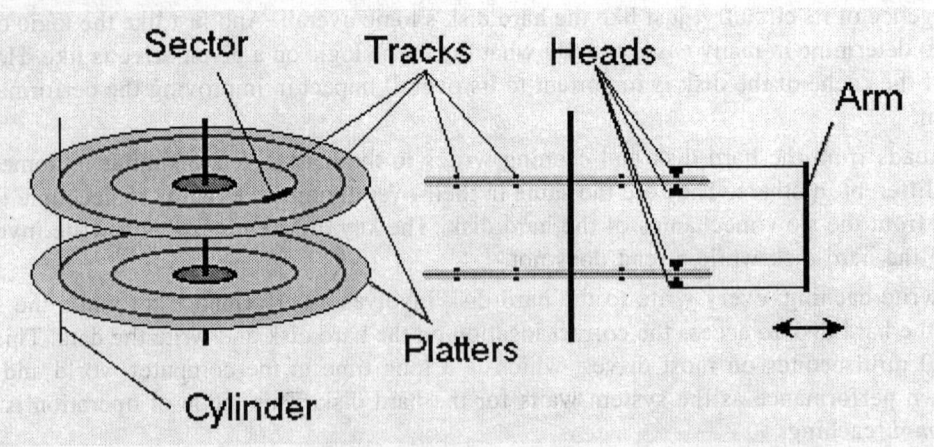

The platters of a hard disk have two sides for recording the data. Every surface of the platter has invisible concentric circles on it, which are written on the surface as magnetic information during

Introduction of Hard Disks

the formatting of the hard disk. These circles are called tracks. All information stored on a hard disk is recorded in tracks. The tracks are numbered, starting from 0, starting at the outside of the platter and increasing as you go in.

About the maximum number of tracks and cylinders, we shall discuss in detail in the next chapters. However for now we can get the knowledge of **physical low level geometry** of maximum numbers of Cylinders, Tracks, Heads (sides) and sectors.

Name	Start From	End Limit	Total Number
Cylinders	0	1023	1024
Heads	0	255	256
Sectors	1	63	63

In the surface of the platter of a hard disk, the data is accessed by moving the heads from the inner to the outer part of the disk. This organization of data allows for easy access to any part of the disk, which is why disks are called random access storage devices.

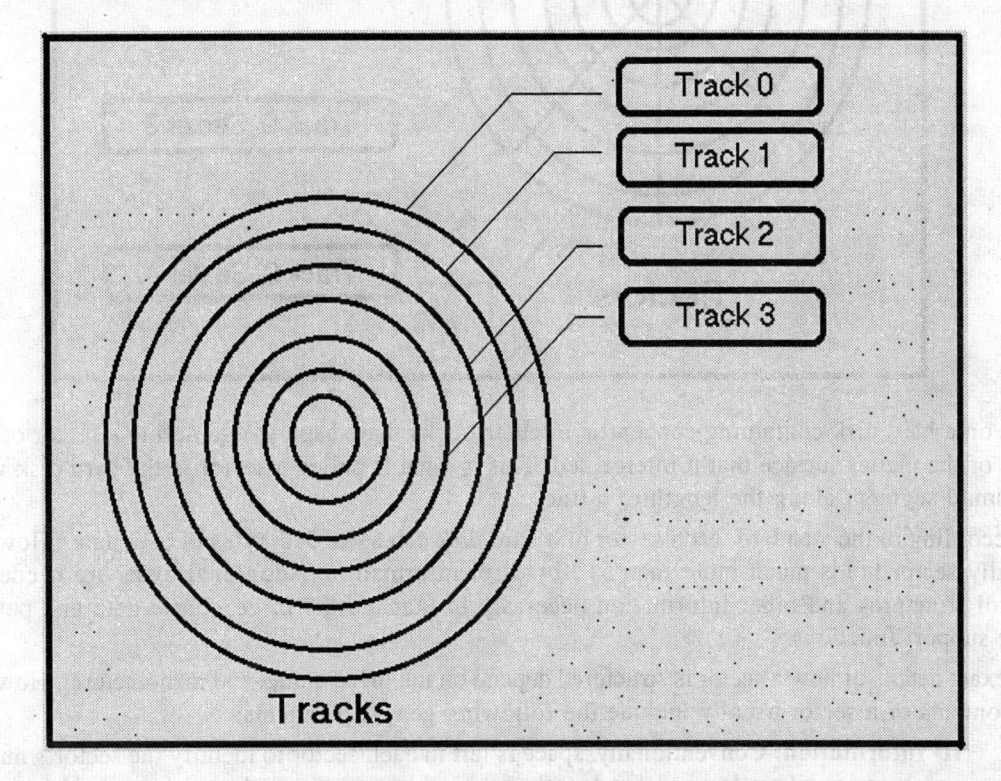

Each track can hold thousands of bytes of data and generally this storage is more than 5000 bytes. Therefore if we make a track the smallest unit of storage on the disk it will be the wastage of disk space, because by doing this the small files having the size less then 5000 bytes will waste the amount of space and generally it is quite possible to having a number of files in the disk which are much smaller than this size.

In this way making a track the smallest unit of storage will cause the small files to waste a large amount of space. Therefore, each track is broken into smaller units called *sectors*. The size of each sector is 512 bytes i.e. a sector can hold 512 bytes of information.

Thus the basic unit of data storage on a hard disk is the sector. The name *sector* refers to a pie-shaped angular section of a circle, bounded on two sides by radii and the third by the perimeter of the circle. You can see a logical figure representing sectors on a track given next.

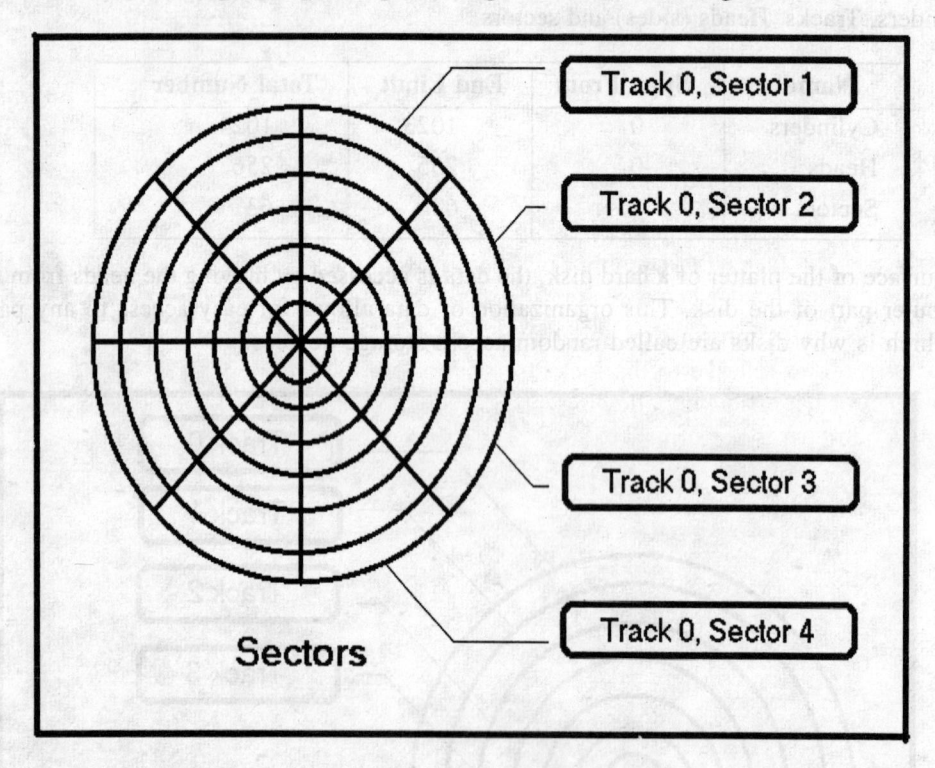

Thus on a hard disk containing concentric circular tracks that shape would define a sector of each track of the platter surface that it intercepted. This is what is called a sector in the hard disk world is a small segment along the length of a track.

As according to the standard, each sector of a hard disk can store 512 bytes of user data. However, actually sector holds much more than 512 bytes of information. Additional bytes are needed for control structures and other information necessary to manage the drive, locate data and perform other support functions.

The exact details of how a sector is structured depend on the drive model and manufacturer. However, the contents of a sector usually include the following general elements:

- **ID Information:** Conventionally, space is left in each sector to identify the sector's number and location. This is used for locating the sector on the disk and also includes status information about the sector in this area. For example, a bit is commonly used to indicate if the sector has been marked defective and remapped.
- **Synchronization Fields:** These are used internally by the drive controller to guide the read process.
- **Data:** The actual data in the sector.

Introduction of Hard Disks

- **Error Correcting Codes (ECC):** Error correcting codes are used to ensure data integrity.
- **Gaps:** Gaps are basically one or more spacers added as necessary to separate other areas of the sector, or provide time for the controller to process what it has read before reading more bits.

In addition to the sectors, each containing the items described, space on each track is also used for servo information. The amount of space taken up by each sector for overhead items is important, because the more bits used for this management, the fewer overall that can be used for data.

This is the reason that the hard disk manufacturers strive to reduce the amount of non-user data information that must be stored on the disk. The percentage of bits on each disk that are used for data, as opposed to other things as described before is known as format efficiency. Therefore the higher format efficiency is an expected feature of a drive.

In the latest approach to get the higher format efficiency now days, the ID fields are removed from the sector format and instead of labeling each sector within the sector header a format map is stored in memory and referenced when a sector must be located.

This map also contains information about the sectors which have been marked bad and relocated where the sectors are relative to the location of servo information and so on. This approach not only improves format efficiency allowing up to 10% more data to be stored on the surface of each platter but also improves performance. Since this critical positioning information is present in high-speed memory, it can be accessed much more quickly.

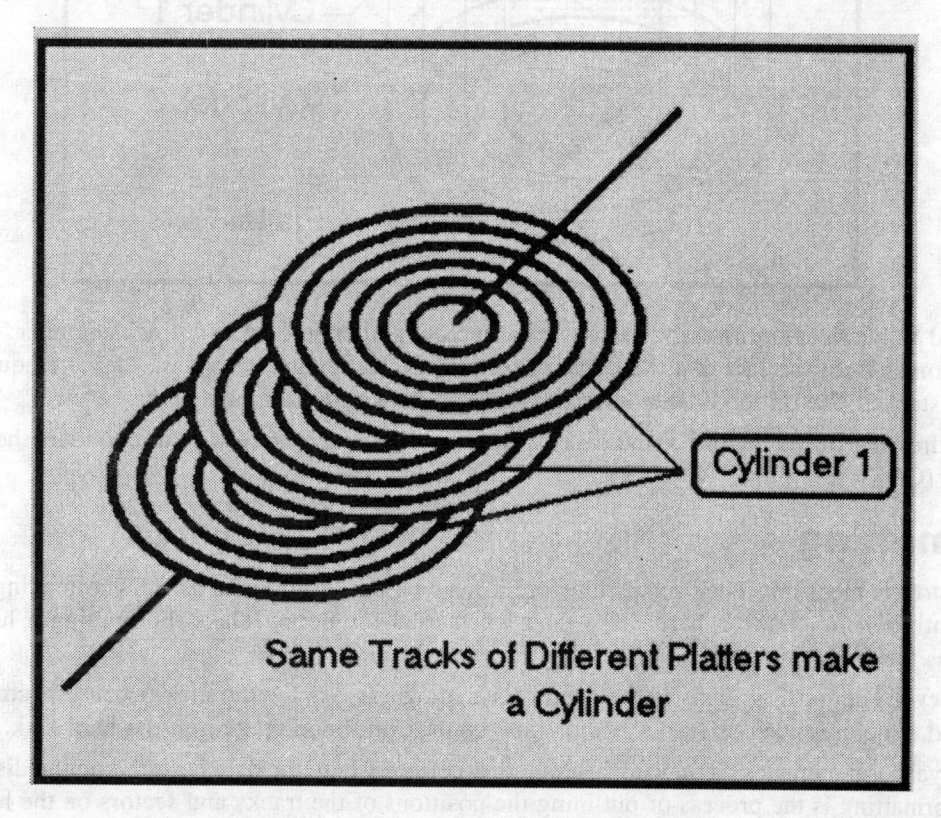

Same Tracks of Different Platters make a Cylinder

Each platter of the hard disk uses two heads (except some special cases) to record and read data, one for the top of the platter and one for the bottom. The heads that access the platters are locked together on an assembly of head arms therefore all the heads move in and out together, so each head is always physically located at the same track number.

This is the reason that it is not possible to have one head at track 0 and another at track 1,000. Because of this arrangement, often the track location of the heads is not referred to as a track number but rather as a cylinder number.

A cylinder is basically the set of all tracks that all the heads are currently located at. If a disk has four platters, in general case it would have eight heads. Now suppose it has cylinders number 720.

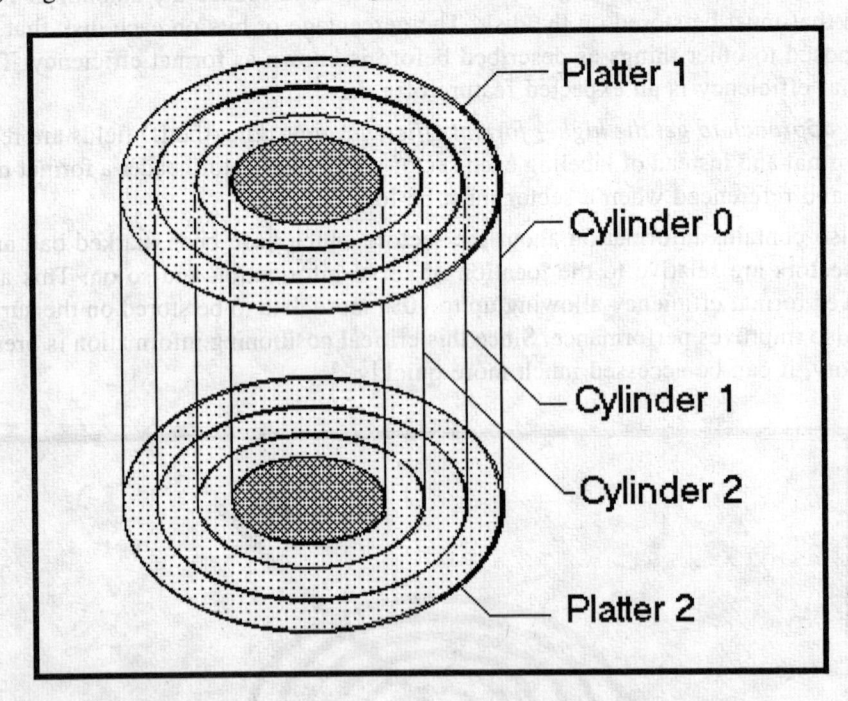

It would be made up of the eight set of tracks, one per platter surface with tracks number 720. The name comes from the fact that these tracks form a skeletal cylinder because they are equal-sized circles stacked one on top of the other in space, as shown in the figure given before.

The addressing of the factors of the disk is traditionally done by referring to cylinders, heads and sectors (CHS).

Formatting

Every storage media must be formatted before it can be used. The utilities used for formatting behave differently when acting on hard disks than when used for floppy disks. Formatting a hard disk involves the following steps:

Low-Level Formatting: This is the actual formatting process for the disk because it creates the physical structures such as tracks, sectors and control information etc., on the hard disk.

Low level format creates the physical format that defines where the data is stored on the disk. Low-level formatting is the process of outlining the positions of the tracks and sectors on the hard disk and writing the control structures that define where the tracks and sectors are.

The first time that a low-level format is performed on a hard disk, the platters of the disk start out empty and that is the last time the platters will be empty for the life of the drive, if you have not used the data wiper or zero-fill utility on it later. The zero-fill utilities are used to wipe out the hard disk platters as like new by erasing all the data on it.

Partitioning: This process divides the disk into logical parts that assign different hard disk volumes or drive letters.

Hard drive partitioning is one of the most effective methods available for organizing hard drives. Partitions provide a more general level of organization than directories and files. They also offer greater security by separating data from operating systems and applications.

Partitions allow you to separate data files, which must be backed up regularly from program and operating system files. Partitioning becomes a necessity for the hard drive if you are willing to load, more than one operating systems in the disk otherwise in most of the cases it is possible that you may lose your data.

The first sector of any hard drive contains a partition table. This partition table only has room to describe four partitions. These are called primary partitions. One of these primary partitions can point to a chain of additional partitions. Each partition in this chain is called a logical partition. We shall discuss the partition basics with logical approach in details, in the next chapters.

High-Level Formatting: It defines the logical structures on the partition and places at the start of the disk any necessary operating system files. This step is also an operating system-level command.

The FORMAT command of DOS that is FORMAT.COM, behaves differently when it is used on a hard disk than when it is used on a floppy disk. Floppy disks have simple, standard geometry and cannot be partitioned, so the FORMAT command is programmed to automatically both low-level and high-level format a floppy disk, if necessary but in case of hard disks, FORMAT will only do a high-level format.

When we have completed low–level formatting, we have a disk with tracks and sectors but nothing written on them. *High-level formatting* is the process of writing the file system structures on the disk that let the disk be used for storing programs and data.

If you are using DOS, the FORMAT command (that is FORMAT.COM), performs this work by writing such structures as the DOS boot record file allocation tables and root directories to the disk. High-level formatting is done after the hard disk has been partitioned.

Formatted and Unformatted Storage Capacity

The total storage of a hard disk depends on, if you are looking at the formatted or unformatted capacity. Some portion of the space on a hard disk is taken up by the formatting information that marks the start and end of sectors, ECC (Error Correction Codes) and other overhead information. For this reason, the difference can be quite significant.

Older drives that were typically low-level formatted by the user often had their size listed in terms of unformatted capacity. For example, take the Seagate ST-412, the first drive used on the original IBM PC/XT in the early 1980s. The "12" in this model number refers to the drive's unformatted capacity of 12.76 MB. Formatted, it is actually a 10.65 MB drive.

Unformatted capacity of a hard disk is generally 19% (19 percent) higher than its formatted capacity. Since nobody can use a drive that is unformatted, the only thing that matters is the formatted capacity and therefore modern drives are always low-level formatted by the manufacturers.

The capacity of a hard disk can be expressed in the following four ways:
- Formatted capacity in millions of bytes
- Formatted capacity in megabytes
- Unformatted capacity in millions of bytes
- Unformatted capacity in megabytes

Now if I have a hard disk with C–H–S = 1024*63*63 (It means that the disk has number of cylinder = 1024, number of heads or sides = 63 number of sectors per track = 63) and every sector having 512 bytes. The formula that will calculate the size of the disk is as follows:

$$\text{Total Size of the Disk (Bytes)} = (\text{Cylinders}) \times (\text{Heads}) \times (\text{Sectors}) \times (\text{Bytes per Sector})$$

By this formula when we calculate the size of the given hard disk in bytes, it will be

$$= 1024 \times 63 \times 63 \times 512$$
$$= 2080899072 \text{ Bytes}$$

Now if I calculate the Size of my disk in millions of bytes, it will be approximately

$$= 2080.899072$$
$$\sim 2081 \text{ millions of byte}$$

Traditionally size in millions of byte is represented by M. Therefore the size of my disk in millions of bytes is approximately 2081 M.

But when I tell the capacity of my hard disk in Megabytes, It will be approximately 1985 and will be written as 1985 Meg.

The reason behind this is that Size of the disk in megabytes is obtained by dividing the size of the disk in Bytes twice by 1024. Thus it comes approximately 1985 Meg.

In this way the general formula to calculate the capacity of disk in Millions of byte will be as follows:

$$\text{Disk Capacity in millions of Byte} = \frac{(\text{Cylinders} \times \text{Heads} \times \text{Sectors} \times \text{Bytes per Sector})}{1,000,000} \text{ M}$$

And general formula for calculating the capacity of the disk in Megabyte will be given as follows:

$$\text{Disk Capacity in Megabytes} = \frac{(\text{Cylinders} \times \text{Heads} \times \text{Sectors} \times \text{Bytes per Sector})}{1024 \times 1024} \text{ Meg}$$

Chapter – 3
Logical Approach to Disks and OS

The hard disk can not run its hardware it self and needs two basic software to run its operations, the BIOS (Basic Input Output System) and The DOS (or Operating System). The disk operating system does not directly talk to the hardware of computer and hard disk but it needs the BIOS in between. That is why the BIOS has taken an important role in the computer.

BIOS

The basic job of BIOS is to provide a standard interface between the hardware or the devices connected to the computer and the DOS. The system BIOS is the lowest-level interface between the hardware of your system and the software that runs on it. It has several significant roles that it plays in the control of access to hard disks such as

- **BIOS Interrupt Routines**
- **Hard Disk Detection and Configuration**
- **Hard Disk Interface Mode Support**

To ensure the interoperability of various hardware and software products, the BIOS of the system is tailored to the needs of its hardware, and provides a standard way of letting software addressing the hardware. These are called BIOS services and are used by many operating system and application programs. They provide a uniform interface to the hard disk, so applications need not to know how to talk to each type of hard disk individually.

Standard IDE/ATA hard disks are configured in the BIOS using various BIOS settings. Modern BIOS programs can detect modern IDE/ATA disks to determine these parameters and automatically configure them. The BIOS controls which types of interface modes can be used with the hard disk, working with the system chipset on the motherboard and the system I/O bus.

The INT 13H Interface and INT 13H Extensions

The primary interface to the BIOS has been the software interrupt 13H which is generally known as INT 13H, where INT stands for interrupt and 13H is the number 19 in hexadecimal notation.

We shall learn and discuss the use of interrupts in programming in detail in the programming phase of this book. The Int13H interface supports many different commands that can be given to the BIOS, which then passes them on to the hard disk. The interrupt 13H include most of the tasks we need to perform with the disk such as reading, writing, formatting etc.

The use and work with Int13H requires the invoking program to know the specific parameters of the hard disk, and provide exact head, cylinder and sector addressing to the routines to allow disk access.

The BIOS uses the geometry for the hard disk as it is set up in the BIOS setup program. The Int13H interface allocates 24 bits for the specification of the geometry of the drive, broken up as follows:

- 10 bits for the cylinder number, or a total of 1,024 cylinders.
- 8 bits for the head number, or a total of 256 heads.
- 6 bits for the sector number, or a total of 63 sectors.

Thus the maximum possible number of sectors in the disk can be

= 1024 * 256 * 63

= 16515072

As we see here that the INT 13H interface can support disks containing up to 16515072 sectors with 512 bytes per sector. Thus the maximum disk size may be,

= 16515072 * 512

= 8455716864 Bytes

~ 8.456 GB

Thus the INT 13H interface can support the disk size approximately up to 8.456 GB (or 7.875 GiB).

Today most of the computer users use the hard disks which is much bigger in capacity then 8 GB that is why, the INT 13H interface has finally come to the end of its usefulness in modern computer systems and has been replaced with a newer interface called INT 13H extensions however INT 13H still may be used by DOS and some other older operating systems, and for other compatibility purposes.

Int13H Extensions

It is really an interesting story that when INT 13H interface was developed, nobody ever expect to get the 8 GB size in hard disk. However today we may feel an 8 GB hard disk much smaller in capacity, even for home user's personal computer.

The older standard has an important limitation that it uses 24 bits of addressing information and as such can only handle drives that contain up to 16515072 sectors with 512 bytes per sector that yields a maximum capacity of 8.456 GB (or 7.875 GiB).

Thus the problem was to widen the access path from 24 bits to something larger but it was not possible to expand the existing INT13H BIOS interface because if we try to do this a lot of older hardware and software would stop working. And practically, there is no hope to get the respectable place in computer world with a lot of older hardware and software not working with your development.

Therefore a new interface was developed to replace Int13H. These routines are called *Int13H* *extensions*. This new interface uses 64 bits instead of 24 bits for addressing and allows a maximum hard drive size of 9.4 * 10^{21} bytes that is 9.4 trillion gigabytes.

We shall learn the use of both, the INT 13H and INT 13H extensions in the programming section of this book. There are a number of other size limitations that took place in the earlier days. Some of the popular logical and physical limits have been described below:

The 2.1 GB limit

This size limit was observed in some older BIOSes which only allocate 12 bits for the field in CMOS RAM that gives the number of cylinders. Therefore this number may be at most **111111111111B** (Maximum possible 12-Bit Binary Number) which is equivalent to **4095**. In this way the maximum disk size with 16 heads, which can be accessed, will be:

= **4095 * 16 * 63 * 512** Bytes

= **2113413120** Bytes are accessible.

The 33.8 GB limit

This hard disk size barrier was noticed in early 1999. Large disks report 16 heads, 63 sectors/track and 16383 cylinders. Many BIOSes compute an actual number of cylinders by dividing the total capacity by 16*63.

For disks larger than 33.8 GB this leads to a number of cylinders larger than 65535. In this particular case, some versions of Award BIOS cannot handle drives that have more than 65,535 cylinders. Now the BIOS crashes or hangs. Since hard disk parameters usually use 16 heads and 63 sectors, this works out to a capacity of about 33.8 GB or 31.5 GiB before trouble occurs.

The solution is to upgrade the BIOS or one can use a jumper to make the disk appear smaller.

ATA Specification for IDE Disks - The 137 GB limit

The old ATA specification does not allow access to a disk that is larger than 137 GB. Actually, it uses only 28 bits to specify a sector number. However, ATA-6 defines an extension with 48-bit sector number.

The limit of the disk size was generated with the combination of at most 65536 cylinders counting from 0 to 65535, 16 heads counting from 0 to15 and 255 sectors per track counting from 1 to 255, the maximum total capacity of disk,

= **65535 * 16 * 255** Sectors

= **267386880** Sectors

= **136902082560** Bytes (Sector of 512 Bytes Each)

~ **137 GB**

Two and Four Disk BIOS IDE Support

Today Most of the modern BIOS programs support hard disk auto detection, which allows the BIOS to interrogate each hard disk to determine its logical geometry, supported transfer modes and other information. This can be done either at setup time or dynamically each time the machine is booted, depending on the BIOS.

The system BIOS provides native support for IDE/ATA hard disks therefore there may be a number of parameters that can be set to tell the BIOS what hard disks are in the system and how to control them. Each hard disk in the system will have its own settings so there is one set for the primary master and one for the primary slave and so on. However SCSI hard disks are configured through their host adapter and built-in SCSI BIOS.

Since the hard disk drives over 8 GB in size cannot be described using traditional IDE/ATA BIOS geometry parameters therefore the dynamic auto detection is the standard way of setting up modern drives, especially in case of older computer systems however user may still set some drive parameters manually.

Following are the settings normally found in the BIOS setup program for configuring IDE/ATA hard disks. Although on modern systems some of the oldest compatibility settings may not even be present any more:

- **Disk Type:** it was originally used to allow the user to pick his hard disk from a predefined list but now this is used to control automatic or manual parameter setup for the drive.
- **Size:** Size of the Hard Disk drive in decimal megabytes. It is calculated from the other parameters like Cylinders, Heads and Sectors etc.
- **Cylinders:** The number of logical cylinders on the disk.
- **Heads:** The number of logical heads on the disk.
- **Sectors:** The number of logical sectors each of 512 bytes, in each logical track on the disk. Usually modern hard disk drives have 63 sectors on a single track.
- **Write Precompensation:** it is a compatibility setting that specifies at which cylinder number write adjustments should be made for very much older drives.
- **Landing Zone (Parking Heads):** Landing Zone is the cylinder where the heads are parked by the BIOS to avoid the data loss or creation of Bad Sectors, when the drive is shut off. As the modern hard disk drives automatically park their heads it is rarely needed today.
- **Translation Mode:** The BIOS translation mode used to support the hard disks over 504 MB.
- **Block Mode:** To Control the BIOS's ability to perform disk transfers in blocks.
- **Programmed I/O (DMA) Mode:** The programmed I/O mode or DMA mode used to perform transfers to and from the hard disk.

32-Bit Transfer Mode: Controls the use of higher-performance 32-bit data transfers.

Limitations in File Systems

Each file system supports a maximum volume size, file size, and number of files per volume. For example, generally FAT16 and FAT32 volumes are limited to 4 GB and 32 GB (Generally) respectively. There are some limitations related to FAT file systems you must know, given below:

- **FAT12:** FAT volumes smaller than 16 MB are formatted as FAT12. It is the oldest FAT type and uses a 12-bit binary to hold cluster numbers. A volume formatted using FAT12 can hold a maximum of 4,086 clusters, which is equal to 2^{12} minus a few reserved values to be used in FAT. (We shall discuss it in detail in the logical structure of the disk given next in this chapter). Therefore FAT12 is most suitable for smaller volumes. It is used on floppy disks and hard disk partitions smaller than about 16 MB.

Logical Approach to Disks and OS

- **FAT16:** The FAT16 uses a 16-bit binary number to hold cluster numbers. A volume using FAT16 can hold a maximum of 65,526 clusters, which is equal to 2^{16} minus a few reserved values to be used in FAT. (We shall discuss it in detail in the logical structure of the disk given next in this chapter). FAT16 is used for hard disk volumes ranging in size from 16 MB to 2,048 MB. FAT16 volumes larger than 2 GB are not accessible from computers running MS-DOS, Windows 95/98/ME and many other operating systems. This limitation occurs because these operating systems do not support cluster sizes larger than 32 KB, which results in the 2 GB limit. (See the Clusters limit given next in this chapter).

- **FAT32:** In theory, the maximum FAT32 volumes may be up to 2048 GB (approximately 2 Terabytes). The FAT32 is supported by Windows 95's OEM SR2 release, as well as Windows 98/ME. FAT32 uses a 28-bit binary cluster number (Remember! not 32, because 4 of the 32 bits are "Reserved"). Thus theoretically FAT32 can handle volumes with over 268 million clusters (Actually 268,435,456 clusters), and will support drives up to 2 TB in size. However to do this the size of the FAT grows very large. (We are going to discuss it in the topics given next in this chapter).

The comparison of FAT Types has been given next, in the table.

File System Attribute	FAT12	FAT16	FAT32
Used For...	Floppies and small hard disk volumes	Small to large hard disk volumes	Medium to very large hard disk volumes
Size of Each FAT Entry	12 Bits	16 Bits (2 Bytes)	32 Bits (4 Bytes)
Maximum Number of Clusters	4,086	65,526	~268,435,456
Cluster Size Used	0.5 KiB to 4 KiB	2 KiB to 64 KiB	4 KiB to 32 KiB
Maximum Volume Size	16,736,256 Bytes	2,147,483,648 Bytes	2,199,023,255,552 Bytes (about 2 Terabytes or 2^{41} Bytes)
Maximum File Size	Less then 16MB (Approximate)	2,147,483,520 Bytes	4,294,967,295 Bytes ($2^{32} - 1$)
Maximum Files and Directories within the Root Directory	128/512(128 for 3½ 1.44MB FDD and 512 for Hard Disk Drives)	(Long file names can reduce the number of available files and Directories in the root Directory.)	65,534(Long file names can reduce the number of available files and Directories in the root Directory.)

- **NTFS:** NTFS stands for New Technology File System. It is used by Windows 2000/XP. In theory, the maximum NTFS partition size is ($2^{64} - 1$) clusters.

The detailed description of NTFS File System is beyond the limit of this book however some limitations of it have been given in the following table:

Description	Limit
Maximum file size	16 Exabytes − 1 KB (2^{64} Bytes − 1 KB)
Maximum volume size	(2^{64} − 1) clusters
Files (and Folders) per volume	4,294,967,295 (2^{32} − 1) Flies and Folders

Cluster

The smallest unit of space on the hard disk for allocation that any software can access is the sector, which contains 512 bytes. It is possible to have an allocation system for the disk where each file is assigned as many individual sectors as it needs. For example, a 1 MB file would require approximately 2,048 individual sectors to store its data.

In case of FAT file system or rather we can say in most of the file systems, individual sectors are not used. There are several performance reasons for this. When DOS writes some information onto the hard disk, it does not allocate the space sector wise, instead it uses a new unit of storage called **cluster**.

FAT was designed many years ago and is a simple file system, and is not capable of managing individual sectors. What FAT does instead is to group sectors into larger blocks that are called clusters or allocation units.

A cluster is the smallest unit of disk space that can be allocated to a file. This is the reason that the clusters are often called allocation units. It may be very difficult to manage the disk when files are broken into 512-byte pieces.

A 20 GB disk volume using 512 byte sectors managed individually would contain over 41 million individual sectors, and keeping track of this many pieces of information is time and resource consuming. However some operating systems do allocate space to files by the sector but they require some advanced intelligence to do this properly.

Clusters are the minimum space allocated by the DOS when storing any information on the disk. Even to store only one byte long information on the disk requires minimum one cluster area on the disk surface.

If one cluster can store 512 bytes of information then to store 513 bytes you will require two clusters. Every file must be allocated an integer number of clusters. This means that if a volume uses clusters that contain 4,096 bytes then a 610 byte file will use one cluster thus 4,096 bytes on the disk but a 4,097 byte file uses two clusters thus 8,192 bytes on the disk.

This is the reason that cluster size is so important to make you sure to maximize the efficient use of the disk. Thus we can understand that the larger cluster sizes result the more wasted space.

The figure given next, shows the properties of a file named BINARY.C and clarifies the fact of the space used by the file in the disk. The actual size of the file is 610 bytes but as the single cluster is of 4,096 bytes, the file uses one cluster (4,096 bytes) in the disk.

Logical Approach to Disks and OS

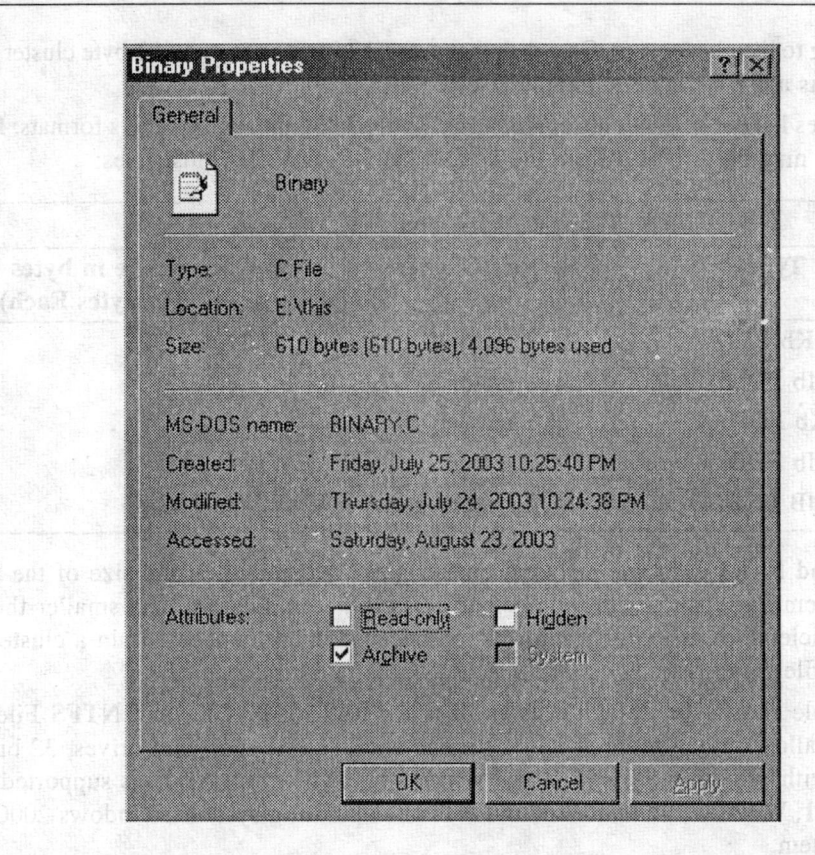

[Screenshot of a "Binary Properties" dialog box showing General tab with: Type: C File; Location: E:\this; Size: 610 bytes (610 bytes), 4,096 bytes used; MS-DOS name: BINARY.C; Created: Friday, July 25, 2003 10:25:40 PM; Modified: Thursday, July 24, 2003 10:24:38 PM; Accessed: Saturday, August 23, 2003; Attributes: Archive checked, Read-only, Hidden, System unchecked.]

A cluster can be made of one or more sectors. It depends on the disk type being used. As a cluster can be made of more than one sector, use of clusters as the allocation unit reduces the size of the File Allocation Table that DOS uses to hold the information of the used and empty disk space.

The cluster size is determined primarily by the size of the disk volume. If not strictly speaking, generally larger volumes use larger cluster sizes. For hard disk volumes, each cluster ranges in size from 4 sectors (2,048 bytes) to 64 sectors (32,768 bytes).

Floppy disks use much smaller clusters, and in some cases use a cluster of size of just 1 sector. The sectors in a cluster are continuous, so each cluster is a continuous block of space on the disk.

The cluster size and thus partition or volume size because they are directly related, has an important impact on performance and disk utilization. The cluster size is determined when the disk volume is partitioned.

There are some utilities like **Partition Magic** available that can alter the cluster size of an existing partition being within the limits of specific conditions but for the general cases, once the partition size and cluster size is selected it is fixed.

As we have discussed earlier that cylinder or track number starts from 0 and the first sector number is always taken as 1 and one more thing you should remember is that the first cluster number is always taken as 2.

Cluster Size

Clusters are used to allocate the storage area for the data area only. FAT and directory area is not allocated according to the cluster size. On a disk that uses 512-byte sectors, a 512-byte cluster contains one sector, whereas a 4-KB cluster contains 8 sectors.

The following tables list the default cluster sizes used by the DOS for various disks formats. However the size of cluster may be different from the default size in some circumstances:

Floppy Disk Drive (FDD)		
Drive Types	**Sectors/Cluster**	**Total Cluster size in bytes (Sectors of 512 bytes Each)**
5.25" 360Kb FDD	2 sectors	1,024
5.25"1.2Mb FDD	1 sector	512
3.5" 720Kb FDD	2 sectors	1,024
3.5"1.44Mb FDD	1 sector	512
3.5"2.88MB FDD	2 sectors	1,024

FAT16, FAT32, and NTFS each use different cluster sizes depending on the size of the partition and each file system has a maximum number of clusters it can support. The smaller the cluster size, the more efficiently a disk stores information because unused space within a cluster cannot be used by other files.

The following table shows the default cluster sizes for **FAT16**, **FAT32**, and **NTFS** File system partition. FAT 32 allows much more efficient storage and use of larger hard drives, 32 bit FAT is only compatible with Windows 95 OSR-2 and Windows 98/ME and. FAT 16 is supported by MS-DOS, Windows 3.1, Windows 95 and Windows NT. The operating systems Windows 2000/XP use the NTFS file system.

Hard Disk Drive (HDD)			
Partition Size	**FAT16 Cluster Size**	**FAT32 Cluster Size**	**NTFS Cluster Size**
7 MB–16 MB	2 KiB	Not supported	512 Bytes
17 MB–32 MB	512 Bytes	Not supported	512 Bytes
33 MB–64 MB	1 KiB	512 Bytes	512 Bytes
65 MB–128 MB	2 KiB	1 KiB	512 Bytes
129 MB–256 MB	4 KiB	2 KiB	512 Bytes
257 MB–512 MB	8 KiB	4 KiB	512 Bytes
513 MB–1,024 MB	16 KiB	4 KiB	1 KiB
1,025 MB–2 GB	32 KiB	4 KiB	2 KiB
2 GB–4 GB	64 KiB	4 KiB	4 KiB
4 GB–8 GB	Not supported	4 KiB	4 KiB
8 GB–16 GB	Not supported	8 KiB	4 KiB
16 GB–32 GB	Not supported	16 KiB	4 KiB
32 GB –2 Terabytes	Not supported	32 KiB	4 KiB

> **Note:** Here 1 KiB has been written for 1 Binary Kilobyte that means that 1 KiB is of 1024 Bytes or we can say two sectors of 512 Bytes are equivalent of 1KiB.

As the size of FAT16 partition increases, the wastage of disk space is also increases. The use of FAT32 reduces the cluster sizes and thus provides an efficient storage. While FAT32 does allow the use of larger hard disks and greatly reduced cluster sizes, there is an important performance consideration in using FAT32 that the huge hard disks with dozens of gigabytes have made FAT32 essential for newer systems. Rather we can say that you often do not have a practical choice between FAT16 and FAT32 any more.

Let us consider a partition of 2,048 MB, the largest that FAT16 can support. If this partition is set up under FAT16, it will result in a file allocation table with 65,526 clusters in it, with each cluster taking up 32 KiB of disk space.

The large cluster size will indeed result a big wastage of disk space. Therefore it will be recommended that FAT32 should be used on this partition, which will result in the cluster size reduced from 32 KiB to 4 KiB.

In fact, this will reduce slack on the disk by an enormous amount which may be up to 30% and potentially free hundreds of megabytes of previously wasted disk space. It is usually the right thing to do in this situation. However it has another side of it. We do not get this reduced cluster size for free.

Since each cluster is smaller, there have to be more of them to cover the same amount of disk. So instead of 65,526 clusters, we will now have 524,208.

Further more, the FAT entries in FAT32 are 32–bits wide (Each entry of 4 Bytes) whereas the entries of FAT16 are of 16–bit (Entry of 2 Bytes each). The end result is that the size of the FAT is 16 times larger for FAT32 than it is for FAT16. The following table summarizes:

FAT 16 and FAT 32 for 2,048 MB Disk Volume		
FAT Type	FAT16	FAT32
Cluster Size	32 KiB	4 KiB
Number of FAT Entries	65,526	524,208
Size of FAT	131052 Bytes (~ 128 KiB)	096832 Bytes (~ 2 MiB)

If we increase the size of the FAT32 volume from 2 GB in size to 8 GB, the size of the FAT increases from around 2 MiB to 8 MiB. The significance of this is not the fact that the FAT32 volume will have to waste several megabytes of space on the disk to hold the FAT. Because only by doing this it is saving far more space than that by reducing the size of FAT. The real problem is that the FAT holds all the cluster pointers for every file in the volume. Having the FAT greatly increase in size can negatively impact system speed.

For this reason it is important to limit the size of the File Allocation Table to a reasonably-sized number. In fact, in most cases it is a matter of finding a balance between cluster size and FAT size. A good illustration of this is the cluster size selections made by FAT32 itself.

Since FAT32 can handle around 268 million maximum clusters, the 4 KiB cluster size is conceptually able to support a disk volume 1 TiB (1,024 GiB) in size but the problem in doing so is that the FAT size then would be reach over 1 GB as according to 268 million times 4 bytes per entry.

For this reason, FAT32 only uses 4 KiB clusters for volumes up to 8 GiB in size, and then larger clusters are used as shown in the table given before, for Cluster Sizes. The maximum partition size supported by FAT32, which is officially declare is 2,048 GiB (2 TiB).

Logical Structure of a Hard Disk

Basically, we can divide the logical structure of the hard disk in the following five logical terms

- MBR (Master Boot Record)
- DBR (DOS Boot Record)
- FAT(s) (File Allocation Tables)
- Root Directory

The following figure represents the conceptual arrangement of these logical terms forming the logical structure of a hard disk:

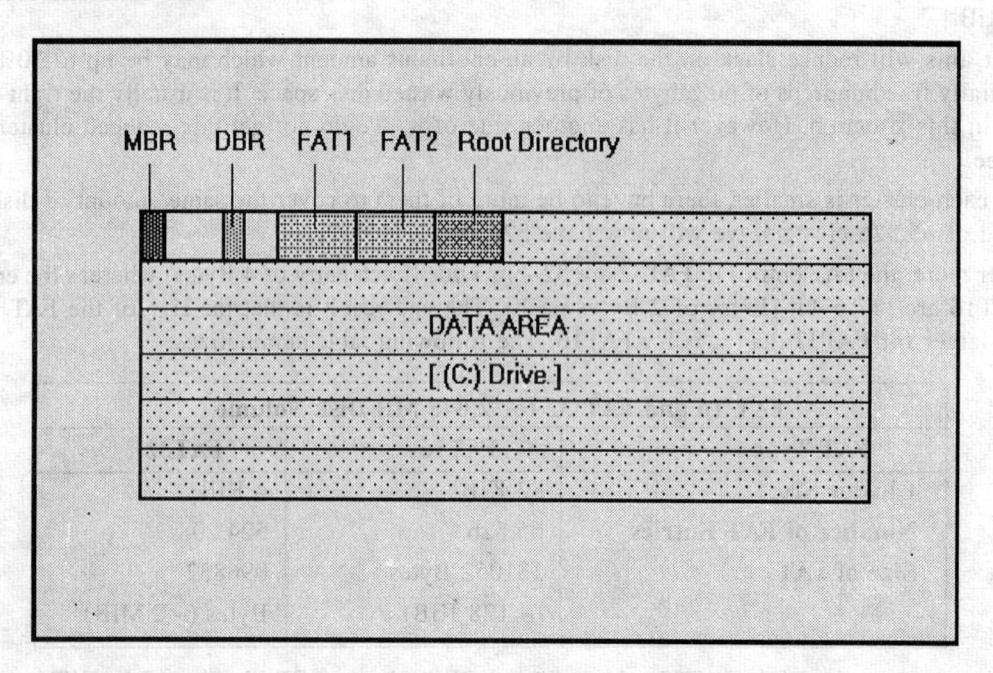

Master Boot Record (MBR) or Master Partition Table (MPT)

The Master Boot Record (MBR) or sometimes referred as The master partition table (MPT), contains a small program to load and start the active (or bootable) partition from the hard disk drive. The Master boot Record contains information about all four primary partitions on the hard disk drive such as the starting sector, ending sector, size of the partition etc.

The MBR is located at Absolute Sector 0 or we can say at cylinder 0, head 0, and sector1 and if there is more than one partition are present in the disk there are Extended Master Boot Records, located at the beginning of each extended partition volume (See the figure given Next).

Logical Approach to Disks and OS

The MBR is created on the hard disk drive by executing FDISK.EXE command of DOS. However there are many other software are available to do the same task. Using the FDISK any one of these partition can be made active or bootable.

This allows the boot sector of the active partition to receive the control when the system is started. Since the floppy has no partitions on it therefore there is no MBR on a Floppy.

Since the DOS uses a single upper case alphabet to name a partition, the maximum number of all type of partitions together allowed by DOS is 24, starting from the drive letter C (C:) to Drive letter Z (Z:). Therefore if even there are more than one physical hard disk drives are present, the total number of partitions of all the drives can not exceed 24.

After the Power-On Self Test (POST), the BIOS loads the MBR (Master Boot Record) from the Hard Disk into memory and then executes it. First the MBR checks the Hard disk for an Active Partition, then it loads the DOS Boot Record (DBR) into memory and turns control over to the Operating System Boot code and then the Operating System Boot Record code loads the rest of the Operating System into Memory.

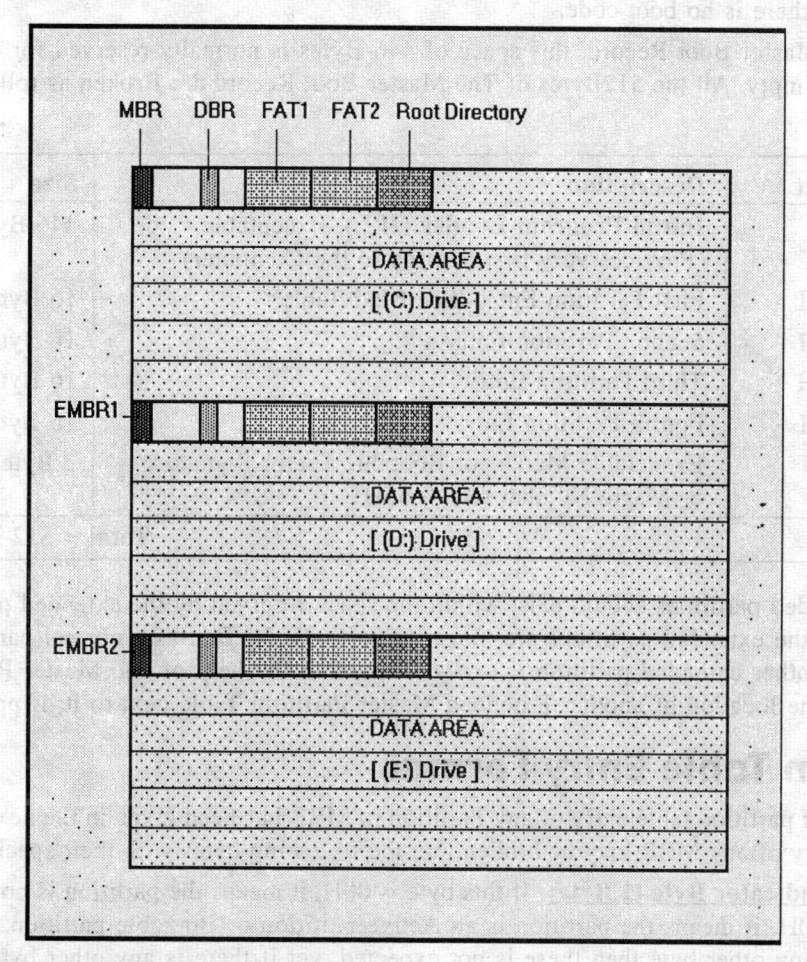

```
         MBR   DBR  FAT1  FAT2  Root Directory

                    DATA AREA
                    [ (C:) Drive ]

EMBR1

                    DATA AREA
                    [ (D:) Drive ]

EMBR2

                    DATA AREA
                    [ (E:) Drive ]
```

Master Boot Record Format

We may partition the Hard Disk Drive into several logical drives which are generally assigned their own drive letter by DOS. Only one partition at a time can be marked as the active (or bootable) Partition.

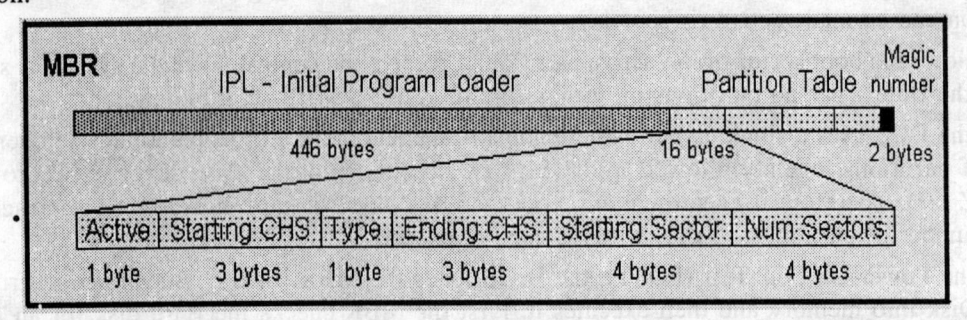

MBR | IPL - Initial Program Loader | Partition Table | Magic number
446 bytes | 16 bytes | 2 bytes

| Active | Starting CHS | Type | Ending CHS | Starting Sector | Num Sectors |
| 1 byte | 3 bytes | 1 byte | 3 bytes | 4 bytes | 4 bytes |

The Master Boot Record has the limit of four entries in the Master Partition Table. However the location of Extended Master Boot Record can be obtained with the help of Master Boot Record that contains Extended Partition Tables, whose format is exactly the same as of the main Partition Table except there is no boot code.

In extended Master Boot Record, this space of 446 Bytes is normally reserved for the boot code and remains empty. All the 512Bytes of The Master Boot Record are Broken as follows, given in the Table:

Offset	Description	Size
000H	**Initial Program Loader (IPL)**, Executable Code (Provides very first booting to the Computer)	446 Bytes
1BEH	First Partition Entry (See Next Table)	16 Bytes
1CEH	Second Partition Entry	16 Bytes
1DEH	Third Partition Entry	16 Bytes
1EEH	Fourth Partition Entry	16 Bytes
1FEH	Executable Marker or Bootable Sector Signature or Magic Number (AAH 55H)	2 Bytes
		Total = 512 Bytes

All the extended partitions should exist within the space reserved by the extended partition entry. Only two of the extended partitions are meant to be used, the first as a normal partition and the second as another extended partition if exists. Thus with the help of one Master Partition Table We can get the location of another Extended Master Partition Table next to it, if present.

Partition Table Entry Format

The format of partition table entry of any Partition in MBR has been given in the next table. Every Partition Entry of any MBR may be broken into the following bytes with their specific meanings:

Boot Type Indicator Byte (1 Byte): If this byte is 00H, it means the partition is not active and if the byte is 80H, it means the partition is an Active partition or Bootable partition. Although the presence of any other byte then these is not expected, yet if there is any other byte is present it may be due to partition table corruption or due to any VIRUS attack in the partition table.

Starting Cylinder – Head – Sector Number of the Partition (3 Bytes): When we calculate the

Logical Approach to Disks and OS 45

CHS (Cylinder, Head, and Sector) of any disk, The Physical CHS are counted as follows:
- The Physical Sector is counted starting from 1.
- The Physical Head is counted from 0.
- The Physical Cylinder is counted from 0 (See the Previous Chapter for Details)

The Byte at offset 01H represents the starting Head Number in hexadecimal System for the partition. 6 Least Significant Bits of Byte at offset 02H make Starting Sector Number of the partition and Combination of remaining 2 Bits (as Two Most Significant Bits) plus 8 Bits of another Byte at offset 03H (Rest 8 least Significant Bits of the 10-Bit Number) make the Starting Cylinder Number of the Partition.

Offset	Meaning	Size	Description
00H	Boot Type Indicator Byte	1 Byte	If Byte is **00H**, the Partition is Inactive and if Byte is **80H**, The Partition is Active (or Bootable)
01H	Head Number of Beginning of the Partition	1 Byte	Starting Head number of the Partition in Hexadecimal System
02H	Sector and Cylinder Number of Beginning of the Partition	2 Bytes	6 Bits of First Byte make Starting Sector Number and Combination of remaining 2 Bits (as Two Most Significant Bits) plus 8 Bits of another Byte (Rest 8 least Significant Bits of the 10-Bit Number) make the Starting Cylinder Number of the Partition
04H	File System indicator Byte	1 Byte	File System Indicator Byte in Hexadecimal system (See the Table given next for Indicators)
05H	Head Number of End of the Partition	1 Byte	Ending Head Number of the Partition in Hexadecimal System
06H	Sector and Cylinder Number of End of the Partition	2 Bytes	6 Bits of First Byte make Ending Sector Number and Combination of remaining 2 Bits (as Two Most Significant Bits) plus 8 Bits of another Byte (Rest 8 least Significant Bits of the 10-Bit Number) make the Ending Cylinder Number of the Partition
08H	Relative Sector number of Beginning of the Partition	4 Bytes	Number of Sectors Between the MBR and the First Sector in the Partition
0CH	Number of Sectors of the Partition	4 Bytes	Number of Sectors in the Partition
Total = 16 Bytes			

The Cylinder and Sector Encoding has been given in the example of a sample partition table study performed next.

File System Indicator Byte (1 Byte): File System Indicator Byte at offset 04H represents the file system of that partition. The table, listing the File System Indicator Byte for various File Systems has been given next in this chapter.

Ending Cylinder – Head – Sector Number of the Partition (3 Bytes): Encoding is same as for Starting Cylinder – Head – Sector Number of the Partition.

Relative Sector number of Beginning of the Partition (4 Bytes): Number of Sectors between the MBR and the First Sector in the Partition in Hexadecimal System.

Number of Sectors of the Partition (4 Bytes): Number of Sectors in the Partition in Hexadecimal system.

It should always be remembered that the Cylinder, Head and Sector numbers are those which should be passed to BIOS. Thus, if BIOS is using translation (LBA mode or INT 13H Extensions Support), the values may not represent the physical CHS values. For large hard drives (Greater than 8.4 GB) the CHS values may be invalid. These values should generally be ignored and the absolute sector values are used instead.

Logical Approach to Disks and OS

The figure given before shows the MBR of a Disk with FAT32 partitions. The highlighted area of 64 bytes in the end of the figure represents the Master Partition Table of the MBR.

The Encoding for the Starting and Ending CHS is as Follows:

- At offset 00H, **80** (Hex) represents that the partition is an Active partition.
- At offset 01H, **01** (Hex) represents the Starting head number = 1.
- The combination of two bytes at offset 02H and 03H form the Starting sector and cylinder number of the partition as per the encoding given next:

00H (Byte At Offset 03H)								01H (Byte At Offset 02H)							
7	6	5	4	3	2	1	0	7	6	5	4	3	2	1	0
0	0	0	0	0	0	0	0	0	0	0	0	0	0	0	1
Bits 7 to 0 For Cylinder Number								Cylinder Bits 9, 8		Sector Bits 5 to 0					
Cylinder Number = 0000000000 (B) = 0								Sector Number = 000001(B)=1							

Thus Starting C-H-S of the partition= 0-0-1.

Similarly the Head number for the Ending of the partition is **FE** (Hex), which is **254** and the Encoding for the Ending Cylinder and Sector number of the partition have been given in the next table:

BDH (Byte At Offset 07H)								BFH (Byte At Offset 06H)							
7	6	5	4	3	2	1	0	7	6	5	4	3	2	1	0
1	0	1	1	1	1	0	1	1	0	1	1	1	1	1	1
Bits 7 to 0 For Cylinder Number								Cylinder Bits 9, 8		Sector Bits 5 to 0					
Cylinder Number = 1010111101 (B) = 701								Sector Number = 111111 (B) = 63							

Thus the Ending C-H-S of the Partition = 701-254-63.

The Byte **0B** (Hex) at offset 04H is the File System Indicator Byte for the Partition. The Byte **0B** (H) Represents that the Partition is having the **FAT32** file system. The table for various file systems and their file system indicator bytes have been given next:

File system Indicator Byte in Hexadecimal	Partition/ File system Description
00H	Unused/Empty Partition-Table Entry (Remember this is not used to designate unused area on the disk, but marks an unused partition table entry)
01H	DOS 12-bit fat (The type **01H** is for partitions up to 15 MB)
02H	XENIX: root file system
03H	XENIX /usr file system (obsolete) (XENIX is an old

	part of Unix V7. Microsoft XENIX Operating System was announced in August 1980. It was a portable and commercial version of the Unix operating system for the Intel 8086, Zilog Z8000, Motorola M68000 and Digital Equipment PDP-11. Microsoft introduced XENIX 3.0 in April 1983. SCO delivered its first XENIX for 8088/8086 in 1983.)
04H	**16-bit FAT, DOS 3.0+ (Partition size < 32M)**(Some old DOS versions have had a bug which required this partition to be located in the 1st physical 32 MB of the hard disk)
05H	**DOS Extended (DOS 3.3+ Extended Volume)** Supports at most 8.4 GB disks. With this type **05H** DOS/Windows will not use the extended BIOS call, even if it is available.)
06H	**16-bit FAT, DOS Big, DOS 3.31+ (Partition Size >= 32M)**
	(Partitions are at most 2 GB for DOS and Windows 95/98 with maximum 65536 clusters with each cluster, at most 32 KB. Windows NT can create up to 4 GB FAT16 partition using 64 KB clusters.)
07H	**OS/2 IFS (Installable File System)** (HPFS is the best known example of this file system. OS/2 only looks at partitions with ID 7 for any installed IFS this is the reason that EXT2 IFS packet includes a special "Linux partition filter" device driver to fool OS/2 into thinking Linux partitions have ID 07).
07H	Advanced Unix
07H	**Windows NT NTFS**
07H	**QNX2.x (pre-1988)**(For the actual file system of partition type 07H, one should inspect the partition boot record)
08H	OS/2 (v1.0 to v1.3 only)
08H	**AIX boot partition** [AIX (Advanced Interactive Executive) is the IBM's version of Unix]
08H	SplitDrive
08H	DELL partition spanning multiple drives
08H	Commodore DOS
08H	**QNX 1.x and 2.x** ("qny" according to QNX partitions)
09H	AIX data partition
09H	**Coherent file system** [Coherent was a UNIX like Operating System for the 286-386-486 systems,

	marketed by Mark Williams Company led by Bob Swartz. It was renowned for its good documentation. It was introduced in 1980 and died 1 Feb 1995. The last versions are V3.2 for 286-386-486 and V4.0 (May 1992, using protected mode) for 386-486 only. It sold for $99 a copy and it is rumored that 40000 copies have been sold. A Coherent partition has to be primary.]
09H	**QNX 1.x and 2.x** ("qnz" according to **QNX Partitions**)
0AH	**OS/2 Boot Manager** (OS/2 is the operating system designed by Microsoft and IBM to be the successor of MS-DOS)
0AH	**Coherent swap partition**
0AH	**OPUS** (Open Parallel Unisys Server)
0BH	**WIN95 OSR2 32-bit FAT** (OSR2 stands for Microsoft's "OEM Service Release 2". It is for Partitions up to 2047GB. Almost always, Windows 95/98/ME have the same File system which is FAT-32, within the same partitions limits)
0CH	**LBA-mapped WIN95 OSR2 32-bit FAT** (It is using **L**ogical **B**lock **A**ddressing – mode of Interrupt 13H extensions therefore we can say that this is the Extended INT 13H equivalent of **0BH**. Almost always, Windows 95/98/ME have the same File system which is FAT-32, within the same partitions limits)
0EH	**LBA-mapped WIN95: DOS 16-bit FAT** or **Logical Block Addressable VFAT** (It is same as **06H** but using LBA-mode of INT 13H)
0FH	**LBA-mapped WIN95: Extended partition** or **Logical Block Addressable VFAT**(It is same as **05H** but using LBA-mode of INT 13H. Windows 95 uses **0EH** and **0FH** as the extended INT13H equivalents of **06H** and **05H**. Windows NT does not recognize the four Windows 95/98/ME types **0BH**, **0CH**, **0EH** and **0FH**)
10H	**OPUS** (Octal Program Updating System)
11H	**Hidden DOS 12-bit FAT** or **OS/2 Boot Manager hidden 12-bit FAT partition** or DOS Seen From

	OS/2 (When OS/2 Boot manager boots a DOS partition, it will hide all primary DOS partitions except the one that is booted, by changing its ID and **01H**, **04H**, **06H** and **07H** becomes **11H**, **14H**, **16H** and **17H**, respectively.
12H	**Compaq Configuration/diagnostics partition** (It is used by Compaq for their configuration utility partition. It is a FAT-compatible partition that boots into their utilities, and can be added to a LILO menu as if it were MS-DOS.)
14H	**(Hidden DOS 16-bit FAT or OS/2 Boot Manager Hidden DOS 16-bit FAT) <32M Partition** (Partition size is less than 32M. ID 14H is resulted from using Novell DOS 7.0 FDISK to delete Linux Native partition.)
15H	Hidden DOS-Extended
16H	**(Hidden DOS 16-bit FAT or OS/2 Boot Manager hidden 16-bit FAT) >=32M Partition**
17H	**OS/2 Boot Manager hidden HPFS partition** or **Hidden IFS (e.g., HPFS)**
17H	Hidden NTFS partition
18H	**AST SmartSleep Partition** or **AST special Windows swap file ("Zero-Volt Suspend" partition)** [AST Research, Inc. (named from first initials of the founders, Albert Wong, Safi Qureshey and Thomas Yuen). Ascentia laptops have a "Zero – Volt Suspend Partition" or `SmartSleep Partition' of size 2MB+memory size.]
19H	**Willowtech Photon COS**(Code 19H is Claimed for Willowtech Photon COS by Willow Schlanger.
1BH	**Hidden WIN95 OSR2 32-bit FAT** or **Hidden Windows 95 FAT32 Partition**
1CH	**LBA-mapped Hidden WIN95 OSR2 32-bit FAT** (It is hidden Windows95 FAT32 partition using LBA-mode of INT 13H Extensions)
1EH	**LBA-mapped Hidden WIN95 16-bit FAT** or **Hidden LBA VFAT partition**
1FH	**LBA mapped Hidden WIN95 Extended** or **Hidden Extended LBA VFAT Partition**
20H	**OFSI**(Willowsoft Overture File System)
21H	**Officially listed as Reserved**(HP Volume Expansion,

	SpeedStor variant.)
21H	**FSO2**(Claimed for **FSO2 (Oxygen File System)** by Dave Poirier)
22H	**FSO2 Extended Partition**(Claimed for Oxygen Extended Partition by Dave Poirier)
23H	Officially listed as Reserved
24H	**NEC DOS 3.x**
26H	Officially listed as Reserved
31H	Officially listed as Reserved
32H	**NOS (Network Operating System)**(32H is being used by the operating system NOS, being developed by Alien Internet Services in Melbourne Australia. The id 32H was chosen not only because of it was one of the few that are left available but also 32k is the size of the EEPROM the OS was originally targeted for.
33H	Officially listed as Reserved
34H	**Officially listed as Reserved**
35H	**JFS on OS/2 or eCS** [35H is used by OS/2 Warp Server for e-Business, OS/2 Convenience Pack (aka version 4.5) and eComStation (eCS, an OEM version of OS/2 Convenience Pack) for the OS/2 implementation of JFS (IBM AIX Journaling File System)]
36H	Officially listed as Reserved
38H	**THEOS v3.2 (2GB partition)**
39H	**Plan 9 partition** (**Plan 9** is an operating system developed at Bell Labs for many architectures. Originally **Plan 9** used an unallocated portion at the end of the disk. 3rd edition of Plan 9 uses partitions of type **39H**, subdivided into sub partitions described in the **Plan 9** partition table in the second sector of the partition.)
39H	**THEOS v4 spanned partition**
3AH	**THEOS v4 (4GB partition)**
3BH	**THEOS v4 Extended partition** (**THEOS** is a multi-user multitasking Operating System for PCs founded by Timothy Williams in 1983.)
3CH	**PartitionMagic recovery partition** (When a **PowerQuest** product like **Partition Magic** or **Drive Image** makes changes to the disk, it first changes the type flag to 3CH so that the Operating System will not try to modify it. At the end of the process, it is

	changed back to what it was at first. Therefore the only time you can see a 3CH type flag, is if the process was interrupted somehow such as power off, user reboot etc. If you change it back manually with a partition table editor or any disk editing program then most of the time everything is okay.)
3DH	**Hidden NetWare**
40H	**Venix 80286** (It is a very old Unix-like operating system for PCs.)
41H	**Linux/MINIX (sharing disk with DR-DOS)** (DR-DOS stands for Digital Research-Disk Operating System.)
41H	**Personal RISC Boot**
41H Partition	**PPC PReP (Power PC Reference Platform) Boot**
42H	**Linux swap (sharing disk with DR-DOS)**
42H	**SFS (Secure File System)** (**SFS** is an encrypted file System driver for DOS on 386+ PCs, written by Peter Gutmann.)
42H	**Windows 2000 Dynamic Extended Partition Marker** (If a partition table entry of type **42H** is present in the legacy partition table, then Windows 2000 ignores the legacy partition table and uses a proprietary partition table and a proprietary partitioning scheme (LDM or DDM). Pure dynamic disks (those not containing any hard-linked partitions) have only a single partition table entry, type **42H** to define the entire disk. Dynamic disks store their volume configuration in a database located in a 1-MB private region at the end of each dynamic disk.)
43H	**Linux native (sharing disk with DR-DOS)**
44H	**GoBack partition** (**GoBack** is a utility that records changes made to the disk, allowing you to view or go back to some earlier state. It takes over disk I/O like a Disk Manager would, and stores its logs in its own partition.)
45H	**Boot-US boot manager** (**Boot-US** (**Ulrich Straub**) **boot manager** can be installed to MBR, a separate primary partition or diskette. When installed to a primary partition this partition gets the ID **45H**. This partition does not contain a file system, it contains only the boot manager and occupies a single cylinder (below 8.4 GB).)

45H	Priam
45H	EUMEL/Elan
46H	EUMEL/Elan
47H	EUMEL/Elan
48H	EUMEL/Elan (EUMEL, later known as Ergos L3, are the multi-user multitasking systems developed by Jochen Liedtke at GMD, using Elan programming Language. It was used at German schools for the computer science education.)
4AH	AdaOS Aquila
4AH	ALFS/THIN lightweight filesystem for DOS
4CH	Oberon partition
4DH	QNX4.x
4EH	QNX4.x 2nd partition
4FH	QNX4.x 3rd partition (QNX is a POSIX (Portable Operating System Interface for Unix)-certified, microkernel, distributed, fault-tolerant Operating System for the 386 and later, including support for the 386EX in embedded applications.)
4FH	Oberon boot/data partition
50H	OnTrack Disk Manager (older versions), Read-Only Partition (Disk Manager is a program of OnTrack to enable people to use IDE disks that are larger than 504MB under DOS. Linux kernel versions older than 1.3.14 do not coexist with DM.)
50H	Lynx RTOS (Real-Time Operating System)(Lynx RTOS gives users the ability to place up to 14 partitions of 2 GB each on both SCSI and IDE drives, for a total of up to 28 GB of file system space.)
50H	Native Oberon
51H	OnTrack Disk Manager (DM6.0 Aux1), Read/Write Partition
51H	Novell
52H	CP/M
52H	Microport SysV/AT or Microport System V/386
53H	OnTrack Disk Manager (DM6.0 Aux3), Write-Only partition
54H	OnTrack Disk Manager 6.0 Dynamic Drive Overlay
55H	EZ-Drive Partition(EZ-Drive is another disk manager like program developed by MicroHouse in 1992. Now It is marketed by StorageSoft.)

56H	**Golden Bow VFeature Partitioned Volume.** (This is also a Disk Manager like Utility software. This is a Non-Standard DOS Volume.)
56H	**DM converted to EZ-BIOS**
57H	**DrivePro** (**DrivePro** was developed by **MicroHouse** in 1992. Now It is marketed by **StorageSoft**.)
57H	**VNDI Partition**
5CH	**Priam EDisk Partitioned Volume**(**Priam EDisk** is Disk Manager type utility software. This is a Non-Standard DOS Volume.)
61H	**SpeedStor** (**Storage Dimensions SpeedStor** Partitioned Volume. This is a Non-Standard DOS Volume. It is Disk Manager type utility software.)
63H	**Unix System V/386, 386/ix, SCO, ISC Unix, UnixWare, Mach, MtXinu BSD 4.3 on Mach, GNU Hurd**
64H	**Novell NetWare 286, 2.xx**
64H	**PC-ARMOUR protected partition** (**64H** is used by **PC-ARMOUR** disk protection by Dr. A. Solomon, intended to keep the disk inaccessible until the right password was given and then an INT 13H hook was loaded above top-of-memory that showed C-H-S = 0-0-2, with a copy of the real partition table, when 0-0-1 was requested).
65H	**Novell NetWare 3.86, 3.xx or 4.xx** (**Novell Netware 3.0** and later versions use one partition per drive. It allocates logical Volumes inside these partitions. The volumes can be split over several drives. The file system used is called **Turbo FAT** and it only very vaguely resembles the DOS FAT file system. **Novell Netware** used to be the main Network Operating System available. **Netware 68** or **S-Net** (1983) was for a Motorola 68000, **Netware 86** for an Intel 8086 or 8088. **Netware 286** was for an Intel 80286 and existed in various versions that were later merged to **Netware 2.2**. **Netware 386** was a rewrite in C for the Intel 386 which was later renamed to **Netware 3.x** (3.0, 3.1, 3.10, 3.11 and 3.12 etc) versions. Its successor **Netware 4.xx** had versions 4.00, 4.01, 4.02, 4.10 and 4.11. Then came Intranetware)
66H	**Novell Netware SMS Partition** (**SMS** stands for Storage Management Services. It is not used now.)
67H	**Novell**

68H	Novell
69H	**Novell Netware 5+** and **Novell Netware NSS Partition** (**NSS** stands for Novell Storage Services.)
70H	DiskSecure Multi-Boot
71H	**Officially listed as reserved**
73H	**Officially listed as reserved**
74H	**Officially listed as reserved**
74H	**Scramdisk partition** (**Scramdisk** is a disk encryption software. It supports container files, dedicated partitions type **74H** and disks hidden in WAV audio files.)
75H	IBM PC/IX
76H	Officially listed as reserved
77H	**M2FS/M2CS partition**
77H	QNX 4.x
78H	**XOSL File System** (**XOSL** Boot loader file system)
78H	QNY 4.x
79H	QNZ 4.x
7EH	**F.I.X.**
7FH	Alt-OS-Development Partition Standard
80H	**Old MINIX, MINIX v1.1 to v1.4a**
81H	**MINIX 1.4b and Later** (**MINIX** is a Unix-like operating system written by Andy Tanenbaum and students at the Vrije University, Amsterdam, around 1989-1991. It runs on PCs (8086 and up), Macintosh, Atari, Amiga, Sparc.
81H	Early Linux
81H	**Mitac Advanced Disk Manager**
82H	Prime
82H	**Solaris x86** (**Solaris** creates a single partition with ID **82H** and then uses Sun disk labels within the partition to split it further.)
82H	**Linux Swap partition**
83H	**Linux Native Partition** or **Linux native file system** or **Linux Ext2fs**(Linux is a Unix-like operating system written by Linus Torvalds and many others on the internet since 1991. It runs on PCs 386 and later and a variety of other hardware. It is distributed under GPL (General Public License). Various file system types like xiafs, ext2, ext3, reiserfs, etc. all use ID **83H**.)

84H	**OS/2 hidden C: drive** or **OS/2-renumbered type 04 partition.**(OS/2-renumbered type 04h partition is related to hiding DOS C: drive)
84H	**Hibernation partition** (Reported for various laptop models, e.g., used on Dell Latitudes (with Dell BIOS) that use the MKS2D utility.)
85H	Linux Extended partition
86H	Old Linux RAID partition super block
86H	**FAT16 volume/stripe set (Windows NT)** or **NTFS volume set** (It is Legacy Fault Tolerant FAT16 volume.)
87H	**HPFS Fault-Tolerant mirrored partition** or **NTFS volume set** or **NTFS volume/stripe set**(Legacy Fault Tolerant NTFS volume. HPFS Fault-Tolerant mirrored partition.)
8AH	**Linux Kernel Partition** (It is used by AiR-BOOT)
8BH	Legacy Fault Tolerant FAT32 volume
8CH	**Legacy Fault Tolerant FAT32 volume** using BIOS Extended INT 13H.
8DH	**Free FDISK hidden Primary DOS FAT12 partition** (**Free FDISK** is the FDISK used by **FreeDOS**. It hides types **01H, 04H, 05H, 06H, 0BH, 0CH, 0EH** and **0FH** by adding decimal Number **140 (8CH).**)
8EH	**Linux Logical Volume Manager partition**
90H	Free FDISK hidden Primary DOS FAT16 partition
91H	Free FDISK hidden DOS extended partition
92H	Free FDISK hidden Primary DOS large FAT16 partition
93H	Hidden Linux native partition
93H	Amoeba file system
94H	**Amoeba bad block table** (Amoeba is a distributed operating system written by Andy Tanenbaum, together with Frans Kaashoek, Sape Mullender, Robert van Renesse and others since 1981. It runs on PCs (386 and up), Sun3, Sparc, 68030. It is free for universities for research and teaching purposes.)
95H	MIT EXOPC native partition
97H	Free FDISK hidden Primary DOS FAT32 partition
98H	Free FDISK hidden Primary DOS FAT32 partition (LBA)
99H	**Mylex EISA SCSI** or **DCE376 logical drive** (It is

	used by the **Mylex DCE376 EISA SCSI** adaptor for partitions which are beyond the 1024 cylinder of a drive.)
9AH	Free FDISK hidden Primary DOS FAT16 partition (LBA)
9BH	Free FDISK hidden DOS extended partition (LBA)
9FH	**BSD/OS**
A0H	**Phoenix NoteBIOS Power Management "Save-to-Disk" partition** or **Laptop hibernation partition** (It is Reported for various laptops like **IBM Thinkpad**, **Phoenix NoteBIOS**, **Toshiba** under names like **zero-volt suspend** partition, **suspend-to-disk** partition, **save-to-disk** partition, **power-management partition**, **hibernation** partition, usually at the start or end of the disk area.)
A1H	**Laptop hibernation partition** (Used as "Save-to-Disk" partition on a NEC 6000H notebook. Types **A0H** and **A1H** are used on systems with **Phoenix BIOS**. The **Phoenix PHDISK** utility is used with these.)
A1H	**HP Volume Expansion (SpeedStor variant)**
A3H	Officially listed as Reserved
A4H	Officially listed as Reserved
A5H	**BSD/386, 386BSD, NetBSD, FreeBSD** (386BSD is a Unix-like operating system, a port of 4.3BSD Net/2 to the PC done by Bill Jolitz around 1991.)
A6H	**OpenBSD** (OpenBSD, led by Theo de Raadt, split off from NetBSD. It tries to emphasize on security.)
A7H	**NEXTSTEP** (**NEXTSTEP** is Based on **Mach 2.6** and features of **Mach 3.0**. It is a true object-oriented operating system and user environment.
A8H	**Mac OS-X** (**Apple's OS-X** uses this type for its file system partition)
A9H	**NetBSD**
AAH	**Olivetti Fat 12 1.44MB Service Partition** (It Contains a bare DOS 6.22 and a utility to exchange types **06H** and **AAH** in the partition table.)
ABH	**Mac OS-X Boot partition** (Apple's OS-X (Darwin Intel) uses this type for its boot partition.)
ABH	**GO! partition**
AEH	**ShagOS file system**
AFH	**ShagOS swap partition**

B0H	**BootStar Dummy** (The boot manager BootStar manages its own partition table, with up to 15 primary partitions. It fills unused entries in the MBR with BootStar Dummy values.)
B1H	**Officially listed as Reserved**
B3H	**Officially listed as Reserved**
B4H	**Officially listed as Reserved**
B6H	**Officially listed as Reserved**
B6H	**Windows NT mirror set (master), FAT16 file system**
B7H	**BSDI file system (secondarily swap), BSDI BSD/386 file system**
B7H	**Windows NT mirror set (master), NTFS file system**
B8H	**BSDI BSD/386 swap partition (secondarily file system)** (BSDI (Berkeley Software Design, Inc.) was founded by former CSRG (UCB Computer Systems Research Group) members. Their operating system, based on Net/2, was called BSD/386.)
BBH	**Boot Wizard hidden**
BEH	**Solaris 8 boot partition**
C0H	**DR-DOS/Novell DOS secured partition**
C0H	CTOS
C0H	**REAL/32 secure small partition**
C0H	**NTFT Partition**
C1H	DR DOS 6.0 LOGIN.EXE-secured 12-bit FAT partition
C2H	**Reserved for DR-DOS 7+**
C2H	Hidden Linux
C3H	**Hidden Linux swap**
C4H	DR DOS 6.0 LOGIN.EXE-secured 16-bit FAT partition
C5H	**DRDOS/secured (Extended)**
C6H	**DRDOS/secured (FAT-16, >= 32M)** (DR-DOS 6.0 will add **C0H** to the partition type for a LOGIN.EXE - secured partition so that User can not avoid the password check by booting from an MS-DOS floppy. Otherwise it seems that the types **C1H**, **C4H**, **C5H**, **C6H** and **D1H**, **D4H**, **D5H**, **D6H** are used precisely like **1H**, **4H**, **5H**, and **6H**.)
C6H	**Corrupted FAT16 volume/stripe set (Windows NT)**(NTFS will add **C0H** to the partition type for disabled parts of a Fault Tolerant set. Thus, one gets types **C6H**, **C7H**.)

C7H	Windows NT corrupted NTFS volume/stripe set
C7H	Syrinx boot
C8H	Officially listed as Reserved
C9H	Officially listed as Reserved
CAH	Officially listed as Reserved
CBH	Reserved for DR-DOS secured FAT32
CCH	Reserved for DR-DOS secured FAT32 (LBA)
CDH	CTOS Memdump
CEH	Reserved for DR-DOS secured FAT16 (LBA)
D0H	REAL/32 secure big partition (REAL/32 is a continuation of DR Multi-user DOS.)
D1H	Old Multi-user DOS secured FAT12
D4H	Old Multi-user DOS secured FAT16 <32M
D5H	Old Multi-user DOS secured extended partition
D6H	Old Multi-user DOS secured FAT16 >=32M
D8H	CP/M-86
DAH	Non-FS Data
DBH	Digital Research CP/M, Concurrent CP/M, Concurrent DOS
DBH	CTOS (Convergent Technologies OS -Unisys)
DBH	KDG Telemetry SCPU boot (KDG Telemetry uses ID **DBH** to store a protected-mode binary image of the code to be run on a 'x86-based SCPU (Supervisory CPU) module from the DT800 range.)
DDH	Hidden CTOS Memdump
DEH	Dell PowerEdge Server utilities (FAT)
DFH	DG/UX virtual disk manager partition
DFH	BootIt EMBRM (The boot manager **BootIt** manages its own partition table, with up to 255 primary partitions.)
E0H	Reserved by **ST Microelectronics** for a file system called ST AVFS.
E1H	DOS access or SpeedStor 12-bit FAT extended partition (It is a SSTOR partition on cylinders more than 1023.)
E2H	DOS Read-Only
E3H	Storage Dimensions
E4H	SpeedStor 16-bit FAT extended partition < 1024 cylinders
E5H	Officially listed as Reserved

	E5H	Tandy DOS with logical sectored FAT
	E6H	Officially listed as Reserved
	EBH	BeOS BFS (BFS1)(BeOS is an operating system that runs on Power PCs)
	EDH	Reserved for Matthias Paul's Sprytix
	EEH	Indication that this legacy MBR is followed by an EFI Header
	EFH	Partition that contains an EFI file system
	F0H	Linux/PA-RISC boot loader
	F1H	Storage Dimensions
	F2H	DOS 3.3+ secondary partition
	F2H	Unisys DOS with logical sectored FAT
	F3H	Officially listed as Reserved
	F4H	SpeedStor large partition
	F4H	Prologue single-volume partition
	F5H	Prologue multi-volume partition (The type **F4H** partition contains one volume, and is not used anymore. The type **F5H** partition contains 1 to 10 volumes called **MD0** to **MD9**. It supports one or more systems. Each volume can have as file system the **NGF** file system or **TwinFS** file system.)
	F6H	Officially listed as Reserved
	F6H	Storage Dimensions SpeedStor
	FAH	MandrakeSoft's **Bochs** x86 emulator
	FBH	VMware File System partition
	FCH	VMware Swap partition (**VMware** offers virtual machines in which one can run **Linux, Windows, FreeBSD.**)
	FDH	Linux raid partition with auto detect using persistent super block
	FEH	SpeedStor more than 1024 cylinders
	FEH	LANstep
	FEH	IBM PS/2 IML (Initial Microcode Load) partition (It is located at the end of the disk.)
	FEH	Windows NT Disk Administrator hidden partition (Windows NT Disk Administrator marks hidden partitions, i.e. present but not to be accessed, as type **FEH**.)
	FEH	Linux Logical Volume Manager partition (old)
	FFH	XENIX Bad Block Table

DOS Boot Record (DBR) / DOS Boot Sector

After the partition table, the DOS Boot Record (DBR) or sometimes called DOS Boot Sector is the second most important information on your hard drive. Most commercial applications for disc-recovery are capable of regenerating destroyed boot-records

The DOS Boot Record (DBR) for the first partition on a hard disk is usually found at Absolute Sector 63 (the 64th sector on the disk drive) or in CHS form we can say C–H–S = 0–1–1 for most drives.

However this location may vary depending upon the SPT (Sectors per Track) of the Drive. For example, on an old 245MB drive having only 31 SPT, the Boot Record was located on the 32nd sector (Absolute Sector 31).

The DBR is created by the FORMAT command of DOS. This program can be executed from a DOS floppy disk (or directly from another volume, following some OS limits) to create the DBR after partitioning is done using the FDISK command.

The sector on which DBR resides becomes logical sector 1 of that particular partition for the DOS. The sector number used by DOS starts from the physical sector on which DBR is located.

First logical sector of each DOS partition will contain a DOS Boot Record (DBR) or DOS Boot Sector. The job of the DBR is to load the operating system from the hard disk drive into the main memory of computer and give the systems control to the loaded program.

For doing this, the DBR contains a small program which is executed by the Master Boot Record (MBR) Executable program. All DOS partitions contain the program code to boot the machine i.e. load the operating system, but only that partition is given control by the Master Boot Record which as specified as active partition, in the partition table entry.

The Boot program in the DBR looks for the two program files IBMBIO.COM or IO.SYS and IBMDOS.COM or MSDOS.SYS, in the root directory of the partition. IBMBIO.COM and IBMDOS.COM are two hidden system program files on the PC-DOS systems or original IBM systems. Whereas IO.SYS and MSDOS.SYS are two hidden system program files on a MS-DOS operating system provided with IBM compatible systems.

After that, the IO.SYS (or IBMBIO.COM) program loads the MSDOS.SYS (or IBMDOS.COM) program and the COMMAND.COM program. This complete process is called "booting" of the computer. If these system files are not available in the directory then this MBR program displays error messages soothing like,

> **"Invalid system disk or Disk I/O error,**
> **Replace the disk, and then press any key…"**

On the screen and waits for the user to put a bootable disk with the above mentioned programs in the floppy drive and press a key.

Since the floppy has no partitions on it therefore it has no MBR or Master Partition Table on its absolute sector 0, instead it contains the DBR on its very first sector.

The following table gives a simple map of a 3½ Inches, 1.44 MB floppy disk's layout after having been formatted with the FAT12 file system. It shows where the Boot Record, both copies of the FAT, the Root Directory and the beginning of the Data Area are located:

Logical Map of 3½ Inches, 1.44 MB floppy disk, Formatted with the FAT12 File System and having 18 Sectors Per Track, 80 Tracks, 2 Sides and 512 bytes per Sector (using 1 Sector per Cluster).

Absolute Sectors	Contents
0	Boot Record
1 – 9	FAT 1
10 – 18	FAT 2
19 – 32	Root Directory
33 – 2879	Data Area

You can also create sub-directories in the Data Area with files that appear to be contained inside them. In Fact, Subdirectories are nothing more than a special file which lists all of the files seemingly contained inside this directory and all the relevant data about each file such as, the location of each file's Starting Cluster, date, time and file size etc.

The DBR also contains some important information about the disk geometry. This information is located in the first sector of every partition, such as:

- Jump Code + NOP
- OEM Name and Version
- Bytes Per Sector
- Sectors Per Cluster
- Reserved Sectors
- Number of Copies of FAT
- Maximum Root Directory Entries (but Not Available for FAT32)
- Number of Sectors in Partition Smaller than 32MB (Therefore Not Available for FAT32)
- Media Descriptor (F8h for Hard Disks)
- Sectors Per FAT (In Older FAT Systems and Not Available for FAT32)
- Sectors Per Track
- Number of Heads
- Number of Hidden Sectors in Partition
- Number of Sectors in Partition
- Number of Sectors Per FAT
- FAT Information Descriptor Flags
- Version of FAT32 Drive
- Cluster Number of the Start of the Root Directory
- Sector Number of the File System Information Sector
- Sector Number of the Backup Boot Sector
- Reserved
- Logical Drive Number of Partition

Logical Approach to Disks and OS

- Extended Signature (29H)
- Serial Number of Partition
- Volume Name of Partition
- FAT Name
- Executable Code
- Executable Marker or Magic Number (AAH 55H)

The first 3 Bytes of DBR contain a JMP instruction to skip the information and make extensions possible because the MBR loads this sector into memory and transfers execution to it. Usually these three bytes are hexadecimal numbers in format something like **E9 XX XX (Hex)** or **EB XX 90 (Hex)**.

Following the initial JMP instruction OEM ID is an 8–Bit Field that is reserved by Microsoft for OEM Identification. The OEM ID describes the program that created the boot record. This is often "**MSWIN4.0**" for Windows 95/98/ME, "**IBM 20.0**" for OS/2 and "**MSDOS5.0**" for MS-DOS 4.0 and later.

The third major component of the boot sector is the BIOS Parameter Block (BPB). The disk parameter block is very important data area for DOS. It helps the DOS to find:

- Bytes Per Sector
- Sectors Per Cluster
- Reserved Sectors
- Number of FAT
- Number of Root Directory Entries

FAT32 DOS Boot Record Format		
Offset	**Description**	**Size**
00H	Jump Code + NOP	3 Bytes
03H	OEM Name and Version	8 Bytes
0BH	Bytes Per Sector	2 Bytes
0DH	Sectors Per Cluster	1 Byte
0EH	Reserved Sectors	2 Bytes
10H	Number of Copies of FAT	1 Byte
11H	Maximum Root Directory Entries (but Not Available for FAT32)	2 Bytes
13H	Number of Sectors in Partition Smaller than 32MB (Therefore Not Available for FAT32)	2 Bytes
15H	Media Descriptor (F8H for Hard Disks)	1 Byte
16H	Sectors Per FAT (In Older FAT Systems and Not Available for FAT32)	2 Bytes
18H	Sectors Per Track	2 Bytes
1AH	Number of Heads	2 Bytes
1CH	Number of Hidden Sectors in Partition	4 Bytes

20H	Number of Sectors in Partition	4 Bytes
24H	Number of Sectors Per FAT	4 Bytes
28H	Flags (Bits 0-4 Indicate Active FAT Copy) (Bit 7 Indicates whether FAT Mirroring is Enabled or Disabled <Clear is Enabled>) (If FAT Mirroring is Disabled, the FAT Information is only written to the copy indicated by bits 0-4)	2 Bytes
2AH	Version of FAT32 Drive (High Byte = Major Version, Low Byte = Minor Version)	2 Bytes
2CH	Cluster Number of the Start of the Root Directory	4 Bytes
30H	Sector Number of the File System Information Sector (Referenced from the Start of the Partition)	2 Bytes
32H	Sector Number of the Backup Boot Sector (Referenced from the Start of the Partition)	2 Bytes
34H	Reserved	12 Bytes
40H	Logical Drive Number of Partition	1 Byte
41H	Unused (Could be High Byte of Previous Entry)	1 Byte
42H	Extended Signature (29H)	1 Byte
43H	Serial Number or 32 – Bit Binary ID of Partition (Binary ID of 32 Bits provided by the OS itself)	4 Bytes
47H	Volume Name of Partition	11 Bytes
52H	FAT Name (FAT32 in this case)	8 Bytes
5AH	Executable Code	420 Bytes
1FEH	Executable Marker or Magic Number (AAH 55H)	2 Bytes

DOS Boot Record Format for FAT12 and FAT16			
Offset	Size	Field	Default
00H	3	Jump	E9 XX XX or EB XX 90 (Hex)
03H	8	OEM ID	MSWIN4.0
BIOS Parameter Block			
0BH	2	Bytes Per Sector	512
0DH	1	Sectors Per Cluster	(See Table of Cluster Sizes)
0EH	2	Reserved Sectors	1
10H	1	Number of FATs	2
11H	2	Number of Root Directory Entries	512/544

13H	2	Total Sectors in Logical Volume (Small, For Logical Volume Size Less than or Equal to 32 MB)	0
15H	1	Media Descriptor Byte	(See the Table of Media Descriptors)
16H	2	Number of Sectors Per FAT	Must Be Calculated
(End of BIOS Parameter Block)			
18H	2	Sectors Per Track	Depends on Hard Disk, Usually 63
1AH	2	Number of Heads	Depends on Hard Disk
1CH	4	Number of Hidden Sectors	
20H	4	Total Sectors in Volume (Large, Logical volume size greater than 32MB)	Size of the partition in terms of Sectors
Extended Boot Record Information (DOS 4.0 and Later)			
24H	1	Physical Drive Number	80H
25H	1	Current Head	0
26H	1	Extended Boot Signature Record	for WinNT, 28H else 29H
27H	4	Volume Serial Number (32 – bit Binary Volume ID)	Random
2BH	11	Volume Label	1
36H	8	File System ID	FAT12, FAT16
Total	62		

- Total Sectors in Logical Volume (Small, For Logical Volume Size Less than or Equal to 32 MB)
- Media Descriptor Byte
- Number of Sectors Per FAT

This information helps us to find the location of FAT and some other important values. Putting wrong information here or corrupting these values makes booting from the hard disk drive impossible. Sometimes having wrong information in the disk parameter block will prevents the booting from hard disk drive as well as from the floppy disk drive.

Bytes per sector are almost always 512. If not so even then it must be an integer power of 2 (e.g. 64, 128, and 256).

The number of Sectors per cluster depends on the size of cluster. (See the Clusters section given in this chapter earlier). Number of Copies of FAT is almost always 2.

Number of Root Directories: It depends on the File system and Volume size. (See File System Limits given before and description of Root Directory given next).

Total number of sectors: Excludes hidden sectors. If it is 0 in the BPB, the field in the extended boot record information is used and vice versa. Note that it is possible to determine if the extended information (DOS 4.0 and later) is available by examining the signature byte at offset 26H.

Any sectors before the boot sector of a logical DOS drive are considered to be 'hidden' sectors. The DOS does not interpret hidden sectors. Normal floppy drives have 0 hidden sectors. Hard drive partitions will have a number reflecting their location on the drive. Note that the whole first head of the first cylinder is usually reserved for the partition table, even though it is only the first sector which is actually used.

Media descriptor: Used to give an indication of the media or disk type. Normal values are 0 for an extended DOS partition and F8H for a hard drive. The values of Media Descriptor Bytes have been given in the following table.

Media Descriptors		
Type	Capacity	Size and type
F0H	2.88 MB	3.5"; 2-Sided, 36 Sectors per Track
F0H	1.44 MB	3.5", 2-Sided, 18 Sectors per Track
F9H	720 KB	3.5", 2-Sided, 9 Sectors per Track
F9H	1.2 MB	5.25", 2-Sided, 15 Sectors per Track
FDH	360 KB	5.25", 2-Sided, 9 Sectors per Track
FFH	320 KB	5.25", 2-Sided, 8 Sectors per Track
FCH	180 KB	5.25", 1-Sided, 9 Sectors per Track
FEH	160 KB	5.25", 1-Sided, 8 Sectors per Track
F8H	————	Fixed Disk

Number of Sectors of FAT: It must be calculated. The method of calculating the size of FAT has been given in the description of FAT given in the chapter.

The DBR of a FAT32 File System has been given in the figure given next:

Sectors Per Track (or Sectors Per Head): Sectors Per Head is the number of sectors grouped under one head. Likewise, Heads per Cylinder reflects the number of cylinders per head. If this partition is a CHS partition, these values must be the same as those returned by BIOS. If they are not the same, you must consider that the disk has been misconfigured and that the partition may be unusable.

Hidden Sectors: As we have already discussed, this is the number of sectors on the physical disk preceding the start of the volume, before the boot sector itself. It is used during the boot sequence in order to calculate the absolute offset to the root directory and data areas. Think of it as the number of sectors between the beginning of this partition and the partition table itself.

This field should be the same as the "number of sectors preceding the partition" in the partition table. Note that it is not necessarily the physical LBA address of the first sector, as secondary partitions may exist.

If the Hidden Sectors are not the same as in the partition table, you may consider the boot sector as corrupted and the partition unusable. Note also that the high word usually contains garbage in old versions of DOS.

Logical Approach to Disks and OS

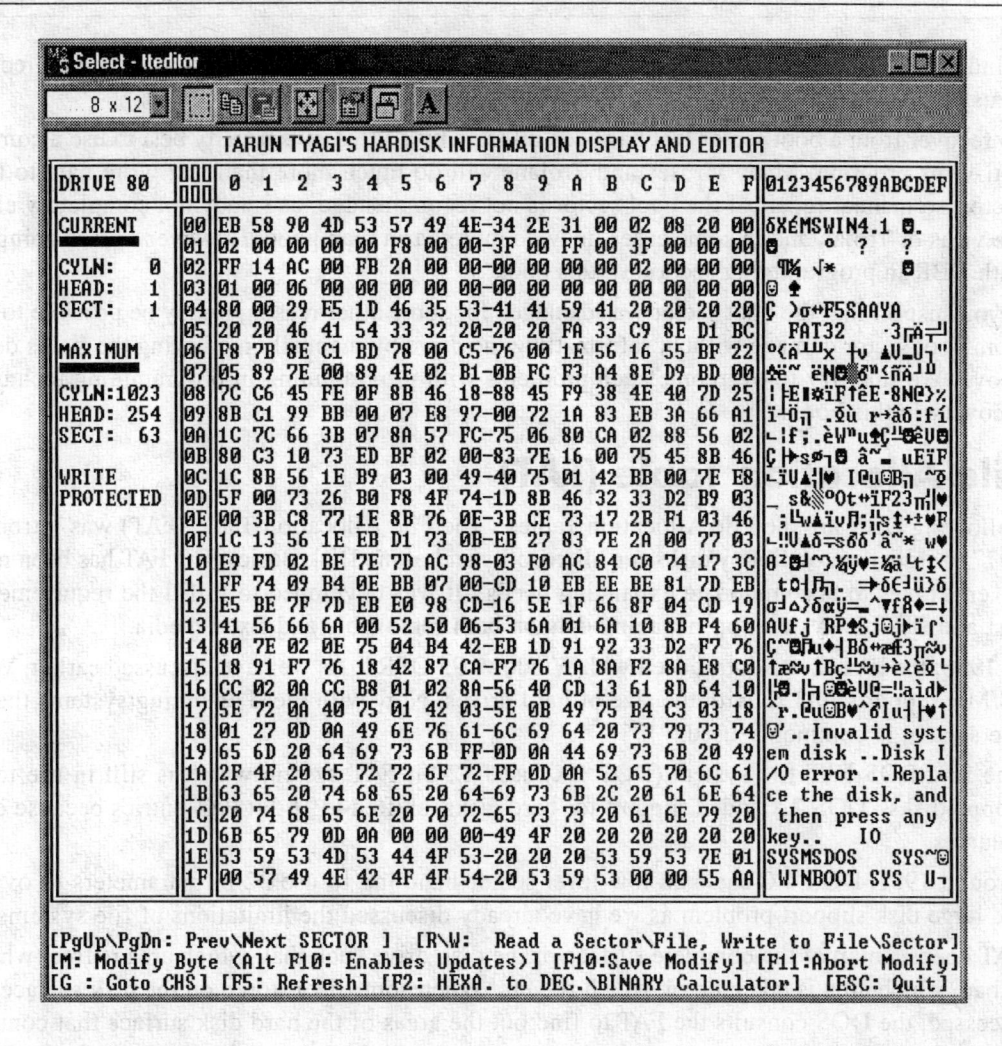

If you suspect that a Boot Sector has become corrupt, you can check several of the fields listed above to see whether the values listed there make sense.

For example, Bytes per Sector will be 512 in the vast majority of cases. You may also expect to see text strings in the executable code section of the boot sector that are appropriate for the operating system that formatted the disk.

For Example, Typical text strings on FAT volumes formatted by MS-DOS include: "Invalid system disk.", "Disk I/O error.", "Replace the disk, and then press any key", "Non-System disk or disk error", "Replace and press any key when ready." and "Disk Boot failure." Text strings on FAT volumes formatted by Windows NT include: "BOOT: Unable to (or Could not) find NTLDR", "I/O error reading disk." and "Please insert another disk."

But remember that you should not regard this list as being all inclusive. If you find other messages in the boot sector, this does not necessarily indicate that there is a problem with the boot sector. Different versions of MS-DOS and Windows NT may sometimes have slightly different message strings in their boot sectors.

On the other hand, if you find no text whatsoever, or if the text is clearly not related to MS-DOS or

Windows NT, you should consider the possibility that your boot sector may have been infected by a virus or that some other form of data corruption may have taken place.

To recover from a boot sector that has been infected by a virus, it is usually best to use a commercial anti-virus program. Many viruses and Trojans will do much more than just write data to the boot sector, so manual repair of the boot sector is not recommended, as it may not completely eliminate the virus or Trojan and in some cases, may do more harm than good. However we are going to deal with DBR in programming section of this book.

If you suspect that the boot sector was damaged for some other reason, it may be possible to recover from boot sector damage without reformatting the drive by manually modifying the fields described above. We shall try to overcome such problems with programming in programming techniques of recovery in this book.

File Allocation Table (FAT)

Following DBR are the File Allocation Tables. The File Allocation Table (FAT) was introduced in 1977 to store data on floppy disks for Microsoft stand-alone Disk Basic. The FAT has been modified several times to accommodate expanding needs. It was developed to fulfill the requirements of a fast and flexible system for managing data on both removable and fixed media.

In 1996, the FAT32 was introduced with Windows 95 OSR2. As we have discussed earlier, Windows 98/ME supports FAT32 with the size of hard drives. Now with these operating systems the FAT32 file system is commonly used.

The first DOS FAT file system (DOS 1.x) used 12-bit FAT system which is still in use today for floppy disks. DOS 2.x added support for hard disks, shifted to 16-bit FAT entries because of larger volumes.

Around 1987, DOS 4.0 changed low-level sector-handling to use 32-bit parameters to over come the large disk support problem as we have already discussed the limitations of file systems.

FAT keeps a map of the complete surface of the disk drive such that, which area is free, which area is bad, which area is taken up by which file etc. When some data stored on the disk surface is to be accessed, the DOS consults the FAT to find out the areas of the hard disk surface that contains the data.

The type of the FAT to be used is decided by the FDISK program during the partition of the hard disk drive. But the actual FAT is written by the FORMAT program of DOS.

The FAT does not keep track of each and every sector on the disk surface instead it manages the disk area in a group of sectors called "cluster" or "allocation unit" (See the Cluster Discussed before, in the same chapter).

A cluster is the smallest unit of hard disk drive space that DOS allocates to a file, it consist of one or more sectors depending on the drive size. The cluster size is decided and fixed by the DOS FORMAT program during the high level formatting of the hard disk drive. (See the "size of clusters" discussion, given before)

Actually, the FAT is an index of the clusters of the entire volume. The FAT has one entry for each cluster. The first two entries in a FAT contain information about the FAT. The third and subsequent entries in the FAT are assigned to clusters of disk space, starting with the first cluster available for use by files.

Because FAT is such an important item, DOS keeps two copies of the FAT, primary FAT or FAT1 and secondary FAT or FAT2 (there are normally two copies, however many new operating systems create more than two copies of FAT).

Each FAT occupies contiguous sectors on the disk, with the 2nd FAT immediately following the1st FAT does not make the DOS use 2nd FAT to correct the problem, instead when the 1st FAT is updated DOS copies it to the 2nd FAT, corrupting the 2nd FAT as well, in the process.

This updating is done every time DOS finds that the 1st and 2nd FAT does not match. So, in case of any corruption of the 1st FAT, one should immediately do the repair by using some disk editor software and comparing the 1st FAT with the 2nd FAT. This should be done before DOS copies the corrupted FAT to the second FAT.

With the introduction of FAT32, both the FAT entries and the sector numbering are now 32-bit. That means that there are now 4,294,967,296 distinct 32-bit values multiplied by 512 bytes per sector yielding 2 terabytes (2,199,023,255,552 bytes) as the maximum possible disk size under FAT32.

The size of the directory entry for each file in FAT 32 is 4 bytes to contain the value of the starting cluster of the file rather than the 2 bytes needed under FAT16. The larger value accommodates the larger number of possible clusters.

Traditionally, each directory entry is a 32-byte record, and this remains the same. In the middle of the directory record there is 10 bytes (bytes 12 to 21) that Microsoft has reserved for its own future use. Two of those bytes are now used to accommodate the extra bytes needed to specify the starting cluster under FAT32.

As we have already discussed that there have been 12 bit, 16 bit, and 32 bit versions of FAT. While 32 bit FAT allows much more efficient storage which may be up to 30% more efficient and use of larger hard drives.

When the File System of an Operating System is invoked by a program to find the contents of a file, the first cluster value, in the directory entry for that file, is read and used to find the FAT chain. The FAT chain is the list of clusters that contain data belonging to a file.

FAT32 Drive Layout	
Offset	**Description**
Start of Partition	Boot Sector
Start of Partition + Number of Reserved Sectors	FAT Tables
Start of Partition + Number of Reserved Sector + (Number of Sectors Per FAT * 2) [Assuming that FAT Mirroring is Enabled, this is almost always true]	Root Directory
Start of Partition + Number of Reserved Sectors + (Number of Sectors Per FAT * 2) + Number of Sectors in root directory	Data Area

FAT entries can contain values that indicate:
- The next cluster in a FAT chain for a given file
- The Free clusters i.e., the clusters which are not in use by any file
- The information of Bad Sectors i.e., the cluster containing one or more sectors that are

physically damaged & should not be used.
- The final cluster of a file

Entries of FAT Table	
Number (Hex.)	**Description**
0	Free cluster
????	Cluster in use, next cluster in chain
FF0-FF6 / FFF0-FFF6	Cluster is reserved
FF7 /FFF7	Cluster contains bad sectors
FF8-FFF / FFF8-FFFF	End of file

Each FAT entry represents a cluster address and contains a pointer to the next cluster address (FAT entry) for the file. The last FAT entry for a file contains the final cluster value instead of a pointer. The first two entries in a FAT contain information about the FAT. These Bytes of the FAT contain a media descriptor byte. This byte can be used to find the type of the disk media of which this FAT entry is.

The third and subsequent entries in the FAT are assigned to clusters of disk space, starting with the first cluster available for use by files. A FAT entry can have any of the values given in the above table, based on the information it wants to convey.

A 000H in 12–Bit FAT or 0000H in 16–Bit FAT indicates that the cluster corresponding to this FAT location is unallocated or is empty. Any value from FF8H to FFFH in 12–Bit FAT or FFF8H to FFFFH in 16 – Bit FAT indicates that this cluster is the last cluster in a chain of clusters of a file.

Value from FF0H to FF7H in 12 – Bit FAT indicates reserved clusters. An FF7H in a 12–Bit FAT or FFF7H in 16–Bit FAT indicates that the cluster corresponding to the location of the FAT is a bad cluster i.e. this is basically a cluster containing bad sectors. This cluster is not used for data storage.

Any other value in the FAT table is a pointer to the next cluster in the file allocation chain.

How Windows detects the Improper – Shutdown

It is very common thing and I hope you have noticed it many times when using windows that if there is any Improperly – Shutdown in your computer, due to any reason like, power failure, software corruption, accidental shutdown etc, when you further restart your computer, the message of Improper – Shutdown is displayed on the screen during the booting process and the Operating System Scans the disk for errors.

The next two figures show the 256 Bytes of the beginning of a 32 – Bit FAT however we only need initial 8 bytes to discuss this.

Actually, when the Windows Operating Systems has loaded itself into Memory i.e. the Windows has started, the 8th Byte (or offset 7H) of FAT becomes 07H or F7H from 0FH or FFH.

Microsoft uses the byte 0FH only for the volume that contains the running Operating System, and the byte FFH for any other volume that it is accessing.

Once Windows starts booting, the 8th Byte is changed to 07H or F7H which will be set back to a 0FH or FFH only if Windows is properly shut down.

Logical Approach to Disks and OS

If there is a power failure, or the Power switch of the computer is accidentally turned OFF or the system is manually rebooted due to some software problem, then this byte will remain as 07H or F7H which informs the Windows Operating System when next time it is booted that there was some kind of improper shut down and then Windows uses it's disk scanning program (Scandisk) to verify the disk for errors.

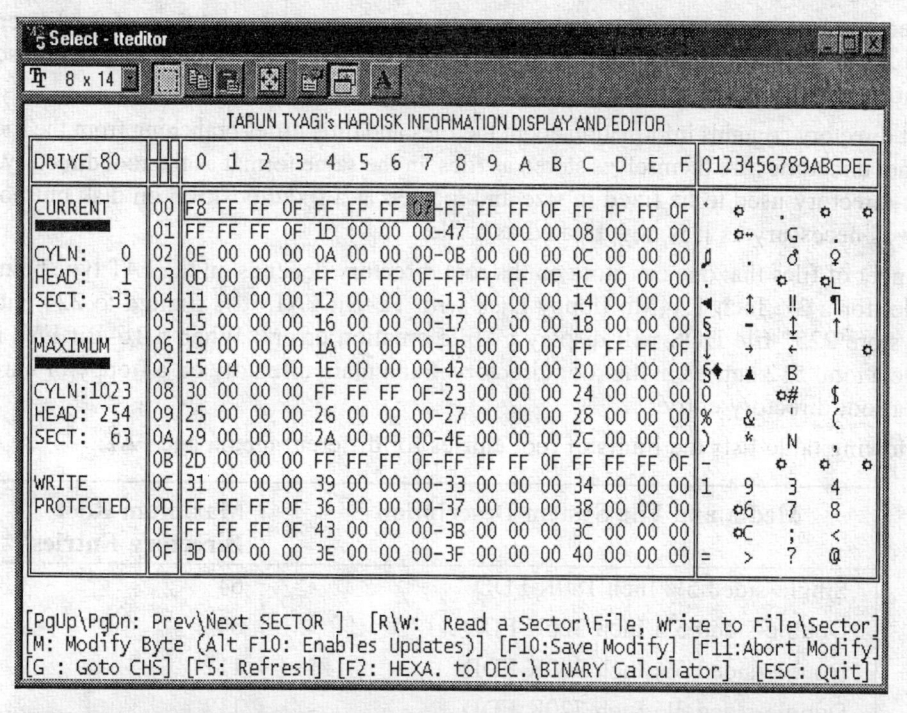

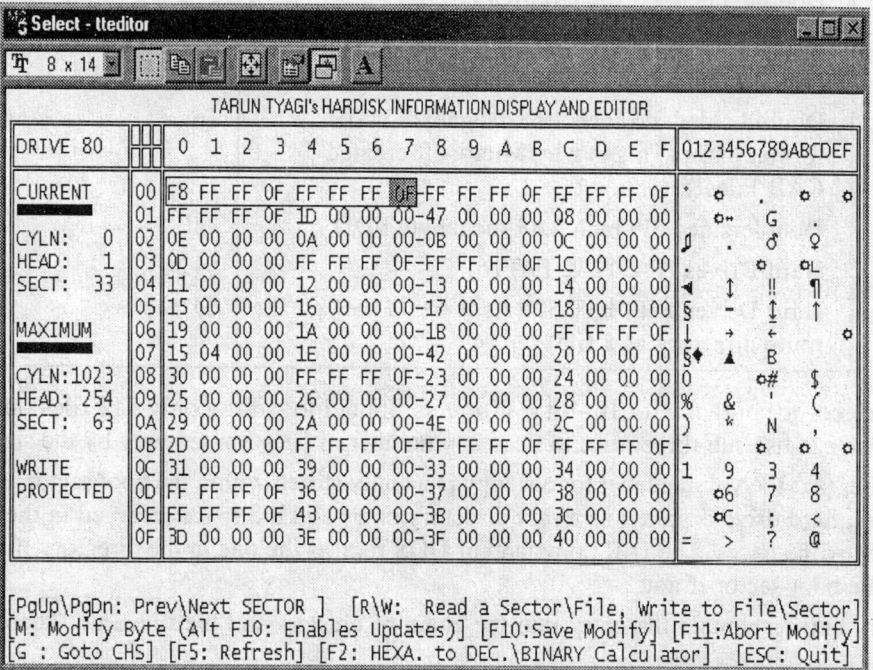

Root Directory

Following the last FAT is the Root Directory. The root directory is like a table of contents for the information stored on the hard disk drive. The location of the Root Directory can easily be established by adding up the values from boot record, as it is positioned following the FATs.

The directory area keeps the information about the file name, date and time of the file creation, file attribute, file size and starting cluster of the particular file. Each directory entry describing this information about a file is a 32 byte information.

The root directory contains information about the files and directories branching from the root directory. All further directories are themselves stored as files, in the same format as the root directory. Previously the root directory used to be fixed in size and located at a fixed position on disk but now it is free to grow as necessary as it is now treated as a file.

The number of files that one can store on the root directory depends on the FAT type being used. For Example, for a 3½ Inch 1.44Mb floppy Disk with 12-Bit FAT, it is limited to 224 entries, if one tries to store 225th file DOS will display a "File creation error". When a 16-Bit FAT is used one can have a total 512 entries in the root directory. Each main directory on a floppy or hard disk, also acts as a root directory entry.

The following table lists the limits of root entries for different media and FAT:

Media and File System Description	Maximum Root Directory Entries
Single-sided 5¼ Inch 180K FDD	64
Double-sided 5¼ Inch 320K FDD	64
Double-sided 5¼ Inch 360K FDD	112
Double-sided 3½ Inch 720K FDD	112
Double-sided 5¼ Inch 1.2-megabyte FDD	224
Double-sided 3½ Inch 1.44-megabyte FDD	224
Double-sided 3½ Inch 1.68-megabyte DMF format disks (This is why Microsoft created CAB Files!)	16
Double-sided 3½ Inch 2.88-megabyte FDD	240
Hard Drives (FAT12 & FAT16)	512
Hard Drives with FAT 32 (As it treats the route directory as a file)	65,536

This does not mean that with 16-Bit FAT one is limited to storing only 512 files on the hard disk drive. One can use sub-directories to store any number of files limited only by the size of the drive.

Remember that the volume label for a floppy is usually stored within the boot sector, but the volume label for a hard drive is stored as a root directory entry and the space reserved in the boot sector is left blank with spaces. The DIR command of DOS returns the one in the directory if present, or the one in the boot sector if not.

Directory entries contain the entry into the chain of clusters and the filename. Therefore the most

Logical Approach to Disks and OS

important Directory Entries are of the root directory, because it contains cluster indexes that points to all Sub–Directories.

All directories contain two entries, "." for Current directory (This Sub Directory) and ".." for parent directory (Parent Directory of this Sub Directory). We can track these entries easily as they will always be positioned in the beginning of a cluster if the cluster contains a directory.

The following table shows the format of a directory entry in the Root Directory. The table given next Shows, how the 32 Bytes of directory entry of a file in Root Directory are sliced to store the various information about it:

Offset	Size	Description
00H	8 Bytes	Filename (Also see the next table for the special meaning of first character of file name)
08H	3 Bytes	Extension
0BH	1 Byte	File attributes(See The Table Of File Attributes)
0CH	10 Bytes	Reserved
16H	2 Bytes	Time Created or Last Updated (See Date–Time Format Table)
18H	2 Bytes	Date Created or Last Updated (See Date–Time Format Table)
1AH	2 Bytes	Starting or First cluster of file (The value 0000H is used in Parent Directory ('..') entries to indicate that the Parent Directory is the Root Directory)
1CH	4 Bytes	File size in Bytes.

Filename contains the name in uppercase and if the size of filename is smaller than the 8 characters the spaces are filled with space characters of ASCII Number 32. Extension field contains the extension of file, in uppercase.

If the Filename is longer than the 8 characters, Windows creates a short filename from a long one by truncating it to six uppercase characters and adding "~1" to the end of the base filename.

If there is already another filename with the same first six characters, the number is incremented. The extension is kept the same, and any character that was illegal in earlier versions of Windows and DOS is replaced with an underscore.

Long filenames are stored in specially formatted 32-Byte Long File Name (LFN) directory entries marked with attribute bytes set to 0FH. For a given file or subdirectory, a group of one or more Long filename directory entries immediately precedes the single 8.3 directory entry on the disk.

Each LFN directory entry contains up to 13 characters of the long filename, and the operating system strings together as many as needed to comprise an entire long filename.

This is the cause, why the long file names decreases the maximum possible number of root directory entries in a File system. **How Windows Supports Long File Names, We shall Discuss in detail, Later in this Chapter.**

The first Byte of the filename may also contain some important information about file. The information given by this byte may be one of as given in the following table:

First Character of File Name	
Value	**Meaning**
00H	Indicates that this directory entry is unused.
05H	Indicates that 1st character of filename is character E5H But actually the file has not been deleted. (See the Meaning of E5H)
E5H	The file has been Erased and this directory entry is a deleted file's directory entry. The data area previously occupied by that file is now free for allocation for another new file.
2EH	This is a Sub-directory. The cluster number field of this entry will contain the cluster number of the directory.
2EH 2EH	Two 2EH in a directory entry indicate the parent directory entry of a Sub-Directory. The cluster number of this entry will contain the cluster number of the parent directory of this directory. The cluster number will be zero 0000H if the parent directory is root directory.

The Attributes is an 8-Bit binary coded field. The following table tells about the Status for flag of attributes for the given file:

Attribute Bits			
Attribute	**Bit**	**Binary**	**Hex**
Read Only File Flag	0	.......?	01H
Hidden File Flag	1	......?.	02H
System File Flag	2	.....?..	04H
Volume Label Flag (Indicates that the entry is a volume label)	3	....?...	08H
Sub-directory (in same format as directory)	4	...?....	10H
Archive Bit (File Modified Since Last Backup)	5	..?.....	20H
Reserved (Contains 0)	6	.0......	-
Reserved (Contains 0)	7	0.......	-

One File may have multiple attributes. For example, a single File may be a Read-Only as well as Hidden-File or a single file may have both attributes, The System-File and The Hidden-File. (See the Example given next for the Encoding of Directory Entries).

Time and Date is a specially coded field of 32-Bits (16-Bits of Time and 16-Bits for Date). The division of these Bits encoding to compose the Time of created or last updated and the Date of created or last updated for a File, has been given in the Following table:

The DOS Date-Time format

Name	Size (Bits)	Value
Hour (24-hour)	5	0..23
Minute	6	0..59
Seconds (Seconds in increment of 2)	5	0..30

Bits Distribution For Time

17th Byte								16th Byte							
15	14	13	12	11	10	9	8	7	6	5	4	3	2	1	0
H	H	H	H	H	M	M	M	M	M	M	S	S	S	S	S

Name	Size (Bits)	Value
Year (from 1980 - meaning year=1980 + Value)	7	0..127
Month	4	1..12
Day	5	1..31

Bits Distribution For Date

19th Byte								18th Byte							
15	14	13	12	11	10	9	8	7	6	5	4	3	2	1	0
Y	Y	Y	Y	Y	Y	Y	M	M	M	M	D	D	D	D	D

Total size	32 Bits

The entry for Time of Create or Last Update of file, which is the 16th and 17th Byte in the directory entry, has the format given in the above table. The encoding is as follows:

- H is binary number for hour, that could range from 0 to 23
- M is a binary number for minute, that could range from 0 to 59
- S is a binary number for seconds in 2 seconds increment

The entry for Data of Create or Last Update of File, which is the 18th and 19th Byte in the directory entry, has the following format:

- Y is binary number between 0 to 127or year 1980 to 2107
- M is binary number for month, this could range from 1 to 12
- D is a binary number for date, this could range from 1 to 31

This directory entry is linked with the FAT entry based on the first cluster value. Once the DOS has the starting cluster value of any file from the Directory, the DOS can find out the complete file using the FAT. The Entry Cluster in the chain is the first cluster that makes up the file. If the attributes' directory flag is set, this field points to a new directory entry.

The entry of Size of file is 4 Bytes. By this we can calculate, how FAT32 supports the maximum size of a file up to 4,294,967,295 Bytes which is about 4 GiB. The 4 Bytes have 32 Bits and the maximum possible File size composed by any 32–Bit Binary could be,

= 11111111 11111111 11111111 11111111 (B) Bytes

= 4,294,967,295 (D) Bytes

~ 4 GiB

Thus the FAT32 supports the maximum File size up to 4 GiB.

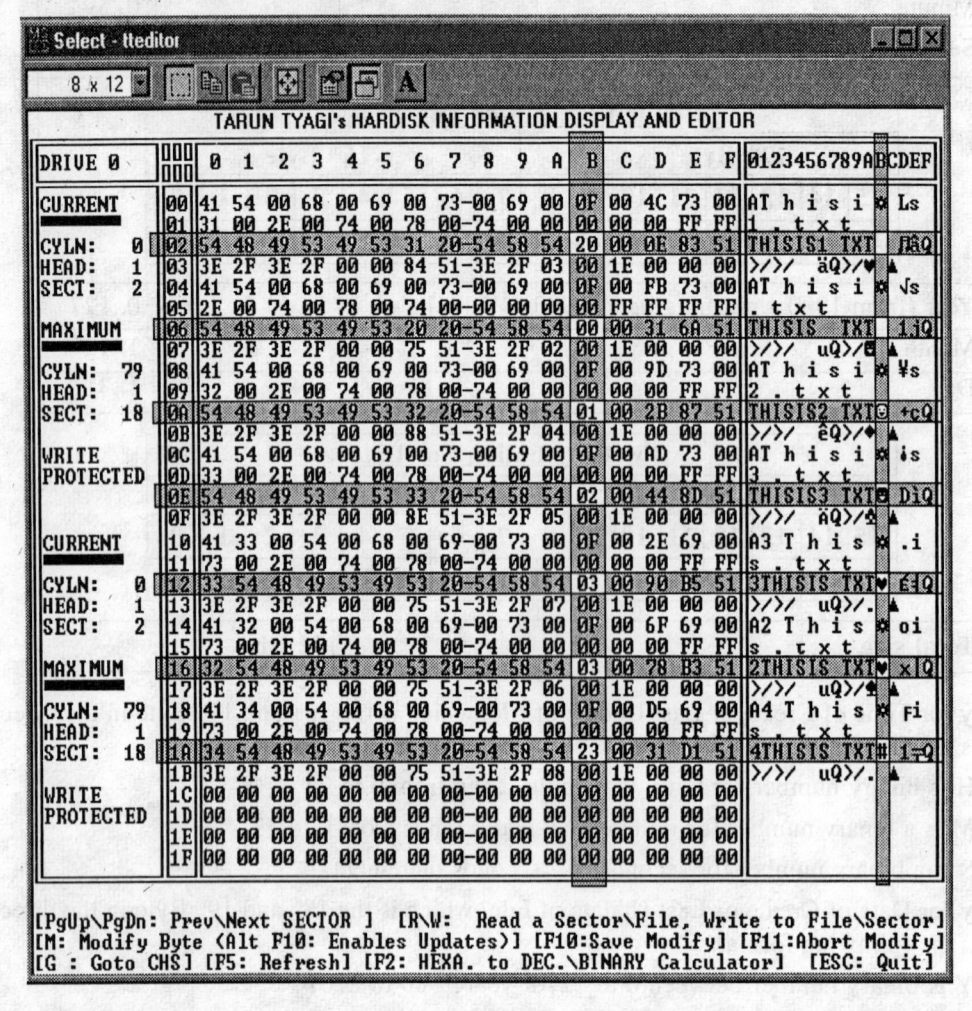

The Size of File and starting cluster of file may be a valuable resource for data recovery in recovering damaged files since we can calculate how many clusters the file is supposed to consist of.

The Figure given before shows the Root Directory entry for seven Different files. The encoding for these entries has been given in the following table:

Encoding For Filename, Extension, Attribute, Starting Cluster and File Size				
Filename	Extension	Attribute	Starting Cluster	Size of File in Bytes
THISIS1	TXT	20H = 00100000B = **Archive**(The	03H, 00H (Read As 00H, 03H To Calculate the	1EH, 00H, 00H, 00H (Read As 00H, 00H, 00H, 1EH to

		6th bit is Set)	Starting Cluster) = 0003H = 3	Calculate File Size) = 0000001EH= 30 Bytes
THISIS	TXT	00H = 00000000B = No Attribute (No Bit is Set)	02H, 00H = 0002H = 2	1EH, 00H, 00H, 00H= 0000001EH = 30 Bytes
THISIS2	TXT	01H = 00000001B = Read-Only	04H, 00H = 0004H = 4	1EH, 00H, 00H, 00H= 0000001EH = 30 Bytes
THISIS3	TXT	02H = 00000010B = Hidden-File	05H, 00H = 0005H = 5	1EH, 00H, 00H, 00H= 0000001EH = 30 Bytes
3THISIS	TXT	03H = 00000011B = Hidden-File + Read-Only	07H, 00H = 0007H = 7	1EH, 00H, 00H, 00H= 0000001EH = 30 Bytes
2THISIS	TXT	03H = 00000011B = Hidden-File + Read-Only	06H, 00H = 0006H = 6	1EH, 00H, 00H, 00H= 0000001EH = 30 Bytes
4THISIS	TXT	23H = 00100011B = Hidden-File+ Read-Only+ Archive	08H, 00H = 0008H = 8	1EH, 00H, 00H, 00H= 0000001EH = 30 Bytes

Long File Name (LFN)

As we have already discussed earlier in Root Directory Discussion, Previously the root directory used to be fixed in size and located at a fixed position on disk but now it is free to grow as necessary as it is now treated as a file.

This is very important to long filenames because each long filename uses multiple directory entries. Adding long filename support to an operating system that uses 8.3 filenames is not as simple as expanding directory entries to hold more than 11 characters.

If this new operating system returns 255-character filenames, many older applications, which expect to receive no more than 11 characters, would crash because a program has to set aside memory to store the filenames it reads, and if it sets aside 16 Bytes for a filename and the operating system copies (say) 32 characters into that space, then other data gets overwritten. A sure way to break an application is to copy random data into its data space.

To overcome this problem, a clever solution was found in Windows 95, to the problem of supporting long filenames while preserving compatibility with previous versions of DOS and Windows applications.

When most applications (except for low-level disk utilities such as the Norton Disk Doctor) query the system for file and subdirectory names, they do so not by reading directory entries directly off the disk, but by using enumeration functions built into the operating system.

As we know that a directory entry is marked with the combination of read-only, hidden, system, and volume label attributes Bits. Likely, if the attribute byte of Directory Entry holds the value 0FH the enumeration functions built into all existing versions of DOS and all Pre-Windows 95 versions of Windows will skip over that directory entry as if it were not there.

Then, the solution was to store two names for every file and subdirectory, a short name that is visible to all applications and a long name that is visible only to Windows 95 (and Later) applications and to applications that have been rewritten to add support for long filenames. Short filenames are stored in 8.3 formats in conventional 32-byte directory entries.

We have already discussed that Windows creates a short filename from a long one by truncating it to six uppercase characters and adding "~1" to the end of the base filename.

If there is already another filename with the same first six characters, the number is incremented. The extension is kept the same, and any character that was illegal in earlier versions of Windows and DOS is replaced with an underscore.

The Long filenames are stored in specially formatted 32-Byte Long File Name (LFN) Directory Entries marked with attribute bytes set to 0FH. For a given file or subdirectory, a group of one or more Long File Name directory entries immediately precedes the single 8.3 directory entry on the disk.

Each Long File Name directory entry contains up to 13 characters of the long filename, and the operating system strings together as many as needed to comprise an entire long filename.

For a Long File Name directory entry, filenames are stored in Unicode format, which requires 2 Bytes per character as opposed to 1 Byte of ASCII. Filename characters are spread among three separate fields:

- The first 10 Bytes (five characters) in length,
- The second 12 Bytes (six characters),
- The third 4 Bytes (two characters).

The lowest five Bits of the first byte of directory entry hold a sequence number that identifies the position of directory entry relative to other Long File Name directory entries associated with the same file.

If a long filename requires three LFN directory entries, the sequence number of the first will be 1, that of the second will be 2, and the sequence number of the third will be 3 and Bit 6 of the first Byte of third entry is set to 1 to indicate that it is the last entry in the sequence.

The attribute field appears at the same location in LFN directory entries as in 8.3 directory entries because the file system does not know which type of directory entry it is dealing with until after it examines the attribute byte. The starting cluster number field also appears at the same location, but in LFN directory entries its value is always 0. The type indicator field also holds 0 in every long filename.

One of the problems with long filenames is that they consume more disk space than short ones. That is not a big deal when long names are stored in subdirectories, because as long as disk space is available, subdirectories can grow to accommodate added directory entries but the maximum number of directory entries available in the root directory is fixed, and long filenames waste space in the root directory which is limited in size.

Now for Example, if the root directory of a hard disks contains at most 512 directory entries, because a 128-character name requires 11 entries, 10 for the long name and 1 for the short name, you could create only 46 files and subdirectories in the root directory if each were given a 128-character name.

The problem goes away for FAT32 also because the root directory under FAT32 can grow as well because in FAT32 system the root directory is treated as a File which can grow in size.

Data Area (or Files Area)

Following the Root Directory the Data Area (or Files Area) starts. Rather we can say that the remainder of the volume after Root Directory is the Data Area.

The data area contains the actual data stored on the disk surface. DOS uses cluster number 2 for the first sector of the data area therefore we should keep it in mind while performing various calculations that the cluster number should start from 2.

When we format a hard disk drive the FORMAT command of DOS does not destroy or overwrite the data on the data area. The FORMAT command only removes the directory entry and FAT entries and it does not touch the actual data area.

This makes the recovery of accidentally formatted hard disk drive possible, which is not possible in all cases of accidentally formatted floppy disk. As in full Format by Windows the Data area of Floppy is filled by F6H characters and all the information is overwritten.

DOS uses a 16-Bit/32-Bit pointer called a "Last Cluster Used" (LCU) pointer to store the last used cluster number. Initially this pointer value is zero, when some information is written on a particular cluster, that cluster number is stored into LCU pointer.

After this, every time if the new information is to be written, DOS searches for a free cluster from the LCU number onwards. This forces new data written on the disk to remain contiguous as the data is written to the new, unused area.

Now understanding of data in case of an accidental deletion would be much easier as the file is in one contiguous area on the disk. Once the end of disk is reached or the system is reset, the LCU pointer value is reset to zero.

But the problem does not last here. It is not practically possible that you only create new files on your disk and you never delete or modify any file from the previously stored ones. Using only LCU has the problems if you do a lot of creation and deletion of files as this will force the new data to move further and further into the inner tracks of the hard disk.

Therefore if any file, which was stored in the disk, is moved or deleted, the clusters in the data area which were occupied by the file are now set as unallocated clusters available in the data area and ready to be written new data on them. By doing this, operating system do not need to move all the data to the inner tracks of the disk.

But a lot of deletion and creation of files fragments the data on the disk and this causes the Fragmentation in the data.

Fragmented and Defragmented Data

We have already discussed that each file in the disk is stored as a linked list of clusters by which the data that is contained in a file and can be located anywhere on the disk. If you have a 10 MB file stored on a disk using 4,096-byte clusters, it is using 2,560 clusters. These clusters can be on different tracks, different platters of the disk, in fact, they can be anywhere.

Though a file can be spread all over the disk, this is far from the preferred situation. The reason is the undesirable slow performance. Hard disks are relatively slow devices, mainly because they have mechanical parts in them. Each time the hard disk has to move the heads to a different track, it takes time that is equivalent to thousands and thousands of processor cycles.

Therefore, we want to minimize the degree to which each file is spread around the disk. In the ideal case, every file would in fact be completely contiguous. That means each cluster it uses would be located one after the other on the disk. This would enable the entire file to be read, if necessary, without a lot of mechanical movement by the hard disk.

Actually, the file system starts out with all or most of its file contiguous but as a result of the creation and deletion of files over a period of time the data on the disk becomes more and more fragmented.

Let us consider a simple example to understand the fragmentation. The table below represents the usage of the 12 clusters. Initially, the table is empty:

cluster 1	cluster 2	cluster 3	cluster 4	cluster 5	cluster 6
cluster 7	cluster 8	cluster 9	cluster 10	cluster 11	cluster 12

Now let us suppose that we create four files, File A, B, C and D in this disk. File A takes 1 cluster, file B takes 4, file C takes 2, and file D takes 3. We store them in the free available space, and they start out all contiguous as shown in the next figure:

A	B	B	B	B	C
C	D	D	D		

After some time let we delete the file C and by doing this, both the clusters which were occupied by file C, are now free or unallocated. This leaves the disk looking like the following figure:

A	B	B	B	B	
	D	D	D		

Now, we create a new File E that needs 3 clusters. But, as there are no contiguous blocks on the disk left that are 3 clusters long, so we have to split E into two fragments, using part of the space formerly occupied by C. Now our disk is going to look like the figure given next:

A	B	B	B	B	E
E	D	D	D	E	

After a slice of time period, let we delete files A and E and create file F which takes up 5 clusters. The disk now looks like the figure given below:

F	B	B	B	B	F
F	D	D	D	F	F

Now we see that the file F ends up being broken into three fragments. This type of data in the disk is called the fragmented data. The example given above is a very simplified example of fragmentation, because the real disks have thousands of files and thousands of clusters, so the problem there is magnified. This gives you the general idea of what happens though.

What a defragmentation program (Like Microsoft's DEFRAG Program, Norton's SpeedDisk) does is to rearrange the disk to get the files back into contiguous form. After running the disk defragmentation utility, the Defragmented data on the disk which we were talking about will look like the figure given below:

B	B	B	B	F	F
F	F	F	D	D	D

The Fragmented and Defragmented data have a lot of importance during the data recovery, in many cases.

Let us consider that we have two crashed disks for Data Recovery, one has fragmented data and one was defragmented recently. And you have to do data recovery by collecting the data from the surface of both the disks as the FAT and Root information of the files is damaged. In such type of cases the percentage of recovery will be proportional to the defragmentation of the data in the disk.

Obviously, the data recovery from the Defragmented disk will be easy and percentage of data recovery will also be high but on the other hand, the data recovery from the fragmented disk will be difficult and time-taking as well as the percentage of recovered data will also be disappointing.

Identifying the cause of data corruption

There are some specific steps which if followed in a sequence, may help us to find the area of corruption. These steps have been described with recovery procedure as follows:

Boot the system with bootable floppy

Boot your system with a bootable floppy or CD of the operating system you were using. Try to read the logical drives C: or D: or whatever. If the drive(s) is accessible, just copy all the data off the drive. Now you can figure out why the disk is not booting properly, with less stress.

Verify the MBR Information

The first and most important piece of data on the hard disk is the MBR and the table that it carries within it, the partition table. The small disk Editing tool named **"TTEDITOR.EXE"** has been given in the disk included with this book. Or you can use any other program to analyze the hard disk.

Diskedit will be the most suitable program to analyze the disk for data recovery purpose. Well, whichever program you feel easy to use is upon you. Try to read MBR and especially its partition table.

As you have seen in the description of **MBR**, discussed in this chapter, In the second half portion of MBR, there is some readable text which displayed as error message by this, if there is something wrong with it. These text messages are displayed something like:

> "Invalid partition table, Setup can not continue"
> "Error loading operating system, Setup can not continue"

If these error messages are not available this indicates the corruption of MBR. There may also some illegal message instead of this like, "Your system has been hacked by....." or any other unexpected message. It indicates that there is something seriously wrong with the MBR, and most probably, it is due to some VIRAL infection.

Now check the partition table of MBR after the initial 446 bytes. If the partition table is blank, you will not see any error message at boot time. DOS ignores a non partitioned drive. If there is not any bootable floppy in drive A:, the system will request for a bootable floppy to be inserted in drive A:.

The important thing to be noticed here is that the partition table should not be blank on a drive that was previously working, so something has erased it. If the partition table is blank, restore the MBR from the backup.

If the backup does not work, even after the successful completion of restoring process, there is physical damage on this sector. Try the programming techniques of data recovery, given in the next chapters to recover the data. If you are not a programmer at all, better to go to any good data recovery center.

If you not have any backup of MBR try to write partition table manually with some disk editing tool, like Diskedit, how ever it is very difficult to do so in some cases.

For those users who are not the programmers and also do not have any backup, may use the method which I have been using since my data recovery project development time, in my college days.

What you have to do is, just search the computer near you, which has almost same size of disk, with same number of partitions and the most important thing the same operating system which was in your computer.

However it works completely, most of the time. But if not so, at least it may help you to access the first partition of your disk. Even your operating system will also boot normally, if it was installed in the first partition and if the other information are not corrupted.

If MBR is okay, Verify DBR

If the MBR is all right, verify the DBR (DOS Boot Record). As we have already discussed, this is the first sector in the DOS partition and contains a small program that loads the hidden files and boots the operating system.

The DBR also contains much important information about the FAT, root directory clusters and size of the partition etc. Use some Diskedit like utility to read the DBR information if the DBR is corrupted or has some illegal information restore the DBR from the Backup.

All the professional software for data recovery, are capable to rewrite the DBR. We shall discuss about, how to rewrite the DBR of the partition with programming, in the next chapters of the book.

You can also rewrite the DBR of the partition with the help of Diskedit by providing appropriate information.

There is also a very easy way to find out the area of corruption. The error messages which are displayed on the screen have some specific cause to be displayed. The description of some important error messages is as follows:

Message	Description
"Sector not found reading drive"	This message can appear during any DOS operation. Generally, it is caused either by fading or the loss of a sector ID.
"Data error reading drive"	This message can appear during any DOS operation. It is caused by failing the data check – CRC (Cyclic Redundancy Check) or ECC (Error Correction Code). This "Data check" refers to the mechanism used to check whether the data read from the disk is reliable.
" 0 hard disk(s) found"	It is displayed if the hard disk is not detected by the BIOS of the computer. Check the power and data cable connections of the hard disk. If connections are all right, the problem may be due to some hardware error of hard disk.
"Hard Drive failure, press F1 to continue"	Same as above
"Invalid drive specification"	It is displayed in the condition when either the system does not recognize the hardware, or there is no partition information, or the device driver of the drive is missing.
"Invalid configuration press F1 to continue"	If the hard disk is available, Either the battery in the motherboard is dead, and the system has lost its configuration SETUP information or the disk is not responding.
"Invalid partition table"	This is the MBR error message. It is displayed when the partition table of the MBR does not have the valid partition information.
"Error loading operating system"	This is the MBR error message. It is displayed due to any type of MBR information corruption.
"Missing operating system"	Same as above.
"Disk boot failure"	It is the DBR error message. Normally, The Hard drive should be accessible if you boot from the floppy. Though it is not bootable but that should not affect the access to the data of the drive.
"non system disk or disk error"	Same as above.
"Bad or missing command interpreter"	This message is displayed due to Bad or Missing Command Interpreter. For example if the operating do not find the **command.com** in current path or the command.com is corrupted.

Chapter – 4
Number Systems

Introduction

It is very common in data recovery programming or any other disk troubleshooting programming to handle the different type of number systems simultaneously to perform a single task or even a very small piece of work such as calculating the specific locations of **Extended MBR**(s) in terms of CHS (Cylinders, Heads and Sectors) and these locations guide the programmer through out the operation(s).

Probably most of the beginning programmers encounter the problem or confusion while converting different type of number systems to one another when attempting to learn assembly language based system level programming and when the use of the binary and hexadecimal number systems is must.

In this chapters we shall discusses many important concepts including the binary, decimal, hexadecimal numbering systems and as well as binary data organization such as conversion of bits, nibbles, bytes, words, and double words etc. and many other related topics of number systems.

Most of the modern computer systems do not represent numeric values using the decimal system but they generally use a binary or 2's complement numbering system.

There are four number bases commonly used in programming, Binary, Octal Decimal and Hexadecimal. However most of the time we shall meet with Binary, Decimal and Hexadecimal number systems. These number systems have been differentiated according to their base number.

Every numbering system has its own base number and representation symbol. I have presented these four numbers in the following table:

Name of Number System	Base Number Representation	Symbol Used for
Binary	2	B
Octal	8	Q or O
Decimal	10	D or None
Hexadecimal	16	H

Decimal Number System

The Decimal Number System uses base 10 and it includes the digits from 0 through 9. Don't get confused, it is the common number system that we use in our daily life to calculate the things. The powers weighted values for each position will be as follows:

Number Systems

(Base 10)^{Number}	10^4	10^3	10^2	10^1	10^0	10^{-1}	10^{-2}	10^{-3}
Value	10000	1000	100	10	1	.1	.01	.001

In this way if I have a decimal number 218 and I want to represent it in above manner the number 218 will be represented in the following manner:

$2 * 10^2 + 1 * 10^1 + 8 * 10^0$
$= 2 * 100 + 1 * 10 + 8 * 1$
$= 200 + 10 + 8$
$= 218$

Now let us take an example of any fractional decimal number. Let we have a number 821.128. Each digit appearing to the left of the decimal point represents a value between zero and nine and the power of ten is represented by its position in the number (starting from 0).

Digits appearing to the right of the decimal point represent a value between zero and nine times an increasing negative power of ten. Let us see how:

$8 * 10^2 + 2 * 10^1 + 1 * 10^0 + 1 * 10^{-1} + 2 * 10^{-2} + 8 * 10^{-3}$
$= 8 * 100 + 2 * 10 + 1 * 1 + 1 * 0.1 + 2 * 0.01 + 8 * 0.001$
$= 800 + 20 + 1 + 0.1 + 0.02 + 0.008$
$= 821.128$

Binary Number System

Today most of the modern computer systems operate using binary logic. The computer represents values using two voltage levels that indicate to either **OFF** or **ON** using 0 and 1. For example the voltage 0V is usually represented by **logic 0** and either +3.3 V or +5V voltage is represented by **logic 1**. Thus with two levels we can represent exactly two different values. These could be any two different values, but by convention we use the values **0** and **1**.

Since there is a correspondence between the logic levels used by the computer and the two digits used in the binary numbering system, it should come as no surprise that computers employ the binary system.

The binary number system works like the decimal number system except the Binary Number System uses the base 2 and includes only the digits **0** and **1** and use of any other digit would make the number an invalid binary number.

The weighted values for each position are represented as follows:

(Base)^{power}	2^7	2^6	2^5	2^4	2^3	2^2	2^1	2^0	2^{-1}	2^{-2}
Value	128	64	32	16	8	4	2	1	.5	.25

The following table shows the representation of binary number against the decimal numbers:

Decimal Number	Binary Number Representation
0	0000
1	0001
2	0010
3	0011
4	0100
5	0101
6	0110
7	0111
8	1000
9	1001
10	1010
11	1011
12	1100
13	1101
14	1110
15	1111

Usually in case of decimal numbers, every three decimal digits are separated with a comma to make larger numbers easier to read. For example, it is much easier to read a number 840,349,823 than 840349823.

Getting the inspiration from the same idea, there is a similar convention for binary numbers so that it may be easier to read binary numbers but in case of binary numbers we will add a space every four digits starting from the least significant digit on the left of the decimal point.

For example if the binary value is 1010011001101011, it will be written as 1010 0110 0110 1011.

Binary to Decimal number Conversion

To convert the binary number to the decimal number, we multiply each digit by its weighted position, and add each of the weighted values together. For example, the binary value 1011 0101 represents:

$$1*2^7 + 0*2^6 + 1*2^5 + 1*2^4 + 0*2^3 + 1*2^2 + 0*2^1 + 1*2^0$$
$$= 1*128 + 0*64 + 1*32 + 1*16 + 0*8 + 1*4 + 0*2 + 1*1$$
$$= 128 + 0 + 32 + 16 + 0 + 4 + 0 + 1$$
$$= 181$$

Decimal to Binary number Conversion

To convert any decimal number to its binary number system the general method is to divide the decimal number by 2, if the remainder is 0, on the side write down a 0. If the remainder is 1, write down a 1.

This process is continued by dividing the quotient by 2 and dropping the previous remainder until the quotient is 0. When performing the division, the remainders which will represent the binary

Number Systems

equivalent of the decimal number, are written beginning at the least significant digit (right) and each new digit is written to more significant digit (the left) of the previous digit.

Let us take an example. Consider the number 2671. The binary conversion for the number 2671 has been given in the following table.

Division	Quotient	Remainder	Binary Number
2671 / 2	1335	1	1
1335 / 2	667	1	11
667 / 2	333	1	111
333 / 2	166	1	1111
166 / 2	83	0	0 1111
83 / 2	41	1	10 1111
41 / 2	20	1	110 1111
20 / 2	10	0	0110 1111
10 / 2	5	0	0 0110 1111
5 / 2	2	1	10 0110 1111
2 / 2	1	0	010 0110 1111
1 / 2	0	1	1010 0110 1111

This table is to clarify every step of the conversion however in practice and to get the ease and speed of conversion you can follow the following manner to get the results.

Let 1980 is any decimal number to be converted into its binary equivalent. Than following the method given in the table we will solve this problem in the following manner:

2	1980	
2	990	0
2	495	0
2	247	1
2	123	1
2	61	1
2	30	1
2	15	0
2	7	1
2	3	1
2	1	1
2	0	1

When we arrange the remainders according to the direction of arrow, we get the **binary number equivalent to the decimal number 1980**

= 0111 1011 1100

Binary Number Formats

Typically we write binary numbers as a sequence of bits. The **"bits"** is short for "binary digits" in a machine. There are defined format boundaries for these bits. These format boundaries have been represented in the following table:

Name	Size in bits	Example
Bit	1	1
Nibble	4	0101
Byte	8	0000 0101
Word	16	0000 0000 0000 0101
Double Word	32	0000 0000 0000 0000 0000 0000 0000 0101

We may add as many leading zeroes as we wish without changing its value in any number base however we normally add leading zeroes to adjust the binary number to a desired size boundary.

For example, we can represent the number **7** as in different cases as shown in the table:

	15 14 13 12	11 10 9 8	7 6 5 4	3 2 1 0
Bit				1 1 1
Nibble				0 1 1 1
Byte			0 0 0 0	0 1 1 1
Word	0 0 0 0	0 0 0 0	0 0 0 0	0 1 1 1

Where the rightmost bit in a binary number is bit position zero and each bit to the left is given the next successive bit number as shown in the above table.

Bit zero is usually referred to as the **Least Significant Bit** or **LSB** and the left most bit is typically called the **Most Significant Bit** or **MSB**. Let us know about these formats of representation:

The Bit

A **Bit** is the smallest unit of data on a binary computer. A single bit is capable of representing only one value, either **0** or **1**. If you are using a bit to represent a Boolean (True/False) value then that bit represents true or false.

The Nibble

The Nibble specially comes in the area of interest when we are talking about the number systems, BCD (Binary Coded Decimal) or/and hexadecimal (base 16) numbers.

A nibble is a collection of bits on a 4-bit boundary. It takes four bits to represent a single BCD or hexadecimal digit. With a nibble, we can represent up to 16 distinct values.

In the case of hexadecimal numbers, the values 0, 1, 2, 3, 4, 5, 6, 7, 8, 9, A, B, C, D, E, and F are represented with four bits. BCD uses ten different digits (0, 1, 2, 3, 4, 5, 6, 7, 8, 9) and requires four bits.

In fact, any sixteen distinct values can be represented with a nibble but hexadecimal and BCD digits are the primary items we can represent with a single nibble. The bit level representation of nibble will be as follows:

b3	b2	b1	b0

The Byte

The **Byte** is the most important data structure used by 80x86 microprocessor. A byte consists of eight bits and is the smallest addressable data item in the microprocessor. The Main memory and I/O addresses in the computer are all byte addresses and thus the smallest item that can be individually accessed by an 80x86 microprocessor programs is an 8-bit value.

To access anything smaller requires that you read the byte containing the data and mask out the unwanted bits. We shall do the programming to do this in the next chapters.

The most important use for a byte is holding a character code. The bits in a byte are numbered from bit zero (b0) through seven (b7) as given follows:

b7	b6	b5	b4	b3	b2	b1	b0

Bit 0 (b0) is the low order bit or least significant bit and bit 7 (b7) is the high order bit or most significant bit of the byte.

As here we see that a byte contains exactly two nibbles where Bits b0 to b3 comprise the low order nibble and bits b4 through b7 form the high order nibble.

Since a byte contains exactly two nibbles, byte values require two hexadecimal digits.

As the traditional modern computer is a byte addressable machine, it turns out to be more efficient to manipulate a whole byte than an individual bit or nibble.

This is the reason that most programmers use a whole byte to represent data types that require no more than 256 items

Since a **Byte** contains eight bits, it can represent 2^8 or 256 different values because the maximum 8-bit binary number may by 1111 1111 that is equivalent to 256(Decimal) therefore generally a byte is used to represent the following:

> - unsigned numeric values in the range 0 to 255
> - signed numbers in the range -128 to +127
> - ASCII character codes
> - And other special data types requiring no more than 256 different values as many data types have fewer than 256 items so eight bits is usually sufficient.

The Word

A word is a group of 16 bits. But traditionally the boundary for a Word is defined as either 16-bits or the size of the data bus for the processor and a Double Word is Two Words. Therefore a Word and a Double Word is not a fixed size but varies from system to system depending on the processor. However for conceptual reading, we will define a word as two bytes.

When we see a word on bit level, it will be numbered as the bits in a word starting from bit zero (b0) through fifteen (b15). The bit level representation will be as follows:

b15	b14	b13	b12	b11	b10	b9	b8	b7	b6	b5	b4	b3	b2	b1	b0

Where **bit 0** is the **LSB** (Least Significant Bit) and **bit 15** is the **MSB** (Most Significant Bit). When there is need to refer the other bits in a word, their bit position number is used to refer them.

In this way a word contains exactly two bytes such that from **Bit b0 to Bit b7** form the low order byte and bits **b8 through b15** form the high order byte. With a word of 16-bits, we can represent 2^{16} (**65536**) different values. These values may be of following:

- The unsigned numeric values in the range of 0 to 65,535.
- The Signed numeric values in the range of -32,768 to +32,767
- Any data type with no more than 65,536 values. In this way words are mostly used for:
    - 16-bit integer data values
    - 16-bit memory addresses
    - Any number system requiring 16 bits or less

The Double Word

A double word is exactly according to its name and is two words. Therefore a double word quantity is 32 bits. The double word can also be divided into a high order word and a low order word, four bytes, or eight nibbles etc.

In this way The Double word can represent all kinds of different data. It may be of following:

- An unsigned double word in the range of 0 to 4,294,967,295,
- A signed double word in the range of -2,147,483,648 to 2,147,483,647,
- A 32-bit floating point value
- Or any other data that requires 32 bits or less.

Octal Number System

The Octal Number System was popular in old computer systems but it is very rarely used today. However we shall take an ideal of Octal System just for knowledge.

The Octal system is based on the binary system with a 3-bit boundary. The Octal Number System uses base 8 and includes only the digits 0 through 7. In this way any other digit would make the number an invalid octal number.

The weighted values for each position are as follows shown in the table:

(base)^{power}	8^5	8^4	8^3	8^2	8^1	8^0
Value	32768	4096	512	64	8	1

Number Systems

Binary to Octal Conversion

To convert from an integer binary number to octal we follow the following two steps:

1. First break the binary number into **3-bit sections from the LSB to the MSB**.
2. And then convert the 3-bit binary number to its octal equivalent.

Let us take an example to better understand it. If we have given any binary number say 11001011010001 to convert into Octal Number System, we shall apply above two steps on this number as follows:

3-bit Section of Binary Number	011	001	011	010	001
Equivalent number	3	1	3	2	1

Thus the Octal Number, Equivalent to The Binary Number 11001011010001 is **31321**.

Octal to Binary Conversion

To convert any integer octal number to its corresponding binary number we follow the following two steps:

1. First convert the decimal number to its 3-bit binary equivalent.
2. And then combine the 3-bit sections by removing the spaces.

Let us take an example. If we have any octal number integer 31321(Q) to convert into its corresponding binary number, we shall apply above two steps as follows:

Equivalent number	3	1	3	2	1
3-bit Section of Binary Number	011	001	011	010	001

Thus the binary equivalent for the octal number 31321(Q) is **011 0010 1101 0001**.

Octal to Decimal Conversion

To convert any octal number to Decimal we multiply the value in each position by its octal weight and add each value.

Let us take an example to better understand this. Let we have any octal number 31321Q to be converted into its corresponding decimal number. Then we will follow the following steps:

$$3*8^4 + 1*8^3 + 3*8^2 + 2*8^1 + 1*8^0$$
$$= 3*4096 + 1*512 + 3*64 + 2*8 + 1*1$$
$$= 12288 + 512 + 192 + 16 + 1$$
$$= 13009$$

Decimal to Octal Conversion

To convert decimal to octal is slightly more difficult. The typical method to convert from decimal to octal is repeated division by 8. For this method we divide the decimal number by 8 and write the remainder on the side as the least significant digit. This process is continued by dividing the quotient by 8 and writing the remainder until the quotient is 0.

When performing the division, the remainders which will represent the octal equivalent of the decimal number are written beginning at the least significant digit (right) and each new digit is written to the next more significant digit (the left) of the previous digit.

Let us better understand it with an example. If we have any decimal number say 13009 (we found this decimal number from the above example and by converting it back to Octal number we can also check the previous example.) then this method has been described in the following table:

Division	Quotient	Remainder	Octal Number
13009 / 8	1626	1	1
1626 / 8	203	2	21
203 / 8	25	3	321
25 / 8	3	1	1321
3 / 8	0	3	**31321**

As you can see, we are back with the original number. That is what we should expect. This table was to understand the procedure. Now let us repeat the same conversion to understand the method that should be followed in practice to get the ease of working and to save the time as well. Both are the same things in fact.

8	13009	
8	1626	1
8	203	2
8	25	3
8	3	1
	0	3

When we arrange the remainders according to the direction of arrow, we get the Octal Number **31321**, which we were expecting.

Hexadecimal Number System

Hexadecimal number are most commonly used in our data recovery or any other type of disk troubleshooting or disk analyzing programming because hexadecimal numbers offer the two features as follows:

- Hexadecimal numbers are very compact
- And it is easy to convert from hex to binary and binary to hex.

When we shall be calculating many important things like Number of Cylinders, Heads and Sectors of a hard disk or we shall be using hard disk editor programs to analyze different characteristics and problems, we shall need the good knowledge of Hex system. The Hexadecimal system is based on the binary system using a Nibble or 4-bit boundary.

The Hexadecimal Number System uses base 16 and includes only the digits 0 through 9 and the letters A, B, C, D, E, and F. We use H with the number to denote any hexadecimal number. The following table shows the representation of various number systems, differentiating them with each other:

Binary	Octal	Decimal	Hex
0000B	00Q	00	00H
0001B	01Q	01	01H
0010B	02Q	02	02H
0011B	03Q	03	03H
0100B	04Q	04	04H
0101B	05Q	05	05H
0110B	06Q	06	06H
0111B	07Q	07	07H
1000B	10Q	08	08H
1001B	11Q	09	09H
1010B	12Q	10	0AH
1011B	13Q	11	0BH
1100B	14Q	12	0CH
1101B	15Q	13	0DH
1110B	16Q	14	0EH
1111B	17Q	15	0FH
1 0000B	20Q	16	10H

This table provides all the information that you may ever need to convert from one number base into another for the decimal values from 0 to 16.

The weighted values for each position for hexadecimal numbers have been shown in the following table:

(Base)^{power}	16^3	16^2	16^1	16^0
Value	4096	256	16	1

Binary to Hexadecimal Conversion

To convert a binary number into hexadecimal format, first of all pad the binary number with leading zeros on the left most side to make sure that the binary number contains multiples of four bits. After that follow the following two steps:

1. First, break the binary number into 4-bit sections from the LSB to the MSB.
2. And then convert the 4-bit binary number to its Hex equivalent.

Let us take an example to better understand the method. Let we have any binary number 100 1110 1101 0011 to be converted into its corresponding hexadecimal number. Then we shall apply above two steps as shown below:

4-bit binary number section	0100	1110	1101	0011
Hexadecimal value	4	E	D	3

Thus the hexadecimal value, corresponding to the binary number **100 1110 1101 0011** is **4ED3**.

Hexadecimal to Binary Conversion

To convert a hexadecimal number into a binary number we follow the following two steps:

1. First, convert the Hexadecimal number to its 4-bit binary equivalent.
2. And then combine the 4-bit sections by removing the spaces.

To better understand the procedure let us take an example of the above hexadecimal number, that is **4ED3** and apply these two steps on it as follows:

Hexadecimal value	4	E	D	3
4-bit binary number section	0100	1110	1101	0011

Thus for the hexadecimal number **4ED3**, we get the corresponding binary number

= **0100 1110 1101 0011**

This is the expected answer.

Hexadecimal to Decimal Conversion

To convert from Hexadecimal to Decimal we multiply the value in each position by its hex weight and add each value.

Let us take an example to better understand the procedure. Assume that we have any hexadecimal number **3ABE** to be converted to its equivalent decimal number. Then the procedure will be as follows:

$$3*16^3 + A*16^2 + B*16^1 + E*16^0$$
$$= 3*4096 + 10*256 + 11*16 + 14$$
$$= 12288 + 2560 + 176 + 14$$
$$= 15038$$

Thus the equivalent decimal number for the hexadecimal number **3ABE** is **15038**.

Decimal to Hexadecimal Conversion

To convert decimal to hexadecimal, the typical method is repeated division by 16. For this method, we divide the decimal number by 16 and write the remainder on the side as the least significant digit.

This process is continued by dividing the quotient by 16 and writing the remainder until the quotient is 0. When performing the division, the remainders which will represent the hex equivalent of the decimal number are written beginning at the least significant digit (right) and each new digit is written to the next more significant digit (the left) of the previous digit.

Let us learn it with example. We take the decimal number 15038 which we got after conversion

Number Systems

above. By this we can also check the above conversion and vice-versa.

Division	Quotient	Remainder	Hex Number
15038 / 16	939	14 (E H)	E
939 / 16	58	11 (B H)	BE
58 / 16	3	10 (A H)	ABE
3 / 16	0	3 (3 H)	**03ABE**

Thus we get hexadecimal number **03ABE** H, equivalent to the decimal number **15038** and in this way we are back with the original number. That is what we should expect.

The table given next can help to get the quick search of Hexadecimal number to decimal number conversion and vice-versa from the range of 0 to 255 decimal numbers.

	0	1	2	3	4	5	6	7	8	9	A	B	C	D	E	F
0	0	1	2	3	4	5	6	7	8	9	10	11	12	13	14	15
1	16	17	18	19	20	21	22	23	24	25	26	27	28	29	30	31
2	32	33	34	35	36	37	38	39	40	41	42	43	44	45	46	47
3	48	49	50	51	52	53	54	55	56	57	58	59	60	61	62	63
4	64	65	66	67	68	69	70	71	72	73	74	75	76	77	78	79
5	80	81	82	83	84	85	86	87	88	89	90	91	92	93	94	95
6	96	97	98	99	100	101	102	103	104	105	106	107	108	109	110	111
7	112	113	114	115	116	117	118	119	120	121	122	123	124	125	126	127
8	128	129	130	131	132	133	134	135	136	137	138	139	140	141	142	143
9	144	145	146	147	148	149	150	151	152	153	154	155	156	157	158	159
A	160	161	162	163	164	165	166	167	168	169	170	171	172	173	174	175
B	176	177	178	179	180	181	182	183	184	185	186	187	188	189	190	191
C	192	193	194	195	196	197	198	199	200	201	202	203	204	205	206	207
D	208	209	210	211	212	213	214	215	216	217	218	219	220	221	222	223
E	224	225	226	227	228	229	230	231	232	233	234	235	236	237	238	239
F	240	241	242	243	244	245	246	247	248	249	250	251	252	253	254	255

In this **Square table** there are 16 rows, starting from 0 to A and there are 16 columns also starting from 0 to A. From this table you can find the decimal value of any hexadecimal number that is in between the range of **0H to FFH**. It means that the decimal value of the number should be in between the range of **0 to 255** decimal numbers.

- **Finding Decimal value for Hexadecimal number from above table:** In the table given above, the number of rows represent the first hexadecimal digit (left Hexadecimal digit) and the number of columns represent the second hexadecimal digit (right hexadecimal digit) of the hexadecimal number.

  Let we have any hexadecimal number say **ACH**, to be converted into the equivalent decimal number. Then we shall see the decimal value in the Cth column of the Ath row in the table and get the decimal value **172,** which is the equivalent decimal number for the hexadecimal number ACH.

- **Finding Hexadecimal Value for the Decimal number from above table:** In the table given above, the number of rows represent the first hexadecimal digit (left Hexadecimal digit) and the number of columns represent the second hexadecimal digit (right hexadecimal digit) of the hexadecimal number thus if you have any decimal number to be converted into equivalent hexadecimal number, search the number in the table and find the equivalent hexadecimal value as follows:

Hex Value for the Decimal Number =
$$(Row\ Number)(Column\ Number)$$

For example if you want to find the equivalent hexadecimal value number for the decimal number **154**, see the location of the number in the table. The number **154** is in the 9th row and A^{th} column of the table. Thus the equivalent hexadecimal value for the decimal number **154** is **9AH**.

ASCII Code

The abbreviation **ASCII** stands for **A**merican **S**tandard **C**ode for **I**nformation **I**nterchange. It is a coding standard for characters, numbers, and symbols that is the same as the first 128 characters of the ASCII character set but differs from the remaining characters. These other characters are usually called special ASCII characters of Extended characters which have been defined by IBM.

The first 32 characters which are ASCII codes 0 through 1FH, form a special set of non-printing characters. These characters are called the control characters because these characters perform various printer and display control operations rather than displaying symbols. These characters have been listed in the ASCII character table given in this chapter. These control characters have following meanings:

NUL (Null):

No character. It is used for filling in time or filling space on the surface (such as surface of platter) of storage device where there are no data. We'll use this character when we'll be doing **programming for data wipers (destructive and non-destructive both) to wipeout the unallocated space** so that deleted data may not be recovered by any one or by any program.

SOH (Start Of Heading):

This character is used to indicate the start of heading, which may contain address or routing information.

STX (Start of Text):

This character is used to indicate the start of text and in this way this is also used to indicate the end of the heading.

ETX (End of Text):

This character is used to terminate the text that was started with **STX**.

EOT (End Of Transmission):

This character indicates the end of the transmission, which may have included one or more "tests" with their headings.

ENQ (Enquiry):
It is a request for a response from a remote station. It is a request for a station to identify itself.

ACK (Acknowledge):
It is a character, transmitted by a receiving device as an affirmation response to a sander. It is used as a positive response to polling messages.

BEL (Bell):
It is used when there is need to call human attention. It may control alarm or attention devices. You can hear a bell tone from the speakers, attached to your computer when you type this character in the command prompt as given below:

    C:\> Echo ^G

Here ^G is printed by the combination of Ctrl + G keys combination.

BS (Backspace):
This character indicates the movement of the printing mechanism or display cursor backward in one position.

HT (Horizontal Tab):
It indicates the movement of the printing mechanism or display cursor forward to the next pre assigned "Tab" or stopping position.

LF (Line Feed):
It indicates the movement of printing mechanism or display cursor to the start of the next line.

VT (Vertical Tab):
It indicates the movement of the printing mechanism or display cursor to the next of a series of pre assigned printing lines.

FF (Form Feed):
It indicates the movement of the printing mechanism or display cursor to the starting position of the next page, from, or screen.

CR (Carriage Return):
It indicates the movement of printing mechanism or display cursor to the starting position of the same line.

SO (Shift Out):
It indicates that the code combinations that follow shall be interpreted as **outside** of the standard character set until a **Shift In** character is reached.

SI (Shift In):

It indicates that the code combinations that follow shall be interpreted according to the standard character set.

DLE (Data Link Escape):

It is a character that shall change the meaning of one or more contiguously following characters. It can provide supplementary control, or permits the sending of data characters having any bit combination.

DC1, DC2, DC3 and DC4 (Device Controls):

These are the characters for the control of ancillary devices or special terminal features.

NAK (Negative Acknowledgement):

It is a character transmitted by a receiving device as a negative response to a sender. It is used as a negative response to polling message.

SYN (Synchronous/ Idle):

it is used by a synchronous transmission system to achieve synchronization when no data is being sent a synchronous transmission system may send **SYN characters** continuously.

ETB (End of Transmission Block):

This character indicates the end of a block of data for communication purpose. It is used for blocking data, where the block structure is not necessarily related to the processing format.

CAN (Cancel):

It indicates that the data that precedes it in a message or block should be disregarded usually because an error has been detected.

EM (End of Medium):

It indicates the physical end of a tape, surface (usually of a disk's platter) or other medium or end of the required of used portion of the medium.

SUB (Substitute):

It is a substitute for a character that is found to be erroneous or invalid.

ESC (Escape):

It is a character intended to provide code extension in that it gives a specified number of continuously following characters an alternate meaning.

FS (File Separator):

This character is used as a file separator character.

GS (Group Separator):

It is used as a group separator character.

RS (Record Separator):
It is used as a record separator character.

US (United Separator):
It is a united separator character.

The second group of 32 ASCII character codes has various punctuation symbols, special characters, and the numeric digits. The most notable characters in this group include the following:
- space character (ASCII code 20H)
- numeric digits 0 through 9 (ASCII codes 30h through 39h)
- mathematical and logical symbols

SP (Space):
It is a non printing character used to separate words or to move the printing mechanism or to display the cursor forward by one position.

The third group of 32 ASCII characters is the group of upper case alphabetic characters. The ASCII codes for the characters **A through Z** lie in the range 41H through 5AH. Since there are only 26 different alphabetic characters, the remaining six codes hold various special symbols.

The fourth group of 32 ASCII character codes is the group of lower case alphabetic symbols, five additional special symbols and another control character **delete**.

DEL (Delete):
It is used to obliterate unwanted characters rather we can say to delete the unwanted characters.

There have been shown two tables next, representing the ASCII codes and Extended Characters. The first table represents all the four group of different type of characters described. This table is data representation and ASCII table as shown next:

Data Representation & ASCII Code Table:

HEX	DEC	CHR	CTRL	HEX	DEC	CHR
00	0	NUL	^@	20	32	SP
01	1	SOH	^A	21	33	!
02	2	STX	^B	22	34	"
03	3	ETX	^C	23	35	#
04	4	EOT	^D	24	36	$
05	5	ENQ	^E	25	37	%
06	6	ACK	^F	26	38	&
07	7	BEL	^G	27	39	'
08	8	BS	^H	28	40	(
09	9	HT	^I	29	41	)
0A	10	LF	^J	2A	42	*
0B	11	VT	^K	2B	43	+

HEX	DEC	CHR	HEX	DEC	CHR
0C	12	FF	^L	2C	44	,
0D	13	CR	^M	2D	45	-
0E	14	SO	^N	2E	46	.
0F	15	SI	^O	2F	47	/
10	16	DLE	^P	30	48	0
11	17	DC1	^Q	31	49	1
12	18	DC2	^R	32	50	2
13	19	DC3	^S	33	51	3
14	20	DC4	^T	34	52	4
15	21	NAK	^U	35	53	5
16	22	SYN	^V	36	54	6
17	23	ETB	^W	37	55	7
18	24	CAN	^X	38	56	8
19	25	EM	^Y	39	57	9
1A	26	SUB	^Z	3A	58	:
1B	27	ESC		3B	59	;
1C	28	FS		3C	60	<
1D	29	GS		3D	61	=
1E	30	RS		3E	62	>
1F	31	US		3F	63	?

HEX	DEC	CHR	HEX	DEC	CHR
40	64	@	60	96	`
41	65	A	61	97	a
42	66	B	62	98	b
43	67	C	63	99	c
44	68	D	64	100	d
45	69	E	65	101	e
46	70	F	66	102	f
47	71	G	67	103	g
48	72	H	68	104	h
49	73	I	69	105	i
4A	74	J	6A	106	j
4B	75	K	6B	107	k
4C	76	L	6C	108	l
4D	77	M	6D	109	m
4E	78	N	6E	100	n
4F	79	O	6F	111	o

Number Systems

50	80	P	70	112	p
51	80	Q	71	113	q
52	82	R	72	114	r
53	83	S	73	115	s
54	84	T	74	116	t
55	85	U	75	117	u
56	86	V	76	118	v
57	87	W	77	119	w
58	88	X	78	120	x
59	89	Y	79	121	y
5A	90	Z	7A	122	z
5B	91	[	7B	123	{
5C	92	\	7C	124	|
5D	93	]	7D	125	}
5E	94	^	7E	126	~
5F	95	_	7F	127	DEL

The next table shows the 128 special ASCII characters set which are often called the Extended ASCII characters:

HEX	DEC	CHR	HEX	DEC	CHR
80	128	Ç	A5	165	Ñ
81	129	ü	A6	166	ª
82	130	é	A7	167	º
83	131	â	A8	168	¿
84	132	ä	A9	169	⌐
85	133	à	AA	170	¬
86	134	å	AB	171	½
87	135	ç	AC	172	¼
88	136	ê	AD	173	¡
89	137	ë	AE	174	«
8A	138	è	AF	175	»
8C	139	ï	B0	176	░
8C	140	î	B1	177	▒
8D	141	ì	B2	178	▓
8E	142	Ä	B3	179	│
8F	143	Å	B4	180	┤

HEX	DEC	CHR	HEX	DEC	CHR
90	144	É	B5	181	┤
91	145	æ	B6	182	╡
92	146	Æ	B7	183	╢
93	147	ô	B8	184	╖
94	148	ö	B9	185	╕
95	149	ò	BA	186	╣
96	150	û	BB	187	║
97	151	ù	BC	188	╗
98	152	ÿ	BD	189	╝
99	153	Ö	BE	190	╜
9A	154	Ü	BF	191	╛
9B	155	¢	C0	192	┐
9C	156	£	C1	193	└
9D	157	¥	C2	194	┴
9E	158	₧	C3	195	┬
9F	159	ƒ	C4	196	├
A0	160	á	C5	197	─
A1	161	í	C6	198	┼
A2	162	ó	C7	199	╞
A3	163	ú	C8	200	╟
A4	164	ñ	C9	201	╚

HEX	DEC	CHR	HEX	DEC	CHR
CA	202	╔	EF	239	∩
CB	203	╦	F0	240	≡
CC	204	╠	F1	241	±
CD	205	═	F2	242	≥
CE	206	╬	F3	243	≤
CF	207	╧	F4	244	⌠
D0	208	╨	F5	245	⌡
D1	209	╤	F6	246	÷
D2	210	╥	F7	247	≈
D3	211	╙	F8	248	°
D4	212	╘	F9	249	·

Hex	Dec	Char	Hex	Dec	Char
D5	213	⊢	FA	250	·
D6	214	⊤	FB	251	√
D7	215	⊧	FC	252	n
D8	216	⊨	FD	253	²
D9	217	⌐	FE	254	■
DA	218	⌐	FF	255	
DB	219	■			
DC	220	▌			
DD	221	▐			
DE	222	▌			
DF	223	▀			
E0	224	α			
E1	225	ß			
E2	226	Γ			
E3	227	π			
E4	228	Σ			
E5	229	σ			
E6	230	μ			
E7	231	τ			
E8	232	Φ			
E9	233	Θ			
EA	234	Ω			
EB	235	δ			
EC	236	∞			
ED	237	φ			
EE	238	ε			

Some important number system terms, often used for Data and Data Storage representation

The table given below represents the various prefix which are used as fractional prefixes and as magnifying prefixes:

Prefix	Decimal	Binary
yocto-	10^{-24}	not used (Fractional Prefix)
zepto-	10^{-21}	not used (Fractional Prefix)
atto-	10^{-18}	not used (Fractional Prefix)
femto-	10^{-15}	not used (Fractional Prefix)
pico-	10^{-12}	not used (Fractional Prefix)
nano-	10^{-9}	not used (Fractional Prefix)
micro-	10^{-6}	not used (Fractional Prefix)
milli-	10^{-3}	not used (Fractional Prefix)
unit	1	1
kilo-	10^{3}	$2^{10} = (1024)^1 = 1,024$
mega-	10^{6}	$2^{20} = (1024)^2 = 1,048,576$
giga-	10^{9}	$2^{30} = (1024)^3 = 1,073,741,824$
tera-	10^{12}	$2^{40} = (1024)^4 = 1,099,511,627,776$
peta-	10^{15}	$2^{50} = (1024)^5 = 1,125,899,906,842,624$
exa-	10^{18}	$2^{60} = (1024)^6 = 1,152,921,504,606,846,976$
zetta-	10^{21}	$2^{70} = (1024)^7 = 1,180,591,620,717,411,303,424$
yotta-	10^{24}	$2^{80} = (1024)^8 = 1,208,925,819,614,629,174,706,176$

Byte:

The most important use for a byte is holding a character code. We have discussed it earlier.

Kilobyte

Technically a kilobyte is 1024 bytes, but it is often used loosely as a synonym for 1000 bytes. In decimal systems, kilo stands for 1000 but in binary systems a kilo is 1024 (2^{10}).

Kilobyte is usually represented by K or Kb. To distinguish between a decimal K (1000) and a binary K (1024), the IEEE (Institute of Electrical and Electronics Engineers) standard has suggested following the convention of using a small k for a decimal kilo and a capital K for a binary kilo but this convention is by no means strictly followed.

Megabyte

Megabyte is used to describe data storage of 1048576 (2^{20}) bytes but when it is used to describe data transfer rates as in MBps, it refers to one million bytes. Megabyte is usually abbreviated as M or MB.

Gigabyte

Gigabyte is used to describe the storage of 1,073,741,824 (2^{30}) bytes and One gigabyte is equal to 1,024 megabytes. Gigabyte is usually abbreviated as G or GB.

Terabyte

Terabyte is 1,099,511,627,776 (2^{40}) bytes which is approximately 1 trillion bytes. Terabyte is

Number Systems

sometimes described as 10^{12} (1,000,000,000,000) bytes which is exactly one trillion.

Petabyte
Petabyte is described as 1,125,899,906,842,624 (2^{50}) bytes. A Petabyte is equal to 1,024 terabytes.

Exabyte
Exabyte is described as 1,152,921,504,606,846,976 (2^{60}) bytes. An Exabyte is equal to 1,024 Petabyte.

Zettabyte
Zettabyte is described as 1,180,591,620,717,411,303,424 (2^{70}) bytes which is approximately 10^{21} (1,000,000,000,000,000,000,000) bytes. A Zettabyte is equal to 1,024 Exabytes.

Yottabyte
Yottabyte is described as 1,208,925,819,614,629,174,706,176 (2^{80}) bytes which is approximately 10^{24} (1,000,000,000,000,000,000,000,000) bytes. A Yottabyte is equal to 1,024 Zettabytes.

Common Data Storage Terms
There are various names used to refer the terms given before, to various groupings of bits of data. Some of the Most commonly used, have been listed in the following table:

Term	Number of Bits
Bit / Digit / Flag	1
Nibble / Nybble	4
Byte / Character	8
Word	16
Double Word / Long Word	32
Very Long Word	64

Chapter – 5
Introduction of C Programming

Introduction

'C' is one of the most popular computer languages in today's computer world. The 'C' programming language was designed and developed by Brian Kernighan and Dennis Ritchie at The Bell Research Labs in 1972.

'C' is a Language specifically created in order to allow the programmer access to almost all of the machine's internals - registers, I/O slots and absolute addresses. At the same time, 'C' allows for as much data handling and programmed text modularization as is needed to allow very complex multi-programmer projects to be constructed in an organized and timely fashion.

Although this language was originally intended to run under UNIX, there has been a great interest in running it under the MS-DOS operating system on the IBM PC and compatibles. It is an excellent language for this environment because of the simplicity of expression, the compactness of the code, and the wide range of applicability.

Also, due to the simplicity and ease of writing a C compiler, it is usually the first high level language available on any new computer, including microcomputers, minicomputers, and mainframes.

Why use C in Data Recovery Programming

In today's world of computer programming, there are many high-level languages are available. These languages are good with many features suited for most programming tasks. Yet, there are several reasons that C is the first choice of the programmers who are willing to do programming for data recovery, system programming, device programming or hardware programming:

- C is a popular language preferred by professional programmers. As a result, a wide variety of C compilers and helpful accessories are available.

- C is a portable language. A C program written for one computer system can be compiled and run on another system with little or no modification. Portability is enhanced by the ANSI standard for C, the set of rules for C compilers.

- C allows a wide use of modules in programming. C code can be written in routines called functions. These functions can be reused in other applications or programs. You need not to do extra efforts in the programming of new application to create the same module that you developed in another application programming before.

  You can use this function in new program without any change or some minor changes. In case of data recovery programming you will find this quality very much helping when you

- need the run the same functions several times in different applications of different program.
- C is a powerful and flexible language. This is the reason why C is used for projects as diverse as operating systems, word processors, graphics, spreadsheets, and even compilers for other languages.
- C is a language of few words, containing only a handful of terms, called keywords, which serve as the base on which the language's functionality is built. These keywords, also called reserved words, make it more powerful and give the wide area of programming and make a programmer feel to do any type of programming in C.

Let me assume that you know nothing in C

I assume that you know nothing about C programming and also not have any idea of programming. I will begin with the most basic concepts of C and take you up to the high level of C programming including the usually intimidating concepts of pointers, structures, and dynamic allocation.

To fully understand these concepts, it will take a good bit of time and work on your part because they are not particularly easy to grasp, but they are very powerful tools.

Programming in C is a tremendous asset in those areas where you may need to use Assembly Language but would rather keep it a simple to write and easy to maintain program. The time saved in coding of C can be tremendous in such cases.

Even though the C language enjoys a good record when programs are transported from one implementation to another, there are differences in compilers that you will find anytime you try to use another compiler.

Most of the differences become apparent when you use nonstandard extensions such as calls to the DOS BIOS when using MS-DOS, but even these differences can be minimized by careful choice of programming constructs.

When it became evident that the C programming language was becoming a very popular language available on a wide range of computers, a group of concerned individuals met to propose a standard set of rules for the use of the C programming language.

The group represented all sectors of the software industry and after many meetings, and many preliminary drafts, they finally wrote an acceptable standard for the C language. It has been accepted by the American National Standards Institute (ANSI), and by the International Standards Organization (ISO).

It is not forced upon any group or user, but since it is so widely accepted, it would be economic suicide for any compiler writer to refuse to conform to the standard.

The programs written in this book are primarily for use on an IBM-PC or compatible computer but can be used with any ANSI standard compiler since it conforms so closely to the ANSI standard.

Let us start

Before you can do anything in any language and start programming, you must know how to name an identifier. An identifier is used for any variable, function, data definition, etc. In the C programming language, an identifier is a combination of alphanumeric characters, the first being a letter of the alphabet or an underline, and the remaining being any letter of the alphabet, any numeric digit, or the underline.

Two rules must be kept in mind when naming identifiers.

1. The case of alphabetic characters is significant. C is a case sensitive language. That means **Recovery** is different from **recovery** and **rEcOveRY** is different from both mentioned before.
2. According to the ANSI-C standard, at least 31 significant characters can be used and will be considered significant by a conforming ANSI-C compiler. If more than 31 are used, all characters beyond the 31st may be ignored by any given compiler

Keywords

There are 32 words defined as keywords in C. These have predefined uses and cannot be used for any other purpose in a C program. They are used by the compiler as an aid to compiling the program. They are always written in lower case. A complete list follows:

auto	double	int	struct
break	else	long	switch
case	enum	register	typedef
char	extern	return	union
const	float	short	unsigned
continue	for	signed	void
default	goto	sizeof	volatile
do	if	static	while

Here we see the magic of C. The wonderful collection of only 32 keywords gives a wide use in different applications. Any computer program has two entities to consider, the data, and the program. They are highly dependent on one another and careful planning of both lead to a well planned and well written program.

Let us begin with a simple C program:

```
/* First Program to learn C */
    #include <stdio.h>
    void main()
    {
        printf("This is a C program\n"); // printing a message
    }
```

Though the program is very simple, a few points are worthy of note. Let us examine the above program. Everything that is inside **/*** and ***/** is considered a **comment** and will be ignored by the compiler. You should not include **comments** within other comments, so something like this is not allowed:

/* this is a /* comment */ inside a comment, which is wrong */

There is also a way of documentation that works within a line. By using **//** we can add small documentation within that line.

Every C program contains a function called **main**. This is the start point of the program. Every function should return a value. In this program the function **main** returns no return value therefore we have written **void main**. We could also write this program as:

```
/*   First Program to learn C */
```

Introduction of C Programming

```
#include <stdio.h>
main()
{
    printf("This is a C program\n");   // printing a message
    return 0;
}
```

Both the program are same and perform the same task. The result of both the program will print the following output on the screen:

This is a C program

#include<stdio.h> allows the program to interact with the screen, keyboard and file system of your computer. You will find it at the beginning of almost every C program.

main() declares the start of the function, while the two curly brackets show the start and finish of the function. Curly brackets in C are used to group statements together as in a function, or in the body of a loop. Such a grouping is known as a compound statement or a block.

printf("This is a C program\n"); prints the words on the screen. The text to be printed is enclosed in double quotes. The **\n** at the end of the text tells the program to print a new line as part of the output. **printf()** function is used for monitor display of the output.

Most of the C programs are in lower case letters. You will usually find upper case letters used in preprocessor definitions which will be discussed later, or inside quotes as parts of character strings.

Compiling the program

Let the name of our program is CPROG.C. To enter and compile the C program, follow these steps:

1. Make the active directory of your C programs and start your editor. For this any text editor can be used, but most C compilers such as Borland's Turbo C++ has an integrated development environment (IDE) that lets you enter, compile, and link your programs in one convenient setting.
2. Write and save the source code. You should name the file CPROG.C.
3. Compile and link CPROG.C. Execute the appropriate command specified by your compiler's manuals. You should get a message stating that there were no errors or warnings.
4. Check the compiler messages. If you receive no errors or warnings, everything should be okay. If there is any error in typing the program, the compiler will catch it and display an error message. Correct the error, displayed in the error message.
5. Your first C program should now be compiled and ready to run. If you display a directory listing of all files named CPROG you will get the four files with different extension described as follows:
    1. CPROG.C, the source code file
    2. CPROG.BAK, the backup file of source file you created with editor
    3. CPROG.OBJ, contains the object code for CPROG.C
    4. CPROG.EXE, the executable program created when you compiled and linked CPROG.C
6. To execute, or run, CPROG.EXE, simply enter cprog. The message, This is a C program is

displayed on-screen.

Now let us examine the following program:

```
/* First Program to learn C */                  // 1
                                                // 2
    #include <stdio.h>                          // 3
                                                // 4
    main()                                      // 5
    {                                           
                                                // 6
        printf("This is a C program\n");        // 7
                                                // 8
        return 0;                               // 9
    }                                           // 10
```

When you compile this program, the compiler displays a message similar to the following:

cprog.c(8) : Error: ';' expected

let us break this error message in parts. cprog.c is the name of the file where the error was found. (8) is line number where the error was found. Error: ';' expected is A description of the error.

This message is quite informative, and tells you that in line 8 of CPROG.C the compiler expected to find a semicolon but didn't. However, you know that the semicolon was actually omitted from line 7, so there is a discrepancy.

Why the compiler reports an error in line 8 when, in fact, a semicolon was omitted from line 7. The answer lies in the fact that C doesn't care about things like breaks between lines. The semicolon that belongs after the **printf()** statement could have been placed on the next line though doing so would be bad programming in practice.

Only after encountering the next command (return) in line 8 is the compiler sure that the semicolon is missing. Therefore, the compiler reports that the error is in line 8.

There may be a number of possibilities of different type of errors. Let us discuss linking error Messages. **Linker errors** are relatively rare and usually result from misspelling the name of a C library function. In this case, you get an Error: undefined symbols: error message, followed by the misspelled name. Once you correct the spelling, the problem should go away.

Printing Numbers

Let us see the following example:

```
// How To print the numbers //
#include<stdio.h>
void main()
{
    int num = 10;
    printf(" The Number Is %d", num);

}
```

The output of the program will be displayed on the screen as follows:
   The Number Is 10

The % sign is used to signal the output of many different types of variables. The character following the % sign is a **d**, which signals the output routine to get a decimal value and output it.

Using Variables

In C, a variable must be declared before it can be used. Variables can be declared at the start of any block of code, but most are found at the start of each function. Most local variables are created when the function is called, and are destroyed on return from that function.

To use variables in your C programs, you must know the following rules when giving the name to variables in C:

- The name can contain letters, digits, and the underscore character (_).
- The first character of the name must be a letter. The underscore is also a legal first character, but its use is not recommended.
- C is case sensitive therefore the variable name num is Different from Num.
- C keywords can't be used as variable names. A keyword is a word that is part of the C language.

The following list contains some examples of legal and illegal C variable names:

Variable Name	Legal or Not
Num	Legal
Ttpt2_t2p	Legal
Tt pt	Illegal: Space is not allowed
_1990_tax	Legal but not advised
Jack_phone#	Illegal: Contains the illegal character #
Case	Illegal: Is a C keyword
1book	Illegal: First character is a digit

The first new thing that stands out is the first line of the body of main():
   int num = 10;

This line defines a variable named 'num' of type **int** and initializes it with the value 10. This might also have been written as:
   int num;   /* define uninitialized variable 'num' */
   /* and after all variable definitions: */
   num = 10;   /* assigns value 10 to variable 'num' */

Variables may be defined at the start of a block (between the braces {and}), usually this is at the start of a function body, but it may also be at the start of another type of block.

Variables that are defined at the beginning of a block default to the '**auto**' status. This means that they only exist during the execution of the block. When the function execution begins, the variables will be created but their contents will be undefined. When the function returns, the variables will be destroyed. The definition could also have been written as:

    auto int num = 10;

Since the definition with or without the **auto** keyword is completely equivalent, the **auto** keyword is obviously rather redundant.

However, sometimes this is not what you want. Suppose you want a function to keep count of how many times it is called. If the variable would be destroyed every time the function returns, this would not be possible.

Therefore it is possible to give the variable what is called **static** duration, which means it will stay intact during the whole execution of the program. For example:

    static int num = 10;

This initializes the variable num to 10 at the beginning of the program execution. From then on the value will remain untouched; the variable will not be re-initialized if the function is called multiple times.

Sometimes it is not sufficient that the variable will be accessible from one function only or it might not be convenient to pass the value via a parameter to all other functions that need it.

But if you need access to the variable from all the functions in the entire source file, this can also done with the **static** keyword, but by putting the definition outside all functions. For example:

```
#include <stdio.h>
static int num = 10;   /* will be accessible from entire source file */
int main(void)
{
    printf("The Number Is: %d\n", num);
    return 0;
}
```

And there are also cases where a variable needs to be accessible from the entire program, which may consist of several source files. This is called a **global variable** and should be avoided when it is not required.

This is also done by putting the definition outside all functions, but without using the **static** keyword:

```
#include <stdio.h>
int num = 10;   /* will be accessible from entire program! */
int main(void)
{
    printf("The Number Is: %d\n", num);
    return 0;
}
```

There is also the **extern** keyword, which is used for accessing global variables in other modules. There are also a few qualifiers that you can add to variable definitions. The most important of them is **const**. A variable that is defined as **const** may not be modified.

There are two more modifiers that are less commonly used. The **volatile** and **register** modifier. The **volatile** modifier requires the compiler to actually access the variable every time it is read. It may

Introduction of C Programming

not optimize the variable by putting it in a register or so. This is mainly used for multithreading and interrupt processing purposes etc.

The **register** modifier requests the compiler to optimize the variable into a register. This is only possible with **auto** variables and in many cases the compiler can better select the variables to optimize into registers, so this keyword is obsolescent. The only direct consequence of making a variable **register** is that its address cannot be taken.

The table of variables, given in the next page describes the storage class of five type of storage classes.

In the table we see the keyword extern is placed in two rows. The extern keyword is used in functions to declare a static external variable that is defined elsewhere.

Variable	Defined as Storage class	Scope	Class	Keyword
Automatic	Keyword is optional	Temporary	In a function	Local
Static	static	Temporary	In a function	Local
Register	register	Temporary	In a function	Local
External	Optional	Permanent	Outside a function	Global (all files)
External	Static	Permanent	Outside a function	Global (one file)

Numeric Variable Types

C provides several different types of numeric variables because different numeric values have varying memory storage requirements. These numeric types differ in the ease with which certain mathematical operations can be performed on them.

Small integers require less memory to store, and your computer can perform mathematical operations with such numbers very quickly. Large integers and floating-point values require more storage space and more time for mathematical operations. By using the appropriate variable types, you ensure that your program runs as efficiently as possible.

C's numeric variables fall into the following two main categories:

- Integer variables
- Floating-point variables

Within each of these categories are two or more specific variable types. Table given next, shows the amount of memory, in bytes, required to hold a single variable of each type.

The type **char** may be equivalent to either **signed char** or **unsigned char**, but it is always a separate type from either of these.

In C there is no difference between storing characters or their corresponding numerical values in a variable, so there is also no need for a function to convert between a character and its numerical value or vice versa. For the other integer types, if you omit **signed** or **unsigned** the default will be **signed**, so e.g. **int** and **signed int** are equivalent.

The type **int** must be greater than or equal to the type **short**, and smaller than or equal to the type **long**. If you simply need to store some values which are not enormously large it's often a good idea to use the type **int**; it usually is the size the processor can deal with the easiest, and therefore the fastest.

With several compilers **double** and **long double** are equivalent. That combined with the fact that most standard mathematical functions work with type **double**, is a good reason to always use the type **double** if you have to work with fractional numbers.

The following table is to better describe the variable types:

Variable Type	Keyword	Bytes Required	Range	Format
Character	char	1	-128 to 127	%c
Integer	int	2	-32768 to 32767	%d
Short integer	short	2	-32768 to 32767	%d
Long integer	long	4	-2,147,483,648 to 2,147,438,647	%ld
Unsigned character	unsigned char	1	0 to 255	%c
Unsigned integer	unsigned int	2	0 to 65535	%u
Unsigned short integer	unsigned short	2	0 to 65535	%u
Unsigned long integer	unsigned long	4	0 to 4,294,967,295	%lu
Single floating-point	float	4	-3.4E38 to 3.4E38	%f
Double floating-point	double	8	-1.7E308 to 1.7E308	%lf
Long double floating-point	long double	10	-1.7E4932 to 1.7E4932	%Lf

Special-purpose types commonly used:

Variable Type	Description
size_t	unsigned type used for storing the sizes of objects in bytes
time_t	used to store results of the time() function
clock_t	used to store results of the clock() function
FILE	used for accessing a stream (usually a file or device)
ptrdiff_t	signed type of the difference between 2 pointers
div_t	used to store results of the div() function
ldiv_t	used to store results of ldiv() function

Introduction of C Programming

fpos_t	used to hold file position information
va_list	used in variable argument handling
wchar_t	wide character type (used for extended character sets)
sig_atomic_t	used in signal handlers
Jmp_buf	used for non-local jumps

To better understand these variables let us take an example:

```c
/* Program to tell the range and size in bytes of the C variable */
#include <stdio.h>
int main()
{
    int a;                  /* simple integer type */
    long int b;             /* long integer type */
    short int c;            /* short integer type */
    unsigned int d;         /* unsigned integer type */
    char e;                 /* character type */
    float f;                /* floating point type */
    double g;               /* double precision floating point */

    a = 1023;
    b = 2222;
    c = 123;
    d = 1234;
    e = 'X';
    f = 3.14159;
    g = 3.1415926535898;

    printf( "\nA char     is %d bytes", sizeof( char ));
    printf( "\nAn int     is %d bytes", sizeof( int ));
    printf( "\nA short    is %d bytes", sizeof( short ));
    printf( "\nA long     is %d bytes", sizeof( long ));

    printf( "\nAn unsigned char  is %d bytes",
            sizeof( unsigned char ));

    printf( "\nAn unsigned int   is %d bytes",
            sizeof( unsigned int ));

    printf( "\nAn unsigned short is %d bytes",
            sizeof( unsigned short ));

    printf( "\nAn unsigned long  is %d bytes",
            sizeof( unsigned long ));

    printf( "\nA float    is %d bytes", sizeof( float ));
```

```c
    printf( "\nA double    is %d bytes\n", sizeof( double ));

    printf("a = %d\n", a);       /* decimal output */
    printf("a = %o\n", a);       /* octal output */
    printf("a = %x\n", a);       /* hexadecimal output */
    printf("b = %ld\n", b);      /* decimal long output */
    printf("c = %d\n", c);       /* decimal short output */
    printf("d = %u\n", d);       /* unsigned output */
    printf("e = %c\n", e);       /* character output */
    printf("f = %f\n", f);       /* floating output */
    printf("g = %f\n", g);       /* double float output */

    printf("\n");

    printf("a = %d\n", a);       /* simple int output */
    printf("a = %7d\n", a);      /* use a field width of 7 */
    printf("a = %-7d\n", a);     /* left justify in field of 7 */

    c = 5;
    d = 8;

    printf("a = %*d\n", c, a);   /* use a field width of 5*/
    printf("a = %*d\n", d, a);   /* use a field width of 8 */

    printf("\n");

    printf("f = %f\n", f);       /* simple float output */
    printf("f = %12f\n", f);     /* use field width of 12 */
    printf("f = %12.3f\n", f);   /* use 3 decimal places */
    printf("f = %12.5f\n", f);   /* use 5 decimal places */
    printf("f = %-12.5f\n", f);  /* left justify in field */

    return 0;
}
```

The Result of program after execution will be displayed as:

```
A char is 1 bytes
An int is 2 bytes
A short is 2 bytes
A long is 4 bytes
An unsigned char is 1 bytes
An unsigned int is 2 bytes
An unsigned short is 2 bytes
An unsigned long is 4 bytes
```

```
A float is 4 bytes
A double is 8 bytes
a = 1023
a = 1777
a = 3ff
b = 2222
c = 123
d = 1234
e = X
f = 3.141590
g = 3.141593
a = 1023
a = 1023
a = 1023
a = 1023
a = 1023
f = 3.141590
f = 3.141590
f = 3.142
f = 3.14159
f = 3.14159
```

Before its use, a variable in a C program, it must be declared. A variable declaration tells the compiler the name and type of a variable and optionally initializes the variable to a specific value.

If your program attempts to use a variable that hasn't been declared, the compiler generates an error message. A variable declaration has the following form:

    typename varname;

typename specifies the variable type and must be one of the keywords. *varname* is the variable name. You can declare multiple variables of the same type on one line by separating the variable names with commas:

    int count, number, start;   /* three integer variables */

    float percent, total;   /* two float variables */

The typedef Keyword

The typedef keyword is used to create a new name for an existing data type. In effect, typedef creates a synonym. For example, the statement

    typedef int integer;

here we see **typedef** creates **integer** as a synonym for **int**. You then can use **integer** to define variables of type **int**, as in this example:

    integer count;

So **typedef** does not create a new data type, it only lets you use a different name for a predefined data type.

Initializing Numeric Variables

When any variable is declared, the compiler is instructed to set aside storage space for the variable. However, the value stored in that space, the value of the variable, is not defined. It might be zero, or it might be some random "garbage" value. Before using a variable, you should always initialize it to a known value. Let us take this example:

    int count;   /* Set aside storage space for count */

    count = 0;   /* Store 0 in count */

This statement uses the equal sign (=), which is C's assignment operator. You can also initialize a variable when it's declared. To do so, follow the variable name in the declaration statement with an equal sign and the desired initial value:

    int count = 0;

    double rate = 0.01, complexity = 28.5;

Be careful not to initialize a variable with a value outside the allowed range. Here are two examples of out-of-range initializations:

    int amount = 100000;

    unsigned int length = -2500;

The C compiler does not catch such errors. Your program may compile and link, but you may get unexpected results when the program is run.

Let us take the following example to calculate the total number of sectors in a Disk:

```c
// Model Program To Calculate Sectors in A Disk //
#include<stdio.h>
#define SECTOR_PER_SIDE 63
#define SIDE_PER_CYLINDER 254
void main()
{
	int cylinder=0;
	clrscr();
	printf("Enter The No. of Cylinders in the Disk \n\n\t");
	scanf("%d",&cylinder);   // Get the value from the user //

	printf("\n\n\t Total Number of Sectors in the disk = %ld",
	(long)SECTOR_PER_SIDE*SIDE_PER_CYLINDER* cylinder);
	getch();
}
```

The output of the program is as follows:

> Enter The No. of Cylinders in the Disk
> **1024**
> Total Number of Sectors in the disk = **16386048**

Introduction of C Programming

In this example we see three new things to learn. **#define** is used to use symbolic constants in the program or in some cases to save time by defining long words in small symbols.

Here we have defined the number of sectors per side that is 63 as SECTOR_PER_SIDE to make the program easy to understand. The same case is true for **#define SIDE_PER_CYLINDER 254**. **scanf()** is used to get the input from the user.

Here we are taking the number of cylinders as input from the user. * is used to multiply two or more value as shown in the example.

getch() function basically gets a single character input from the keyboard. By typing **getch();** here we stop the screen until any key is hit from the keyboard.

Operators

An *operator* is a symbol that instructs C to perform some operation, or action, on one or more operands. An *operand* is something that an operator acts on. In C, all operands are expressions. C operators are of following four categories:
- The assignment operator
- Mathematical operators
- Relational operators
- Logical operators

Assignment Operator

The *assignment operator* is the equal sign (=). The use of equal sign in programming is different from its use in regular mathematical algebraic relations. If you write

   x = y;

In a C program, it does not mean "x is equal to y." Instead, it means "**assign the value of y to x.**" In a C assignment statement, the right side can be any expression, and the left side must be a variable name. Thus, the form is as follows:

   variable = expression;

During the execution, *expression* is evaluated, and the resulting value is assigned to *variable*.

Mathematical Operators

C's mathematical operators perform mathematical operations such as addition and subtraction. C has two unary mathematical operators and five binary mathematical operators. The ***unary* mathematical operators** are so named because they take a single operand. C has two unary mathematical operators.

The increment and decrement operators can be used only with variables, not with constants. The operation performed is to add one to or subtract one from the operand. In other words, the statements **++x;** and **—y;** are the equivalents of these statements:

   x = x + 1;
   y = y - 1;

***binary* mathematical operators** take two operands. The first four binary operators, which include the common mathematical operations found on a calculator (+, -, *, /), are familiar to you. The fifth operator Modulus returns the remainder when the first operand is divided by the second operand. For example, 11 modulus 4 equals 3 (11 is divided by 4, two times and 3 left over).

Relational Operators

C's relational operators are used to compare expressions. An expression containing a relational operator evaluates to either true (1) or false (0). C has six relational operators.

Logical Operators

Logical operators of C let you combine two or more relational expressions into a single expression that evaluates to either true or false. Logical operators evaluate to either true or false, depending on the true or false value of their operands.

If x is an integer variable, expressions using logical operators could be written in the following ways:

(x > 1) && (x < 5)
(x >= 2) && (x <= 4)

Operator	Symbol	Description	Example
Assignment operators			
equal	=	assign the value of y to x	x = y
Mathematical operators			
Increment	++	Increments the operand by one	++x, x++
Decrement	——	Decrements the operand by one	——x, x——
Addition	+	Adds two operands	x + y
Subtraction	-	Subtracts the second operand from the first	x - y
Multiplication	*	Multiplies two operands	x * y
Division	/	Divides the first operand by the second operand	x / y
Modulus	%	Gives the remainder when the first operand is divided by the second operand	x % y
Relational operators			
Equal	= =	Equality	x = = y
Greater than	>	Greater than	x > y
Less than	<	Less than	x < y
Greater than	>=	Greater than or equal to	x >= y
Less than or equal to	<=	Less than or equal to	x <= y
Not equal	!=	Not equal to	x != y
Logical operators			
AND	&&	True (1) only if both *exp1* and *exp2* are true;	exp1 && exp2

OR	||	false (0) otherwise True (1) if either *exp1* or *exp2* is true; false (0) only if both are false	exp1 || exp2
NOT	!	False (0) if *exp1* is true; true (1) if *exp1* is false	!exp1

Things to remember about logical expressions

x * = y	is same as	x = x * y
y - = z + 1	is same as	y = y - z + 1
a / = b	is same as	a = a / b
x + = y / 8	is same as	x = x + y / 8
y % = 3	is same as	y = y % 3

The Comma Operator

The comma is frequently used in C as a simple punctuation mark, to separate variable declarations, function arguments, etc. In certain situations, the comma acts as an operator.

You can form an expression by separating two sub expressions with a comma. The result is as follows:

- Both expressions are evaluated, with the left expression being evaluated first.
- The entire expression evaluates to the value of the right expression.

For example, the following statement assigns the value of b to x, then increments a, and then increments b:

    x = (a++, b++);

C operator precedence (Summary of C operators)

Rank and Associativity	Operators
1 (left to right)	() [] -> .
2 (right to left)	! ~ ++ — * *(indirection)* & *(address-of)* *(type)*sizeof + *(unary)* - *(unary)*
3 (left to right)	* *(multiplication)* / %
4 (left to right)	+ -
5 (left to right)	<< >>
6 (left to right)	< <= > >=
7 (left to right)	= = !=
8 (left to right)	& *(bitwise* AND*)*
9 (left to right)	^
10 (left to right)	|

11	(left to right)	&&
12	(left to right)	||
13	(right to left)	?:
14	(right to left)	= += -= *= /= %= &= ^= |= <<= >>=
15	(left to right)	,
() is the function operator; [] is the array operator.		

Let us take an example of use of operators:

```
/* Use Of Operators */
int main()
{
      int    x = 0, y = 2, z = 1025;
      float  a = 0.0, b = 3.14159, c = -37.234;

      /* incrementing */
      x = x + 1;          /* This increments x */
      x++;                /* This increments x */
      ++x;                /* This increments x */
      z = y++;            /* z = 2, y = 3 */
      z = ++y;            /* z = 4, y = 4 */

      /* decrementing */
      y = y - 1;          /* This decrements y */
      y--;                /* This decrements y */
      --y;                /* This decrements y */
      y = 3;
      z = y--;            /* z = 3, y = 2 */
      z = --y;            /* z = 1, y = 1 */

      /* arithmetic op */
      a = a + 12;         /* This adds 12 to a          */
      a += 12;            /* This adds 12 more to a     */
      a *= 3.2;           /* This multiplies a by 3.2   */
      a -= b;             /* This subtracts b from a    */
      a /= 10.0;          /* This divides a by 10.0     */

      /* conditional expression */
      a = (b >= 3.0 ? 2.0 : 10.5      /* This expression */
      if (b >= 3.0)                   /* And this expression */
           a = 2.0;                   /* are identical, both */

      else
           a = 10.5;                  /* will cause the same */
                                      /* result.             */
```

```
            c = (a > b ? a : b);  /* c will have the max of a or b */
            c = (a > b ? b : a);  /* c will have the min of a or b */
       printf("x=%d, y=%d, z= %d\n", x, y, z);
           printf("a=%f, b=%f, c= %f", a, b, c);

       return 0;
}
```

and the result of this program will be displayed on the screen as:

> x=3, y=1, z=1
> a=2.000000, b=3.141590, c=2.000000

Something more about *printf()* and *Scanf()*

Consider the following two *printf* statements

       printf("\t %d\n", num);

       printf("%5.2f", fract);

in the first printf statement **\t** requests for the tab displacement on the screen the argument **%d** tells the compiler that the value of **num** should be printed as decimal integer. **\n** causes the new output to start from new line.

In second printf statement **%5.2f** tells the compiler that the output must be in floating point, with five places in all and two places to the right of the decimal point. More about the backslash character has been shown in the following table:

Constant	Meaning
'\a'	Audible alert (bell)
'\b'	Backspace
'\f'	Form feed
'\n'	New line
'\r'	Carriage return
'\t'	Horizontal tab
'\v'	Vertical tab
'\''	Single quote
'\"'	Double quote
'\?'	Question mark
'\\'	Backslash
'\0'	Null

Let us consider the following scanf statement

scanf("%d", &num);

The data from the keyboard is received by **scanf** function. In the above format, the **&** (ampersand) symbol before each variable name is an operator that specifies the address of variable name.

By doing this, the execution stops and waits for the value of the variable **num** to be typed. When the integer value is entered and return key is pressed, the computer proceeds to the next statement. The **scanf** and **printf** format codes are listed in the following table:

Code	Reads...
%c	Single character
%d	Decimal integer
%e	Floating point value
%f	Floating point value
%g	Floating point value
%h	Short integer
%i	Decimal, hexadecimal or octal integer
%o	Octal integer
%s	String
%u	Unsigned decimal integer
%x	Hexadecimal integer

Control Statements

A program consists of a number of statements which are usually executed in sequence. Programs can be much more powerful if we can control the order in which statements are run.

Statements fall into three general types:
- Assignment, where values, usually the results of calculations, are stored in variables.
- Input / Output, data is read in or printed out.
- Control, the program makes a decision about what to do next.

This section will discuss the use of control statements in C. We will show how they can be used to write powerful programs by;
- Repeating important sections of the program.
- Selecting between optional sections of a program.

The if else *Statement*

This is used to decide whether to do something at a special point, or to decide between two courses of action.

The following test decides whether a student has passed an exam with a pass mark of 45

```
if (result >= 45)
     printf("Pass\n");
else
     printf("Fail\n");
```

Introduction of C Programming

It is possible to use the if part without the else.
```
if (temperature < 0)
        print("Frozen\n");
```

Each version consists of a test, in the bracketed statement following the **if**. If the test is true then the next statement is obeyed. If it is false then the statement following the **else** is obeyed if present. After this, the rest of the program continues as normal.

If we wish to have more than one statement following the **if** or the **else**, they should be grouped together between curly brackets. Such a grouping is called a compound statement or a block.
```
if (result >= 45)
{       printf("Passed\n");
        printf("Congratulations\n");
}
else
{       printf("Failed\n");
        printf("Better Luck Next Time\n");
}
```

Sometimes we wish to make a multi-way decision based on several conditions. The most general way of doing this is by using the **else if** variant on the **if** statement.

This works by cascading several comparisons. As soon as one of these gives a true result, the following statement or block is executed, and no further comparisons are performed. In the following example we are awarding grades depending on the exam result.
```
if (result <=100 && result >= 75)
        printf("Passed: Grade A\n");
else if (result >= 60)
        printf("Passed: Grade B\n");
else if (result >= 45)
        printf("Passed: Grade C\n");
else
        printf("Failed\n");
```

In this example, all comparisons test a single variable called result. In other cases, each test may involve a different variable or some combination of tests. The same pattern can be used with more or fewer **else if**'s, and the final alone **else** may be left out.

It is up to the programmer to devise the correct structure for each programming problem. To better understand the use of **if else** let us see the example
```
#include <stdio.h>
int main()
{
        int num;
        for(num = 0 ; num < 10 ; num = num + 1)
        {
```

```
            if (num == 2)
            printf("num is now equal to %d\n", num);

            if (num < 5)
            printf("num is now %d, which is less than 5\n", num);
            else
            printf("num is now %d, which is greater than 4\n", num);
    }   /* end of for loop */
    return 0;
}
```

Result of the program

```
num is now 0, which is less than 5
num is now 1, which is less than 5
num is now equal to 2
num is now 2, which is less than 5
num is now 3, which is less than 5
num is now 4, which is less than 5
num is now 5, which is greater than 4
num is now 6, which is greater than 4
num is now 7, which is greater than 4
num is now 8, which is greater than 4
num is now 9, which is greater than 4
```

The switch *Statement*

This is another form of the multi way decision. It is well structured, but can only be used in certain cases where;

- Only one variable is tested, all branches must depend on the value of that variable. The variable must be an integral type. (int, long, short or char).
- Each possible value of the variable can control a single branch. A final, catch all, default branch may optionally be used to trap all unspecified cases.

Example given below will clarify things. This is a function which converts an integer into a vague description. It is useful where we are only concerned in measuring a quantity when it is quite small.

```
estimate(number)
int number;
/* Estimate a number as none, one, two, several, many */
{ switch(number) {
    case 0 :
        printf("None\n");
        break;
```

Introduction of C Programming

```
                case 1 :
                printf("One\n");
                break;
        case 2 :
                printf("Two\n");
                break;
        case 3 :
        case 4 :
        case 5 :
                printf("Several\n");
                break;
                default :
                printf("Many\n");
                break;
        }
}
```

Each interesting case is listed with a corresponding action. The break statement prevents any further statements from being executed by leaving the switch. Since case 3 and case 4 have no following break, they continue on allowing the same action for several values of number.

Both if and switch constructs allow the programmer to make a selection from a number of possible actions. Let us see an example:

```
#include <stdio.h>
int main()
{
        int num;
        for (num = 3 ; num < 13 ; num = num + 1)
        {
                switch (num)
                {
                        case 3 :
                                printf("The value is three\n");
                                break;
                        case 4 :
                                printf("The value is four\n");
                                break;
                        case 5 :
                        case 6 :
                        case 7 :
                        case 8 :
                                printf("The value is between 5 and 8\n");
                                break;
                        case 11 :
                                printf("The value is eleven\n");
                                break;
```

```
                default :
                    printf("It is one of the undefined values\n");
                    break;
            } /* end of switch */
    } /* end of for loop */
    return 0;
}
```

The output of the program will be

> The value is three
> The value is four
> The value is between 5 and 8
> The value is between 5 and 8
> The value is between 5 and 8
> The value is between 5 and 8
> It is one of the undefined values
> It is one of the undefined values
> The value is eleven
> It is one of the undefined values

The break *Statement*

We have already met break in the discussion of the switch statement. It is used to exit from a loop or a switch, control passing to the first statement beyond the loop or a switch.

With loops, break can be used to force an early exit from the loop, or to implement a loop with a test to exit in the middle of the loop body. A break within a loop should always be protected within an **if** statement which provides the test to control the exit condition.

The continue *Statement*

This is similar to break but is encountered less frequently. It only works within loops where its effect is to force an immediate jump to the loop control statement.

- In a **while** loop, jump to the test statement.
- In a **do while** loop, jump to the test statement.
- In a **for** loop, jump to the test, and perform the iteration.

Like a break, continue should be protected by an **if** statement. You are unlikely to use it very often. To better understand the use of **break** and **continue** let us examine the following program:

```
#include <stdio.h>
int main()
{
int value;
    for(value = 5 ; value < 15 ; value = value + 1)
```

Introduction of C Programming

```
    {
        if (value == 8)
            break;
        printf("In the break loop, value is now %d\n", value);
    }

    for(value = 5 ; value < 15 ; value = value + 1)
    {
        if (value == 8)
            continue;

        printf("In the continue loop, value is now %d\n", value);
    }
    return 0;
}
```

The output of the program will be as follows:

> In the break loop, value is now 5
> In the break loop, value is now 6
> In the break loop, value is now 7
> In the continue loop, value is now 5
> In the continue loop, value is now 6
> In the continue loop, value is now 7
> In the continue loop, value is now 9
> In the continue loop, value is now 10
> In the continue loop, value is now 11
> In the continue loop, value is now 12
> In the continue loop, value is now 13
> In the continue loop, value is now 14

Loops

The other main type of control statement is the loop. Loops allow a statement, or block of statements, to be repeated. Computers are very good at repeating simple tasks many times. The loop is C's way of achieving this.

C gives you a choice of three types of loop, **while**, **do-while** and **for**.

- The **while** loop keeps repeating an action until an associated test returns false. This is useful where the programmer does not know in advance how many times the loop will be traversed.
- The **do while** loops is similar, but the test occurs after the loop body is executed. This ensures that the loop body is run at least once.
- The **for** loop is frequently used, usually where the loop will be traversed a fixed number of

times. It is very flexible, and novice programmers should take care not to abuse the power it offers.

The while *Loop*

The while loop repeats a statement until the test at the top proves false. As an example, here is a function to return the length of a string. Remember that the string is represented as an array of characters terminated by a null character '\0'.

```
int string_length(char string[])
{       int i = 0;
        while (string[i] != '\0')
                i++;
        return(i);
}
```

The string is passed to the function as an argument. The size of the array is not specified, the function will work for a string of any size.

The **while** loop is used to look at the characters in the string one at a time until the null character is found. Then the loop is exited and the index of the null is returned.

While the character is not null, the index is incremented and the test is repeated. We'll go in depth of **arrays** later. Let us see an example for while loop:

```
#include <stdio.h>
int main()
{
    int count;
    count = 0;
    while (count < 6)
    {
        printf("The value of count is %d\n", count);
        count = count + 1;
    }
    return 0;
}
```

and the result is displayed as follows:

```
The value of count is 0
The value of count is 1
The value of count is 2
The value of count is 3
The value of count is 4
The value of count is 5
```

Introduction of C Programming

The do while Loop

This is very similar to the while loop except that the test occurs at the end of the loop body. This guarantees that the loop is executed at least once before continuing.

Such a setup is frequently used where data is to be read. The test then verifies the data, and loops back to read again if it was unacceptable.

```
do
{
        printf("Enter 1 for yes, 0 for no :");
          scanf("%d", &input_value);
} while (input_value != 1 && input_value != 0)
```

To better understand the do while loop let us see the following example:

```
#include <stdio.h>
int main()
{
int i;
    i = 0;
    do
    {
       printf("The value of i is now %d\n", i);
         i = i + 1;
    } while (i < 5);
    return 0;
}
```

The result of the program is displayed as follows:

```
The value of i is now 0
The value of i is now 1
The value of i is now 2
The value of i is now 3
The value of i is now 4
```

The for Loop

The for loop works well where the number of iterations of the loop is known before the loop is entered. The head of the loop consists of three parts separated by semicolons.

- The first is run before the loop is entered. This is usually the initialization of the loop variable.
- The second is a test, the loop is exited when this returns false.
- The third is a statement to be run every time the loop body is completed. This is usually an increment of the loop counter.

The example is a function which calculates the average of the numbers stored in an array. The function takes the array and the number of elements as arguments.

```
float average(float array[], int count)
{
        float total = 0.0;
            int i;
            for(i = 0; i < count; i++)
                        total += array[i];

            return(total / count);
}
```

The for loop ensures that the correct number of array elements are added up before calculating the average.

The three statements at the head of a **for** loop usually do just one thing each, however any of them can be left blank. A blank first or last statement will mean no initialization or running increment. A blank comparison statement will always be treated as true. This will cause the loop to run indefinitely unless interrupted by some other means. This might be a return or a break statement.

It is also possible to squeeze several statements into the first or third position, separating them with commas. This allows a loop with more than one controlling variable. The example below illustrates the definition of such a loop, with variables hi and lo starting at 100 and 0 respectively and converging.

The for loop gives a variety of shorthand to be used in it. Watch out the following expression, in this expression the single loop contains two for loops in it. Here **hi—** is same as **hi = hi - 1** and **lo++** is same as **lo = lo + 1**,

   for(hi = 100, lo = 0; hi >= lo; hi—, lo++)

The **for** loop is extremely flexible and allows many types of program behavior to be specified simply and quickly. Let us see an example of **for** loop

```
#include <stdio.h>
int main()
{
int index;
    for(index = 0 ; index < 6 ; index = index + 1)
        printf("The value of the index is %d\n", index);
    return 0;
}
```

Result of the program is displayed as follows:

The value of the index is 0
The value of the index is 1
The value of the index is 2
The value of the index is 3
The value of the index is 4
The value of the index is 5

The goto Statement

C has a goto statement which permits unstructured jumps to be made. To use a **goto** statement, you simply use the reserved word **goto** followed by the symbolic name to which you wish to jump. The name is then placed anywhere in the program followed by a colon. You can jump nearly anywhere within a function, but you are not permitted to jump into a loop, although you are allowed to jump out of a loop.

This particular program is really a mess but it is a good example of why software writers are trying to eliminate the use of the **goto** statement as much as possible. The only place in this program where it is reasonable to use the **goto** is, where the program jumps out of the three nested loops in one jump. In this case it would be rather messy to set up a variable and jump successively out of each of the three nested loops but one **goto** statement gets you out of all three in a very concise manner.

Some persons say the **goto** statement should never be used under any circumstances, but this is narrow minded thinking. If there is a place where a **goto** will clearly do a neater control flow than some other construct, feel free to use it, however, as it is in the rest of the program on your monitor. Let us see the example:

```
#include <stdio.h>
int main()
{
int dog, cat, pig;
    goto real_start;
    some_where:
    printf("This is another line of the mess.\n");
    goto stop_it;
/* the following section is the only section with a useable goto */
    real_start:
    for(dog = 1 ; dog < 6 ; dog = dog + 1)
    {
        for(cat = 1 ; cat < 6 ; cat = cat + 1)
        {
            for(pig = 1 ; pig < 4 ; pig = pig + 1)
            {
                printf("Dog = %d  Cat = %d  Pig = %d\n", dog, cat, pig);
                if ((dog + cat + pig) > 8 ) goto enough;
            }
        }
    }
    enough: printf("Those are enough animals for now.\n");
/* this is the end of the section with a useable goto statement */
    printf("\nThis is the first line of the code.\n");
    goto there;
    where:
    printf("This is the third line of the code.\n");
    goto some_where;
    there:
    printf("This is the second line of the code.\n");
```

```
        goto where;
    stop_it:
        printf("This is the last line of this mess.\n");
        return 0;
}
```

Let us see the results displayed

```
Dog = 1  Cat = 1  Pig = 1
Dog = 1  Cat = 1  Pig = 2
Dog = 1  Cat = 1  Pig = 3
Dog = 1  Cat = 2  Pig = 1
Dog = 1  Cat = 2  Pig = 2
Dog = 1  Cat = 2  Pig = 3
Dog = 1  Cat = 3  Pig = 1
Dog = 1  Cat = 3  Pig = 2
Dog = 1  Cat = 3  Pig = 3
Dog = 1  Cat = 4  Pig = 1
Dog = 1  Cat = 4  Pig = 2
Dog = 1  Cat = 4  Pig = 3
Dog = 1  Cat = 5  Pig = 1
Dog = 1  Cat = 5  Pig = 2
Dog = 1  Cat = 5  Pig = 3
Those are enough animals for now.

This is the first line of the code.
This is the second line of the code.
This is the third line of the code.
This is another line of the mess.
This is the last line of this mess.
```

Pointers

Sometimes we want to know where a variable resides in memory. A pointer contains the address of a variable that has a specific value. When declaring a pointer, an asterisk is placed immediately before the pointer name.

The address of the memory location where the variable is stored can be found by placing an ampersand in front of the variable name.

```
        int num;        /* Normal integer variable      */
        int *numPtr;    /* Pointer to an integer variable */
```

The following example prints the variable value and the address in memory of that variable.

   printf("The value %d is stored at address %X\n", num, &num);

To assign the address of the variable num to the pointer numPtr, you assign the address of the variable, num, as in the example given next:

   numPtr = #

To find out what is stored at the address pointed to by **numPtr**, the variable needs to be dereferenced. Dereferencing is achieved with the asterisk that the pointer was declared with.

   printf("The value %d is stored at address %X\n", *numPtr, numPtr);

All variables in a program reside in memory. The statements given below request that the compiler reserve 4 bytes of memory on a 32-bit computer for the floating-point variable x, then put the value 6.5 in it.

   float x;
   x = 6.5;

As the address location in memory of any variable is obtained by placing the operator & before its name therefore &x is the address of x. C allows us to go one stage further and define a variable, called a *pointer* that contains the address of other variables. Rather we can say that pointer points to other variable. For example:

   float x;
   float* px;
   x = 6.5;
   px = &x;

defines px to be a pointer to objects of type float, and sets it equal to the address of x. Thus, *px refers to the value of x:

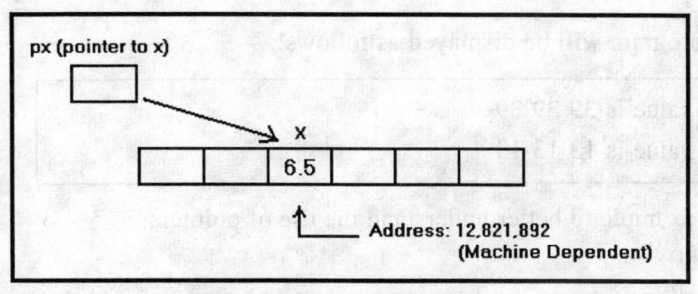

Pointer use for a variable

Let us examine the following statements:

```
int var_x;
int* ptrX;
var_x = 6;
ptrX = &var_x;
*ptrX = 12;
printf("value of x : %d", var_x);
```

The first line causes the compiler to reserve a space in memory for an integer. The second line tells the compiler to reserve space to store a pointer.

A pointer is a storage location for an address. The third line should remind you the *scanf* statements. The address "&" operator tells compiler to go to the place it stored **var_x**, and then give the address of the storage location to **ptrX**.

The asterisk * in front of a variable tells the compiler to dereference the pointer, and go to memory. Then you can make assignments to variable stored at that location. You can reference a variable and access its data through a pointer. Let us see an example of pointers:

```
/* illustration of pointer use */
#include <stdio.h>
int main()
{
int index, *pt1, *pt2;
    index = 39;            /* any numerical value */
    pt1 = &index;          /* the address of index */
    pt2 = pt1;

    printf("The value is %d %d %d\n", index, *pt1, *pt2);

    *pt1 = 13;             /* this changes the value of index */

    printf("The value is %d %d %d\n", index, *pt1, *pt2);

    return 0;
}
```

The output of the program will be displayed as follows:

> The value is 39 39 39
> The value is 13 13 13

Let us see another example to better understand the use of pointers:

```
#include <stdio.h>
#include <string.h>
int main()
{
char strg[40], *there, one, two;
int  *pt, list[100], index;
    strcpy(strg, "This is a character string.");

/* the function strcpy() is to copy one string to another. we'll read
about strcpy() function in String Section later */
    one = strg[0];         /* one and two are identical */
    two = *strg;
    printf("The first output is %c %c\n", one, two);
```

```
        one = strg[8];            /* one and two are identical */
        two = *(strg+8);
        printf("The second output is %c %c\n", one, two);
        there = strg+10;  /* strg+10 is identical to &strg[10] */
        printf("The third output is %c\n", strg[10]);
        printf("The fourth output is %c\n", *there);
        for (index = 0 ; index < 100 ; index++)
            list[index] = index + 100;
            pt = list + 27;
        printf("The fifth output is %d\n", list[27]);
        printf("The sixth output is %d\n", *pt);
        return 0;
}
```

The output of the program will be like this:

> The first output is **T T**
> The second output is **a a**
> The third output is **c**
> The fourth output is **c**
> The fifth output is **127**
> The sixth output is **127**

Arrays

An array is a collection of variables of the same type. Individual array elements are identified by an integer index. In C the index begins at zero and is always written inside square brackets.

We have already met single dimensioned arrays which are declared like this

    int results[20];

Arrays can have more dimensions, in which case they might be declared as

    int results_2d[20][5];

    int results_3d[20][5][3];

Each index has its own set of square brackets. An array is declared in the main function, usually has details of dimensions included. It is possible to use another type called a pointer in place of an array. This means that dimensions are not fixed immediately, but space can be allocated as required. This is an advanced technique which is only required in certain specialized programs.

As an example, here is a simple function to add up all of the integers in a single dimensioned array.

```
int add_array(int array[], int size)
{
    int i;
    int total = 0;
    for(i = 0; i < size; i++)
```

```
            total += array[i];
        return(total);
}
```

The program given next will make a string, access some data in it, print it out. Access it again using pointers, and then print the string out. It should print "Hi!" and "012345678" on different lines. Let us see the coding of the program:

```
#include <stdio.h>
#define STR_LENGTH   10
void main()
{
        char Str[STR_LENGTH];
        char* pStr;
        int i;
        Str[0] = 'H';
        Str[1] = 'i';
        Str[2] = '!';
        Str[3] = '\0';   // special end string character NULL

        printf("The string in Str is : %s\n", Str);

        pStr = &Str[0];
        for (i = 0; i < STR_LENGTH; i++)
        {
            *pStr = '0'+i;
            pStr++;
        }
        Str[STR_LENGTH-1] = '\0';
        printf("The string in Str is : %s\n", Str);
}
```

[] (square braces) are used to declare the array. The line of the program char Str[STR_LENGTH]; declares an array of ten characters. These are ten individual characters, which are all put together in memory into the same place. They can all be accessed through our variable name **Str** along with a [n] where n is the element number.

It should always be kept in mind when talking about array that when C declares an array of ten, the elements you can access are numbered 0 to 9. Accessing the first element corresponds to accessing the 0th element. So in case of Arrays always count from 0 to size of array - 1.

Next notice that we put the letters "Hi!" into the array, but then we put in a '\0' you are probably wondering what this is. "\0" stands for NULL and represents the end of string. All character strings need to end with this special character '\0'. If they do not, and then someone calls printf on the string, then printf would start at the memory location of your string, and continue printing tell it encounters '\0' and thus you will end up with a bunch of garbage at the end of your string. So make sure to terminate your strings properly.

Character Arrays

A *string constant*, such as

"I am a string"

is an array of characters. It is represented internally in C by the ASCII characters in the string, i.e., "I", blank, "a", "m",…or the above string, and terminated by the special null character "\0" so programs can find the end of the string.

String constants are often used in making the output of code intelligible using printf:

printf("Hello, world\n");

printf("The value of a is: %f\n", a);

String constants can be associated with variables. C provides the character type variable, which can contain one character (1 byte) at a time. A character string is stored in an array of character type, one ASCII character per location.

Never forget that, since strings are conventionally terminated by the null character "\0", we require one extra storage location in the array.

C does not provide any operator which manipulates entire strings at once. Strings are manipulated either via pointers or via special routines available from the standard *string* library **string.h**.

Using character pointers is relatively easy since the name of an array is a just a pointer to its first element. Consider the program given next:

```c
#include<stdio.h>
void main()
{
      char text_1[100], text_2[100], text_3[100];
      char *ta, *tb;
      int i;

      /* set message to be an arrray     */
      /* of characters; initialize it    */
      /* to the constant string "..."    */
      /* let the compiler decide on      */
      /* its size by using []            */

      char message[] = "Hello, I am a string; what are you?";
      printf("Original message: %s\n", message);
      /* copy the message to text_1      */
      i=0;
      while ( (text_1[i] = message[i]) != '\0' ) i++;
      printf("Text_1: %s\n", text_1);
      /* use explicit pointer arithmetic */
      ta=message;
      tb=text_2;
      while ( ( *tb++ = *ta++ ) != '\0' )
      printf("Text_2: %s\n", text_2);
}
```

The output of the program will be as follows:

> Original message: Hello, I am a string; what are you?
> Text_1: Hello, I am a string; what are you?
> Text_2: Hello, I am a string; what are you?

The standard "string" library contains many useful functions to manipulate strings, which we will learn in the **string** section later.

Accessing the Elements

To access an individual element in the array, the index number follows the variable name in square brackets. The variable can then be treated like any other variable in C. The following example assigns a value to the first element in the array.

    x[0] = 16;

The following example prints the value of the third element in an array.

    printf("%d\n", x[2]);

The following example uses the scanf function to read a value from the keyboard into the last element of an array with ten elements.

    scanf("%d", &x[9]);

Initializing Array Elements

Arrays can be initialized like any other variables by assignment. As an array contains more than one value, the individual values are placed in curly braces, and separated with commas. The following example initializes a ten dimensional array with the first ten values of the three times table.

    int x[10] = {3, 6, 9, 12, 15, 18, 21, 24, 27, 30};

This saves assigning the values individually as in the following example.

    int x[10];
    x[0] = 3;
    x[1] = 6;
    x[2] = 9;
    x[3] = 12;
    x[4] = 15;
    x[5] = 18;
    x[6] = 21;
    x[7] = 24;
    x[8] = 27;
    x[9] = 30;

Looping through an Array

As the array is indexed sequentially, we can use the **for** loop to display all the values of an array. The following example displays all the values of an array:

```c
#include <stdio.h>
int main()
{
    int x[10];
    int counter;

    /* Randomise the random number generator */
    srand((unsigned)time(NULL));

    /* Assign random values to the variable */
    for (counter=0; counter<10; counter++)
        x[counter] = rand();

    /* Display the contents of the array */
    for (counter=0; counter<10; counter++)
    printf("element %d has the value %d\n", counter, x[counter]);
    return 0;
}
```

though the output will print the different values every time, result will be displayed something like this:

```
element 0 has the value 17132
element 1 has the value 24904
element 2 has the value 13466
element 3 has the value 3147
element 4 has the value 22006
element 5 has the value 10397
element 6 has the value 28114
element 7 has the value 19817
element 8 has the value 27430
element 9 has the value 22136
```

Multidimensional Arrays

An array can have more than one dimension. By allowing the array to have more than one dimension provides greater flexibility. For example, spreadsheets are built on a two dimensional array; an array for the rows, and an array for the columns.

The following example uses a two dimensional array with two rows, each containing five columns:

```c
#include <stdio.h>
int main()
{
    /* Declare a 2 x 5 multidimensional array */
    int x[2][5] = { {1, 2, 3, 4, 5},
```

```
                        {2, 4, 6, 8, 10} };
    int row, column;
    /* Display the rows */
    for (row=0; row<2; row++)
    {
        /* Display the columns */
        for (column=0; column<5; column++)
            printf("%d\t", x[row][column]);
        putchar('\n');
    }
    return 0;
}
```

The output of this program will be displayed as follows:

1	2	3	4	5
2	4	6	8	10

Strings

A string is a group of characters, usually letters of the alphabet, In order to format your print display in such a way that it looks nice, has meaningful names and titles, and is aesthetically pleasing to you and the people using the output of your program.

In fact, you have already been using strings in the examples of the previous topics. But it is not the complete introduction of strings. There are many possible cases in the programming, where the use of formatted strings helps the programmer to avoid the too many complications in the program and too many bugs of course.

A complete definition of a string is a series of **character** type data terminated by a null character ('\0').

When C is going to use a string of data in some way, either to compare it with another string, output it, copy it to another string, or whatever, the functions are set up to do what they are called to do until a null is detected.

There is no basic data type for a string in C Instead; strings in C are implemented as an array of characters. For example, to store a name you could declare a character array big enough to store the name, and then use the appropriate library functions to manipulate the name.

The following example displays the string on the screen, entered by user:

```
#include <stdio.h>
int main()
{
    char name[80];         /* Create a character array called name */
    printf("Enter your name: ");
    gets(name);
    printf("The name you entered was %s\n", name);
    return 0;
```

The execution of the program will be:

> Enter your name: **Tarun Tyagi**
> The name you entered was **Tarun Tyagi**

Some Common String Functions

The standard string.h library contains many useful functions to manipulate strings. Some of the most useful functions have been exampled here.

The strlen Function

The **strlen** function is used to determine the length of a string. Let us learn the use of **strlen** with example:

```
#include <stdio.h>
#include <string.h>
int main()
{
    char name[80];
    int length;
    printf("Enter your name: ");
    gets(name);
    length = strlen(name);
    printf("Your name has %d characters\n", length);
    return 0;
}
```

And the execution of the program will be as follows:

> Enter your name: **Tarun Subhash Tyagi**
> Your name has **19** characters
> Enter your name: **Preeti Tarun**
> Your name has **12** characters

The strcpy Function

The **strcpy** function is used to copy one string to another. Let us learn the use of this function with example:

```
#include <stdio.h>
#include <string.h>
int main()
{
    char first[80];
```

```
    char second[80];
    printf("Enter first string: ");
    gets(first);
    printf("Enter second string: ");
    gets(second);
    printf("first: %s, and second: %s Before strcpy()\n "
                                            , first, second);
    strcpy(second, first);
    printf("first: %s, and second: %s After strcpy()\n",
                                            first, second);
    return 0;
}
```

and the output of the program will be as:

> Enter first string: **Tarun**
> Enter second string: **Tyagi**
> first: **Tarun**, and second: **Tyagi** Before strcpy()
> first: **Tarun**, and second: **Tarun** After strcpy()

The strcmp Function

The **strcmp** function is used to compare two strings together. The variable name of an array points to the base address of that array. Therefore, if we try to compare two strings using the following, we would be comparing two addresses, which would obviously never be the same as it is not possible to store two values in the same location.

    if (first == second) /* **It can never be done to compare strings** */

The following example uses the **strcmp** function to compare two strings:

```
#include <string.h>
int main()
{
    char first[80], second[80];
        int t;
    for(t=1;t<=2;t++)
    {
        printf("\nEnter a string: ");
        gets(first);
        printf("Enter another string: ");
        gets(second);
        if (strcmp(first, second) == 0)
            puts("The two strings are equal");
    else
        puts("The two strings are not equal");
    }
```

```
        return 0;
}
```

And the execution of the program will be as follows:

> Enter a string: **Tarun**
> Enter another string: **tarun**
> The two strings are not equal
> Enter a string: **Tarun**
> Enter another string: **Tarun**
> The two strings are equal

The strcat Function

The **strcat** function is used to join one string to another. Let us see how? With the help of example:

```
#include <string.h>
int main()
{
        char first[80], second[80];
        printf("Enter a string: ");
        gets(first);
        printf("Enter another string: ");
        gets(second);
        strcat(first, second);
        printf("The two strings joined together: %s\n", first);
        return 0;
}
```

And the execution of the program will be as follows:

> Enter a string: **Data**
> Enter another string: **Recovery**
> The two strings joined together: **DataRecovery**

The strtok Function

The **strtok** function is used to find the next token in a string. The token is specified by a list of possible delimiters.

The following example reads a line of text from a file and determines a word using the delimiters, space, tab, and new line. Each word is then displayed on a separate line:

```
#include <stdio.h>
#include <string.h>
int main()
```

```c
{
    FILE *in;
    char line[80];
    char *delimiters = " \t\n";
    char *token;
    if ((in = fopen("C:\\text.txt", "r")) == NULL)
    {
        puts("Unable to open the input file");
        return 0;
    }

    /* Read each line one at a time */
    while(!feof(in))
    {
        /* Get one line */
        fgets(line, 80, in);
        if (!feof(in))
        {
            /* Break the line up into words */
            token = strtok(line, delimiters);
            while (token != NULL)
            {
                puts(token);
                /* Get the next word */
                token = strtok(NULL, delimiters);
            }
        }
    }
    fclose(in);
    return 0;
}
```

It above program, **in = fopen("C:\\text.txt", "r")**, opens and existing file **C:\\text.txt**. If the does not exist in the specified path or for any reason, the file could not be opened, an error message is displayed on screen. Consider the following example, which uses some of these functions:

```c
#include <stdio.h>
#include <string.h>
void main()
{
    char line[100], *sub_text;

    /* initialize string */
    strcpy(line,"hello, I am a string;");
    printf("Line: %s\n", line);
```

```c
    /* add to end of string */
    strcat(line," what are you?");
    printf("Line: %s\n", line);

    /* find length of string */
    /* strlen brings back      */
    /* length as type size_t */
    printf("Length of line: %d\n", (int)strlen(line));

    /* find occurence of substrings */
    if ( (sub_text = strchr ( line, 'W' ) )!= NULL )
    printf("String starting with \"W\" ->%s\n", sub_text);
    if ( ( sub_text = strchr ( line, 'w' ) )!= NULL )
    printf("String starting with \"w\" ->%s\n", sub_text);
    if ( ( sub_text = strchr ( sub_text, 'u' ) )!= NULL )
        printf("String starting with \"w\" ->%s\n", sub_text);
}
```

The output of the program will be displayed as follows:

> Line: hello, I am a string;
> Line: hello, I am a string; what are you?
> Length of line: 35
> String starting with "w" ->what are you?
> String starting with "w" ->u?

Functions

The best way to develop and maintain a large program is to construct it from smaller pieces each of which are easier to manage (a technique sometimes referred to as Divide and Conquer). Functions allow the programmer to modularize the program.

Functions allow complicated programs to be parceled up into small blocks, each of which is easier to write, read, and maintain. We have already encountered the function **main** and made use of **printf** from the standard library. We can of course make our own functions and header files. A function has the following layout:

return-type function-name (**argument list** if necessary)
{
    local-declarations;
    statements ;
    return **return-value;**
}

If **return-type** is omitted, C defaults to **int**. The **return-value** must be of the declared type. All variables declared within functions are called local variables, in that they are known only in the function to which they have been defined.

Some functions have a parameter list that provides a communication method between the function, and the module that called the function. The parameters are also local variables, in that they are not available outside of the function. The programs covered so far all have main, which is a function.

A function may simply perform a task without returning any value, in which case it has the following layout:

```
void function-name ( argument list if necessary )
{
        local-declarations ;
        statements;
}
```

Arguments are always passed by value in C function calls. This means that local **copies** of the values of the arguments are passed to the routines. Any change made to the arguments internally in the function is made only to the local copies of the arguments.

In order to change or define an argument in the argument list, this argument must be passed as an address. You use regular variables if the function does not change the values of those arguments. You MUST use pointers if the function changes the values of those arguments. Let us learn with examples:

```
#include <stdio.h>
void exchange ( int *a, int *b )
{
        int temp;
        temp = *a;
        *a = *b;
        *b = temp;
        printf(" From function exchange: ");
        printf("a = %d, b = %d\n", *a, *b);
}
void main()
{
        int a, b;
        a = 5;
        b = 7;
        printf("From main: a = %d, b = %d\n", a, b);
        exchange(&a, &b);
        printf("Back in main: ");
        printf("a = %d, b = %d\n", a, b);
}
```

And the output of this program will be displayed as follows:

> From main: a = 5, b = 7
> From function exchange: a = 7, b = 5
> Back in main: a = 7, b = 5

Let us see another example. The following example uses a function called square which writes the square of the numbers between 1 and 10.

```c
#include <stdio.h>
int square(int x);   /* Function prototype */
int main()
{
    int counter;
    for (counter=1; counter<=10; counter++)
        printf("Square of %d is %d\n", counter, square(counter));
    return 0;
}
/* Define the function 'square' */
int square(int x)
{
    return x * x;
}
```

The output of this program will be displayed as follows:

```
Square of 1 is 1
Square of 2 is 4
Square of 3 is 9
Square of 4 is 16
Square of 5 is 25
Square of 6 is 36
Square of 7 is 49
Square of 8 is 64
Square of 9 is 81
Square of 10 is 100
```

The function prototype square declares a function that takes an integer parameter and returns an integer. When the compiler reaches the function call to square in the main program, it is able to check the function call against the function's definition.

When the program reaches the line that calls the function square, the program jumps to the function and executes that function before resuming its path through the main program. Programs that do not have a return type should be declared using void. Thus Parameters to the function may be **Pass By Value** or **Pass By Reference.**

A Recursive function is a function that calls itself. And this process is called recursion.

Pass By Value Functions

The square function's parameters in the previous example are passed by value. This means that only a copy of the variable has been passed to the function. Any changes to the value will not be reflected back to the calling function.

The following example uses **pass-by-value** and changes the value of the passed parameter, which has no effect on the calling function. The function count_down has been declared as void as there is no return type.

```c
#include <stdio.h>
void count_down(int x);
int main()
{
    int counter;
    for (counter=1; counter<=10; counter++)
        count_down(counter);
    return 0;
}
void count_down(int x)
{
    int counter;
    for (counter = x; counter > 0; counter-)
    {
        printf("%d ", x);
        x-;
    }
    putchar('\n');
}
```

The output of the program will be displayed as follows:

```
1
2 1
3 2 1
4 3 2 1
5 4 3 2 1
6 5 4 3 2 1
7 6 5 4 3 2 1
8 7 6 5 4 3 2 1
9 8 7 6 5 4 3 2 1
10 9 8 7 6 5 4 3 2 1
```

Let us see another **C Pass By Value** Example to better understand it. The following example converts a number between 1 and 30,000 typed by the user into words.

```c
#include <stdio.h>
void do_units(int num);
void do_tens(int num);
void do_teens(int num);
```

```c
int main()
{
    int num, residue;
    do
    {
        printf("Enter a number between 1 and 30,000: ");
        scanf("%d", &num);
    } while (num < 1 || num > 30000);
    residue = num;
    printf("%d in words = ", num);
    do_tens(residue/1000);
    if (num >= 1000)
        printf("thousand ");
    residue %= 1000;
    do_units(residue/100);
    if (residue >= 100)
    {
        printf("hundred ");
    }
    if (num > 100 && num%100 > 0)
        printf("and ");
    residue %=100;
    do_tens(residue);
    putchar('\n');
    return 0;
}

void do_units(int num)
{
    switch(num)
    {
    case 1:
        printf("one ");
        break;
    case 2:
        printf("two ");
        break;
    case 3:
        printf("three ");
        break;
    case 4:
        printf("four ");
        break;
    case 5:
        printf("five ");
        break;
```

```c
        case 6:
            printf("six ");
            break;
        case 7:
            printf("seven ");
            break;
        case 8:
            printf("eight ");
            break;
        case 9:
            printf("nine ");
        }
}

void do_tens(int num)
{
        switch(num/10)
        {
        case 1:
            do_teens(num);
            break;
        case 2:
            printf("twenty ");
            break;
        case 3:
            printf("thirty ");
            break;
        case 4:
            printf("forty ");
            break;
        case 5:
            printf("fifty ");
            break;
        case 6:
            printf("sixty ");
            break;
        case 7:
            printf("seventy ");
            break;
        case 8:
            printf("eighty ");
            break;
        case 9:
            printf("ninety ");
        }
```

```c
        if (num/10 != 1)
            do_units(num%10);
}
void do_teens(int num)
{
    switch(num)
    {
    case 10:
        printf("ten ");
        break;
    case 11:
        printf("eleven ");
        break;
    case 12:
        printf("twelve ");
        break;
    case 13:
        printf("thirteen ");
        break;
    case 14:
        printf("fourteen ");
        break;
    case 15:
        printf("fifteen ");
        break;
    case 16:
        printf("sixteen ");
        break;
    case 17:
        printf("seventeen ");
        break;
    case 18:
        printf("eighteen ");
        break;
    case 19:
        printf("nineteen ");
    }
}
```

and the output of the program will be as follows:

> Enter a number between 1 and 30,000: **12345**
> **12345** in words = **twelve thousand three hundred and forty five**

Call-by-reference

To make a function **call-by-reference**, instead of passing the variable itself, pass the address of the variable. The address of the variable can be taken by using the & operator. The following calls a swap function passing the address of variables instead of the actual values.

>   swap(&x, &y);

Dereferencing

The problem we have now is that the function swap has been passed the address rather than the variable, so we need to dereference the variables so that we are looking at the actual values rather than the addresses of the variables in order to swap them.

Dereferencing is achieved in C by using the pointer (*) notation. In simple terms, this means placing a * before each variable before using it in order that it refers to the value of the variable rather than its address. The following program illustrates **passing-by-reference** to swap two values.

```c
#include <stdio.h>
void swap(int *x, int *y);
int main()
{
    int x=6, y=10;
    printf("Before the function swap, x = %d and y = %d\n\n", x, y);
    swap(&x, &y);
    printf("After the function swap, x = %d and y = %d\n\n", x, y);
    return 0;
}

void swap(int *x, int *y)
{
    int temp = *x;
    *x = *y;
    *y = temp;
}
```

Let us see the output of the program:

>   Before the function swap, x = 6 and y = 10
>   After the function swap, x = 10 and y = 6

Functions may be **recursive** that is a function may call itself. Each call to itself requires that the current state of the function is pushed onto the stack. It is important to remember this fact as it is easy to create a stack overflow, i.e. the stack has run out of space to place any more data.

The following example calculates the Factorial of a number using recursion. A factorial is a number multiplied by every other integer below itself, down to 1. For example, the factorial of the number 6 is:

>   Factorial 6 = 6 * 5 * 4 * 3 * 2 * 1

Therefore the factorial of 6 is 720. It can be seen from the above example that factorial 6 = 6 * factorial 5. Similarly, factorial 5 = 5 * factorial 4, and so on.

The following is the general rule for calculating factorial numbers.

factorial(n) = n * factorial(n-1)

The above rule terminates when n = 1, as the factorial of 1 is 1. Let us try to better understand it with the help of example:

```
#include <stdio.h>
long int factorial(int num);
int main()
{
    int num;
    long int f;
    printf("Enter a number: ");
    scanf("%d", &num);
    f = factorial(num);
    printf("factorial of %d is %ld\n", num, f);
    return 0;
}
long int factorial(int num)
{
    if (num == 1)
        return 1;
    else
        return num * factorial(num-1);
}
```

Let us see the output of the execution of this program:

> Enter a number: **7**
> factorial of **7** is **5040**

Memory Allocation in C

The C compiler has a memory allocation library, defined in malloc.h. Memory is reserved using the malloc function, and returns a pointer to the address. It takes one parameter, the size of memory required in bytes.

The following example allocates space for the string, "hello world".

    ptr = (char *)malloc(strlen("Hello world") + 1);

The extra one byte is required to take into account the string termination character, '\0'. The (char *) is called a cast, and forces the return type to be char *.

As data types have different sizes, and malloc returns the space in bytes, it is good practice for portability reasons to use the sizeof operator when specifying a size to allocate.

The following example reads a string into the character array buffer and then allocates the exact amount of memory required and copies it to a variable called "ptr".

```c
#include <string.h>
#include <malloc.h>
int main()
{
    char *ptr, buffer[80];
    printf("Enter a string: ");
    gets(buffer);
    ptr = (char *)malloc((strlen(buffer) + 1) * sizeof(char));
    strcpy(ptr, buffer);
    printf("You entered: %s\n", ptr);
    return 0;
}
```

The output of the program will be as follows:

> Enter a string: **India is the best**
> You entered: **India is the best**

Reallocating Memory

It is possible many times while you are programming that you want to reallocate memory. This is done with the **realloc** function. The **realloc** function takes two parameters, the base address of memory you want to resize, and the amount of space you want to reserve and returns a pointer to the base address.

Suppose we have reserved space for a pointer called msg and we want to reallocate space to the amount of space it already takes up, plus the length of another string then we could use the following.

   msg = (char *)realloc(msg, (strlen(msg) + strlen(buffer) + 1)*sizeof(char));

The following program illustrates the use of malloc, realloc and free. The user enters a series of strings that are joined together. The program stops reading strings when an empty string is entered.

```c
#include <string.h>
#include <malloc.h>
int main()
{
    char buffer[80], *msg;
    int firstTime=0;
    do
    {
        printf("\nEnter a sentence: ");
        gets(buffer);
        if (!firstTime)
        {
            msg = (char *)malloc((strlen(buffer) + 1) * sizeof(char));
            strcpy(msg, buffer);
            firstTime = 1;
```

Introduction of C Programming

```
        }
        else
        {
                msg = (char *)realloc(msg, (strlen(msg) +
                       strlen(buffer) + 1) * sizeof(char));
                       strcat(msg, buffer);
        }
        puts(msg);
    } while(strcmp(buffer, ""));
    free(msg);
    return 0;
}
```

The output of the program will be as follows:

> Enter a sentence: **Once upon a time**
> **Once upon a time**
> Enter a sentence: **there was a king**
> **Once upon a timethere was a king**
> Enter a sentence: **the king was**
> **Once upon a timethere was a kingthe king was**
> Enter a sentence: **Once upon a timethere was a kingthe king was**

Releasing Memory

When you have finished with memory that has been allocated, you should never forget to free the memory as it will free up resources and improve speed. To release allocated memory, use the free function.

  free(ptr);

Structures

As well as the basic data types, C has a structure mechanism that allows you to group data items that are related to each other under a common name. This is commonly referred to as a User Defined Type.

The keyword **struct** starts the structure definition, and a tag gives the unique name to the structure. The data types and variable names added to the structure are members of the structure. The result is a structure template that may be used as a type specifier. The following is a structure with a tag of month.

```
struct month
{
    char name[10];
    char abbrev[4];
    int days;
};
```

A structure type is usually defined near to the start of a file using a **typedef** statement. **typedef** defines and names a new type, allowing its use throughout the program. **typedef** usually occur just after the #define and #include statements in a file.

The **typedef** keyword may be used to define a word to refer to the structure rather than specifying the **struct** keyword with the name of the structure. It is usual to name the **typedef** in capital letters. Here are the examples of structure definition.

```
typedef struct {
      char name[64];
      char course[128];
      int age;
      int year;
} student;
```

This defines a new type student variables of type student can be declared as follows.

       student st_rec;

Notice how similar this is to declaring an int or float. The variable name is **st_rec**, it has members called name, course, age and year. Similarly,

```
typedef struct element
{
      char data;
      struct element *next;
} STACKELEMENT;
```

A variable of the user defined type struct element may now be declared as follows.

       STACKELEMENT *stack;

Consider the following structure:
```
struct student
{
      char *name;
      int grade;
};
```

A pointer to struct student may be defined as follows.

       struct student *hnc;

When accessing a pointer to a structure, the member pointer operator, -> is used instead of the dot operator. To add a grade to a structure,

       s.grade = 50;

You could assign a grade to the structure as follows.

       s->grade = 50;

As with the basic data types, if you want the changes made in a function to passed parameters to be persistent, you have to pass by reference (pass the address). The mechanism is exactly the same as the basic data types. Pass the address, and refer to the variable using pointer notation.

Introduction of C Programming

Having defined the structure, you can declare an instance of it and assign values to the members using the dot notation. The following example illustrates the use of the month structure.

```c
#include <stdio.h>
#include <string.h>
struct month
{
    char name[10];
    char abbreviation[4];
    int days;
};
int main()
{
    struct month m;
    strcpy(m.name, "January");
    strcpy(m.abbreviation, "Jan");
    m.days = 31;
    printf("%s is abbreviated as %s and has %d days\n", m.name,
    m.abbreviation, m.days);
    return 0;
}
```

The output of the program will be as follows:

> January is abbreviated as Jan and has 31 days

All ANSI C compilers allow you to assign one structure to another, performing a member-wise copy. If we had month structures called m1 and m2, then we could assign the values from m1 to m2 with the following:

- Structure with Pointer Members.
- Structure Initializes.
- Passing a Structure to a Function.
- Pointers and Structures.

Structures with Pointer Members in C

Holding strings in a fixed size array is inefficient use of memory. A more efficient approach would be to use pointers. Pointers are used in structures in exactly the same way they are used in normal pointer definitions. Let us see an example:

```c
#include <string.h>
#include <malloc.h>
struct month
{
    char *name;
    char *abbreviation;
    int days;
```

```
};
int main()
{
        struct month m;
        m.name = (char *)malloc((strlen("January")+1) * sizeof(char));
        strcpy(m.name, "January");
        m.abbreviation = (char *)malloc((strlen("Jan")+1) * sizeof(char));
        strcpy(m.abbreviation, "Jan");
        m.days = 31;
        printf("%s is abbreviated as %s and has %d days\n",
            m.name, m.abbreviation, m.days);
        return 0;
}
```

The output of the program will be as follows:

> January is abbreviated as Jan and has 31 days

Structure Initializers in C

To provide a set of initial values for the structure, Initialisers may be added to the declaration statement. As months start at 1, but arrays start at zero in C, an extra element at position zero called junk, has been used in the following example.

```
#include <stdio.h>
#include <string.h>
struct month
{
        char *name;
        char *abbreviation;
        int days;
} month_details[] =
{
        "Junk", "Junk", 0,
        "January", "Jan", 31,
        "February", "Feb", 28,
        "March", "Mar", 31,
        "April", "Apr", 30,
        "May", "May", 31,
        "June", "Jun", 30,
        "July", "Jul", 31,
        "August", "Aug", 31,
        "September", "Sep", 30,
        "October", "Oct", 31,
        "November", "Nov", 30,
        "December", "Dec", 31
```

Introduction of C Programming

```
};
int main()
{
    int counter;
    for (counter=1; counter<=12; counter++)
    printf("%s is abbreviated as %s and has %d days\n",
            month_details[counter].name,
                month_details[counter].abbreviation,
                    month_details[counter].days);
    return 0;
}
```

And the output will be displayed as follows:

> January is abbreviated as Jan and has 31 days
> February is abbreviated as Feb and has 28 days
> March is abbreviated as Mar and has 31 days
> April is abbreviated as Apr and has 30 days
> May is abbreviated as May and has 31 days
> June is abbreviated as Jun and has 30 days
> July is abbreviated as Jul and has 31 days
> August is abbreviated as Aug and has 31 days
> September is abbreviated as Sep and has 30 days
> October is abbreviated as Oct and has 31 days
> November is abbreviated as Nov and has 30 days
> December is abbreviated as Dec and has 31 days

Passing Structures to Functions in C

Structures may be passed as a parameter to a function, just as any of the basic data types. The following example uses a structure called date that has is passed to an isLeapYear function to determine if the year is a leap year.

Normally you would only pass the day value, but the whole structure is passed to illustrate passing structures to functions.

```
#include <stdio.h>
#include <string.h>
struct month
{
    char *name;
    char *abbreviation;
    int days;
} month_details[] =
{
```

```c
            "Junk",      "Junk",  0,
            "January",   "Jan",   31,
            "February",  "Feb",   28,
            "March",     "Mar",   31,
            "April",     "Apr",   30,
            "May",       "May",   31,
            "June",      "Jun",   30,
            "July",      "Jul",   31,
            "August",    "Aug",   31,
            "September", "Sep",   30,
            "October",   "Oct",   31,
            "November",  "Nov",   30,
            "December",  "Dec",   31
};
struct date
{
        int day;
        int month;
        int year;
};
int isLeapYear(struct date d);
int main()
{
        struct date d;
        printf("Enter the date (eg: 11/11/1980): ");
        scanf("%d/%d/%d", &d.day, &d.month, &d.year);
        printf("The date %d %s %d is ", d.day, month_details[d.month].name,
                d.year);
        if (isLeapYear(d) == 0)
            printf("not ");
        puts("a leap year");
        return 0;
}
int isLeapYear(struct date d)
{
        if ((d.year % 4 == 0 && d.year % 100 != 0) ||
                    d.year % 400 == 0)
            return 1;
        return 0;
}
```

And the Execution of the program will be as follows:

> Enter the date (eg: 11/11/1980): **9/12/1980**
> **The date 9 December 1980 is a leap year**

The following example dynamically allocates an array of structures to store students names and grade. The grades are then displayed back to the user in ascending order.

```c
#include <string.h>
#include <malloc.h>
struct student
{
        char *name;
        int grade;
};

void swap(struct student *x, struct student *y);
int main()
{
        struct student *group;
        char buffer[80];
        int spurious;
        int inner, outer;
        int counter, numStudents;
        printf("How many students are there in the group: ");
        scanf("%d", &numStudents);
        group = (struct student *)malloc(numStudents * sizeof(struct
                student));
        for (counter=0; counter<numStudents; counter++)
        {
                spurious = getchar();
                printf("Enter the name of the student: ");
                gets(buffer);
                group[counter].name = (char *)malloc((strlen(buffer)+1) *
                        sizeof(char));
                strcpy(group[counter].name, buffer);
                printf("Enter grade: ");
                scanf("%d", &group[counter].grade);
        }
        for (outer=0; outer<numStudents; outer++)
                for (inner=0; inner<outer; inner++)
                        if (group[outer].grade <
                        group[inner].grade)
                                swap(&group[outer], &group[inner]);
        puts("The group in ascending order of grades ...");
        for (counter=0; counter<numStudents; counter++)
        printf("%s achieved Grade %d \n",
                group[counter].name,
                group[counter].grade);
        return 0;
}
```

```
void swap(struct student *x, struct student *y)
{
    struct student temp;
    temp.name = (char *)malloc((strlen(x->name)+1) * sizeof(char));
    strcpy(temp.name, x->name);
    temp.grade = x->grade;
    x->grade = y->grade;
    x->name = (char *)malloc((strlen(y->name)+1) * sizeof(char));
    strcpy(x->name, y->name);
    y->grade = temp.grade;
    y->name = (char *)malloc((strlen(temp.name)+1) * sizeof(char));
    strcpy(y->name, temp.name);
}
```

The execution of the output will be as follows:

> How many students are there in the group: **4**
> Enter the name of the student: **Anuraaj**
> Enter grade: **7**
> Enter the name of the student: **Honey**
> Enter grade: **2**
> Enter the name of the student: **Meetushi**
> Enter grade: **1**
> Enter the name of the student: **Deepti**
> Enter grade: **4**
> The group in ascending order of grades ...
>
> **Meetushi** achieved Grade **1**
> **Honey** achieved Grade **2**
> **Deepti** achieved Grade **4**
> **Anuraaj** achieved Grade **7**

Union

A *union* allows you a way to look at the same data with different types, or to use the same data with different names. *Unions* are similar to structures. A union is declared and used in the same ways that a structure is.

A union differs from a structure in that only one of its members can be used at a time. The reason for this is simple. All the members of a union occupy the same area of memory. They are laid on top of each other.

Unions are defined and declared in the same fashion as structures. The only difference in the declarations is that the keyword **union** is used instead of **struct**. To define a simple union of a char

variable and an integer variable, you would write the following:
```
union shared {
      char c;
      int i;
};
```

This union, shared, can be used to create instances of a union that can hold either a character value c or an integer value i. This is an OR condition. Unlike a structure that would hold both values, the union can hold only one value at a time.

A union can be initialized on its declaration. Because only one member can be used at a time and only one can be initialized. To avoid confusion, only the first member of the union can be initialized. The following code shows an instance of the shared union being declared and initialized:

>   union shared generic_variable = {'@'};

Notice that the generic_variable union was initialized just as the first member of a structure would be initialized.

Individual union members can be used in the same way that structure members can be used by using the member operator (.). However, there is an important difference in accessing union members.

Only one union member should be accessed at a time. Because a union stores its members on top of each other, it's important to access only one member at a time.

The union Keyword

```
union tag {
      union_member(s);
      /* additional statements may go here */
} instance;
```

The union keyword is used for declaring unions. A union is a collection of one or more variables (*union_members*) that have been grouped under a single name. In addition, each of these union members occupies the same area of memory.

The keyword union identifies the beginning of a union definition. It's followed by a tag that is the name given to the union. Following the tag are the union members enclosed in braces.

An *instance*, the actual declaration of a union, also can be defined. If you define the structure without the instance, it's just a template that can be used later in a program to declare structures. The following is a template's format:

```
union tag {
      union_member(s);
      /* additional statements may go here */
};
```

To use the template, you would use the following format:

>   union *tag instance*;

To use this format, you must have previously declared a union with the given tag.

```c
/* Declare a union template called tag */
union tag {
      int num;
      char alps;
}

/* Use the union template */
union tag mixed_variable;
/* Declare a union and instance together */
union generic_type_tag {
      char c;
      int i;
      float f;
      double d;
} generic;

/* Initialize a union. */
union date_tag {
      char full_date[9];
      struct part_date_tag {
            char month[2];
            char break_value1;
            char day[2];
            char break_value2;
            char year[2];
      } part_date;
}date = {"09/12/80"};
```

Let us better understand it with the help of examples:
```c
#include <stdio.h>
int main()
{
      union
      {
            int value;   /* This is the first part of the union */
            struct
            {
                  char first; /* These two values are the second part of
                  it */
                  char second;
            } half;
      } number;
      long index;
      for (index = 12 ; index < 300000L ; index += 35231L)
      {
```

```
            number.value = index;
            printf("%8x %6x %6x\n", number.value, number.half.first,
            number.half.second);
        }
        return 0;
}
```

And the output of the program will be displayed as follows:

c	c	0
89ab	ffab	ff89
134a	4a	13
9ce9	ffe9	ff9c
2688	ff88	26
b027	27	ffb0
39c6	ffc6	39
c365	65	ffc3
4d04	4	4d

A practical use of a union in data recovery

Now let us see a practical use of union is data recovery programming. Let us take a little example. The following program is the small model of bad sector scanning program for a floppy disk drive (a:) however it is not the complete model of bad sector scanning software.

Let us examine the program:

```
#include<dos.h>
#include<conio.h>
int main()
{
        int rp, head, track, sector, status;
        char *buf;
        union REGS in, out;
        struct SREGS s;
        clrscr();
/* Reset the disk system to initialize to disk */
printf("\n Resetting the disk system....");
for(rp=0;rp<=2;rp++)
{
        in.h.ah = 0;
        in.h.dl = 0x00;
        int86(0x13,&in,&out);
}
printf("\n\n\n Now Testing the Disk for Bad Sectors....");
```

```c
/* scan for bad sectors */
for(track=0;track<=79;track++)
{
    for(head=0;head<=1;head++)
    {
        for(sector=1;sector<=18;sector++)
        {
            in.h.ah = 0x04;
            in.h.al = 1;
            in.h.dl = 0x00;
            in.h.ch = track;
            in.h.dh = head;
            in.h.cl = sector;
            in.x.bx = FP_OFF(buf);
            s.es = FP_SEG(buf);
            int86x(0x13,&in,&out,&s);
            if(out.x.cflag)
            {
                status=out.h.ah;
                printf("\n track:%d  Head:%d   Sector:%d   Status ==0x%X",track,head,sector,status);
            }
        }
    }
}
printf("\n\n\nDone");
return 0;
}
```

Now let us see what its output will look like if there are bad sector in the floppy disk:

```
Resetting the disk system....

Now Testing the Disk for Bad Sectors....
track:0      Head:0     Sector:4   Status ==0xA
track:0      Head:0     Sector:5   Status ==0xA
track:1      Head:0     Sector:4   Status ==0xA
track:1      Head:0     Sector:5   Status ==0xA
track:1      Head:0     Sector:6   Status ==0xA
track:1      Head:0     Sector:7   Status ==0xA
track:1      Head:0     Sector:8   Status ==0xA
track:1      Head:0     Sector:11  Status ==0xA
track:1      Head:0     Sector:12  Status ==0xA
```

```
track:1     Head:0    Sector:13   Status ==0xA
track:1     Head:0    Sector:14   Status ==0xA
track:1     Head:0    Sector:15   Status ==0xA
track:1     Head:0    Sector:16   Status ==0xA
track:1     Head:0    Sector:17   Status ==0xA
track:1     Head:0    Sector:18   Status ==0xA
track:1     Head:1    Sector:5    Status ==0xA
track:1     Head:1    Sector:6    Status ==0xA
track:1     Head:1    Sector:7    Status ==0xA
track:1     Head:1    Sector:8    Status ==0xA
track:1     Head:1    Sector:9    Status ==0xA
track:1     Head:1    Sector:10   Status ==0xA
track:1     Head:1    Sector:11   Status ==0xA
track:1     Head:1    Sector:12   Status ==0xA
track:1     Head:1    Sector:13   Status ==0xA
track:1     Head:1    Sector:14   Status ==0xA
track:1     Head:1    Sector:15   Status ==0xA
track:1     Head:1    Sector:16   Status ==0xA
track:1     Head:1    Sector:17   Status ==0xA
track:1     Head:1    Sector:18   Status ==0xA
track:2     Head:0    Sector:4    Status ==0xA
track:2     Head:0    Sector:5    Status ==0xA
track:14    Head:0    Sector:6    Status ==0xA
Done
```

It may be a little bit difficult to understand functions and interrupts used in this program to verify the disk for bad sectors and resetting the disk system etc. but you need not to worry, we are going to learn all these things in BIOS and interrupt programming sections later in the next coming chapters.

File Handling in C

File access in C is achieved by associating a stream with a file. C communicates with files using a new data type called a file pointer. This type is defined within stdio.h, and written as FILE *. A file pointer called output_file is declared in a statement like

    FILE *output_file;

The File Modes of *fopen* Function

Your program must open a file before it can access it. This is done using the fopen function, which returns the required file pointer. If the file cannot be opened for any reason then the value **NULL** will be returned. You will usually use fopen as follows

```
if ((output_file = fopen("output_file", "w")) == NULL)
        fprintf(stderr, "Cannot open %s\n",
                    "output_file");
```

fopen takes two arguments, both are strings, the first is the name of the file to be opened, the second is an access character, which is usually one of **r, a** or **w** etc. Files may be opened in a number of modes, as shown in the following table.

	File Modes
r	Open a text file for reading.
w	Create a text file for writing. If the file exists, it is overwritten.
a	Open a text file in append mode. Text is added to the end of the file.
rb	Open a binary file for reading.
wb	Create a binary file for writing. If the file exists, it is overwritten.
ab	Open a binary file in append mode. Data is added to the file.
r+	Open a text file for reading and writing.
w+	Create a text file for reading and writing. If the file exists, it is overwritten.
a+	Open a text file for reading and writing at the end.
r+b or rb+	Open binary file for reading and writing.
w+b or wb+	Create a binary file for reading and writing. If the file exists, it is overwritten.
a+b or ab+	Open a text file for reading and writing at the end.

The update modes are used with **fseek**, **fsetpos** and rewind functions. The fopen function returns a file pointer, or **NULL** if an error occurs.

The following example opens a file, **tarun.txt** in **read-only** mode. It is good programming practice to test the file exists.

```
if ((in = fopen("tarun.txt", "r")) == NULL)
{
    puts("Unable to open the file");
    return 0;
}
```

Closing Files

Files are closed using the **fclose** function. The syntax is as follows:

fclose(in);

Reading Files

The **feof** function is used to test for the end of the file. The functions **fgetc**, **fscanf**, and **fgets** are used to read data from the file.

The following example lists the contents of a file on the screen, using **fgetc** to read the file a character at a time.

```c
#include <stdio.h>
int main()
{
    FILE *in;
    int key;
    if ((in = fopen("tarun.txt", "r")) == NULL)
    {
        puts("Unable to open the file");
        return 0;
    }
    while (!feof(in))
    {
        key = fgetc(in);
        /* The last character read is the end of file
        marker so don't print it */
        if (!feof(in))
            putchar(key);
    }
    fclose(in);
    return 0;
}
```

The **fscanf** function can be used to read different data types from the file as in the following example, providing the data in the file is in the format of the format string used with **fscanf**.

> **fscanf(in, "%d/%d/%d", &day, &month, &year);**

The **fgets** function is used to read a number of characters from a file. **stdin** is the standard input file stream, and the **fgets** function can be used to control input.

Writing to Files

Data can be written to the file using **fputc** and **fprintf**. The following example uses the **fgetc** and **fputc** functions to make a copy of a text file.

```c
#include <stdio.h>
int main()
{
    FILE *in, *out;
    int key;
    if ((in = fopen("tarun.txt", "r")) == NULL)
    {
        puts("Unable to open the file");
        return 0;
    }
    out = fopen("copy.txt", "w");
```

```
    while (!feof(in))
    {
        key = fgetc(in);
        if (!feof(in))
            fputc(key, out);
    }
    fclose(in);
    fclose(out);
    return 0;
}
```

The **fprintf** function can be used to write formatted data to a file.

fprintf(out, "Date: %02d/%02d/%02d\n", day, month, year);

Command Line Arguments with C

The ANSI C definition for declaring the **main( )** function is either:

int main()   or   **int main(int argc, char **argv)**

The second version allows arguments to be passed from the command line. The parameter argc is an argument counter and contains the number of parameters passed from the command line. The parameter argv is the argument vector which is an array of pointers to strings that represent the actual parameters passed.

The following example allows any number of arguments to be passed from the command line and prints them out. argv[0] is the actual program. The program must be run from a command prompt.

```
#include <stdio.h>
int main(int argc, char **argv)
{
    int counter;
    puts("The arguments to the program are:");
    for (counter=0; counter<argc; counter++)
        puts(argv[counter]);
    return 0;
}
```

If the program name was **count.c**, it could be called as follows from the command line.

count 3

or

count 7

or

count 192 etc.

The next example uses the file handling routines to copy a text file to a new file. For example the command line argument could be called as:

txtcpy   one.txt   two.txt

```c
#include <stdio.h>
int main(int argc, char **argv)
{
    FILE *in, *out;
    int key;
    if (argc < 3)
    {
        puts("Usage: txtcpy source destination\n");
        puts("The source must be an existing file");
        puts("If the destination file exists, it will be overwritten");
        return 0;
    }
    if ((in = fopen(argv[1], "r")) == NULL)
    {
        puts("Unable to open the file to be copied");
        return 0;
    }
    if ((out = fopen(argv[2], "w")) == NULL)
    {
        puts("Unable to open the output file");
        return 0;
    }
    while (!feof(in))
    {
        key = fgetc(in);
        if (!feof(in))
        fputc(key, out);
    }
    fclose(in);
    fclose(out);
    return 0;
}
```

Bitwise Manipulators

At a hardware level, data is represented as binary numbers. The binary representation of the number 59 is 111011. Bit 0 is the least significant bit, and in this case bit 5 is the most significant bit.

Each bit set is calculated as 2 to the power of the bit set. Bitwise operators allow you to manipulate integer variables at bit level. The following shows the binary representation of the number **59**.

binary representation of the number 59						
bit	5	4	3	2	1	0
2 power n	32	16	8	4	2	1
set	1	1	1	0	1	1

With three bits, it is possible to represent the numbers 0 to 7. The following table shows the numbers 0 to 7 in their binary form.

Binary	Digits
000	0
001	1
010	2
011	3
100	4
101	5
110	6
111	7

The following table lists the bitwise operators that may be used to manipulate binary numbers.

Binary	Digits
&	Bitwise AND
|	Bitwise OR
^	Bitwise Exclusive OR
~	Bitwise Complement
<<	Bitwise Shift Left
>>	Bitwise Shift Right

Bitwise AND

The bitwise AND is True only if both bits are set. The following example shows the result of a bitwise AND on the numbers 23 and 12.

```
10111   (23)
01100   (12)  AND
00100   (result = 4)
```

You can use a mask value to check if certain bits have been set. If we wanted to check whether bits 1 and 3 were set, we could mask the number with 10 (the value if bits 1 and 3) and test the result against the mask.

```
#include <stdio.h>
int main()
{
    int num, mask = 10;
    printf("Enter a number: ");
    scanf("%d", &num);
    if ((num & mask) == mask)
```

```
            puts("Bits 1 and 3 are set");
    else
            puts("Bits 1 and 3 are not set");
    return 0;
}
```

Bitwise OR

The bitwise OR is true if either bits are set. The following shows the result of a bitwise OR on the numbers 23 and 12.

> 10111 (23)
> 01100 (12) OR
> 11111 (result = 31)

You can use a mask to ensure a bit or bits have been set. The following example ensures bit 2 is set.

```
#include <stdio.h>
int main()
{
    int num, mask = 4;
    printf("Enter a number: ");
    scanf("%d", &num);
    num |= mask;
    printf("After ensuring bit 2 is set: %d\n", num);
    return 0;
}
```

Bitwise Exclusive OR

The bitwise Exclusive OR is True if either bits are set, but not both. The following shows the result of a bitwise Exclusive OR on the numbers 23 and 12.

> 10111 (23)
> 01100 (12) Exclusive OR (XOR)
> 11011 (result = 27)

The Exclusive OR has some interesting properties. If you Exclusive OR a number by itself, it sets itself to zero as the zeros will remain zero and the ones can't both be set so are set to zero.

As a result of this, if you Exclusive OR a number with another number, then Exclusive OR the result with the other number again, the result is the original number. You can try this with the numbers used in the above example.

    23 XOR 12 = 27
    27 XOR 12 = 23
    27 XOR 23 = 12

This feature can be used for encryption. The following program uses an encryption key of 23 to illustrate the property on a number entered by the user.

```c
#include <stdio.h>
int main()
{
    int num, key = 23;
    printf("Enter a number: ");
    scanf("%d", &num);
    num ^= key;
    printf("Exclusive OR with %d gives %d\n", key, num);
    num ^= key;
    printf("Exclusive OR with %d gives %d\n", key, num);
    return 0;
}
```

Bitwise Compliment

The bitwise Compliment is a one's compliment operator that toggles the bit on or off. If it is 1, it will be set to 0, if it is 0 it will be set to 1.

```c
#include <stdio.h>
int main()
{
    int num = 0xFFFF;
    printf("The compliment of %X is %X\n", num, ~num);
    return 0;
}
```

Bitwise Shift Left

The Bitwise Shift Left operator shifts the number left. The most significant bits are lost as the number moves left, and the vacated least significant bits are zero. The following shows the binary representation of 43.

0101011 (decimal 43)

By shifting the bits to the left, we lose the most significant bit (in this case, a zero), and the number is padded with a zero at the least significant bit. The following is the resulting number.

1010110 (decimal 86)

Bitwise Shift Right

The Bitwise Shift Right operator shifts the number right. Zero is introduced to the vacated most significant bits, and the vacated least significant bits are lost. The following shows the binary representation of the number 43.

0101011 (decimal 43)

By shifting the bits to the right, we lose the least significant bit (in this case, a one), and the number is padded with a zero at the most significant bit. The following is the resulting number.

0010101 (decimal 21)

The following program uses the Bitwise Shift Right and Bitwise AND to display a number as a 16-bit binary number. The number is shifted right successively from 16 down to zero and Bitwise ANDed with 1 to see if the bit is set. An alternative method would be to use successive masks with the Bitwise OR operator.

```c
#include <stdio.h>
int main()
{
    int counter, num;
    printf("Enter a number: ");
    scanf("%d", &num);
    printf("%d is binary: ", num);
    for (counter=15; counter>=0; counter--)
        printf("%d", (num >> counter) & 1);
    putchar('\n');
    return 0;
}
```

Functions for Binary – Decimal Conversions

The two functions given next are for Binary to Decimal and Decimal to Binary conversion. The function given next to convert a decimal number to corresponding binary number supports up to 32 – Bit Binary number. You can use this or program given before for conversion as per your requirements.

Function for Decimal to Binary conversion:

```c
void Decimal_to_Binary(void)
{
    int input =0;
    int i;
    int count = 0;
    int binary [32];  /* 32 Bit, MAXIMUM 32 elements */
    printf ("Enter Decimal number to convert into Binary :");
    scanf ("%d", &input);
    do
    {
        i = input%2;            /* MOD 2 to get 1 or a 0*/
        binary[count] = i;      /* Load Elements into the Binary
                                   Array */
        input = input/2;        /* Divide input by 2 to decrement
                                   via binary */
        count++;                /* Count how many elements are needed*/
    }while (input > 0);

    /* Reverse and output binary digits */
    printf ("Binary representation is: ");
    do
    {
```

```
                printf ("%d", binary[count - 1]);
                count—;
        }       while (count > 0);
        printf ("\n");
}
```

Function for Binary to Decimal conversion:

The following function is to convert any Binary number to its corresponding Decimal number:

```
void Binary_to_Decimal(void)
{
        char binaryhold[512];
        char *binary;
        int i=0;
        int dec = 0;
        int z;
        printf ("Please enter the Binary Digits.\n");
        printf ("Binary digits are either 0 or 1 Only ");
        printf ("Binary Entry : ");
        binary = gets(binaryhold);
        i=strlen(binary);
        for (z=0; z<i; ++z)
        {
                dec=dec*2+(binary[z]=='1'? 1:0); /* if Binary[z] is equal
                to 1,
                then 1 else 0 */
        }
        printf ("\n");
        printf ("Decimal value of %s is %d", binary, dec);
        printf ("\n");
}
```

Debugging and Testing

Syntax Errors

Syntax refers to the grammar, structure and order of the elements in a statement. A syntax error occurs when we break the rules, such as forgetting to end a statement with a semicolon. When you compile the program, the compiler will produce a list of any syntax errors that it may encounter.

A good compiler will output the list with a description of the error, and may provide a possible solution. Fixing the errors may result in further errors being displayed when recompiled. The reason for this is that the previous errors changed the structure of the program meaning further errors were suppressed during the original compilation.

Similarly, a single mistake may result in several errors. Try putting a semicolon at the end of the main function of a program that compiles and runs correctly. When you recompile it, you will get a huge list of errors, and yet it's only a misplaced semicolon.

As well as syntax errors, compilers may also issue warnings. A warning is not an error, but may cause problems during the execution of your program. For example assigning a double-precision floating point number to a single-precision floating point number may result in a loss of precision. It is not a syntax error, but could lead to problems. In this particular example, you could show intent by casting the variable to the appropriate data type.

Consider the following example where x is a single-precision floating point number, and y is a double-precision floating point number. y is explicitly cast to a float during the assignment, which would eliminate any compiler warnings.

    x = (float)y;

Logic Errors

Logic errors occur when there is an error in the logic. For example, you could test that a number is less than 4 and greater than 8. That could not possibly ever be true, but if it is syntactically correct the program will compile successfully. Consider the following example:

    if (x < 4 && x > 8)
        puts("Will never happen!");

The syntax is correct, so the program will compile, but the puts statement will never be printed as the value of x could not possibly be less than four and greater than eight at the same time.

Most logic errors are discovered through the initial testing of the program. When it doesn't behave as you expected, you inspect the logical statements more closely and correct them. This is only true for obvious logical errors. The larger the program, the more paths there will be through it, the more difficult it becomes to verify that the program behaves as expected.

Testing

In software development process, errors can be injected at any stages during development. This is because of verification methods of earlier phases of development of software are manual. Hence the code developed during the coding activity is likely to have some requirement errors and design errors, in addition to errors introduced during the coding activity. During testing, the program to be tested is executed with a set of test cases, and the output of the program for the test cases is evaluated to determine if the programming is performing is expected.

Thus, testing is the process of analyzing a software item to detect the difference between existing and required conditions (i.e., bugs) and to evaluate the features of the software items. So, Testing is the process of analyzing a program with the intent of finding errors.

Some testing principles

- Testing can not show the absence of defects, only their presence.
- The earlier an error is made, the costlier it is.
- The later an error is detected, the costlier it is.

Now let us discuss some testing techniques:

White Box Testing

White box testing is a technique whereby all paths through the program are tested with every possible value. This approach requires some knowledge of how the program should behave. For example, if your program accepted an integer value between 1 and 50, a white box test would test the program with all 50 values to ensure it was correct for each, and then test every other possible value that an integer may take and test that it behaved as expected. Considering the number of data items a typical program may have, the possible permutations make white box testing extremely difficult for large programs.

White box testing may be applied to safety critical functions of a large program, and much of the rest tested using black box testing, discussed below. Because of the number of permutations, white box testing is usually performed using a test harness, where ranges of values are fed to the program rapidly through a special program, logging exceptions to the expected behavior. White box testing is sometimes referred to as structural, clear, or open box testing.

Black Box Testing

Black box testing is similar to white box testing, except rather than testing every possible value, selected values are tested. In this type of test, the tester knows the inputs and what the expected outcomes should be, but not necessarily how the program arrived at them. Black box testing is sometimes referred to as functional testing.

The test cases for black box testing are normally devised as soon as the program specifications are complete. The test cases are based on equivalence classes.

Equivalence Classes

For each input, an equivalence class identifies the valid and invalid states. There are generally three scenarios to plan for when defining equivalence classes.

If the input specifies a range or a specific value, there will be one valid state, and two invalid states defined. For example, if a number must be between 1 and 20, the valid state is between 1 and 20, there will be an invalid state for less than 1, and an invalid state greater than 20.

If the input excludes a range or specific value, there will be two valid states, and one invalid state defined. For example, if a number must not be between 1 and 20, the valid states are less than one and greater than 20, and the invalid state is between 1 and 20.

If the input specifies a Boolean value, there will be just two states, one valid and one invalid.

Boundary Value Analysis

Boundary value analysis only considers the values at the boundary of the inputs. For example, in the case of a number being between 1 and 20, the test cases may be 1, 20, 0, and 21. The thinking behind it is that if the program works as expected with these values, the other values will also work as expected.

The following table gives an overview of the typical boundaries you may want to identify.

Introduction of C Programming

Testing Ranges	
Input type	**Test Values**
Range	• x[lower_bound]-1 • x[lower_bound] • x[upper_bound] • x[upper_bound]+1
Boolean	• True • False

Devising a Test Plan

Identify the equivalence classes, and for each class identify the boundaries. Having identified the boundaries for the class, write a list of valid and invalid values on the boundary, and what the expected behavior should be. The tester can then run the program with the boundary values, and indicate what happened when the boundary value was tested against the required outcome.

The following might be a typical test plan used to check for an age being entered where the acceptable values are in the range of 10 to 110.

Equivalence Class	
Valid	**Invalid**
Between 10 and 110	> 110 < 10

Having defined our equivalence class, we can now devise a test plan for, age.

Test Plan			
Value	**State**	**Expected Result**	**Actual Result**
10	Valid	Continue execution to get name	
110	Valid	Continue execution to get name	
9	Invalid	Ask for age again	
111	Invalid	Ask for age again	

The "**Actual Result**" column is left blank, as it will be completed when testing. If the result is as expected, the column will be ticked. If not, a comment indicating what occurred should be entered.

Chapter – 6

Introduction to Computer Basics

Introduction

Some times, in some cases when you are trying to recover the data or you are performing any data and disk troubleshooting task (or it may be any other system related task) it is very convenient to use **DEBUG** command of DOC.

Also it may be possible for some particular cases that you feel it easy to do that particular task with the help of **DEBUG** then with programming. Let us take an example. The following coding of **debug** will be sufficient to make the back up of **DBR**. Just type the followings lines:

```
DEBUG  BKDBR.BIN
L   100   2   0   1
R   CX
200
W
Q
```

Here you can see that only by typing the above few lines you can avoid to write a program. Let us see another example of coding that loads the backup copy of DBR to the disk

Always remember! Do not try this without the complete knowledge. Be sure what you are going to do. A careless use of the following Instructions may cause a big data loss as the misuse of Instruction may cause all your information of the disk inaccessible.

```
DEBUG  BKDBR.BIN
W   100   2   0   1
Q
```

By seeing the coding of this example you can easily guess how much it may help you when you need it most. Also it is not possible to do programming in every situation. However within a limit of simple cases of the problem, to use assembly Instructions, you have to just copy the **debug.exe/ debug.com** in your boot disk and start writing the code.

The functioning and the described examples in this chapter and in this book are compatible with x86 Intel Processor Family architecture only.

First of all we need to get a little knowledge of computer architecture basics to understand the terms used in the coming sections while describing the functioning and examples in different steps. Let us know some computer architecture basics:

Basic Concepts

Central Processor

This part is also known as central processing unit or CPU, which in turn is made up by the control unit and the arithmetic and logic unit. Its functions consist in reading and writing the contents of the memory cells, to forward data between memory cells and special registers, and decode and execute the Instructions of a program. The processor has a series of memory cells which are used very often and thus, are part of the CPU.

These cells are known with the name of registers. A processor may have one or two dozens of these registers. The arithmetic and logic unit of the CPU realizes the operations related with numeric and symbolic calculations.

Typically these units only have capacity of performing very elemental operations such as, the addition and subtraction of two whole numbers, whole number multiplication and division, handling of the registers' bits and the comparison of the content of two registers. Personal computers can be classified by what is known as word size, this is, the quantity of bits which the processor can handle at a time.

Central Memory

It is a group of cells, fabricated with semi-conductors, used for general processes, such as the execution of programs and the storage of information for the operations. Each one of these cells may contain a numeric value and they have the property of being direction able. This is that they can distinguish one from another by means of a unique number or an address for each cell. The generic name of these memories is Random Access Memory or RAM.

The main disadvantage of this type of memory is that the integrated circuits lose the information they have stored when the electricity flow is interrupted. This was the reason for the creation of memories whose information is not lost when the system is turned off. These memories receive the name of Read Only Memory or ROM.

In order for the PC to process information, it is necessary that this information be in special cells called registers. The registers are groups of 8 or 16 flip-flops.

A flip-flop is a device capable of storing two levels of voltage, a low one, regularly 0.5 volts, and another one, commonly of 5 volts. The low level of energy in the flip-flop is interpreted as off or 0, and the high level as on or 1. These states are usually known as bits, which are the smallest information unit in a computer.

A group of 16 bits is known as word; a word can be divided in groups of 8 bits called bytes, and the groups of 4 bits are called nibbles.

CPU Registers

The CPU has 4 internal registers, each one of 16 bits. The first four, AX, BX, CX, and DX are general use registers and can also be used as 8 bit registers, if used in such a way it is necessary to refer to them for example as: AH and AL, which are the high and low bytes of the AX register. This nomenclature is also applicable to the BX, CX, and DX registers.

The registers known by their specific names:

Register	Specific Name
AX	Accumulator
BX	Base register
CX	Counting register
DX	Data register
DS	Data segment register
ES	Extra segment register
SS	Battery segment register
CS	Code segment register
BP	Base pointers register
SI	Source index register
DI	Destination index register
SP	Battery pointer register
IP	Next Instruction pointer register
F	Flag register

However we'll use these register in **interrupts programming through C** in the next chapters in detail but learning the basics of assembly language here will be good ideal and it will help us through out the programming of disk operations etc.

It is possible to visualize the values of the internal registers of the CPU using the **Debug** program. To begin working with **Debug**, type the following prompt in your computer:

C:/>Debug <Enter>

On the next line a dash will appear, this is the indicator of Debug, at this moment the Instructions of **Debug** can be introduced using the following command:

- r <Enter>

All the contents of the internal registers of the CPU are displayed. An alternative of viewing them is to use the "r" command using as a parameter the name of the register whose value wants to be seen. For example:

-rbx <Enter>

This Instruction will only display the content of the **BX** register and the Debug indicator changes from "-" to ":"

When the prompt is like this, it is possible to change the value of the register which was seen by typing the new value and <Enter>, or the old value can be left by pressing Enter without typing any other value.

It is possible to change the value of the flag register, and use it as a control structure in our programs as we will see later. Each bit of the register has a special name and meaning, the following list describes the value of each bit, on or off and its relation with the operations of the processor:

Overflow

NV = there is no overflow

OV = there is an overflow

Direction
UP = forward
DN = backward

Interrupts
DI = deactivated
EI = activated

Sign
PL = positive
NG = negative

Zero
NZ = it is not zero
ZR = it is zero

Auxiliary Carry
NA = there is no auxiliary carry
AC = there is auxiliary carry

Parity
PO = uneven parity
PE = even parity

Carry
NC = there is no carry
CY = there is carry

Assembler structure

In assembly language code lines have two parts, the first one is the name of the Instruction which is to be executed, and the second one are the parameters of the command. For example:

ADD ah, bh

Here "ADD" is the command to be executed; in this case an addition, and "ah" as well as "bh" are the parameters.

The name of the Instructions in language is made up of two, three or four letters. These Instructions are also called mnemonic names or operation codes, since they represent a function the processor will perform. There are some commands which do not require parameters for their operation, as well as others that only require just one parameter.

Sometimes Instructions are used as follows:

ADD al,[170]

The brackets in the second parameter indicate to us that we are going to work with the content of the memory cell number 170 and not with the 170 value; this is known as direct direction.

Now we are ready to code for our first program with the help of **debug**. We are going to create a program that works to illustrate what we have been seeing, and what we will do is to add two values that we will directly introduce into the program.

The first step is to initiate the Debug, this step only consists of typing **debug** <Enter> on the operative system prompt.

To assemble a program on the Debug, the **"a"** (assemble) command is used. When this command is used, the address where you want the assembling to begin can be given as a parameter, if the parameter is omitted the assembling will be initiated at the locality specified by **CS:IP**, usually 0100h, which is the locality where programs with .COM extension must be initiated. And it will be the place we will use since only Debug can create this specific type of programs.

Even though at this moment it is not necessary to give the **"a"** command a parameter, it is recommendable to do so to avoid problems once the **CS:IP** Registers are used, therefore we type:

    -a0100 <Enter>

When this is done something like this will appear on the screen: **0C1B:0100** and the cursor is positioned to the right of these numbers, note that the first four digits, in hexadecimal system, can be different, but the last four must be 0100, since it is the address we indicated as a **begin**. Now we can introduce the Instructions:

    0C1B:0100 **mov ax,0002**; puts the 0002 value on the ax register

    0C1B:0103 **mov bx,0004**; puts the 0004 value on the bx register

    0C1B:0106 **add ax,bx**; the content of bx is added to the content of ax

    0C1B:0108 **int 20**; provoques the termination of the program.

    0C1B:010A

It is not necessary to write the comments which go after the **";"**. Once the last command has been typed, **int 20**, <Enter> is pressed without writing anything more, to see the Debugger prompt again.

The last written line is not properly an assembler Instruction, instead it is a call for an operative system interruption, these interruptions save us a great deal of lines and are very useful to access operative system functions.

To execute the program we wrote, the **"g"** command is used, and when used we will see a message that says: **"Program terminated normally"**. Naturally with a message like this one we can not be sure the program has done the addition, but there is a simple way to verify it, by using the **"r"** command of the Debug we can see the contents of all the registers of the processor, simply type:

    -r <Enter>

Each register with its respective actual value will appear on the screen like this:

    AX=0006 BX=0004 CX=0000 DX=0000 SP=FFEE BP=0000 SI=0000 DI=0000

    DS=0C1B ES=0C1B SS=0C1B CS=0C1B IP=010A   NV UP EI PL NZ NA PO NC

    0C1B:010A OF DB

The possibility that the registers contain different values exists, but **AX** and **BX** must be the same, since they are the ones we just modified.

Another way to see the values, while the program is executed, is to use the address where we want the execution to end and show the values of the registers as a parameter for **"g"**, in this case it would be: **g108**, this Instruction executes the program, it stops on the **108** address and shows the contents of the registers.

A follow up of what is happening in the registers can be done by using the **"t"** command (trace), the function of this command is to execute line by line what was assembled, showing each time the contents of the registers.

To exit **Debug** use the **"q"** (quit) command.

Advantages of the Assembler

The first reason to work with assembler is that it provides the opportunity of knowing more the operation of your PC, which allows the development of software in a more consistent manner.

The second reason is the total control of the computer, which you can have with the use of the assembler. Another reason is that the assembly based programs are quicker and in some cases they are smaller, and have larger capacities than ones created with other languages.

Let me keep my promise!!

In the earlier part of this chapter we were using some instructions as example, to make the backup of **DBR** and to load the backup of **DBR** to its original location when it is needed. First we examine the Instruction to make the backup.

```
C:\>DEBUG    A:\BKDBR.BIN   <Enter>
   File not found
   - L   100   2   0   1    <Enter>
   - R   CX           <Enter>
   CX  0000
   : 200       <Enter>
   - W         <Enter>
   Writing 00200 bytes
   - Q   <Enter>
```

In this example let us start studying from the first line. The command **DEBUG A:\BKDBR.BIN** Initializes the debug command with creating a file in **A:** floppy drive named as **BKDBR.BIN** if it is not already present there. That's why we got the message "**File not found**" in the starting.

In our second Instruction **L 100 2 0 1,** The L (load) command is to load the DBR of the instructed drive. Let us learn how? In this Instruction the number **100** is the address of the buffer, where the DBR will be stored, next number **2** is used for the drive **C(C :)**. The drive numbers are given as follows:

Drive Letter	Number Used
A:	0
B:	1
C:	2
D:	3
.	.
.	.
and so on	.

The next number **0** is the starting sector number of the number of sectors to be read. Here we are using **0** to read the 1st sector i.e. **DBR** sector. The next number that is **1** is used to inform the number of sectors to be read.

Here we have given **1** because we only want to read one sector. However we can use the numbers and locations of starting and ending sectors according to our needs in different type of other operations. Therefore it will load one sector staring from 1st sector of the drive **C:** to the memory location **100**.

And **R CX** Instruction is used to change or to define the length of the data we want to write in **BKDBR.BIN** file. This Instruction will show the current value of the **CX** register and allow you to make any change. We typed **200** here because the **DEBUG** command uses hexadecimal system and the size of **DBR** in hexadecimal is **200**(h) bytes that is 512 bytes in Decimal system.

W command tells the **DEBUG** to write the 200(h) bytes from location 100 to the **BKDBR.BIN** file. And finally we use the Instruction **Q** to quit the **DEBUG** and go back to the DOS prompt.

Warning!!!   Warning!!!   Warning!!!

It is strictly recommended that you should know what and how are you doing in the procedure of restoring DBR of any disk. If accidentally you store the illegal or DBR of any other Disk, it is possible in most of the cases that the complete data of the disk may become inaccessible.

when you type the first Instruction of the coding that is:

DEBUG A:\BKDBR.BIN <Enter>

File must be in the given location where you are starting the DEBUG program. Now if you get the error message "File not found" before the DEBUG prompt then immediately stop the process by using the Q (quit) command. Because it means that the BKDBR.BIN file could not be found or opened by the DEBUG program and if you continue this process some junk information will be written on DBR and it will make the complete partition inaccessible.

Now let us see what we did in the coding of the Instructions for **restoring the DBR** from the backup file we made named **BKDBR.BIN**. The commands of **DEBUG** to restore the backup are as follows:

```
C:\> DEBUG  A:\BKDBR.BIN <Enter>
-     W 100 2 0 1 <Enter>
-     Q <Enter>
```

This Instruction will write **1 sector** of information from the **BKDBR.BIN** file in floppy drive (**a:**) in the memory location **100** to the first sector that is **sector 0** of **2nd drive** that is **drive(C:)**.

Storing and loading the programs

It would not seem practical to type an entire program each time it is needed, and to avoid this it is possible to store a program on the disk, with the enormous advantage that by being already assembled it will not be necessary to run Debug again to execute it.

The steps to save a program that it is already stored on memory are:

Introduction of Computer Basics

- Obtain the length of the program subtracting the final address from the initial address, naturally in hexadecimal system.
- Give the program a name and extension.
- Put the length of the program on the CX register.
- Order Debug to write the program on the disk.

Using the following program as an example, we will have a clearer idea of how to take these steps. When the program is finally assembled it would look like this:

```
0C1B:0100 mov ax,0002
0C1B:0103 mov bx,0004
0C1B:0106 add ax,bx
0C1B:0108 int 20
0C1B:010 A
-h 10a 100
020a 000a
-n test.com
-rcx
CX 0000
:000a
-w
Writing 000A bytes
```

To obtain the length of a program the **"h"** command is used, since it will show us the addition and subtraction of two numbers in hexadecimal. To obtain the length of ours, we give it as parameters the value of our program's final address (10A), and the program's initial address (100). The first result the command shows us is the addition of the parameters and the second is the subtraction.

The **"n"** command allows us to name the program. The **"rcx"** command allows us to change the content of the CX register to the value we obtained from the size of the file with **"h"**, in this case 000a, since the result of the subtraction of the final address from the initial address.

Lastly, the **"w"** command writes our program on the disk, indicating how many bytes it wrote. Also, to save an already loaded file two steps are necessary:

- Give the name of the file to be loaded.
- Load it using the **"l"** (load) command.

To obtain the correct result of the following steps, it is necessary that the above program be already created.

Inside Debug we write the following:

```
-n test.com
-l
-u 100 109
0C3D:0100 B80200 MOV AX,0002
```

    0C3D:0103 BB0400 **MOV BX,0004**
    0C3D:0106 01D8 **ADD AX,BX**
    0C3D:0108 CD20 **INT 20**

The last **"u"** command is used to verify that the program was loaded on memory. What it does is that it disassembles the code and shows it disassembled. The parameters indicate to **DEBUG** from where and to where to disassemble. **DEBUG** always loads the programs on memory on the address 100H, otherwise indicated.

Segments

The architecture of the x86 processors forces to the use of memory segments to manage the information, the size of these segments is of 64kb.

The reason of being of these segments is that, considering that the maximum size of a number that the processor can manage is given by a word of 16 bits or register, it would not be possible to access more than 65536 localities of memory using only one of these registers, but now, if the memory is divided into groups or segments, each one of 65536 localities, and we use an address on an exclusive register to find each segment, and then we make each address of a specific slot with two registers, and it is possible for us to access a quantity of 4294967296 bytes of memory.

In order for the assembler to be able to manage the data, it is necessary that each piece of information or Instruction be found in the area that corresponds to its respective segments. The assembler accesses this information taking into account the localization of the segment, given by the DS, ES, SS and CS registers and inside the register the address of the specified piece of information. It is because of this that when we create a program using the Debug on each line that we assemble, something like this appears:

    1CB0:0102 **MOV AX,BX**

Where the first number, **1CB0**, corresponds to the memory segment being used, the second one refers to the address inside this segment, and the Instructions which will be stored from that address follow.

The assembler adjusts the size of the segments taking as a base the number of bytes each assembled Instruction needs, since it would be a waste of memory to use the whole segments. For example, if a program only needs 10kb to store data, the data segment will only be of 10kb and not the 64kb it can handle.

Data movement

I am listing some assembly language Instructions for data operations here for your knowledge and convenience, when we'll be doing programming with the help of interrupts and other BIOS operations we'll need its basics.

Detailed introduction and thorough study of assembly language is beyond the limit of this book. Though the knowledge of basics of assembly is necessary to proceed in the further important programming chapters yet if you feel it difficult to understand all the Instructions, you need not to worry but it is recommended that you should gain the basic idea of Instructions.

In any program it is necessary to move the data in the memory and in the CPU registers and there are several ways to do this. it can copy data in the memory to some register, from register to register, from a register to a stack, from a stack to a register, to transmit data to external devices as well as vice versa.

Introduction of Computer Basics

This movement of data is subject to rules and restrictions. The following are some of them:

- It is not possible to move data from one memory location to another directly. It is necessary to first move the data of the source location to a register and then from the register to the destination locality.
- It is not possible to move a constant directly to a segment register; it first must be moved to a register in the CPU.
- It is possible to move data blocks by means of the **MOVS** Instructions, which copies a chain of bytes or words. **MOCSB** which copies n bytes from one location to another and **MOVSW** copies n words from one location to another. The last two Instructions take the values from the defined addresses by DS:SI as a group of data to move and ES:DI as the new localization of the data.

To move data there are also structures called batteries, where the data is introduced with the push Instruction and are extracted with the pop Instruction. In a stack the first data to be introduced is the last one we can take, this is, if in our program we use these Instructions:

    PUSH AX
    PUSH BX
    PUSH CX

To return the correct values to each register at the moment of taking them from the stack it is necessary to do it in the following order:

    POP CX
    POP BX
    POP AX

For the communication with external devices the out command is used to send information to a port and the in command to read the information received from a port.

The syntax of the OUT command is:

    OUT DX,AX

Where DX contains the value of the port which will be used for the communication and AX contains the information which will be sent.

The syntax of the IN command is:

    IN AX,DX

Where AX is the register where the incoming information will be kept and DX contains the address of the port by which the information will arrive.

MOV Instruction

Used to Data transfer between memory cells, registers and the accumulator. Syntax is as follows:

    MOV Destination, Source

The different movements of data allowed for this Instruction are shown in the table given next:

S. No.	Destination	Source
1.	memory	accumulator
2.	accumulator	memory
3.	segment register	memory/register
4.	memory/register	segment register
5.	Register	register
6.	Register	memory
7.	memory	register
8.	Register	immediate data
9.	memory	immediate data

Let us see an example:

    MOV AX,0006

    MOV BX,AX

    MOV AX,4C00

    INT 21

This program moves the value of 0006H to the AX register, then it moves the content of AX (0006h) to the BX register, and lastly it moves the 4C00h value to the AX register to end the execution with the 4C option of the 21h interruption. We'll take a brief introduction of interrupt 13H and interrupt 21H later.

Interruptions

An *interrupt* is a hardware facility that causes the CPU to suspend execution, save its status, and transfer to a specific location. The transfer location specifies the address of a program that is intended to take action in response to the interrupt. The program that is executed as a result of the interrupt is called an *interrupt-handling* program.

For example, if DOS wants to send some information to the BIOS or BIOS wants to send some information to the computer system, DOS or BIOS generate interrupts. Whenever an interrupt is generated, computer suspends whatever it is doing and first takes care of the operation which has generated the interrupt.

Each device capable of generating interrupt is given a unique interrupt number to identify which device is generating these interrupts. We shall discuss all the functions and sub functions of **interrupt 13H, Extensions of interrupt 13H** and **interrupt 21H** within this book.

Basically, the interruptions may be of following three types:

1. Internal hardware interruptions
2. External hardware interruptions
3. Software interruptions

Internal Hardware interruptions

Internal interruptions are generated by certain events which come up during the execution of a program. This type of interruptions is managed on their totality by the hardware and it is not possible to modify them.

A clear example of this type of interruptions is the one which actualizes the counter of the computer internal clock, the hardware makes the call to this interruption several times during a second in order to maintain the time up to date.

Though we cannot directly manage this interruption, since we cannot control the time updating by means of software yet it is possible to use its effects on the computer to our benefit. For example to create a virtual clock updated continuously we only have to write a program which reads the actual value of the counter and to translate it into an understandable format for the user.

External Hardware Interruptions

External interruptions are generated by peripheral devices, such as keyboards, printers, communication cards, etc. They are also generated by coprocessors. It is not possible to deactivate external interruptions.

These interruptions are not sent directly to the CPU but they are sent to an integrated circuit whose function is to exclusively handle this type of interruptions

Software Interruptions

Software interruptions can be directly activated by the assembler invoking the number of the desired interruption with the INT Instruction.

The use of interruptions helps us in the creation of programs and by using them our programs gets shorter. It is easier to understand them and they usually have a better performance mostly due to their smaller size. This type of interruptions can be separated in two categories: the operative system DOS interruptions and the BIOS interruptions.

The difference between the two is that the operative system interruptions are easier to use but they are also slower since these interruptions make use of the BIOS to achieve their goal, on the other hand the BIOS interruptions are much faster but they have the disadvantage that since they are part of the hardware, they are very specific and can vary depending even on the manufacturer brand of the circuit.

The election of the type of interruption to use will depend solely on the characteristics you want to give your program.

> Since we shall use interrupts for data recovery programming with the help of C language via **Interrupt handling with C,** we shall discuss only **Interrupt 13H, Interrupt 13H Extensions** and some **Interrupt 21H** routines, specially. It is not so important to discuss all of the other interrupts and their functions because in **C language,** easier functions are available to perform most of those tasks. However, the knowledge of **Interrupt 13H and its Extensions** is necessary for data recovery programming.

Let us take a brief introduction of Interrupt 20H and Interrupt 21H. The value written in brackets (like 0x20) indicates, how to use

INT 20H (0x20)   →   Terminate process

Call with: CS   =   segment address of program segment prefix

Returns: Nothing

Comments:

It terminates the current process. This is one of several methods that a program can use to perform a final exit. You can also use functions (**00H** or **31H** or **4CH**) of **INT 21H** or simply **INT 27H** to perform a final exit where functions **31H** and **4CH** of **INT 21H** are generally preferred because they allow a return code to be passed to the parent process.

It is recommended that if you have used File Control Blocks (FCBs) to write any file, you should close the file first otherwise you may lose the data because in the action of final exit all the memory that was taken by the process is released, File buffers are flushed and any open handles for files or devices owned by the process are closed.

Therefore if you have open handles for file you may lose the data.

INT 21H (0x21)

Function 00H (0x00) → Terminate process

Call with: AH = 00H
CS = segment address of program segment prefix

Returns: Nothing

Comments:

This interrupt terminates the current process. This is one of several methods that a program can use to perform a final exit. For more information see INT 20H.

INT 21H (0x21)

Function 03H (0x03) → Auxiliary input

Call with: AH = 03H
Returns: AL = 8-bit input data

Comments:

It reads a character from the standard auxiliary device. The default is the first serial port (COM1).

If the auxiliary device sends data faster than your program can process it, characters may be lost. There is no way for a user program to read the status of the auxiliary device or to detect I/O errors such as lost characters, through this function call.

INT 21H (0x21)

Function 04H (0x04) → Auxiliary output

Call with: AH = 04H
DL = 8-bit data for output

Returns: Nothing

Comments

This function of INT 21H outputs a character to the standard auxiliary device. The default is the first serial port (COM1). Strings can also be sent to the auxiliary device by performing a write (INT 21H Function 40H) using the predefined handle for the standard auxiliary device (00034) or using a handle obtained by opening the logical device AUX.

INT 21H (0x21)

Function 05H (0x05) → Printer output

Call with:	AH	=	05H
	DL	=	8-bit data for output
Returns:	Nothing		

Comments:

This function sends a character to the standard list device. The default device is the printer on the first parallel port (LPT1). Strings can also be sent to the printer by performing a write (INT 21H Function 40H) using the predefined handle for the standard printer device (0004H) or using a handle obtained by opening the logical device PRN or LPT1.

INT 21H (0x21)

Function 0DH (0x0D or 13) → Disk reset

Call with:	AH	=	0DH
Returns:	Nothing		

Comments:

This function flushes all file buffers. The function does not update the disk directory for any files that are still open.

INT 21H (0x21)

Function 0EH (0x0E or 14) → Select disk

Call with:	AH	=	0EH
	DL	=	drive code (0 = A, 1= B, etc.)
Returns:	AL	=	number of logical drives in system

Comments:

Selects the specified drive to be current or default, disk drive and returns the total number of logical drives in the system.

The applications should limit themselves to the drive letters A-Z (0 = A, 1 = B, etc.). Logical drives means, the total number of block devices such as floppy disk and hard-disk drives etc. Generally A single physical hard-disk drive is partitioned into two or more logical drives.

INT 21H (0x21)

Function 0FH (0x0F or 15) → Open file

Call with: AH = 0FH
DS: DX = segment: offset of file control block

Returns: If function successful and file found
AL = 00H
And FCB filled in by MS-DOS is as follows:

> Drive field (offset 00H) =1 for drive A, 2 for drive B, etc. Current block field (offset 0CH) = 00H Record size field (offset 0EH) = 0080H Size field (offset 10H) = file size from directory Data field (offset 14H) = date stamp from directory Time field (offset 16H) = time stamp from directory

If function unsuccessful and file not found
AL = 0FFH

Comments:

Opens a file and makes it available for subsequent read/write operation. If the program is going to use a record size other than 128 bytes, it should set the record-size field at FCB offset 0EH after the file is successfully opened and before any other disk operation.

INT 21H (0x21)

Function 10H (0x10 or 16) → Close file

Call with: AH = 10H
DS: DX = segment: offset of file control block

Returns: If function successful (directory update successful)
AL = 00H
If function unsuccessful (file not found in directory)
AL = FFH

Comments:

It is used to close a file. It closes a file, flushes all MS-DOS internal disk buffers associated with the file to disk, and updates the disk directory if the file has been modified or extended.

INT 21H (0x21)

Function 11H (0x11 or 17) → Find first file

Call with: AH = 11H
DS: DX = segment: offset of file control block

Introduction of Computer Basics

Returns: If function successful and matching file found

AL = 00H

And buffer at current disk transfer area (DTA) address filled in as an unopened normal FCB or extended FCB, depending on which type of FCB was input to function.

If function unsuccessful (no matching filename found)

AL = FFH

Comments:

It searches the current directory on the designated drive for a matching filename. You can use wildcards (? and *). This function returns first matching filename.

INT 21H (0x21)

Function 12H (0x12 or 18) → Find next file

Call with: AH = 12H

DS: DX = segment: offset of file control block

Returns: If function successful and matching filename found

AL = 00H

And buffer at current disk transfer area (DTA) address set up as an unopened normal FCB or extended FCB, depending on which type of FCB was originally input to INT21H function 11H.

If function unsuccessful and matching filenames not found

AL = FFH

Comments:

This is the companion of the previous function. If INT 21H Function 11H has been successful, it returns the next matching filename, if any. This function assumes that the FCB used as input has been properly initialized by a previous call to INT 21H Function 11H and possible subsequent calls to INT 21H Function 12H and that the filename or extension being searched for contained at least one wildcard character.

INT 21H (0x21)

Function 13H (0x13 or 19) → Delete file

Call with: AH = 13H

DS: DX = segment: offset of file control block

Returns: If function is successful and file or files deleted

AL = 00H

If function is unsuccessful and no matching files were found or at least one matching file was read-only,

AL = FFH

Comments:

It deletes all matching files from the current directory on the default or specified disk drive. You can also use wildcards (? and *).

INT 21H (0x21)

Function 14H (0x14 or 20) → Sequential read

Call with:	AH	=	14H
	DS: DX	=	segment: offset of previously opened file control block
Returns:	AL	=	00H if read successful
			01H if end of file
			02H if segment wrap
			03H if partial record read at end of file

Comments:

This function reads the next sequential block of data from a file, then increments the file pointer appropriately. The number of bytes of data to be read is specified by the record-size field (offset 0EH) of the file control block (FCB).

The record is read into memory at the current disk transfer area (DTA) address, specified by the most recent call to INT 21H Function 1AH. If the size of the record and the location of the buffer are such that a segment overflow or wraparound would occur, the function fails with a return code of 02H.

INT 21H (0x21)

Function 15H (0x15 or 21) → Sequential write

Call with:	AH	=	15H
	DS: DX	=	segment: offset of previously opened file control block
Returns:	AL	=	00H, if write successful
			01H, if disk is file
			02H, if segment wrap

Comments:

This function writes the next sequential block of data into a file, then increments the file pointer appropriately. The number of bytes of data to be written is specified by the record size-field (offset 0EH) of the file control block (FCB).

INT 21H (0x21)

Function 16H (0x16 or 22) → Create file

Call with:	AH	=	16H
	DS: DX	=	segment: offset of unopened file control block

Returns: If function is successful and file was created or truncated

AL = 00H

And FCB filled in by MS-DOS as follows:

Drive field (offset 00H)	= 1 for drive A, 2 for drive B, etc.
Current block field (offset 0CH)	= 00H
Record size field (offset 0EH)	= 0080H
Size field (offset 10H)	= file size from directory
Date field (offset 14H)	= date stamp from directory
Time field (offset 16H)	= time stamp from directory

If function unsuccessful (directory full)

AL = FFH

Comments:

This function creates a new directory entry in the current directory or truncates any existing file with the same name to zero length. Also opens the file for subsequent read/write operations. This function must be used with caution because an existing file with the specified name is truncated to zero length and all data in that file is irretrievably lost.

INT 21H (0x21)

Function 17H (0x17 or 23) → Rename file

Call with: AH = 17H

DS: DX = segment: offset of special file control block

Returns: If function is successful and one or more files renamed

AL = 00H

If function is unsuccessful and no matching files, or new filename matched an existing file

AL = FFH

Comments:

This function changes the name of all matching files in the current directory on the disk in the specified drive.

You can also use wild cards with this. The special file control block has a drive code, filename, and extension in the usual position (bytes 0 through 0BH) and a second filename starting 6 bytes after the first (offset 11H).

INT 21H (0x21)

Function 19H (0x19 or 25) → Get current disk

Call with: AH = 19H

Returns: AL = drive code (0 for A drive, 1 for B drive etc.)

Comments:

This function returns the drive code of the current or default disk drive.

INT 21H (0x21)

Function 1AH (0x1A or 26) → Set DTA address

Call with: AH = 1AH
DS: DX = segment: offset of disk transfer area.

Returns: Nothing

Comments:

This function specifies the address of the disk transfer area (DTA) to be used for subsequent FCB-related function calls.

INT 21H (0x21)

Function 1BH (0x1B or 27) → Get default drive data

Call with: AH = 1BH

Returns: If function successful

AL = sectors per cluster
DS: DX = segment offset of media ID byte
CX = size of physical sector in bytes
DX = number of clusters for default drive

If function unsuccessful (invalid drive or critical error)

AL = FFH

Comments:

This function obtains selected information about the default disk drive and a pointer to the media identification byte from its file allocation table.

The media ID byte has the following meanings:

Media Descriptor ID	Medium
0F0H	3.5-inch Floppy Disk, double-sided, 18 sectors (or other)
0F8H	fixed disk
0F9H	5.25-inch Floppy Disk, double-sided, 15 sectors
0F9H	3.5-inch Floppy Disk, double-sided, 9 sectors
0FCH	5.25-inch Floppy Disk, single-sided, 9 sectors
0FDH	5.25-inch Floppy Disk, double-sided, 9 sectors
0FDH	8-inch Floppy Disk, single sided, single density

0FEH	5.25-inch Floppy Disk, single-sided, 8 sectors
0FEH	8-inch Floppy Disk, Single Sided, Single Density
0FEH	8-inch Floppy Disk, Double Sided, Double Density
0FFH	5.25-inch Floppy Disk, double-sided, 8 sectors

INT 21H (0x21)

Function 1CH (0x1C or 28) → Get drive data

Call with: AH   =   1CH
               DL   =   Drive Code

Returns: If function is successful
            AL   =   sectors per cluster
            DS: BX   =   segment: offset of media ID byte
            CX   =   size of physical sector in bytes
            DX   =   number of clusters for default or specified drive
            If function is unsuccessful and invalid drive or critical error
            AL   =   FFH

Comments:

This function obtains allocation information about the specified disk drive and a pointer to the media identification byte from its file allocation table. Refer the media descriptor ID byte table, given in INT 21H, Function 1BH, for Media ID information.

INT 21H (0x21)

Function 21H (0x21 or 33) → Random read

Call with: AH   =   21H
            DS: DX   =   segment: offset of previously opened file control block

Returns: AL   =   00H if read successful
            01H if end of file
            02H if segment wrap, read canceled
            03H if partial record read at end of file

Comments:

This function reads a selected record from a file into memory. The record is read into memory at the current disk transfer area address, specified by the most recent call to INT 21H Function 1AH.

INT 21H (0x21)

Function 22H (0x22 or 34) → Random write

Call with: AH   =   22H

	DS: DX	=	segment: offset of previously opened file control block
Returns:	AL	=	00H if write successful
			01H if disk full
			02H if segment wrap, write canceled

Comments:

This function writes the data from memory into a selected record in a file.

INT 21H (0x21)

Function 23H (0x23 or 35) → Get file size

Call with:	AH	=	23H
	DS: DX	=	segment: offset of unopened file control block
Returns:	If function is successful and matching filename found		
	AL	=	00H
	And FCB relative-record field (offset 21H) set to the number of records in the file, rounded up if necessary to the next complete record		
	If function is unsuccessful and no matching file found		
	AL	=	FFH

Comments:

This function searches for a matching file in the current directory; if one is found, updates the FCB with the size of the file in terms of number of records. There is no default record size for this function therefore an appropriate value must be placed in the FCB record size field (offset 0EH) before calling this function.

INT 21H (0x21)

Function 24H (0x24 or 36) → Set relative record number

Call with:	AH	=	24H
	DS: DX	=	segment: offset of previously opened file control block
Returns:	AL is destroyed (other register not affected)		
	FCB relative-record field (offset 21H) updated		

Comments:

This function sets the relative-record number field of a file control block (FCB) to correspond to the current file position as recorded in the opened FCB.

INT 21H (0x21)

Function 25H (0x25 or 37) → Set interrupt vector

Call with: AH   =   25H
             AL   =   interrupt number
             DS:DX = segment: offset of interrupt handling routine
Returns: Nothing

Comments:

This function Initialize a CPU interrupt vector to point to an interrupt handling routine. It should be used in preference to direct editing of the interrupt-vector table by well-behaved applications.

INT 21H (0x21)

Function 26H (0x26 or 38) → Create new Program Segment Prefix (PSP)

Call with: AH   =   26H
             DX   =   segment: of new program segment prefix (PSP)
Returns: Nothing

Comments:

This function copies the program segment prefix (PSP) of the currently executing program to a specified segment address in free memory, then updates the new PSP to make it usable by another program.

INT 21H (0x21)

Function 27H (0x27 or 39) → Random block read

Call with: AH   =   27H
             CX   =   number of records to read
             DS:DX = segment: offset of previously opened file control block
Returns: AL   =   00H if all requested records read
                      01H if end of file
                      02H if segment wrap
                      03H if partial record read at end of file
             CX   =   actual number of records read

Comments:

This function reads one or more sequential records from a file into memory, starting at a designated file location. If the size and location of the buffer are such that a segment overflow or wraparound would occur, the function fails with a return code of 02H and if a partial record is read at the end of file, the remainder of the record is padded with zeros.

INT 21H (0x21)

Function 28H (0x28 or 40) → Random block write

Call with:	AH	=	28H
	CX	=	number of records to write
	DS: DX	=	segment: offset of previously opened file control block
Returns:	AL	=	00H if all requested records written
			01H if disk full
			02H if segment wrap
	CX	=	actual number of records written

Comments:

This function writes one or more sequential records from memory to a file, starting at a designated file location. If the size and location of the buffer are such that a segment overflow or wraparound would occur, the function fails with a return code 02H.

INT 21H (0x21)

Function 29H (0x29 or 41) → Parse filename

Call with:	AH	=	29H
	AL	=	flags to control parsing
	Bit 0	=	1, if leading separators will be scanned off (ignored).
		=	0, if leading separators will not be scanned off
	Bit 1	=	1, if drive ID byte in FCB will be modified only if a drive was specified in the string being parsed.
		=	0, if the drive ID byte in FCB will be modified regardless, if no drive specifier is present in the parsed string, FCB drive code field is set to 0 (default)
	Bit 2	=	1, if filename field in FCB will be modified only if a filename is specified in the string being parsed.
		=	0, if filename field in FCB will be modified regardless, if no filename is presenting the parsed string, FCB filename is set to ASCIIZ blanks.
	Bit 3	=	1, if extension field in FCB will be modified, only if an Extension is specified in the string being parsed.
		=	0, if extension field in FCB will be modified regardless, if no extension is present in the parsed string, FCB extension is set to ASCIIZ blanks.
	DS: SI	=	segment: offset of string

	ES: DI	=	segment: offset of file control block
Returns:	AL	=	00H, if no wildcard characters Encountered 01H, if parsed string contained wildcard characters FFH, if drive specifier invalid
	DS: SI	=	segment: offset of first character after parsed filename
	ES: DI	=	segment: offset of formatted unopened file control block

Comments:

This function parses a text string into the various fields of a file control block (FCB).

This function regards the characters (: . ; , = + tab space) as separator characters and regards all control characters and characters (: . ; , = + tab space < > | / " [ ])as terminator characters.

INT 21H (0x21)

Function 2AH (0x2A or 42) → Get day and date

Call with:	AH	=	2AH
Returns:	CX	=	year (1980 through 2099)
	DH	=	month (1 through 12)
	DL	=	day (1 through 31)
	AL	=	day of the week (0 = Sunday, 1= Monday, etc.)

Comments:

This function obtains the system day of the month, day of the week, month and year.

INT 21H (0x21)

Function 2BH (0x2B or 43) → Set date

Call with:	AH	=	2BH
	CX	=	year (1980 through 2099)
	DH	=	month (1 through 12)
	DL	=	day (1 through 31)
Returns:	AL	=	00H if date set successfully
			FFH if date not valid (ignored)

Comments:

This function initializes the system clock driver to a specific date but the system time remains unchanged.

INT 21H (0x21)

Function 2CH (0x2C or 44) → Get time

Call with:	AH	=	2CH

Returns:	CH	=	hours (0 through 23)
	CL	=	minutes (0 through 59)
	DH	=	seconds (0 through 59)
	DL	=	hundredths of seconds (0 through 99)

Comments:

This is used to obtain the time of day from the system real-time clock driver, converted to hours, minutes, seconds, and hundredths of seconds.

INT 21H (0x21)

Function 2DH (0x2D or 45) → Set time

Call with:	AH	=	2DH
	CH	=	hours (0 through 23)
	CL	=	minutes (0 through 59)
	DH	=	seconds (0 through 59)
	DL	=	hundredths of seconds (0 through 99)
Returns:	AL	=	00H, if time set successfully
			FFH, if time not valid (ignored)

Comments:

This function initializes the system real-time clock to a specified hour, minute, second, and hundredth of second. The system date is not affected.

INT 21H (0x21)

Function 2EH (0x2E or 46) → Set verify flag

Call with:	AH	=	2EH
	AL	=	00H, if turning off verify flag
			01H, if turning on verify flag
	DL	=	00H
Returns:	Nothing		

Comments:

This function turns off or turns on the operating-system flag for automatic read-after-write verification of data. The default setting of the verify flag is OFF because read-after-write verification slows disk operations.

INT 21H (0x21)

Function 2FH (0x2F or 47) → Get DTA address

Call with:	AH	=	2FH

Introduction of Computer Basics

Returns: ES: BX = segment: offset of disk transfer area

Comments:

This function obtains the current address of the disk transfer area (DTA) for FCB file read/write operations.

INT 21H (0x21)

Function 31H (0x31 or 49) → Terminate and Stay Resident (TSR)

Call with: AH = 31H
AL = return code
DX = amount of memory in paragraphs, to reserve

Returns: Nothing

Comments:

This function terminates the execution of the currently executing program by passing a return code to the parent process but reserves part or all of the memory of the program so that it will be overlaid by the next transient program to be loaded. This function should be used in preference to INT 27H because it supports CS to contain the segment of the program segment prefix.

INT 21H (0x21)

Function 33H (0x33 or 51) → Get or set break flag, get boot Drive

Call with: If getting break flag
AH = 33H
AL = 00H

If setting break flag
AH = 33H
AL = 01H
DL = 00H if turning break flag OFF
01H if turning break flag ON

If getting boot drive
AH = 33H
AL = 05H

Returns: If called with AL = 00H or 01H
DL = 00H break flag is OFF
01H break flag is ON

If called with AL = 05H

DL = boot drive (1 = A, 2 = B, etc.)

Comments:

This function obtains or changes the status of the operating system's break flag, which influences Ctrl-C checking during function calls.

INT 21H (0x21)

Function 35H (0x35 or 53) ➔ Get interrupt vector

Call with:	AH	=	35H
	AL	=	interrupt number
Returns:	ES: BX	=	segment: offset of interrupt handler

Comments:

This function obtains the address of the current interrupt-handler routine for the specified machine interrupt.

INT 21H (0x21)

Function 36H (0x36 or 54) ➔ Get drive allocation Information

Call with:	AH	=	36H
	DL	=	drive code (0 default, 1 = A, etc.)
Returns:	If function successful		
	AX	=	sector per cluster
	BX	=	number of available cluster
	CX	=	bytes per sector
	DX	=	cluster per drive
	If function unsuccessful (drive invalid)		
	AX	=	FFFFH

Comments:

This function obtains selected information about a disk drive.

This function is very important in data recovery and disk troubleshooting programming from which the drive's capacity and remaining free space and many other important things can be calculated.

INT 21H (0x21)

Function 38H (0x38 or 56) ➔ Get or set country Information

Call with: If getting country information

Introduction of Computer Basics

	AH	=	38H
	AL	=	0, to get current country information
			1-FEH, to get information for countries with code <255
			FFH, to get information for countries with code >=255
	BX	=	country code, if AL = FFH
	DS:DX	=	segment: offset of buffer for returned information

If setting current country code

	AH	=	38H
	AL	=	1-FEH, country code for countries with code <255
			FFH, for countries with code >=255
	BX	=	country code, if AL = 0FFH
	DX	=	FFFFH

Returns: If function is successful

Carry flag = clear

And, if getting internationalization information

BX = country code

DS: DX = segment: offset of buffer holding internationalization Information.

If function is unsuccessful

Carry flag = set

AX = error code

Comments:

This function obtains international information for the current or specified country or sets the current country code.

INT 21H (0x21)

Function 39H (0x39 or 57) → Create directory

Call with: AH = 39H

DS: DX = segment: offset of ASCIIZ pathname

Returns: If function successful

Carry flag = clear

If function unsuccessful

Carry flag = set

AX = error code

Comments:

This function creates a directory using the specified drive and path.

> ASCIIZ is known as the sequence of ASCII characters terminated be, Null or Zero, Byte.

INT 21H (0x21)

Function 3AH (0x3A or 58) → Delete directory

Call with:	AH	=	3AH
	DS: DX	=	segment: offset of ASCIIZ pathname
Returns:	If function successful		
	Carry flag	=	clear
	If function unsuccessful		
	Carry flag	=	set
	AX	=	error code

Comments:

This function removes a directory using the specified drive and path. If any element of the pathname does not exist or directory is not empty or access is denied or specified directory is also current directory, the function of deleting the directory fails.

INT 21H (0x21)

Function 3BH (0x3B or 59) → Set current directory

Call with:	AH	=	3BH
	DS: DX	=	segment: offset of ASCIIZ pathname
Returns:	If function successful		
	Carry flag	=	clear
	If function unsuccessful		
	Carry flag	=	set
	AX	=	error code

Comments:

This function sets the current or default directory using the specified drive and path. If the specified path or any element of the path does not exist, the function fails.

INT 21H (0x21)

Function 3CH (0x3C or 60) → Create file

Call with:	AH	=	3CH
	CX	=	file attribute, where attribute significance bits may be Combined. Significance of bits is given in the following Table:

Bit(s)	Significance (if set)
0	Read-only
1	Hidden
2	System
3	Volume label
4	Reserved (0)
5	Archive
6 – 15	Reserved (0)

        DS: DX = segment: offset of ASCIIZ pathname

Returns: If function successful

        Carry flag = clear

        AX = handle

        If function unsuccessful

        Carry flag = set

        AX = error code

Comments:

If an ASCIIZ pathname is given, this function creates a new file in the designated or default directory on the designated or default disk drive. If the specified file already exists, it is truncated to zero length. In either case, the file is opened and a handle is returned that can be used by the program for subsequent access to the file.

If any element of the pathname does not exists or file is being created in root directory and root directory is full or access is denied or a file with read – only attribute is already in the specified directory, the function of creating file fails.

INT 21H (0x21)

Function 3DH (0x3D or 61) → Open file

Call with: AH = 3DH

                AL = access mode

Access mode bits significance is given in the following table:

Bits	Significance
0 – 2	Access Mode 000 = read access 001 = write access 010 = read/write access
3	Reserved (0)

4 – 6	Sharing Mode 000 = compatibility mode 001 = deny a 11010 = deny write 011 = deny read 100 = deny none
7	Inheritance flag 0 = child process inherits handle 1 = child does not inherit handle

DS: DX   =   segment: offset of ASCIIZ pathname

Returns: If function successful

Carry flag   =   clear

AX   =   handle

If function unsuccessful

Carry flag   =   set

AX   =   error code

Comments:

If an ASCIIZ pathname is given, this function opens the specified file in the designated or default directory on the designated or default disk drive. A handle is returned which can be used by the program for subsequent access to the file.

INT 21H (0x21)

Function 3EH (0x3E or 62) → Close file

Call with: AH   =   3EH

BX   =   handle

Returns: If function successful

Carry flag   =   clear

If function unsuccessful

Carry flag   =   set

AX   =   error code

Comments:

This function flushes all internal buffers associated with the file to disk, closes the file, and releases the handle for reuse, of previously open or created with success of a given handle. If the file was modified, the time and date stamp and file size are updated in the directory entry of the file.

INT 21H (0x21)

Function 3FH (0x3F or 63) → Read file or device

Call with: AH   =   3FH
              BX   =   handle
              CX   =   number of bytes to read
              DS: DX =   segment: offset of buffer

Returns: If function successful
              Carry flag   =   clear
              AX   =   byte transferred
              If function unsuccessful
              Carry flag   =   set
              AX   =   error code

Comments:

This function transfers data at the current file-pointer position from the file into the buffer and then updates the file pointer position for a given valid file handle from a previous open or create operation, a buffer address, and a length in bytes.

INT 21H (0x21)

Function 40H (0x40 or 64) → Write file or device

Call with: AH   =   40H
              BX   =   handle
              CX   =   number of bytes to write
              DS: DX =   segment: offset of buffer

Returns: If function successful
              Carry flag   =   clear
              AX   =   byte transferred
              If function unsuccessful
              Carry flag   =   set
              AX   =   error code

Comments:

This function transfers data from the buffer into the file and then updates the file pointer position for given valid file handle from a previous open or create operation, a buffer address, and a length in bytes. If the function is called with CX = 0, the file is truncated or extended to the current file pointer position.

INT 21H (0x21)

Function 41H (0x41 or 65) → Delete file

Call with:	AH	=	41H
	DS: DX	=	segment: offset of ASCIIZ pathname
Returns:	If function successful		
	Carry flag	=	clear
	If function unsuccessful		
	Carry flag	=	set
	AX	=	error code

Comments:

This function deletes a file from the default or specified disk and directory. The function deletes a file by replacing the first character of its filename in the root directory with the character E5H (0xE5) and making the file's clusters as available for the new data in the file allocation table. Till then actual data stored in those clusters is not overwritten.

INT 21H (0x21)

Function 42H (0x42 or 66) → Set file pointer

Call with:	AH	=	42H
	AL	=	method code
			00H absolute offset from start of file
			01H signed offset from current file pointer
			02H signed offset from end of file
	BX	=	handle
	CX	=	most significant half of offset
	DX	=	least significant half of offset
Returns:	If function is successful		
	Carry flag	=	clear
	DX	=	most significant half of resulting file pointer
	AX	=	least significant half of resulting file pointer
	If function is unsuccessful		
	Carry flag	=	set
	AX	=	error code

Comments:

This function sets the file pointer location relative to the start of file, end of file, or current file position.

INT 21H (0x21)

Function 43H (0x43 or 67) → Get or set file attributes

Call with:	AH	=	43H
	AL	=	00H to get attributes
			01H to set attributes
	CX	=	file attribute, if AL=01H. Bits can be combined
	DS: DX	=	segment: offset of ASCIIZ pathname
Returns:	If function successful		
	Carry flag	=	clear
	CX	=	file attribute
	If function unsuccessful		
	Carry flag	=	set
	AX	=	error code

Comments:

This function obtains or alters the attributes of file (read-only, hidden, system, or archive) or directory. For the significance of bits for different attributes refer Bits significance table given before.

INT 21H (0x21)

Function 44H (0x44 or 68) → Input/Output Control (I/O Ctrl)

This function provides a direct path of communication between an application program and a device driver. It allows a program to obtain hardware-dependent information and to request operations that are not supported by other MS-DOS function calls.

The sub functions of Input and output Control have been given in the following table:

Sub function	Operation Name
00H	Get Device Information
01H	Set Device Information
02H	Receive Control Data from Character Device Driver
03H	Send Control Data to Character Device Driver
04H	Receive Control Data from Block Device Driver
05H	Send Control Data to Block Device Driver
06H	Check Input Status
07H	Check Output Status
08H	Check If Block Device Is Removable

09H	Check If Block Device Is Remote	
0AH (10)	Check If Handle Is Remote	
0BH (11)	Change Sharing Retry Count	
0CH (12)	Generic I/O Control for Character Devices	

Value	Description
CL = 45H	Set Iteration Count
CL = 4AH	Select Code Page
CL = 4CH	Start Code Page Preparation
CL = 4DH	End Code Page Preparation
CL = 5FH	Set Display Information
CL = 65H	Get Iteration Count
CL = 6AH	Query Selected Code Page
CL = 6BH	Query Prepare List
CL = 7FH	Get Display Information

0DH (13)	Generic I/O Control for Block Devices

Value	Description
CL = 40H	Set Device Parameters
CL = 41H	Write Track
CL = 42H	Format and Verify Track
CL = 47H	Set Access Flag
CL = 60H	Get Device Parameters
CL = 61H	Read Track
CL = 62H	Verify Track
CL = 67H	Get Access Flag

0EH (14)	Get Logical Drive Map
0FH (15)	Set Logical Drive Map

INT 21H (0x21)

Function 44H (0x44 or 68), sub function 00H (0x00)

I/O Ctrl → get device information

Call with:
- AH = 44H
- AL = 00H
- BX = handle
- Carry flag = clear

Introduction of Computer Basics 217

| | DX | = | device information word |

If function unsuccessful
Carry flag = set
AX = error code

Comments:

This sub function returns a device information word for the file or device associated with the specified handle.

INT 21H (0x21)

Function 44H (0x44 or 68), sub function 01H (0x01)

I/O Ctrl → set device information

Call with: AH = 44H
AL = 01H
BX = handle
DX = device information word

Returns: If function successful
Carry flag = clear
If function unsuccessful
Carry flag = set
AX = error code

Comments:

This sub function of function 44H of INT 21H, sets certain flags for a handle associated with a character device. This sub function may not be used for a handle that is associated with a file.

INT 21H (0x21)

Function 44H (0x44 or 68), Sub function 02H (0x02)

I/O Ctrl → read control data character device driver

Call with: AH = 44H
AL = 02H
BX = handle
CX = number of bytes to read
DS: DX = segment: offset of buffer

Returns: If function is successful

	Carry flag	=	clear
	AX	=	bytes read

And buffer contains control data from driver

If function is unsuccessful

	Carry flag	=	set
	AX	=	error code

Comments:

It reads control data from a character-device driver. The length and contents of the data are specified to each device driver and do not follow any standard format. This function does not necessarily result in any input from the physical device.

INT 21H (0x21)

Function 44H (0x44 or 68), Sub function 03H (0x03)

I/O Ctrl → write control data character-device driver

Call with:	AH	=	44H
	AL	=	03H
	BX	=	handle
	CX	=	number of bytes to write
	DS: DX	=	segment: offset of data
Returns:	If function successful		
	Carry flag	=	clear
	AX	=	bytes transferred
	If function unsuccessful		
	Carry flag	=	set
	AX	=	error code

Comments:

This sub function transfers control data from an application to a character-device driver. The length and contents of the data are specific to each device driver and do not follow any standard format. This function does not necessarily result if any output to the physical device.

INT 21H (0x21)

Function 44H (0x44 or 68), Sub function 04H (0x04)

I/O Ctrl → Read control data block-device driver

Call with:	AH	=	44H

Introduction of Computer Basics

	AL	=	04H
	BL	=	device code (0= default, 1=A, 2=B, etc.)
	CX	=	number of bytes to read
	DS: DX	=	segment: offset of buffer
Returns:	If function successful		
	Carry flag	=	clear
	AX	=	bytes transferred
	And buffer contains control data from device driver		
	If function unsuccessful		
	Carry flag	=	set
	AX	=	error code

Comments:

This sub function transfers control data from a block-device driver directly into an application program's buffer. The length and contents of the data are specific to each device driver and do not follow any standard format. This function does not necessarily result in input from the physical device.

INT 21H (0x21)

Function 44H (0x44 or 68), Sub function 05H (0x05)

I/O Ctrl → write control data block-device driver

Call with:	AH	=	44H
	AL	=	05H
	BL	=	device code (0= default, 1=A, 2=B, etc.)
	CX	=	number of bytes to write
	DS: DX	=	segment: offset of data
Returns:	If function successful		
	Carry flag	=	clear
	AX	=	bytes transferred
	If function unsuccessful		
	Carry flag	=	set
	AX	=	error code

Comments:

This sub function transfers control data from an application program directly to a block-device driver. The length and contents of the control data are specific to each device driver and do not follow any standard format. This function does not necessarily result any output to the physical device.

INT 21H (0x21)

Function 44H (0x44 or 68), Sub function 06H (0x06)

I/O Ctrl → check input status

Call with:
- AH = 44H
- AL = 06H
- BX = handle

Returns: If function successful
- Carry flag = clear

And for a device:
- AL = 00H, if device not ready
- FFH, if device ready

For a file:
- AL = 00H, if file pointer at EOF
- FFH, if file pointer not at EOF

If function unsuccessful
- Carry flag = set
- AX = error code

Comments

It returns a code indicating whether the device or files associated with a handle is ready for input.

INT 21H (0x21)

Function 44H (0x44 or 68), Sub function 07H (0x07)

I/O Ctrl → check output status

Call with:
- AH = 44H
- AL = 07H
- BX = handle

Returns: If function successful
- Carry flag = clear

And for a device:
- AL = 00H, if device not ready
- FFH, if device ready

For a file:
- AL = FFH

If function unsuccessful

Introduction of Computer Basics

	Carry flag	=	set
	AX	=	error code

Comments:

It returns a code indicating whether the device associated with a handle is ready for output.

INT 21H (0x21)

Function 44H (0x44 or 68), Sub function 08H (0x08)

I/O Ctrl → check if block device is removable

Call with: AH = 44H
AL = 08H
BL = drive number (0 = default, 1=A, 2=B, etc.)

Returns: If function successful
Carry flag = clear
AL = 00H, if medium is removable
= 01H, if medium is not removable

If function unsuccessful
Carry flag = set
AX = error code

Comments:

This sub function checks whether the specified block device contains a removable storage medium, such as a floppy disk. If a file is not found as expected on a particular drive, a program can use this sub function to determine whether the user should be prompted to insert another disk.

INT 21H (0x21)

Function 44H (0x44 or 68), Sub function 09H (0x09)

I/O Ctrl → check if block device is remote

Call with: AH = 44H
AL = 09H
BL = drive number (0 = default, 1=A, 2=B, etc.)

Returns: If function successful
Carry flag = clear
DX = device attribute word
bit 12 = 0, if drive is local
= 1, if drive is remote

If function unsuccessful
Carry flag = set
AX = error code

Comments:

This sub function checks whether the specified block device is local (attached to the computer running the program) or remote (redirected to a network server).

INT 21H (0x21)

Function 44H (0x44 or 68), Sub function 0AH (0x0A or 10)

I/O Ctrl → check if handle is remote

Call with: AH = 44H
AL = 0AH
BX = handle

Returns: If function successful
Carry flag = clear
DX = attribute word for file or device
bit 15 = 0 if local
1 if remote
If function unsuccessful
Carry flag = set
AX = error code

Comments:

It checks whether the specified handle refers to a file or device that is local (located on the PC that is running program) or remote (located on a network server).

INT 21H (0x21)

Function 44H (0x44 or 68), Sub function 0BH (0x0B or 11)

I/O Ctrl → change sharing retry count

Call with: AH = 44H
AL = 0BH
CX = delays per retry (default = 1)
DX = number of retries (default = 3)

Introduction of Computer Basics 223

Returns: If function successful
              Carry flag   =   clear
              If function unsuccessful
              Carry flag   =   set
              AX   =   error code

Comments:

This sub function sets the number of times MS-DOS retries a disk operation after a failure caused by a file-sharing violation before it returns an error to the requesting process. This sub function is not available unless the file sharing module is loaded.

INT 21H (0x21)

Function 44H (0x44 or 68), Sub function 0CH (0x0C or 12)

I/O Ctrl → generic I/O control for character devices

Call with: AH = 44H
              AL = 0CH
              BX = handle
              CH = category (major) code:

00H	=	unknown
01H	=	COM1, COM2, COM3, OR COM4
03H	=	CON (keyboard and display)
05H	=	LPT1, LPT2, OR LPT3

              CL = function (minor) code:

45H	=	Set Iteration Count
4AH	=	Select Code Page
4CH	=	Start Code Page Preparation
4DH	=	End Code Page Preparation
5FH	=	Set Display Information
65H	=	Get Iteration Count
6AH	=	Query Selected Code Page
6BH	=	Query Prepare List
7FH	=	Get Display Information

              DS: DX = segment: offset of parameter block

Returns: If function successful
             Carry flag   =   clear
             And if called with CL = 65H, 6AH, 6BH or 7FH
             DS: DX =   segment: offset of parameter block
             If function unsuccessful
             Carry flag   =   set
             AX   =   error code

Comments:

It provides a general-purpose mechanism for communication between application programs and character-device drivers.

INT 21H (0x21)

Function 44H (0x44 or 68), Sub function 0DH (0x0D or 13)

I/O Ctrl → generic I/O control for block devices

Call with: AH   =   44H
                   AL   =   0DH
                   BL   =   drive code (0 =default, 1=A, 2=B, etc.)
                   CH   =   category (major) code:
                                       08H = disk drive
                   CL   =   function (minor) code:

40H	=	Set Drive Parameters
41H	=	Write Track
42H	=	Format and Verify Track
47H	=	Set Access Flag
60H	=	Get Device Parameters
61H	=	Read Track
62H	=	Verify track
67H	=	Get Access Flag

             DS: DX=   segment: offset of parameter block

Returns: If function successful
             Carry flag   =   clear
             And if called with CL = 60H or 61H
             DS: DX   =   segment: offset of parameter block
             If function unsuccessful

Introduction of Computer Basics 225

Carry flag	=	set
AX	=	error code

Comments:

This sub function provides a general-purpose mechanism for communication between application programs and block-device drivers. Allows a program to inspect or change device parameters for a logical drive and to read, write, format, and verify disk tracks in a hardware-independent manner.

INT 21H (0x21)

Function 44H (0x44 or 68), Sub function 0EH (0x0E or 14) I/O Ctrl → get logical drive map

Call with: AH = 44H
AL = 0EH
BL = drive code (0 = default, 1=A, 2=B, etc.)

Returns: If function successful

Carry flag = clear
AL = mapping code
    00H, if only one logical drive code assigned to the block device
    01H-1AH logical drive code (1=A, 2=B, etc.) mapped to the block device

If function unsuccessful

Carry flag = set
AX = error code

Comments:

It returns the logical drive code that was most recently used to access the specified block drive.

INT 21H (0x21)

Function 44H (0x44 or 68), Sub function 0FH (0x0F or 15)

I/O Ctrl → set logical drive map

Call with: AH = 44H
AL = 0FH
BL = drive code (0 = default, 1=A, 2=B, etc.)

Returns: If function successful

Carry flag = clear

	AL	=	mapping code
			00H, if only one logical drive code assigned to the block device
			01H-1AH, logical drive code (1=A, 2=B, etc.) mapped to the block device
	If function unsuccessful		
	Carry flag	=	set
	AX	=	error code

Comments:

This sub function sets the next logical drive code that will be used to reference a block device.

INT 21H (0x21)

Function 45H (0x45 or 69) → Duplicate handle

Call with:	AH	=	45H
	BX	=	handle to be duplicated
Returns:	If function successful		
	Carry flag	=	clear
	AX	=	new handle
	If function unsuccessful		
	Carry flag	=	set
	AX	=	error code

Comments:

This function returns a new handle that refers to the same device or file at the same position for given handle for a currently open device or file.

INT 21H (0x21)

Function 46H (0x46 or 70) → Redirect handle

Call with:	AH	=	46H
	BX	=	handle for file or device
	CX	=	handle to be redirected
Returns:	If function successful		
	Carry flag	=	clear
	If function unsuccessful		
	Carry flag	=	set
	AX	=	error code

Comments:

If there are two given handles, this function makes the second handle refer to the same device or file at the same location as the first handle. The second handle is then said to be redirected.

INT 21H (0x21)

Function 47H (0x47 or 71) → Get current directory

Call with:	AH	=	47H
	DL	=	drive code (0 =default, 1=A, 2=B, etc.)
	DS: SI	=	segment: offset of 64-byte buffer
Returns:	If function is successful		
	Carry flag	=	clear
	And buffer is filled in with full pathname from root of current directory.		
	If function is unsuccessful		
	Carry flag	=	set
	AX	=	error code

Comments:

This function obtains an ASCIIZ string that describes the path from the root to the current directory, and the name of that directory.

INT 21H (0x21)

Function 48H (0x48 or 72) → Allocate memory block

Call with:	AH	=	48H
	BX	=	number of paragraphs of memory needed
Returns:	If function successful		
	Carry flag	=	clear
	Ax	=	base segment address of allocated block
	If function unsuccessful		
	Carry flag	=	set
	AX	=	error code
	BX	=	size of largest available block (paragraphs)

Comments:

It allocates a block of memory and returns a pointer to the beginning of the allocated area.

INT 21H (0x21)

Function 49H (0x49 or 73) → Release memory block

| Call with: | AH | = | 49H |

	ES	=	segment of block to be released
Returns:	If function successful		
	Carry flag	=	clear
	If function unsuccessful		
	Carry flag	=	set
	AX	=	error code

Comments:

This function is used to Release a memory block and makes it available for use by other programs.

The function will fail or can cause unpredictable system errors if the program release a memory block that does not belong to it or the segment address passed in register ES is not a valid base address for an existing memory block.

INT 21H (0x21)

Function 4AH (0x4A or 74) → Resize memory block

Call with:	AH	=	4AH
	BX	=	desired new block size in paragraphs
	ES	=	segment of block to be modified
Returns:	If function successful		
	Carry flag	=	clear
	If function unsuccessful		
	Carry flag	=	set
	AX	=	error code
	BX	=	maximum block size available (paragraphs)

Comments:

This function dynamically shrinks or extends a memory block, according to the needs of an application program.

INT 21H (0x21)

Function 4BH (0x4B or 75) → Execute program (EXEC)

Call with:	AH	=	4BH
	AL	=	sub function
			00H = Load and Execute Program
			03H = Load Overlay
	ES: BX	=	segment: offset of parameter block
	DS: DX	=	segment: offset of ASCIIZ program pathname
Returns:	If function successful		

Carry flag = clear
Registers are preserved in the usual fashion.
If function unsuccessful
Carry flag = set
AX = error code

Comments:

This function allows an application program to run another program, regaining control when it is finished. Can also be used to load overlays, although this is use is uncommon.

INT 21H (0x21)

Function 4CH (0x4C or 76) → Terminate process with Return code

Call with: AH = 4CH
AL = return code
Returns: Nothing

Comments:

This function terminates the current process, passing a return code to the parent process. This is one of several methods that a program can use to perform a final exit.

INT 21H (0x21)

Function 4DH (0x4D or 77) → Get return code

Call with: AH = 4DH
Returns: AH = exit type

00H,	if normal termination by INT 20H, INT
21H	Function 00H, or INT 21H Functions 4CH
01H	if termination by user's entry of Ctrl-C 02H if termination by critical-error handler
03H	if termination by INT21H Function 31H or INT 27H

AL = return code passed by child process (0 if child terminated by INT 20H, INT 21H Function 00H, or INT 27H)

Comments:

This function is used by a parent process, after the successful execution of an EXEC call (INT 21H Function 4BH), to obtain the return code and termination type of a child process.

INT 21H (0x21)

Function 4EH (0x4E or 78) → Find first file

Call with: AH = 4EH
CX = search attribute (bits may be combined)
DS: DX = segment: offset of ASCIIZ pathname

Returns: If function successful and matching file found

Carry flag = clear

And search results returned in current disk transfer area as given next:

Byte(s)	Description
00H-14H	Reserved (0)
15H	Attribute of matched file or directory

16H-17H	File time
	  bits 00H-04H = 2-second increments (0-29)
	  bits 05H-0AH = minutes (0-59)
	  bits 0BH-0FH = hours (0-23)

18H-19H	File date
	  bits 00H-04H = day (1-31)
	  bits 05H-08H = month (1-12)
	  bits 09H-0FH = year (relative to 1980)

1AH-1DH	File size
1EH-2AH	ASCIIZ filename and extension

If function is unsuccessful

Carry flag = set
AX = error code

Comments:

This function searches the default or specified directory on the default or specified drive for the first matching file for a given file specification in the form of an ASCIIZ string. For bit significance of attributes, refer bits significance table given before.

INT 21H (0x21)

Function 4FH (0x4F or 79) → Find next file

Call with: AH = 4FH
Returns: If function is successful and matching file found

Carry flag = clear

Introduction of Computer Basics 231

        If function is unsuccessful
        Carry flag   =   set
        AX   =   error code

Comments:

If there is a previous successful call to INT 21H Function 4EH, this function finds the next file in the default or specified directory on the default or specified drive that matches the original file specification.

INT 21H (0x21)

Function 54H (0x54 or 84) → Get verify flag

Call with: AH = 54H
Returns: AL = current verify flag value
                          00H if verify off
                          01H if verify on

Comments:

This function obtains the current value of the system verify (read-after-write) flag.

INT 21H (0x21)

Function 57H (0x57 or 87) → Get or set file date and time

Call with: If getting date and time
                AH = 57H
                AL = 00H
                BX = handle
            If setting date and time
                AH = 57H
                AL = 01H
                BX = handle
                CX = time
                          bits 00H-04H = 2-second increments (0-29)
                          bits 05H-0AH = minutes (0-59)
                          bits 0BH-0FH = hours (0-23)
                DX = date
                          bits 00H-04H = day (1-31)
                          bits 05H-08H = month (1-12)
                          bits 09H-0FH = year (relative to 1980)

Returns: If function successful
Carry flag	=	clear and, if called with AL = 00H
CX	=	time
DX	=	date

If function unsuccessful
Carry flag	=	set
AX	=	error code

Comments:

This function obtains or modifies the date and time stamp in the root directory entry of file.

INT 21H (0x21)

Function 59H (0x59 or 89) → Get extended error Information

Call with:
AH	=	59H
BX	=	00H

Returns: AX = extended error code

Table of error codes has been given below:

Error Code	Error
01H	function number invalid
02H	file not found
03H	path not found
04H	too many open files
05H	access denied
06H	handle invalid
07H	memory control blocks destroyed
08H	insufficient memory
09H	memory block address invalid
0AH (10)	environment Invalid
0BH (11)	format invalid
0CH (12)	access code invalid
0DH (13)	data invalid
0EH (14)	unknown unit
0FH (15)	disk drive invalid
10H (16)	attempted to remove current directory
11H (17)	not same device
12H (18)	no more files

13H (19)	disk write-protected
14H (20)	unknown unit
15H (21)	drive not ready
16H (22)	unknown command
17H (23)	data error (CRC)
18H (24)	bad request structure length
19H (25)	seek error
1AH (26)	unknown media type
1BH (27)	sector not found
1CH (28)	printer out of paper
1DH (29)	write fault
1EH (30)	read fault
1FH (31)	general failure
20H (32)	sharing violation
21H (33)	lock violation
22H (34)	disk change invalid
23H (35)	FCB unavailable
24H (36)	sharing buffer exceeded
25H-31H	reserved
32H (50)	unsupported network request
33H (51)	remote machine not listening
34H (52)	duplicate name on network
35H (53)	network name not found
36H (54)	network busy
37H (55)	device no longer exists on network
38H (56)	net BIOS command limit exceeded
39H (57)	error in network adapter hardware
3AH (58)	incorrect response from network
3BH (59)	unexpected network error
3CH (60)	remote adapter incompatible
3DH (61)	print queue full
3EH (62)	not enough space for print file
3FH (63)	print file canceled
40H (64)	network name deleted
41H (65)	network access denied
42H (66)	incorrect network device type
43H (67)	network name not found

44H (68)	network name limit exceeded
45H (69)	net BIOS session limit exceeded
46H (70)	file sharing temporarily paused
47H (71)	network request not accepted
48H (72)	print or disk redirection paused
49H-4FH	reserved
50H (80)	file already exists
51H (81)	reserved
52H (82)	cannot make directory
53H (83)	fail on INT 24H (critical error)
54H (84)	too many redirections
55H (85)	duplicate redirection
56H (86)	invalid password
57H (87)	invalid parameter
58H (88)	network device fault
59H (89)	function not supported by network
5AH (90)	required system component not installed

BH = error class

01H	if out of resource (such as storage or handles)
02H	if not error, but temporary situation (such as locked region in file) that can be expected to end
03H	if authorization problem
04H	if internal error in system software
05H	if hardware failure
06H	if system software failure not the fault of the active process (such as missing configuration files)
07H	if application program error
08H	if file or item not found
09H	if file or item of invalid type or format
0AH (10)	if file or item locked
0BH (11)	if wrong disk in drive, bad spot on disk, or storage medium problem
0CH (12)	if item already exists
0DH (13)	unknown error

BL = recommend action

	01H	Retry reasonable number of times, then prompt user to select abort or ignore
	02H	retry reasonable number of times with delay between retries, then prompt user to select abort or ignore
	03H	get correct information from user (typically caused by incorrect file name or device specification)
	04H	abort application with cleanup (i.e., terminate the program in as orderly a manner as possible: releasing locks, closing files, etc.)
	05H	perform immediate exit without cleanup
	06H	ignore error
	07H	retry after user intervention to remove cause of error

        CH   =   error locus
                          01H unknown
                          02H block device (disk or disk emulator)
                          03H network
                          04H serial device
                          05H memory
        ES: DI   =   ASCIIZ volume label of disk to insert, if AX = 0022H (invalid disk change)

Comments:

This function obtains detailed error information after a previous unsuccessful INT 21H function call, including the recommended remedial action.

INT 21H (0x21)

Function 5AH (0x5A or 90) → Create temporary file

Call with: AH   =   5AH
                     CX   =   attribute (bits may be combined)
                     DS: DX   =   segment: offset of ASCIIZ path
Returns: If function is successful
                     Carry flag   =   clear
                     AX   =   handle
                     DS: DX   =   segment: offset of complete ASCIIZ pathname
                If function is unsuccessful
                     Carry flag   =   set
                     AX   =   error code

Comments:

This function creates a file with a unique name, in the current or specified directory on the default or specified disk drive, and returns a handle that can be used by the program by the program for subsequent access to the file. The name generated for the file is also returned in a buffer specified by the program.

If any element of the pathname does not exist or the file is being created in the root directory, and the root directory is full the function fails.

INT 21H (0x21)

Function 5BH (0x5B or 91) → Create new file

Call with: AH   =   5BH
　　　　　　　　CX   =   attribute (bits may be combined)
　　　　　　　　DS: DX =   segment: offset of ASCIIZ pathname

Returns: If function is successful
　　　　　　　　Carry flag   =   clear
　　　　　　　　AX   =   handle
　　　　　　　　If function is unsuccessful
　　　　　　　　Carry flag   =   set
　　　　　　　　AX   =   error code

Comments:

This function creates a file in the designated or default directory on the designated or default drive, and returns a handle that can be used by the program for subsequent access to the file for a given ASCIIZ pathname.

If a file with the same name and path already exists or any element of the specified path does not exist or the file is being created in the root directory, and the root directory is full or the user has insufficient access rights, the function fails.

INT 21H (0x21)

Function 5CH (0x5C or 92) → Lock or unlock file region

Call with: AH   =   5CH
　　　　　　　　AL   =   00H if locking region
　　　　　　　　　　　　　01H if unlocking region
　　　　　　　　BX   =   handle
　　　　　　　　CX   =   high part of region offset
　　　　　　　　DX   =   low part of region offset
　　　　　　　　SI   =   high part of region length

Introduction of Computer Basics

	DI	=	low part of region length
Returns:	If function successful		
	Carry flag	=	clear
	If function unsuccessful		
	Carry flag	=	set
	AX	=	error code

Comments:

This function locks or unlocks the specified region of a file. This function is not available unless the file-sharing module (such as SHARE.EXE) is loaded.

INT 21H (0x21)

Function 5EH (0x5E or 94), sub function 00H (0x00)

➔ Get machine name

Call with:	AH	=	5EH
	AL	=	00H
	DS: DX	=	segment: offset of buffer to receive string
Returns:	If function is successful		
	Carry flag	=	clear
	CH	=	00H if name not defined
			<> 00H if name defined
	CL	=	netBIOS name number (if CH <> 0)
	DX: DX	=	segment: offset of identifier (if CH <> 0)
	If function is unsuccessful		
	Carry flag	=	set
	AX	=	error code

Comments:

This sub function returns the address of an ASCIIZ string identifying the local computer. This function call is only available when the Microsoft Network is running.

INT 21H (0x21)

Function 5FH (0x5F or 95), sub function 02H (0x02)

➔ Get redirection list entry

Call with:	AH	=	5FH
	AL	=	02H

	BX	=	redirection list index
	DS: SI	=	segment: offset of 16-byte buffer to receive local device name
	ES: DI	=	segment: offset of 128-byte buffer to receive network name
Returns:	If function successful		
	Carry flag	=	clear
	BH	=	device status flag
	Bit 0	=	0 if device valid
		=	1 if not valid
	BL	=	device type
			03H, if printer
			04H, if drive
	CX	=	stored parameter value
	DX	=	destroyed
	BP	=	destroyed
	DS: SI	=	segment: offset of ASCIIZ local device name
	ES: DI	=	segment: offset of ASCIIZ network name
	If function unsuccessful		
	Carry flag	=	set
	AX	=	error code

Comments:

This sub function allows inspection of the system redirection list, which associates local logical names with network files, directories, or printers. This function call is only available when Microsoft Networks is running and the file-sharing module has been loaded.

INT 21H (0x21)

Function 5FH (0x5F or 95), sub function 03H (0x03)

→ Redirect device

Call with:	AH	=	5FH
	AL	=	03H
	BL	=	device type
			03H, if printer
			04H, if drive
	DS: SI	=	segment: offset of ASCIIZ local device name
	ES: DI	=	segment: offset of ASCIIZ network name, followed by ASCIIZ password
Returns:	If function successful		

Carry flag	=	clear
If function unsuccessful		
Carry flag	=	set
AX	=	error code

Comments:

Establishes redirection across the network by associating a local device name with a network name. This function call is only available when Microsoft Networks is running and the file-sharing module (SHARE.EXE) has been loaded.

INT 21H (0x21)

Function 5FH (0x5F or 95), sub function 04H (0x04)

→ Cancel device redirection

Call with:	AH	=	5FH
	AL	=	04H
	DS: SI	=	segment: offset of ASCIIZ local device name
Returns:	If function successful		
	Carry flag	=	clear
	If function unsuccessful		
	Carry flag	=	set
	AX	=	error code

Comments:

This sub function cancels a previous redirection request by removing the association of a local device name with a network name. This function call is only available when Microsoft Networks is running and the file-sharing module such as SHARE.EXE has been loaded.

INT 21H (0x21)

Function 67H (0x67 or 103) → Set handle count

Call with:	AH	=	67H
	BX	=	number of desired handles
Returns:	If function is successful		
	Carry flag	=	clear
	If function is unsuccessful		
	Carry flag	=	set
	AX	=	error code

Comments:

This function sets the maximum number of files and devices that may be opened simultaneously using handles by the current process.

INT 21H (0x21)

Function 6CH (0x6C or 108) → Extended open file

Call with: AH = 6CH
             AL = 00H
             BX = open mode

Bit(s)	Significance
0-2	Access type 000 = read-only 001 = write-only 010 = read/write
3	Reserved (0)
4-6	Sharing mode 000 = compatibility 001 = deny read/write (deny all) 010 = deny write 011 = deny read 100 = deny none
7	Inheritance 0 = child process inherits handle 1 = child does not inherit handle
8-12	Reserved (0)
13	Critical error handling 0 = execute INT 24H 1 = return error to process
14	Write-through 0 = writes may be buffered and deferred 1 = physical write at request time
15	Reserved (0)

  CX = file attribute (bits may be combined; if ignored if open **refer Bits Significance table.**

  DX = open flag

Introduction of Computer Basics

Bit(s)	Significance
0-3	Action if file exists 0000 = fail 0001 = open file 0010 = replace file
4-7	Action if file does not exists 0000 = fail 0001 = create file
8-15	Reserved (0)

          DS: SI   =   segment: offset of ASCIIZ pathname

Returns: If function successful

          Carry flag   =   clear
          AX   =   handle
          CX   =   action taken

              1 = file existed and was opened
              2 = file did not exists and was created
              3 = file existed and was replaced

          If function unsuccessful

          Carry flag   =   set
          AX   =   error code

Comments:

This function opens, creates or replaces a file in the designated or default directory on the designated or default disk drive for a given ASCIIZ pathname and returns a handle that can be used by the program for subsequent access to the file. If any element of the pathname does not exist or the file is being created in the root directory and the root directory is full or the file is being created and a file with the same name and the read-only attribute already exists in the specified directory or the user has insufficient access rights, the function fails.

Chapter – 7
Necessary DOS Commands

Introduction

While we try to recover the data from the disk, it depends on the case of data loss that how much effort is required to recover the loss. In many cases it is possible that if we have the sufficient knowledge of some important DOS (Disk Operating System) commands, we may recover data with fewer efforts.

In some cases it may be possible that we can recover data without programming only by use of these commands with a tricky mind.

I assume that you do not know anything about DOS and its commands. In this chapter of DOS commands introduction we'll learn only about those command which may help us for recovering our data. First of all we'll give a glance to the evolution of MS – DOS.

Brief History

The MS – DOS operating system is based on the Intel 8086 family of microprocessor. MS – DOS has evolved from a simple program loader into a sophisticated, stable operating system for personal computers.

Microsoft Disk Operating System (MS-DOS) Version 1.0

IBM developed this computer in the early 1980s. Microsoft developed MS-DOS 1.0. Released in August 1981, it consisted of 4000 lines of assembly language source code and ran in 8 kilobytes of memory.

Shortly after that, in 1982, MS-DOS version 1.1 was released and worked with double sided 320kb floppy disks. Versions of DOS marketed by IBM are called IBM-DOS or PC-DOS.

MS-DOS Version 2.0

When IBM began development of a 10-megabyte hard disk, Microsoft began work on the development of version 2.0 of DOS, which would be designed to support the hard disk. Up to this point, DOS 1.0, in keeping with its heritage, had been designed for a floppy disk environment. One of the major limitations in DOS 1.0 is that its directory is limited to a maximum of 64 files.

MS-DOS version 2.0 was so designed to include a hierarchically designed file system. A hierarchical file system is significant in that any directory can contain both files and other subdirectories. Hierarchical file systems were already in use in the UNIX operating system, which was used as the development platform of the MS-DOS/IBM-DOS operating system. In effect some of the underlying concepts of MS-DOS are similar to their counterparts in UNIX.

MS-DOS Version 3.0 to 5.0

Version 3.0 was released in August of 1984 to support the IBM PC/AT. Version 3.1 was released in November 1984 and contained networking support. The January 1986 version 3.2 supported 3.5-inch disks. In 1987 IBM version 3.3 followed, with the principal purpose of supporting the IBM PS/2 line of computers.

The MS-DOS version 3.3 added many new features and commands. Compaq version 3.31 of DOS allowed for hard disk partitions larger than 32 megabytes.

MS-DOS version 4.01 also reads partitions greater then 32 megabytes. Originally issued as MS-DOS 4.0, some minor bugs resulted in upgraded version 4.01 being issued with various fixes. This version added full screens, a menu-driven interface called DOS SHELL, and extra support for Expanded Memory Specifications.

Version 5.0 was designed as a replacement for all preceding versions of DOS. With DOS 5.0 both IBM and Microsoft were selling the same DOS even the documentation was similar. Memory requirements were significantly reduced. Significant enhancements were made to the support for expanded and extended memory.

The DOS editor "EDIT" was included with this version of DOS. The DOS SHELL is completely new. QBASIC was introduced to replace BASICA and GWBASIC. This version offered a way to recover data that had been accidentally lost at least some of the time.

MS-DOS Version 6.0

Version 6.0 included many new programs to enhance the performance of DOS. They included:

- Microsoft Double Space, an integrated disk compression program that increased available disk space by compressing files
- Microsoft Mem Maker, a memory-optimization program that makes it easy to move device drivers and memory-resident programs from conventional memory into the upper memory area
- An enhanced EMM386.EXE device driver that provides access to more upper memory blocks
- Enhanced loadhigh and devicehigh commands that enable you to specify the memory region in which to load a program
- Microsoft Backup, a program that makes it easy to back up your data
- Microsoft Anti-Virus, a program that can identify and remove may different computer viruses
- Microsoft Undelete, an enhanced program that enables you to choose one or three levels of protection in case you accidentally delete a file,
- The ability to include more than one configuration in the CONFIG.SYS file. The ability to bypass startup commands when you turn on your computer
- MS-DOS Help, a complete online reference to MS-DOS commands

MS-DOS Version 7.0 (Windows 95)

DOS is provided with Windows 95 for backward compatibility with DOS and Windows 3.x applications. Let us see the evolution of MS – DOS to Windows in the following table:

MS – DOS Version	Notes and Comments
MS- DOS 1.0	First operating system on IBM PC in 1981
MS- DOS 1.25	Double sided disk support and bug fixes added
MS- DOS 2.0	Introduced with IBM PC/XT in 1983 and having the support of hierarchical file structure and hard disks added.
MS- DOS 2.01	2.0 with international support
MS- DOS 2.11	2.01 with bug fixes
MS- DOS 2.25	Support for Extended Character sets
MS- DOS 3.0	Support for 1.2MB floppy disks and larger hard disks added
MS- DOS 3.1	Support for Microsoft networks added
MS- DOS 3.2	Support for 3.5 inches disks added
MS- DOS 3.3	Generalized code page (font) support
MS- DOS 4.0	Support for logical volumes larger then 32 MB and Visual shell
Windows 1.0	Graphical user interface for MS – DOS
Windows 2.0	Compatibility with OS/2, Presentation Manager
Windows 95	Used Version 4.00.950
Windows 95 Se	Used Version 4.00.1111
Windows 98	Used Version 4.10.1998
Windows 98 Second Edition	Used Version 4.10.2222
Windows Millennium	Used Version 4.90.3000
Windows NT	Used Version 4.0
Windows 2000	Used Version 5.00.2195
Windows XP	Used Version 5.1.2600

Necessary Commands

Let us learn some important commands that may be useful while we are trying to recover data by programming and non programming techniques:

ATTRIB

The ATTRIB command is used to display, set, or remove one or more of the four attributes, read-only, archive, system, and hidden that can be assigned to files and directories. It is typically used to remove read-only, hidden, and system attributes so a file can be moved or deleted or also to set them so that it can not be.

Syntax:

To display the attribute settings of all files in the current directory:

ATTRIB

To display the attributes of a directory:

    ATTRIB   *directoryname*

To display the attributes of a file:

    ATTRIB   *filename*

To set or remove attributes of a file or directory:

    ATTRIB [+ | - R] [+ | - A] [+ | - S] [+ | - H] [*directory|filename*] [/S]

+ Sets an attribute, - Clears an attribute.

R	Read-only file attribute.
A	Archive file attribute.
S	System file attribute
H	Hidden file attribute.
/S	Processes files in all directories in the specified path.

The **Read-Only** attribute allows a file to be accessed but not modified. The **System** attribute is normally reserved for files that are necessary for DOS or Windows to load properly. Files and directories with the **Hidden** attribute set are not normally displayed in directory listings or Open Files dialogue boxes.

The usual reason for hiding folders is because they are important to system or program operation and should not be deleted or moved in casual tidy-up operations. Hidden and System folders will often also have the Read-Only attribute set.

Multiple attributes can be set or cleared by combining switches, separated by spaces. Although both files and directories can have attributes assigned and cleared using ATTRIB, there are differences in the way they behave - the most obvious of which is that wildcards (? and *) can be used to display or change the attributes for a group of files whereas directories must be named in full. We are going to know in details about wildcards and shortcuts later in this chapter.

Setting a file attribute to System, Hidden, or Read-Only, will prevent the file from being deleted or moved using DEL, ERASE, or MOVE commands but will not protect the files from DELTREE or FORMAT. Although a directory's Read-Only attribute can be set, this seems to serve little purpose.

Firstly, the attribute only applies to the directory and not the files within it. Also setting a folder to read-only does not prevent it being deleted however in Windows explorer it will cause a warning notice to be displayed before the folder is deleted or moved.

To display the attributes of a file named *"readme"*:

    ATTRIB   **readme**

To assign the Read-Only attribute to the file *"readus.txt"*, use:

    ATTRIB readus.txt   **+R**

To remove the System and Hidden attributes from *"data19.txt"*:

    ATTRIB   -S   -H   **data19.txt**

To hide the directory *"c:\mynotes"*

ATTRIB   +H   c:\mynotes

To hide the files, but not the directories in the C:

ATTRIB   +H   c:*.*

CD (or CHDIR)

Changes (or displays) the current directory on the specified drive.

Syntax:

To display the current directory:

CD   [drive:]

To change the current directory:

CD   path

Path Changes the current directory to **path**. Each drive has its own "current directory" which remains "current" until it is changed thus changing the current directory of drive c: will not affect the current directory status of any other drive. To change to the current directory on a different drive, just enter the drive letter and colon.

If the current drive is c:, to enter the directory *"c:\windows\java"*

CD   \windows\java

If the current directory is already *"c:\windows"*, all that is necessary is:

CD   java

To change the current directory *"c:\windows\java"* to the parent directory *"c:\windows"*:

CD..

Suppose you are currently in director *"c:\windows\java\notes\klip\"*, now if you directly want to jump to the windows directory, just increase the two more dots (..) you we did in the previous case, like this

CD....

If the current directory on the c: drive is **"c:\windows\notes"** and the current directory on the e: drive is **"e:\movie"**, then to copy all files from **"e:\movie"** to **"c\windows\notes"**:

COPY   e:*.*   c:

To copy all files from *"e:\downloads"* to the root directory of c:

COPY   e:*.*   c:\

CHKDSK

CHKDSK is used to check the status of a disk, fix some disk errors, and display a status report showing any errors found in the file allocation table (FAT) and directory structure. CHKDSK also displays a summary of disk usage. If errors are found on the disk, CHKDSK displays a warning message.

Syntax:

CHKDSK   [path]   [/F]   [/V]

Path   Specifies the drive and directory to check.

/F   Fixes errors on the disk.

/V   Displays the full path and name of every file on the disk

SCANDISK can reliably detect and fix a much wider range of disk problems and is generally preferred to the somewhat dated CHKDSK. The /F switch (for fixing any errors found) should not be used while any program is running other than DOS and CHKDSK itself.

CHKDSK cannot be used on drives created using SUBST, nor can it be used on network drives. In win98, CHKDSK does not check the disk, though still provides some basic data

> You should not scan the disk with CHKDSK or SCANDISK or any other disk scanning program if your disk is crashed or there is any logical error in your boot sectors like MBR, DBR, FAT or root directories are corrupted. It may make you data information distorted and can make it difficult to recover. Not only this you may not recover data completely.

CLS

Clears the screen leaving only the command prompt and cursor.

Syntax:
CLS

COMMAND

Starts a new copy of the Command Interpreter.

Syntax:
COMMAND [path] [device] [/Switches]

Path	Drive and directory containing command.com. This must be specified unless command.com is in the root directory.
Device	Device to use for command input and output. By default this is the keyboard and monitor
/P	Makes the new Command Interpreter permanent.
/E:x	Sets the initial environment size [bytes]. x should be set between 256 and 32,768 bytes. The default is: 256 bytes.
/L:y	Internal buffers length [bytes]. y should be set between 128 and 1,024 bytes. This switch is only accepted if the Command Interpreter is permanent. The /P switch must also be set.
/U:z	Input buffer length [bytes]. z should be set between 128 and 255 bytes. The default is: ? This switch is only accepted if the Command Interpreter is permanent. the /P switch must also be set.
/MSG	Stores all error messages in memory. This switch is only accepted if the Command Interpreter is permanent. The /P switch must also be set.
/LOW	Forces COMMAND to keep in low memory
/Y	Steps through the batch program specified by /C or /K
/C command	Executes **command** and exits. This must be the last switch on the command line.

/K command Executes **command** and continues running. This must be the last switch on the command line.

COPY

The prime use of COPY is to copy one or more files to another location but it can also be used to combine (append and concatenate) files and to type directly to a file, printer, or other device.

Syntax:

COPY   [/A | /B]   source   [/A | /B]   [+ source [/A | /B] [+ ...]]
                                       [destination   [/A | /B]]   [/V] [/Y | /-Y]

source   The file(s) to be copied. Although this must be a single parameter, it may include multiple files specified using wildcards (* or ?). It may also be a valid device (e.g. **CON**)

like **COPY CON NOTES.TXT**

now write or copy the text and come out by entering the key **Ctrl+Z**.

destination   The directory and/or filename for the new file(s). If **destination** is not specified **source** is copied to the current directory with the same name and creation date as the original. If **source** is in the current directory, an error message is displayed stating that the "file cannot be copied to itself".

file /A   Forces COPY to treat the file as an ASCII text file.

file /B   Forces COPY to treat the file as a binary file.

/V   Verifies that new files can be read.

/Y   No warning prompt before overwriting a file.

/-Y   Displays a warning and requires confirmation before overwriting a file.

When used from the command line, if a file specified in **destination** already exists in the specified location, COPY will, by default, display a warning message and require confirmation before overwriting the old file. On the other hand, when COPY is used in a batch file, any existing files will be overwritten without warning.

This default behavior can be modified by presetting the /Y | /-Y switch in the COPYCMD environment variable and overruled by using the /Y | /-Y switch on the command line.

COPY does not copy files that are 0 bytes long; instead, it deletes such files. Use XCOPY to copy these files. **Source** and/or **Destination** may be an appropriate device (such as CON, COM*x* or LPT*x* where *x* is 1,2,3 exc.) rather than a file.

Depending on context, Copy treats files as binaries or ASCII text files. By default:

- When copying files from one location to another (ASCII or not), COPY assumes binary mode,
- When concatenating files, COPY assumes ASCII mode,
- When source or destination is a device (other than a disk), copy assumes ASCII mode.

When operating in binary mode, COPY determines the file's starting location from the File Allocation

Necessary DOS Commands

Table and copies the number of bytes allocated to that file from that point.

When in ASCII mode, data is copied until an End-Of-File (ASCII character no. 26; Ctrl-Z) character is reached. This character is NOT copied, but COPY adds an EOF character before closing the new file.

This convoluted procedure enables COPY to concatenate files and to work with non-file input (like keyboard). On the few occasions that the default mode is inappropriate, it may be over-ridden by adding the /A or /B switch to source and/or destination files as required.

To copy "**note.txt**" in the current drive and directory to the directory "**mynotes**":

    COPY note.txt c:\mynotes

or

    COPY note.txt c:\mynotes

In the first case, if the "**mynotes**" directory doesn't exist, "**note.txt**" is copied to a file named "**mynotes**" in the root directory of drive C. In the second case, an "Invalid Directory" error message will be displayed. To copy all the files in the "**mynotes**" directory to a directory named "**mynotes backup**" on drive D:

    COPY c;\mynotes*.* d:\mynotes backup

To make a copy of "**note.txt**" in the current drive and directory and call it "**program note.txt**"

    COPY note.txt "program note.txt"

DEBUG

DEBUG is a method of looking at portions of your computer and writing assembly code to perform certain tasks on your computer. MS-DOS 2.x - 4.x used DEBUG.COM and MS-DOS 5.x and beyond used DEBUG.EXE for this.

DEBUG.EXE is one of those little programs that, in the hands of a skilled user, is an amazingly powerful tool with which one can view and edit the contents of memory both short term(RAM) and long term (hard/floppy/tape media). One can also compile (and, up to a point, decompile) assembly language code.

DEBUG is a byte editor that enables files to be viewed and modified at the byte level. It is generally recommended as there is no "undo" command, so make a backup before playing with it. Be sure that you know what you are doing when using the DEBUG utility.

This is a powerful programmer's tool that can be used to gain access to your computer at the hardware level. If you are not careful, you could cause such damage as erasing your hard disk or locking up your keyboard.

Syntax:

DEBUG	[filename]
DEBUG	[[drive:] [path] filename [testfile-parameters]]
[drive:][path]filename	Specifies the file you want to test
testfile-parameters	Specifies command-line information required by the file you want to test.

How to start DEBUG

DEBUG can be started in one of two ways.

Method one:

At the DOS prompt you enter

DEBUG (return)

DEBUG will respond with the hyphen (-) prompt. When the prompt appears DEBUG is waiting for you to enter one of its many one letter commands. Starting DEBUG this way will allow you to work on the internal hardware of the computer and view the contents of all of the memory location in RAM. You can also load in as many as 128 sectors of a floppy or Hard disk and view, edit or move the contents to another location.

DEBUG sets up a work area in memory of 65,535 (decimal) one byte locations which is equal to FFFF bytes in Hex. The first 256 (decimal) or 100 Hex bytes of this area are set aside for what is called the Program Segment Prefix (PSP) of a program and must not be altered in any way. Whenever we load sectors or data in memory with DEBUG, it must be put at a location starting at offset 100.

An example of a debug command is shown on the following line.

> DEBUG
> L 0100 0 0 80 (return)

In this command, We are telling debug to load into memory starting at offset 100, 80 (Hex) sectors from the A drive starting with sector 0. 80 Hex sectors is equal to 128 decimal sectors, so if each sector on the disk, stores 512 bytes then the total number of bytes loaded into memory is (512 X 128) or 65,540 bytes (Maximum).

Method Two:

At the DOS prompt you enter

> DEBUG \path\filename (return)

DEBUG will then load itself into memory along with the file that is specified in the path and filename field of the command line and put the first byte of the file at offset 100 of the work area.

By starting DEBUG this way, we are able to view, edit or move a COM program or an ASCII text file. This is a very convenient way to DEBUG or fix a COM program.

MS-DOS will allow only two types of programs to run under its control and they must end with the extensions of EXE or COM. The difference in these two program types is in the way DOS handles the maintenance portions of the program.

This maintenance area, often called the Program Segment Prefix (PSP), is a 256 byte block of memory that must be set aside by the program and is needed by DOS to return control back to the operating system when the program terminates.

Without going into a lot of details, we shall point out the major difference between these two types of programs.

COM Extension

COM programs are very small and compact programs that cannot be larger than 65K bytes in size. The PSP of a COM program is located in the first 100 Hex (256 Dec) locations of the program. The first instruction of the COM program must start at offset 100 in memory.

DOS creates the PSP for the COM program, which means we don't have to be concerned with this when we assemble a program. All the data, code, and the stack area are in the same segment of memory (1 segment is 64K).

EXE Extension

The EXE programs can be any size from 200 bytes to 640k bytes. The PSP must be setup by the programmer, when the program is assembled. The programmer determines where the first instruction is in the program. The EXE program uses separate segments for the data, code and stack area in memory.

From the comparison of EXE and COM file properties, you can see it is much more difficult to assemble an EXE program than it is a COM program. The debug utility program was designed to work only with a COM program by setting up the PSP area each time we enter debug.

Once in DEBUG, we can start assembly of a program at offset 100 and not be concerned with PSP or where the data, code, and stack is located. It is possible to look at an EXE program with DEBUG if we rename the program with a different extension before we load it into memory.

After DEBUG starts, type ? to display a list of debugging commands. To get out of DEBUG you need to "Q" and enter. To execute the DEBUG routine you need to do "G" and enter.

Let us see an example:

    DEBUG
    D40:00   <return>   <return>

Information about your computer ports would be displayed if any port is absent or not responding the status of that port will be shown as 00.

Now enter **Q** to return.

    Q   <return>

Once DEBUG has been called, the somewhat cryptic "DEBUG prompt", a hyphen (-), is displayed. At the prompt, the following "DEBUG commands" are valid:

Command	Parameters	Action
?		This list of DEBUG commands.
A	[address]	Assemble
C	range address	Compare
D	[start address [end address | L range]]	Displays a segment of memory. By default **start address** is offset 100 of the first free segment of memory, or offset 100 of the segment containing a file loaded by DEBUG. The default **end address** is 017F (a range of 128 bytes).
E	address [list]	Enter
F	range list	Fill
G	[=address] [addresses]	Go
H	value1 value2	Hex
I	Port	Input

L	-	Loads a previously "named" (by **N command**) file into memory where it can be viewed /edited.
L	Number	Used with commands accepting a "range" argument to denote a number of bytes. Typically used in arguments as: **start address L number**. If **number** should take **end address** past the end of the segment, then **number** is truncated so the **end address** is the last byte of the segment.
M	range address	Move
N	[path] filename [arglist]	"Names" a file for DEBUG. A file must be "named" before it can be loaded for viewing/editing.
O	port byte	Output
P	[=address] [number]	Proceed
Q		Exit DEBUG.
R	[register]	Register
S	range list	Search
T	[=address] [value]	Trace
U	[range]	Unassembled
W	[address] [drive] [first sector] [number]	Write
XA	[#pages]	Allocate expanded memory
XD	[handle]	de-allocate expanded memory
XM	[Lpage] [Ppage] [handle]	Map expanded memory pages
XS		Display expanded memory status

DEL (or ERASE)

Deletes named files. DEL and ERASE are synonymous.

Syntax:

To delete a file:

    DEL [path] filename [/P]

Filename   Name of file to delete.

/P   Forces confirmation before deleting each file.

To delete all files in a directory with confirmation:

    DEL path or

    DEL path *.*

To delete all files in a directory without confirmation:

>   **DEL path \?*.***

DEL only accepts **one** parameter specifying what is to be deleted. However this parameter can be written using wildcards so that multiple files are deleted. If more than one parameter is detected, the command aborts and an error message is displayed.

DEL will be interpreted with a long file name with spaces as multiple parameters, causing an error. Enclosing the long file name with spaces in inverted commas solves the problem. Let us see an example:

>   **D:\>del   note 2.txt**

Too many parameters - 2.txt

>   **D:\>del   "note 2.txt"**

>   **D:\>_**

DEL does not delete files that have read-only, hidden, and/or system attributes set. To delete such files, one can use **DELTREE** or modify the necessary attributes with **ATTRIB** command.

DELTREE

Deletes Files and Directories, and all the Subdirectories and files in it.

Syntax:

To delete a directory and all the subdirectories and files contained therein:

>   **DELTREE [/Y] directory**

directory   The directory to be deleted.

/Y   Suppresses prompts for confirmation before deletion.

To delete all the files and subdirectories but leave the directory itself:

>   **DELTREE [/Y] directory*.***

To delete a file:

>   **DELTREE [/Y] filename**

The DELTREE command deletes all files contained in a directory or subdirectory, regardless of whether files are marked as hidden, system, or read-only.

The DELTREE command supports wildcards, but they should be used with some caution. If you specify a wildcard that matches both directory names and filenames, both the directories and files will be deleted.

Before specifying wildcards with the DELTREE command, use the DIR /A command to view the files and directories you will delete. It is also safest to specify the full path to avoid any surprises from ambiguous specification. Let us see some examples.

To delete the NOTES directory on drive C, including all files and subdirectories of the NOTES directory:

>   **DELTREE c:\notes**

To delete all the files and subdirectories in the NOTES directory leaving an empty directory NOTES for future use, and avoiding the prompt for confirmation:

>   **DELTREE /Y c:\notes*.***

To delete the read-only file **recover.doc** in the **c:\data** directory without resetting the attributes:

DELTREE /Y c:\data\recover.doc

DOSKEY

DOSKEY is a TSR designed to assist working from the command line by making it easier to edit the command line, by remembering previous commands, and being able to record macros.

Syntax:

To load DOSKEY:

DOSKEY [/Switches]

Switches	what it does
/B:*xxx*	Sets the size of the buffer for macros and commands. The minimum value of *xxx* is 256 and the default is 512 (bytes). If DOSKEY is already running, it must be reloaded (with /R) when changing the buffer size.
/E:On|Off	Enables|Disables the display of commands when a macro plays. **E**(Echo) is **On** by default.
/F:filename	Retrieves **filename** - a text file containing a list of macros in the form **Macroname=Text**
/H	Displays all commands stored in memory. (This list will not be redirected to a file).
/I|O	Specifies whether text is entered in Insert or Overstrike mode by default. In either case the alternative mode can be selected by using <Insert> but the default is reset as soon as <Enter> is used. The default mode is Overstrike.
/K:*xx*	Sets the size of the keyboard type-ahead buffer. The default is 15 (characters). If DOSKEY is already running, it must be reloaded (with /R) when changing the buffer size.
/L	Sets the maximum size of the line edit buffer. The default is 128 (characters).
/M	Displays a list of all DOSKEY macros currently in the buffer. This list can be redirected to a text file using standard Dos redirection (>)
/R	Installs a new instance of DOSKEY. If DOSKEY is already running, the buffer is cleared of both macros and the Command Line history. Note that installing a new instance of DOSKEY does not remove the previous instance. Thus each use of /R takes another 5K of conventional/upper memory.
Macroname	The name of the macro. This is a string of one or more characters possibly modified by the Ctrl and/or Alt keys.
Text	The text string to be assigned to **Macroname**. This will typically be one or more DOS commands along with appropriate parameters and/or switches.

To create a DOSKEY macro:

Necessary DOS Commands

    DOSKEY Macroname=Text

To run a macro:

    Macroname

DOSKEY Commands	What it does
Left/Right cursor	Moves the cursor back/forward one character.
Ctrl + Left/Right cursor	Moves the cursor back/forward one word.
Home/End	Moves the cursor to beginning/end of line.
Up/Down cursor	To scroll up (and back) through the list of stored commands. Each press of the "up" key recalls the previous command and displays it on the command line.
Page Up/Down	Recalls the oldest/most recent command in the buffer
F1	Copies the next character from the Template to the Command Line
F2 + key	Copies text from the Template up to (but not including) **key**.
F3	Copies the Template from the present character position to the Command Line.
F4 + key	Deletes the characters from the present character position up to (but not including) **key**.
F5	Copies the current command to the Template and clears the Command Line.
F6	Places an end-of-file character (^Z) at the current position of the Command Line.
F7	Displays a numbered list of the command history.
Alt-F7	Deletes all commands stored in the buffer.
Chars + F8	Entering one or more characters **Chars** followed by F8 will display the most recent command beginning with **Chars**. Pressing F8 again will display the next most recent command beginning with **Chars**, and so on.
F9 + *Command#*	Displays the designated command on the command line.
Alt-F10	Deletes all macro definitions.

To delete a macro:

    DOSKEY Macroname=

DOSKEY Special Characters

The following special characters can be used in macros to control command operations:

Characters	What is does
$G	Redirects output – equivalent to the redirection symbol >
GG	Appends output to the end of a file - equivalent to the append symbol >>
$L	Redirects input - equivalent to the symbol <
$B	Sends macro output to a command - equivalent to the pipe symbol |
$T	Separates commands when creating macros or typing commands on the DOSKEY command line
$$	Use for the $ sign
$1 to $9	Represents any command-line parameters that can be specified when the macro is run. Comparable with the %1. to %9 characters in batch programs
$*	Represents command-line information that can be specified when macroname is written. $* is similar to the replaceable parameters $n except that everything typed on the command line after macroname is substituted for the $* in the macro.

DIR

Displays the list of Files and Subdirectories in a Directory.

Syntax:

   DIR   [drive:]   [path]   [filename]   [/Switches]

Switch	What Is does
none	By default, DIR displays: • a header comprising the disk's volume label and serial number; • a list of all files and subdirectories in the current directory in the order they are listed in the FAT except those marked 'hidden' and/or 'system'. Along with each file/directory is its size, date/time of last modification, and long file name; • a footer comprising the total number of files listed, their cumulative size, and the free space (in bytes) remaining on the disk.
/A [attributes]	Displays files with and without specified attributes. Multiple attributes can be specified with no spaces between them.**attributes** (Using the "-" as a prefix specifies "not") D Directories R Read-only files H Hidden files A Files modified since last back-up S System files
/O [sortorder]	List files in sorted order. If order of sorting is not specified, directories

	are listed alphabetically followed by files, also listed alphabetically. Any combination of sorting order keys can be specified and files will be sorted in the order of the keys. **sortorder** (Using "-" as a prefix reverses the order)
	N By name (alphabetic)
	S By size (smallest first)
	E By extension (alphabetic)
	D By date & time (earliest first)
	G Group directories first
	A By Last Access Date (earliest first)
/S	Displays Files in the specified Directory and all its Subdirectories
/W	Wide list format. File and Directory names are listed in 5 columns
/B	Bare format. Files and Directories are listed in a single column without header, summary, or any details.
/L	Output is in lowercase.
/P	Pauses with each screen, full of information. Press any key to see the next screen.
/V	Forces to Verbose mode. This displays attributes, date last accessed, and disk space allocated for each file, in addition to the standard information.
/Z	Long file names are not displayed in the file listing.
/4	Displays the date as four digits rather than two.

The DIR command only accepts one path as a parameter. Long file and Directory names that include a space must be enclosed in inverted commas. You can also use wildcards such as * and ? to display a listing of a subset of files and subdirectories.

DIR can be used with the standard period (.) shortcuts to show higher level directories. If more periods are used than are required to show the root directory, the directories and files.

When using redirection to send the output of DIR command to a file or another command, it is often useful to use **/A:-D** to list only files, and **/B** to avoid extraneous information such as files sizes, headers and summary information. Also when the output of a DIR command is redirected via a pipe, a temporary file is created which is automatically deleted once the operation is completed.

By default, this temporary file is located in the directory specified by the "TEMP" environmental variable but, if this is not specified or cannot be found, it will be created in the current directory of the current drive. If the DIR command also refers to the current directory, any such temporary files will be picked up and included in the listing.

DISKCOPY

DISKCOPY is used to duplicate floppy disks. Any data on the destination disk is overwritten.

Syntax:

DISKCOPY drive1: [drive2:] [/1] [/V] [/M]

drive1	Drive containing disk to be copied from and to, if the computer has only one floppy drive.
drive2	Drive containing disk to be copied to if different from **drive1**.
/1	Copies only the first side of the disk.
/V	Verifies that the information is copied correctly.
/M	Force multi-pass copy using memory only.

DISKCOPY is designed to duplicate standard floppy disks by making a byte-by-byte copy of the source disk to the destination disk. DISKCOPY do not work with hard drives, CDs, network drives, or Zip, Jazz, etc. type drives. Also it should be kept in mind Source and destination disks must be of the same type, size, and capacity. If they are not, an error message is displayed:

EDIT

It is a simple full-screen DOSased ASCII text editor.

Syntax

EDIT [/B] [/H] [/R] [/S] [/nnn] [filename(s)]

/B	Forces monochrome mode.
/H	Displays the maximum number of lines possible for your hardware.
/R	Load file(s) in read-only mode.
/S	Forces the use of short filenames.
nnn	Load binary file(s), wrapping lines to **nnn** characters wide.
filename(s)	Specifies initial files(s) to load. Wildcards can also be used.

To see the list of shortcut keys you can see the "Help" menu of editor.

EXIT

In case of DOS of windows environment, EXIT command is used to quit the DOS shell else if talking generally, Quits the MS-DOS command interpreter (COMMAND.COM) and returns to the program that started the command interpreter, if one exists.

Syntax

EXIT

FC

Compares two files or sets of files and displays the differences between them.

Syntax:

FC [/Switches] file1 file2

Switch	What It does
/B	Performs a binary comparison. The two files are compared byte by byte and there is no attempt to resynchronize the files after finding a mismatch. This is the default mode for comparing files when **file1** has an extension of .EXE, .COM, .SYS, .OBJ, .LIB and .BIN or similar to it.

/L	Compares files as ASCII. The two files are compared line by line and FC attempts to resynchronize the files after finding a mismatch. This is the default mode for comparing files when **file1** does not have an extension of .EXE, .COM, .SYS, .OBJ, .LIB and .BIN or similar to it.	
/LBn	Sets the number of lines for the internal line buffer. If the files being compared have more than this number of consecutive differing lines, FC cancels the comparison. Default value of **n** is 100	
/nn	The number of consecutive lines that must match before the files are declared resynchronized. If the number of matching lines in the files is less than this number, the matching lines are displayed as differences. Default value of **nn**: 2.	
/N	Displays the line numbers on an ASCII comparison.	
/A	Abbreviates the output of an ASCII comparison. Only the first and last line for each set of differences is displayed as opposed to the default of every different line.	
/C	Disregards the case of letters.	
/T	Does not expand tabs to spaces. By default, tabs are treated as spaces with 1 tab = 8 spaces.	
/W	Compresses tabs and multiple spaces to a single space for the comparison.	

If **file1** includes a wildcard, all applicable files are compared to **file2**. If **file2** also includes a wildcard, it is compared with the corresponding **file1**. In most cases, binary files are compared to see if they are the same or not. To simply see if two binary files are identical, it is often quickest to compare them as ASCII files using the /LB1 switch to cut the output to a minimum.

Let us see an example of the significant differences in processing times. By trying the following examples you will be able to understand how to use FC in Time saving and batter way:

```
FC  c:\windows\command\xcopy.exe  c:\windows\command\attrib.exe
FC  c:\windows\command\xcopy.exe  c:\windows\command\attrib.exe  /L
FC  c:\windows\command\xcopy.exe  c:\windows\command\attrib.exe  /L  /LB1
```

FDISK

FDISK is a menu driven utility used to configure and/or display information about the partitions on a hard disk. You Should know What you are doing in FDISK environment and you should be sure for doing that otherwise it may delete or change your partitions' information and you may suffer the loss of partitions(s) i.e. data.

Before a hard disk can be recognized by DOS, a Master Boot Record (MBR) must be established. FDISK is the MS-DOS utility used to create an MBR by defining the size and nature of a hard drive's partitions. The MBR defines areas of the disk to be:

- A Primary Partition and/or
- An Extended Partition.

An Extended Partition has to be designated as containing one or more Logical DOS Drives. If you remove partitions, you will destroy everything on them, or, at the least, make it very difficult to recover any data. We'll learn more about Fdisk in the Recovery programming section of this book.

FIND

The FIND command is used to search for a text string in a file or files. After searching the specified files, FIND displays any lines of text that contain the string.

Syntax:

FIND [/V] [/C] [/N] [/I] "string" "filename1" "filename2" "filename ..."

Switch	What It Does
/V	Displays all lines NOT containing the specified string.
/C	Displays only a count of lines containing the string. If used with /V, FIND displays a count of the lines that do not contain the specified string.
/N	Displays line numbers with the lines. If /C and /N are used together, /N is ignored.
/I	Ignores the case of characters in **string**. By default FIND is case sensitive and searches for an exact character match.
string	The text string to be found. **String** must be in inverted commas.
filename	The file(s) to be searched. If **filename** does not contain spaces, it does not need to be enclosed in inverted commas.

If **filename** is not specified, FIND searches the text input from the standard source which is usually the keyboard, a pipe, or a redirected file. Wildcards are not accepted in **filename**. Also as inverted commas are used to delimit **string**, they cannot be used within **string** as part of the search pattern.

To include inverted commas within string, it is necessary to use the "special character" of double inverted commas ("") which FIND interprets as inverted commas in the search string. Let us see some examples:

To display all lines from the file "NOTES.TXT" that contains the string "homework":
   FIND "homework" notes.txt

If the string contains inverted commas, these must be doubled:
   FIND "The result of ""B.E. Final year"" has not been displayed." Result.doc

FORMAT

Formats a disk for use with MS-DOS. Always remember that the data stored in the disk will be erased after the format. Be careful and be sure before using the format command and always remember to see which drive letter you are entering in FORMAT command.

Syntax:

FORMAT drive: [/Switches]

Switch	What It does
/V[:label]	Specifies a volume label. If the /V switch is omitted, or label is not specified, a prompt for a volume label is displayed after formatting is completed. If no volume label is required, the prompt can be avoided by specifying: /V:"" If a label is specified and more than one disk is formatted in a session, all of the disks will be given the same volume label.

/Q	Forces the Quick format of a previously formatted disk. The file allocation table (FAT) and root directory of the disk is deleted but it is not scanned for bad areas.
/S	Copies system files to the formatted disk to make it a boot disk.
/B	Allocates space on the formatted disk for system files.
/F:size	Formats a disk to a capacity other than that for which the drive was designed. Size can be: 360, 720, 1.2, 1.44, and 2.88.
/T:tracks	Specifies the number of tracks per disk side.
/N:sectors	Specifies the number of sectors per track.
/1	Formats a single side of a floppy disk.
/4	Formats a 5.25-inch 360K floppy disk in a high-density drive.
/8	Formats eight sectors per track
/C	Tests clusters that are currently marked "bad." By default, if a disk contains clusters that have been marked as "bad", FORMAT does not retest the clusters; it simply leaves them marked "bad".

By default, and unless the **/Q** switch is used; each sector on the disk is checked during the formatting process to ensure that the sector can properly store data.

If a bad sector is located, it is marked and is not used. When formatting is complete, a message is displayed showing the total disk space, any space marked as defective, the space used and the space available for files. FORMAT cannot be used on a virtual drive created using the SUBST command.

A fast way to reformat a floppy is:

    ren /? | format /q/v:"" > nul

The **ren /?** part feeds, along with a load of redundant material, an "enter", followed by a "n, enter" in response to FORMAT's prompts. The **>nul** prevents the display of the somewhat messy mixed up output of the two commands.

LABEL

The LABEL command is used to create, change, or delete the volume label of a disk. The volume label of a disk is displayed as part of the directory listing along with the volume serial number, if exists.

Syntax:

    LABEL   [drive:]   [label]

Drive: The location of the disk to be named.
Label: The new volume label.
None: Displays current disk label, if they exist. Prompts to enter a new label or delete the existing one

MD (or MKDIR)

Creates a directory. **MD** and **MKDIR** are synonymous do the same tasks.

Syntax:

MD [path] directoryname

MORE

The MORE command reads standard input from a pipe or redirected file and displays one screen of information at a time. This command is commonly used to view long files, directory output, etc.

Syntax:

MORE   [path] filename

MORE < [path] filename

command | MORE [path] [filename]

command   a command whose output is to be displayed.

Filename   file(s) to display one screen at a time

MORE filename and **MORE < filename** are synonymous and equivalent to **TYPE filename | MORE**. In all these cases filename is displayed a screenful at a time. Pressing "Enter" displays the next screen. The display can be terminated at any time by pressing Ctrl-C. MORE automatically wraps text to fit the screen.

Let us consider an example of a big text file named BIGFILE.TXT. Now the following three commands will do the same task:

TYPE bigfile.txt | MORE

MORE bigfile.txt

MORE < bigfile.txt

MOVE

Moves files and directories from one location to another on the same or different drives.

Syntax:

MOVE [/Y | /-Y] [path] filename   destination

/Y   Suppresses prompting to confirm creation of a directory or overwriting of the destination. This is the default when MOVE is used in a batch file.

/-Y .   Forces a prompt to confirm creation of a directory or overwriting of the destination. This is the default when MOVE is used from the command line.

If more than one file is listed to be moved, destination path must be a directory and the files will retain their original names.

RD (or RMDIR)

Removes (deletes) an empty directory. **RD** and **RMDIR** are synonymous and do the same tasks.

Syntax:

RD [path] directoryname

If there is a backslash (\ ) before the first directory name in path, that directory is considered a subdirectory of the root directory on the current drive. If there is no backslash before the first directory name in path, the directory is considered a subdirectory of the current directory.

Also RD will only delete an empty directory. If RD is used on a directory containing files and/or subdirectories, Error message is displayed by the computer.

SCANDISK

Runs the SCANDISK disk-repair program.

Syntax

To check and repair the current drive:

> SCANDISK

> **You should not scan the disk with CHKDSK or SCANDISK or any other disk scanning program if your disk is crashed or there is any logical error in your boot sectors like MBR, DBR, FAT or root directories are corrupted. It may make you data information distorted and can make it difficult to recover. Not only this you may not recover data completely.**

Generally the DOS version of Scandisk does not run while Windows is running. Rather than signaling an error, it automatically transfers control to the Windows version of Scandisk

TYPE

The TYPE command is used to display the contents of an ASCII text file on screen.

Syntax:

> **TYPE filename**

To display text files one screen at a time, pipe the output from a TYPE command to MORE. Let us see some examples:

To display the contents of ROMI.TXT:

> **TYPE romi.txt**

If the file is too long to fit on a single screen:

> **TYPE romi.txt | MORE**

XCOPY

This command is one of the most important commands when you want to make the backup of your important data or even you want to make the image of entire drive to Copy files and directory trees.

XCOPY is similar to the COPY command except that it has many more switches that allow considerable control over exactly what is copied when using wildcards.

Syntax:

> **XCOPY source [destination] [/Switches]**

source   The file(s) and Directories to be copied. Wildcards (* or ?) may be used.

destination   The path and/or name(s) of new files. If **destination** is omitted, the files are copied to the current directory. If **destination** refers to a directory that does not exist, the directory is created. By default, XCOPY will confine its operation to files in the **source** directory.

Switch	What it does
/E	Copies the complete subdirectory structure of **source** and all files therein.
/S	Copies the complete subdirectory structure of **source** and all files therein but does not copy empty subdirectories.
/T	Copies the subdirectory structure of **source** but does not copy any files and does not copy empty subdirectories. To include empty subdirectories, use with the /E switch.
/A	Only copies files with the archive attribute set.
/M	Only copies files with the archive attribute set, turning off the archive attribute of the source files.
/H	Includes files with hidden and system attributes set.
/K	Copies files without resetting the read-only attribute, if set.
/R	Overwrites read-only files.
/U	Only copies files in **source** that already exist in **destination**. Can be used with /D to update files with more recent versions.
/D:date	Only copies files with a 'last modified date' the same as, or later than, **date**. If **date** is not specified, all files are copied except for same-named files in the destination directory that have a more recent 'last modified date' than the one in **source**.
/I	Forces **destination** to be treated as a directory. The file/directory prompt is suppressed.
/Y	Overwrites existing files without prompting.
/-Y	Prompts before overwriting existing files.
/W	Displays a prompt before starting to copy files.
/P	Prompts for confirmation before creating each destination file.
/F	Displays full source and destination file names while copying.
/Q	Does not display file names or any other messages while copying.
/C	Continues copying even if errors occur.
/L	Displays files to be copied but does not actually copy them.
/N	Copy using the generated short names. This is necessary when copying from a VFAT volume to a FAT volume.
/V	Verifies that new files are readable.

By default XCOPY will not copy files which have **system** or **hidden** attributes set and also copies of **read-only** files do not have the read-only attribute set, and all copied files have their **archive** attribute set. By default, XCOPY prompts before overwriting files in destination with files in source of the same name.

XCOPY also prompts for instructions if there is ambiguity whether destination is a directory or file. An ambiguity is seen when destination does not refer to an existing directory or end in a "\ ". For example a destination of **name.ext** could be either a file or a directory. Let us learn it better by the following examples.

To copy all files and subdirectories from the **notes** directory to the disk in drive a:

    xcopy c:\notes a: /s

or

    xcopy c:\notes*.* a: /s

To copy all files and subdirectories from the **notes** directory created or modified since **9 dec 2002** to the disk in drive **a**:

    xcopy c:\notes a: /s /d:9/12/02

Making the "Drive Image"

If you want to make the backup of your entire drive to another or you want to make image of your data of drive "including Operating System and other installed software" to another hard disk, just try this:

    C:\> Xcopy * D: \I\E\C\H

Here **D:** is supposed to be the Active partition of another hard disk. This will copy the whole data of the **source** drive (Including installed Operating System, Software, Document etc.) as image to the **Destination** Drive.

And after this if you boot your computer with the **destination** drive, it will work same as the **source** drive was working and it will show all the data that you were having in the **source** drive.

Specification Shortcuts, Wildcards and Redirection

Shortcuts

A number of DOS commands recognize certain shortcuts when navigating between directories. The best known of these are:

Shortcut	Why to use it
.	to refer to the current directory
..	to refer to the parent directory
\	to refer to the root directory of the current drive.
drive:	to refer to the current directory on *drive*

Let us try to understand it with the help of examples. If the current directory on the c: drive is **c:\windows\java\notes**, then **dir c:** at the a:\> prompt will list the files in **c:\windows\java\notes**

1.   If the current drive and directory is **c:\data\docs\letters**, then:

Command	.	..	...	\
CD or CHDIR	Nothing. Current directory stays as: **c:\windows \java\notes**	Change to parent directory: **c:\windows \java**	Change to parent's parent directory: **c:\windows**	Change to root directory: **c:**
DIR	Displays contents of current directory: **c:\windows \java\notes**	Displays contents of parent directory: **c:\windows \java**	Displays contents of parent's parent directory: **c:\windows**	Displays contents of root directory: **c:**

2. If the current drive and directory is **c:**, then:

Command	.	..	...	\
CD(ChDir)	Nothing - current directory stays as: **c:**	Error message: "Invalid Directory"	Error message: "Invalid Directory"	Nothing. Current directory stays as: **c:**
DIR	Displays contents of current directory: **c:**	Error message: "Invalid Directory" and extension less files of current directory	Displays directories root directory: **c:**	Displays contents of

Wildcards

Many DOS commands like, ATTRIB, COPY, DEL, DELTREE, etc., accept the use of the "wildcards" (* and ?). Generally terms, * refers to multiple characters and ? refers to a single character in a file or directory name.

This is the reason we can not use these characters in the name of any file. These Special characters are / \ : * ? < > " | which should not be tried to insert in a file name. Following table shows the use of wildcards:

Wildcard	What it does
.	All files with all extensions.
data.*	All files with "data" anywhere in its name.
array.	All files with names ending with "array"
note?.cpp	All files named "note" plus one character and with .CPP extensions. This file may be note1.cpp, but not note.cpp.
?t*.*	All files with an "t" as second letter in their names

It should be noted that not all commands handle wildcards in exactly the same way. For example DIR * and DIR *.* are considered synonymous but DEL * would delete only files without an extension.

A space enclosed by inverted commas (" ") is accepted as a valid file specification by EDIT and DEL yet in rather different ways.

EDIT will open a file using the name of the current directory. Thus if the current directory is D:\windows\java\notes, **EDIT** " " will create a file in that directory called "notes".

DEL recognizes " " as *.* and will prompt for confirmation before deleting all files in the directory. As with EDIT, the number of spaces between the inverted commas does not seem significant but if there are no spaces an error message is displayed saying that a required parameter missing.

Unlike EDIT, a path can be included and, if it is, no spaces between inverted commas are required. i.e. to delete all files in the current directory:

    DEL ./"" works, but **DEL** "" gives an error message.

COPY also sees " " as *.* and, like DEL, accepts a path with it. Unlike DEL, there must always be a space between the inverted commas, even when a path is included

Redirection

A number of DOS commands send output to the screen and/or require input from the user. Redirection is a mechanism whereby the output of a command can be fed either to some other device for example, a printer or file, or to another program or command.

There are four redirection functions:

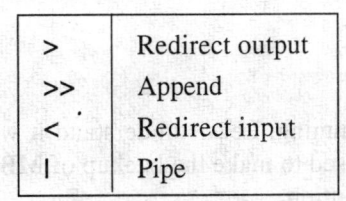

>	Redirect output
>>	Append
<	Redirect input
|	Pipe

>

Redirects a command's output from the "standard output device" (usually the monitor) to another device (e.g. printer) or a file.

Syntax:

To redirect output to a device:

    Command > Device

To redirect output to a file:

    Command > Filename

Acceptable **Device** names are, **CON** (Monitor), **PRN** (LPT1 - assumed to be the printer), **LPT1 - 3** (Parallel Ports - usually connected to a printer), **COM 1 - 4** (Serial Ports) and **NUL** (an electronic void).

If anything other than a recognized device is specified, it is assumed to be the name of a file. If a file alrcady exists with the specified **Filename**, it is overwritten without any Warnings. Let us see some Examples to better understand it.

Probably the most common uses of this redirection function is to send directory listings to the printer or to save them as a file. To print out a sorted directory listing of all files in the Windows directory:

DIR c:\windows /o/a > PRN

To create a file containing the directory listing of the same directory:

DIR c:\windows /o/a > d:\windows.txt

>>

Appends the output from a command to the specified file.

Syntax:

Command >> Filename

If **Filename** does not exist, it is created. If **Filename** does exist, the output from the command is added to it, unlike the > function where the original contents are overwritten. Let us better understand it with example.

To add the directory listing of the files in the c:\windows\system directory to that created before:

DIR c:\windows\system /o/a >> d:\windows.txt

<

Directs input to a command from a source other than the default. The default source usually being the keyboard.

Syntax:

Command < Datasource

It is used generally in batch programming. Let us understand it with the example. The following procedure of **DEBUG** command is used to make the backup of **MBR** where MBR.BIN is the name of backup file created after this execution.

```
debug mbr.bin
A
MOV DX, 6000
MOV ES, DX
XOR BX, BX
MOV DX, 0080
MOV CX, 0001
MOV AX, 0201
INT 13
INT 20
<Enter>(type nothing)
G
R CX
200
W 6000:0000
Q
```

To this with help of batch file we make two batch files, one containing the command instruction to start **DEBUG** command and other to store other instructions which will be fed to the **DEBUG** command as input. This File will be the **datasource** for the first file. Let us see how:

    C:\ **mbr.bat**

Now let us see what this **MBR.BAT** has in it.

MBR.BAT
DEBUG mbr.bin < ttsource.bat

And obviously the second file named **TTSOURCE.BAT** will work as **datasource** for this and will be having following instructions in it:

TTSOURCE.BAT
A
MOV DX, 6000
MOV ES, DX
XOR BX, BX
MOV DX, 0080
MOV CX, 0001
MOV AX, 0201
INT 13
INT 20
<enter> (Type Nothing)
G
R CX
200
W 6000:0000
Q

|

The **pipe** redirects the output of a program or command to a second program or command.

Syntax

    Command1 | Command2

Let us see an example of typing a long text file:

    type file.txt |more

Chapter – 8
Disk-BIOS Functions and Interrupts Handling With C

Introduction

In this chapter we shall discuss the important Disk-BIOS functions and other important functions which give us the freedom to uses and handle interrupts in our program with C, with the easy and short method. These functions are the back – bone of the data recovery and disk troubleshooting programming. These are the functions that make The C language a "High – level Assembly Language".

biosdisk and _bios_disk Functions

These two functions are the most important function for our purpose of data recovery and disk troubleshooting programming. We'll use these functions most of the time.

These two are the BIOS disk drive services and have been defined in **bios.h** where **biosdisk** operates below the level of files on raw sectors. **If these functions are used even in a little bit lack of care, it can destroy the file contents and directories on a hard disk.** Both **biosdisk** and **_bios_disk** functions, use **interrupt 0x13** to issue disk operations directly to the BIOS. The **_bios_disk** function is declared in the program in the following manner:

   unsigned _bios_disk(unsigned cmd, struct diskinfo_t *dinfo);

And the declaration for the bios disk function is as follows:

   int biosdisk(int cmd, int drive, int head, int track,
       int sector, int nsects, void *buffer);

The meaning of these parameters has been described in the following table:

Parameter	Function	What It Is or what it does
cmd	Both	Indicates the operation to perform such as read, write, verify etc.(See the description of cmd, given next)
dinfo	_bios_disk	Points to a diskinfo_t structure that contains the remaining Parameters required by the operation.(see the description of diskinfo_t structure, given next)

Disk-BIOS Functions and Interrupts Handling With C

drive	biosdisk	Specifies which disk drive is to be used(0 for a:, 1for b: and 0x80 for first physical hard disk, 0x81 for second and so on.)
head track sector	biosdisk	These specify the starting sector location from which the Operation is to be started.
nsects	biosdisk	Number of sectors to read, write, verify etc.
buffer	biosdisk	Memory address where data is to be read or written

In both of these functions, the data is read into and written from buffer at 512 bytes per sector that is the logical size of sector of a hard disk and the value returned by both functions is the value of the AX register set by the INT 0x13H BIOS call.

If the function is successful, High byte = 0, that means the successful completion and low byte contains the number of sectors read, written or verified and so on.

But if there is any error and function is not successful, the value of High byte will be one of the following error codes which are described in the following table:

Value	Description
0x00	Successful completion (Not an Error!!)
0x01	Bad command
0x02	Address mark not found
0x03	Attempt to write to write-protected disk
0x04	Sector not found
0x05	Reset failed (hard disk)
0x06	Disk changed since last operation
0x07	Drive parameter activity failed
0x08	Direct memory access (DMA) overrun
0x09	Attempt to perform DMA across 64K boundary(data Boundary error or >80H sectors)
0x0A	Bad sector detected
0x0B	Bad track detected
0x0C	Unsupported track
0x0D	Invalid number of sectors on format (PS/2 hard disk)
0x0E	Control data address mark detected (hard disk)
0x0F	DMA arbitration level out of range (hard disk)
0x10	Bad CRC/ECC on disk read
0x11	CRC/ECC corrected data error (Not an error actually)
0x20	Controller has failed
0x31	No media in drive (IBM/MS INT 13 extensions)
0x32	Incorrect drive type stored in CMOS (Compaq)
0x40	Seek operation failed

0x80	Attachment failed to respond
0xAA	Drive not ready (hard disk only)
0xB0	Volume not locked in drive (INT 13 extensions)
0xB1	Volume locked in drive (INT 13 extensions)
0xB2	Volume not removable (INT 13 extensions)
0xB3	Volume in use (INT 13 extensions)
0xB4	Lock count exceeded (INT 13 extensions)
0xB5	Valid eject request failed (INT 13 extensions)
0xBB	Undefined error occurred (hard disk only)
0xCC	Write fault occurred
0xE0	Status register error
0xFF	Sense operation failed

The table given next represents the operation commands to be performed by **cmd** parameter. First of all we shall see the common operations of both the functions.

biosdisk	_bios_disk	What it does
0	_DISK_RESET	Resets disk system, forcing the drive controller to do a hard reset. Ignore all other parameters
1	_DISK_STATUS	Returns the status of the last disk operation. Ignores all other parameters
2	_DISK_READ	Reads one or more disk sectors into memory
3	_DISK_WRITE	Writes one or more disk sectors from memory
4	_DISK_VERIFY	Verifies one or more sectors
5	_DISK_FORMAT	Formats a track

Though you are free to use either cmd = 0, 1, 2, 3, 4,5 or cmd = _DISK_RESET, _DISK_STATUS, _DISK_READ, _DISK_WRITE, _DISK_VARIFY, _DISK_FORMAT and both the options have the same effect, but it is recommended that you should have a habit to use words option such as cmd = _DISK_FORMAT instead of cmd = 5 because it may help you to avoid errors that may take place if you have typed a wrong command number for cmd.

In the declaration of biosdisk or _bios_disk function if we give the cmd = _DISK_RESET the function reset the disk system by ignoring the all other parameters and _DISK_STATUS returns the status of the last disk operation, ignoring the all other parameters.

For cmd =_DISK_READ, _DISK_WRITE, or _DISK_VERIFY (2, 3 or 4), **biosdisk** and **_bios_disk** functions also use other parameters shown below:

Disk-BIOS Functions and Interrupts Handling With C

Parameter	What It Does
head track sector	These three specify the location of starting sector for the specified operation. (minimum possible values may be head = 0, track = 0 and sector =1)
nsectors	This specifies the number of sectors to read or write
buffer	It points to the buffer where data is to be read and written

If the value of cmd is = 5 (_DISK_FORMAT), biosdisk and _bios_disk use the following parameters as according to the description in the table. It is always recommended that you should take care while you are using _DISK_FORMAT and you should know what you are going to with. Lack of knowledge or even a small mistake may make you to face a big loss of data.

Parameter	What It Does
head track	These specify the location of the track to format
buffer	It points to a table of sector headers to be written on the named track

There are some additional values of cmd which are used **only by biosdisk** functions. These values of cmd are allowed only for the XT, AT, PS/2, and compatibles. Values have been described in the table given next:

cmd	What it does
6	Formats a track and sets bad sector flags
7	Formats the drive beginning at a specific track
8	Returns the current drive parameters in first 4 bytes of buffer
9	Initializes drive-pair characteristics
10	Does a long read (512 plus 4 extra bytes per sector)
11	Does a long write (512 plus 4 extra bytes per sector)
12	Does a disk seek
13	Alternates disk reset
14	Reads sector buffer
15	Writes sector buffer
16	Tests whether the named drive is ready
17	Recalibrates the drive
18	Controller RAM diagnostic
19	Drive diagnostic
20	Controller internal diagnostic

diskinfo_t Structure

diskinfo_t structure is used by _bios_disk function. The description of the structure is as follows:

```
struct diskinfo_t {
    unsigned drive, head, track, sector, nsectors;
    void far *buffer;
            };
```

Where **drive** specifies the disk drive which is to be used. Always remember that for the hard disks, the physical drive is specified, not the disk partition. If you want to operate partitions, the application program must also interpret the partition table information of that disk itself.

The value of **head**, **track** and **sector** specify the location of the starting sector for the operation. nsectors specifies the number of sectors to be read or written and buffer points to the buffer where data is read and written. Depending on the value of cmd, the other parameters in the diskinfo_t structure might or might not be needed.

The value for the specification of disk drive to be used in the **biosdisk** and **_bios_disk** functions has been given in the following table:

drive Value	Disk drive to use
0	First floppy-disk drive
1	Second floppy-disk drive
2	Third floppy-disk drive
....	(and so on)
0x80	First hard-disk drive
0x81	Second hard-disk drive
0x82	Third hard-disk drive
....	(and so on)

Enough theory! Now let us see some practical things and some example of these functions. The following example reads the sectors of the both sides of four tracks of the floppy and stores the contents to the file, specified by the user. It does not matter, if you have deleted the files from your disk because the program is directly reading the surface of the disk.

To see the deleted data, it is a better ideal that you take a fully formatted floppy disk and copy some text files such as your **.c** programs coding or other text files (so that you can understand the contents of the files) occupying approximately 73KB(data stored in four tracks, two sides and 18 sectors in each track. Each sector is of 512bytes). The program has been developed to demonstrate the example. However you can alter and develop it to ready to recover data.

```
/* Program to read 4·tracks (0, 1, 2 and 3) of a floppy and write the
contents to specified file */
#include <bios.h>
#include <stdio.h>
#include<conio.h>
void main(void)
{
     int head,track;
     int result,i,sector;
```

```c
        char filename[80];
        char *buffer;
        struct diskinfo_t dinfo;
        static char dbuf[512];
        FILE *tt;
        clrscr();
        /// Check if drive is Ready or Not \\\
        if(!(biosdisk(4,0,0,0,0,1,buffer) & 0x02))
        {
            printf(" Drive A: Not Ready:\n Insert disk into Drive A: and
            press any key\n");
            getch();
        }

        /* Get the file name to store the data of the Sectors of the disk
        */
        printf("\nEnter the Destination File name with full Path to store
        the data \n\n >");
        gets(filename);
        if((tt= fopen(filename, "wb"))==NULL)
        {
            printf("Could not open the File!!!");
            getch();
        }
        for(track=0;track<4;track++)
        {
            for(head=0;  head<=1;head++)
            {
                for(sector=1;sector<=18;sector++)
                {
                    dinfo.drive =   0;      /* drive number for A: */
                    dinfo.head  =   head;   /* disk head number */
                    dinfo.track =   track;  /* track number */
                    dinfo.sector =  sector; /* sector number */
                    dinfo.nsectors =  1; /* sector count */
                    dinfo.buffer = dbuf; /* data buffer */
                    /// Show the Status \\\
                    gotoxy(10,10); printf("Reading Data from: Head=%d
                        Track=%d Sector=%d",
                        head, track, sector);
                    fprintf(tt,"\n Data read from: Head=%d   Track=%d
                        Sector=%d\n",
                        head, track, sector);
                    /// Read the Specified Sectors       \\\
                    result = _bios_disk(_DISK_READ, &dinfo);
                    /// Store the contents in the Specified file \\\
```

```
                    if ((result & 0xff00) == 0)
                    {
                        for(i=0;i<512;i++)
                            fprintf(tt,"%c",dbuf[i] & 0xff);
                    }

                    /* Print Error message on screen and in file for
                    Error while Reading a sector */
                    else
                    {
                        printf("\n Can not read at Head= %d   Track=
                        %d Sector= %d\n",head,track,sector);
                        fprintf(tt,"\n Can not read at Head= %d   Track=
                        %d Sector =%d\n",head,track,sector);
                    }
                }
            }
        }
        fclose(tt);
}
```

The example shows the use of the functions, **biosdisk** and **_bios_disk.** The **biosdisk** function check if the disk is ready or not and address mark is found. The **_bios_disk** function reads the sectors of the both sides up to four tracks. The sequence of reading (or writing) at the surface of the disk should be as follows:

Step no.	Reading Sequence

1.	Read Track **0**
	 {
	     Read Head **0**
	     {
	         Read Sectors **from 1 to 18**
	     }
	 }

2.	Read Track **0**
	 {
	     Read Head **1**
	     {
	         Read Sectors **from 1 to 18**
	     }
	 }

3.	Read Track **1**
	{
	    Read Head **0**
	    {
	        Read Sectors **from 1 to 18**
	    }
	}	

4.	Read Track **1**
	{
	    Read Head **1**
	    {
	        Read Sectors **from 1 to 18**
	    }
	}	

5.	Read Track **2**
	{
	    Read Head **0**
	    {
	        Read Sectors **from 1 to 18**
	    }
	}	

	.......And So On.............	

absread and abswrite Functions

These Functions have been defined in **Dos.h**. The **absread** function reads absolute disk sectors and the **abswrite** function writes absolute disk sectors. The function **absread** uses DOS **interrupt 0x25** to read specific disk sectors and the function **abswrite** uses DOS **interrupt 0x26** to write specific disk sectors.

Absolute read or write operations proceeds in sequential manner by incrementing sector(s) step by step and are completely free of the head and track numbers etc. it is the job of BIOS of the computer to translate the absolute sectors to the respective track, Head and Sector numbers.

Absolute read and write operations are recommended in such programs where we are going to perform read/write operation on the entire disk and we want to avoid extra coding and looping in our program to increase the speed of the program to fastest.

Both of the functions **absread** and **abswrite**, ignore the logical structure of a disk and pay no attention to files, FATs, or directories. These functions directly perform absolute read and absolute write operation on the surface of the disk, This is the reason that if used improperly, **abswrite** can overwrite files, directories, and FATs.

The declaration of the **absread** function is as follows:

   int absread(int drive, int nsects, long lsect, void *buffer);

and the **abswrite** function is declared as follows:

   int abswrite(int drive, int nsects, long lsect, void *buffer);

Where the meaning of parameters is as follows:

Param.	What It Is/Does
drive	Drive number to read (or write): 0 = A, 1 = B, etc.
nsects	Number of sectors to read (or write)
lsect	Beginning logical sector number
buffer	Memory address where the data is to be read (or written)

On success, both of the functions return 0. When there is any error, both return -1 and set error no. to the value of the AX register returned by the system call.

> *The number of sectors for read or write operation is limited to 64K or the size of the buffer, whichever is smaller. However we will learn the use of Huge memory in next chapters to exceed out of the memory limit 64K, to develop a very fast program.*

Interrupt Handling with C

C is sometimes called a high level assembly language because it can call the different interrupts using some of its some defined functions. Some important functions are as follows:

- **int86:** Invokes MS-DOS interrupts.
- **int86x:** Invokes MS-DOS interrupt with segment register values.
- **intdos:** invokes MS-DOS service using registers other than DX and AL
- **intdosx:** invokes MS-DOS service with segment register values.
- **segread:** Reads Segment registers

We shall discuss these functions in detail. First of all we discuss some predefined structure and unions that are frequently or necessarily used with these functions.

SREGS Structure

This structure has been defined in **dos.h** and it is a structure of the segment registers passed to and filled in by the functions, **int86x, intdosx** and **segread**. The declaration of the structure is as follows:

```
struct SREGS {
      unsigned int    es;
      unsigned int    cs;
      unsigned int    ss;
      unsigned int    ds;
};
```

REGS union

REGS is the union of two structures. The union REGS has been defined **dos.h** and it is used to pass information to and from the functions, **int86, int86x, intdos** and **intdosx**. The declaration of the union is as follows:

```
union REGS {
      struct    WORDREGS    x;
      struct    BYTEREGS    h;
};
```

BYTEREGS and WORDREGS Structures

The BYTEREGES and WORDREGS structures have been defined in **dos.h** and these are used for storing byte and word registers. The **WORGREGS** structure allows the user to access the registers of CPU as **16-bit quantities** where **BYTEREGES** structure gives the access to the individual **8-bit registers.**

The BITEREGS structure is declared as follows:

```
struct BYTEREGS   {
      unsigned char    al, ah, bl, bh;
      unsigned char    cl, ch, dl, dh;
};
```

And the WORDREGS structure is declared as follows:

```
struct WORDREGS   {
      unsigned int    ax, bx, cx, dx;
      unsigned int    si, di, cflag, flags;
};
```

int86 and int86x functions

These functions are the general 8086 software interrupt interfaces defined in dos.h. Registers are set to the desired values and these functions are called to invoke the MS-DOS interrupts. The declaration of the **int86** function is as follows:

> **int int86(int intno, union REGS *inregs,**
> **union REGS *outregs);**

int86x is the variation of **int86** function. It is declared as follows:

> **int int86x(int intno, union REGS *inregs,**
> **union REGS *outregs, struct SREGS *segregs);**

Both the functions **int86** and **int86x** execute an 8086 software interrupt specified by the argument **intno** Or we can say interrupt to generate is specified by **intno.**

With **int86x** function access is possible **only to ES and DS** and **not to CS and SS** so you can invoke an 8086 software interrupt that takes a value of DS different from the default data segment and/or takes an argument in ES.

These functions copy register values from **inregs** into the registers before execution of the software interrupt. The function int86x also copies the segregs->ds and segregs->es values into the corresponding registers before executing the software interrupt. This feature allows programs that use far pointers or a large data memory model to specify which segment is to be used for the software interrupt.

The functions copy the current register values to outregs, status of the carry flag to the x.cflag field in outregs and the value of the 8086 flags register to the x.flags field in outregs, after the software interrupt returns. The function int86x also restores DS and sets the segregs->es and segregs->ds fields to the values of the corresponding segment registers.

In both functions **inregs** and **outregs** can point to the same structure and both functions return the value of AX after completion of the software interrupt. If the carry flag is set, it usually indicates that an error has occurred.

The REGS union elements used in C, equivalent to Assembly language have been in the table given next:

16-bit		8-bit	
C language	Assembly language	C language	Assembly language
inregs.x.ax	AX	inregs.h.al	AL
		inregs.h.ah	AH
inregs.x.bx	BX	inregs.h.bl	BL
		inregs.h.bh	BH
inregs.x.cx	CX	inregs.h.cl	CL
		inregs.h.ch	CH
inregs.x.dx	DX	inregs.h.dl	DL
		inregs.h.dh	DH
inregs.x.si	SI		
inregs.x.di	DI		
inregs.x.cflag	CF		

Let us see the examples of **int86** and **int86x** functions. The Following Program Scans the every sector of the floppy disk and prints the status of every sector on the screen.

```
/* Program To Scan Every Sector Of The Floppy Disk and Print the Status
*/
#include<dos.h>
#include<conio.h>
void main()
{
        int  head,track,sector,i;
        char  *buf;
        union REGS inregs, outregs;
        struct SREGS sregs;
        clrscr();
        /// Initializing Disk By Resetting Disk System \\\
        gotoxy(10,2); printf("Initializing The Disk...");
```

```c
    for(i=0;i<3;i++)
    {
        inregs.h.ah=0x00;      // Function Number
        inregs.h.dl=0x00;      // Floppy Disk
        int86(0x13,&inregs,&outregs);
    }
    gotoxy(10,2); printf("The Status of the Disk is as....\n");

    /*Scan the Floppy Disk from 0 to 79 Tracks (Total Tracks 80) */
    for(track=0;track<=79;track++)
    for(head=0;head<=1;head++)
    for(sector=1;sector<=18;sector++)
    {
        inregs.h.ah = 0x04;    /// function Number
        inregs.h.al = 1;       /// Number of sectors
        inregs.h.dl = 0x00;    /// Floppy Disk
        inregs.h.ch = track;
        inregs.h.dh = head;
        inregs.h.cl = sector;
        inregs.x.bx = FP_OFF(buf);
        sregs.es    = FP_SEG(buf);
        int86x(0x13,&inregs,&outregs,&sregs);

        //// Print The Status of the Scanned Sector \\\\
        switch(outregs.h.ah)
        {
            case 0x00:
                cprintf("STATUS:    No Error!!");
                break;
            case 0x01:
                cprintf("STATUS:    Bad command")
                break;
            case 0x02:
                cprintf("STATUS:    Address mark not found");
                break;
            case 0x03:
                cprintf("STATUS:    Attempt to write to write-protected
                disk");
                break;
            case 0x04:
                cprintf("STATUS:    Sector not found");
                break;
            case 0x05:
                cprintf("STATUS:    Reset failed (hard disk)");
                break;
            case 0x06:
```

```c
                cprintf("STATUS:    Disk changed since last
        operation");
                break;
        case 0x07:
                cprintf("STATUS:    Drive parameter activity failed");
                break;
        case 0x08:
                cprintf("STATUS:    Direct memory access (DMA)
        overrun");
                break;
        case 0x09:
                cprintf("STATUS:    Attempt to perform DMA across
        64K boundary");
                break;
        case 0x0A:
                cprintf("STATUS:    Bad sector detected");
                break;
        case 0x0B:
                cprintf("STATUS:    Bad track detected");
                break;
        case 0x0C:
                cprintf("STATUS:    Media type not found");
                break;
        case 0x0D:
                cprintf("STATUS:    Invalid number of sectors on
        format (hard disk)");
                break;
        case 0x0E:
                cprintf("STATUS:    Control data address mark detected
        (hard disk)");
                break;
        case 0x0F:
                cprintf("STATUS:    DMA arbitration level out of range
        (hard disk)");
                break;
        case 0x10:
                cprintf("STATUS:    Bad CRC/ECC on disk read");
                break;
        case 0x11:
                cprintf("STATUS:    CRC/ECC corrected data error");
                break;
        case 0x20:
                cprintf("STATUS:    Controller has failed");
                break;
        case 0x31:
                cprintf("STATUS:    No media in drive (IBM/MS INT
```

```
                13H extensions)");
                break;
        case 0x32:
                cprintf("STATUS:   Incorrect drive type stored in
                CMOS (Compaq)");
                break;
        case 0x40:
                cprintf("STATUS:   Seek operation failed");
                break;
        case 0x80:
                cprintf("STATUS:   Attachment failed to respond (Disk
                Timed-out)");
                break;
        case 0xAA:
                cprintf("STATUS:   Drive not ready (hard disk only)");
                break;
        case 0xB0:
                cprintf("STATUS:   Volume not locked in drive (INT
                13H extensions)");
                break;
        case 0xB1:
                cprintf("STATUS:   Volume locked in drive (INT 13H
                extensions)");
                break;
        case 0xB2:
                cprintf("STATUS:   Volume not removable (INT 13H
                extensions)");
                break;
        case 0xB3:
                cprintf("STATUS:   Volume in use (INT 13H
                extensions)");
                break;
        case 0xB4:
                cprintf("STATUS:   Lock count exceeded (INT 13H
                extensions)");
                break;
        case 0xB5:
                cprintf("STATUS:   Valid eject request failed (INT
                13H extensions)");
                break;
        case 0xBB:
                cprintf("STATUS:   Undefined error occurred (hard
                disk only)");
                break;
        case 0xCC:
                cprintf("STATUS:   Write fault occurred");
```

```
                    break;
            case 0xE0:
                    cprintf("STATUS:     Status register error");
                    break;
            case 0xFF:
                    cprintf("STATUS:     Sense operation failed");
                    break;
            default: cprintf("STATUS:     UNKNOWN Status CODE");
        }
        printf("\nCurrent position= Track:%d Head:%d Sector:%d \n",
        track,head,sector);
    }
    gotoxy(10,24);printf("Scanning Completed!! Press Any Key TO Exit..");
    getch();
}
```

The program shows the example of use of functions **int86** and **int86x** functions. In this Program the **int86** function is initializing the disk by resetting the disk system, using function 00H of INT 13H. The **int86x** function is verifying every sector of the floppy (1.44Mb, 3½ floppy disk) from both sides, up to 0 to 79 tracks (total 80 tracks) using the function 04H of INT 13H.

segread Function

This function has been defined in dos.h. This function reads the segment registers. The declaration of the function is as follows:

    void segread(struct SREGS *segp);

where segread puts the current values of the segment registers into the structure *segp. Nothing is returned by the function and the call is intended for use with intdosx and int86x. let us see an example:

```
#include <stdio.h>
#include <dos.h>
void main()
{
    struct SREGS segs;
    segread(&segs);
    printf("Current segment register settings\n\n");
    printf("CS: %X    DS: %X\n", segs.cs, segs.ds);
    printf("ES: %X    SS: %X\n", segs.es, segs.ss);
    getch();
}
```

And the output of the program will be something like this:

Current segment register settings
CS: EED   DS: 10BA
ES: 10BA SS: 10BA

intdos and intdosx Functions

These functions have been defined in dos.h. These are the general DOS interrupt interfaces. The function **intdos** invokes MS-DOS service registers then DX and AL where the function **intdosx** invokes MS-DOS service with segment register values.

The Declaration of the **intdos** function is as follows:

    int intdos(union REGS *inregs, union REGS *outregs);

and the declaration of **intdosx** function is as:

    int intdosx(union REGS *inregs, union REGS *outregs, struct SREGS *segregs);

The functions **intdos** and **intdosx** execute DOS interrupt **0x21** to invoke a specified DOS function. The value of **inregs->h.ah** specifies the DOS function to be invoked. The function **intdosx** also copies the **segregs ->ds** and **segregs ->es** values into the corresponding registers before invoking the DOS function and then restores DS.

This feature of the functions allows the programs that use far pointers or a large data memory model specify which segment is to be used for the function execution. With **intdosx** function you can invoke a DOS function that takes a value of DS different from the default data segment and/or takes an argument in ES.

Both the functions return the value of AX after completion of the DOS function call and if the carry flag is set (**outregs -> x.cflag != 0**), it indicates that an error occurred.

After the interrupt 0x21 returns the functions copy the current register values to **outregs,** status of the carry flag to the **x.cflag** field in **outregs** and value of the 8086 flags register to the **x.flags** field in **outregs.** Both **inregs** and **outregs** can point to the same structure. Let us see the examples of these functions.

The example of the use of **intdos** function has been given below. This program obtains the selected information about the floppy (1.44Mb, 3½ inch floppy disk) disk drive. This program provides the allocation information of a floppy disk.

```
/* The get drive allocation information for disk usage */
#include <dos.h>      /* for intdos() and union REGS */
#include <stdio.h>    /* for printf() */
union REGS inregs, outregs;
void main()
{
        inregs.h.ah = 0x36;    /* get disk free space function number */
        inregs.h.dl = 0x01;    /* drive A: */
        intdos(&inregs, &outregs);
        printf("%d sectors/cluster,\n%d clusters,\n%d bytes/sector, \n%d
        total clusters",
        outregs.x.ax,outregs.x.bx,
        outregs.x.cx, outregs.x.dx);
        getch();
}
```

And output of the program will be like this:

> 1 sectors/cluster,
> 1933 clusters,
> 512 bytes/sector,
> 2843 total clusters

Now let us see an example of the function **intdosx**. The following example shows the use of **intdosx** function. The program outputs a string to the standard output.

```c
/* The program to output 'string' to the standard output.*/
#include <dos.h>
union REGS inregs, outregs;
struct SREGS segregs;
char far *string = "this string is not in the default data segment$";
void main()
{
        inregs.h.ah = 0x09;         /* function number */
        inregs.x.dx = FP_OFF(string);/*DS:DX is far address of 'string */
        segregs.ds = FP_SEG(string);
        intdosx(&inregs, &outregs, &segregs);
        getch();
}
```

And the output of the program will be as follows:

> this string is not in the default data segment

Here we are printing the given string with the function **intdosx,** by function 09H of INT 21H. It should always be kept in mind that the given string should always end with the character "$".

How to know the Physical Hard Drive Number

The physical hard drive number is a very important thing and should be written exact. The illegal drive specification may cause a major data loss. We must be confident about the drive number during the data recovery or disk troubleshooting programming. How to know the drive number of any disk with different arrangements of disks can be estimated by the examples given next.

According to a **most generalized** Myth, The physical drive numbers are provided according to the attachment status of the disk however in some or special cases it may be dependent for your Operating system's Boot procedure or boot settings.

The most generalized idea for the Physical drive number provided by BIOS has been given here but even then you must confirm with the help of any disk editing tool or with the programs given in the next chapters, about the configuration of the disk. After being sure you should take any decision about running such programs which may corrupt or harm the data, if used illegally or in lack of knowledge.

Generally, If the two disks are attached to the system, one is primary master and another is secondary master, the first preference will be given to the primary master (and then to primary slave if available)

Disk-BIOS Functions and Interrupts Handling With C

and then to secondary master (and then to secondary slave if available and so on) and the physical number will be given according to their preferences.

Let us assume that your system supports the maximum four hard disks at a time. The all four hard disks may be connected as given Next:

Primary Master
Primary Slave
Secondary Master
Secondary Slave

Now let us consider some cases for drive number of physical drives. Here I assume that you have connected the disks with proper jumper settings as mentioned by the disk manufacturer, and in proper Master–Slave settings:

- **If all four Hard Disks are connected to the system:** if all four disks are connected to the system the physical drive numbers will be as follows:

Primary/Secondary (Master/Slave)	Status	Physical Drive Number and Description
Primary Master	Disk is Present	Physical Drive Number will be **80H.** In this case the Hard Disk is called the **First Hard Disk**.
Primary Slave	Disk is Present	Physical Drive Number will be **81H.** In this case the Hard Disk is called the **Second Hard Disk**.
Secondary Master	Disk is Present	Physical Drive Number will be **82H.** In this case the Hard Disk is called the **Third Hard Disk**.
Secondary Slave	Disk is Present	Physical Drive Number will be **83H.** In this case the Hard Disk is called the **Fourth Hard Disk**.

- **If three Hard Disks are connected to the system:** if three Hard Disks are connected to the system the physical drive numbers will be as according to their attachment preferences. The following examples represent some of the arrangements:

Primary/Secondary (Master/Slave)	Status	Physical Drive Number and Description
Primary Master	Disk is Present	Physical Drive Number will be **80H.** In this case the Hard Disk is called the **First Hard Disk**.
Primary Slave	Disk is Present	Physical Drive Number will be **81H.** In this case the Hard Disk is called the **Second Hard Disk**.

Primary/Secondary (Master/Slave)	Status	Physical Drive Number and Description
Secondary Master	Disk is Present	Physical Drive Number will be **82H.** In this case the Hard Disk is called the **Third Hard Disk.**
Secondary Slave	**Disk Not Present**	————————

Primary/Secondary (Master/Slave)	Status	Physical Drive Number and Description
Primary Master	**Disk Not Present**	————————
Primary Slave	Disk is Present	Physical Drive Number will be **80H.** In this case the Hard Disk is called the **First Hard Disk.**
Secondary Master	Disk is Present	Physical Drive Number will be **81H.** In this case the Hard Disk is called the **Second Hard Disk.**
Secondary Slave	Disk is Present	Physical Drive Number will be **82H.** In this case the Hard Disk is called the **Third Hard Disk.**

Primary/Secondary (Master/Slave)	Status	Physical Drive Number and Description
Primary Master	Disk is Present	Physical Drive Number will be **80H.** In this case the Hard Disk is called the **First Hard Disk.**
Primary Slave	**Disk Not Present**	————————
Secondary Master	Disk is Present	Physical Drive Number will be **81H.** In this case the Hard Disk is called the **Second Hard Disk.**
Secondary Slave	Disk is Present	Physical Drive Number will be **82H.** In this case the Hard Disk is called the **Third Hard Disk.**

Primary/Secondary (Master/Slave)	Status	Physical Drive Number and Description
Primary Master	Disk is Present	Physical Drive Number will be **80H.** In this case the Hard Disk is called the **First Hard Disk.**
Primary Slave	Disk is Present	Physical Drive Number will be **81H.** In this case the Hard Disk is called the **Second Hard Disk.**

| Secondary Master | Disk Not Present | — |
| Secondary Slave | Disk is Present | Physical Drive Number will be **82H**. In this case the Hard Disk is called the **Third Hard Disk**. |

- **If two Hard Disks are connected to the system:** Similarly, if two Hard Disks are connected to the system the physical drive numbers will be as according to their attachment preferences. Following example illustrates it:

Primary/Secondary (Master/Slave)	Status	Physical Drive Number and Description
Primary Master	Disk is Present	Physical Drive Number will be **80H**. In this case the Hard Disk is called the **First Hard Disk**.
Primary Slave	**Disk Not Present**	—
Secondary Master	Disk Not Present	—
Secondary Slave	Disk is Present	Physical Drive Number will be **81H**. In this case the Hard Disk is called the **Second Hard Disk**.

- **If Single Hard Disk is connected to the system:** Need not to think, if there is only one disk available, the physical drive number will be **80H**.

Interrupt 13H (INT 13H), ROM BIOS Disk Driver Functions

The description of **INT 13H** functions has been given here. These functions should be learnt with care, as the misuse of these functions or use in lack of care or lack of knowledge, may cause big loss of data or many other problems. However if used in a appropriate and proper way these functions help to minimize the coding of your program and to make your programming simple and easy as well as.

INT 13H (0x13)

Function 00H (0x00) → Reset disk system

Call with   AH = 00H
               DL = drive
                           00H-7FH floppy disk
                           80H-FFH fixed disk

Returns: If function is successful

Carry flag	=	clear
AH	=	00H

If function is unsuccessful

Carry flag	=	set
AH	=	status

Comments:

Reset the disk controller, recalibrates its attached drives. The read/write arm is moved to cylinder 0 and prepares for the disk I/O.

This function should be called after a failed floppy disk Read, write, Verify, or Format request before retrying the operation. If the function is called with a fixed disk drive (i.e. selecting DL>=80H), the floppy disk controller and then the fixed disk controller are reset.

INT 13H (0x13)

Function 01H (0x01) → Get disk system status

Call with:	AH	=	01H
	DL	=	drive
			00H-7FH floppy disk
			80H-FFH fixed disk
Returns:	AH	=	00H
	AL	=	status of previous disk operation (See the table given before for error and status codes description).

Comments:

Returns the status of the most recent disk operation

INT 13H (0x13)

Function 02H (0x02) → Read sector

Call with:	AH	=	02H
	AL	=	number of sectors
	CH	=	cylinder
	CL	=	sector
	DH	=	head
	DL	=	drive
			00H-7FH floppy disk
			80H-FFH fixed disk
	ES:BX	=	segment: offset of buffer
Returns:	If function successful		

Carry flag	=	clear
AH	=	00H
AL	=	number of sectors transferred
If function unsuccessful		
Carry flag	=	set
AH	=	status

Comments:

This function reads one or more sectors from disk into memory. On fixed disks, the upper 2 bits of the 10-bit cylinder number are placed in the upper 2 bits of register CL.

INT 13H (0x13)

Function 03H (0x03) → Write sector

Call with:	AH	=	03H
	AL	=	number of sectors
	CH	=	cylinder
	CL	=	sector
	DH	=	head
	DL	=	drive
			00H-7FH floppy disk
			80H-FFH fixed disk
	ES: BX	=	segment: offset of buffer
Returns:	If function successful		
	Carry flag	=	clear
	AH	=	00H
	AL	=	number of sector transferred
	If function unsuccessful		
	Carry flag	=	set
	AH	=	status

Comments:

This function writes one or more sectors from memory to disk. On fixed disks, the upper 2 bits of the 10-bit cylinder number are placed in the upper 2 bits of register CL.

INT 13H (0x13)

Function 04H (0x04) → Verify sector

Call with:	AH	=	04H

AL	=	number of sectors
CH	=	cylinder
CL	=	sector
DH	=	drive
		00H-7FH floppy disk
		80H-FFH fixed drive
ES: BX	=	segment: offset of buffer

Returns: If function is successful

Carry flag	=	clear
AH	=	00H
AL	=	number of sectors verified

If function is unsuccessful

Carry flag	=	set
AH	=	status

Comments:

This function verifies the address fields of one or more sectors. No data is transferred to or from memory by this operation. On fixed disks, the upper 2 bits of the 10-bit cylinder number re placed in the upper 2 bits of register CL.

This function can be used to test whether a readable media is in a floppy disk drive. The requesting program should reset the floppy disk system (INT 13H Function 00H) and retry the operation three times before assuming that a readable floppy disk is not present. It is recommended in most of the floppy initialization operations.

INT 13H (0x13)

Function 05H (0x05) → Format track

Call with:

AH	=	05H
AL	=	interleave (PC/XT fixed disks)
CH	=	cylinder
DH	=	head
DL	=	drive
		00H-7FH floppy disk
		80H-FFH fixed disk
ES: BX	=	segment: offset of address field list
		(Except PC/XT fixed disk)

Returns: If function successful

Carry flag	=	clear
AH	=	00H

If function unsuccessful

Carry flag	=	set
AH	=	status (see the status table given earlier)

Comments:

Initialize disk sector and tracks address fields on the specified track. On floppy disks, the address field list consists of a series of 4-byte entries, one entry per sector. The Format has been given in the following table. On fixed disks, the upper 2-bits of the 10-bits cylinder number are placed in the upper 2 bits of register CL.

Byte	Contents		
0	Cylinder		
1	Head		
2	Sector		
3	Sector-size code		
		Value	Description
		00H	128 Byte per sector
		01H	256 Byte per sector
		02H	512 Byte per sector
		03H	1024 Byte per sector

INT 13H (0x13)

Function 06H (0x06) → Format bad track

Call with:	AH	=	06H
	AL	=	interleave
	CH	=	cylinder
	DH	=	head
	DL	=	drive
			80H-FFH fixed disk
Returns:	If function successful		
	Carry flag	=	clear
	AH	=	00H
	If function unsuccessful		
	Carry flag	=	set
	AH	=	status

Comments:

This function is defined for PC/XT fixed disk drives only. It initializes a track, writing disk address fields and data sectors and setting bad sector flags.

INT 13H (0x13)

Function 07H (0x07) → Format drive

Call with: AH = 07H
           AL = interleave
           CH = cylinder
           DL = drive
                80H-FFH fixed disk

Returns: If function successful
           Carry flag = clear
           AH = 00H
           If function unsuccessful
           Carry flag = set
           AH = status (see the status table given earlier)

Comments:

This function is defined for PC/XT fixed disk drives only. It formats the entire drive, writing disk address fields and data sectors, starting at the specified cylinder.

INT 13H (0x13)

Function 08H (0x08) → Get drive parameters

Call with: AH = 08H
           DL = drive
                00H-7FH floppy disk
                80H-FFH fixed disk

Returns: If function successful
           Carry flag = clear
           BL = drive type (PC/AT and PS/2 floppy disk)

Value	Description
01H	360KB, 40 track, 5.25"
02H	1.2MB, 80 track, 5.25"
03H	720KB, 80 track, 3.5"
04H	1.44MB, 80 track, 3.5"

           CH = low 8 bits of maximum cylinder number
           CL = bits 6-7 high order 2 bits of maximum cylinder number bits 0-5 maximum sector number

Disk-BIOS Functions and Interrupts Handling With C

DH	=	maximum head number
DL	=	number of drives
ES: DI	=	segment: offset of disk drive parameter table

If function unsuccessful

Carry flag	=	set
AH	=	status

Comments:

This function returns various parameters for the specified drive. The value returned in register DL reflects the true number of physical drives attached to the adapter for the requested drive.

INT 13H (0x13)

Function 09H (0x09) → Initialize fixed disk characteristics

Call with:

AH	=	09H
DL	=	drive

80H-FFH fixed disk

On the PC/XT Vector for INT 41H must point to disk parameter block or, on the PC/AT and PS/2

Vector for INT 41H must point to disk parameter block for drive 0

Vector for INT 46H must point to disk parameter block for drive 1

Returns: If function successful

Carry flag	=	clear
AH	=	00H

If function unsuccessful

Carry flag	=	set
AH	=	status

Comments:

This function initializes the fixed disk controller for subsequent I/O operations, using the values found in the ROM BIOS disk parameter block(s). The function is supported on fixed disk only. The parameter block format for PC and PC/XT fixed disks is as follows:

Byte	Contents
00H-01H	Maximum number of cylinders
02H	Maximum number of heads
03H-04H	Starting reduced write current cylinder
05H-06H	Starting write pre compensation cylinder
07H	Maximum ECC burst length

08H	Drive option		
	Bit(s)	Significance (if set)	
	0 – 2	drive option	
	3 – 5	reserved (0)	
	6	disable ECC entries	
	7	disable disk-access retries	
09H	Standard time-out value		
0AH	Time-out value for format drive		
0BH	Time-out value for check drive		
0CH-0FH	Reserved		

The parameter block format for PC/AT and PS/2 fixed disks is as given next:

Byte(s)	Contents		
00H_01H	maximum number of cylinders		
02H	maximum number of heads		
03H-04H	Reserved		
05H-06H	starting write pre compensation cylinder		
07H	maximum ECC burst length		
08H	Drive options		
	Bit(s)	Significance (if set)	
	0 – 2	not used	
	3	more than 8 heads	
	4	not used	
	5	manufacturer's defect map present at maximum cylinder +1	
	6 – 8	nonzero (10, 01,or 11) if retries disabled	
09H-0BH	Reserved		
0CH-0DH	landing zone cylinder		
0EH	sector per track		
0FH	Reserved		

INT 13H (0x13)

Function 0A H (0x0A or 10) → Read sector long

Call with:	AH	=	0AH
	AL	=	number of sectors
	CH	=	cylinder
	CL	=	sector
	DH	=	head
	DL	=	drive
			80H-FFH fixed disk
	ES: BX	=	segment: offset of buffer
Returns:	If function successful		
	Carry flag	=	clear
	AH	=	00H
	AL	=	number of sectors transferred
	If function unsuccessful		
	Carry flag	=	set
	AH	=	status

Comments:

This function reads a sector or sectors from disk into memory along with a 4 byte Error Correcting Code (ECC) code for each sector. Unlike the normal Read sector function (INT 13H (0x13) Function 02H), ECC errors are not automatically corrected. Multi sector transfers are terminated after any sector with a read error.

This function is supported on fixed disks only. The upper 2 bits of the 10-bit cylinder number are placed in the upper 2 bits of register CL.

INT 13H (0x13)

Function 0BH (0x0B or 11) → Write sector long

Call with:	AH	=	0BH
	AL	=	number of sectors
	CH	=	cylinder
	CL	=	sector
	DH	=	head
	DL	=	drive
			80H-FFH fixed disk
	ES: BX	=	segment: offset of buffer
Returns:	If function successful		

Carry flag	=	clear
AH	=	00H
AL	=	number of sectors transferred
If function unsuccessful		
Carry flag	=	set
AH	=	status

Comments:

This function writes a sector(s) from memory to disk. Each sector's worth of data must be followed by its 4-byte ECC code. The upper 2 bits of the 10-bit cylinder number are placed in the upper 2 bits of register CL. This function is supported on fixed disks only.

INT 13H (0x13)

Function 0CH (0x0C or 12) → Seek

Call with:	AH	=	0CH
	CH	=	lower 8 bits of cylinder
	CL	=	upper 2 bits of cylinder in bits 6-7
	DH	=	head
	DL	=	drive
			80H-FFH fixed disk
Returns:	If function successful		
	Carry flag	=	clear
	AH	=	00H
	If function unsuccessful		
	Carry flag	=	set
	AH	=	status

Comments:

This function positions the disk read/write heads to the specified cylinder without transferring any data. The upper 2 bits of the cylinder number are placed in the upper 2 bits of register CL. This function is supported on fixed disks only.

INT 13H (0x13)

Function 0DH (0x0D or 13) → Reset fixed disk system

Call with:	AH	=	0DH
	DL	=	drive
			80H-FFH fixed disk
Returns:	If function successful		

	Carry flag	=	clear
	AH	=	00H
If function unsuccessful			
	Carry flag	=	set
	AH	=	status (see INT 13H Function 01H)

Comments:

This function resets the fixed disk controller, recalibrates attached drives, moves the read/write arm to cylinder 0, and prepares for subsequent disk I/O.

INT 13H (0x13)

Function 0EH (0x0E or 14) → Read sector buffer

Call with: AH = 0EH
ES: BX = segment: offset of buffer
Returns: If function successful
Carry flag = clear
If function unsuccessful
Carry flag = set
AH = status

Comments:

This function transfers the contents of the internal sector buffer of the fixed disk adapter to the system memory. No data is read from the physical disk drive.

INT 13H (0x13)

Function 0FH (0x0F or 15) → Write sector buffer

Call with: AH = 0FH
ES: BX = segment: offset of buffer
Returns: If function successful
Carry flag = clear
If function unsuccessful
Carry flag = set
AH = status

Comments:

This function transfers data from system memory to internal sector buffer of the fixed adapter. No data is written to the physical disk drive. This function should be called to initialize the contents of the sector buffer before formatting the drive with INT 13H Function 05H.

INT 13H (0x13)

Function 10H (0x10 or 16) → Get drive status

Call with: AH   =   10H
             DL   =   drive
                           80H-FFH fixed disk
Returns: If function successful
             Carry flag   =   clear
             AH   =   00H
             If function unsuccessful
             Carry flag   =   set
             AH   =   status

Comments:

This function tests whether the specified fixed disk drive is operational and returns the drive's status. This function is supported on fixed disks only.

INT 13H (0x13)

Function 11H (0x11 or 17) → Recalibrate drive

Call with: AH   =   11H
             DL   =   drive
                           80H-FFH fixed disk
Returns: If function successful
             Carry flag   =   clear
             AH   =   00H
             If function unsuccessful
             Carry flag   =   set
             AH   =   status

Comments:

This function causes the fixed disk adapter to recalibrate itself for the specified drive, positioning the read/write arm to cylinder 0, and returns the drive's status. This function is supported on fixed disks only.

INT 13H (0x13)

Function 12H (0x12 or 18) → Controller RAM diagnostic

Call with: AH   =   12H

Returns: If function successful
              Carry flag   =   clear
              If function unsuccessful
              Carry flag   =   set
              AH   =   status

Comments:

This function causes the fixed disk adapter to carry out a built-in diagnostic test on its internal sector buffer, indicating whether the test was passed by the returned status.

INT 13H (0x13)

Function 13H (0x13 or 19) → Controller drive diagnostic

Call with: AH   =   13H
Returns: If function successful
              Carry flag   =   clear
              If function unsuccessful
              Carry flag   =   set
              AH   =   status

Comments:

This function causes the fixed adapter to run internal diagnostic tests of the attached drive, indicating whether the test was passed by the returned status.

INT 13H (0x13)

Function 14H (0x14 or 20) → Controller internal diagnostic

Call with: AH   =   14H
Returns: If function successful
              Carry flag   =   clear
              AH   =   00H
              If function unsuccessful
              Carry flag   =   set
              AH   =   status

Comments:

This function causes the fixed disk adapter to carry out a built-in diagnostic self-test, indicating whether the test was passed by the returned status.

INT 13H (0x13)

Function 15H (0x15 or 21) → Get disk type

Call with: AH = 15H
DL = drive
    00H-7FH floppy disk
    80H-FFH fixed disk

Returns: If function successful
Carry flag = clear
AH = drive type code

00H	if no drive present
01H	if floppy disk drive without change-line support
02H	if floppy disk drive with change-line support
03H	if fixed disk

And, if fixed disk (AH =03H)
CX: DX = number of 512-byte sectors
If function unsuccessful
Carry flag = set
AH = status

Comments:

This function returns a code indicating the type of floppy or fixed disk referenced by the specified drive code.

INT 13H (0x13)

Function 16H (0x16 or 22) → Get disk change status

Call with: AH = 16H
DL = drive
    00H-7FH floppy disk

Returns: If change line inactive and disk has not been changed
Carry flag = clear
AH = 00H
If change line active and disk may have been changed
Carry flag = set
AH = 06H

Disk-BIOS Functions and Interrupts Handling With C

Comments:

This function returns the status of the change line, indicating whether the disk in the drive may have been replaced since the last disk access. If this function returns with the carry flag set, the disk has not necessarily been changed and the change line can be activated by simply unlocking and locking the disk drive door without removing the floppy disk.

INT 13H (0x13)

Function 17H (0x17 or 23) → Set disk type

Call with: AH   =   17H
              AL   =   floppy disk type code

Value	Description
00H	Not used
01H	320/360 KB floppy disk in 360 KB drive
02H	320/360 KB floppy disk in 1.2 MB drive
03H	1.2 MB floppy disk in 1.2 MB drive
04H	720 KB floppy disk in 720 KB drive

              SL   =   drive
                          00H-7FH floppy disk

Returns: If function successful
            Carry flag   =   clear
            AH   =   00H
            If function unsuccessful
            Carry flag   =   set
            AH   =   status

Comments:

This function selects a floppy disk type for the specified drive.

INT 13H (0x13)

Function 18H (0x18 or 24) → Set media type for format

Call with: AH   =   18H
              CH   =   number of cylinders
              CL   =   sector per track
              DL   =   drive
                          00H-7FH floppy disk

Returns: If function successful

Carry flag	=	clear
AH	=	00H
ES: DI	=	segment: offset of disk parameter table for media type

If function unsuccessful

Carry flag	=	set
AH	=	status

Comments:

This function selects media characteristics for the specified drive therefore A floppy disk must be present in the drive.

INT 13H (0x13)

Function 19H (0x19 or 25) → Park heads

Call with:

AH	=	19H
DL	=	drive
		80H-FFH fixed disk

Returns: If function successful

Carry flag	=	clear
AH	=	00H

If function unsuccessful

Carry flag	=	set
AH	=	status

Comments:

This function moves the read/write arm to a track that is not used for data storage, so that data will not be damaged when the drive is turned off.

INT 13H (0x13)

Function 1AH (0x1A or 26) → Format ESDI drive

Call with:

AH	=	1AH
AL	=	Relative Block Address (RBA) defect table count
		0, if no RBA table
		>0, if RBA table used
CL	=	format modifier bits

Bit(s)	Significance (if set)
0	Ignore primary defect map
1	Ignore secondary defect map
2	Update secondary defect map
3	Perform extended surface analysis
4	Generate periodic interrupt
5-7	Reserved (must be 0)

            DL   =   drive
                          80H-FFH fixed disk
            ES: BX =   segment: offset of RBA table

Returns: If function successful
            Carry flag =   clear
            AH   =   00H
            If function unsuccessful
            Carry flag =   set
            AH   =   status (see INT 13H Function 01H)

Comments:

This function initialize disk sector and track address fields on a drive attached to the ESDI Fixed Disk Drive Adapter. The operation of this function is called a **low level format** and prepares the disk for physical read/write operations at the sector level. The drive must be subsequently partitioned with the FDISK command and then given a high level format with the FORMAT command to install a file system.

Chapter – 9

Handling Large Hard Disks

In the previous chapter, we discussed the BIOS-Disk functions and the use of interrupts to access the physical media of the hard disks. We used INT 13H functions there to access the hard disks.

The INT 13H interface supports many different commands such as reading, writing, formatting and verifying etc. that can be given to the BIOS, which then passes them on to the hard disk. As it has been used by DOS for a long time, INT13H has been the standard for many years.

The INT 13H allocates 24 bits for the specification of the geometry of the drive and requires the invoking program to know the specific parameters of the hard disk, and provide exact head, cylinder and sector addressing to the routines to allow disk access.

The BIOS uses the geometry for the hard disk as it is set up in the BIOS setup program. The 24 bits, allocated by the INT 13H interface for the specification of the drive geometry are broken up as follows:

- 10 bits for the cylinder number. Thus the maximum limit of total cylinders may be up to 1,024 cylinders.
- 8 bits for the head number. Thus the maximum limit of total heads is up to 256.
- 6 bits for the sector number. Thus a maximum total of sectors may be up to 63 sectors.

Thus the maximum sectors supported by this approach may be up to, 1024 * 256 * 63 = 16515072.

This means that the INT13H interface can support disks containing up to approximately 16.5 million sectors, which at 512 bytes per sector leads a maximum of 8.46 GB. That is exactly I want to explain. Thus by using all these functions or INT 13H, we can access the disks up to 8.46 GB only.

That is why, in recent years that the limitations of this old interface have caused it to be abandoned in favor of a new way of addressing hard disks, as described next in this chapter.

First of all, let me tell you a Story!

Eleven years ago, when I was in seventh standard, in my school, I heard about the hard disk with the capacity of 42 MB, perhaps it was WDA-L42 of IBM. It was really difficult for me and my friends to imagine such a big capacity of hard disk, that time.

The INT 13H methodology was developed about twenty years ago from today. You can now understand that an 8 GB hard disk was much bigger to fit even in dreams in that age. But today, if we talk about an 8 GB hard disk to any personal computer users, he may not like to use it saying it small in storage capacity.

This is the reason that INT 13H interface has finally come to the end of its usefulness in modern

Handling Large Hard Disks

systems. INT 13H used 24 bits to allocate the disk geometry and unfortunately it was not possible to expand the existing INT 13H BIOS interface because if it was done, a lot of older hardware and software would stop working, and you can understand that the today's computer market can never bear such a big change with millions of older software and hardware products to stop working.

Keeping this condition in mind, INT 13H has been replaced with a newer interface called INT 13H extensions. However INT 13H still may be used by DOS and some other older operating systems and for other compatibility purposes.

The new INT 13H interface uses 64 bits instead of 24 bits for addressing and allows a maximum hard drive size of 9.4 * 1021 bytes which is in fact 9.4 trillion gigabytes or 9400000000000 Gigabytes. I hope now we are relaxed for some time until this limit is broken.

Some Important functions of the Extension for Interrupt 13H has been described next. You can use these function in programming in the same way as you were using the functions of INT 13H. This is also a reason that these functions are called the extensions of INT 13H.

INT 13H Extensions:

INT 13H (0x13)

Function 1BH (0x1B or 27) → Get Manufacturing Header (ESDI Fixed Disk)

Call with:	AH	=	1BH
	AL	=	number of sector(s) to read
	DL	=	drive
	ES: BX	=	buffer for manufacturing header (defect list)
Returns:	If function successful		
	Carry flag	=	clear
	AH	=	00H
	If function unsuccessful		
	Carry flag	=	set
	AH	=	status

Comments:

This function is used to get the manufacturing header of the fixed disk. The first sector read contains the manufacturing header with the number of defect entries and the beginning of the defect map; the remaining sectors contain the remainder of the defect map. Manufacturing header format (Defect Map Record format) can be found in IBM 70MB, 115MB Fixed Disk Drives Technical Reference.

INT 13H (0x13)

Function 1BH (0x1B or 27) → Get Pointer to SCSI Disk Information Block (Future Domain SCSI Controller)

Call with:	AH	=	1BH

	DL	=	hard drive ID
Returns:	If function successful		
	Carry flag	=	clear
	AH	=	01H
	If function unsuccessful		
	Carry flag	=	set
	AH	=	status
	ES:BX	=	SCSI disk information block

Comments:

This function is used to get the pointer to SCSI Disk Information Block. This also sets a non-resettable flag which prevents some controller messages from being displayed.

INT 13H (0x13)

Function 1CH (0x1C or 28) → Get Pointer to Free Controller Ram (Future Domain SCSI Controller)

Call with:	AH	=	1CH
	DL	=	hard drive ID for any valid SCSI hard disk
Returns:	If function successful		
	Carry flag	=	clear
	AH	=	01H
	If function unsuccessful		
	Carry flag	=	set
	AH	=	status
	ES:BX	=	first byte of free RAM on controller

Comments:

This function is used to get the free controller Ram. ES:BX points to the first byte of free RAM on the controller, available for other uses. ES contains the segment at which the controller resides. The two memory-mapped I/O ports of the controller are at offsets 1C00H and 1E00H.

INT 13H (0x13)

Function 1C08H (0x1C08) → Get Command Completion Status (ESDI Fixed Disk)

Call with:	AX	=	1C08H
	DL	=	drive
	ES:BX	=	buffer for Command Complete Status Block
Return:	If function successful		
	Carry flag	=	clear

	AH	=	01H
	If function unsuccessful		
	Carry flag	=	set
	AH	=	status

Comments:

This Function is used to get the Command Completion Status. If the function is successful the carry flag is clear and if unsuccessful carry flag is set.

INT 13H (0x13)

Function 1C09H (0x1C09) → Get Device Status (ESDI Fixed Disk)

Call with:	AX	=	1C09H
	DL	=	drive
	ES:BX	=	buffer for Device Status Block
Return:	If function successful		
	Carry flag	=	clear
	AH	=	01H
	If function unsuccessful		
	Carry flag	=	set
	AH	=	status

Comments:

This Function is used to get the Device Status. If the function is successful the carry flag is clear and if unsuccessful carry flag is set.

INT 13H (0x13)

Function 1C0AH (0x1C0A) → Get Device Configuration (ESDI Fixed Disk)

Call with:	AX	=	1C0AH
	DL	=	drive
	ES:BX	=	buffer for Drive Configuration Status Block
Return:	If function successful		
	Carry flag	=	clear
	AH	=	01H
	If function unsuccessful		
	Carry flag	=	set
	AH	=	status

Comments:

This Function is used to get the Device Configuration for the disk. If the function is successful, carry flag is clear and AH register is 01H else Carry flag is set and AH register Returns the Status. The following table shows the Format of ESDI Drive Configuration Status Block:

Offset	Size	Description
00H	Byte	09H
01H	Byte	number of words in block (06H)
02H	Byte	flags
03H	Byte	number of spare sectors per cylinder
04H	Double Word	total number of usable sectors
08H	Word	total number of cylinders
0AH	Byte	tracks per cylinder
0BH	Byte	sectors per track

INT 13H (0x13)

Function 1C0BH (0x1C0B) → Get Adapter Configuration (ESDI Fixed Disk)

Call with: AX   =   1C0BH
                   ES:BX   =   buffer for Controller Configuration Status Block

Return: If function successful
               Carry flag   =   clear
               AH   =   01H
               If function unsuccessful
               Carry flag   =   set
               AH   =   status

Comments:

This Function is used to get the Adapter Configuration. If the function is successful the carry flag is clear and AH is 01H, if unsuccessful carry flag is set and AH returns the status.

INT 13H (0x13)

Function 1C0CH (0x1C0C) → Get POS Information (ESDI Fixed Disk)

Call with: AX   =   1C0CH
                   ES:BX   =   buffer for POS Information Status Block

Return: If function successful
               Carry flag   =   clear
               AH   =   01H
               If function unsuccessful
               Carry flag   =   set

Handling Large Hard Disks

AH	=	status

Comments:

This Function is used to get the POS Information. If the function is successful the carry flag is clear and AH is 01H, if unsuccessful carry flag is set and AH returns the status.

INT 13H (0x13)

Function 1C0EH (0x1C0E) → Translate RBA to ABA (ESDI Fixed Disk)

Call with:	AX	=	1C0EH
	CH	=	low 8 bits of cylinder number
	CL	=	sector number (high two bits of cylinder number in bits 6 and 7)
	DH	=	head number
	DL	=	drive number
	ES:BX	=	ABA (Absolute Block Address) number
Return:	If function successful		
	Carry flag	=	clear
	AH	=	01H
	If function unsuccessful		
	Carry flag	=	set
	AH	=	status

Comments:

This Function translates the RBA (Relative Block Address) to ABA (Absolute Block Address). If the function is successful carry flag is clear and AH register is 01H, else Carry Flag is set and AH returns the status.

INT 13H (0x13)

Function 20H (0x20 or 32) → Get Current Media Format (Compaq ATAPI Removable Media Device)

Call with:	AH	=	20H
	DL	=	drive number
Return:	If Function Successful,		
	Carry Flag	=	clear
	AL	=	media type
	AH	=	00H
	If Function Unsuccessful,		
	CF	=	set
	AH	=	error code

Comments:

This Function is used to get the current media format. Values for Compaq/ATAPI diskette media type have been given in the following table:

Value	Media
03H	720K (1M unformatted)
04H	1.44M (2M unformatted)
06H	2.88M (4M unformatted)
0CH	360K
0DH	1.2M
0EH	Toshiba 3mode
0FH	NEC 3mode (1024 bytes per sectors)
10H	ATAPI Removable Media Device

INT 13H (0x13)

Function 21H (0x21 or 33) → Read Multiple Disk Sectors (PS and PS/2, Hard Disks)

Call with:	AH	=	21H
	AL	=	number of sectors to Read
	CH	=	low byte of 12-bit cylinder number
	CL	=	starting sector (bits 0 to 5) and bits 8 and 9 of cylinder (bits 6 and 7)
	DH	=	head number (bits 0 to 5) and bits 10 and 11 of cylinder (bits 6 and 7)
	DL	=	drive number
	ES:BX	=	Data buffer to be read
Return:	If Function Successful,		
	Carry flag	=	clear
	ES:BX	=	Filled Data Buffer
	If Function Unsuccessful,		
	Carry flag	=	set
	AH	=	status

Comments:

The Function is used to read the multiple Disk sectors Using Multiple Block Mode, which generates an interrupt only after the end of transferring a group of sectors rather than after each sector.

Handling Large Hard Disks

INT 13H (0x13)

Function 22H (0x22 or 34) → Write Multiple Disk Sectors (PS and PS/2, Hard Disks)

Call with:	AH	=	22H
	AL	=	number of sectors to be written
	CH	=	low byte of 12-bit cylinder number
	CL	=	starting sector (bits 0 to 5) and bits 8 and 9 of cylinder (bits 6 and 7)
	DH	=	head number (bits 0 to 5) and bits 10 and 11 of cylinder (bits 6 and 7)
	DL	=	drive number
	ES:BX	=	buffer containing data to be written
Return:	If function Successful,		
	Carry Flag	=	clear
	AH	=	01H
	If function Unsuccessful,		
	Carry Flag	=	Set
	AH	=	Status

Comments:

The Function is used to write the multiple Disk sectors using Multiple Block Mode, which generates an interrupt only after the end of transferring a group of sectors rather than after each sector.

INT 13H (0x13)

Function 22H (0x22 or 34) → Enable/Disable Cache (QuickCache II v4.20)

Call with:	AH	=	22H
	AL	=	new state (00H, if disabled and 01H, if enabled)
Return:	If Function Successful,		
	AX	=	0000H
	If Function Unsuccessful,		
	AX	=	status

Comments:

This Function Enables and/or disables caching of all drives. If the function is successful the AX register is 0000H else returns the status.

INT 13H (0x13)

Function 23H (0x23 or 35) → Set Controller Features Register (PS and PS/2, Hard Disk)

Call with:	AH	=	23H
	AL	=	feature number
	DL	=	drive number
Return:	If Function Successful,		
	Carry Flag	=	Clear
	If Function Unsuccessful,		
	Carry Flag	=	Set
	AH	=	Status

Comments:

This Function is used to set the controller feature register. If the function is successful the carry flag is clear and if unsuccessful carry flag is set and AH register returns the status.

INT 13H (0x13)

Function 24H (0x24 or 36) → Set Multiple – Transfer Mode (Hard Disk, PS and PS/2)

Call with:	AH	=	24H
	AL	=	number of sectors per block
	DL	=	drive number
Return:	If Function Successful,		
	Carry Flag	=	Clear
	If Function Unsuccessful,		
	Carry Flag	=	Set
	AH	=	Status

Comments:

This Function is used to set Multiple – Transfer Mode. If you want to disable the Multiple – Transfer Mode, set the number of sectors to 0. The maximum value for the block size (Such as 2,4,6,8 and 16 etc.) depends on the fixed disk drive type.

The value is stored in byte 15H of the fixed disk drive parameter table that is created by POST (Power On Self-Test). The byte at address 0040H:0074H is set to status of operation. The Values for PS/1 hard disk feature number have been listed in the following table:

Handling Large Hard Disks

Value	Description
01H	Select 8-bit data transfers instead of 16-bit
02H	Enable write cache
22H	Write Same, user-specified area
33H	Disable retries
44H	Set number of ECC bytes for read long/write long
54H	Set cache segments
55H	Disable look ahead
66H	Disable reverting to power-on defaults
77H	Disable error correction
81H	Select 16-bit data transfers (default)
82H	Disable write cache
88H	Enable error correction (default)
99H	Enable retries (default)
AAH	Enable look ahead
BBH	Set ECC length for read long/write long to four bytes
CCH	Enable reverting to power-on defaults
DDH	Write Same, entire disk

INT 13H (0x13)

Function 24H (0x24 or 36) → Set Sectors (QuickCache II v4.20)

Call with: AX = 24H
            BX = New number of sector buffers in cache
Return: If Function Successful,
            AX = 0000H
            If Function Unsuccessful,
            AX = Status

Comments:

This Function is used to set the Sectors. If the function is successful AX register is 0000H else AX returns the Status.

INT 13H (0x13)

Function 25H (0x25 or 37) → Identify Drive (Hard Disk, PS and PS/2)

Call with: AH = 25H
            DL = Drive number
            ES:BX = Buffer of 512 bytes for reply packet
Return: If Function Successful,

Carry Flag = Clear
Buffer filled with drive information block
If Function Unsuccessful,
Carry Flag = Set
AH = Status

Comments:

This Function is used to identify the Drive. The byte at address 0040h:0074h is set to the status of the operation. IBM officially classifies this function as optional. The Bit fields for general drive configuration have been given in the following table:

Bit(s)	Description
0	Reserved (0)
1	Hard sectored
2	Soft sectored
3	Not MFM encoded
4	Head switch time greater than 15msec
5	Spindle motor control option implemented
6	Fixed drive
7	Removable cartridge drive
8	Disk transfer rate is less than or equal to 5Mbs
9	Disk transfer rate is greater than 5Mbs but less than or equal to 10Mbs
10	Disk transfer rate is greater than 10Mbs
11	Rotational speed tolerance is greater than 0.5%
12	Data strobe offset option available
13	Track offset option available
14	Format speed tolerance gap required
15	Reserved for non-magnetic drives (0)

The description of Format of Drive information block as given in the ATA (AT Attachment) Specification has been given in the next table:

Offset	Size	Description
00H	WORD	General drive configuration
02H	WORD	Number of cylinders
04H	WORD	Reserved
06H	WORD	Number of heads
08H	WORD	Number of unformatted bytes per track
0AH	WORD	Number of unformatted bytes per sector

Handling Large Hard Disks

0CH	WORD	Number of sectors per track
0EH	6 BYTES	Vendor unique
14H	20 BYTES	Serial number in ASCII, (0000H=not specified)
28H	WORD	Buffer type
2AH	WORD	Buffer size in 512 byte increments (0000H=not specified)
2CH	WORD	Number of ECC bytes passed on Read/Write Long commands 0000H = not specified
2EH	8 BYTES	Firmware revision in ASCII, 0000H=not specified
36H	40 BYTES	Model number in ASCII, 0000H=not specified
5EH	WORD	Bits 15-8 Vendor Unique, bits 7-0, (if 00H = Read/Write Multiple commands not Implemented, else xxH = Maximum number of sectors that can be transferred per interrupt on Read and Write Multiple Commands)
60H	WORD	0000H = Cannot perform Doubleword I/O, 0001H = Can perform Doubleword I/O.
62H	WORD	Bit 15-9 (0=reserved), bit 8 (1=DMA Supported), Bit 7-0 Vendor Unique.
64H	WORD	Reserved
66H	WORD	Bits 15-8 PIO data transfer cycle timing mode, Bits 7-0 Vendor Unique
68H	WORD	Bits 15-8 DMA data transfer cycle timing mode, Bits 7-0 Vendor Unique
6AH	WORD	Bits 15-1 reserved, bit 0 (1=the fields reported in translation mode are valid, 0=the fields reported in translation mode may be valid)
6CH	WORD	Number of current cylinders
6EH	WORD	Number of current heads
70H	WORD	Number of current sectors per track
72H	DWORD	Current capacity in sectors
76H	WORD	Reserved
78H	136 BYTES	Not defined
100H	64 BYTES	Vendor unique
140H	96 BYTES	Reserved

INT 13H (0x13)

Function 25H (0x25 or 37) → Set Flush Interval (QuickCache II v4.20)

Call with: AH   =   25H
                 BX   =   Interval of Flush

Return: If Function Successful,
    AH   =   0000H
    If Function Unsuccessful,
    AH   =   status

Comments:

This Function is used to set the Flush Interval. If the function is successful the AH is 0000H else AH returns the status.

INT 13H (0x13)

Function 26H (0x26 or 38) → QuickCache II v4.20 Uninstall

Call with: AH   =   26H
Return: If Function Successful,
    AX   =   0000H
    If Function Unsuccessful,
    AX   =   status

Comments:

AX returns status from 0001H to 00FFH for interrupt vector which was hooked by another TSR

INT 13H (0x13)

Function 27H (0x27 or 39) → Installation Check (QuickCache II v4.20)

Call with: AH   =   27H
    BX   =   0000H
Return: BH   =   Major Version
    BL   =   Binary Minor Version
    If installed,
    AX   =   0000H
    BX   =   Non-zero

Comments:

If installed, AX Register is 0000H and BX returns Non-zero value.

INT 13H (0x13)

Function 28H (0x28 or 40) → Set Automatic Dismount (QuickCache II v4.20)

Call with: AH   =   28H
    AL   =   New State
Return: If Function Successful,
    AX   =   0000H

Handling Large Hard Disks

       If Function Unsuccessful,
       AX   =   Status

Comments:

Call function with AL = 00H to Disable and with AL = 01H to Enable.

INT 13H (0x13)

Function 29H (0x29 or 41) → No Operation (QuickCache II v4.20)

Call with: AH   =   29H
Return: AX   =   0000H

INT 13H (0x13)

Function 2AH (0x2A or 42) → Set Buffer Size (QuickCache II v4.20)

Call with: AH   =   2AH
                AL   =   Buffer Size
Return: If Function Successful,
                AX   =   0000H
                If Function Unsuccessful,
                AX   =   Status

Comments:

This Function is used to set the buffer size. If the function is successful the AX is 0000H, if unsuccessful AX returns the status.

INT 13H (0x13)

Function 2BH (0x2B or 43) → Drive Access Sounds (QuickCache II v4.20)

Call with: AH   =   2BH
                AL   =   new state (00h disabled, 01h enabled)
Return: If Function Successful,
                AX   =   0000H
                If Function Unsuccessful,
                AX   =   Status

Comments:

If the function is successful the AX is 0000H, if unsuccessful AX returns the status. Call function with AL = 00H to Disable and AL = 01H to Enable Drive Access Sounds.

INT 13H (0x13)

Function 2CH (0x2C or 44) → Set Buffered Write (QuickCache II v4.20)

Call with: AH   =   2CH

	AL	=	new state

Return: If Function Successful,
AX = 0000H
If Function Unsuccessful,
AX = Status

Comments:

This function enables or disables delayed writes for all drives. Use AH=38H to change a single drive. Use AL = 00H to Disable and 01H to Enable.

INT 13H (0x13)

Function 2DH (0x2D or 45) → Set Buffered Read (QuickCache II v4.20)

Call with: AH = 2Dh
AL = new state (00h disabled, 01h enabled)
Return: If Function Successful,
AX = 0000H
If Function Unsuccessful,
AX = Status

Comments:

This function enables or disables read-ahead for all drives. Use AL = 00H to Disable and AL = 01H to Enable. Use AH=37H to change a single drive.

INT 13H (0x13)

Function 2EH (0x2E or 46) → Set Flush Count (QuickCache II v4.20)

Call with: AH = 2EH
BX = Flush count
Return: If Function Successful,
AX = 0000H
If Function Unsuccessful,
AX = Status

Comments:

This Function is used to set the Flush Count. If the function is successful the AX is 0000H, if unsuccessful AX returns the status.

INT 13H (0x13)

Function 2FH (0x2F or 47) → Force Immediate Incremental Flush (QuickCache II v4.20)

Call with: AH = 2FH

Return: If Function Successful,
AX = 0000H
If Function Unsuccessful,
AX = Status

Comments:
If the function is successful the AX is 0000H, if unsuccessful AX returns the status.

INT 13H (0x13)

Function 30H (0x30 or 48) → Get Information (QuickCache II v4.20)

Call with: AH = 30H
AL = Information Number (See Table in Comments)
DS:DX = buffer for info

Return: If Function Successful,
AX = 0000H
If Function Unsuccessful,
AX = Status

Comments:
This Function is used to get the different type of information about system, specified by AL. If the function is successful the AX is 0000H, if unsuccessful AX returns the status. AX = 8000H indicates the invalid Information specifier. Information numbers to be specified to AL, have been listed in the following table:

Value	Description
00H	System information
01H	Drive information
02H	Access frequency (Array of 30 words)
03H	Drive Index (Array of 32 bytes indicating BIOS drive for DOS drive)

INT 13H (0x13)

Function 31H (0x31 or 49) → Reserve Memory (QuickCache II v4.20)

Call with: AH = 31H
BX = Number of paragraphs of conventional memory to reserve for Applications.

Return: If Function Successful,
AX = 0000H
If Function Unsuccessful,
AX = Status

Comments:

This Function is used to reserve the memory for applications. If the function is successful the AX is 0000H, if unsuccessful AX returns the status.

INT 13H (0x13)

Function 32H (0x32 or 50) → Enable Caching For Specific Drive (QuickCache II v4.20)

Call with:	AH	=	32H
	AL	=	drive number
Return:	If Function Successful,		
	AX	=	0000H
	If Function Unsuccessful,		
	AX	=	Status

Comments:

This Function is used to enable caching for specific drive. For example, call Function with AL = 00H for A: and so on. If the function is successful the AX is 0000H, if unsuccessful AX returns the status.

INT 13H (0x13)

Function 33H (0x33 or 51) → Disable Caching For Specific Drive (QuickCache II v4.20)

Call with:	AH	=	33H
	AL	=	drive number
Return:	If Function Successful,		
	AX	=	0000H
	If Function Unsuccessful,		
	AX	=	Status

Comments:

This Function is used to disable caching for specific drive. For example, call Function with AL = 00H for A: and so on. If the function is successful the AX is 0000H, if unsuccessful AX returns the status.

INT 13H (0x13)

Function 34H (0x34 or 52) → Lock/Unlock Sector(s) (QuickCache II v4.20)

Call with:	AH	=	34H
	AL	=	Locking/Unlocking function number (See the Table Given in Comments)

Handling Large Hard Disks

Return: If Function Successful,
AX = 0000H
If Function Unsuccessful,
AX = Status

Comments:

This Function is used to call lock/unlock functions of sectors, specified by AL. If the function is successful the AX is 0000H, if unsuccessful AX returns the status. The different function numbers to be called with AL have been given in the following table:

Value	Function
00H	End sector locking/unlocking
01H	Lock all accessed sectors into cache
02H	Unlock all accessed sectors and discard from cache

INT 13H (0x13)

Function 35H (0x35 or 53) → Set Lock Pool Size (QuickCache II v4.20)

Call with: AH = 35H
BX = Number of sectors in lock pool
Return: If Function Successful,
AX = 0000H
If Function Unsuccessful,
AX = Status

Comments:

This Function is used to set lock pool size. If the function is successful the AX is 0000H, if unsuccessful AX returns the status.

INT 13H (0x13)

Function 36H (0x36 or 54) → Set Trace Buffer Size

Call with: AH = 36H
AL = New size of trace buffer
Return: If Function Successful,
AX = 0000H
If Function Unsuccessful,
AX = Status

Comments:

This Function is used to set the Trace Buffer Size. If the function is successful the AX is 0000H, if unsuccessful AX returns the status. This Function is usually called with Function 24H of INT 13H with AL=05H.

INT 13H (0x13)

Function 37H (0x37 or 55) → Set Buffered Reads For Specific Drive (QuickCache II v4.20)

Call with:	AH	=	37H
	AL	=	New state
	DL	=	Drive number
Return:	If Function Successful,		
	AX	=	0000H
	If Function Unsuccessful,		
	AX	=	Status

Comments:

This Function is used to set buffered reads for specific Drive. If AL = 00H the State is enable, else disable. If the function is successful the AX is 0000H, if unsuccessful AX returns the status.

INT 13H (0x13)

Function 38H (0x38 or 56) → Set Buffered Writes for Specific Drive (QuickCache II v4.20)

Call with:	AH	=	38H
	AL	=	New state
	DL	=	Drive number
Return:	If Function Successful,		
	AX	=	0000H
	If Function Unsuccessful,		
	AX	=	Status

Comments:

This Function is used to set buffered writes for specific Drive. If AL = 00H the State is enable, else disable. If the function is successful the AX is 0000H, if unsuccessful AX returns the status.

INT 13H (0x13)

Function 39H (0x39 or 57) → Set Read Buffer Size for Specific Drive (QuickCache II v4.20)

Call with:	AH	=	39H
	AL	=	New size of read buffer
	DL	=	Drive number
Return:	If Function Successful,		
	AX	=	0000H
	If Function Unsuccessful,		

Handling Large Hard Disks

	AX	=	Status

Comments:

This Function is used to set the Read Buffer size for Specific Drive such as DL = 00H for A: and so on. If the function is successful the AX is 0000H, if unsuccessful AX returns the status.

INT 13H (0x13)

Function 3AH (0x3A or 58) → Set Write Buffer Size for Specific Drive (QuickCache II v4.20)

Call with:	AH	=	3AH
	AL	=	New size of Write buffer
	DL	=	Drive number
Return:	If Function Successful,		
	AX	=	0000H
	If Function Unsuccessful,		
	AX	=	Status

Comments:

This Function is used to set the write Buffer size for Specific Drive such as DL = 00H for A: and so on. If the function is successful the AX is 0000H, if unsuccessful AX returns the status.

INT 13H (0x13)

Function 3DH (0x3D or 61) → Enable/Disable Cylinder Flush for Drive (QuickCache II v4.20)

Call with:	AH	=	3DH
	AL	=	New state
	DL	=	drive number
Return:	If Function Successful,		
	AX	=	0000H
	If Function Unsuccessful,		
	AX	=	Status

Comments:

This Function is used to Enable/Disable Cylinder flush for Specific Drive such as DL = 00H for A: and so on. If the function is successful the AX is 0000H, if unsuccessful AX returns the status. If AL register is set to 01H, state is enable, else disable.

INT 13H (0x13)

Function 3EH (0x3E or 62) → Set Single-Sector Bonus (QuickCache II v4.20)

Call with:	AH	=	3EH

	AL	=	New value for bonus
Return:	If Function Successful,		
	AX	=	0000H
	If Function Unsuccessful,		
	AX	=	Status

Comments:

This Function is used to set the Single-Sector Bonus. If the function is successful the AX is 0000H, if unsuccessful AX returns the status.

INT 13H (0x13)

Function 3FH (0x3F or 63) → Set Bonus Thrashold (QuickCache II v4.20)

Call with:	AH	=	3FH
	AL	=	New value for bonus threshold
Return:	If Function Successful,		
	AX	=	0000H
	If Function Unsuccessful,		
	AX	=	Status

Comments:

This Function is used to set the Bonus Threshold. If the function is successful the AX is 0000H, if unsuccessful AX returns the status.

INT 13H (0x13)

Function 41H (0x41 or 65) → Installation Check (IBM/MS INT 13H Extensions)

Call with:	AH	=	41H
	BX	=	55AAH
	DL	=	Drive number (80H-FFH)
Return:	If Extensions Supported and Function Successful,		
	Carry Flag	=	Clear
	BX	=	AA55H
	AH	=	Major version of extensions (See the table in Comments)
	AL	=	Internal use
	CX	=	API subset support bitmap (See the Table in Comments)
	DH	=	Extension version (v2.0 and later)
	If Extension not Supported or Function Unsuccessful,		
	Carry Flag	=	set

Handling Large Hard Disks

           AH   =   01H (Function Invalid)

Comments:

This function checks whether the IBM/MS INT 13H Extensions are installed and supported. Values for major versions of extensions have been given in the following table:

Value	Major Version of Extension
01H	1.x
20H	2.0 / EDD-1.0
21H	2.1 / EDD-1.1
30H	EDD-3.0

The Bit fields for IBM/MS INT 13H Extensions API support bitmap have been given in the table given next:

Bit(s)	Description
0	Extended disk access functions (AH=42H, 43H, 44H, 47h and 48H) supported.
1	Removable drive controller functions (AH=45H, 46H, 48H, 49H, and INT15/AH =52H) supported.
2	Enhanced disk drive (EDD) functions (AH=48H and AH=4EH) supported. Extended drive parameter table is valid.
3-15	Reserved (0)

INT 13H (0x13)

Function 42H (0x42 or 66) → Extended Read (IBM/MS INT 13H Extensions)

Call with: AH   =   42H
            DL   =   Drive number
            DS:SI   =   Disk address packet (See the table in comments)
Return: If Function Successful,
            Carry Flag =   Clear
            AH   =   00H
            If Function Unsuccessful,
            Carry Flag =   Set
            AH   =   error code

Comments:

This function is the extension for disk read function. If the function is successful carry flag is clear and AH register is 00H, else Carry flag is set and AH returns the error code. The block count field of disk address packet is set to number of blocks successfully transferred. The Format of disk address packet has been given next:

Offset	Size	Description
00H	BYTE	Size of Packet (10H)
01H	BYTE	Reserved (0)
02H	WORD	Number of blocks to transfer
04H	DWORD	Transfer buffer
08H	QWORD	Starting absolute block number (LBA)

INT 13H (0x13)

Function 43H (0x43 or 67) → Extended Write (IBM/MS INT 13H Extensions)

Call with: AH   =   43H
             AL   =   write flags (See the table in comments)
             DL   =   drive number.
             DS:SI =   disk address packet

Return: If Function Successful,
             Carry Flag   =   clear
             AH   =   00H
             If Function Unsuccessful,
             Carry Flag   =   set
             AH   =   error code

Comments:

This function is the extension for disk write function. If the function is successful carry flag is clear and AH register is 00H, else Carry flag is set and AH returns the error code.

The block count field of disk address packet is set to number of blocks successfully. The information of write flags for different versions has been given in the following table:

Version 1.0 and 2.0		Version 2.1 and later	
Value	Description	Value	Description
Bit 0	Verify Write	00H and 01H	Write without Verify
Bits 1 to 7	Reserved (0)	02H	Write with verify

INT 13H (0x13)

Function 44H (0x44 or 68) → Verify Sectors (IBM/MS INT 13H Extensions)

Call with: AH   =   44H

Handling Large Hard Disks 329

	DL	=	drive number
	DS:SI	=	disk address packet
Return:	If Function Successful,		
	Carry Flag	=	Clear
	AH	=	00H
	If Function Unsuccessful,		
	Carry Flag	=	Set
	AH	=	error code

Comments:

This function is the extension for Verify Sectors function. If the function is successful carry flag is clear and AH register is 00H, else Carry flag is set and AH returns the error code. The block count field of disk address packet is set to number of blocks successfully

INT 13H (0x13)

Function 45H (0x45 or 69) → Lock/Unlock Drive (IBM/MS INT 13H Extensions)

Call with:	AH	=	45H
	AL	=	Operation Number (See the Table in comments)
	DL	=	Drive number
Return:	If Function Successful,		
	Carry Flag	=	Clear
	AH	=	00H
	AL	=	Lock State (00H = Unlocked)
	If Function Unsuccessful,		
	Carry Flag	=	Set
	AH	=	Error code

Comments:

This function is used to Lock/Unlock the drive. This function is required to be supported for any removable drives numbered 80H or higher. Up to 255 locks may be placed on a drive, and the media will not be physically unlocked until all locks have been removed.

If the function is successful carry flag is clear and AH register is 00H, else Carry flag is set and AH returns the error code.

Operation numbers for different Lock/Unlock operation of the drive have been given in the following table:

Value	Function
00H	Lock media in drive
01H	Unlock media
02H	Check lock status

INT 13H (0x13)

Function 46H (0x46 or 70) → Eject Media (IBM/MS INT 13H Extensions)

Call with:	AH	=	46H
	AL	=	00H (reserved)
	DL	=	Drive number
Return:	If Function Successful,		
	Carry Flag	=	Clear
	AH	=	00H
	If Function Unsuccessful,		
	Carry Flag	=	Set
	AH	=	error code

Comments:

This function is to eject media. If the function is successful carry flag is clear and AH register is 00H, else Carry flag is set and AH returns the error code.

INT 13H (0x13)

Function 47H (0x47 or 71) → Extended Seek (IBM/MS INT 13H Extensions)

Call with:	AH	=	47H
	DL	=	Drive number
	DS:SI	=	Disk address packet
Return:	If Function Successful,		
	Carry Flag	=	Clear
	AH	=	00H
	If Function Unsuccessful,		
	Carry Flag	=	Set
	AH	=	error code

Comments:

This function is the extension for seek function. If the function is successful carry flag is clear and AH register is 00H, else Carry flag is set and AH returns the error code. The block count field of disk address packet is set to number of blocks successfully.

INT 13H (0x13)

Function 48H (0x48 or 72) → Get Drive Parameters (IBM/MS INT 13H Extensions)

Call with:	AH	=	48H

Handling Large Hard Disks

	DL	=	Drive (80H-FFH)
	DS:SI	=	Buffer for drive parameters
Return:	If Function Successful,		
	Carry Flag	=	Clear
	AH	=	00H
	DS:SI	=	Buffer filled
	If Function Unsuccessful,		
	Carry Flag	=	Set
	AH	=	Error code

Comments:

This function is used to get the drive parameters. If the function is successful carry flag is clear and AH register is 00H with DS:SI of Filled buffer, else Carry flag is set and AH returns the error code.

INT 13H (0x13)

Function 49H (0x49 or 73) → Extended Media Change (IBM/MS INT 13H Extensions)

Call with:	AH	=	49H
	DL	=	Drive number (any drive number, see Comments)
Return:	If media has not been changed,		
	Carry Flag	=	Clear
	AH	=	00H
	If media may have been changed,		
	Carry Flag	=	Set
	AH	=	06H (Error code for media change)

Comments:

This function is the extension for media change function. If the function is successful carry flag is clear and AH register is 00H, else Carry flag is set and AH returns the error code.

The main difference in this function and function AH = 16H of INT 13H is that we may specify any drive number, where Function 16H allows only drive number 00H to 7FH of floppy disks.

INT 13H (0x13)

Function 4AH (0x4A or 74) → Initiate disk Emulation (Bootable CD-ROM)

Call with:	AH	=	4AH
	AL	=	00H
	DS:SI	=	Specification packet (see the Table in comments)
Return:	If Function Successful,		
	Carry Flag	=	Clear

If Function unsuccessful,

Carry Flag = Set
AX = Status Code

Comments:

This Function is used to initiate the disk emulation. If the function is successful carry flag is clear, else carry flag is set and AX register returns status code and drive will not be in emulation mode.

The Format of Bootable CD-ROM Specification Packet has been given in the following table:

Offset	Size	Description
00H	BYTE	Size of packet in bytes (13H)
01H	BYTE	Boot media type
02H	BYTE	**Drive Number**
		<table><tr><th>Drive Number</th><th>Drive Description</th></tr><tr><td>00H</td><td>Floppy image</td></tr><tr><td>80H</td><td>Bootable hard disk</td></tr><tr><td>81H to FFH</td><td>Non bootable or no Emulation</td></tr></table>
03H	BYTE	CD-ROM controller number
04H	DWORD	Logical Block Address of disk image to Emulate
08H	WORD	**Device Specification**
		<table><tr><th>Value</th><th>Description</th></tr><tr><td>(IDE) Bit 0</td><td>Drive is slave instead of master</td></tr><tr><td>(SCSI) Bits 0 to 7</td><td>LUN (Logical Unit Number) and PUN (Physical Unit Number)</td></tr><tr><td>Bits 8 to 15</td><td>Bus Number</td></tr></table>
0AH	WORD	Segment of 3Kb buffer for caching CD-ROM reads
0CH	WORD	Load segment for initial boot image (if 0000H, load at segment 07C0H)
0EH	WORD	Number of 512-byte virtual sectors to load (only valid for Function 4CH of INT 13H)
10H	BYTE	Low byte of cylinder count (for Function 08H of INT 13H)
11H	BYTE	Sector count, high bits of cylinder count (for Function 08H of INT 13H)
12H	BYTE	Head count (for Function 08H of INT 13H)

The Bit fields for Bootable CD-ROM boot media type have been given in the following table:

Bit(s)	Description		
3-0	**Media type**		
	Value	Description	
	0000	No emulation.	
	0001	1.2M diskette.	
	0010	1.44M diskette.	
	0011	2.88M diskette.	
	0100	Hard disk (drive C:)	
	Other	Reserved	
5-4	Reserved (0)		
6	Image contains ATAPI driver		
7	Image contains SCSI driver(s)		

INT 13H (0x13)

Function 4B00H (0x4B00) → Terminate Disk Emulation (Bootable CD-ROM)

Call with: AX = 4B00H
  DL = Drive number (or 7FH to terminate all emulations)
  DS:SI = Empty specification packet

Return: If Function Successful,
  Carry Flag = Clear
  If Function Unsuccessful,
  Carry Flag = Set
  AX = Status code
  DS:SI = Specification packet filled

Comments:

This Function is used to terminate the disk emulation. If you want to terminate all emulations, call the function with DL = 7FH. If the Function is successful, the carry flag is clear, else carry flag is set and AX register returns status code and the drive remains in emulation mode.

INT 13H (0x13)

Function 4B01H (0x4B01) → Get Status (Bootable CD-ROM)

Call with: AX = 4B01H
  DL = Drive number
  DS:SI = Empty specification packet

Return: If Function Successful,
            Carry Flag   =   Clear
If Function Unsuccessful,
            Carry Flag   =   Set
            AX   =   Status code
            DS:SI   =   Specification packet filled

Comments:

The Function is used to get the status. If the Function is successful, the carry flag is clear, else carry flag is set and AX register returns status code

INT 13H (0x13)

Function 4CH (0x4C or 76) → Initiate Disk Emulation and Boot (Bootable CD-ROM)

Call with: AH   =   4CH
                  AL   =   00H
                  DS:SI   =   Specification packet
Return: If Function Successful, Nothing
               If Function Unsuccessful,
               Carry Flag   =   Set
               AX   =   Status code

Comments:

This Function is used to Initiate the disk Emulation and boot the system. If the function is successful, returns nothing else the carry flag is set and AX register returns the status code.

INT 13H (0x13)

Function 4D00H (0x4D00) → Return Boot Catalog (Bootable CD-ROM)

Call with: AX   =   4D00H
                  DS:SI   =   Command packet (See the Table in comments)
Return: If Function Successful,
               Carry Flag   =   Clear
               If Function Unsuccessful,
               Carry Flag   =   Set
               AX   =   Status code

Comments:

This function is used to return the boot catalog. If the Function is successful, the carry flag is clear, else carry flag is set and AX register returns status code. The Format of Bootable CD-ROM of "Get Boot Catalog" command packet has been given in the following table:

Offset	Size	Description
00H	BYTE	Size of packet in bytes (08H)
01H	BYTE	Number of sectors of boot catalog to read
02H	DWORD	Buffer for boot catalog
06H	WORD	First sector in boot catalog to transfer

INT 13H (0x13)

Function 4EH (0x4E or 78) → Set Hardware Configuration (IBM/MS INT 13H Extensions v2.1)

Call with: AH = 4EH
            AL = Function Number (See the Table in comments)
            DL = Drive number

Return: If Function Successful,
            Carry Flag = Clear
            AH = 00H
            If Function Unsuccessful,
            Carry Flag = Set
            AH = error code
            AL = Status

Comments:

This Function is used to set the hardware configuration. The function numbers for AL to call this Function have been given in the following table:

Value	Description
00H	Enable prefetch
01H	Disable prefetch
02H	Set maximum PIO transfer mode
03H	Set PIO mode 0
04H	Set default PIO transfer mode
05H	Enable INT 13H DMA maximum mode
06H	Disable INT 13H DMA

DMA and PIO modes are mutually exclusive therefore selecting DMA disables PIO for either the specified device or all devices on that controller and selecting PIO disables DMA

INT 13H (0x13)

Function 5001H (0x5001) → Send Packet Command (Enhanced Disk Drive Spec v3.0)

Call with: AX = 5001H

	DL	=	Drive number
	ES:BX	=	Command packet (See the Table in comments)
Return:	If Function Successful,		
	Carry Flag	=	Clear
	AH	=	00H
	If Function Unsuccessful,		
	Carry Flag	=	Set
	AH	=	error code

Comments:

This function is used to send the packet commands. If the function is successful carry flag is clear and AH register is 00H, else Carry flag is set and AH returns the error code. The Format of Enhanced Disk Drive Spec v3.0 command packet has been given in the following table:

Offset	Size	Description
00H	WORD	Signature B055H
02H	BYTE	Length of packet in bytes
03H	BYTE	Reserved (0)
04H	N BYTEs	Formatted packet data

INT 13H (0x13)

Function 5501H (0x5501) → Inquiry (Seagate ST01/ST02)

Call with:	AX	=	5501H
	DH	=	Number of bytes to transfer
	DL	=	Drive Number
	ES:BX	=	Buffer for results
Return:	ES:BX buffer, filled with the Inquiry results.		

Comments:

This function is used to send inquiry. The ST01/ST02 BIOS does not return any success or failure indication for the function therefore all the commands must be assumed to have been successful.

The ST01/ST02 BIOS always maps its drives after the previous BIOS drives without changing the BIOS drive count at 0040H:0075H. This command is identical to the SCSI Inquiry command

INT 13H (0x13)

Function 5502H (0x5502) → Reserved (Seagate ST01/ST02)

INT 13H (0x13)

Function 5503H (0x5503) → Set DTQ (Device Type Qualifier) (Seagate ST01/ST02)

Call with:	AX	=	5503H

Handling Large Hard Disks

	DH	=	DTQ byte (See the table in comments)
	DL	=	Drive Number
Return:	Nothing		

Comments:

This function is used to set the DTQ (Device Type Qualifier). The Function returns nothing. The Bit fields for DTQ byte have been shown in the following table:

Bit(s)	Description
0	Seagate installation software present
1	Selected drive has been installed
2	Host Adapter checks parity on the selected drive
3	Selected drive is ST225N
4	Selected drive is paired ST225N/NP
5	Reserved
6	SCSI drive attached
7	Reserved

INT 13H (0x13)

Function 5504H (0x5504) → Return Identification (Seagate ST01/ST02)

Call with:	AX	=	5504H
	DL	=	Drive Number
Return:	AX	=	4321H
	BL	=	selected drive number (00H, 01H)
	BH	=	number of drives attached to Host Adapter

Comments:

Function is used to return the identification of the drive(s).

INT 13H (0x13)

Function 5505H (0x5505) → Park Heads (Seagate ST01/ST02)

Call with:	AX	=	5505H
	DL	=	Drive Number
	DH	=	Sub function (see the comments)
Return:	Nothing		

Comments:

The function is used to park the heads of the disk. It was used in the old hard disk disks however the modern hard disks do not need any external program to park their heads.

The Sub function 00H parks the heads (SCSI Stop command) and Sub function 01H un-park the heads (SCSI Start command) of the disk.

INT 13H (0x13)

Function 5506H (0x5506) → SCSI Bus Parity (Seagate ST01/ST02)

Call with:	AX	=	5506H
	DL	=	Drive Number
	DH	=	Sub function Number (See Comments)
Return:	AL	=	Status (00H parity checking disabled, 01H parity checking enabled)

Comments:

Call the function with the following sub function number for DH:

Value	Description
00H	Disable parity check
01H	Enable parity check
02H	Return current parity setting

INT 13H (0x13)

Function 5507H (0x5507) To Function 550DH (0x550D) → Reserved Functions (Seagate ST01/ST02)

Call with: AX   =   5507H   to   AX   =   550DH

Comments:

These Functions have been officially listed as "Reserved"

INT 13H (0x13)

Function A0H (0xA0 or 160) → Get Resident Code Segment (Super PC-Kwik v3.20 and Later)

Call with:	AH	=	A0H
	SI	=	4358H
Return:	AX	=	Segment of Resident Code

Comments:

This function is used to get the resident code segment. AX returns the segment of resident code.

INT 13H (0x13)

Function A1H (0xA1 or 161) → Flush Cache (Super PC-Kwik v3.20 and Later)

Call with: AH   =   A1H

Handling Large Hard Disks

```
                SI       =    4358H
Return:   Carry Flag     =    Clear
          AH             =    00H (v5.10)
```

Comments:

The Function is used to flush the cache.

INT 13H (0x13)

Function A3H (0xA3 or 163) → Disable Cache (Super PC-Kwik v3.20 and Later)

```
Call with:  AH           =    A3H
            SI           =    4358H
Return:     Carry Flag   =    Clear
```

Comments:

Function is used to disable the cache.

INT 13H (0x13)

Function A4H (0xA4 or 164) → Enable Cache (Super PC-Kwik v3.20 and Later)

```
Call with:  AH           =    A4H
            SI           =    4358H
Return:     Carry Flag   =    Clear
```

Comments:

This function is used to enable cache.

INT 13H (0x13)

Function EEH (0xEE or 238) → Set 1024-Cylinder Flag (SWBIOS)

```
Call with:  AH           =    EEH
            DL           =    Drive Number
Return:     Carry Flag   =    Clear
            AH           =    00H
```

Comments:

The Function is used to Set 1024 – Cylinder flag. The flag is cleared by all INT 13H calls except AH=EEH and AH=EFH. Disk Manager also supports these calls. This function is equivalent to calling Function AH=EFH with CX=0400H for the software which supports that call.

This function is also supported by HyperDisk v4.01 and later, and PC-Cache v5.5 and later, in order to allow caching of drives using SWBIOS to access more than 1024 cylinders.

INT 13H (0x13)

Function EFH (0xEF or 239) → Set Cylinder Offset (Ontrack Drive Rocket)

Call with:	AH	=	EFH
	CX	=	Cylinder offset for next INT 13H call
	DL	=	Drive Number
Return:	Carry Flag	=	Clear
	AH	=	00H

Comments:

The Function is used to set Cylinder offset. For software which supports this call, the Function AH=EEH is equivalent to calling this function with CX=0400H. The cylinder offset is reset to 0 by all INT 13H called except AH=EEH and AH=EFH.

INT 13H (0x13)

Function F9H (0xF9 or 249) → Installation Check (SWBIOS)

Call with:	AH	=	F9H
	DL	=	Drive Number
Return:	If Function Successful,		
	Carry Flag	=	Clear
	DX	=	Configuration Word (see comments)
	If Function Unsuccessful,		
	Carry Flag	=	Set

Comments:

This Function is used for installation Check. If the Function is successful carry flag is clear and DX returns the configuration word, else carry flag is set.

Bit 15 is set if other SWBIOS extensions are available. Disk Manager also supports these calls.

INT 13H (0x13)

Function FEH (0xFE or 254) → Get Extended Cylinder Count (SWBIOS)

Call with:	AH	=	FEH
	DL	=	Drive Number
Return:	Carry Flag	=	Clear
	DX	=	Number of Cylinders beyond 1024 on drive

Comments:

This function is used to get the extended Cylinder count. The function AH = 08H of INT 13H will return a cylinder count truncated to 1024. BIOS without this extension would return count modul 1024. Disk Manager also supports these calls

Handling Large Hard Disks

INT 13H (0x13)

Function FFH (0xFF or 255) → **Officially Private Function (IBM SurePath BIOS)**

INT 13H (0x13)

Function FFFFH (0xFFFF) → **Set Turbo Mode (UNIQUE UX Turbo Utility)**

Call with: AX = FFFFH
BH = AAH
BL = Sub Function Number (See the table in Comments)

Return: If installed,
AX = 1234H

Comments:

This function is used to set the Turbo Mode. The Sub function numbers to call the function with BL have been given in the following table:

Value	Description
00H	Installation check
01H	Turn on Turbo mode
02H	Turn off Turbo mode
03H	Set Turbo mode according to hardware switch
04H	Set disk access to Turbo mode
05H	Set disk access to Normal mode

How to use INT 13H Extensions in C Programming

We can call the Extension Functions of INT 13H with the same C functions (int86(), int86x() etc.), which we were using in the earlier chapters. Let us learn it by an example.

The following example gives the focus to the three functions (Check Extensions present, extended read and extended write). However we are not going to use extended write function in this chapter.

The program first checks if extensions are supported or not if the extensions are present for INT 13H, It reads the absolute sector 0 (thus MBR) of the disk. The coding of the program proceeds in the following manner:

```
/* Program to access sectors beyond 8.46 GB using INT 13 BIOS extensions
*/
#include<stdio.h>
#include<dos.h>

/* Assigns the identifier to the data type */
typedef unsigned char Byte;
typedef unsigned int Word;
```

```c
typedef unsigned long DWord;

/* disk_packet structure is loaded in DS:SI and command executed */
struct disk_packet
{
    Byte size_pack;        // Size of packet must be 16 or 16+
    Byte reserved1;        // Reserved
    Byte no_of_blocks;     // Number of blocks for transfer
    Byte reserved2;        // Reserved
    /*  Address in Segment:Offset format */
    Word offset;           //offset address
    Word segment;          //segment address

/* To Support the Disk Even of Capacity of 1152921504.607 GB */
    DWord lba1;
    DWord lba2;
}disk_pack;

/* Function to check if the Extensions are supported */
void check_ext_present()
{
    union REGS inregs, outregs;  /* Input Registers and Output */
    inregs.h.ah=0x41;            /* Function to Check Extension Present */
    inregs.x.bx=0x55AA;
    inregs.h.dl=0x80; /* Drive No for first Hard Disk */
    int86(0x13,&inregs,&outregs); /*Call interrupt */
    if(outregs.x.cflag)
    {
        /*  Extension Not Supported  */
        printf("\nBios extension not supported");
        exit(1);
    }
    if(outregs.x.bx==0xAA55)
    if(outregs.x.cx & 0x1)
    /*  Extension Present    */
    printf("\nExtended I/O supported");
}

/*  Function to read the Sector */
void read_sectors(void *buffer)
{
    union REGS inregs, outregs; /* Input and Output Registers */
    struct SREGS segregs;       // Segment Registers
    disk_pack.size_pack=16;     // Set size to 16
    disk_pack.no_of_blocks=1;   // One block
    disk_pack.reserved1=0;      // Reserved Word
```

```c
        disk_pack.reserved2=0;                  // Reserved Word
        disk_pack.segment=FP_SEG(buffer);       // Segment of buffer
        disk_pack.offset=FP_OFF(buffer);        // Offset of buffer
        /*   request for MBR of hard disk 1 */
        /* Read Absolute sector 0   */
        disk_pack.lba1=0;      /*  LBA address, Contains first 32 bits */
        /*  We normally require( drives < 2.1 T.B) to set only this    */
        disk_pack.lba2=0;  // Last 32 bit address
        inregs.h.ah=0x42;  // Function to read
        inregs.h.dl=0x80;  // Drive Number for First Hard Disk
        inregs.x.si=FP_OFF(&disk_pack); /*Make DS:SI point to disk_pack */
        segregs.ds = FP_SEG(&disk_pack);
        /* Call Interrupt */
        int86x(0x13,&inregs,&outregs,&segregs);
        if(outregs.x.cflag)
            printf("\n\nError %d\n",outregs.h.ah);
            else
            printf("\n\nI hope Everything is all Right");
}

//// Write Sector Function \\\\
void write_sector()
{
        /*  It will be written in the same way as read_sectors function,
        except Function Number, which will be 0x43 in this function. We'll
        discuss extended write function in next chapters.
        Before Using this Function please check and verify what are you
        going to do. You should have the proper knowledge of what you are
        going to do. Use of this function in lack of knowledge or carelessly
        may destroy your data. */
}

/// Main Function \\\\
void main()
{
        int i=0;
        /*   buffer to hold MBR   */
        Byte mbr[512];
        clrscr();

/*   check for BIOS extension present    */
        check_ext_present();
        /*   read sector   */
        read_sectors(&mbr);
        printf("\n\n Data of MBR \n");
        printf("•••••••••••••••••\n\n\n");
```

```
        while(i++<512)
        {
            /*   display the MBR buffer   */
            printf("%c",mbr[i]);
        }
}
```

And the Output of the Program will be displayed on the Screen as follows:

Extended I/O supported

I hope Everything is all Right

Data of MBR

[garbled binary data output] ...Invalid partition table. Setup cannot continue. Error loading operating system. Setup cannot continue. ...

Comments on Coding of the program

typedef Assigns the identifier to the data type such that **typedef unsigned char Byte;** assigns identifier **Byte** for the data type **char.** Similarly identifier **Word** is assigned to **int** and **DWord** is assigned to **long.**

The **disk_packet** structure is loaded in DS:SI and the command (such as extended read, extended write or verify etc.) is executed. See the functions of **IBM/MS INT 13H Extensions** (Function 41H to Function 49H) given before.

The **check_ext_present**() function checks if the extensions are available/supported or not. The function is called with BX=55AAH (**inregs.x.bx=0x55AA;**) and if extensions are supported the BX register is set to AA55H. (See Function 41H given before)

The Function **read_sectors** is used to read the absolute sector of the disk, specified by **disk_pack.lba1**. In this program we have given **disk_pack.lba1=0**, thus we are going to read the absolute sector 0 (See the Note Below) thus going to read the **MBR** of the disk.

The **write_sector** function is also same as the **read_sectors** function and will be written in the same way but with the different Function options. We shall use it in the next chapters.

Note:

We read the disk sectors in the following two ways:
1. Relative Sector Read (or Write)
2. Absolute Sector Read (or Write)

Handling Large Hard Disks

In Relative Sector Read we read the disk sectors in accordance with CHS (Cylinder, Head and Sector) geometry of the disk. In relative sector read the MBR of the disk (First Sector of the disk) is on Cylinder 0, head 0 and Sector 1.

In the Absolute reading of the disk sectors, we need not to specify the Cylinder or Head numbers in our program. The absolute sectors are counted from absolute sector 0.

Thus if we are going to read the MBR of the disk (First sector of the disk), we are going to read absolute sector 0. It is the work of BIOS to convert the absolute sector number to its corresponding Cylinder, Head and Sector number.

As in absolute sector reading (or writing), we have to calculate only the absolute sectors within the loop in the operations such as entire disk reading or writing, whereas in case of relative sector reading (or writing), we need to run three loops at a time for calculating CHS therefore **absolute sector reading/writing is much faster than relative sector reading/writing.**

For example, if we have any hard disk with the 16 heads (sides), 12 Cylinders and with 63 sectors, the table given next, shows the procedure and difference of both the reading methods and thus shows how absolute sector approach may make our time taking programs (such as entire disk reading/ writing or entire disk wiping programs etc.) to run much faster:

Relative Sectors Reading	Absolute Sector reading
Cylinder =0, Head =0, Sector = 1	Absolute Sector = 0
Cylinder =0, Head =0, Sector = 2	Absolute Sector = 1
Cylinder =0, Head =0, Sector = 3	Absolute Sector = 2
.	.
.	.
.	.
Cylinder =0, Head =0, Sector = 62	Absolute Sector = 61
Cylinder =0, Head =0, Sector = 63	Absolute Sector = 62
Cylinder =0, Head =1, Sector = 1	Absolute Sector = 63
Cylinder =0, Head =1, Sector = 2	Absolute Sector = 64
Cylinder =0, Head =1, Sector = 3	Absolute Sector = 65
Cylinder =0, Head =1, Sector = 4	Absolute Sector = 66
.	.
.	.
.	.
Cylinder =0, Head =1, Sector = 63	Absolute Sector = 125
Cylinder =0, Head =2, Sector = 1	Absolute Sector = 126
Cylinder =0, Head =2, Sector = 2	Absolute Sector = 127
Cylinder =0, Head =2, Sector = 3	Absolute Sector = 128
.	.

Cylinder =0, Head =15, Sector = 63	Absolute Sector = 1007
Cylinder =1, Head =0, Sector = 1	Absolute Sector = 1008
Cylinder =1, Head =0, Sector = 2	Absolute Sector = 1009
Cylinder =1, Head =0, Sector = 3	Absolute Sector = 1010
.	.
.	.
.	.
Cylinder =1, Head =0, Sector = 63	Absolute Sector = 1070
Cylinder =1, Head =1, Sector = 1	Absolute Sector = 1071
Cylinder =1, Head =1, Sector = 2	Absolute Sector = 1072
Cylinder =1, Head =1, Sector = 3	Absolute Sector = 1073
.	.
.	.
.	.
Cylinder =1, Head =15, Sector = 63	Absolute Sector = 2015
Cylinder =2, Head =0, Sector = 1	Absolute Sector = 2016
Cylinder =2, Head =0, Sector = 2	Absolute Sector = 2017
Cylinder =2, Head =0, Sector = 3	Absolute Sector = 2018
.	.
.	.
.	.
Cylinder =11, Head =15, Sector = 60	Absolute Sector = 12092
Cylinder =11, Head =15, Sector = 61	Absolute Sector = 12093
Cylinder =11, Head =15, Sector = 62	Absolute Sector = 12094
Cylinder =11, Head =15, Sector = 63	Absolute Sector = 12095

The information of partition table of MBR, which is displayed by any disk MBR analyzing tool, has been given below:

Part. Type	Boot	Starting location Side Cylinder Sector			Ending Location Side Cylinder Sector			Relative Sectors	Number of Sectors
FAT32	Yes	1	0	1	254	701	63	63	11277567
FAT32	No	0	702	1	254	1023	63	11277630	28724220
Unused	No	0	0	0	0	0	0	0	0
Unused	No	0	0	0	0	0	0	0	0

In the above information, the relative sector numbers for the starting of both partitions are **63** and **11277630** respectively, which are free from partitions and counted according to the number of sectors, available in disk.

Chapter – 10

Data Recovery From Corrupted Floppy

The Floppy is one of the most unreliable sources for data storage. If you go to any organization which uses computer systems and ask to its employees about the problems generated by floppy disks, you will very commonly hear the problem that the employee of the organization was having some important data in his floppy and now the floppy is not readable by the computer and a messages is displayed something like,

"Can not read the disk"

"Track 0 Bad"

"Invalid Drive or Capacity"

"The disk is not formatted. Do you want to format it now?"

This is the everyday problem for the organizations which uses computer systems and floppy. The problem becomes critical when you come to know that there was no backup made or backup available for the data which seems to be lost in the corrupted floppy disk.

The biggest hell of the problem is supposed to come when you make backup in the floppy for your critical information, rescue disks of Antivirus program to overcome the virus attack or boot records or other backups (there may be number of possibilities) in a floppy and when you want to reuse the backup from the floppy it gives a reading error.

In such condition you are about to lose your important information and data or even in some cases when you feel the lack of backups and recovery program for you computer boot information and Virus attack rescue programs etc., you may suffer a big loss of data in form of OS crash occurred due to the lack of information, stored in the floppy that is not readable by the computer now.

In such cases it becomes most important requirement to recover the data from the floppy that has been declared bad by your computer system.

Why the floppy is not readable

The most common problem that causes a floppy to show such type of error messages is the corruption of its DOS boot record (DBR) of floppy, which helps the computer to know the logical identification of the floppy.

The DBR is a small program stored in **track 0, head 0** and **sector 1** and containing important information about the floppy such as:
- Number of bytes per sector
- Sector per cluster

- Number of FATs
- Maximum number of root directories etc.

> Since Floppy has no logical partition system therefore there is no MBR available in floppy. The First Sector of Floppy holds the DBR. This is also a main difference to compare logical structure of hard disk with a floppy.

When we read the boot sector information of a floppy with the help of any disk editing program, it will display information like as in the figure given next.

The following figure shows the 512 Bytes information of the DBR of a 1.44MB, 3½ Inch floppy.

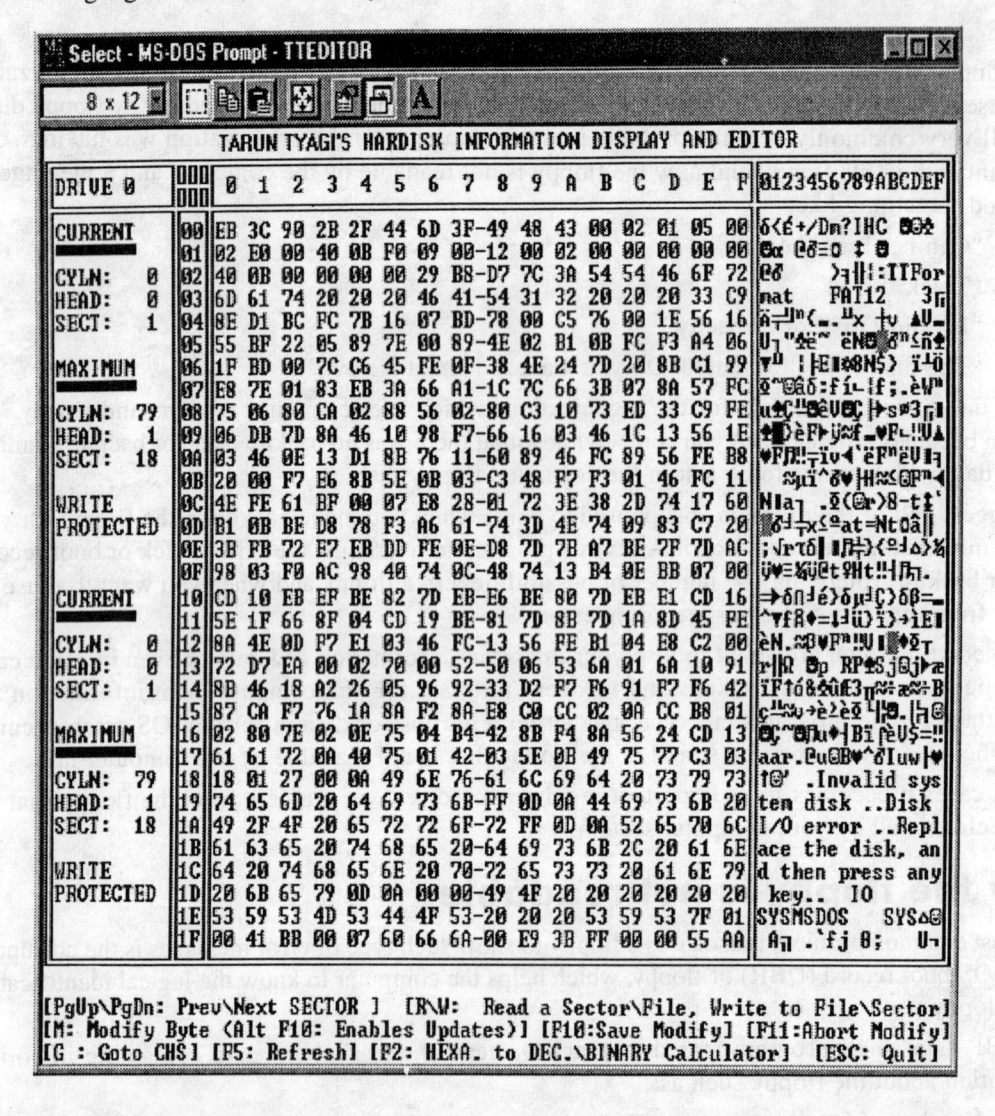

If this information is corrupted any how or it becomes unreadable, the floppy disk causes such reading error messages. It may be due to physical or logical corruption of the first sector of the disk.

Data Recovery From Corrupted Floppy

The Logical corruption includes the cases when the information of the first sector of the floppy is changed, there occurs any logical bad sector or the DBR of the floppy is corrupted due to any other reason.

The Physical corruption is supposed to take place in case of, if there are physical bad sectors (means the sector 1 is physically damaged) on the first sector of the floppy disk. The problem becomes more serious when you find that floppy is having more than one bad sector in track 0.

How to recover

As we have learnt both the causes of corruption I hope now you are able to understand the problem. It is not a very difficult thing to recover the data from logical corruption however the recovery from the physical corruption needs slightly more efforts to do.

Method – 1

Store the boot image of any fresh floppy

If the problem is logical, now we understand that how can we recover the data. What we need to do is just to get the appropriate Boot record from another floppy of same size and capacity and to paste it to the first sector of the unreadable floppy. Though the problem was created due to the bad boot record, it should work now.

There are two steps involved in this procedure by following which we are recovering our data from an unreadable floppy:

- Making the image of DOS Boot Record of a good floppy
- Pasting the boot image to the first sector of unreadable floppy

Making the image of DOS Boot Record of a good floppy

To store the image of boot record of fresh floppy, the program must do the following three tasks:

- Read exactly first 512 bytes of the good floppy
- Check for the successful read operation (Most important)
- Store these 512 bytes to the specified filename and destination path

The sector of floppy is 512 bytes and it is necessary to copy the exact image of the sector. It is most important and necessary step in case of any type of operations applied on floppy to check whether the operation was successful or not.

There may be any initialization problem even with the good and fresh floppy disk. That is why in most of the cases when the operation is performed on floppy disks, first of all initialization of floppy disks is performed in the programming with the reset disk operation (Function 00 H of INT 13H).

If Even after initialization the recently inserted floppy disk or changed floppy disk causes any reading error you are advised to run the program again, most probably it may work this time.

The following program is to perform these specified tasks. Let us see how it proceeds:

```
/* Store The Boot Image to a file from a Fresh Floppy Disk */
#include <bios.h>
#include <stdio.h>
int main(void)
```

```c
{
    struct diskinfo_t dinfo;
    union REGS regs;
    int result;
    int count=0, i;
    char fname[80];
    static char dbuf[512];
    FILE *fp;
    dinfo.drive  =   0x00;     /* drive number for A: */
    dinfo.head   =   0;        /* disk head number */
    dinfo.track  =   0;        /* track number */
    dinfo.sector =   1;        /* sector number */
    dinfo.nsectors = 1;        /* sector count */
    dinfo.buffer = dbuf;       /* data buffer */
    clrscr();
    gotoxy(10,3);cprintf("Enter The File Name And Path To
        Store Boot Image");
    gotoxy(5,5);
    gets(fname);
    fp=fopen(fname,"wb");
    if((fp=fopen(fname,"wb"))==NULL)
    {
        highvideo();
        gotoxy(10,10);cprintf("File Could Not Be created");
        getch();
        exit(0);
    }
    gotoxy(10,9);
    cprintf("Attempting to read from Floppy disk drive :\n");
    /// Initialize the Disk System \\\
    for(i=0; i<3; i++)
    {
        regs.h.ah = 0x00;   /* Reset Disk System */
        regs.h.dl = 0x00;   /* Floppy Disk a: */
        int86(0x13, &regs, &regs);
    }
    result = _bios_disk(_DISK_READ, &dinfo);
    if ((result & 0xff00) == 0)
    {
        while(count<512)
        {
            fprintf(fp,"%c",dbuf[count] & 0xff );
            count++;
        }
        fclose(fp);
```

```c
            gotoxy(10,14);cprintf("Disk read from Floppy disk drive
    : successful.\n");
}
else
{
    gotoxy(10,14);
    cprintf("Cannot read drive A, status = 0x%02x\n", result);
    switch(result)
    {
        case 0x00:
            cprintf("\n\n STATUS:   No Error!!");
            break;
        case 0x01:
            cprintf("\n\n STATUS:   Bad command");
            break;
        case 0x02:
            cprintf("\n\n STATUS:   Address mark not found");
            break;
        case 0x03:
            cprintf("\n\n STATUS:   Attempt to write to write-
            protected disk");
            break;
        case 0x04:
            cprintf("\n\n STATUS:   Sector not found");
            break;
        case 0x06:
            cprintf("\n\n STATUS:   Disk changed since last
            operation");
            break;
        case 0x08:
            cprintf("\n\n STATUS:   Direct memory access (DMA)
            overrun");
            break;
        case 0x09:
            cprintf("\n\n STATUS:   Attempt to perform DMA
            across 64K boundary");
            break;
        case 0x0C:
            cprintf("\n\n STATUS:   Media type not found");
            break;
        case 0x10:
            cprintf("\n\n STATUS:   Bad CRC/ECC on disk read");
            break;
        case 0x20:
            cprintf("\n\n STATUS:   Controller has failed");
```

```c
                    break;
            case 0x31:
                    cprintf("\n\n STATUS:    No media in drive (IBM/MS
                    INT 13H extensions)");
                    break;
            case 0x32:
                    cprintf("\n\n STATUS:    Incorrect drive type stored
                    in CMOS (Compaq)");
                    break;
            case 0x40:
                    cprintf("\n\n STATUS:    Seek operation failed");
                    break;
            case 0x80:
                    cprintf("\n\n STATUS:    Attachment failed to
                    respond(Disk Timed-out)");
                    break;
            case 0xB0:
                    cprintf("\n\n STATUS:    Volume not locked in drive
                    (INT 13H extensions)");
                    break;
            case 0xB1:
                    cprintf("\n\n STATUS:    Volume locked in drive (INT
                    13H extensions)");
                    break;
            case 0xB2:
                    cprintf("\n\n STATUS:    Volume not removable (INT
                    13H extensions)");
                    break;
            case 0xB3:
                    cprintf("\n\n STATUS:    Volume in use (INT 13H
                    extensions)");
                    break;
            case 0xB4:
                    cprintf("\n\n STATUS: Lock count exceeded (INT 13H
                    extensions)");
                    break;
            case 0xB5:
                    cprintf("\n\n STATUS:    Valid eject request failed
                    (INT 13H extensions)");
                    break;
            default: cprintf("\n\n STATUS:    UNKNOWN Status CODE
            For Floppy Errors");
        }
    }
    return 0;
}
```

Data Recovery From Corrupted Floppy 353

Comments on Program coding:

In the program coding given earlier, basically we are proceeding to perform the following tasks step by step:

- **dinfo** points to the **diskinfo_t** structure that contains the information of parameters required by the operation performed by the **_bios_disk** function.
- Since we want to read first sector of the disk therefore the location of the sector will be as follows:

Parameter	What it means
dinfo.drive = **0x00**	It indicates the drive **0** that is floppy disk drive (**a:**)
dinfo.head = 0	It points to head number **0**
dinfo.track = 0	It points to track **0**
dinfo.sector = 1	First sector of the floppy that is sector **1**
dinfo.sector = 1	Number of sectors to consider for read operation = **1**
dinfo.buffer = **dbuf**	Data buffer for the operation

- Open a file stream of user given file name and path to store the boot image information of exact 512 bytes. The file name and path is stored in the character array **fname**.
- Initialize the disk system using the **interrupt 13H (function 00h)** where **regs.h.ah = 0x00** points to the function 00 H and **regs.h.dl = 0x00** is used for **a: floppy**. And **int86(0x13, &regs, &regs)** invokes MS-DOS interrupt service **INT 13 H**.
- **_bios_disk(_DISK_READ, &dinfo)** reads the specified sector of the floppy disk.
- The status returned is stored in **result** that is used to display the message for successful operation or to display an error message on the screen if any error occurs.

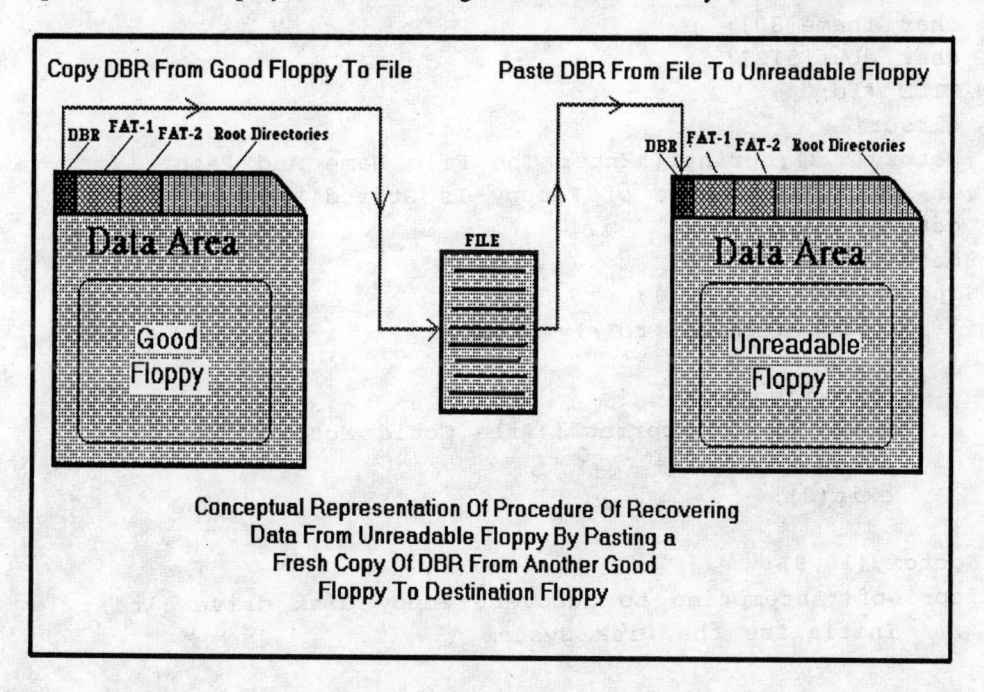

Conceptual Representation Of Procedure Of Recovering Data From Unreadable Floppy By Pasting a Fresh Copy Of DBR From Another Good Floppy To Destination Floppy

Pasting the boot image to the first sector of unreadable floppy

For pasting the boot image from the file to the first sector of the unreadable floppy we have to perform the following three main tasks in our program:

- Read exact 512 bytes information of boot record of fresh floppy from previously saved file.
- Write this information to the first sector of the floppy which is currently unreadable.
- Check for the successful completion of write operation (Most Important).

As the sector of floppy is 512 bytes and it is necessary to paste the exact boot image to the sector. It is most important and necessary step in case of any type of operations applied on floppy to check whether the operation was successful or not.

There may be any initialization problem with the floppy disk during the operation therefore you must initialize the disk by resetting the disk system(using function 00H of INT 13H).

If Even after initialization the recently inserted floppy disk or changed floppy disk causes any reading error you are advised to run the program again, most probably it may work this time.

The following program is to perform these specified tasks. Let us see how it proceeds:

```
/* Load Boot Image to the unreadable Floppy   */
#include <bios.h>
#include <stdio.h>
int main(void)
{
        struct diskinfo_t dinfo;
        union REGS regs;
        int result;
        int count=0, i;
        char fname[80];
        char dbuf[512];
        FILE *fp;
        clrscr();
        gotoxy(5,3);cprintf("Enter The File Name And Path,
        In Which Boot image of Floppy Is Stored");
        gotoxy(5,5);
        gets(fname);
        fp=fopen(fname,"rb");
        if((fp=fopen(fname,"rb"))==NULL)
        {
            highvideo();
            gotoxy(10,10);cprintf("File Could Not Be Opened");
            getch();
            exit(0);
        }
        gotoxy(10,9);
        cprintf("Attempting to Recover Floppy disk drive :\n");
        /// Initialize the Disk System \\\
```

Data Recovery From Corrupted Floppy

```c
        for(i=0; i<3; i++)
        {
            regs.h.ah = 0x00;    /* Reset Disk System */
            regs.h.dl = 0x00;    /* Floppy Disk a: */
            int86(0x13, &regs, &regs);
        }
        while(count<512)
        {
            fscanf(fp,"%c",&dbuf[count]);
            count++;
        }
        dinfo.drive   = 0x00;     /* drive number for A: */
        dinfo.head    = 0;        /* disk head number */
        dinfo.track   = 0;        /* track number */
        dinfo.sector  = 1;        /* sector number */
        dinfo.nsectors = 1;       /* sector count */
        dinfo.buffer  = dbuf;     /* data buffer */
        result = _bios_disk(_DISK_WRITE, &dinfo);
        if ((result & 0xff00) == 0)
        {
            fclose(fp);
            gotoxy(10,14);cprintf("Successful!!! I Hope Floppy May Work
            Now.\n");
        }
        else
        {
            gotoxy(10,14);
            cprintf("Cannot read drive A, status = 0x%02x\n",result);
            gotoxy(10,16);
            switch(result)
            {
                case 0x00:
                    cprintf("\n\n STATUS:   No Error!!");
                    break;
                case 0x01:
                    cprintf("\n\n STATUS:   Bad command");
                    break;

                case 0x02:
                    cprintf("\n\n STATUS:   Address mark not found");
                    break;
                case 0x03:
                    cprintf("\n\n STATUS:   Attempt to write to write-
                    protected disk");
                    break;
```

```c
        case 0x04:
            cprintf("\n\n STATUS:    Sector not found");
            break;
        case 0x06:
            cprintf("\n\n STATUS:    Disk changed since last
            operation");
            break;
        case 0x08:
            cprintf("\n\n STATUS:    Direct memory access (DMA)
            overrun");
            break;
        case 0x09:
            cprintf("\n\n STATUS:    Attempt to perform DMA
            across 64K boundary");
            break;
        case 0x0C:
            cprintf("\n\n STATUS:    Media type not found");
            break;
        case 0x10:
            cprintf("\n\n STATUS:    Bad CRC/ECC on disk read");
            break;
        case 0x20:
            cprintf("\n\n STATUS:    Controller has failed");
                break;
        case 0x31:
            cprintf("\n\n STATUS:    No media in drive (IBM/MS
            INT 13H extensions)");
            break;
        case 0x32:
            cprintf("\n\n STATUS:    Incorrect drive type stored
            in CMOS (Compaq)");
            break;
        case 0x40:
            cprintf("\n\n STATUS:    Seek operation failed");
            break;
        case 0x80:
            cprintf("\n\n STATUS:    Attachment failed to
            respond(Disk Timed-out)");
            break;
        case 0xB0:
            cprintf("\n\n STATUS:    Volume not locked in drive
            (INT 13H extensions)");
            break;
        case 0xB1:
            cprintf("\n\n STATUS:    Volume locked in drive (INT
            13H extensions)");
```

```
                        break;
            case 0xB2:
                        cprintf("\n\n STATUS:    Volume not removable (INT
                        13H extensions)");
                        break;
            case 0xB3:
                        cprintf("\n\n STATUS:    Volume in use (INT 13H
                        extensions)");
                        break;
            case 0xB4:
                        cprintf("\n\n STATUS:    Lock count exceeded (INT
                        13H extensions)");
                        break;
            case 0xB5:
                        cprintf("\n\n STATUS:    Valid eject request failed
                        (INT 13H extensions)");
                        break;
            default: cprintf("\n\n STATUS:    UNKNOWN Status CODE
            For Floppy Errors");
        }
    }
    return 0;
}
```

Comments on Program coding:

In the program coding given earlier, basically we are proceeding to perform the following tasks step by step:

- **dinfo** points to the **diskinfo_t** structure that contains the information of parameters required by the operation performed by the **_bios_disk** function.
- As we are going to write the information on the first sector of the disk therefore the location of the sector will be as follows:

Parameter	What it means
dinfo.drive = **0x00**	It indicates the drive **0** that is floppy disk drive (**a:**)
dinfo.head = **0**	It points to head number **0**
dinfo.track = **0**	It points to track **0**
dinfo.sector = **1**	First sector of the floppy that is sector **1**
dinfo.sector = **1**	Number of sectors to consider for write operation = **1**
dinfo.buffer = **dbuf**	Data buffer for the operation

- Open the file in which the boot image information of 512 bytes of a fresh floppy was stored by the previous program. The file name and path is stored in the character array **fname**.

- Initialize the disk system using the **interrupt 13H (function 00h)** where **regs.h.ah = 0x00** points to the function 00 H and **regs.h.dl = 0x00** is used for **a: floppy**. And **int86(0x13, &regs, &regs)** invokes MS-DOS interrupt service **INT 13 H**.
- **_bios_disk(_DISK_WRITE, &dinfo)** writes the boot information from the specified file to the first (specified) sector of the floppy disk.
- The status returned is stored in **result** that is used to display the message for successful operation or to display an error message on the screen if any error occurs.

Let us do it with single program

I hope, now you have understood the concept behind such type of data recovery from the floppy disk. After this let us imagine a single program which gives the same results that we got with the help of previously discussed two programs.

We were doing the following tasks with the recently discussed programs:

1. Store the Boot information from a good floppy disk to a file
2. Paste this information to the first sector of the currently unreadable floppy

The file which we were using to store the boot image was working as intermediate bridge to connect the operations of both the program. But if we define this boot information in our program coding itself, we need not to create a file as well as we need not to read the boot information of the floppy from the file.

In our next program we are telling our program about what it has to write in the first sector of the unreadable floppy disk and thus we are able to avoid two different programs to do the same task and we can recover our data in the same way as before from the new single program.

The program thus becomes simple with less coding and we are able to reduce the probability of occurrence of file read, write or creation errors. We are doing the following four important tasks in this program:

- Define the DOS boot record information in hexadecimal system to be written in the first sector of currently unreadable floppy.
- Reset the disk system to initialize the floppy disk (INT 13H, Function 00H).
- Write the DOS Boot Record to the first sector of floppy
- Check for the successful completion of operation and error, if occurred.

> *Don't think the program difficult to write and understand by seeing the 512 bytes hexadecimal information of* **dbuf[512]**. *Later, We'll discuss the easy way to write this information for your program coding.*

Let us examine the program:

```
/* Single Program to load Default Boot Image To Unreadable Floppy Disk
*/
#include <bios.h>
#include <stdio.h>
int main(void)
{
    struct diskinfo_t dinfo;
```

```c
    union REGS regs;
    int result, i;
    /* Boot Image to Be Loaded in the Floppy Disk Drive */
    static char dbuf[512]=
    {
        0xEB,0x3E,0x90,0x2B,0x29,0x6E,0x70,0x32,0x49,0x48,0x43,0x0,0x2,
        0x1,0x1,0x0,0x2,0xE0,0x0,0x40,0xB,0xF0,0x9,0x0,0x12,0x0,0x2 ,
        0x0,0x0,0x0,0x0,0x0,0x0,0x0,0x0,0x0,0x0,0x0,0x29,
        0x24,0x3B,0xDB,0x16,0x4E,0x4F,0x20,0x4E,0x41,0x4D,0x45,
        0x20,0x20,0x20,0x20,0x46,0x41,0x54,0x31,0x32,0x20,0x20,
        0x20,0xF1,0x7D,0xFA,0x33,0xC9,0x8E,0xD1,0xBC,0xFC,0x7B,0x16,0x7,
        0xBD,0x78,0x0,0xC5,0x76,0x0,0x1E,0x56,0x16,0x55,0xBF,0x22,0x5,
        0x89,0x7E,0x0,0x89,0x4E,0x2,0xB1,0xB,0xFC,0xF3,0xA4,0x6,
        0x1F,0xBD,0x0,0x7C,0xC6,0x45,0xFE,0xF,0x8B, 0x46,0x18,0x88,
        0x45,0xF9,0xFB,0x38,0x66,0x24,0x7C,0x4,0xCD,0x13,0x72,0x3C,
        0x8A,0x46,0x10,0x98,0xF7,0x66,0x16,0x3,0x46,0x1C,0x13,0x56,
        0x1E,0x3,0x46,0xE,0x13,0xD1,0x50,0x52,0x89,0x46,0xFC,0x89,0x56,
        0xFE,0xB8,0x20,0x0,0x8B,0x76,0x11,0xF7,0xE6,0x8B,0x5E,0xB,0x3,
        0xC3,0x48,0xF7,0xF3,0x1,0x46,0xFC, 0x11,0x4E,0xFE,0x5A,0x58,
        0xBB,0x0,0x7,0x8B,0xFB,0xB1,0x1,0xE8,0x94,0x0,0x72,0x47,0x38,
        0x2D,0x74,0x19,0xB1,0xB,0x56,0x8B,0x76,0x3E,0xF3,0xA6,0x5E,
        0x74,0x4A,0x4E,0x74,0xB,0x3,0xF9,0x83,0xC7,0x15,0x3B,0xFB,0x72,
        0xE5,0xEB,0xD7,0x2B,0xC9,0xB8,0xD8,0x7D,0x87,0x46,0x3E,0x3C,
        0xD8,0x75,0x99,0xBE,0x80,0x7D,0xAC,0x98,0x3,0xF0,0xAC,0x84,
        0xC0,0x74,0x17,0x3C,0xFF,0x74,0x9,0xB4,0xE,0xBB,0x7,0x0,0xCD,
        0x10,0xEB,0xEE,0xBE,0x83,0x7D,0xEB,0xE5,0xBE,0x81,0x7D,0xEB,
        0xE0,0x33,0xC0,0xCD,0x16,0x5E,0x1F,0x8F,0x4,0x8F,0x44,0x2,0xCD,
        0x19,0xBE,0x82,0x7D,0x8B,0x7D,0xF,0x83,0xFF,0x2,0 x72,0xC8,
        0x8B,0xC7,0x48,0x48,0x8A,0x4E,0xD,0xF7,0xE1,0x3,0x46,0xFC,
        0x13,0x56,0xFE,0xBB,0x0,0x7,0x53,0xB1,0x4,0xE8,0x16,0x0,0x5B,
        0x72,0xC8,0x81,0x3F,0x4D,0x5A,0x75,0xA7,0x81,0xBF,0x0,0x2,0x42,
        0x4A,0x75,0x9F,0xEA,0x0,0x2,0x70,0x0,0x50,0x52,0x51,0x91,0x92,
        0x33,0xD2,0xF7,0x76,0x18,0x91,0xF7,0x76,0x18,0x42, 0x87,0xCA,
        0xF7,0x76,0x1A,0x8A,0xF2,0x8A,0x56,0x24,0x8A,0xE8,0xD0,0xCC,
        0xD0,0xCC,0xA,0xCC,0xB8,0x1,0x2,0xCD,0x13,0x59,0x5A,0x58,0x72,
        0x9,0x40,0x75,0x1,0x42,0x3,0x5E,0xB,0xE2,0xCC,0xC3,0x3,0x18,0x1,
        0x27,0xD,0xA,0x49,0x6E,0x76,0x61,0x6C,0x69,0x64,0x20,0x73,0x79,
        0x73,0x74,0x65,0x6D,0x20,0x64,0x69,0x73,0x6B,0xFF,0xD,
        0xA,0x44,0x69,0x73,0x6B,0x20,0x49,0x2F,0x4F,0x20,0x65,0x72,
        0x72,0x6F,0x72,0xFF,0xD,0xA,0x52,0x65,0x70,0x6C,0x61,0x63,0x65,
        0x20,0x74,0x68,0x65,0x20,0x64,0x69,0x73,0x6B,0x2C,0x20,0x61,
        0x6E,0x64,0x20,0x74,0x68,0x65,0x6E,0x20,0x70,0x72,0x65,
        0x73,0x73,0x20,0x61,0x6E,0x79,0x20,0x6B,0x65,0x79,0xD,0xA,
        0x0,0x49,0x4F,0x20,0x20,0x20,0x20,0x20,0x20,0x53,0x59,0x53,0x4D,
        0x53,0x44,0x4F,0x53,0x20,0x20,0x20,0x53,0x59,0x53,0x80,0x1,0x0,
        0x57,0x49,0x4E,0x42,0x4F,0x4F,0x54,0x20,0x53,0x59,0x53,0x0,0x0,
        0x55,0xAA};
    clrscr();
    dinfo.drive =   0x00;      /* drive number for A: */
    dinfo.head   =   0;        /* disk head number */
```

```c
                dinfo.track   =  0;     /* track number */
                dinfo.sector  =  1;     /* sector number */
                dinfo.nsectors = 1;     /* sector count */
                dinfo.buffer = dbuf;    /* data buffer */
            gotoxy(10,9);
            cprintf("Attempting to read from Floppy disk drive :\n");
            /// Initialize the Disk System    \\\
            for(i=0; i<3; i++)
            {
                regs.h.ah = 0x00;   /* Reset Disk System */
                regs.h.dl = 0x00;   /* Floppy Disk a: */
                int86(0x13, &regs, &regs);
            }
            result = _bios_disk(_DISK_WRITE, &dinfo);
            if ((result & 0xff00) == 0)
            {
                gotoxy(10,14);
                cprintf("Disk Write Status :successful.\n");
            }
            else
            {
                gotoxy(10,14);
                cprintf("Cannot read drive A, status = 0x%02x\n", result);
                gotoxy(10,16);
                switch(result)
                {
                    case 0x00:
                        cprintf("\n\n STATUS:    No Error!!");
                        break;
                    case 0x01:
                        cprintf("\n\n STATUS:    Bad command");
                        break;
                    case 0x02:
                        cprintf("\n\n STATUS:    Address mark not
                        found");
                        break;
                    case 0x03:
                        cprintf("\n\n STATUS:    Attempt to write to
                        write-protected disk");
                        break;
                    case 0x04:
                        cprintf("\n\n STATUS:    Sector not found");
                        break;
                    case 0x06:
                        cprintf("\n\n STATUS:    Disk changed since
                        last operation");
```

```
                    break;
            case 0x08:
                    cprintf("\n\n STATUS:    Direct memory access
                    (DMA) overrun");
                    break;
            case 0x09:
                    cprintf("\n\n STATUS:    Attempt to perform
                    DMA across 64K boundary");
                    break;
            case 0x0C:
                    cprintf("\n\n STATUS:    Media type not found");
                    break;
            case 0x10:
                    cprintf("\n\n STATUS: Bad CRC/ECC on disk
                    read");
                    break;
            case 0x20:
                    cprintf("\n\n STATUS:    Controller has failed");
                    break;
            case 0x31:
                    cprintf("\n\n STATUS:    No media in drive (IBM/
                    MS INT 13H extensions)");
                    break;
            case 0x32:
                    cprintf("\n\n STATUS:    Incorrect drive type
                    stored in CMOS (Compaq)");
                    break;
            case 0x40:
                    cprintf("\n\n STATUS: Seek operation failed");
                    break;
            case 0x80:
                    cprintf("\n\n STATUS:    Attachment failed to
                    respond(Disk Timed-out)");
                    break;
            case 0xB0:
                    cprintf("\n\n STATUS: Volume not locked in
                    drive (INT 13H extensions)");
                    break;
            case 0xB1:
                    cprintf("\n\n STATUS:    Volume locked in drive
                    (INT 13H extensions)");
                    break;
            case 0xB2:
                    cprintf("\n\n STATUS:    Volume not removable
                    (INT 13H extensions)");
                    break;
```

```
                    case 0xB3:
                        cprintf("\n\n STATUS:    Volume in use (INT
                        13 extensions)");
                        break;
                    case 0xB4:
                        cprintf("\n\n STATUS:    Lock count exceeded
                        (INT 13H extensions)");
                        break;
                    case 0xB5:
                        cprintf("\n\n STATUS:    Valid eject request
                        failed (INT 13H extensions)");
                        break;
                        default: cprintf("\n\n STATUS:    UNKNOWN Status
                        CODE
                        For Floppy Errors");
                }
        }
        return 0;
}
```

Comments on Program coding:

In this program coding, basically we are proceeding to perform the following these tasks step by step:

- Static character data buffer **dbuf[512]** is provided the information of 512 bytes in hexadecimal system, which is to be written in the first sector of unreadable floppy. **dbuf[512]** tells the computer during the operation that what information is to be written in the first sector of floppy. (See the Next Program)
- **dinfo** points to the **diskinfo_t** structure that contains the information of parameters required by the operation performed by the **_bios_disk** function.
- As we are going to write the information on the first sector of the disk therefore the location of the sector will be as follows:

Parameter	What it means
dinfo.drive = **0x00**	It indicates the drive **0** that is floppy disk drive (**a:**)
dinfo.head = 0	It points to head number **0**
dinfo.track = 0	It points to track **0**
dinfo.sector = 1	First sector of the floppy that is sector **1**
dinfo.sector = 1	Number of sectors to consider for write operation = **1**
dinfo.buffer = **dbuf**	Data buffer for the operation

- Initialize the disk system using the **interrupt 13H (function 00h)** where **regs.h.ah = 0x00** points to the function 00 H and **regs.h.dl = 0x00** is used for **a: floppy**. And **int86(0x13, &regs, &regs)** invokes MS-DOS interrupt service **INT 13 H.**

Data Recovery From Corrupted Floppy

- **_bios_disk(_DISK_WRITE, &dinfo)** writes the boot information from the specified file to the first (specified) sector of the floppy disk.

The status returned is stored in **result** that is used to display the message for successful operation or to display an error message on the screen if any error occurs.

Storing the boot Image in HEXADECIMAL Characters to use in our previous Program

It will be a very difficult job to write all 512 the characters of floppy's DOS Boot Record manually in hexadecimal system without any error in the program we recently discussed. If we can write it accurately even than it will be a difficult and time taking task to do this. Let us use some tricky mind to store the data for data buffer **dbuf[512]** in a file.

We know that in C programming the hexadecimal characters are represented with **0x** such that if hexadecimal character is A9 H, we shall write this in our C program as 0xA9. Our next program is doing the same. It will store the data that we need to write in our previous program, as the data of data buffer **dbuf[512]**.

What you have to do is just to take a fresh and new floppy to make the image of its DBR and copy the output of this program from the destination file specified and paste this data in your program. Do some formatting if required. Let us see how it works:

```
/*  Program to make the boot Image of the Floppy Disk In HEX Character
*/
#include <bios.h>
#include <stdio.h>
int main(void)
{
        struct diskinfo_t dinfo;
        union REGS regs;
        int result,i;
        int count=0;
        char fname[80];
        static char dbuf[512];
        FILE *fp;
        dinfo.drive   =   0x00;        /* drive number for A: */
        dinfo.head    =   0;           /* disk head number    */
        dinfo.track   =   0;           /* track number        */
        dinfo.sector  =   1;           /* sector number       */
        dinfo.nsectors =  1;           /* sector count        */
        dinfo.buffer  =   dbuf;        /* data buffer         */
        clrscr();
        gotoxy(10,3);cprintf("Enter The File Name And Path To Store The Boot Image in HEX System");
        gotoxy(5,5);
        gets(fname);
        fp=fopen(fname,"wb");
        if((fp=fopen(fname,"wb"))==NULL)
        {
```

```c
            highvideo();
            gotoxy(10,10);cprintf("File Could Not Be created");
            getch();
            exit(0);
        }
        /// Initialize the Disk System     \\\
        for(i=0; i<3; i++)
        {
            regs.h.ah = 0x00;    /* Reset Disk System */
            regs.h.dl = 0x00;    /* Floppy Disk a: */
            int86(0x13, &regs, &regs);
        }
        gotoxy(10,9);  cprintf("Attempting to read from Floppy disk drive :\n");
        result = _bios_disk(_DISK_READ, &dinfo);
        if ((result & 0xff00) == 0)
        {
            gotoxy(10,14);
            cprintf("Disk read from Floppy disk drive : successful.\n");
            while(count<512)
            {
                fprintf(fp,"0x%X, ",dbuf[count] & 0xff );
                count++;
            }
            fclose(fp);
        }
        else
        {
            gotoxy(10,14);
            cprintf("Cannot read drive A, status = 0x%02x\n",
                result);
        }
        return 0;
}
```

Comments on coding of the program:

Thus the data is stored in the specified file. Just copy the data to your program and do some required formatting. You should never forget the following tips through out the procedure:

- Make it sure that the operation of the program was successful and the data which has been stored in the destination file is the appropriate.
- You should check the operation through out for occurrence of expected errors.
- You must initialize the Floppy disk in, with the program before reading its boot sector. You may use function 00H of INT 13H for this purpose.

Method – 2
What to do if <u>Method – 1</u> doesn't work?

If the **Method – 1** does not work and the unreadable disk is not allowing the program to re-write the boot information on its first sector you should try this second method. The reason behind the failure of First Method may be the physical corruption of first sector of the floppy disk.

In this second method we are going to copy all the data of the surface of the unreadable Floppy to a single file temporarily and then we shall paste this image directly on the surface of the another good disk.

The procedure involves the following two important steps:
- Sector-by-Sector Copy all the data of the surface of floppy's media to a single file temporarily.
- Paste the data previously stored in file, to a new fresh floppy as it is, on the same sectors.

Copy all the data of media surface to a single file

To store all the data of the surface of media of floppy, the program must do the following three tasks:
- Initialize the disk properly with the help of function 00H of INT 13H.
- Read the Sector-by-Sector information of the surface and store to a single file.
- Check for the successful read operation (Most important)

It is very common to have any initialization problem with a floppy disk which leads many unsuccessful read messages. That is why the disk must be initialized before the read write operation with the help of programming.

It is most important and necessary step in case of any type of operations applied on floppy to check whether the operation was successful or not.

If Even after initialization the recently inserted floppy disk or changed floppy disk causes any reading error you are advised to run the program again, most probably it may work this time.

The following program is to perform these specified tasks. Let us see how it proceeds:

```
/* Program to store the data of physical surface of the floppy disk to
a file */
#include <bios.h>
#include <stdio.h>
void main(void)
{
        int head,track;
        union REGS regs;
        int result,i,sector;
        char filename[80];
        struct diskinfo_t dinfo;
        static char dbuf[512];
        FILE *tt;
        clrscr();
        printf("\n Enter The Name of file with Path to store The Data
        Temporarily\n");
```

```c
      gets(filename);
      if((tt=fopen(filename,"wb"))==NULL)
      {
            printf("Could Not Create The File,
            Press any Key To EXIT");
            getch();
            exit(0);
      }
      printf("\n Initializing Floppy Disk System...\n");
      /// Initialize the Disk System \\\
      for(i=0; i<3; i++)
      {
            regs.h.ah = 0x00;    /* Reset Disk System */
            regs.h.dl = 0x00;    /* Floppy Disk a:    */
            int86(0x13, &regs, &regs);
      }
      for(track=0;track<=79;track++)
      {
            for(head=0;head<=1;head++)
            {
                  for(sector=1;sector<=18;sector++)
                  {
                        dinfo.drive  =  0;    /* drive number for A: */
                        dinfo.head   =  head; /* disk head number*/
                        dinfo.track  =  track; /* track number */
                        dinfo.sector =  sector;   /* sector number */
                        dinfo.nsectors = 1;/* sector count   */
                        dinfo.buffer = dbuf; /* data buffer    */
                        result = _bios_disk(_DISK_READ, &dinfo);
                        if ((result & 0xff00) == 0)
                        {
                              for(i=0;i<512;i++)
                              fprintf(tt,"%c",dbuf[i] & 0xff);
                        }
                        else
                        {
                              printf("Cannot read drive A, status =
                              0x%02x\t%d\t%d\t%d\n",
                              result,head,track,sector);
                        }
                        printf("Reading Track= %d  Head= %d  Sector= %d\n",
                        track,head,sector);
                  }
            }
      }
}
```

Comments on Program coding:

In the program coding given earlier, basically we are proceeding to perform the following tasks step by step:

- Character array **filename[80]** stores the user defined path and file name of the file in which we are going to store the data temporarily.
- **dinfo** points to the **diskinfo_t** structure that contains the information of parameters required by the operation performed by the **_bios_disk** function.
- Initialize the disk system using the **interrupt 13H (function 00h)** where **regs.h.ah = 0x00** points to the function **00 H** and **regs.h.dl = 0x00** is used for **a: floppy**. And **int86(0x13, &regs, &regs)** invokes MS-DOS interrupt service **INT 13 H**.
- As we are going to read all the information of the surface of disk, The parameters of **_bios_disk** will be as follows:

Parameter	What it means
dinfo.drive = 0x00	It indicates the drive **0** that is floppy disk drive (**a:**)
dinfo.head = head	It points to head number **0 and 1** as floppy has two sides(two heads)
dinfo.track = track	It points to track **0 to 79** as there are **80 tracks** on each side of floppy.
dinfo.sector = sector	It points to sector **1 to 18** as there are **18 sectors** in each track.
dinfo.sector = 1	Number of sectors to consider for read operation = **1**
dinfo.buffer = dbuf	Data buffer for the operation

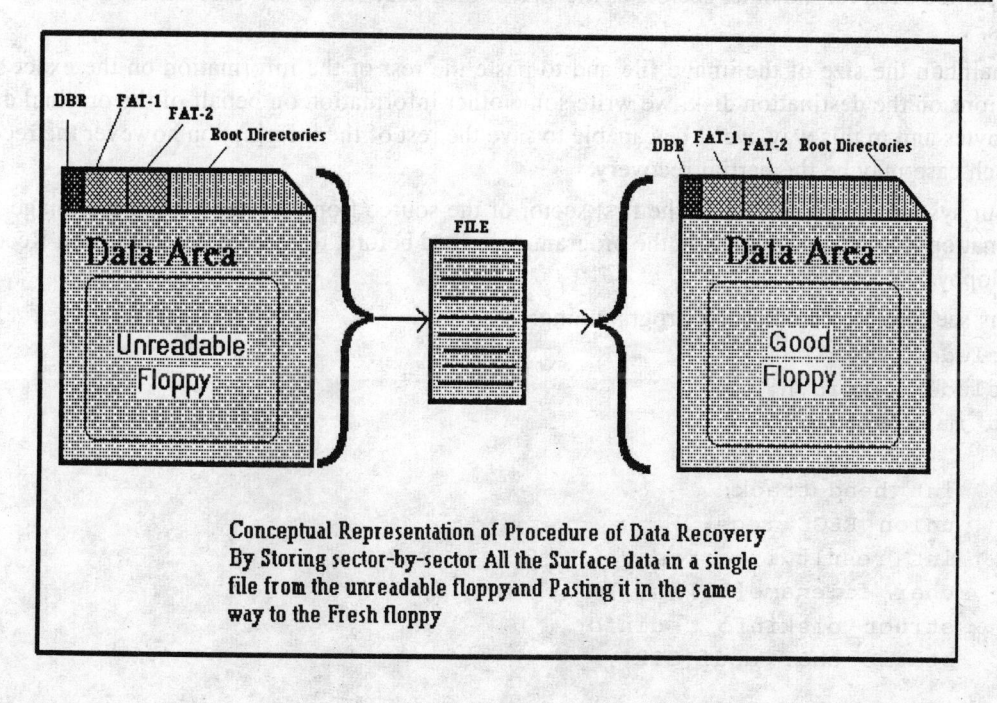

Conceptual Representation of Procedure of Data Recovery
By Storing sector-by-sector All the Surface data in a single
file from the unreadable floppy and Pasting it in the same
way to the Fresh floppy

- **_bios_disk(_DISK_READ, &dinfo)** reads the data from the physical surface of floppy disk from the sector specified by **dinfo**.
- The status returned is stored in **result** that is used to display the message for successful operation or to display an error message on the screen if any error occurs.

Always remember that the size of the file that holds the image of the floppy disk's data must be exact 1,474,560 bytes because the floppy has 80 tracks (0 to 79), 2 sides or heads (head 0 and head 1), each track has 18 sectors on it and each sector holds the 512 bytes of data, thus

Total bytes = (Number of tracks) * (Number of Heads) *
(Number of Sectors per Track) * 512

= 80*2*18*512

= 1,474,560 Bytes

Thus, if there is any error in reading at any sector of the floppy disk, it will change the size of the file from 1,474,560 Bytes, which will make the entire information completely or partially of no use for the destination disk on which we are going to write the disk image sector by sector from this file.

This is so because the Computer reads the information of any file on the surface of the media of the floppy disk within the sector range as it has been allocated in its allocation unit. Now if the sectors of the data of the files are changed, the complete file information is changed.

Thinking for the solution of sector(s) reading error

It is possible with the bad or unreadable floppy that it may have such bad area on its surface that we may not be able to read the information from the surface of the disk.

In this condition the information of this sector(s) will we skipped and the image of the floppy will be distorted even for the other sectors as the size of the image file in this case differs from 1,474,560 Bytes.

To maintain the size of the image file and to paste the rest of the information on the exact sector locations on the destination disk, we write some other information on behalf of the original data of 512 bytes and in this way, we'll be capable to save the rest of the information however the recovery in such case may be the partial recovery.

If your system also fails to read the first sector of the source floppy, after pasting the image to the destination floppy you should run the program described before, to rewrite the DOS Boot Record of the floppy.

Let us see how we can do it by programming:

```c
#include <bios.h>
#include <stdio.h>
void main(void)
{
    int head,track;
    union REGS regs;
    int result,i,sector;
    char filename[80];
    struct diskinfo_t dinfo;
    static char dbuf[512];
```

```c
/*Information of 512 Bytes to fill space of Bad Sector */
/// I used 512 zeros to fill the space of 512 bytes \\\
static char dbuf2[512] =
                    "00000000000000000000000000000000"
                    "00000000000000000000000000000000"
                    "00000000000000000000000000000000"
                    "00000000000000000000000000000000"
                    "00000000000000000000000000000000"
                    "00000000000000000000000000000000"
                    "00000000000000000000000000000000"
                    "00000000000000000000000000000000"
                    "00000000000000000000000000000000"
                    "00000000000000000000000000000000"
                    "00000000000000000000000000000000"
                    "00000000000000000000000000000000"
                    "00000000000000000000000000000000"
                    "00000000000000000000000000000000"
                    "00000000000000000000000000000000"
                    "00000000000000000000000000000000";
FILE *tt;
clrscr();
printf("\n Enter The Name of file with Path to store The
Data Temporarily\n");
gets(filename);
if((tt=fopen(filename,"wb"))==NULL)
{
    printf("Could Not Create The File, Press any Key To EXIT");
    getch();
    exit(0);
}
printf("\n Initializing Floppy Disk System...\n");
/// Initialize the Disk System \\\
for(i=0; i<3; i++)
{
    regs.h.ah = 0x00;    /* Reset Disk System */
    regs.h.dl = 0x00;    /* Floppy Disk a: */
    int86(0x13, &regs, &regs);
}
for(track=0;track<=79;track++)
{
    for(head=0;head<=1;head++)
    {
        for(sector=1;sector<=18;sector++)
        {
            dinfo.drive =  0;      /* drive number for A: */
            dinfo.head  =  head;   /* disk head number */
            dinfo.track =  track;  /* track number */
```

```
                dinfo.sector = sector;   /* sector number */
                dinfo.nsectors =  1; /* sector count */
                dinfo.buffer = dbuf; /* data buffer */
                result = _bios_disk(_DISK_READ, &dinfo);
                if ((result & 0xff00) == 0)
                {
                        for(i=0;i<512;i++)
                        fprintf(tt,"%c",dbuf[i] & 0xff);
                }
                else
                {
                        printf("Cannot read drive A, status =
                        0x%02x\t%d\t%d\t%d\n", result, head, track,
                        sector);
                        /* If Sector is not Readable, occupy 512 bytes
                        by dbuf2 */
                        fwrite(dbuf2,512,1,tt);
                }
                printf("Reading Track= %d  Head= %d  Sector= %d\n",
                track, head, sector);
            }
        }
    }
}
```

Comments on Program coding:

In the coding of the program, every step is same as in previous program except the data buffer **dbuf2[512]**, which we are using to handle the error generated by bad sector during the Disk reading operation and to maintain the size of the image file.

By doing this, we are filling the space of the information, which we failed to read from the bad sector and now we are writing the pseudo information of 512 bytes so that we may maintain the accuracy of disk image.

Paste the Data from the file to the physical surface of fresh floppy:

In this step, we paste the data stored in the file by the previous program, to the physical surface of the fresh floppy, sector by sector in the same way by which we copied it to the file.

The program proceeds with the following main steps:

- Open the file in which we stored the surface data of the unreadable floppy temporarily.
- Initialize the disk system properly by the resetting function **00H** of **INT 13H**.
- Write the information on the sectors of the fresh floppy from the file
- Display the write status simultaneously to find or avoid the occurrence of errors.

Data Recovery From Corrupted Floppy

The program source code has been given below. Let us examine how it works:

```c
/* Program to write the data on the sectors of the surface of fresh
floppy from the file, created by the previous program */
#include <bios.h>
#include <stdio.h>
void main(void)
{
    int head,track;
    union REGS regs;
    int result,i,sector;
    int count =0;
    char filename[80];
    struct diskinfo_t dinfo;
    static char dbuf[512];
    FILE *fp;
    clrscr();
    printf("\n Enter The Name of file with Path to store The
    Data Temporarily\n");
    gets(filename);
    if((fp=fopen(filename,"rb"))==NULL)
    {
        printf("Could Not Create The File, Press any Key To EXIT");
        getch();
        exit(1);
    }
    /// Initialize the Disk System \\\
    for(i=0; i<3; i++)
    {
        regs.h.ah = 0x00;      /* Reset Disk System    */
        regs.h.dl = 0x00;      /* Floppy Disk a:       */
        int86(0x13, &regs, &regs);
    }
    for(track=0;track<=79;track++)
    {
        for(head=0;head<=1;head++)
        {
            for(sector=1;sector<=18;sector++)
            {
                count =0;
                while(count<512  )
                {
                    fscanf(fp,"%c",&dbuf[count]);
                    count++;
                }
                dinfo.drive =   0x00;    /* drive number for A:*/
```

```
                    dinfo.head    =    head;    /* disk head number */
                    dinfo.track   =    track;   /* track number */
                    dinfo.sector  =    sector;  /* sector number */
                    dinfo.nsectors =   1;       /* sector count*/
                    dinfo.buffer  = dbuf;       /* data buffer */
                    result= _bios_disk(_DISK_WRITE, &dinfo);
                    if ((result & 0xff00) == 0)
                    printf("Successful write on Track = %d, Head = %d,
                    Sector = %d.\n", track, head, sector);
                    else
                    printf("Cannot read drive A, status = 0x%02x\n",
                    result);
            }
        }
    }
}
```

Comments on Program coding:

In the program coding given earlier, basically we are proceeding to perform the following tasks step by step:

- Character array **filename[80]** holds the path and file name of the file in which we stored the data of the surface of unreadable floppy temporarily.
- **dinfo** points to the **diskinfo_t** structure that contains the information of parameters required by the operation performed by the **_bios_disk** function.
- Initialize the disk system using the **interrupt 13H (function 00h)** where **regs.h.ah = 0x00** points to the function **00 H** and **regs.h.dl = 0x00** is used for **a: floppy**. And **int86(0x13, &regs, &regs)** invokes MS-DOS interrupt service **INT 13 H**.
- As we are going to write the information directly to sectors of the surface of disk, The parameters of **_bios_disk** will be as follows:

Parameter	What it means
dinfo.drive = 0x00	It indicates the drive **0** that is floppy disk drive (**a:**)
dinfo.head = head	It points to head number **0 and 1** as floppy has two sides(two heads)
dinfo.track = track	It points to track **0 to 79** as there are **80 tracks** on each side of floppy.
dinfo.sector = sector	It points to sector **1 to 18** as there are **18 sectors** in each track.
dinfo.sector = 1	Number of sectors to consider for write operation = **1**
dinfo.buffer = dbuf	Data buffer for the operation

- **_bios_disk(_DISK_WRITE, &dinfo)** writes the data on the sectors of the physical surface

Data Recovery From Corrupted Floppy 373

of floppy disk, specified by **dinfo**.

- The status returned is stored in **result** that is used to display the message for successful operation or to display an error message on the screen if any error occurs.

> If after the <u>Method – 2</u> your new floppy does not work, you may further apply <u>Method – 1</u> on your new floppy, which you used as destination disk during the <u>Method – 2</u>.
>
> Not only this but also the number of hits and trials may vary depending upon the corruption of the disk. But you need not to worry if even after you are not getting the satisfactory results.
>
> You can try file by file recovery or can try many more tips which you will learn in the next. Here we shall implement the idea of collecting the file information from Root Directories, in our programming to recover the data.

Thinking for Logical Recovery for Deleted or lost Data:

All the previous cases we discussed in this chapter for recovery, were to recover the data in such cases where we were expecting that only the DBR is corrupted and the sectors in track 0, having FAT1, FAT2 and Root directories are readable.

But if the problem is due to the corruption of FAT or the data has been deleted from the disk or you want to recover the data directly by reading its information from the Root directory, we need to read the information such as, Filename, starting cluster, size of the file, Attribute etc. from its Root directory entry.

As we have already discussed about Root Directory in earlier chapters that there is the information of 32 Bytes for each file or directory. These 32 Bytes are divided as follows:

Number of Bytes	Information Description
8 Bytes	Filename
3 Bytes	Extension
1 Byte	Attribute
10 Bytes	Reserved
2 Bytes	Time, Created or Last Updated
2 Bytes	Date, Created or Last Updated
2 Bytes	Starting Cluster
4 Bytes	File Size

We recover the data by reading the information of the file(s) from the Root Directory and then integrate the file to the destination path and recover the file. Our next program performs the following steps to recover the data:

- Read the Root Directory entries and Display them on the screen with all information such as File/Directory name, Extension of the File, Starting cluster size of the files in Bytes.

- Read the Files and Directories information in the Subdirectories and display them if required.
- Confirm the File name to be recovered and continue recovery.
- Calculate the CHS (Cylinder, Head, and Sector) info for the Specified file to be recovered.
- Integrate the data of the file from the data area of the disk and save the recovered file to the specified destination file name in specified path.

This Program does not care if the boot information of the floppy is readable or not. Therefore you can recover even deleted data from the corrupted floppy disk too. Let us see the coding of the program:

```c
/* Program to recover the data from the Floppy disk by Reading file
information from the Root Directory */
#include<stdio.h>
#include<bios.h>
#include<dos.h>
void main()
{
    void Display_Information(unsigned int,unsigned int, unsigned int);
    unsigned int track=0,head=1,sector=2;
    Display_Information(track,head,sector);
}  /*End of main */
void Display_Information(unsigned int track,
    unsigned int head,
    unsigned int sector)
{
    void recover(unsigned int *,unsigned int);
    char buf[512]; // Buffer of 512 Bytes char ch;
    struct diskinfo_t finfo;   //Structure, Used by _bios_disk
    unsigned int result,i,j, count=0;  /* Unsigned Integers Defined */
    unsigned int file_no; /* Unsigned Integer for File Number */
    struct
    {
        unsigned int name[8],ext[3];   /* File Name for DOS in 8.3
        (Eight Dot Three) Format */
        unsigned int attribute;  // File/Directory Attribute
        unsigned int start;      // Starting Cluster of the File
        long unsigned int size; // Size of the File in Bytes
    }root[32];                   /* 32 Bytes Information of
                                File/Directory in Root Directory */
    clrscr();
    do
    {
        file_no=0;
        finfo.drive  =  0x00;     /* drive number for A: */
        finfo.head   =  head;     /* disk head number    */
        finfo.track  =  track;    /* track number        */
        finfo.sector=  sector;    /* sector number       */
        finfo.nsectors=1;         /* sector count        */
```

```c
        finfo.buffer = buf;        /* data buffer          */
        result = _bios_disk(_DISK_READ, &finfo); /* Read the
                                                    Sector  */
        if( (result & 0xff00) != 0) /* If Read Error, Display
                                        Error Message and Exit*/
        {
                printf("Read error");
                getch();
                exit(0); // Go Back to DOS
        }
        /// Information Display Screen Format \\\
        clrscr();
        gotoxy(9,1);
        cprintf("DISPLAY CYLN: %u, HEAD: %u, SECTOR: %u",
        track, head, sector);
        gotoxy(9,2);
        cprintf("FNO  NAME      EXT ATTRIBUTE   START     SIZE");
        gotoxy(7,3);
        cprintf("————————————————————————");
        /* One Sector At a time. Every File/DIR entry Takes
        32 Byte */
        for(i=0;i<512;i+=32)
        {
                for(j=0;j<8;j++)
                {
                        /// Find The File/Dir Name \\\
                        root[file_no].name[j]=buf[j+i];
                }
                for(j=8;j<11;j++)
                {
                        /// Find the Extension \\\
                        root[file_no].ext[j-8]=buf[i+j];
                }
                j=11;
                root[file_no].attribute=buf[i+j];
                /// Attribute/// Starting Cluster \\\
                root[file_no].start=(0xff & buf[27+i])*16*16 + (0xff
                & buf[26+i]);
                /// Calculate the Size \\\
                root[file_no].size =(long unsigned int)(0xff &
                buf[31+i])*16*16*16*16*16*16*16*16;
                root[file_no].size+=(long unsigned int)(0xff &
                buf[30+i])*16*16*16*16;
                root[file_no].size+=(long unsigned int)(0xff &
                buf[29+i])*16*16;
                root[file_no].size+=(long unsigned int)(0xff &
```

```c
                    buf[28+i]);
                if((root[file_no].start == 0) ||
                    (root[file_no].attribute == 15))
                    continue;
                else
                {
                    gotoxy(8,i/32+4);
                    cprintf("%2u",file_no); /* Display File Number */
                    for(j=0;j<8;j++)
                    {
                        gotoxy(14+j,i/32+4);
                        cprintf("%c",root[file_no].name[j]);
                        /* Display File Name */
                    }
                    for(j=0;j<3;j++)
                    {
                        gotoxy(26+j,i/32+4);
                        cprintf("%c",root[file_no].ext[j]);
                        /* Display Extension */
                    }
                    gotoxy(30,i/32+4);
                    cprintf("%u",root[file_no].attribute);
                    /* Display Attribute */
                    if(root[file_no].attribute==16)
                    {
                        gotoxy(33,i/32+4);
                        cprintf("<DIR>"); /* Display if Directory
                                                Attribute */
                    }
                    else
                    {
                        gotoxy(33,i/32+4);
                        cprintf("<FILE>"); /*The Entry is of a file*/
                    }
                    gotoxy(44,i/32+4);
                    cprintf("%-5u",    root[file_no].start);
                    /* Display Starting Cluster */
                    gotoxy(58,i/32+4);
                    cprintf("%-10lu", root[file_no].size);
                    /* Fize of the File */
                }
            file_no++;
        }
    gotoxy(10,21);
    cprintf("Press 'M' : To see list of more files ");
    gotoxy(10,22);
```

Data Recovery From Corrupted Floppy

```
            cprintf("Press 'R' :To recover a file from the above list");
            ch=getch();
            switch(ch)
            {
                case 'm':    // "Press M/m to See the More Listings" Option
                case 'M':
                if(sector<18)
                sector++;
                else if(sector==18)
                {    sector=1;
                    if(head==0) head=1;
                    else if(head==1)
                    {    head=0;
                        if(track<70) track++;
                        else if(track==79)
                        track=0;
                    }
                }
                count++;
                break;
                case 'r':    // "Press R/r to Recover any File" option
                case 'R':
                //  "Recover File" Function recover(root,sizeof(root[0]));
                break;
                default:
                exit(0);
            }
    }while((ch=='M' || ch=='m') && count<12);
}
```

> Remember that the file name starting with σ (E5H) represents that the file has been deleted and therefore the first character of the filename has been replaced with σ (See the root directory description in the earlier chapters).

And the output of the program is displayed like this:

		DISPLAY CYLN: 0, HEAD: 1, SECTOR: 2			
FNO	NAME	EXT	ATTRIBUTE	START	SIZE
0	WE		32 <FILE>	15	1800
1	**σ2_INFO**	**C**	**32 <FILE>**	**5**	**4700**
2	THELP	CFG	32 <FILE>	2	22
3	THELP	COM	32 <FILE>	3	11072
4	TIMEIT	CPP	32 <FILE>	39	1186

5	TOUCH	COM	32 <FILE>	42	5124
6	TRY1	CPP	32 <FILE>	53	1581
7	TURBOC	CFG	32 <FILE>	57	30
8	AA	CPP	32 <FILE>	58	260
9	ABC	CPP	32 <FILE>	59	1036
10	ASSIGN1	CPP	32 <FILE>	62	4257
11	CH24_2	CPP	32 <FILE>	71	834
12	**σBSDISK1**	**C**	**32 <FILE>**	**73**	**911**
13	**σH24_25**	**C**	**32 <FILE>**	**75**	**594**
14	**σBSDISK**	**C**	**32 <FILE>**	**77**	**840**

Press 'M' : To see list of more files
Press 'R' : To recover a file from the above list **R**

DISPLAY CYLN: 0, HEAD: 1, SECTOR: 2

FNO	NAME	EXT	ATTRIBUTE	START	SIZE
0	WE		32 <FILE>	15	1800
1	**σ2_INFO**	**C**	**32 <FILE>**	**5**	**4700**
2	THELP	CFG	32 <FILE>	2	22
3	THELP	COM	32 <FILE>	3	11072
4	TIMEIT	CPP	32 <FILE>	39	1186
5	TOUCH	COM	32 <FILE>	42	5124
6	TRY1	CPP	32 <FILE>	53	1581
7	TURBOC	CFG	32 <FILE>	57	30
8	AA	CPP	32 <FILE>	58	260
9	ABC	CPP	32 <FILE>	59	1036
10	ASSIGN1	CPP	32 <FILE>	62	4257
11	CH24_2	CPP	32 <FILE>	71	834
12	**σBSDISK1**	**C**	**32 <FILE>**	**73**	**911**
13	**σH24_25**	**C**	**32 <FILE>**	**75**	**594**
14	**σBSDISK**	**C**	**32 <FILE>**	**77**	**840**

Enter FNO. of the file you want to recover **1**
You want to recover _2_INFO .C
Cylinder = 1, Head = 0, Sector = 1   Integrating........
Enter Path and Filename to recover the file:
c:\windows\desktop\H2_INFO.C
Recovery Done !!!

Comments on coding:

The function **Display_Information** is to read the file and directory information and from the root directory. In the Structure we are reading the 32 bytes information for every file or directory with **root[32]**.

The unsigned integer arrays **name[8]** and **ext[3]** are for File or Directory name for DOS in 8.3 (Eight Dot Three) Format. Similarly one byte is for attribute and two bytes for starting cluster. **long unsigned int size;** is to store the size of the file of four bytes.

The **_bios_disk** function reads the sector, specified by the structure **finfo** and the status of the operation is stored in **result**.

From the every information of 512 bytes read by the **_bios_disk** function, till the root directory area ends, we collect the information of the files and directories stored in the disk and display them on the screen.

The integer **file_no** is stores the number of the file or directory in the list, starting from 0. Generally the size of root directory is of 14 sectors and root directory generally starts from Cylinder =0, Head = 0 and Sector =2 in case of 1.44MB and 3½ floppy disk.

If user gives the character 'M' or 'm' as input, the information of next sector is displayed if the choice by user is 'R' or 'r' the recovery functions are called. The coding of the function **recover()** has been given below:

```
/* Function To Start Recovery for The Specified File */
void recover(unsigned int *root,unsigned int len)
{
    void clear_the_line(unsigned int r);   /* Function to Clear a Row
    on the Screen */
    /* Function to Integrate The Specified File */
    void integrate(long unsigned int,unsigned int,
    unsigned int,unsigned int);
    unsigned int file_no,i;
    char ch;
    unsigned int *loc;
    unsigned int cylinder,head,sector;
    unsigned int start;
    long unsigned int size;
    clear_the_line(21);  /* Clear The Row Number 21   */
    clear_the_line(22);  /* Clear The Row Number 22   */
    clear_the_line(23);  /* Clear The Row Number 23   */
    clear_the_line(24);  /* Clear The Row Number 24   */
    gotoxy(10,21);
    cprintf("Enter FNO. of the file you want to recover");
    scanf("%u",&file_no);         /* Get the File No. to be
    Recovered */
    loc=(root+(len*file_no/2));
    /* Confirm the file Name to be recovered    */gotoxy(10,22);
    cprintf("You want to recover");
    for(i=0;i<8;i++)
```

```
        {
            gotoxy(30+i,22);
            cprintf("%c",*(loc+i));   /* File name */
        }
        gotoxy(38,22);
        cprintf(".");
        for(i=0;i<3;i++)
        {
            gotoxy(39+i,22);
            cprintf("%c",*(loc+8+i));   /* File Extension */
        }
        start=*(loc+12);
        /// Sorry, You Selected a Directory \\\
        if(*(loc+11)==16)
        {
            gotoxy(5,23);
            cprintf("Is A directory. Do you want to see the contents
            of this directory Y/N");
            ch=getch();
            if(ch==27)
            main();
            if(ch=='y' || ch=='Y')
            {
                /* Calculate Geometry */
                calculate(start,&cylinder,&head,&sector);
                /* Display Directory Contents*/
                Display_Information(cylinder,head,sector);
            }
            else
            /* Ask for A file again and Continue Recovery */
            recover(root,len);
        }
        else
        {
            size=*(loc+13);
            /* Calculate for CHS info */
            calculate(start,&cylinder,&head,&sector);
            /* Integrate The File */
            integrate(size,cylinder,head,sector);
        }
}
```

Comments on coding:

The function **recover()** is to get the user input to start the recovery. The file number given as input by the user to recover the file, is stored in **file_no**.

If the entered number is for the Directory entry, **Display_Information()** shows the contents of that directory, else The file name and extension of file number **file_no** is displayed on the screen to confirm the file to be recovered.

To recover the specified file, the functions **calculate()** and **integrate()** are called within the function. The coding of the function **calculate()** has been given below:

```
/* Function To calculate the CHS Geomatry For The Recovery */
void calculate(unsigned int start,unsigned int *cylinder,
unsigned int *head,unsigned int *sector)
{
        unsigned int temp;
        *cylinder=0;
        *head=1;
        *sector=14;
        if(start<5)
        *sector=14+start;
        else
        {
            temp= (start-4)/18;
            if(temp>0)
            {
                if(temp%2==0)
                *head=0;
                else
                *head=1;
                *cylinder+=1+temp/2;
            }
            else
            {
                *head=0;
                *cylinder=1;
            }
            *sector=(start-4)%18;
        }
        /// Display The CHS of The File to Be Recovered \\\
        gotoxy(10,23);
        cprintf("Cylinder = %u, Head = %u, Sector = %u",
        *cylinder,*head,*sector);
}
```

Comments on coding:

The function **calculate()** is to calculate the Cylinder, Head and Sector information for the file to be recovered. After calculation the Cylinder, Head and Sector numbers are displayed on the screen.

The coding for the function **integrate()** has been given below:

```
/* Integrate File and Save the Recovered File To the Specified Path
```

```c
and File name */
void integrate(long unsigned int size,
unsigned int cylinder,
unsigned int head,
unsigned int sector)
{
      void clear_the_line(unsigned int);
      /*   Function to Verify The Sector for Errors */
      int verify_the_sector(unsigned int, unsigned int,
      unsigned int);
      int status;
      char buf[512],*Filename_with_path;
      struct diskinfo_t dinfo;
      unsigned int result;
      FILE *fp;
      unsigned int left,i;
      unsigned int sec;
      /* Enter The Destination Path and File Name to Save the Recovered
      file */
      gotoxy(2,24);
      cprintf("Enter Path and Filename to recover the file: ");
      fflush(stdin);
      gets(Filename_with_path);
      fp=fopen(Filename_with_path,"wb");
      /* If Error Occured Display Error Message and get input Path and
      File Name Again */
      if(fp==NULL)
      {
           gotoxy(5,25);
           cprintf("Error in opening the file");
           getch();
           clear_the_line(24);
           gotoxy(0,25);
           cprintf("                         ");
           integrate(size,cylinder,head,sector); /* Enter the Destination
           Again     */
      }
      /*   If Everything is all right, Integrate and write */
      gotoxy(50,23);
      cprintf("Integrating........");
      left= size%512;
      sec = size/512;
      sec++;
      while(sec>0)
      {
           dinfo.drive =   0x00;      /* drive number for A: */
```

```c
            dinfo.head   =   head;     /* disk head number  */
            dinfo.track  =   cylinder; /* track number      */
            dinfo.sector =   sector;   /* sector number     */
            dinfo.nsectors=1;          /* sector count      */
            dinfo.buffer = buf;        /* data buffer       */
            result = _bios_disk(_DISK_READ, &dinfo);
            /* If there is Error While Reading any Sector */
            if( (result & 0xff00) != 0)
            {
                gotoxy(5,25);
                cprintf("read error Cylinder %u, Head %u, Sector %u",
                cylinder, head, sector);
            }
            else
            {
                if(sec==1)
                {
                    for(i=0;i<left;i++)
                    fputc(buf[i],fp);   /* Write The Integrated
                    Information to the File */
                }
                else
                {
                    fwrite(buf,512,1,fp);
                }
                /// Varify The Sector For Error \\\
                status=verify_the_sector(cylinder,head,sector);
                if(status!=10)
                sec—;
            }
            if(sector<18)
            sector++;
            else if(sector==18)
            {   sector=1;
                if(head==0)  head=1;
                else if(head==1)
                {   head=0;
                    if(cylinder<70) cylinder++;
                    else if(cylinder==79)
                    cylinder=0;
                }
            }
        }
    fclose(fp);
    gotoxy(1,25);
```

```
        cprintf("           Recovery Done !!!                              ");
        getch();
}
```

Comments on coding:

The function **integrate()** is the actual module of performing the recovery of the user specified file, in this recovery program.

The file name with the destination path to store the recovered file is stored in the character pointer ***Filename_with_path**. If there is any error in opening the destination file, error message is displayed and user is prompt again to enter the destination.

The function **_bios_disk(_DISK_READ, &dinfo);** reads the data of the file from the data area of the disk sector by sector, specified by the structure **dinfo** and stored in the data buffer **buf**. This data of 512 bytes is written to the destination file. This is repeated until the complete file is integrated.

The function **status=verify_the_sector(cylinder,head,sector);** verifies the sector to be read. If the **status = 10**, it represents a bad (0xA) sector. The coding of the function has been given below:

```
/// Verify the Sector. (No Data is Transferred here) \\\
int verify_the_sector(unsigned int c,unsigned int h,unsigned int s)
{
        int status;
        char *buf;
        union REGS in, out;
        struct SREGS sg;
        in.h.ah = 0x04;              /* Function Number                  */
        in.h.al = 1;                 /* Number of Sectors to Verify */
        in.h.dl = 0x00;              /* Drive Number for A:              */
        in.h.ch = c;                 /* Cylinder Number                  */
        in.h.dh = h;                 /* Head Number                      */
        in.h.cl = s;                 /* Sector Number                    */
        in.x.bx = FP_OFF(buf);       /* Offset                           */
        sg.es   = FP_SEG(buf);       /* Segment                  */
        int86x(0x13,&in,&out,&sg);   /* Call the Function 4H of INT 13H */
        if(out.x.cflag)
        {
                status=out.h.ah;
        }
        return(status);
}
```

Comments on Coding:

The function **verify_the_sector()**, verifies sector to be read by the **_bios_disk()** function and returns the status of the operation. The function uses INT 13H and function 4H to verify the sector.

***buf** is the data buffer, 0x04 is the function number specified by **in.h.ah = 0x04;** and **in.h.al = 1;** instructs to verify the one sector at a time. **in.h.dl = 0x00;** is used for the drive number for floppy drive A:, **c,h**, and **s** are Cylinder, Head and Sector numbers.

The function **int86x()** is used to invoke INT 13H (function 4H) with segment register values. The status of the operation is returned by the integer **status**.

The function **clear_the_line()** clears the specified row on the screen. The coding of the function is as follows:

```
/* Function to clear the Line on the Screen, for Specified Row Number*/
void clear_the_line(unsigned int row)
{
      unsigned int column;
      /* There are 80 Columns in a Row (Line) */
      for(column=1;column<=80;column++)
      {
            gotoxy(column,row);
            cprintf(" ");          /* Clear With " "*/
      }
}
```

Comments on coding:

The function is used to clear the specified row on the screen. The function is called with the number of row, which is to be cleared from the screen.

Chapter – 11
Making Backups

Why Backups?

"The prevention is always better than the cure". Making backups is also an important part of prevention of data disaster, which may help us to overcome the disk crash or any other type of data loss. In this chapter, we shall discuss how we can recover the data even after some serious disk crashes, just only with the help of previously made backups.

The recovery done by the previously stored backups is, almost always up to 100 percent, however the several type of disk crash may cause the variation in the recovery results in some particular cases.

Recovering data with the help of backups is quite easy, fast and reliable and can give the best results whereas the data recovery without backups is a difficult, complicated may be a lot of time taking process and even then we are in fear of not getting the 100 percent data in several cases.

When and what to Back up

There are several different areas on the disk which should be backed up once or at different intervals of time. The following table gives the idea of complete back up measures and helps to find out that when and what to back up:

What to Backup	When to be Backed up
Backup of MBR	Once after FDISK. The MBR is Created By the FDISK command of DOS. You can take backup of MBR After FDISK, however even after the FORMAT of partitions created by FDISK, The MBR remains Unchanged.
Backup of DBR	Back up the DBRs for each logical drive once, after FORMAT.
Backup of FAT and Directory entries.	FAT and Directory Entries are changed every time when you create of delete files or directories. Therefore it is recommended that you should take backup daily.
Backup of User Data	Should be taken regularly. This type of backup causes the disk imaging to take place. However it is time taking yet most of the companies which have very sensitive data in their disks like to spend their time on disk imaging because by doing this they can backup all of the information described above.

Besides this you should make an Emergency Boot Floppy for the system. If there is any type of disaster with the data in you hard disk, you can boot your system with the help of this floppy and analyze the disk for errors.

Backup of MBR (Master Boot Record) and its use

The Master Boot Record (MBR) or sometimes referred as The master partition table (MPT), contains a small program to load and start the active (or bootable) partition from the hard disk drive. The Master boot Record contains information about all four primary partitions.

For a Detailed study about MBR, refer the chapter, "**Logical Approach to Disks and OS**", Discussed earlier in this book.

The MBR is located at Absolute Sector 0 or we can say at cylinder 0, head 0, and sector1. It is created on the hard disk drive by executing FDISK.EXE command of DOS.

Why Backup MBR?

MBR allows the boot sector of the active partition to receive the control when the system is started.

After the Power-On Self Test (POST), the BIOS loads the MBR (Master Boot Record) from the Hard Disk into memory and then executes it. First the MBR checks the Hard disk for an Active Partition, then it loads the DOS Boot Record (DBR) into memory and turns control over to the Operating System Boot code and then the Operating System Boot Record code loads the rest of the Operating System into Memory.

There for we can say that if the MBR of the Disk is corrupted, the hard disk is almost dead and the system is completely unable to boot or Run the Operating system. In such condition, all the data stored in the hard disk, becomes inaccessible. Generally The Error Messages are displayed as follows:

"Invalid partition table"

"Error loading operating system"

"Missing operating system"

What Can Be Recovered with the Backup of MBR?

The back up of MBR may help you to get rid of the above Error messages. With the backup, the Following problems can be rectified:

- Error Loading Operating system, due to Corrupted **IPL (Initial Program Loader)**
- Lost Primary Partition(s)
- Corrupted Partition information
- Invalid Magic Number

Writing the Program to make Backup of MBR:

```c
/* Program to make Backup of MBR */
#include <bios.h>
#include <stdio.h>
int main(void)
{
    struct diskinfo_t dinfo; /* Structure to Hold the
    information of disk Parameters */
    int result;
```

```c
    int count=0;
    char filename[80];      /* Stores the File name given by User */
    static char dbuf[512];  /* Data Buffer of 512 Bytes */
    FILE *fp;
    dinfo.drive  =  0x80;   /* drive number for First Hard Disk */
    dinfo.head   =  0;      /* disk head number */
    dinfo.track  =  0;      /* track number                     */
    dinfo.sector =  1;      /* sector number                    */
    dinfo.nsectors = 1;     /* sector count                     */
    dinfo.buffer = dbuf;    /* data buffer                      */
    printf("\n Enter The Filename and path to store the Backup of MBR
     \n ");
    gets(filename);
    // Open The File to Store the MBR Backup \\
    if((fp=fopen(filename,"wb"))==NULL)
    {
        printf("Could not Create File, Press any key to
        Exit...");
        getch();
        exit(0);
    }
    printf("Attempting to read from Hard disk drive :\n");
    //// Read the Specified Disk Sector \\\\
    result = _bios_disk(_DISK_READ, &dinfo);
    if ((result & 0xff00) == 0)
    {
        printf("Disk read from hard disk drive : successful.\n");
        /// Write 512 Bytes Of MBR to the File \\\\
        while(count<512)
        {
            fprintf(fp,"%c",dbuf[count] & 0xff );
            count++;
        }
        fclose(fp);
    }
    else
    printf("Cannot read Hard Disk drive, status = 0x%02x\n", result);
    return 0;
}
```

Comments on Program coding:

In the program coding given earlier, basically we are proceeding to perform the following tasks step by step:

- **dinfo** points to the **diskinfo_t** structure that contains the information of parameters required

Making Backups

by the operation performed by the **_bios_disk** function.

- Since we want to read first sector of the disk therefore the location of the sector will be as follows:

Parameter	What it means
dinfo.drive = **0x80**	It indicates the Physical drive **80H** that is the first Hard disk drive.
dinfo.head = **0**	It points to head number **0**
dinfo.track = **0**	It points to track **0**
dinfo.sector = **1**	First sector of the floppy that is sector **1**
dinfo.sector = **1**	Number of sectors to consider for read operation = **1**
dinfo.buffer = **dbuf**	Data buffer for the operation

- Open a file stream of user given file name and path to store the backup of MBR of exact 512 bytes. The file name and path is stored in the character array **filename**.
- **_bios_disk(_DISK_READ, &dinfo)** reads the first sector of the hard disk (80H), specified by **dinfo**.
- The status returned, is stored in **result** that is used to display the message for successful operation or to display an error message on the screen if any error occurs.

Program to Restore the MBR from Backup:

If the MBR is corrupted any how, the program given next helps to restore the MBR Back.

It should always be kept in mind that the illegal use or use in lack of knowledge may of this program, may destroy your data information in the hard disk and may make the entire data inaccessible. You should be sure of what you are going to do. Otherwise you may more complicate the problem.

The Coding of the program is as follows:

```
/*   Program to Restore the Backup of MBR From the Backup File */
#include <bios.h>
#include <stdio.h>
int main(void)
{
    struct diskinfo_t dinfo;
    int result;
    int count=0;
    char filename[80];   /* Stores the File name given by User */
    static char dbuf[512];    /* Data Buffer of 512 Bytes */
    FILE *fp;
    /* Get the user Input for MBR Backup file Path */
    printf("\n Enter The Filename and path of Backup File of MBR \n
");
    gets(filename);
    if((fp=fopen(filename,"rb"))==NULL)
    {
```

```c
        printf("Could not open Backup File, Press any key to Exit...");
        getch();
        exit(1);
    }
    /* MBR data should be of Exact 512 Bytes */
    while(count<512)
    {
        fscanf(fp,"%c",&dbuf[count]);
        count++;
    }
    fclose(fp);
    printf("Attempting to Write to Hard disk drive :\n");
    dinfo.drive =  0x80;/* drive number for First Hard Disk */
    dinfo.head  =  0;   /* disk head number           */
    dinfo.track =  0;   /* track number               */
    dinfo.sector   =  1; /* sector number             */
    dinfo.nsectors =  1; /* sector count              */
    dinfo.buffer = dbuf; /* data buffer               */
    result = _bios_disk(_DISK_WRITE, &dinfo);
    if ((result & 0xff00) == 0)
    {
        printf("Restoring the Backup of MBR to The Disk Sector:
        successful.\n");
    }
    else
    printf("Cannot Write on Hard Disk drive, status = 0x%02x\n", result);
    return 0;
}
```

Comments on Program coding:

In the program coding given above, basically we are proceeding to perform the following tasks step by step:

- **dinfo** points to the **diskinfo_t** structure that contains the information of parameters required by the operation performed by the **_bios_disk** function.
- Since we want to write on first sector of the disk therefore the location of the sector will be as follows:

Parameter	What it means
dinfo.drive = **0x80**	It indicates the Physical drive **80H** that is the first Hard disk drive.
dinfo.head = **0**	It points to head number **0**
dinfo.track = **0**	It points to track **0**
dinfo.sector = **1**	First sector of the floppy that is sector **1**
dinfo.sector = **1**	Number of sectors to consider for read operation = **1**
dinfo.buffer = **dbuf**	Data buffer for the operation

- The file name and path of Backup of MBR, given by the user, is stored in the character array **filename**. It should be kept in mind that the MBR information should of Exact 512 bytes.

- **_bios_disk(_DISK_WRITE, &dinfo)** writes the data on the first sector of the hard disk (80H), specified by **dinfo**.

- The status returned, is stored in **result** that is used to display the message for successful operation or to display an error message on the screen if any error occurs.

Backup of DBR (DOS Boot Record) and its use

After the partition table, the DOS Boot Record (DBR) or sometimes called DOS Boot Sector is the second most important information on your hard drive.

For a Detailed study about DBR, refer the chapter, "**Logical Approach to Disks and OS**", Discussed earlier in this book.

First logical sector of each DOS partition will contain a DOS Boot Record (DBR) or DOS Boot Sector. The job of the DBR is to load the operating system from the hard disk drive into the main memory of computer and give the system's control to the loaded program.

The DOS Boot Record (DBR) for the first partition on a hard disk is usually found at Absolute Sector 63 (the 64th sector on the disk drive) or in CHS form we can say C–H–S = 0–1–1 for most drives.

However this location may vary depending upon the SPT (Sectors per Track) of the Drive. For example, on an old 245MB drive having only 31 SPT, the Boot Record was located on the 32nd sector (Absolute Sector 31).

The DBR is created by the FORMAT command of DOS, after partitioning is done using the FDISK command. The sector on which DBR resides becomes logical sector 1 of that particular partition for the DOS. The sector number used by DOS starts from the physical sector on which DBR is located.

The DBR contains a small program which is executed by the Master Boot Record (MBR) Executable program. All DOS partitions contain the program code to boot the machine i.e. load the operating system, but only that partition is given control by the Master Boot Record which as specified as active partition, in the partition table entry.

Why Backup DBR:

The DBR contains some important information about the disk geometry. This information is located in the first sector of every partition, such as:

- Jump Code + NOP
- OEM Name and Version
- Bytes Per Sector
- Sectors Per Cluster
- Reserved Sectors
- Number of Copies of FAT
- Maximum Root Directory Entries (but Not Available for FAT32)
- Number of Sectors in Partition Smaller than 32MB (Therefore Not Available for FAT32)
- Media Descriptor (F8H for Hard Disks)

- Sectors Per FAT (In Older FAT Systems and Not Available for FAT32)
- Sectors Per Track
- Number of Heads
- Number of Hidden Sectors in Partition
- Number of Sectors in Partition
- Number of Sectors Per FAT
- FAT Information Descriptor Flags
- Version of FAT32 Drive
- Cluster Number of the Start of the Root Directory
- Sector Number of the File System Information Sector
- Sector Number of the Backup Boot Sector
- Reserved
- Logical Drive Number of Partition
- Extended Signature (29H)
- Serial Number of Partition
- Volume Name of Partition
- FAT Name
- Executable Code
- Executable Marker or Magic Number (AAH 55H)

Generally, the following error messages are displayed on the screen:

"Disk boot failure"
"Non system disk or disk error"
"Invalid system disk or Disk I/O error"
"Replace the disk, and then press any key…"

What can be recovered with the Backup of DBR?

The back up of DBR may help you to get rid of the above Error messages. These Error Messages On the screen wait for the user to put a bootable disk with the above mentioned programs in the floppy drive and press a key.

The drive should be accessible if you boot the system from the bootable floppy or CD. Although the hard disk is not bootable, yet generally that should not affect access to the data of the disk drive. After booting the system with the bootable disk you can access the data.

By restoring the backup of DBR You can overcome the problems generated, as mentioned above.

Programs for Making and Restoring Backups of DBR:

The programs for making the Backups of DBR's and restoring them are almost similar to the programs of MBR backup and to restore.

For example, if you are going to write the programs for making backup of DBR of First logical drive of the disk and to restore it back, the parameters specified by **dinfo** structure will be changed as follows:

Parameter	What it means
dinfo.drive = **0x80**	It indicates the Physical drive **80H** that is the first Hard disk drive.
dinfo.head = **1**	It points to head number **1**
dinfo.track = **0**	It points to track **0**
dinfo.sector = **1**	First sector of the floppy that is sector **1**
dinfo.sector = **1**	Number of sectors to consider for read operation = **1**
dinfo.buffer = **dbuf**	Data buffer for the operation

Here we see that only the location of the sector to read/write is changed. Here the C-H-S is given as 0-1-1 as the DBR of first logical drive is stored here.

Complete Disk Imaging

This type of backup is getting more and more popular now days and most preferred by such organizations which have very sensitive data in their systems. They people can not take any chance of even a single percent of data loss.

Such organizations take their backups as entire disk image regularly. Though it is some time taking but gives you surety that you will miss nothing. Due to its increasing popularity, programmers have tried their best to make the disk imaging software more and more faster to minimize the time period taken by the imaging process.

Disk imaging is a good Idea because just by spending some tens of minutes you can get the ease of mind that you have backup of everything in your pocket. All of the factors like MBR, BDR, FATs, Root Directories are copied to the destination disk as it is.

What we need for disk imaging is an Identical (or almost Identical) destination hard disk, to our source hard disk in which we have our valuable data. One thing is always kept in mind that the destination disk should not be smaller then the source disk.

After taking the complete image, if you boot the system with the destination disk, in which you have taken the disk image, generally you will get all the data as it is.

Writing the program for complete disk imaging

The program for disk imaging has been given next. The Program uses the INT 13H extensions therefore it can support large disks too.

The program makes the image of first physical hard disk drive (0x80) to the second physical hard disk drive (0x81) therefore before making the backup image you should keep it in mind that all the data in destination disk (0x81) will be overwritten by the data of source disk (0x80) in sector by sector pattern.

The coding of the program has been given next:

```
/* Program to make the Image of First Hard Disk (0x80) to the second
Hard Disk (0x81) */
#include<stdio.h>
#include<dos.h>
#include<conio.h>
/* Structure to be used by getdrivegeometry function using INT 13H
```

Extension, Function Number 0x48. */
```c
struct geometry
{
    unsigned    int size ;   /* (call) size of Buffer */
    unsigned    int flags ;  /* Information Flags    */
    unsigned    long cyl ;   /* Number of Physical Cylinders on Drive*/
    unsigned    long heads ; /* Number of Physical Heads on Drive */
    unsigned long spt ;      /* Number of Physical Sectors Per Track */
    unsigned long sectors[2] ; /* Total Number of Sectors on Drive */
    unsigned int bps ;       /* Bytes Per Sector */
} ;

/* Structure of Disk Address packet format, To be used by the Functions,
readabsolutesectors and writeabsolutesectors   */
struct diskaddrpacket
{
    char packetsize ; /* Size of Packet, generally 10H */
    char reserved ;   /* Reserved (0)                 */
    int blockcount ;  /* Number of Blocks to Transfer  */
    char far *bufferaddress ; /* address to Transfer Buffer */
    unsigned long blocknumber[2]; /* Starting Absolute Block Number*/
} ;

///// Function to get Drive Parameters \\\\\
unsigned long getdrivegeometry (int drive)
{
    union REGS i, o ;
    struct SREGS s ;
    struct geometry g = { 26, 0, 0, 0, 0, 0, 0, 0 };i.h.ah = 0x48 ;
    /* Function Number 0x48 of INT 13H Extensions See the Comments
    Below    */
    i.h.dl = drive;    /* Drive Number          */
    i.x.si = FP_OFF ( (void far*)&g ) ;
    s.ds = FP_SEG ( (void far*)&g ) ;
    /* Invoke the specified function number of INT 13H extension with
    Segment Register Values*/
    int86x ( 0x13, &i, &o, &s ) ;
    printf("\n Head = %lu, Sectors Per Track = %lu, Cylinder = %lu\n",
    g.heads, g.spt, g.cyl);
    /* If get drive Geometry function Fails, Display Error Message
    and Exit*/
    if(g.spt==0)
    {
        printf("\n Get Drive Geometry Function Fails....");
        printf("\n Extensions Not Supported, Press any Key to Exit...");
        getch();
```

Making Backups

```c
            exit(1);
    }
    return *g.sectors;   /* Return The Number of Sectors on Drive */
}

////// Start Of Main \\\\\\
void main()
{
    unsigned long loop=0, Sectors_in_HDD1=0, Sectors_in_HDD2=0;
    unsigned char buffer[61440]; /* Data buffer of 61440
    Bytes to Read/Write   120 Sectors of 512 Bytes at a time to save
    time. */
    char choice;
    clrscr();
    /*  If total no. of hard disks attached is less than two Display
    Error Message and Exit.    */
    if(((char)peekb(0x0040, 0x0075))<2)
    {
        printf("\n\n You Must Have At least Two Hard Disks
        Attached to your Computer To Run This");
        printf("\n Program. Press any Key to Exit... ");
        getch();
        exit(1);
    }
    /// Get parameters of First Hard Disk (0x80) \\\
    Sectors_in_HDD1 = getdrivegeometry (0x80);
    printf(" Total Sectors in First Hard Disk = %lu\n\n",
    Sectors_in_HDD1);
    /// Get Parameters of Second Hsrd Disk (0x81) \\\
    Sectors_in_HDD2 = getdrivegeometry (0x81);

    printf(" Total Sectors in Second Hard Disk = %lu\n\n",
    Sectors_in_HDD2);
    /// First Confirm, Then Proceed \\\
    printf("\n All The Data in Second Hard Disk will be lost !!!");
    printf("\n Press \'Y\' to Continue, Else any key to
    Exit...    ");
    choice = getche();
    switch(choice)
    {
        case 'y':
        case 'Y':
        break;
        default:
        exit(0);
    }
```

```c
            /* Destination should not be smaller than the Source */
            if(Sectors_in_HDD2<Sectors_in_HDD1)
            {
                printf("\n\n Destination Disk should not be Smaller than Source
                Disk");
                printf("\n Press any Key to Exit...");
                getch();
                exit(0);
            }
            /* If Everything is okay, copy All the Sectors of the Source Disk
            to Destination Hard Disk */
            gotoxy(10,15);printf("Copying Absolute Sector: ");
            for(loop=0;loop<=Sectors_in_HDD1;loop=loop+120)
            {
                readabsolutesectors ( 0x80, loop, 120, buffer );
                writeabsolutesectors ( 0x81, loop, 120, buffer );
                gotoxy(36,15); printf("%ld",loop);
                if(kbhit())
                {
                    exit(0);
                }
            }
            //// Show the Message of Completion \\\
            printf("\n\n Disk Imaging is Now Completed, Press any Key To
            Exit...");
            getch();
} //// End of main
```

Comments on Coding:

In the coding of the program given earlier, for disk Imaging We are proceeding by performing the Following tasks:

- The Structure, **geometry** is used by **getdrivegeometry** function using **INT 13H Extension, Function Number 0x48**. For a Detailed description on INT 13H Extensions, refer the chapter "Handling large hard disks", Discussed earlier in this book.

The Data Types representing several parameters of the disk have the following meanings:

Data Type	Size in Bytes	Description
unsigned int **size**	2 Bytes	Size of Buffer
unsigned int **flags**	2 Bytes	Information Flags
unsigned long **cyl**	4 Bytes	Number of Physical Cylinders on Drive
unsigned long **heads**	4 Bytes	Number of Physical Heads on Drive
unsigned long **spt**	4 Bytes	Number of Physical Sectors Per Track
unsigned long **sectors[2]**	8 Bytes	Total Number of Sectors on Drive
unsigned int **bps**	2 Bytes	Bytes Per Sector

- The structure **diskaddrpacket** is used by the functions **readabsolutesectors** and **writeabsolutesectors**. The format of disk address packet has been given in the following table:

Data Type	Size in Bytes	Description
char **packetsize**	1 Byte	Size of Packet, generally 10H
char **reserved**	1 Byte	Reserved (0)
int **blockcount**	2 Bytes	Number of Blocks to Transfer
char far ***bufferaddress**	4 Bytes	address to Transfer Buffer
unsigned long **blocknumber[2]**	4 Bytes	Starting Absolute Block Number

The **getdrivegeometry** function is used to get the parameters of specified Drive. The Function **getdrivegeometry** uses function number 0x48 of INT 13H Extensions.

The meaning of parameters has been described in the table given next:

Parameter	What it means
i.h.ah = 0x48	Function Number 0x48 of INT 13H Extensions
i.h.dl = drive	Drive Number
i.x.si = FP_OFF ((void far*)&g)	ds:si address to buffer for drive parameters as discussed earlier
s.ds = FP_SEG ((void far*)&g)	ds:si address to buffer for drive parameters as discussed earlier

The **int86x(0x13, &i, &o, &s)** function invokes the interrupt 13H with segment register Values. The **getdrivegeometry** function returns the total number on drive.

- In the **main()** function, **(char)peekb(0x0040, 0x0075);** (the function **peekb** is Defined in DOS.H) returns the number of hard disks attached to the system.

    The number of hard disks connected to the system is represented by the byte stored at memory location **0040H:0075H (Segment 0040H: Offset 0075H)**. If the number of hard disks connected to the system is less then two program shows the error message and exits.

    Sectors_in_HDD1 = getdrivegeometry (0x80); gets the parameters of first hard disk (0x80) and returns the total number of sectors on first hard disk.

    Similarly **Sectors_in_HDD2 = getdrivegeometry (0x81);** gets the parameters of second hard disk (0x81) and returns the total number of sectors on second hard disk.

    After confirmation by the user to continue with imaging, first check the condition that the size of source hard disk should not be greater then the size of the destination hard disk. If the destination is smaller, Display the error message and exit.

    If everything is going right, copy the sectors of the source disk to the destination disk. Here we are reading and writing **61440 Bytes (120 sectors with each of 512 Bytes)** at a time to make the imaging process faster.

    If you want to use more sectors at a time, even beyond the limit of 64K, you can do it by

using **"huge Pointer"** in large memory model. The Example of Specification is as follows:
   char huge array[100000L];

- The Function, **readabsolutesectors (0x80, loop, 120, buffer)**; reads the 120 sectors of first hard disk (0x80), starting from the sector number specified by unsigned long integer **loop** and store the data in data buffer.

- The Function, **writeabsolutesectors (0x81, loop, 120, buffer)**; writes the data of data buffer to 120 sectors of second hard disk (0x81), starting from the sector number specified by unsigned long integer **loop.**

The coding of the functions **readabsolutesectors ( )** and **writeabsolutesectors ( )** have been given next:

```
//// Function to read absolute sector(s) \\\\
int readabsolutesectors ( int drive,
unsigned long sectornumber,
int numofsectors,
void *buffer )
{
      union REGS i, o ;
      struct SREGS s ;
      struct diskaddrpacket pp ;
      pp.packetsize = 16 ;        /* packet size = 10H      */
      pp.reserved = 0 ;    /* Reserved = 0              */
      pp.blockcount = numofsectors ; /* Number of sectors to read*/
      /* for Data buffer */
      pp.bufferaddress = (char far*) MK_FP ( FP_SEG((void far*)buffer),
      FP_OFF((void far*)buffer));
      pp.blocknumber[0] = sectornumber ; /* Sector number to read*/
      pp.blocknumber[1] = 0 ; /* Block number */
      i.h.ah = 0x42 ;      /* Function Number*/
      i.h.dl = drive ;     /* Physical Drive Number */
      i.x.si = FP_OFF ( (void far*)&pp ) ; /*ds:si for buffer Parameters*/
      s.ds = FP_SEG ( (void far*)&pp ) ;        /* ds:si for buffer
                                                   Parameters */
      /* Invoke the specified Function of INT 13H with segment  register
      values   */
      int86x ( 0x13, &i, &o, &s ) ;
      if ( o.x.cflag==1)
      return 0 ;   /*failure    */
      else
      return 1 ;   /* success  */
}

//// Function to Write Absolute Sector(s) \\\\
int writeabsolutesectors (int drive, unsigned long sectornumber, int numofsectors,void *buffer )
{
```

```c
    union REGS i, o ;
    struct SREGS s ;
    struct diskaddrpacket pp ;
    pp.packetsize = 16 ;         /* Packet Size = 10H      */
    pp.reserved = 0 ;    /* Reserved   = 0         */
    pp.blockcount = numofsectors ; /* Number of Sectors to be written*/
    /* for Data buffer   */
    pp.bufferaddress = (char far*) MK_FP ( FP_SEG((void far*)buffer),
    FP_OFF((void far*)buffer));
    pp.blocknumber[0] = sectornumber ;/* Sector number to be written*/
    pp.blocknumber[1] = 0 ; /* Block number = 0   */
    i.h.ah = 0x43 ;              /* Function Number   */
    i.h.al = 0x00 ;              /* Write Flags, see comments */
    i.h.dl = drive ;             /* Physical Drive number*/
    /* ds:si for buffer Parameters */
    i.x.si = FP_OFF ( (void far*)&pp ) ;
    /* ds:si for buffer Parameters */
    s.ds = FP_SEG ( (void far*)&pp ) ;
    /* Invoke the specified Function of INT 13H with segment  register
    values */
    int86x ( 0x13, &i, &o, &s ) ;
    if ( o.x.cflag==1)
    return 0 ;    /* failure */
    else
    return 1 ;    /* success  */
}
```

Comments on Coding:

The parameters used by both the function have the following meanings:

Parameter	Size in Bytes	Description
pp.packetsize = 16 ;	1 Byte	Size of packet = 10H
pp.reserved = 0 ;	1 Byte	Reserved = 0
pp.blockcount = **numofsectors** ;	2 Bytes	Number of sectors to read
pp.bufferaddress = **(char far*) MK_FP (FP_SEG((void far*) buffer), FP_OFF ((void far*)buffer));**	———	for Data buffer or Transfer Buffer
pp.blocknumber[0] = **sectornumber ;**	4 Bytes	Sector number to read/write (generally, we need only this). Only alone This can support up to 2.1 Terabytes.

pp.blocknumber[1] = 0 ;	4 Bytes	Block number. Use this, If accessing the disk of greater then 2.1 Terabytes in size.
i.h.ah = 0x42 ; <u>or</u> i.h.ah = 0x43 ;	2 Bytes	Function Number of INT 13H Extensions
i.h.al = 0x00 ;	1 Byte	Write Flags used in write function only, 00H, 01H are used for Write Without Verify and 02H is used for write with verify
i.h.dl = **drive** ;	2 Bytes	Physical Drive Number
i.x.si = FP_OFF ((void far*)&pp) ;	——	ds:si for buffer Parameters
s.ds = FP_SEG ((void far*)&pp) ;	——	ds:si for buffer Parameters
int86x (0x13, &i, &o, &s) ;	——	Invoke the specified Function of INT 13H with segment register values

Chapter – 12
Reading and Modifying MBR with Programming

Master Boot Record (MBR) or Master Partition Table (MPT)

The Master Boot Record (MBR) or sometimes referred as The master partition table (MPT), is created on the hard disk drive by executing FDISK.EXE command of DOS.

The MBR contains a small program to load and start the active (or bootable) partition from the hard disk drive. The Master boot Record contains information about all four primary partitions on the hard disk drive such as the starting sector, ending sector, size of the partition etc.

The MBR is located at Absolute Sector 0 or we can say at cylinder 0, head 0, and sector1 and if there is more than one partition are present in the disk there are Extended Master Boot Records, located at the beginning of each extended partition volume.

For detailed description refer the chapter "**Logical Approach to Disks and OS**", discussed earlier in this book.

Master boot record format

We may partition the Hard Disk Drive into several logical drives which are generally assigned their own drive letter by DOS). Only one partition at a time can be marked as the active (or bootable) Partition.

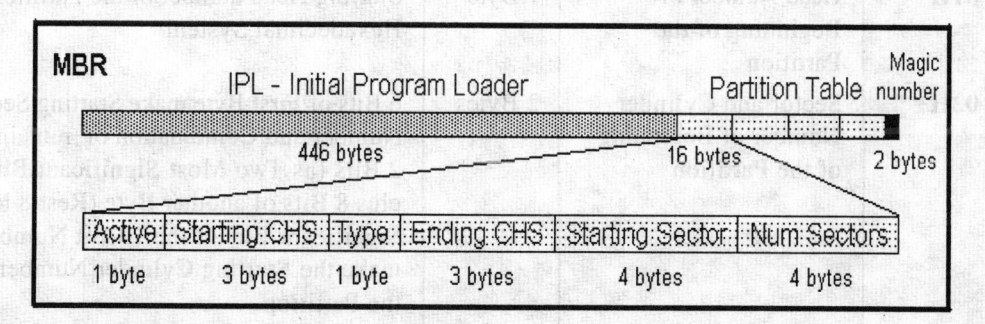

The Master Boot Record has the limit of four entries in the Master Partition Table. However the location of Extended Master Boot Record can be obtained with the help of Master Boot Record that contains Extended Partition Tables, whose format is exactly the same as of the main Partition Table except there is no boot code and this space of 446 Bytes is normally reserved for the boot code and remains empty.

All the 512Bytes of The Master Boot Record are Broken as follows, given in the Table:

Offset	Description	Size
000H	**Initial Program Loader (IPL)**, Executable Code (Provides very first booting to the Computer)	446 Bytes
1BEH	First Partition Entry (See Next Table)	16 Bytes
1CEH	Second Partition Entry	16 Bytes
1DEH	Third Partition Entry	16 Bytes
1EEH	Fourth Partition Entry	16 Bytes
1FEH	Executable Marker or Bootable Sector Signature or Magic Number (AAH 55H)	2 Bytes
		Total = 512 Bytes

All the extended partitions should exist within the space reserved by the extended partition entry. Only two of the extended partitions are meant to be used, the first as a normal partition and the second as another extended partition if exists.

Thus with the help of one Master Partition Table We can get the location of another Extended Master Partition Table next to it, if present.

Partition Table Entry Format

The format of partition table entry of any Partition in MBR has been given in the next table. Every Partition Entry of any MBR may be broken into the following bytes with their specific meanings:

Offset	Meaning	Size	Description
00H	Boot Type Indicator Byte	1 Byte	If Byte is **00H,** the Partition is Inactive and if Byte is **80H**, The Partition is Active (or Bootable)
01H	Head Number of Beginning of the Partition	1 Byte	Starting Head number of the Partition in Hexadecimal System
02H	Sector and Cylinder Number of Beginning of the Partition	2 Bytes	6 Bits of First Byte make Starting Sector Number and Combination of remaining 2 Bits (as Two Most Significant Bits) plus 8 Bits of another Byte (Rest 8 least Significant Bits of the 10-Bit Number) make the Starting Cylinder Number of the Partition
04H	File System indicator Byte	1 Byte	File System Indicator Byte in Hexadecimal system

Reading and Modifying MBR with Programming

05H	Head Number of End of the Partition	1 Byte	Ending Head Number of the Partition in Hexadecimal System
06H	Sector and Cylinder Number of End of the Partition	2 Bytes	6 Bits of First Byte make Ending Sector Number and Combination of remaining 2 Bits (as Two Most Significant Bits) plus 8 Bits of another Byte (Rest 8 least Significant Bits of the 10-Bit Number) make the Ending Cylinder Number of the Partition
08H	Absolute Sector number of Beginning of the Partition	4 Bytes	Number of Sectors Between the MBR and the First Sector in the Partition
0CH	Absolute Sector number of End of the Partition	4 Bytes	Number of Sectors in the Partition
		Total = 16 Bytes	

Writing program to read the partition table of MBR

The program to read all four partition entries from partition table of MBR has been given next. The program displays all the parameters of partition information, written in partition table of MBR.

The coding of the program is as follows:

```
/* Program To Read MBR Partition Table */
# include <bios.h>
/* structure to read the partition entry from partition table */
struct partition
{
      unsigned char bootable ;   /* Active Partition Byte */
      unsigned char start_side ;/* Starting Head          */
      unsigned int start_sec_cyl ; /* combination of
                             Starting sector and cylinder number */
      unsigned char parttype ;  /* File system Indicator Byte   */
      unsigned char end_side ;  /* Ending Head */
      unsigned int end_sec_cyl ;   /* combination of Starting sector and
                             cylinder number */
      unsigned long part_beg ;  /* Relative Sector Number */
      unsigned long plen ;      /* Partition length in sectors  */
} ;

/* Structure to read MBR */
struct part
{
      unsigned char master_boot[446] ; /* IPL (Initial Program Loader)*/
      struct partition pt[4] ;    /* Partition table */
      int lasttwo ;               /* Magic Number    */
```

```c
} ;
struct part p ;
void main()
{
    clrscr();
    /* Read First Sector of first hard disk */
    biosdisk ( 2, 0x80, 0, 0, 1, 1, &p ) ;
    display();      /* Display the information of MBR Partition Table*/
    getch();
}

/*    Function to Display the Information Of partition table of MBR */
display()
{
    unsigned int s_sec, s_trk, e_sec, e_trk, i, t1, t2 ;
    char type[20], boot[5] ;
    printf("\n\nPart.  Boot  Starting location Ending Location Relative Number of");
    printf("\nType     Side Cylinder Sector    Side Cylinder Sector     Sectors     Sectors\n");
    for ( i = 0 ; i <= 3 ; i++ )
    {
        if ( p.pt[i].bootable == 0x80 )
            strcpy ( boot, "Yes" ) ;
        else
            strcpy ( boot, "No" ) ;
        switch ( p.pt[i].parttype )
        {
            case 0x00 :
                strcpy ( type, "Unused" ) ; break ;
            case 0x1 :
                strcpy ( type, "FAT12" ) ; break ;
            case 0x2 :
                strcpy ( type, "Xenix" ) ; break ;
            case 0x3 :
                strcpy ( type, "Xenix:usr" ) ; break ;
            case 0x4 :
                strcpy ( type, "FAT16<32M" ) ; break ;
            case 0x5 :
                strcpy ( type, "DOS-Ext." ) ; break ;
            case 0x6 :
                strcpy ( type, "FAT16>32M" ) ; break ;
            case 0x7 :
                strcpy ( type, "NTFS" ) ; break ;
            case 0x0b :
```

```
                    strcpy ( type, "FAT32" ) ; break ;
        case 0x0c :
                    strcpy ( type, "FAT32-LBA" ) ; break ;
        case 0x0d :
                    strcpy ( type, "VFAT16" ) ; break ;
        case 0x0e :
                    strcpy ( type, "VFAT16-LBA" ) ; break ;
        case 0x0f :
                    strcpy ( type, "VFAT EXT" ) ; break ;
        case 0x17 :
                    strcpy ( type, "HPFS" ) ; break ;
        case 0x81 :
                    strcpy ( type, "Old LINUX" ) ; break ;
        case 0x82 :
                    strcpy ( type, "LinuxSwap" ) ; break ;
        case 0x83 :
                    strcpy ( type, "LinuxNative" ) ; break ;
        case 0x85 :
                    strcpy ( type, "Linux Ext." ) ; break ;
        default :
                    strcpy ( type, "Unknown" ) ; break ;
    }
    s_sec = ( p.pt[i].start_sec_cyl & 0x3f ) ; /* starting Sector
    of the partition */
    t1    = ( p.pt[i].start_sec_cyl & 0xff00 ) >> 8 ;
    t2    = ( p.pt[i].start_sec_cyl & 0x00c0 ) << 2 ;
    s_trk = t1 | t2 ;  /* Starting Cylinder */
    e_sec = ( p.pt[i].end_sec_cyl & 0x3f ) ; /*Ending Sector */
    t1    = ( p.pt[i].end_sec_cyl & 0xff00 ) >> 8 ;
    t2    = ( p.pt[i].end_sec_cyl & 0x00c0 ) << 2 ;
    e_trk = t1 | t2 ; /* ending Cylinder */
    printf ( "\n%6s %3s", type, boot ) ;
    printf ( "%4d %6d %8d", p.pt[i].start_side, s_trk,s_sec ) ;
    printf ( "%7d %6u %8u", p.pt[i].end_side,   e_trk, e_sec ) ;
    printf ( "    %10lu    %10lu", p.pt[i].part_beg,
    p.pt[i].plen ) ;
    }
    return 0;
}
```

The information given by the output of the program is displayed something like as given below:

Part. Type	Boot	Starting location			Ending Location			Relative Sectors	Number of Sectors
		Side	Cylinder	Sector	Side	Cylinder	Sector		
FAT32	Yes	1	0	1	254	701	63	63	11277567
VFAT EXT	No	0	702	1	254	1023	63	11277630	28724220
Unused	No	0	0	0	0	0	0	0	0
Unused	No	0	0	0	0	0	0	0	0

Comments on coding:

The structure **partition** is used to read the various parameters of partition entry of partition in partition table of MBR. The structure **part** is used to read MBR information.

The function **display()** displays the information of MBR Partition Table parameters on the screen. As we see the output of the program, the starting and ending cylinder and sector number are displayed as follows:

    Starting Sector   =   **1**
    Starting Cylinder =   **0**
    Ending Sector   =   **63**
    Ending Cylinder   =   **701**

These sector and cylinder numbers are calculated from the combination of two bytes. The following tables show that how these numbers are calculated:

00H (Byte At Offset 03H)								01H (Byte At Offset 02H)							
7	6	5	4	3	2	1	0	7	6	5	4	3	2	1	0
0	0	0	0	0	0	0	0	0	0	0	0	0	0	0	1
Bits 7 to 0 For Cylinder Number								Cylinder Bits 9, 8		Sector Bits 5 to 0					
Cylinder Number = 0000000000 (B) = 0								Sector Number = 000001(B)=1							

Thus Starting C-H-S of the partition= 0-0-1.

Similarly, the Encoding for the Ending Cylinder and Sector number of the partition have been given in the next table:

BDH (Byte At Offset 07H)								BFH (Byte At Offset 06H)							
7	6	5	4	3	2	1	0	7	6	5	4	3	2	1	0
1	0	1	1	1	1	0	1	1	0	1	1	1	1	1	1
Bits 7 to 0 For Cylinder Number								Cylinder Bits 9, 8		Sector Bits 5 to 0					
Cylinder Number = 1010111101 (B) = 701								Sector Number = 111111 (B) = 63							

Thus the Ending C-H-S of the Partition = 701-254-63.

Program to find all logical partitions and their information

The program we discussed earlier was to read the partition information from the partition table of MBR. But just only by reading the MBR, we can not get the information of other logical partitions which are in extended partition of the disk.

We have already discussed that the Master Boot Record has the limit of four entries in the Master Partition Table. However the location of Extended Master Boot Record can be obtained with the help of Master Boot Record that contains Extended Partition Tables, whose format is exactly the same as of the main Partition Table.

All the extended partitions should exist within the space reserved by the extended partition entry. Only two of the extended partitions are meant to be used, the first as a normal partition and the second as another extended partition if exists.

Thus with the help of one Master Partition Table We can get the location of another Extended Master Partition Table next to it, if present.

The following program is for finding all the logical partitions and their partition entry information, reading MBR and Extended MBRs from the disk. The coding of the program is as follows:

```c
/*    Program to read the parameters of all logical partition present
in the disk */
#include<dos.h>
char        buffer[512], report_par[20];
unsigned    drive_num =0x80;
unsigned long   star_sec[20],   sec;

/* Structure of Disk Address packet format, to be used by the
readabsolutesectors Function */
struct diskaddrpacket
{
        char packetsize ; /* Size of Packet, generally 10H */
        char reserved ;   /* Reserved (0) */
        int blockcount ;  /* Number of Blocks to Transfer */
        char far *bufferaddress ; /* address to Transfer Buffer */
        unsigned long blocknumber[2] ; /* Starting Absolute Block Number*/
} ;
void main()
{
        int no_par,i;
        clrscr();
        no_par = 0;
        All_partition_information(star_sec,&no_par,&sec,buffer, report_par);
        printf(" \n\n Total Partitions in Disk = %d\n ", no_par);
        for(i=0;i<no_par;i++)
        {
```

```
            printf("\nStarting Sector Number of Partition %d = %lu ",
            i+1, star_sec[i]);
    }
    printf("\n");
    getch();
}
```

The Output of the program will be displayed as similar to this:

> Partition 1 - **FAT32**
> Partition 2 - **FAT32**
> Partition 3 - **FAT32**
>
> Total Partitions in Disk = **3**
>
> Starting Sector Number of Partition 1 = **63**
> Starting Sector Number of Partition 2 = **11277693**
> Starting Sector Number of Partition 3 = **25623738**

Comments on coding:

The structure **diskaddrpacket** is used to read Disk Address packet format, to be used by the **readabsolutesectors** function.

The function **All_partition_information( )** is used to find all the parameters of all partitions from the partition entry.

Although in this program, we have displayed only the File system and relative sector information of all available logical partitions in the disk, you can also print the information of other parameters of partition information by using the function **All_partition_information( )** with some more printf.

The coding of the function is as follows:

```
/*    Function to Find all logical partitions' information reading their
partition entry */
All_partition_information(unsigned long *star_sec,
unsigned *no_par,
long *sec, char *buffer,
unsigned char *report_par )
{
    unsigned long fat_check;
    unsigned long *sectors_part;
    static long     se_p;
    int  temp_var1,active_offset,active_pos=0,i, extended_pos=0,
    partloc1;
    unsigned long b_sec,se;
    unsigned char active_par;
    long    relative_sec;
```

```c
        long no_sectors;
        if(*sec==0 || *sec==1)
        se_p=0;
        do{
            se=*sec;
            /* Read absolute sector specified by *sec   */
            readabsolutesectors(drive_num,*sec,1,buffer);
            /*   ***** check for active partition *****   */
            if(*sec==se && *no_par==0)    /*if primary partition */
            {
                *sec=se=0;
                for(active_offset=446;active_offset<=494;
                active_offset+=16)
                {
                    active_par=buffer[active_offset];
                    if(active_par==0x80)    /* check for active
                                                partition */
                    break;
                    else
                    active_pos++;  /* position of active partition */
                }
                /* for extended partition */
                for(active_offset=450;active_offset<=511;
                active_offset+=16)
                {
                    active_par=buffer[active_offset];
                    if(active_par==0x05 | active_par==0x0F)
                    /*check for extended partition */
                    break;
                    else
                    extended_pos++;  /*position of extended partition*/
                }
                if(active_pos==4)
                active_pos=1;
                if(extended_pos==4)
                extended_pos=1;
                partloc1=0x1C0+extended_pos*16;
            }
            else
            {
                active_pos=0;
                extended_pos=1;
                partloc1=0x1D0;
                if(se_p!=0)
                {
                    *sec=se=se_p;   /*starting of extended partition*/
```

```c
            }
    }
    /* Relative Sectors in partition */
    relative_sec= *(unsigned long *)(buffer+454+active_pos*16);
    /* Number of Sectors in Partition */
    no_sectors=*(long *)(buffer+458+active_pos*16);
    /* Identify the File System Indicator Byte */
    if( buffer[0x1C2+active_pos*16]==0x04 ||
        buffer[0x1C2+active_pos*16]==0x05 ||
        buffer[0x1C2+active_pos*16]==0x06 ||
        buffer[0x1C2+active_pos*16]==0x0B ||
        buffer[0x1C2+active_pos*16]==0x0C ||
        buffer[0x1C2+active_pos*16]==0x0E ||
        buffer[0x1C2+active_pos*16]==0x0F ||
        buffer[0x1C2+active_pos*16]==0x07)
    {
        switch(buffer[0x1C2+active_pos*16])
            {
                /* For NTFS Partition */
                case 0x07:      report_par[*no_par]='N';
                printf("\n      Partition -%d     = NTFS",
                *no_par+1);
                break;
                /* For FAT32 Partition */
                case 0x0B:
                case 0x0C:      report_par[*no_par]='3';
                printf("\n      Partition -%d     = FAT32",
                *no_par+1);
                break;
                /* For FAT16 Partition */
                case 0x04:
                case 0x06:
                case 0x0E:      report_par[*no_par]='1';
                printf("\n      Partition -%d     = FAT16",
                *no_par+1);
                break;
            }   // End of the Switch
        b_sec=*sec+relative_sec;
        sectors_part[*no_par]=no_sectors; /* Array to store
        Number of sectors of partitions */
    } //End of if Condition
    else
    {   /* if partition indicator not match */
        if(*sec==0)
        { no_par=0;
            break;
```

```c
                }
                if((fat_check!=0x3631)&&(fat_check!=0x3233))
                b_sec=*sec=0;
            }
            if((b_sec!=0)&&(sec!=0))
            {
                star_sec[*no_par]=b_sec;
                (*no_par)++;
            }
            else
            break;
            /* checking if extended partition exist*/
            if(buffer[0x1C2+extended_pos*16]==0x05 ||
            buffer[0x1C2+extended_pos*16]==0x0F  )
            {
                    temp_var1=(unsigned )buffer[partloc1];
                    *sec=temp_var1 & 0x003F;       /* sector of extended
                                                    partition */
                    if(*sec!=0)
                    {
                        se_p=se+relative_sec+no_sectors;
                        *sec=se_p;
                    }
                    else
                    { *sec=-1;
                        break;
                    }
            } //close of if statement
            else
            {
                if(*sec>0)
                *sec=-1;
                break;
            }
    } while(1); // close of do-while loop
    /*  check for other non active primary partitions on sector 0 */
    if(*sec==0)
    {
        for(i=0;i<4;i++)
        {
            active_par=buffer[446+i*16];
            /* Identify the file system indicator Byte */
            if((buffer[0x1C2+i*16]==(char)0x06 ||
            buffer[0x1C2+i*16]==(char)0x0B  ||
            buffer[0x1C2+i*16]==(char)0x0C  ||
            buffer[0x1C2+i*16]==(char)0x07  ||
```

```
                    buffer[0x1C2+i*16]==(char)0x0E ||
                    buffer[0x1C2+i*16]==(char)0x04) && active_par!=0x80)
                {
                    switch(buffer[0x1C2+active_pos*16])
                    {
                        /* For NTFS Partition */
                        case 0x07:      report_par[*no_par]='N';
                        printf("\n        Partition -%d    = NTFS",
                        *no_par+1);
                        break;
                        /* For FAT32 Partition */
                        case 0x0B:
                        case 0x0C:      report_par[*no_par]='3';
                        printf("\n        Partition -%d    = FAT32",
                        *no_par+1);
                        break;
                        /* For FAT16 Partition */
                        case 0x04:
                        case 0x06:
                        case 0x0E:      report_par[*no_par]='1';
                        printf("\n        Partition -%d    = FAT16",
                        *no_par+1);
                        break;
                    } // End of switch
                    /* relative sectors Number of Partition */
                    relative_sec=*(long *)(buffer+454+i*16);
                    no_sectors=*(long *)(buffer+458+i*16);
                    /* number of sectors in partition*/
                    sectors_part[*no_par]=no_sectors;
                    /* Array to store Number of sectors of partitions*/
                    *sec=star_sec[*no_par]=relative_sec;
                    (*no_par)++;
                }
            } //loop close of for(i=0;i<4;i++)
        } //loop close of if(*sec==0)
        return;
}
```

Comments on coding:

The function starts reading the partitions information from the MBR and then reads the Extended MBRs if required. The function **readabsolutesectors** reads the absolute sector, specified by *sec.

sectors_part[*no_par] is the array to store the number of sectors of partitions. The partition number is specified by ***no_par** starting from 0.

no_sectors is the number of sectors in partition and **relative_sec** is the relative sector number for

Reading and Modifying MBR with Programming

that partition.

star_sec[*no_par] is the array to store the stating sector numbers of partitions. The partition number is specified by ***no_par** starting from 0.

star_cyl, star_hea and **star_sec** are the arrays which keep the information of starting of each partition in terms of CHS. **star_cyl** stores the information of starting cylinders, **star_hea** stores the information of starting heads and **star_sec** stores the information of starting sectors of partitions.

For the description of **readabsolutesectors** function refer the chapters given earlier in this book.

Modify MBR by Programming

The sample program to show, how we can modify the values of MBR partition table entry has been given below. The program modifies the values second partition entry of MBR partition table.

The coding of the program has been given below:

```
/*    Program to modify the values of partition table entry  of MBR  */
# include <bios.h>
/*    structure to read the partition entry from partition table */
struct partition
{
       unsigned char bootable ;    /* Active Partition Byte */
       unsigned char start_side ;     /* Starting Head    */
       unsigned int start_sec_cyl ; /* combination of Starting sector and
                           cylinder number   */
       unsigned char parttype ;    /* File system Indicator Byte    */
       unsigned char end_side ;    /* Ending Head   */
       unsigned int end_sec_cyl ;   /* combination of Starting sector and
                           cylinder number   */
       unsigned long part_beg ;    /* Relative Sector Number */
       unsigned long plen ;        /* Partition length in sectors */
} ;

/* Structure to read MBR */
struct part
{
       unsigned char master_boot[446] ; /* IPL (Initial Program Loader)*/
       struct partition pt[4] ;        /*   Partition table*/
       int lasttwo ;                   /* Magic Number    */
} ;
struct part p ;
void main()
{
       unsigned int t1,t2;
       clrscr();
       biosdisk ( 2, 0x80, 0, 0, 1, 1, &p ) ;
       display();     /* display the partition Table information */
```

```
        getch();
        /* Let us assume that we want to modify the partition information
        of second partition entry from partition table of MBR, with these
        values */
        p.pt[1].bootable = 0x80;     /* Active Boot Partition         */
        p.pt[1].parttype = 0x7;      /* NTFS Partition                */
        p.pt[1].start_side = 0;      /* Starting Head = 0             */
        p.pt[1].end_side = 31;       /* Ending Head == 31             */
        p.pt[1].part_beg = 808416;   /* Relative Sector = 808416      */
        p.pt[1].plen = 405216;       /* Total Sectors in Partition
                                        = 405216                      */
        /* Write New Information to MBR *\
        /* To write the values to MBR partition table, Uncomment the biosdisk
        function given below          */
        //biosdisk ( 3, 0x80, 0, 0, 1, 1, &p ) ;
        display();      /* Display the Modified Information */
        getch();
}
```

Comments on coding:

The program given above is a sample program to show how we can modify the values of partition table entry of MBR. If you want to modify the values of partition entry for such logical partitions, which lie in extended partition, you have to modify the values in partition table of Extended MBR.

The values which have been given here to modify the partition table entry are just for demonstrate, how to modify. Never modify partition table with illegal or illogical values. By doing so the entire partition may become inaccessible.

The structure **partition** is used to read the partition entry from partition table and structure **part** to read MBR. To actually make the modifications in partition table uncomment the **biosdisk( )** function.

If you want to modify the values of starting and ending, sectors and cylinder numbers of the partition, calculate the values, as described in the comments of the program to read and display the partition table of MBR, discussed in the starting of this chapter.

Chapter – 13

Reading and Modifying DBR with Programming

DOS Boot Record (DBR) / DOS Boot Sector

After the partition table, the DOS Boot Record (DBR) or sometimes called DOS Boot Sector is the second most important information on your hard drive.

For a Detailed study about DBR, refer the chapter, **"Logical Approach to Disks and OS"**, Discussed earlier in this book.

First logical sector of each DOS partition will contain a DOS Boot Record (DBR) or DOS Boot Sector. The job of the DBR is to load the operating system from the hard disk drive into the main memory of computer and give the system's control to the loaded program.

The DOS Boot Record (DBR) for the first partition on a hard disk is usually found at Absolute Sector 63 (the 64th sector on the disk drive) or in CHS form we can say C–H–S = 0–1–1 for most drives.

However this location may vary depending upon the SPT (Sectors per Track) of the Drive. For example, on an old 245MB drive having only 31 SPT, the Boot Record was located on the 32nd sector (Absolute Sector 31).

Since the floppy has no partitions on it therefore it has no MBR or Master Partition Table on its first sector, instead it contains the DBR on its very first sector.

The DBR is created by the FORMAT command of DOS, after partitioning is done using the FDISK command. The sector on which DBR resides becomes logical sector 1 of that particular partition for the DOS. The sector number used by DOS starts from the physical sector on which DBR is located.

The DBR contains a small program which is executed by the Master Boot Record (MBR) Executable program. All DOS partitions contain the program code to boot the machine i.e. load the operating system, but only that partition is given control by the Master Boot Record which is specified as active partition, in the partition table entry.

If the DBR is corrupted any how, the drive should be accessible if you boot the system from the bootable floppy or CD. Although the hard disk is not bootable (if the DBR of Active partition is corrupted), yet generally that should not affect access to the data of the disk drive. After booting the system with the bootable disk you can access the data.

Reading DBR of Floppy and Small Volumes

The table given next represents the format of DBR of Floppy. The Partitions having FAT12 File System or FAT16 File system with less than or equal to 32MB size also have the similar DBR format.

DOS Boot Record Format for FAT12 and FAT16			
Offset	Size	Field	Default
00H	3	Jump	E9 XX XX or EB XX 90 (Hex)
03H	8	OEM ID	MSWIN4.0
BIOS Parameter Block			
0BH	2	Bytes Per Sector	512
0DH	1	Sectors Per Cluster	(See Table of Cluster Sizes)
0EH	2	Reserved Sectors	1
10H	1	Number of FATs	2
11H	2	Number of Root Directory Entries	512/544
13H	2	Total Sectors in Logical Volume (Small, For Logical Volume Size Less than or Equal to 32 MB)	0
15H	1	Media Descriptor Byte	(See the Table of Media Descriptors)
16H	2	Number of Sectors Per FAT	Must Be Calculated
(End of BIOS Parameter Block)			
18H	2	Sectors Per Track	Depends on Hard Disk, Usually 63
1AH	2	Number of Heads	Depends on Hard Disk
1CH	4	Number of Hidden Sectors	
20H	4	Total Sectors in Volume (Large, Logical volume size greater than 32MB)	Size of the partition in terms of Sectors
Extended Boot Record Information (DOS 4.0 and Later)			
24H	1	Physical Drive Number	80H
25H	1	Current Head	0
26H	1	Extended Boot Signature Record	for WinNT, 28H else 29H
27H	4	Volume Serial Number (32 – bit Binary Volume ID)	Random
2BH	11	Volume Label	1
36H	8	File System ID	FAT12, FAT16
Total	62		

Reading and Modifying DBR with Programming

The following program has been written to read the DBR of Floppy and different parameters of the disk. However, you can also use it for FAT12 and Small FAT16 volumes of Hard Disks by specifying the appropriate Sector location of DBR and Physical Drive Number.

```c
/* Display boot parameters of floppy */
# include <dos.h>
# include <stdio.h>
main( )
{
      struct boot
      {
            unsigned char code[3] ;           /* Jump Code                */
            unsigned char system_id[8] ;      /* OEM Name and Version*/
            int bytes_per_sec ;               /* Bytes Per Sector   */
            char sec_per_clus ;               /* Sectors Per Cluster */
            int res_sec ;                     /* Reserved Sectors   */
            char fat_copies ;                 /* Number of FATs     */
            int root_dir_entry ;              /* Number of Root Directory
                                                 Entries   */
            unsigned int no_sects ;           /* Number of Sectors in Logical
                                                 Volume   */
            unsigned char format_id ;         /* Media Descriptor Byte */
            int sec_per_fat ;                 /* Sectors Per FAT    */
            int sec_per_trk ;                 /* Sectors Per Track    */
            int no_sides ;                    /* Number of Heads      */
            int no_sp_res_sect ;              /* Number of Hidden Sectors */
            unsigned char rest_code[482] ;    /* Rest of the code */
      } ;
      struct boot b ;
      char temp[4] ;
      int val, drive ;
      val = absread(0, 1, 0, &b) ; /* Use For Floppy Disk*/
      if ( val == -1 )
      {
            printf ( "Disk read Error...bad sector\n" ) ;
            exit ( 1 ) ;
      }
      clrscr ( ) ;
      printf ( "System ID                  = %s\n", b.system_id ) ;
      printf ( "Bytes per sector           = %d\n", b.bytes_per_sec ) ;
      printf ( "Sectors per cluster        = %d\n", b.sec_per_clus ) ;
      printf ( "Reserved sectors           = %d\n", b.res_sec ) ;
      printf ( "FAT copies                 = %d\n", b.fat_copies ) ;
      printf ( "Root directory entries     = %d\n", b.root_dir_entry ) ;
      printf ( "No. of sectors on disk     = %u\n", b.no_sects ) ;
      printf ( "Media Descriptor Byte      = %X\n", b.format_id ) ;
```

```
    printf ( "Sectors per FAT      = %d\n", b.sec_per_fat ) ;
    printf ( "Sectors per track    = %d\n", b.sec_per_trk ) ;
    printf ( "No. of sides         = %d\n", b.no_sides ) ;
    printf ( "No. of reserved sectors = %d\n", b.no_sp_res_sect ) ;
    return 0;
}
```

If you run this program to test the DBR of 1.44M, 3½ Inch Floppy disk having 70 tracks, two sides, 18 sectors per track and 512 bytes in a sector, The Output of the Program will be displayed similar to as follows:

System ID	= +1<*uIHC
Bytes per sector	= 512
Sectors per cluster	= 1
Reserved sectors	= 1FAT
copies	= 2
Root directory entries	= 224
No. of sectors on disk	= 2880
Media Descriptor Byte	= F0
Sectors per FAT	= 9
Sectors per track	= 18
No. of sides	= 2
No. of reserved sectors	= 0

Reading the DBR of Large Volumes

The Partition volumes which are greater than 32MB in size have some different format of DBR than the DBR for less then or Equal to 32MB Volumes.

It is so to provide the support to large Volumes of the disk (For a Detailed description on it, refer the chapter "**Logical Approach to Disks and OS**", Discussed earlier in this book).

The format of DOS Boot Record of a FAT32 volume has been given in the following table:

FAT32 DOS Boot Record Format		
Offset	Description	Size
00H	Jump Code + NOP	3 Bytes
03H	OEM Name and Version	8 Bytes
0BH	Bytes Per Sector	2 Bytes
0DH	Sectors Per Cluster	1 Byte
0EH	Reserved Sectors	2 Bytes
10H	Number of Copies of FAT	1 Byte
11H	Maximum Root Directory Entries (but Not Available for FAT32)	2 Bytes

Reading and Modifying DBR with Programming

13H	Number of Sectors in Partition Smaller than 32MB (Therefore Not Available for FAT32)	2 Bytes
15H	Media Descriptor (F8H for Hard Disks)	1 Byte
16H	Sectors Per FAT (In Older FAT Systems and Not Available for FAT32)	2 Bytes
18H	Sectors Per Track	2 Bytes
1AH	Number of Heads	2 Bytes
1CH	Number of Hidden Sectors in Partition	4 Bytes
20H	Number of Sectors in Partition	4 Bytes
24H	Number of Sectors Per FAT	4 Bytes
28H	Flags (Bits 0-4 Indicate Active FAT Copy) (Bit 7 Indicates whether FAT Mirroring is Enabled or Disabled <Clear is Enabled>) (If FAT Mirroring is Disabled, the FAT Information is only written to the copy indicated by bits 0-4)	2 Bytes
2AH	Version of FAT32 Drive (High Byte = Major Version, Low Byte = Minor Version)	2 Bytes
2CH	Cluster Number of the Start of the Root Directory	4 Bytes
30H	Sector Number of the File System Information Sector (Referenced from the Start of the Partition)	2 Bytes
32H	Sector Number of the Backup Boot Sector (Referenced from the Start of the Partition)	2 Bytes
34H	Reserved	12 Bytes
40H	Logical Drive Number of Partition	1 Byte
41H	Unused (Could be High Byte of Previous Entry)	1 Byte
42H	Extended Signature (29H)	1 Byte
43H	Serial Number or 32 – Bit Binary ID of Partition (Binary ID of 32 Bits provided by the OS itself)	4 Bytes
47H	Volume Name of Partition	11 Bytes
52H	FAT Name (FAT32 in this case)	8 Bytes
5AH	Executable Code	420 Bytes
1FEH	Executable Marker or Magic Number (AAH 55H)	2 Bytes

The following program is to read the DBR of large Volumes, which are greater than 32MB in size:

```
/* Program to display boot parameters of Large Disk Volume */
# include "dos.h"
# include "stdio.h"
void main()
{
    struct boot
```

```c
{
    unsigned char code[3] ;              /* Jump Code                    */
    unsigned char system_id[8] ;         /* OEM name & Version           */
    int bytes_per_sec ;                  /* Bytes Per Sector             */
    char sec_per_clus ;                  /* Sectors Per Cluster          */
    unsigned int res_sec ;               /* Number of Reserved Sectors   */
    char fat_copies ;                    /* Number of FATs               */
    unsigned int root_dir_entry ;        /* Number of Root Directory Entry*/
    unsigned int no_sects ;              /* Number of Sectors in Logical
                                            Volume (if Volume is <= 32MB)*/
    unsigned char Media_id ;             /* Media Descriptor Byte        */
    unsigned int sec_per_fat ;           /* Sector Per FAT               */
    unsigned int sec_per_trk ;           /* Sectors Per Track            */
    unsigned int no_sides ;              /* Number of Heads              */
    unsigned long no_sp_res_sect ;       /* Number of Hidden Sectors     */
    unsigned long long_sec_num ;         /* Total Sectors in Logical
                                            Volume ( Size >32MB)         */
    unsigned long num_sec_per_FAT;       /* Sectors Per FAT              */
    unsigned int binary_flags;           /* Binary Flags */
    unsigned char version_of_FAT1;       /* First Byte of FAT Version    */
    unsigned char version_of_FAT2;       /* Second Byte of FAT Version   */
    unsigned long root_dir_start_cluster; /* Root Directory Starting
                                             Cluster Number              */
    unsigned int   sec_num_of_file_sys;  /* Sector Number of File
                                            System Information
                                            Sector */
    unsigned int   sec_num_of_backup_boot_sec; /* Sector Number
                                                  of Backup Boot Sector  */
    unsigned char reserved[12];          /* Reserved */
    unsigned char logical_drive_number;  /* Physical Drive Number
                                            of Logical Volume*/
    unsigned char unused_byte;           /* Unused Byte                  */
    unsigned char hex_extd_boot_signature; /* Extended Boot
                                              Signature(29H)*/
    unsigned long binary_volume_ID;      /* Binary Volume ID */
    unsigned char volume_label[11];      /* Volume Label   */
    unsigned char FAT_name[8];           /* FAT Name       */
    unsigned char rest_code[420] ;       /* Rest 420 Bytes of The
                                            DBR */
    unsigned char magic_number[2];       /* Magic Number   */
} ;
struct boot b ;
char temp[4] ;
int val, drive,i;
val = biosdisk( 2, 0x80, 1,0,1,1, &b ) ;
/* For First Hard Disk */
```

```c
if ( val == -1 )
{
    printf ( "Disk read Error...bad sector\n" ) ;
    exit ( 1 ) ;
}
clrscr ( ) ;
printf ( " Jump Instruction Code           = ");
for(i=0;i<=2;i++)
{
    printf("%X",b.code[i]);
}
printf("(H)\n ");
printf ( "OEM name and version    = %s\n ", b.system_id ) ;
printf ( "Bytes per sector        = %u\n ", b.bytes_per_sec ) ;
printf ( "Sectors per cluster     = %u\n ", b.sec_per_clus ) ;
printf ( "Reserved sectors        = %u\n ", b.res_sec ) ;
printf ( "FAT copies              = %d\n ", b.fat_copies ) ;
printf ( "Root directory entries  = %u\n ", b.root_dir_entry );
printf ( "No. of sectors on disk  = %u\n ", b.no_sects ) ;
printf ( "Media Descriptor Byte   = %X(H)\n", b.Media_id ) ;
printf ( "Sectors per FAT         = %u\n ", b.sec_per_fat ) ;
printf ( "Sectors per track       = %u\n ", b.sec_per_trk ) ;
printf ( "No. of sides            = %u\n ", b.no_sides ) ;
printf ( "No. of reserved (Hidden) sectors= %lu\n ",
                               b.no_sp_res_sect ) ;
printf ( "==========  For Large(>32MB) Disks  ========\n");
printf ( "No. of sectors,(if Volume is >32MB) = %lu\n ",
b.long_sec_num) ;
printf ( "Number of Sectors Per FAT    = %lu\n ",
                               b.num_sec_per_FAT );
printf ( "Root Directory Starting Cluster    = %lu\n ",
                        b.root_dir_start_cluster);
printf ( "File System Information Sector  = %u\n ",
                        b.sec_num_of_file_sys);
printf ( "Sector Number of Backup Boot Sector  = %u\n ",
                        b.sec_num_of_backup_boot_sec);
printf ( "Physical Drive Number   = %X(H)\n",
                        b.logical_drive_number);
printf ( "Extended Boot Signature = %X(H)\n",
                        b.hex_extd_boot_signature);
printf ( "32-Bit Binary Volume ID = ");
             Decimal_to_Binary(b.binary_volume_ID,32);
printf ( " (B)\n ");
printf ( "Volume Label            = ");
for(i=0;i<=10;i++)
```

```c
        {
            printf ( "%c",b.volume_label[i]);
        }
        printf ( "\n FAT name                 = ");
        for(i=0;i<=7;i++)
        {
            printf ( "%c",b.FAT_name[i]);
        }
        printf ( "\n ");
        printf ( "Magic Number      = %X%X(H)",
                                    b.magic_number[0],b.magic_number[1]);
        getch();
}
 //////// Decimal to Binary Conversion Function \\\\\\\\
Decimal_to_Binary(unsigned long input)
{
        unsigned long i;
        int count = 0;
        int binary [32];        /* 32 Bit MAX only 32 elements total    */
        do
        {
            i = input%2;        /* MOD 2 to get 1 or a 0*/
            binary[count] = i;  /* Load Elements into the Binary Array*/
            input = input/2;    /* Divide input by 2 to decrement via
                                    binary */
            count++;            /* Count how many elements are needed */
        }while (input > 0);
        /* Reverse and output binary digits */
        do
        {
            printf ("%d", binary[count - 1]);
            count--;
        } while (count > 0);
        return 0;
}
```

When the program is run to read the DBR of a large volume, The Output of the Program is displayed as follows:

Jump Instruction Code	= EB5890 (H)
OEM name and version	= MSWIN4.1
Bytes per sector	= 512
Sectors per cluster	= 8
Reserved sectors	= 32

FAT copies	= 2
Root directory entries	= 0
No. of sectors on disk	= 0
Media Descriptor Byte	= F8 (H)
Sectors per FAT	= 0
Sectors per track	= 63
No. of sides	= 255
No. of reserved (Hidden) sectors	= 63
=========== For Large (>32MB) Disks ===========	
No. of sectors, (if Volume is >32MB)	= 11277567
Number of Sectors per FAT	= 11003
Root Directory Starting Cluster	= 2
File System Information Sector	= 1
Sector Number of Backup Boot Sector	= 6
Physical Drive Number	= 80 (H)
Extended Boot Signature	= 29 (H)
32-Bit Binary Volume ID.	=
11010101000110000111011100101 (B) Volume Label	= SAAYA
FAT name	= FAT32
Magic Number	= 55AA (H)

In the output of the program we see that the following parameters are shown zero:
- Root Directory Entry
- Number of Sectors on Disk
- Number Sectors Per FAT

These parameters are so because these values are set to zero, if the partition volume is greater then 32MB in size and the actual information is found in the Extended Volume Information Block of the DBR.

For Example, in the initial part of the DBR information, the number of Sectors per FAT is 0 and in the Extended Volume Information Block of DBR the Number of Sectors per FAT is 11003, which is the Actual Value for this large Volume.

The DBR of the Volume has the important information about the disk parameters, which can be used to link the all data information for programming purpose. For Example, if you want to access the DBRs of other Partition volume on the disk, you can calculate it by number of sectors, written in DBR and other related information.

If you want to access the Disk with cluster approach, you can make calculations with the help of Sectors per cluster, sectors per FAT and other information.

If you are using the hard disk larger than 8.4 GB (See the chapter, "**Logical Approach to Disks and OS**", Discussed earlier in this book), use extensions to access all the DBR's of the disk beyond 8.4 GB. Refer the Extended read-write functions, given in the previous chapters.

How to Recover DBR with Programming

You can recover the DBR of the disk volume up to 100 percent by using some tricky approach and logical calculations. As we discussed about logical approaches of file systems in the chapter, "**Logical Approach to Disks and OS**", earlier in this book, the every information in DBR is written within being some limit or rule.

Every parameter written in the DBR has some Specific meaning and written so by following some specific rule and reason. That is why the information of DBR if lost, can be Re-linked or rewritten manually if you follow these rule and use the tricky mind to find out what and how to cure.

For example, the table given next describes the number of sectors per cluster for different file systems, by using which you can find the number of sectors per cluster for your disk. Let us assume that you had a volume of approximately 10GB in your disk and the operating system which you were using was Windows 98.

Now, if any how the "Sectors per cluster" information of the DBR of the volume is corrupted. Let us try to find out which file system and how many sectors per clusters you had in the volume of your disk.

As the operating system in you disk was windows 98, which supports only FAT file system, therefore the File system of your Volume was FAT. Now let us think about the size of the volume, which was approximately 10GB.

We know that the 10GB Partition is not Supported by FAT16 (See the table given next) therefore the File system of the volume should be FAT32.

Now let us try to calculate the number of sectors per cluster for the volume. As we see in the table that the partition within the range of 8GB to 16GB has one cluster of 8 sectors.

Hard Disk Drive (HDD)			
Partition Size	FAT16 Cluster Size	FAT32 Cluster Size	NTFS Cluster Size
7 MB–16 MB	2 KiB	Not supported	512 Bytes
17 MB–32 MB	512 Bytes	Not supported	512 Bytes
33 MB–64 MB	1 KiB	512 Bytes	512 Bytes
65 MB–128 MB	2 KiB	1 KiB	512 Bytes
129 MB–256 MB	4 KiB	2 KiB	512 Bytes
257 MB–512 MB	8 KiB	4 KiB	512 Bytes
513 MB–1,024 MB	16 KiB	4 KiB	1 KiB
1,025 MB–2 GB	32 KiB	4 KiB	2 KiB
2 GB–4 GB	64 KiB	4 KiB	4 KiB
4 GB–8 GB	Not supported	4 KiB	4 KiB
8 GB–16 GB	Not supported	8 KiB	4 KiB
16 GB–32 GB	Not supported	16 KiB	4 KiB
32 GB–2 Terabytes	Not supported	32 KiB	4 KiB

Therefore, now we can conclude that in the volume, The File system was FAT32 with 8 sectors per

Reading and Modifying DBR with Programming

cluster. Similarly we can assemble the other information of the DBR using other logical approaches described in the previous chapters of this book.

The following program has been written to rewrite the information of disk parameters in DBR of 1.44Mb, 3½ inch floppy disk, with 80 tracks, 2 heads (sides) and 18 sectors per track.

```c
/* Program to Rewrite the parameters of 1.44MB, 3½ inch floppy disk to
its DBR */
# include "dos.h"
# include "stdio.h"
struct boot
{
    unsigned char code[3] ;         /* Jump Code                      */
    unsigned char system_id[8] ;    /* OEM ID and Version             */
    int bytes_per_sec ;             /* Bytes Per Sector               */
    char sec_per_clus ;             /* Number of Sectors Per Cluster*/
    int res_sec ;                   /* Reserved Sectors               */
    char fat_copies ;               /* Number of FATs                 */
    int root_dir_entry ;            /* Number of Root Directory Entries*/
    unsigned int no_sects ;         /* Number of Total Sectors        */
    unsigned char format_id ;       /* Media Descriptor Byte          */
    int sec_per_fat ;               /* Sectors Per FAT                */
    int sec_per_trk ;               /* Sectors Per FAT                */
    int no_sides ;                  /* Number of Sides(Heads)         */
    int no_sp_res_sect ;            /* Number of Hidden Sectors       */
    unsigned char rest_code[482] ;  /* Rest 482 Bytes code of DBR     */
} ;
struct boot b ;
main( )
{
    int val ;
    val = absread(0, 1, 0, &b);     /* Use For Floppy Disk */
    if ( val == -1 )
    {
        printf ( "\n Disk read Error...bad sector\n" ) ;
        exit ( 1 ) ;
    }
    clrscr ( ) ;
    display_info();
    getch();
    printf("\n Now Recovering BDR of Floppy.....\n");
    Recover_with_values();
    printf ( "\n Disk Recovered Successfully." ) ;
    display_info();
    return 0;
}
/* Function To Change the Parameters of DBR */
```

```c
Recover_with_values()
{
    int val =0;
    /* Jump Code of 3 Bytes For Floppy */
        b.code[0] =   0xEB;
        b.code[1]= 0x3E;
        b.code[2]= 0x90 ;
    /* System Id of 8 Bytes            */
    strcpy(b.system_id, "+05PSIHC");
    /* Bytes Per Sector = 512          */
        b.bytes_per_sec = 512;
    /* Sector per Cluster for 1.44M 3.5" Floppy = 1    */
        b.sec_per_clus = 1;
    /* Number of Reserved Sectors = 1      */
        b.res_sec =1;
    /* Number of FAT Copies = 2            */
        b.fat_copies =2;
    /* Number of Root Directory Entry = 224 */
        b.root_dir_entry =224;
    /* Number of Sectors on Disk = 2880     */
        b.no_sects =2880;
    /* Media Descriptor Byte For Floppy = F0 (H) */
        b.format_id =0xF0;
    /* Sectors Per FAT = 9                 */
        b.sec_per_fat =9;
    /* Sectors Per Track = 18              */
        b.sec_per_trk =18;
    /* Number of Sides = 2                 */
        b.no_sides =2;
    /* Number of Special Reserved Sectors (or Hidden Sectors) = 0*/
        b.no_sp_res_sect =0;
    /* Use For Floppy Disk*/
    val = abswrite ( 0, 1, 0, &b );
    if ( val == -1 )
    {
        printf ( "\n Disk Write Error...bad sector\n" ) ;
        printf ( " Disk was not Recovered." ) ;
        exit ( 1 ) ;
    }
    return 0;
}
display_info()
{
    printf ( "\n Jump Code (Hex)        = %X%X%X (H)\n",
        b.code[0],b.code[1],b.code[2]);
```

```
        printf ( " System ID              = %s\n",
           b.system_id ) ;
        printf ( " Bytes per sector       = %d\n",
           b.bytes_per_sec ) ;
        printf ( " Sectors per cluster    = %d\n",
           b.sec_per_clus ) ;
        printf ( " Reserved sectors       = %d\n",
           b.res_sec ) ;
        printf ( " FAT copies             = %d\n",
           b.fat_copies ) ;
        printf ( " Root directory entries = %d\n",
           b.root_dir_entry ) ;
        printf ( " No. of sectors on disk = %u\n",
           b.no_sects ) ;
        printf ( " Media Descriptor Byte  = %X\n",
           b.format_id ) ;
        printf ( " Sectors per FAT        = %d\n",
           b.sec_per_fat ) ;
        printf ( " Sectors per track      = %d\n",
           b.sec_per_trk ) ;
        printf ( " No. of sides           = %d\n",
           b.no_sides ) ;
        printf ( " No. of reserved sectors= %d\n",
           b.no_sp_res_sect ) ;
        return 0;
}
```

Comments on coding:

The structure **boot** is used to access the DBR, to read-write the parameters of the disk. The function **display_info(),** displays the various parameters of the disk, reading from the DBR. The function **Recover_with_values()** is used to modify and recover the parameters of DBR of Floppy.

The values used by the function **Recover_with_values(),** are for parameters of 1.44MB, 3 ½ inch floppy disk's DBR. The description of these values has been given in the table given next:

Value	Description
b.code[0] = **0xEB**;	Jump Code of 3 Bytes For specified
b.code[1] = **0x3E**;	Floppy, has been given **EB 3E 90**(H)
b.code[2] = **0x90** ;	
strcpy(b.system_id,"**+05PSIHC**");	System Id of 8 Bytes. It is calculated with current date and time of the system, however almost anything works.
b.bytes_per_sec = **512**;	Bytes Per Sector = **512**
b.sec_per_clus = **1**;	Number of Sectors per Cluster for 1.44M 3.5" Floppy is **1**

b.res_sec	=	1;	Number of Reserved Sectors = **1**
b.fat_copies	=	**2**;	Number of FAT Copies = **2**
b.root_dir_entry	=	**224**;	Number of Root Directory Entries for the specified floppy disk = **224**
b.no_sects	=	**2880**;	Number of Sectors on Disk = **2880**
b.format_id	=	**0xF0**;	Media Descriptor Byte For the specified Floppy = **F0** (H)
b.sec_per_fat	=	**9**;	Number of Sectors Per FAT = **9**
b.sec_per_trk	=	**18**;	Number of Sectors Per Track = **18**
b.no_sides	=	**2**;	Number of Sides = **2**
b.no_sp_res_sect	=	**0**;	Number of Special Reserved Sectors (or Hidden Sectors) = **0**

Chapter – 14

Programming for "Raw File" Recovery

Raw File Recovery

There are many specific file types which have some specific sequence or combination of characters written in the starting and ending of the file. We can analyze these combinations easily with the help of any disk editing program. We can also use **EDIT** command of DOS to study the structure of file in ASCII format.

The specific sequence or combination of character which is present in the starting of the file is usually called the **header** and the sequence or combination of characters which is stored in the ending of the file is called the **footer** of the file.

If we have lost our data in such type of disk crash that no FAT or Root Directory information is available to recover the data, we can use headers and footers to search these specific file types. The header indicates the starting of the file of that particular type and the footer indicates the end of file of that particular file type.

Here we are using the raw structure of particular file type to recover the data therefore the recovery technique is called **Raw File Recovery.** The surface of the disk is searched sector be sector to find the header and footer information.

Although the Raw File Recovery may have a wide area of application, but there are some specific cases of recovery where it may help a lot. For example, by mistake if you have run any data wiping program in the disk which had some important files but till you stop the program, all the information of MBR, DBR, FAT, and Root directory including Operating system files are wiped out.

In such case even format recovery programs may not help you to recover the data. Here you can use Raw file Recovery to recover the files of those specific file types by searching the headers and footers.

Not only this, even you can recover data in such cases, where you have got such a hard disk in which you have deleted all the logical partitions of the disk, recreated the partitions of different size then before and even you have installed the operating system.

Now you get remembrance, that you had some important data in the disk before partitioning and formatting it. If you have just installed the operating system, there are a lot of chances for the file to be recovered.

The factors that affect the performance of Raw File Recovery are, Fragmented data and the amount of data overwritten by some another other data. However you can your self find more and more areas of application for raw file recovery.

The procedure or almost the rules to search the files with raw file recovery program consider the

following conditions:
- Search the header of the file or multiple file types simultaneously in the sectors of the disk.
- If header of any file type is found, save the data in a file and check the following four conditions to close and save the file

    (a) The footer of that file type is found

    (b) The another header of the same file type is found

    (c) The header of another file type is found

    (d) No another header or footer for the defined file types in the program is found and the size of the file in which you are storing the data reaches to the maximum size limit, which you defined for the file size, in your program.

The information should be stored in the file including the data of the sectors in which you found the header and footers of the file type.

Headers and footers of some important file types

The headers and footers of some important file types have been given in the table given next. The footers given in the table are either in the end of the file of specified file type or are in the ending Offsets of the file such that you can use them as footers to recover the data.

You can also search yourself for headers and footers, different from these file types, by using the **EDIT** command of DOS or by using any disk editing tool. I have used the hexadecimal system to represent the information to make it easy to understand.

Extension	Header (Hex)	Footer (Hex)
DOC	D0 CF 11 E0 A1 B1 1A E1 6D 65 6E 74 2E	57 6F 72 64 2E 44 6F 63 75
XLS	D0 CF 11 E0 A1 B1 1A E1	FE FF FF FF 00 00 00 00 00 00 00 00 57 00 6F 00 72 00 6B 00 62 00 6F 00 6F 00 6B 00
PPT	D0 CF 11 E0 A1 B1 1A E1	50 00 6F 00 77 00 65 00 72 00 50 00 6F 00 69 00 6E 00 74 00 20 00 44 00 6F 00 63 00 75 00 6D 00 65 00 6E 00 74
ZIP	50 4B 03 04 14	50 4B 05 06 00
JPG	FF D8 FF E0 00 10 4A 46 49 46 00 01 01	D9 ("Better To Use File size Check")
GIF	47 49 46 38 39 61 4E 01 53 00 C4	21 00 00 3B 00
PDF	25 50 44 46 2D 31 2E	25 25 45 4F 46

Writing a program for Raw File Recovery

The coding of the program for Raw File Recovery of Microsoft Word files (.DOC Extension) has been given next. The program searches for the files in the sectors of the disk and saves the recovered file automatically by creating the name of file automatically.

The path specified by the user to save the files is used as destination path to save the recovered data. If the destination directory does not exist, program can create the destination up to one directory level.

The recovery program given here supports even the large size disks to search and recover the data. The program has been written to search the data in the second physical hard disk.

```c
/* Raw File Recovery Program to Recover the Microsoft Word Files */
#include<stdio.h>
#include<dos.h>
/* Structure to be used by getdrivegeometry function using INT 13H
Extension, Function Number 0x48.  */
struct geometry
{
      unsigned    int size ;   /* (call) size of Buffer   */
      unsigned    int flags ;  /* Information Flags       */
      unsigned    long cyl ;   /* Number of Physical Cylinders on Drive*/
      unsigned    long heads ;/* Number of Physical Heads on Drive */
      unsigned    long spt ;   /* Number of Physical Sectors Per Track */
      unsigned    long sectors[2] ; /* Total Number of Sectors on Drive*/
      unsigned    int bps ;    /* Bytes Per Sector        */
} ;

/*    Structure of Disk Address packet format, to be used by the
readabsolutesectors Function */
struct diskaddrpacket
{
      char packetsize ; /* Size of Packet, generally 10H */
      char reserved ;       /* Reserved (0)                    */
      int blockcount ;      /* Number of Blocks to Transfer   */
      char far *bufferaddress ;  /* address to Transfer Buffer  */
      unsigned long blocknumber[2] ; /* Starting Absolute Block Number*/
} ;

///// Function to get Drive Parameters \\\\\
unsigned long getdrivegeometry (int drive)
{
      union REGS i, o ;
      struct SREGS s ;
      struct geometry g = { 26, 0, 0, 0, 0, 0, 0, 0 } ;
      i.h.ah = 0x48 ;       /* Function Number 0x48     */
      i.h.dl = drive;       /* Drive Number              */
      i.x.si = FP_OFF ( (void far*)&g ) ;
```

```c
        s.ds = FP_SEG ( (void far*)&g ) ;
        /*   Invoke the specified function number of INT 13H extension
        with Segment Register Values */
        int86x ( 0x13, &i, &o, &s ) ;
        printf("\n Head = %lu, Sectors Per Track = %lu, Cylinder = %lu\n",
        g.heads,g.spt,g.cyl);
        /*   If get drive Geometry function Fails, Display Error Message
        and Exit  */
        if(g.spt==0)
        {
              printf("\n Get Drive Geometry Function Fails....");
              printf("\n Extensions Not Supported, Press any Key to Exit...");
              getch();
              exit(1);
        }
        return *g.sectors;   /* Return The Number of Sectors on Drive*/
}
unsigned long  file_size=0, i=0;
unsigned long  start_file=0, end_file=0;
unsigned long  Sectors_in_HDD2=0, loop=0;
char           buffer[512], filename[80], temp[8];
char           path[80];
unsigned int   result,num=0;

/* Header of Microsoft Word Files */
char header[10] =    {0xD0,0xCF,0x11,0xE0,0xA1,0xB1,0x1A,0xE1};

/* Footer of Microsoft Word Files */
char DOC_footer[14] = {0x57,0x6F,0x72,0x64,0x2E,0x44,0x6F,0x63,
                       0x75,0x6D,0x65,0x6E,0x74};

/// Start Of main \\\
void main()
{
        clrscr();
        /*  If total no. of hard disks attached is less then two, Display
        Error Message and Exit. */
        if(((char)peekb(0x0040,  0x0075))<2)
        {
              printf("\n\n You Must Have At least Two Hard Disks Attached
                 to your Computer To Run This");
              printf("\n Program. This Program has been developed to recover
                 the Data of Second Hard Disk.");
              printf("\n Press any Key to Exit... ");
              getch();
              exit(1);
        }
```

```c
    Sectors_in_HDD2=getdrivegeometry (0x81);
    printf("\n Total Sectors in second Hard Disk = %lu",
    Sectors_in_HDD2);
    printf("\n\n \"You must save the recovered files in another Hard
    Disk, Not in the Same Disk,");
    printf("\n in which you are searching the lost data.\"");
    printf("\n\n Enter The Destination Path to save the Recovered
    Files...\n ");
    gets(path);
    /* check if destination directory exists or Not */
    if(access(path, 0) != 0)
    {
        /* if Destination directory does not exist, create the Directory
        up to one level            */
        if(mkdir(path)!=0)
        {
            printf("\n Could Not Create Directory \"%s\"", path);
            printf("\n Check Path..., Press any key to exit...");
            getch();
            exit(1);
        }
    }
    strcat(path,"\\Ptt");
    /* Function to Hide (and show) Cursor on the screen */
    show_hide_cursor ( 32, 0 );
    gotoxy(15,18);cprintf("[ %d ] Files  Recovered...", num);
    /* search for the data until the ending sector of the disk */
    while(loop<Sectors_in_HDD2)
    {
        /* Read one Sector (Sector No. = loop) */
        readabsolutesectors ( 0x81, loop, 1, buffer );
        gotoxy(19,16);cprintf("Scanning Sector Number = % ld", loop);
        if(kbhit())
        {
            show_hide_cursor ( 6, 7 ); /* Retrieve the cursor before
            Exit the program */
            exit(0);
        }
        /* if specified header is found */
        if((memcmp ( buffer, header,7))==0)
        {
            /* logic to provide the file name to automatically
            create the files to save the recovered data        */
             strcpy(filename, path);
            itoa(num,temp,10);
            strcat(filename, temp);
```

```c
strcat(filename,".DOC");
start_file=loop; /* starting sector of file */
gotoxy(5,19);cprintf("File Found..., Saving As %s",
filename);
num++;
////////////// File Close Conditions \\\\\\\\\\\\\\
file_size=0;
while( file_size<5000000)
{
    loop++;
    file_size+=512;
    readabsolutesectors ( 0x81, loop, 1, buffer );
    gotoxy(19,16);cprintf("Scanning Sector Number = %
    ld" , loop);
    /* if file size reaches up to maximum size of 5MB*/
    if(file_size>=5000000)
    {
        end_file=loop; /* Ending Sector of File */
        Recover_the_file();/* write the data to file*/
        break;
    }
    /* if footer of DOC file is found */
    for(i=0;i<512;i++)
    {
        if( memcmp(buffer+i,DOC_footer,12)==0 )
        {
            end_file=loop;   /* Ending Sector of
            File */
            Recover_the_file();/* write the data to
            file */
            break;
        }
    }
    /* if another header is found */
    if( memcmp(buffer,header,7)==0 )
    {
        loop=loop-1;
        end_file=loop; /* Ending Sector of File */
        Recover_the_file();/* write the data to file*/
        break;
    }
    if(kbhit())
    {
        show_hide_cursor ( 6, 7 );
        exit(0);
    }
```

Programming for "Raw File" Recovery

```
            }
        }
        loop++;
    }       /////////While Loop Ends Here
    /* display message for completion of search and recovery */
    if(loop>=Sectors_in_HDD2 )
    {
        gotoxy(17,23);cprintf("The Saving of files in the Disk is
        Completed !!");
        gotoxy(17,24);cprintf("Press Any Key to Exit...");
        show_hide_cursor ( 6, 7 );
        getch();
    }
}
```

Comments on coding:

The structure **geometry** is used by **getdrivegeometry** function using **INT 13H Extension**, Function Number **0x48** to get the various parameters of the disk.

The structure **diskaddrpacket** is for Disk Address packet format, to be used by the **readabsolutesectors** Function.

The Function **getdrivegeometry (int drive)** is to get Drive Parameters of the disk specified physical drive number **drive**.

(char) peekb(0x0040, 0x0075) is used to find the number of hard disks connected to the computer, stored at memory location represented by **segment 0040H:offset 0075H**. If total number of hard disks attached is less then two Display Error Message and Exit.

Sectors_in_HDD2=getdrivegeometry (0x81); finds the various parameters of the second physical hard disk (0x81) and returns the total number of sectors of the disk.

The statement **if(access(path, 0) != 0)** checks the accessibility of the path given by the user. If destination directory does not exist, the destination is created up to one level and if the given path checked by condition **if(mkdir(path)!=0)** is illegal, error message is displayed.

The file names of automatically created files to save the recovered data are created such that the first three characters of the files are given **PTT** by **strcat(path,"\\Ptt");** function. It is done so to avoid the duplicate file names in the destination directory. Therefore the file names of recovered files are given in format of "**PTTxxxxx.DOC**"

The Function **show_hide_cursor (32, 0);** is used to Hide the Cursor from the screen where **show_hide_cursor (6, 7);** retrieves the cursor back to screen.

The function **readabsolutesectors (0x81, loop, 1, buffer);** Reads one Sector of the second physical hard disk specified by sector number **loop**.

If the header of the file is found, **start_file = loop;** sets the **start_file** to starting sector number of the file to be recovered. The program follows the three conditions given next, to find the ending sector of the file:

- If file size reaches up to maximum size of 5MB
- If footer of DOC file is found

- If another header is found

The long integer **end_file** is set to the ending sector number of the file by **end_file=loop;** if any one condition out of three is satisfied. Now the data of the sectors, starting from sector number **start_file** to sector number **end_file** is saved to the file with the function **Recover_the_file( )**.

The coding of the function **Recover_the_file( )** has been given next:

```
/* Function to save the data of the sectors starting from sector number
start_file to sector number end_file */
Recover_the_file()
{
      FILE *fp;
      if((fp=fopen(filename, "wb"))==NULL)
      {
            gotoxy(10,23);printf("Error Opening File %s", filename);
            getch();
            exit(1);
      }
      for(i=start_file;i<=end_file;i++)
      {
            gotoxy(19,16);cprintf("Scanning Sector Number = %ld", i);
            readabsolutesectors ( 0x81, i, 1, buffer );
            fwrite(buffer,512,1, fp);
      }
      fclose(fp);
      gotoxy(15,18);cprintf("[ %d ] Files Recovered...",num);
      gotoxy(5,19);cprintf("                                                  ");
      return;
}
```

The coding of the function **readabsolutesectors** has been given next. The function uses the **INT 13H Extension and function number 42H** to read the sectors.

For the detailed description of the function, refer the chapter **"Making Backups"** discussed earlier in this book. The coding of the function is as follows:

```
//// Function to read absolute sector(s) \\\\
int readabsolutesectors ( int drive,
unsigned long sectornumber,
int numofsectors,
void *buffer )
{
      union REGS i, o ;
      struct SREGS s ;
      struct diskaddrpacket pp ;
      pp.packetsize = 16 ;        /* packet size = 10H          */
      pp.reserved = 0 ;           /* Reserved = 0               */
      pp.blockcount = numofsectors ; /* Number of sectors to read*/
```

```
        /* for Data buffer             */
    pp.bufferaddress = (char far*) MK_FP ( FP_SEG((void far*)buffer),
    FP_OFF((void far*)buffer));
    pp.blocknumber[0] = sectornumber ; /* Sector number to read*/
    pp.blocknumber[1] = 0 ;   /* Block number           */
    i.h.ah = 0x42 ;           /* Function Number*/
    i.h.dl = drive ;          /* Physical Drive Number */
    /*  ds:si for buffer Parameters     */
    i.x.si = FP_OFF ( (void far*)&pp ) ;
    /*  ds:si for buffer Parameters     */
    s.ds = FP_SEG ( (void far*)&pp ) ;
    /* Invoke the specified Function of INT 13H with segment register
    values          */
    int86x ( 0x13, &i, &o, &s ) ;
    if ( o.x.cflag==1)
        return 0 ; //failure
    else
        return 1 ; // success
}
```

The following function is used to hide or to show the cursor on the screen. The function uses **Interrupt 10H, Function 01H** to set the cursor type. The coding is as follows:

```
show_hide_cursor( ssl, esl )
int ssl, esl ;
{
    union REGS i, o ;
    i.h.ah = 1 ;
    i.h.ch = ssl ;
    i.h.cl = esl ;
    i.h.bh = 0 ;
    int86 ( 16, &i, &o ) ;
    return;
}
```

show_hide_cursor(32, 0) hides the cursor and **show_hide_cursor(6, 7)** retrieves the cursor back. **ssl** is starting line for cursor and **esl** is ending line for cursor.

The little description of **Function 01H** of **INT 10H** is as follows:

INT 10H (16 or 0x10)

Function 01H (or 0x01) → Set Cursor Type

Call with:　　AH　　　　=　　　　01H
　　　　　　　CH bits 0-4　=　　　　starting line for cursor

CL bits 0-4	=	ending line for cursor

Returns: Nothing.

Comments:

The function is used to set the cursor type by selecting the starting and ending lines for the blinking hardware cursor in text display mode. In the graphics modes, the hardware cursor is not available.

Chapter – 15

Programming for Data Wipers

Introduction

We have already that discussed when we delete any file from the disk, the information is not erased completely from the drive but it is marked as available for new data to be written over it.

When we format a drive, all the information of files and directories of the drive such as FATs and Root Directory Entries are wiped out but data area remains unchanged and nothing from data area of the disk is erased.

The data which is deleted or formatted using the operating system remains on the data area as it is and can be recovered with some data recovery efforts and data recovery software.

Therefore the need to fully eliminate data from a drive leads the requirement for such a program that wipes out the data from the disk completely. For doing this it is not sufficient to just delete the files or just to format the drive but the data on the disk must be overwritten by some other data.

The programs which are used to wipe out the data completely from the disk are known as the data wiping programs. These programs write random characters on the data area to overwrite data and to wipe out all the information previously saved on the disk.

When the data becomes completely unrecoverable

To wipe out the data, the data area of the disk should be overwritten by some other data on it but the problem does not end here. To further complicate things, the tendency of magnetic drives to remember data that has been overwritten requires that data also be over-written several times by random sequences of data so that it may not be recovered even with sophisticated data recovery tools.

It is so because the technologies which can recover data even after the use of some simple data wipers are available today.

Some data erasure products perform binary zeros and binary ones overwriting on data. Writing a series of binary zeros and binary ones achieves the deepest overwrite effect as these values are the minimum and maximum magnetic values respectively.

Although this is the theory of an ideal data wiping program, but generally, the data over writing by random ASCII character is sufficient. The reason to say so is that the recovery by sophisticated recovery tools and technology can not be used to recover the data of any organization for a routine data recovery because these technologies are very much expensive and cost in millions even for single recovery. Not only this but also these technologies are available only in few countries around the world.

We shall discuss only the simple data overwriting to wipe the data from the disk. However you can further modify the same programs to write the random characters only with some little efforts. Data wiped out by this idea can also not be recovered by any data recovery software.

Why data wiping is so important

When we discuss about the data recovery techniques we assure the user that the data can be recovered with some general or some specific data recovery efforts. But data recovery is not always a desired and expected feature for everyone.

There may be a lot of people or organizations that are always willing to erase the data of their disk in such a way that it should not be recovered by any how. In such cases very sensitive data might previously stored on the disk, which if goes in wrong hands may harm the organization or user by misusing the information.

As we know that the requirement of more and more space in hard disks is increasing day by day. As the result of this, the older small capacity drives are replaced by new large capacity disks on a large scale every year in almost every organization. If these older disks are got by some wrong hands, it may create a very serious problem for that organization.

According to news published by CNET News.com, on January 16, 2003, Massachusetts Institute of Technology students Simon Garfinkel and Abbi Shelat have been purchasing old hard drives, in the name of research, from the Web and other second-hand sales to uncover the huge amounts of personal information people do not bother to erase.

After buying 158 drives for around US$1000, they managed to collect over 5000 credit card number, medical records, detailed personal and corporate financial information and several gigabytes of e-mails, source codes and other information.

The pair of these students has compiled their findings into a report entitled "**Remembrance of Data Passed: A Study of Disk Sanitation**" published in the February edition of IEEE Security and Privacy.

The main points that have come out of the research are that the second-hand market for hard drives is filled with personal information making it very easy for a malicious buyer to assume the identity of someone else.

Writing program for Non–Destructive data wiper

The non-destructive data wiper is a kind of data wiping program by using which we can wipe out the entire "unallocated space" of the disk volume, without harming the data which is stored in disk, in any way.

The scope of such data wiper is in the cases, where you want to wipe out all the unallocated space of the disk volume while the allocated data stored in the volume should remain untouched. This type of data wiping program also wipes out the data area of deleted files.

The program coding for a type of non – destructive data wiping program has been given next:

```
///// Program for a Non Destructive Data Wiper \\\\\
#include <stdio.h>
unsigned int file_num=0;   /* Provides File Number During the Auto
                              Creation of Temporary Data files */
float status=0;            /* How Much Disk space is still Written */
static char dbuf[40000];   /* Data Buffer to write Temporary Files with*/
char file_extension[5]=".ptt";/* Unique Extensions for Temporary Files*/
char temp[5];              /* File Number converted to String */
```

```c
char filename[40];           /* Temporary File name    */
void main()
{
    unsigned int i=0;
    clrscr();
    while(i<40000)
    {
        dbuf[i] = ' ';
        i++;
    }
    gotoxy(10,14);cprintf("          MB Still Written...");
    while(1)
    {
        /*  Logic to create temporary files automatically with unique
        name */
        strcpy(filename,"TTPT");
        itoa(file_num,temp,10);
        strcat(filename,temp);
        strcat(filename,file_extension);
        file_num++;
        write_to_temp(filename);
    }
} //// End of Main \\\\

///// Function to write the data to temporary file \\\\\
write_to_temp(char *filename)
{
    unsigned int i, count=1;
    float buf_status=0;
    FILE *tt;
    if((tt=fopen(filename,"wb"))==NULL)
    {
        fclose(tt);
        printf("\n Error occurred while creating temporary file, ");
        printf("\n Removing temporery Files After KEY BOARD HIT");
        getch();
        remove_temp_file();/* Remove All temporary files */
    }
    while(1)
    {
        for(i=0;i<50;i++)
        {
            fprintf(tt,"%s",dbuf);
        }
        buf_status = (float)((40000*50*count)/512);
        status= status+(40000*50);
```

```
            count++;
            gotoxy(10,14);
            cprintf("%.0f",(float)(status/1000000));
            if(kbhit())
            {
                fclose(tt);
                printf("\n Removing Temperory Files, Please Wait...");
                remove_temp_file();
            }
            if(buf_status>=10000)
            {
                fclose(tt);
                return;
            }
        }
    }
}

/* Function to Delete the Temporary files automatically */
remove_temp_file()
{
    int i=0;
    for(i=0;i<=file_num;i++)
    {
        strcpy(filename,"TTPT");
        itoa(i,temp,10);
        strcat(filename,temp);
        strcat(filename,file_extension);
        remove(filename);
    }
    exit(1);
    return 0;
}
```

Comments on logic and the coding of the program:

In this program basically we follow the following two steps to wipe the unallocated space of the disk:

- **Create temporary data files automatically:** First we create temporary files with unique names and having some data in them until the disk volume is full with these temporary data files. By doing this, all the unallocated data area of the logical drive is occupied by the data of the temporary files and all unallocated data is overwritten.

  For doing this, I chose the names of temporary files in the **TTPT**xxxx**.PTT** format, which means, the first four characters of the temporary files are **TTPT** and the extension of the files is **.PTT**. It is done so to provide the temporary files the unique filenames.

  I have set the maximum size of the single temporary file, equivalent to approximately 11,718 sectors data however you can define it according to you. I chose space character " " (ASCII character 32) to fill the data in temporary files. However random characters may also be used instead of space.

- **Remove all temporary files:** When the logical drive is full with temporary files, it indicates that all the unallocated data area is now overwritten. Now all the temporary files created by the program are removed automatically. And thus wiped out unallocated space is achieved.

In the coding of the program, the character array **filename** stores the file name to generate temporary files automatically, with different names.

The function **write_to_temp(filename);** fills the temporary file up to 11,718 sectors (because there is no occurrence of 10,000 sectors in specified group writing of buffer) equivalent data with help of data buffer **dbuf** of 40,000 bytes. 50 times data buffer is written at a time to speed up the writing.

The temporary files are created until the disk volume is full and file creation error occurs. The function **remove_temp_file()** removes all temporary file, created by the program.

In this way all the unallocated space is wiped out without harming the data of the disk volume.

Writing program for Destructive Data Wiper:

Destructive data wiping programs are those which write directly on the surface of the disk. This type of data wiping programs work on lower level than file system and operating system, which means that all the data and other logical information including OS, File systems, Directory entry and everything written on the disk is wiped out.

These data wiping programs directly wipe the sectors of the surface of the disk, and wipe out everything written on it. As all the data of the disk including operating system is lost, these programs as called destructive data wiping programs.

These types of wiping programs are preferred in such cases, where user is willing to overwrite everything on the disk, including Operating system and all the data on the disk.

However there are some more benefits of this type of data wiping programs. As these destructive data wiping programs work completely free from OS and File system and write directly on the surface of the disk, they are reasonably faster than the non-destructive data wipers.

Also, if any how logical bad sectors on the disk are created due to illegal storage of some random data, these logical bad sectors are also wiped out completely with the data of the disk.

The coding for a destructive data wiping program has been given next. The program has been written to support large size disks too. The program wipes the data of second physical hard disk connected to the computer.

```
///// Coding for a destructive data wiping program \\\\\
#include<stdio.h>
#include<dos.h>
/*    Structure to be used by getdrivegeometry function using INT 13H
Extension, Function Number 0x48.   */
struct geometry
{
        unsigned      int size ;    /* (call) size of Buffer    */
        unsigned      int flags ;   /* Information Flags         */
        unsigned      long cyl ;    /* Number of Physical Cylinders on Drive*/
        unsigned      long heads ;  /* Number of Physical Heads on Drive*/
        unsigned long spt ;     /* Number of Physical Sectors Per Track*/
```

```c
        unsigned long sectors[2] ; /* Total Number of Sectors on Drive*/
        unsigned int bps ;    /* Bytes Per Sector */
} ;

/*    Structure of Disk Address packet format, To be used by the
writeabsolutesectors Function        */
struct diskaddrpacket
{
        char packetsize ;            /* Size of Packet, generally 10H */
        char reserved ;              /* Reserved (0)                  */
        int blockcount ;             /* Number of Blocks to Transfer */
        char far *bufferaddress ;  /* address to Transfer Buffer   */
        unsigned long blocknumber[2] ; /* Starting Absolute Block Number*/
} ;

///// Function to get Drive Parameters \\\\\
unsigned long getdrivegeometry (int drive)
{
        union REGS i, o ;
        struct SREGS s ;
        struct geometry g = { 26, 0, 0, 0, 0, 0, 0, 0 } ;
        i.h.ah = 0x48 ;      /* Function Number 0x48 of INT 13H Extensions*/
        i.h.dl = drive;      /* Drive Number           */
        i.x.si = FP_OFF ( (void far*)&g ) ;
        s.ds = FP_SEG ( (void far*)&g ) ;
        /*Invoke the specified function number of INT 13H extension with
        Segment Register Values    */
        int86x ( 0x13, &i, &o, &s ) ;
        printf("\n Head = %lu, Sectors Per Track = %lu, Cylinder = %lu\n",
        g.heads,g.spt,g.cyl);
        /*   If get drive Geometry function Fails, Display Error Message
        and Exit */
        if(g.spt==0)
        {
            printf("\n Get Drive Geometry Function Fails....");
            printf("\n Extensions Not Supported, Press any Key to Exit...");
            getch();
            exit(1);
        }
        return *g.sectors;   /* Return The Number of Sectors on Drive*/
}

void main()
{
        unsigned long loop=0, Sectors_in_HDD2=0;
        unsigned char buffer[61440]; /* Data buffer of 61440 bytes
        Equivalent to 120 Sectors */
```

```c
    unsigned long i=0;
    char choice;
    clrscr();
    /* If total no. of hard disks attached is less then two Display
    Error Message and Exit. */
    if(((char)peekb(0x0040, 0x0075))<2)
    {
        printf("\n\n You Must Have At least Two Hard Disks Attached
        to your Computer To Run This");
        printf("\n Program. This Program has been developed to Wipe
        the Data of Second Hard Disk.");
        printf("\n Press any Key to Exit... ");
        getch();
        exit(1);
    }
    Sectors_in_HDD2 = getdrivegeometry (0x81);
    printf(" Total Sectors in Second Hard Disk = %lu\n\n",
    Sectors_in_HDD2);
    ///// First Confirm, then Proceed \\\\\
    printf("\n It is A Data Wiping Program, and Writes on the Surface
    of the Disk,");
    printf("\n After running this program, Data can not be recovered
    by any Software,");
    printf("\n All The Data in Second Hard Disk will be lost !!!");
    printf("\n Press \'Y\' to Continue, Else any key to Exit...    ");
    choice = getche();
    switch(choice)
    {
        case 'y':
        case 'Y':
        break;
        default:
        exit(0);
    }
    gotoxy(10,15);cprintf("Initializing, Please Wait...");
    for(i=0;i<61440;i++)
    {
        buffer[i]='\0';
    }
    gotoxy(10,15);cprintf("                                        ");
    gotoxy(10,15);
    printf("Currently Wiping Absolute Sector: ");
    for(loop=0;loop<=Sectors_in_HDD2;loop=loop+120)
    {
        writeabsolutesectors (0x81, loop, 120, buffer);
        gotoxy(44,15); printf("%ld",loop);
```

```
            if(kbhit())
            {
                exit(0);
            }
        }
        ///// Display Message when completed \\\\\
        printf("\n\n Data wiping is Now Completed, All the Data in Second Hard Disk is now");
        printf("\n Completely Erased, Press any Key to Exit...");
        getch();
}

//// Function to Write Absolute Sector(s) \\\\
int writeabsolutesectors ( int drive, unsigned long sectornumber, int numofsectors, void *buffer )
{
        union REGS i, o ;
        struct SREGS s ;
        struct diskaddrpacket pp ;
        pp.packetsize = 16 ;            /* Packet Size = 10H */
        pp.reserved = 0 ;               /* Reserved    = 0   */
        pp.blockcount = numofsectors ;/* Number of Sectors to be writte*/
        /*   for Data buffer */
        pp.bufferaddress = (char far*) MK_FP ( FP_SEG((void far*)buffer), FP_OFF((void far*)buffer));
        pp.blocknumber[0] = sectornumber ; /* Sector number to be written*/
        pp.blocknumber[1] = 0 ;    /* Block number = 0       */
        i.h.ah = 0x43 ;            /* Function Number        */
        i.h.al = 0x00 ;            /* Write Flags            */
        i.h.dl = drive ;           /* Physical Drive  number */
        i.x.si = FP_OFF ( (void far*)&pp ) ; /* ds:si for buffer Parameters*/
        s.ds = FP_SEG ( (void far*)&pp ) ;   /* ds:si for buffer Parameters*/
        /* Invoke the specified Function of INT 13H with segment register values */
        int86x ( 0x13, &i, &o, &s ) ;
        if ( o.x.cflag==1)
        return 0 ; //failure
        else
        return 1 ; // success
}
```

Comments on coding:

The structure **geometry** is used by **getdrivegeometry** function using **INT 13H Extension**, Function Number **0x48** to get the various parameters of the disk.

The structure **diskaddrpacket** is for Disk Address packet format, to be used by the

writeabsolutesectors Function.

The Function **getdrivegeometry (int drive)** is to get Drive Parameters of the disk specified physical drive number **drive**. **buffer [61440]** is the data buffer of 61440 bytes, Equivalent to 120 Sectors.

(char) peekb(0x0040, 0x0075) is used to find the number of hard disks connected to the computer, stored at memory location represented by **segment 0040H:offset 0075H**. If total number of hard disks attached is less then two Display Error Message and Exit.

writeabsolutesectors (0x81, loop, 120, buffer) function is used to write the data of data buffer on 120 sectors at a time starting from the absolute sector number specified by **loop**.

I chose '**\0**' (NULL character, ASCII code 0) to write on the sectors to overwrite the data. However you can use random characters to overwrite the data.

For detailed description on Functions **writeabsolutesectors** and **getdrivegeometry** refer the chapters given earlier in this book.

Wiping Data Area of specific file

We discussed about the data wiping programs which wipe the data of unallocated space of the disk or wipe the entire disk. But if user is willing to wipe the data every time when he deletes the data, it may be a time taking process to wipe the entire unallocated space of the disk.

We need this type of data wiping programs to wipe the data area only occupied by that particular file. For doing this, we get the help from FAT and Root directory entries, to find the data area occupied by that particular files.

Even in case of floppy, if the data is not fragmented, we can do so only with the help of Root directory information. The Following table shows the information stored by a root directory entry with 32 bytes, for any file:

Offset	Size	Description
00H	8 Bytes	Filename (Also see the next table for the special meaning of first character of file name)
08H	3 Bytes	Extension
0BH	1 Byte	File attributes(See The Table Of File Attributes)
0CH	10Bytes	Reserved
16H	2 Bytes	Time Created or Last Updated (See Date–Time Format Table)
18H	2 Bytes	Date Created or Last Updated (See Date–Time Format Table)
1AH	2 Bytes	Starting or First cluster of file (The value 0000H is used in Parent Directory ('..') entries to indicate that the Parent Directory is the Root Directory)
1CH	4 Bytes	File size in Bytes.

As we see in the table of contents of root directory entry, we are capable to find the starting and ending cluster of the files. The first Byte of the filename may also contain some important information about file. The information given by this byte may be one of the given below:

First Character of File Name	
Value	**Meaning**
00H	Indicates that this directory entry is unused.
05H	Indicates that 1st character of filename is character E5H But actually the file has not been deleted. (See the Meaning of E5H)
E5H	The file has been Erased and this directory entry is a deleted file's directory entry. The data area previously occupied by that file is now free for allocation for another new file.
2EH	This is a Sub-directory. The cluster number field of this entry will contain the cluster number of the directory.
2EH 2EH	Two 2EH in a directory entry indicate the parent directory entry of a Sub–Directory. The cluster number of this entry will contain the cluster number of the parent directory of this directory. The cluster number will be zero 0000H if the parent directory is root directory.

Let us try this information to wipe the data of any file stored in 1.44Mb, 3 ½ inch floppy disk, with the help of root directory information. Assuming that the data in the floppy disk is not fragmented, the program given next wipes the data of specified file from its data area:

```
/*      Program to wipe the data area of specified file in floppy disk */
#include<stdio.h>
#include<dos.h>
///// Structure to read 32 bytes of File Entry in Root Directory \\\\\
struct root
{
        unsigned char filename[8];    /* File name Entry of 8 Bytes */
        unsigned char extension[3];   /* Extension of File of 3 Bytes*/
        unsigned char attribute;      /* File Attribute Byte    */
        unsigned char reserved[10];   /* Reserved Bytes 10      */
        unsigned int time;            /* Time, 2 Bytes          */
        unsigned int date;            /* Date, 2 Bytes          */
        unsigned int starting_cluster;/* Starting Cluster of File, 2 Bytes*/
        unsigned long file_size;      /* File Size in Bytes, 4 Bytes */
};

/*      Should be taken this to read all Root Directory Entries */
//struct root entry[224];
/* Structure to read all 16 File entries in one Sector of Root Directory*/
struct one_root_sector
{
        struct root entry[16];
};
struct   one_root_sector one;
void main()
{
        int result, i, num_sectors,j;
```

Programming for Data Wipers

```c
char wipe_buf[512]; /* Data Buffer to be used to wipe
out the data Area of file*/
clrscr();
result= absread(0x00, 1, 19, &one); /* Read Absolute Sector 19
(First Sector of Root Directory)   */
if (result != 0)
{
    perror("Error in Reading Sector, Press any key to Exit...");
    getch();
    exit(1);
}
/* Display Files' Information after Reading from Root Directory*/
printf(" FILE NO.   FILENAME   EXTENSION   STARTING CLUSTER FILESIZE
\n\n");
for(i=1;i<16;i++)
{
    printf("\n %5d      %8.8s      %3.3s      %5u       %10lu ",
    i, one.entry[i].filename, one.entry[i].extension,
    one.entry[i].starting_cluster, one.entry[i].file_size);
}
//// Get User Input To Delete The File \\\\
printf("\n\n Enter The File Number, you Want to Delete and Wipe
out Completely  ");
scanf("%d", &i);
if(i<1 || i>15)
{
    printf(" \"%d\" is an Invalid Choice..., Press any Key to
    Exit...", i);
    getch();
    exit(1);
}
///// First Confirm, Then Continue \\\\\\
printf("\n You are About to wipe-out, The File \"%.8s.%s\"",
one.entry[i].filename, one.entry[i].extension);
printf("\n Do you Want to Continue...(Y/N)    ");
switch(getche())
{
    case 'y':
    case 'Y':
    break;
    default:
    exit(0);
}
///// Calculate The Size of File in Sectors \\\\\
num_sectors = one.entry[i].file_size/512;
if((one.entry[i].file_size%512)>0)
```

```c
    {
        num_sectors = num_sectors+1;
    }
    /* Data buffer of 512 bytes with 512 NULL characters */
    for(j=0;j<512;j++)
    {
        wipe_buf[j] = '\0';
    }
    ///// Starting Sector of the File \\\\\
    j= one.entry[i].starting_cluster+31;
    /* Wipe out the data Area Until the Sectors of file End */
    while(j!=(one.entry[i].starting_cluster + num_sectors+31)  )
    {
        if((abswrite(0x00, 1, j, &wipe_buf))!=0)
        {
            printf("\n Error Writing on Disk Sectors");
            getch();
            exit(0);
        }
        j++;
    }
    printf("\n\n   File \"%.8s.%.3s\" Deleted !!!" ,
    one.entry[i].filename, one.entry[i].extension);
    one.entry[i].attribute = 0;/* Set the File Attribute to 0*/
    one.entry[i].time = 0;    /* Wipe The Time information of File*/
    one.entry[i].date = 0;    /* Wipe The Date information of File*/
    one.entry[i].starting_cluster = 0; /* Set the Starting cluster
                                          to 0 */
    one.entry[i].file_size = 0;        /* Set the file Size to 0 */
    one.entry[i].filename[0]=0xE5;     /* Give the Deleted file Status
                                          to the File */
    ///// Write above information in the root Directory \\\\\\
    result= abswrite(0x00, 1, 19, &one);
    if (result != 0)
    {
        perror("Error in Reading Sector, Press any key to Exit...");
        getch();
        exit(1);
    }
}
```

Comments on logic and coding of program:

The structure **root** is used to read 32 bytes of File Entry in Root Directory and Structure **one_root_sector** reads all 16 File entries in one Sector of Root Directory

If you want to read all the sectors of root directory information you should take it as **struct root**

entry[224]; however I have written the program to analyze the **16 entries** of only **one sector** of root directory.

The Starting Sector of the File has been calculated as follows:

j= one.entry[i].starting_cluster+31;

It is done so because the data area of the 1.44 MB, 3 ½ inch floppy disk starts after the first 32 sectors of the floppy disk. And in the specified capacity floppy disk, one cluster is of one sector.

The following table shows the logical map of 1.44MB, 3½ inch floppy disk:

Logical Map of 3½ Inches, 1.44 MB floppy disk, Formatted with the FAT12 File System and having 18 Sectors Per Track, 80 Tracks, 2 Sides and 512 bytes per Sector (using 1 Sector per Cluster).	
Absolute Sectors	**Contents**
0	Boot Record
1 – 9	FAT 1
10 – 18	FAT 2
19 – 32	Root Directory
33 – 2879	Data Area

The out put of the program is displayed as follows:

FILE NO.	FILENAME	EXTENSION	STARTING CLUSTER	FILESIZE
1	ALLPARTS	C	19	11131
2	CUTPASTE	C	41	442
3	FLOPYDBR	C	42	1413
4	HDD_DBR	C	45	4094
5	REC_DBR	C	53	2785
6	MBR_BACK	C	59	1172
7	PASTEMBR	C	62	1181
8	PARTBOOT	C	65	2685
9	TTPARBOO	C	71	3220
10	TT_IMAGE	C	78	3826
11	TEMPFLP	C	86	4992
12	TEMPWIPE	C	96	3234
13	NOW_RAW	C	103	5416
14	DATAWIPE	C	114	2029
15	LOW_WIPE	C	118	3385

Enter The File Number, you Want to Delete and Wipe out Completely   **8**

You are About to wipe-out, The File **"PARTBOOT.C"**
Do you Want to Continue...(Y/N) **Y**
File **"PARTBOOT.C** " Deleted !!!

Here we deleted and wiped the data of file **PARTBOOT.C**. When we see the contents of the floppy with DIR command, the file **PARTBOOT.C** is not displayed there. When we further execute the program the entry of the deleted file is showed as follows:

FILE NO.	FILENAME	EXTENSION	STARTING CLUSTER	FILESIZE
1	ALLPARTS	C	19	11131
1	ALLPARTS	C	19	11131
2	CUTPASTE	C	41	442
3	FLOPYDBR	C	42	1413
4	HDD_DBR	C	45	4094
5	REC_DBR	C	53	2785
6	MBR_BACK	C	59	1172
7	PASTEMBR	C	62	1181
8	σARTBOOT	C	0	0
9	TTPARBOO	C	71	3220
10	TT_IMAGE	C	78	3826
11	TEMPFLP	C	86	4992
12	TEMPWIPE	C	96	3234
13	NOW_RAW	C	103	5416
14	DATAWIPE	C	114	2029
15	LOW_WIPE	C	118	3385

Here, the character "σ" (0xE5), represents that the file has been deleted. (see the table for First Character of File Name).

If you want to write the same program for hard disk drive, you must also use the FAT with root directory to get the information of the data area of any file. It is so because, the rate of fragmented data in the hard disk drives, increases with time as the older files are deleted and new file are created. Then it is not necessary for all the data clusters of any file in the drive to stay one after one continuously in the data area. By accessing FAT, you can access all of those clusters.

Chapter – 16
Developing More Utilities for Disks

Introduction

In this chapter we shall discuss, how to use the information of MBR, DBR, FAT and Root Directories to develop utility programs which may help us in managing the data, in optimizing the storage or in may disk troubleshooting tasks.

Usually, these programs are solution to some specific problem. Some utility programs and their programming have been discussed in this chapter.

Hiding Partitions

Generally, the partition hiding utility is used by those users who work on such computer system which is used by users. If there are many users for same the computer, there may be a great possibility, that data of another user may be read, stolen, or deleted.

In such case, where user has some important data or some confidential information in the same computer, he may be willing to hide the partition in which he has his data in such a way that the partition should not be accessed by the Operating system, so that the may not be accessed by other user.

When the user wants to work on the system, he can access the partition back, just by unhiding the partition. Generally these types of events take place in the professional institutions, where the computers are used by many students but senior students are always worried about their important data or project work. As in lack of knowledge, the new student may harm or even delete their data.

How the partition becomes hidden

The following table represents the format of partition in partition table of MBR:

Offset	Meaning	Size	Description
00H	Boot Type Indicator Byte	1 Byte	If Byte is **00H**, the Partition is Inactive and if Byte is **80H**, The Partition is Active (or Bootable)
01H	Head Number of Beginning of the Partition	1 Byte	Starting Head number of the Partition in Hexadecimal System
02H	Sector and Cylinder Number of Beginning of	2 Bytes	6 Bits of First Byte make Starting Sector Number and Combination of

	the Partition		remaining 2 Bits (as Two Most Significant Bits) plus 8 Bits of another Byte (Rest 8 least Significant Bits of the 10-Bit Number) make the Starting Cylinder Number of the Partition
04H	**File System indicator Byte**	1 Byte	**File System Indicator Byte in Hexadecimal system** (for complete list of partition indicator bytes, refer the chapter **"Logical Approach to Disks and OS"** discussed earlier in this book)
05H	Head Number of End of the Partition	1 Byte	Ending Head Number of the Partition in Hexadecimal System
06H	Sector and Cylinder Number of End of the Partition	2 Bytes	6 Bits of First Byte make Ending Sector Number and Combination of remaining 2 Bits (as Two Most Significant Bits) plus 8 Bits of another Byte (Rest 8 least Significant Bits of the 10-Bit Number) make the Ending Cylinder Number of the Partition
08H	Absolute Sector number of Beginning of the Partition	4 Bytes	Number of Sectors Between the MBR and the First Sector in the Partition
0CH	Absolute Sector number of End of the Partition	4 Bytes	Number of Sectors in the Partition
Total = 16 Bytes			

At the offset 04H, in every partition entry, there is a file system indicator byte. This indicator byte represents the type of file system of that partition. If the value of this byte is changed, the identity of the partition is changed.

For example, the value of partition indicator byte for "DOS 12-Bit FAT" is 0x01. If this value is changed to 0x11, The identity of file system in the partition table entry is changed to "Hidden DOS 12-Bit FAT" (for complete list of partition indicator bytes, refer the chapter **"Logical Approach to Disks and OS"** discussed earlier in this book).

The table given next shows some more examples of file system indicator byte for some partition types:

Partition type indicator Byte	**Description of File System of Partition**
0x01	DOS 12–bit FAT
0x11	Hidden DOS 12–bit FAT
0x04	DOS 16–bit FAT (<=32MB)
0x14	Hidden DOS 16–bit FAT (<=32MB)

Developing More Utilities for Disks

0x05	DOS Extended
0x15	Hidden DOS Extended
0x06	DOS 16–bit big (> 32MB)
0x16	Hidden DOS 16–bit big (> 32MB)
0x07	NTFS
0x17	Hidden NTFS
0x0B	Windows FAT32
0x1B	Hidden Windows FAT32
0x0C	Windows FAT32 (LBA)
0x1C	Hidden Windows FAT32 (LBA)
0x0E	Windows FAT16 (LBA)
0x1E	Hidden Windows FAT16 (LBA)
0x0F	Windows Extended
0x1F	Hidden Windows Extended

Here we see that the corresponding hidden partition for any file system is found by adding the value 0x10 to its system indicator byte.

Although it is not the hard and fast rule for hiding the partition yet it works even for most of the file system. The reason behind it is that when we change the value of partition indicator byte, the identity of file system in the partition table entry is changed. And it is very rare that the new file system is also supported by the same operating system.

Writing program to hide partition

The program given next is used to hide the partition using the partition entry of that partition from partition table of MBR. If you want to hide other logical partitions in the extended volume you should access the extended MBRs.

The coding of the program has been given next:

```
/* Program to hide the partition using Partition table entry of that
Partition from MBR   */
#include <bios.h>
#include <stdio.h>
int main(void)
{
    struct diskinfo_t dinfo;
    int result, tohide;
    int i;
    static char dbuf[512];/* Data Buffer to read-Write the Sector
    information     */
    clrscr();
    dinfo.drive  =   0x80; /* drive number for First Hard Disk */
    dinfo.head   =   0;    /* disk head number */
    dinfo.track  =   0;    /* track number        */
```

```c
        dinfo.sector   =   1; /* sector number        */
        dinfo.nsectors =   1; /* sector count         */
        dinfo.buffer = dbuf;  /* data buffer          */
        /* Read the First Sector of the Disk */
        result = _bios_disk(_DISK_READ, &dinfo);
        if ((result & 0xff00) == 0)
        {
            printf("The Partition Codes of Four Partition Entries are,
             0x%02x, 0x%02x, 0x%02x And 0x%02x.\n",
             dbuf[450] & 0xff, dbuf[466] & 0xff,
             dbuf[482] & 0xff, dbuf[498] & 0xff);
            textcolor(15);
            gotoxy(5,5);cprintf("Partition Entry in MBR is as follows:");
            gotoxy(10,7);cprintf("1. ");   showtype(dbuf[450] & 0xff);
            gotoxy(10,8);cprintf("2. ");   showtype(dbuf[466] & 0xff);
            gotoxy(10,9);cprintf("3. ");   showtype(dbuf[482] & 0xff);
            gotoxy(10,10);cprintf("4. ");  showtype(dbuf[498] & 0xff);
            /* get the User Input for Hiding the Partition */
            gotoxy(1,15);
            printf("Enter The partition no. you want to hide, Or Press
             any other key to Exit...  ");
            tohide=getche();
            switch(tohide)
            {
                case '1': /* Hide First Partition in partition Table  */
                dbuf[450]    = dbuf[450] +16;
                result = _bios_disk(_DISK_WRITE, &dinfo);
                break;
                case '2': /* Hide second Partition in partition Table */
                dbuf[466]    = dbuf[466]+16;
                result = _bios_disk(_DISK_WRITE, &dinfo);
                break;
                case '3': /* Hide third Partition in partition Table  */
                dbuf[482]    = dbuf[482] +16;
                result = _bios_disk(_DISK_WRITE, &dinfo);
                break;
                case '4': /* Hide Fourth Partition in partition Table */
                dbuf[498]    = dbuf[498]+16;
                result = _bios_disk(_DISK_WRITE, &dinfo);
                break;
                default:
                exit(0);
            }
            if ((result & 0xff00) == 0)
            {
                printf("\n\nThe New Partition Codes of Four Partition
```

```
                    Entries are, 0x%02x, 0x%02x, 0x%02x And 0x%02x.\n",
                    dbuf[450] & 0xff, dbuf[466] & 0xff,
                    dbuf[482] & 0xff, dbuf[498] & 0xff);
                    getch();
            }
            else
            {
                    printf("Cannot Change the Byte, status = 0x%02x\n",
                    result);
                    getch();
            }
    }
    return 0;
}
```

Comments on coding:

The program reads file system indicator bytes of all four partition entries in partition table of MBR. The function **showtype( )** is used to show the name of file system for the corresponding value of file system indicator byte.

The user selects the partition to hide from the menu displayed on the screen and then 16 (0x10) is added to the value of file system indicator byte of that partition to hide it.

The coding of the function **showtype( )** is as follows:

```
/* Function to show the name of file system corresponding to the value
of file system indicator byte */
showtype(i)
{
        switch (i)
        {
            case 0x00 :cprintf("Empty"); break;
            case 0x01 :cprintf("DOS 12-bit FAT"); break;
            case 0x02 :cprintf("XENIX root"); break;
            case 0x03 :cprintf("XENIX usr"); break;
            case 0x04 :cprintf("DOS 16-bit <32M"); break;
            case 0x05 :cprintf("Extended"); break;
            case 0x06 :cprintf("DOS 16-bit >=32M"); break;
            case 0x07 :cprintf("OS/2 HPFS"); break;
            case 0x08 :cprintf("AIX"); break;
            case 0x09 :cprintf("AIX bootable"); break;
            case 0xa  :cprintf("OS/2 Boot Manag"); break;
            case 0xb  :cprintf("Win95/98/ME FAT32"); break;
            case 0xc  :cprintf("Win95/98/ME FAT32 (LBA)"); break;
            case 0xd  :cprintf("Win95 FAT16"); break;
            case 0xe  :cprintf("Win95 FAT16 (LBA)"); break;
            case 0xf  :cprintf("Win95 Extended"); break;
```

```
                case 0x11 :cprintf("Hidden FAT-12");break;
                case 0x12 :cprintf("Compaq Diagnostics");break;
                case 0x14 :cprintf("Hidden FAT-16 (<32)");break;
                case 0x15 :cprintf("Hidden Extended");break;
                case 0x16 :cprintf("Hidden FAT-16");break;
                case 0x17 :cprintf("NTFS"); break;
                case 0x40 :cprintf("Venix 80286"); break;
                case 0x51 :cprintf("Novell?"); break;
                case 0x52 :cprintf("Microport"); break;
                case 0x63 :cprintf("GNU HURD"); break;
                case 0x64 :
                case 0x65 :cprintf("Novell Netware"); break;
                case 0x75 :cprintf("PC/IX"); break;
                case 0x80 :cprintf("Old MINIX"); break;
                case 0x81 :cprintf("Linux/MINIX"); break;
                case 0x82 :cprintf("Linux swap"); break;
                case 0x83 :cprintf("Linux native"); break;
                case 0x85 :cprintf("Linux Extended"); break;
                case 0x93 :cprintf("Amoeba"); break;
                case 0x94 :cprintf("Amoeba BBT"); break;
                case 0xa5 :cprintf("BSD/386"); break;
                case 0xa6 :cprintf("OpenBSD"); break;
                case 0xa7 :cprintf("NEXTSTEP"); break;
                case 0xb7 :cprintf("BSDI fs"); break;
                case 0xb8 :cprintf("BSDI swap"); break;
                case 0xc7 :cprintf("Syrinx"); break;
                case 0xdb :cprintf("CP/M"); break;
                case 0xe1 :cprintf("DOS access"); break;
                case 0xe3 :cprintf("DOS R/O"); break;
                case 0xf2 :cprintf("DOS secondary"); break;
                case 0xff :cprintf("BBT"); break;
                default   :cprintf("UNKOWN");
        }
        return 0;
}
```

Writing program to Unhide the Partition

The program to unhide the hidden partition works just opposite to the program which hides the program. In this program we subtract 16 (0x10) from the value of file system indicator byte of the hidden partition.

The coding of the program in as follows:

```
/* Program to unhide the partition hidden by the previous program */
#include <bios.h>
#include <stdio.h>
```

Developing More Utilities for Disks

```c
int main(void)
{
    struct diskinfo_t dinfo;
    int result, tohide;
    int i;
    static char dbuf[512];/* Data buffer            */
    clrscr();
    dinfo.drive  =  0x80;      /* drive number for First Hard Disk*/
    dinfo.head   =  0;   /* disk head number */
    dinfo.track  =  0;   /* track number               */
    dinfo.sector  =  1; /* sector number              */
    dinfo.nsectors =  1;       /* sector count            */
    dinfo.buffer = dbuf;       /* data buffer             */
    result = _bios_disk(_DISK_READ, &dinfo);
    if ((result & 0xff00) == 0)
    {
        printf("The Partition Codes of Four Partition Entries are,
        0x%02x, 0x%02x, 0x%02x And 0x%02x.\n",
        dbuf[450] & 0xff, dbuf[466] & 0xff,
        dbuf[482] & 0xff, dbuf[498] & 0xff);
        textcolor(15);
        gotoxy(5,5);
        cprintf("Partition Entry in MBR is as follows:");
        gotoxy(10,7);cprintf("1. ");   showtype(dbuf[450] & 0xff);
        gotoxy(10,8);cprintf("2. ");   showtype(dbuf[466] & 0xff);
        gotoxy(10,9);cprintf("3. ");   showtype(dbuf[482] & 0xff);
        gotoxy(10,10);cprintf("4. ");   showtype(dbuf[498] & 0xff);
        /* Get the Use input to unhide the partition */
        gotoxy(1,15);printf("Enter The partition no., Which to unhide,
        Or Press any other key to Exit...  ");
        tohide=getche();
        switch(tohide)
        {
            /* Unhide first partition of partition table    */
            case '1':
                dbuf[450]  = dbuf[450] -16;
                result = _bios_disk(_DISK_WRITE, &dinfo);
                break;
            /* Unhide second partition of partition table    */
            case '2':
                dbuf[466]  = dbuf[466]-16;
                result = _bios_disk(_DISK_WRITE, &dinfo);
                break;
            /* Unhide third partition of partition table    */
            case '3':
                dbuf[482]  = dbuf[482] -16;
```

```c
                    result = _bios_disk(_DISK_WRITE, &dinfo);
                    break;
            /* Unhide fourth partition of partition table    */
            case '4':
                    dbuf[498]   = dbuf[498]-16;
                    result = _bios_disk(_DISK_WRITE, &dinfo);
                    break;
            default:
                    exit(0);
        }
        if ((result & 0xff00) == 0)
        {
                printf("\n\nThe New Partition Codes of Four Partition
                Entries are, 0x%02x, 0x%02x, 0x%02x And 0x%02x.\n",
                dbuf[450] & 0xff, dbuf[466] & 0xff,
                dbuf[482] & 0xff, dbuf[498] & 0xff);
                getch();
        }
        else
        {
                printf("Cannot Change the Byte, status = 0x%02x\n",
                result);
                getch();
        }
    }
    return 0;
}
```

Comments on Program

Be careful while giving the partition number to unhide. If the number of partition is entered wrong by mistake, the file system information of that partition will be changed and partition may become inaccessible. However the program previously discussed to hide the partitions, may help you to cure the file system indicator byte of that partition.

Writing program to delete Partition

The program to delete partition is used for troubleshooting purpose. For example, assume that you had the FAT32 file system partitions in your disk. Now you decided to install the LINUX operating system in your disk simultaneously.

If any how, the installation of operating system is interrupted in between, at the stage when the modifications were being made to the partition table of the MBR. In such cases there are a lot of possibilities that the partition, in which you were going to install the other operating system, becomes inaccessible.

In this case the disk space of the lost partition becomes useless due to being inaccessible. However if we delete the partition information of that partition from partition table any how, we can again

Developing More Utilities for Disks

make this space usable using FDISK command of DOS.

The program to delete the partition entry from the partition table of MBR has been given next:

```c
/* Program to delete the second partition entry from the partition table
of MBR */
# include <bios.h>
/* structure to read the partition entry from partition table */
struct partition
{
      /* Active Partition Byte */
      unsigned char bootable ;
      /* Starting Head */
      unsigned char start_side ;
      /* combination of Starting sector and cylinder number */
      unsigned int start_sec_cyl ;
      /* File system Indicator Byte  */
      unsigned char parttype ;
      /* Ending Head */
      unsigned char end_side ;
      /* combination of Starting sector and cylinder number */
      unsigned int end_sec_cyl ;
      /* Relative Sector Number */
      unsigned long part_beg ;
      /* Partition length in sectors */
      unsigned long plen ;
} ;

/* Structure to read-write MBR */
struct part
{
      /* IPL (Initial Program Loader) */
      unsigned char master_boot[446] ;
      /*   Partition table */
      struct partition pt[4] ;
      /* Magic Number */
      int lasttwo ;
} ;
struct part p ;
void main()
{
      unsigned int t1,t2;
      clrscr();
      biosdisk ( 2, 0x80, 0, 0, 1, 1, &p ) ;
      display(); /* display the information of Partition table */
      getch();
      p.pt[1].bootable  = 0;
```

```
        p.pt[1].start_side = 0 ;
        p.pt[1].start_sec_cyl = 0 ;
        p.pt[1].parttype = 0;
        p.pt[1].end_side = 0;
        p.pt[1].end_sec_cyl = 0;
        p.pt[1].part_beg = 0;
        p.pt[1].plen = 0;
        printf("\n\n\n After Deleting the Second Partition Entry From MBR
        Partition Table,");
        printf("\n The Partition Table will Be Changed as Follows: ");
        /*  To Delete Second Partition Information from partition table
        of MBR Remove the forward slashes from the biosdisk( ) function.
        Do not use Carelessly, Partition information of Second Partition
        of Partition Table will be Erased Completely. */
        //////   biosdisk ( 3, 0x80, 0, 0, 1, 1, &p ) ;
        display(); /* Display the information of partition table after
        modification */
        getch();
}
```

Comments on program:

Uncomment the **biosdisk (3, 0x80, 0, 0, 1, 1, &p)** function to delete the second partition from the partition table of MBR.

To delete the partition, all the parameters of it, are set to 0 in partition table entry in MBR. Always remember that if you delete the extended partition, all the logical partitions of that extended partition will also become inaccessible.

The Function **display( )** is used to display the partition table of MBR. The coding of the function is as follows:

```
/* Function to display partition table of MBR */
display()
{
        unsigned int s_sec, s_trk, e_sec, e_trk, i, t1, t2 ;
        char type[20], boot[5] ;
        printf("\n\nPart.  Boot   Starting location   Ending Location
        Relative  Number of");
        printf("\nType Side Cylinder Sector   Side Cylinder Sector   Sectors
        Sectors\n");
        for ( i = 0 ; i <= 3 ; i++ )
        {
            if ( p.pt[i].bootable == 0x80 )
                strcpy ( boot, "Yes" ) ;
            else
                strcpy ( boot, "No" ) ;
            switch ( p.pt[i].parttype )
            {
```

```c
            case 0x00 :
                    strcpy ( type, "Unused" ) ; break ;
            case 0x1 :
                    strcpy ( type, "FAT12" ) ; break ;
            case 0x2 :
                    strcpy ( type, "Xenix" ) ; break ;
            case 0x3 :
                    strcpy ( type, "Xenix:usr" ) ; break ;
            case 0x4 :
                    strcpy ( type, "FAT16<32M" ) ; break ;
            case 0x5 :
                    strcpy ( type, "DOS-Ext." ) ; break ;
            case 0x6 :
                    strcpy ( type, "FAT16>32M" ) ; break ;
            case 0x7 :
                    strcpy ( type, "NTFS" ) ; break ;
            case 0x0b :
                    strcpy ( type, "FAT32" ) ; break ;
            case 0x0c :
                    strcpy ( type, "FAT32-LBA" ) ; break ;
            case 0x0d :
                    strcpy ( type, "VFAT16" ) ; break ;
            case 0x0e :
                    strcpy ( type, "VFAT16-LBA" ) ; break ;
            case 0x0f :
                    strcpy ( type, "FAT EXT" ) ; break ;
            case 0x17 :
                    strcpy ( type, "HPFS" ) ; break ;
            case 0x81 :
                    strcpy ( type, "Old LINUX" ) ; break ;
            case 0x82 :
                    strcpy ( type, "LinuxSwap" ) ; break ;
            case 0x83 :
                    strcpy ( type, "LinuxNative" ) ; break ;
            case 0x85 :
                    strcpy ( type, "Linux Ext." ) ; break ;
            default :
                    strcpy ( type, "Unknown" ) ; break ;
    }
    s_sec = ( p.pt[i].start_sec_cyl & 0x3f ) ;
    t1    = ( p.pt[i].start_sec_cyl & 0xff00 ) >> 8 ;
    t2    = ( p.pt[i].start_sec_cyl & 0x00c0 ) << 2 ;
    s_trk = t1 | t2 ;
    e_sec = ( p.pt[i].end_sec_cyl & 0x3f ) ;
    t1    = ( p.pt[i].end_sec_cyl & 0xff00 ) >> 8 ;
```

```
            t2    = ( p.pt[i].end_sec_cyl & 0x00c0 ) << 2 ;
            e_trk = t1 | t2 ;
            printf ( "\n%6s %3s", type, boot ) ;
            printf ( "%4d %6d %8d", p.pt[i].start_side, s_trk,s_sec ) ;
            printf ( "%7d %6u %8u", p.pt[i].end_side,  e_trk, e_sec ) ;
            printf ( "  %10lu  %10lu", p.pt[i].part_beg,p.pt[i].plen ) ;
      }
      return 0;
}
```

Formatting "Track 0 Bad" floppy

This program is used to format those floppies which have bad sectors on their track 0 and when are formatted with DOS or windows, display error messages like "Track 0 BAD". However you can also use it to format normal floppies.

The coding of the program has been given in the disk included with this book with the name "**TTFORMAT.C**". The working logic of the program is same as the program published in **PCQUEST** computer magazine, in February 2003 edition.

In this program, we try to make this type of floppies reusable by formatting them. The program sounds that you can handle the floppy disk even with some bad sectors on it. However, if the first sector of the disk is bad, the floppy can not be formatted.

The program rewrites all the DBR, FAT and Root Directory information. If there are bad sectors on the surface of the disk, they are marked as bad in FAT.

In the coding of the program, the structure **BPB** is used to writer the BIOS Parameter Block of the DBR. The structure **boot_sector** is used to write the DBR of the disk. The structure **address_field** is used for interacting with number of cylinder, heads, and sectors per track and with the size of the sector.

Different functions used in the coding of the program and their description have been given in the table given next.

Function	Description
Random_VolumeID( )	This function provides the volume ID of the disk. (How DOS generates the serial number of the floppy has been discussed next to this table)
sector_no_to_physical( )	This function is used to Convert the number of sectors into tracks, Heads and sectors
format_term( )	To terminate the formatting and exit the program
write_boot_info( )	Writes the boot sector of the disk
set_media_type_for_format( )	The function is used to Set Media Type For format using function 18H of INT 13H
volume_label( )	The function gets the volume label to write

Developing More Utilities for Disks

	volume label of the disk
format( )	Wipes the surface of the disk during formatting as well as handling the bad sectors count.
get_drive_parameters( )	The Function uses INT 13H, Function 08H to get drive parameters.
mark_bad( )	Holds the information of bad cluster to mark in FAT
ask_for_continue( )	Function to confirm before formatting the disk
check_bad( )	Function to check if the returned status is error code for BAD sector
error( )	This function Displays Error message for Corresponding error code
lock_volume( )	The function is used to lock the Drive using INT 21H, function 44H and Sub function 0DH
unlock_volume( )	The function is used to unlock the Drive using INT 21H, function 44H and Sub function 0DH
physical_to_sector_no( )	Function is used to Calculate number of sectors from track, head and sector number

The Volume Serial Number of the Floppy disk is calculated by the DOS according to current date and time of the system clock.

The first part of the serial number is calculated by the sum of the time (seconds and hundredths of a second) and the date (month and day). The second part of the serial number is equal to the sum of the time (hours and minutes) and date (year).

All the calculations are performed in hexadecimal system. For example, let us assume that you formatted the floppy in DOS environment at 11:16:28:65 on 10/23/2003. Now let us calculate the serial number of the disk.

The time in (seconds and Hundredths of seconds) format is

    = (28 and 65)

    = (1CH and 41H)

    Write it as **1C41**

Similarly, date in (month and day) format is

    = (10 and 23)

    = (0AH and 17H)

    Write it as **0A17**

Similarly, time in (hours and minutes) format is,

    = (11 and 16)

    = (0BH and 10H)

    Write it as **0B10**

And the year will be

= 2003

= **07D3**

Now, let us calculate the serial number of the floppy disk, according to the description given before. The first part of the serial number well be **(1C41 + 0A17) = 2658** and the second part of the serial number will be **(0B10 + 07D3) = 12E3**.

Writing the Disk Editing Tool

The coding of the disk editing program has been given in the disk included with this book, with the file name **"TTEDITOR.C"**. You can use this program to analyze the hard disks or floppy disks surface. Even most of the study while writing this book, I have used **TTEDITOR** to analyze the disk surface or perform the disk modifications.

Some of the important tasks, this editing program can perform are as follows:

- Read per sector information of the surface of hard disks and floppy disks.
- Write the backup of any sector to file.
- Restore the data of the sector from the file.
- Modify the single byte
- Hexadecimal to Decimal and Binary calculator.

The program uses biosdisk( ) and _bios_disk( ) function to access the disks. If you want to analyze the disk beyond the 8.4 GB, Modify the program with the use of Extensions of INT 13H. The description of the functions, used in the program has been given in the following table:

Function	Description
bkground( )	creates the back ground and frame of first screen
clsline( )	Used to clear the complete row from the screen specified by row number.
refresh( )	Function to recall all the display functions on the screen
writetofile( )	Function to write the data of a sector to user defined file.
writetosector( )	Function to restore the sector from specified file.
msgdisp( )	Function to display messages on the screen.
modify( )	Function to modify a single byte of any sector, specified by user.
frame( )	Function to draw the frame structure of sector display
dispmax( )	Display maximum CHS number of the disk (Valid Up to 8.4 GB Disk)
display( )	Display the sector and information on the screen.
hextodec( )	Function to Calculate hexadecimal number to corresponding decimal and binary numbers.

Appendix – I
Important C Functions and Header iles

alloc.h

brk	calloc	coreleft	farcalloc
farcoreleft	farfree	farheapcheck	farheapcheckfree
farheapchechnode	farheapfillfree	farheapwalk	farmalloc
farrealloc	free	heapcheck	heapcheckfree
realloc	sbrk		

assert.h

assert			

bcd.h

abs	acos	asin	atan
cos	cosh	exp	log
log10	pow	pow10	real
sin	sinh	sqrt	tan
tanh			

bios.h

_bios_disk	_bios_equip	_bios_keybrd	_bios_memsize
_bios_printer	_bios_serialcom	_bios_timeofday	bioscom
biosdisk	biosequip	bioskey	biosmemory
biosprint	biostime		

complex.h

abs	acos	arg	asin
atan	conj	cos	cosh
exp	imag	log	Log10
norm	polar	pow	Pow10
real	sin	sinh	sqrt
tan	tanh		

conio.h

cgets	clreol	clrscr	cprintf
cputs	cscanf	delline	getch
getche	getpass	gettext	gettextinfo
gotoxy	highvideo	insline	inp
inport	inportb	inpw	kbhit
lowvideo	movetext	normvideo	outp
outport	outportb	outpw	putch
puttext	_setcursortype	textattr	textbackground
textcolor	textmode	ungetch	wherex
wherey	window		

ctype.h

_ftolower	_ftoupper	isalnum	isalpha
isascii	iscntrl	isdigit	isgraph
islower	isprint	ispunct	isspace
isupper	isxdigit	toascii	tolower
toupper			

dir.h

chdir	findfirst	findnext	fnmerge
fnsplit	getcurdir	getcwd	getdisk
mkdir	mktemp	rmdir	searchpath
setdisk			

Appendix-I: Important C Functions and Header Files

direct.h

| _chdrive | _getdcwd | _getdrive | |

dirent.h

| closedir | opendir | readdir | rewindir |

dos.h

absread	abswrite	allocmem	bdos
bdosptr	_chain_intr	country	ctrlbrk
delay	disable	_dos_allocmem	_dos_close
_dos_creat	_dos_creatnew	dosexterr	_dos_findfirst
_dos_findnext	_dos_freemem	_dos_getdate	_dos_getdiskfree
_dos_getdrive	_dos_getfileattr	_dos_getftime	_dos_gettime
_dos_getvect	_dos_keep	_dos_open	_dos_read
_dos_setblock	_dos_setdate	_dos_setdrive	_dos_setfileattr
_dos_setftime	_dos_settime	_dos_setvect	dostounix
_dos_write	_emit_	enable	FP_OFF
FP_SEG	freemem	geninterrupt	getcbrk
getdate	getdfree	_getdrive	getdta
getfat	getfatd	getftime	getpsp
gettime	getvect	getverify	_harderr
harderr	_hardresume	hardresume	_hardretn
hardretn	inp	inport	inportb
int86	int86x	intdos	intdosx
intr	keep	MK_FP	nosound
outp	outport	outportb	_OvrInitEms
_OvrInitExt	parsfnm	peek	peekb
poke	pokeb	randbrd	randbwr
segread	setblock	setcbrk	setdate
setdta	settime	setvect	setverify
sleep	sound	unixtodos	unlink

errno.h
fcntl.h

_fmode	O_APPEND	O_BINARY	O_CHANGED
O_CREAT	O_DENYALL	O_DENYNONE	O_DENYREAD
O_DENYWRITE	O_DEVICE	O_EXCL	O_NOINHERIT
O_RDONLY	O_RDWR	O_TEXT	O_TRUNC
O_WRONLY			

float.h

| _clear87 | _fpreset | _control87 | _status87 |

fstream.h
generic.h
graphics.h

arc	bar	bar3d	circle
cleardevice	clearviewport	closegraph	detectgraph
drawpoly	ellipse	fillellipse	fillpoly
floodfill	getarccoords	getaspectratio	getbkcolor
getcolor	getdefaultpalette	getdrivername	getfillpattern
getfillsettings	getgraphmode	getimage	getlinesettings
getmaxcolor	getmaxmode	getmaxx	getmaxy
getmodename	getmoderange	getpalette	getpalettesize
getpixel	gettextsettings	getviewsettings	getx
gety	graphdefaults	grapherrormsg	_graphfreemem
_graphgetmem	graphresult	imagesize	initgraph
installuserdriver	installuserfont	line	linerel
lineto	moverel	moveto	outtext
outtextxy	pieslice	putimage	putpixel
rectangle	registerbgidriver	registerfarbgidriver	registerbgifont
registerfarbgifont	restorecrtmode	sector	setactivepage
setallpalette	setaspectratio	setbkcolor	setcolor
setfillpattern	setfillstyle	setgraphbufsize	setgraphmode
setlinestyle	setpalette	setrgbpalette	settextjustify
settextstyle	setusercharsize	setviewport	setvisualpage
setwritemode	textheight	textwidth	

Appendix-I: Important C Functions and Header Files

io.h

access	chmod	_chmod	chsize
close	_close	creat	_creat
creatnew	creattemp	dup	dup2
eof	filelength	getftime	ioctl
isatty	lock	locking	lseek
mktemp	open	_open	read
_read	remove	rename	setftime
setmode	sopen	tell	umask
unlink	unlock	write	_write

iomanip.h
iostream.h
limits.h
locale.h

localeconv	setlocale		

malloc.h

stackavail			

math.h

abs	acos,	acosl	asin,
asinl	atan,	atanl	atan2,
atan2l	atof,	_atold	cabs,
cabsl	ceil,	ceill	cos,
cosl	cosh,	coshl	exp,
expl	fabs,	fabsl	floor,
floorl	fmod,	fmodl	frexp,
frexpl	hypot,	hypotl	labs
ldexp,	ldexpl	log,	logl
log10,	log10l	matherr,	_matherrl
modf,	modfl	poly,	polyl
pow,	powl	pow10,	pow10l
sin,	sinl	sinh,	sinhl
sqrt,	sqrtl	tan,	tanl
tanh,	tanhl		

mem.h

_fmemccpy	_fmemchr	_fmemcmp	_fmemcpy
_fmemicmp	_fmemmove	_fmemset	_fmovmem
_fsetmem	memccpy	memchr	memcmp
memcpy	memicmp	memmove	memset
movedata	movmem	setmem	

memory.h
new.h

set_new_handler			

process.h

abort	_cexit	_c_exit	execl
execle	execlp	execlpe	execv
execve	execvp	execvpe	exit
_exit	getpid	spawnl	spawnle
spawnlp	spawnlpe	spawnv	spawnve
spawnvp	spawnvpe	system	

search.h

bsearch	lfind	lsearch	qsort

setjmp.h

longjmp	setjmp		

share.h
signal.h

raise	signal		

Appendix-I: Important C Functions and Header Files

stdarg.h
stddef.h
stdio.h

clearer	fclose	fcloseall	fdopen
feof	ferror	fflush	fgetc
fgetchar	fgetpos	fgets	fileno
flushall	fopen	fprintf	fputc
fputchar	fputs	fred	freopen
fscanf	fseek	fsetpos	ftell
fwrite	getc	getchar	gets
getw	perror	printf	putc
putchar	puts	putw	remove
rename	rewind	rmtmp	scanf
setbuf	setvbuf	sprintf	sscanf
strerror	_strerror	tempnam	tmpfile
tmpnam	ungetc	unlink	vfprintf
vfscanf	vsprintf	vsscanf	

stdiostr.h
stdlib.h

abort	abs	atexit	atof
atoi	atol	bsearch	calloc
div	ecvt	exit	_exit
fcvt	free	_fulpath	gcvt
getnev	itoa	labs	ldiv
lfind	_lrotl	_lrotr	lsearch
ltoa	_makepath	malloc	max
mblen	mbtowc	mbstowcs	min
putenv	qsort	rand	random
randomize	realloc	_rotl	_rotr
_searchenv	_splitpath	srand	strtod
strtol	_strtold	strtoul	swab
system	time	ultoa	wctomb
wcstombs			

stream.h
string.h

_fmemccpy	_fmemchr	_fmemcmp	_fmemcpy
_fmemicmp	_fmemset	_fstrcat	_fstrchr
_fstrcmp	_fstrcpy	_fstrcspn	_fstrdup
_fstricmp	_fstrlen	_fstrlwr	_fstrncat
_fstrncmp	_fstrnicmp	_fstrncpy	_fstrnset
_fstrpbrk	_fstrrchr	_fstrrev	_fstrset
_fstrspn	_fstrstr	_fstrtok	_fstrupr
memccpy	memchr	memcmp	memcpy
memicmp	memmove	memset	movedata
movmem	setmem	stpcpy	strcat
strchr	strcmp	strcmpi	strcpy
strcspn	strdup	_strerror	strerror
stricmp	strlen	strlwr	strncat
strncmp	strncmpi	strncpy	strnicmp
strnset	strpbrk	strrchr	strrev
strset	strspn	strstr	strtok
strxfrm	strupr		

strstrea.h
sys/locking.h
sys/stat.h

fstat	stat		

sys/timeb.h

ftime			

systypes.h
time.h

asctime	clock	ctime	difftime
gmtime	localtime	mktime	stime
strftime	_strdate	_strtime	time
tzset			

utime.h

utime			

values.h
varargs.h

Important C Functions

abort()	Abort Process and Return Error
abs()	Calculate Absolute Value of Integer
absread()	Read Disk Sectors
abswrite()	Write Disk Sectors
access()	Check File Permission Setting
acos()	Calculate Arc Cosine
alloca()	Allocate Memory Block on Stack
allocmem()	Allocate DOS Memory Segment
asctime()	Convert Time from Structure to String
asin()	Calculate Arc Sine
assert()	Diagnostic Message Generator
atan()	Calculate Arc Tangent
atan2()	Calculate Arc Tangent of y/x
atexit()	Register Exit Function
atof()	Convert String to Double
atoi()	Convert String to Integer
atol()	Convert String to Long
bdos()	Invoke DOS Function, Short Form
bdosptr()	MS-DOS System Call
bioscom()	Communications I/O
biosdisk()	Hard Disk / Floppy I/O
biosequip()	Check Equipment
bioskey()	Keyboard Interface
biosmemory()	Return Memory Size
biosprint()	Printer I/O
biostime()	Return the Time of Day
brk()	Change Data-Segment Space Allocation
bsearch()	Perform Binary Search
cabs()	Calculate Absolute Value of Complex Number

calloc()	Allocate and Zero Memory
ceil()	Calculate Ceiling of Value
cgets()	Get a Character String from the Console
chdir()	Change Current Working Directory
chmod()	Change File Permission Setting
_chmod()	Change Access Mode of File
_clear87()	Get and Clear 8087/80287 Status Word
clearerr()	Clear Error Indicator for a Stream
close()	Close File
_close()	Close a File Handle
coreleft()	Return a Measure of Unused Memory
cos()	Calculate Cosine
cosh()	Calculate Hyperbolic Cosine
country()	Return Country-Dependent Information
cprintf()	Formatted Write to Console
cputs()	Write a String to the Console
creat()	Create a New File
_creat()	Create a New File
creatnew()	Create a New File
creattemp()	Create a New File or Rewrite an Existing One
cscanf()	Read Formatted Data from Console
ctime()	Convert Time from Long Integer to String
ctrlbrk()	Set Control-Break Handler
difftime()	Find the Difference between Two Times
disable()	Disable Interrupts
dosexterr()	Get DOS Extended Error Values
dostounix()	Convert Date and Time to UNIX Time Format
dup()	Create Second Handle for Open File
dup2()	Reassign a File Handle
ecvt()	Convert Double to String
enable()	Enable Interrupts
eof()	Test for End of File
exec...()	An Overview of the Eight Exec Functions
execl()	Execute Program Using: Arg List
execle()	Execute Program Using: Arg List, Environment
execlp()	Execute Program Using: Arg List, PATH
execlpe()	Execute Program Using: Arg List, PATH, Environment

execv()	Execute Program Using: Arg Array
execve()	Execute Program Using: Arg Array, Environment
execvp()	Execute Program Using: Arg Array, PATH
execvpe()	Execute Program Using: Arg Array, PATH, Environment
exit()	Terminate Process after Cleanup
_exit()	Terminate Process without Cleanup
exp()	Calculate Exponential
fabs()	Calculate Absolute Value of Floating-Point
farcalloc()	Allocate Memory from Far Heap
farcoreleft()	Return Measure of Unused Memory in Far Heap
farfree()	Free a Block from Far Heap
farmalloc()	Allocate Memory from Far Heap
farrealloc()	Adjust Allocated Block in Far Heap
fclose()	Close a Stream
fcloseall()	Close All Open Streams
fcvt()	Convert Double to String
fdopen()	Open a Stream Using a Handle
feof()	Detect Stream End-of-File (Macro)
ferror()	Test for Error on a Stream (Macro)
fflush()	Flush a Stream
fgetc()	Read a Character from a Stream
fgetchar()	Read a Character from Stdin
fgets()	Read a String from Stream
filelength()	Return File Length
fileno()	Get File Handle Associated with Stream (Macro)
findfirst()	Search Disk Directory
findnext()	Fetch Files That Match findfirst()
floor()	Calculate Floor of Value
flushall()	Flush All Streams and Clear All Buffers
fmod()	Calculate Floating-Point Remainder
fnmerge()	Make New File Name
fnsplit()	Split a Full Path Name into Its Components
fopen()	Open a File
FP_OFF()	Get or Set Offset Portion of a Far Pointer (Macro)
FP_SEG()	Get or Set Segment Portion of a Far Pointer (Macro)
_fpreset()	Reinitialize Floating-Point Math Package
fprintf()	Write Formatted Data to Stream

fputc()	Write a Character to a Stream
fputs()	Write a String to Stream
fread()	Read Unformatted Data from Stream
free()	Deallocate Memory Block
freemem()	Free a Previously Allocated DOS Memory Block
freopen()	Reassign a File Pointer
frexp()	Get Mantissa and Exponent of Floating-Point Value
fscanf()	Read Formatted Data from Screen
fseek()	Reposition File Pointer to Given Location
fstat()	Get Information about Open File
ftell()	Get Current File Pointer Position
fwrite()	Write Unformatted Data to Stream
gcvt()	Convert Double to String
geninterrupt()	Generate Software Interrupt
getc()	Read a Character from a Stream (Macro)
getchar()	Read a Character from 'Stdin'
getch()	Get a Character from the Console without Echo
getche()	Get a Character from Console with Echo
getcwd()	Get Path Name of Current Working Directory
getenv()	Get a Value from the Environment Table
getpid()	Get Process ID
getcbrk()	Get Control-Break Setting
getcurdir()	Get Current Directory
getdate()	Get Date
getdfree()	Get Disk Free Space
getdisk()	Get Current Drive
getdta()	Get Disk Transfer Address
getfat()	Get File Allocation Table Information
getfatd()	Get File Allocation Table Information
getftime()	Get File Date and Time
getpass()	Read a Password
getpsp()	Get the Program Segment Prefix
gets()	Read a Line from 'Stdin'
gettime()	Get System Time
getvect()	Get Interrupt Vector Entry
getverify()	Get Verify State
getw()	Read an Integer from a Stream

Function	Description
gsignal()	Software Signals
harderr()	Establish a Hardware Error Handler
hardresume()	Hardware Error Handler Function
hardretn()	Hardware Error Handler Function
hypot()	Calculate the Hypotenuse of a Right Triangle
inport()	Input from Hardware Port
inportb()	Input from Hardware Port
intr()	Alternate 8086 Software Interrupt Interface
int86()	Execute 8086 Software Interrupt
int86x()	Set Segment Registers and Execute Software Interrupt
intdos()	Invoke DOS Function, Long Form
intdosx()	Set Seg Regs and Invoke DOS Function, Long Form
ioctl()	Control I/O Device
isalnum()	Test for Alphanumeric Character (Macro)
isalpha()	Test for Alphabetic Character (Macro)
isascii()	Test for ASCII Character (Macro)
isatty()	Check for Character Device
iscntrl()	Test for Control Character
isdigit()	Test for Digit
isgraph()	Test for Printable Character Except Space
islower()	Test for Lowercase
isprint()	Test for Printable Character
ispunct()	Test for Punctuation Character
isspace()	Test for White-Space Character
isupper()	Test for Uppercase
isxdigit()	Test for Hexadecimal Digit
itoa()	Convert Integer to String
kbhit()	Check Keyboard Input Buffer for Character Waiting
keep()	Exit and Remain Resident
labs()	Calculate Absolute Value of Long Integer
ldexp()	Convert Mantissa and Exponent to Floating Point
lfind()	Linear Search for Key
localtime()	Convert Time from Int to Structure—Local Correction
lock()	Set File Sharing Locks
log()	Calculate Natural Logarithm
log10()	Calculate Base 10 Logarithm
longjmp()	Restore Program State

lsearch()	Linear Search for Key; Add Key If Not Found
lseek()	Reposition File Pointer to Specified Location
ltoa()	Convert Long to String
malloc()	Allocate Memory Block
matherr()	Handle Math Error
_matherr()	Floating-Point Error Handling Routine
memccpy()	Copy Characters from Buffer
memchr()	Find Character in Buffer
memcmp()	Compare Characters from Two Buffers
memcpy()	Copy Characters between Buffers
memicmp()	Compare Characters in Two Buffers
memmove()	Move a Block of Bytes
memset()	Initialize Buffer
mkdir()	Create a New Directory
MK_FP()	Make a Far Pointer
mktemp()	Create a Unique File Name
modf()	Split Floating Point into Mantissa and Exponent
movedata()	Copy Characters to a Different Segment
movmem()	Move a Block of Bytes
open()	Open a File
_open()	Open a File For Reading or Writing
outport()	Output to a Hardware Port
outportb()	Output to a Hardware Port
parsfnm()	Parse File Name
peek()	Examine Memory Location
peekb()	Examine Memory Location
perror()	Print Error Message
poke()	Store Value at a Given Memory Location
pokeb()	Store Value at a Given Memory Location
poly()	Generate a Polynomial from Arguments
pow()	Calculate X Raised to the Yth Power
pow10()	Power Function
printf()	Write Formatted String to Stdout
putc()	Write a Character to Stream
putchar()	Write a Character to Stdout
putch()	Write a Character to the Console
putenv()	Create New Environment Variables

Appendix-I: Important C Functions and Header Files

puts()	Write String to Stdout
putw()	Write an Integer to Stream
qsort()	Perform Quick Sort
rand()	Get Pseudorandom Integer
randbrd()	Random Block Read
randbwr()	Random Block Write
read()	Read Data from File
_read()	Read Data from a File
realloc()	Reallocate Memory Block
rename()	Rename a File or Directory
rewind()	Reposition File Pointer to Beginning of Stream
rmdir()	Remove a Directory
sbrk()	Reset Break Value for Calling Process
scanf()	Read Formatted Data from Stdin
searchpath()	Search the DOS Path
segread()	Return Current Values of Segment Registers
setblock()	Modify Size of DOS Memory Segment
setbuf()	Control Stream Buffering
setcbrk()	Set Control-Break Setting
setdate()	Set MS-DOS Date
setdisk()	Set Current Disk Drive
setdta()	Set Disk Transfer Address
setftime()	Set File Date and Time
setjmp()	Save Program State
setmem()	Assign a Value to Memory
setmode()	Set File-Translation Mode
settime()	Set System Time
setvbuf()	Control Stream Buffering and Buffer Size
setvect()	Set Interrupt Vector Entry
setverify()	Set Verify State
sin()	Calculate Sine
sinh()	Calculate Hyperbolic Sine
sleep()	Suspend Execution for Interval
spawn...()	An Overview of the Eight Spawn Functions
spawnl()	Execute Program Using: Arg List
spawnle()	Execute Program Using: Arg List, Environment
spawnlp()	Execute Program Using Arg List, PATH

spawnlpe()	Execute Program Using Arg List, PATH, Environment
spawnv()	Execute Program Using Arg Array
spawnve()	Execute Program Using Arg Array, Environment
spawnvp()	Execute Program Using Arg Array, PATH
spawnvpe()	Execute Program Using Arg Array, PATH, Environment
sprintf()	Write Formatted Data to String
sqrt()	Calculate Square Root
srand()	Set Random Starting Point
sscanf()	Read Formatted Data from String
ssignal()	Implement Software Signals
stackavail()	Return Size of Available Stack Memory
stat()	Get File-Status Information on Named File
_status87()	Get 8087/80287 Floating-Point Status Word
stime()	Set Time
strcat()	Append a String
strchr()	Find a Character in a String
strcmp()	Compare Two Strings, Case Sensitive
strcmpi()	Compare Two Strings, Case Insensitive
stricmp()	Compare Two Strings, Case Insensitive
strcpy()	Copy One String to Another
strcspn()	Scan One String for Another
strdup()	Duplicate String
strerror()	Save System Error Message
strlen()	Get String Length
strlwr()	Convert String to Lower Case
strncat()	Append Specified Number of Characters to a String
strncmp()	Compare n Characters of Two Strings, Case Sensitive
strnicmp()	Compare n Characters of Strings, Case Insensitive
strncpy()	Copy a Specified Number of Characters
strnset()	Initialize n Characters of String
strpbrk()	Scan String for Character from Character Set
strrchr()	Scan String for Last Occurrence of Character
strrev()	Reverse Characters in String
strset()	Set All Characters in String
strspn()	Find First Substring
strstr()	Find Substring
strtod()	Convert String to Double

Function	Description
strtol()	Convert String to Long Decimal Integer
strtok()	Finds Next Token in String
strupr()	Convert String to Uppercase
swab()	Swap Bytes
system()	Execute DOS Command
tan()	Calculate Tangent
tanh()	Calculate Hyperbolic Tangent
tell()	Get Current File Pointer Position
time()	Get Current System Time as Long Integer
toascii()	Convert character to ASCII Character
tolower()	Convert character To Lowercase, If Appropriate
_tolower()	Convert character to Lowercase
toupper()	Convert character to Uppercase, If Appropriate
_toupper()	Convert character to Uppercase
tzset()	Set External Time Variables, Environment Variables
ultoa()	Convert Unsigned Long to String
ungetc()	Push Character Back onto the Stream
ungetch()	Push Back the Last Character Read from the Console
unixtodos()	Convert Date and Time to DOS Format
unlink()	Delete a File
unlock()	Release File-Sharing Locks
va_arg()	Access Variable Number of Arguments, ANSI C Style
vfprintf()	Write Formatted Data to Stream
vfscanf()	Perform Formatted Input from a Stream
vprintf()	Write Formatted Data to Stdout
vscanf()	Perform Formatted Input from Stdin
vsprintf()	Write Formatted Data to String
vsscanf()	Perform Formatted Input from String
write()	Write Data to a File
_write()	Write Data to a File

Appendix – II
Glossary of Data Recovery Terms

ABEND: The abnormal termination of a computer program.

ABIOS: The ABIOS is a protected-mode BIOS which is used by OS/2.

Access: To locate the desired data.

Access Arm: The disk-drive component used to position read/write heads over a specified track.

Accessibility: The extent to which computers are easy to use and available to a wide range of users, including people with one or more physical disabilities.

Access Methods: The technique and/or program code for moving data between main storage and Input/Output devices.

Access Time: The time interval between when data is called for or requested to be stored in a storage device and when delivery or storage is completed.

Address Bus: The electrical pathway used to transmit the storage locations for data or instructions.

Address Translation: The process of changing the address of an item of data or an instruction to the address in main storage at which it is to be loaded or reloaded.

ADP: Automatic data processing.

Anticipatory Retrieval: A technique for optimizing the reading of data from a slow storage device by fetching more data than is immediately required and by retaining it in faster medium until it is actually needed.

ANSI: American National Standards Institute.

API: A set of routines that an application program uses to request and carry out lower-level services performed by the operating system.

Architecture: The structure of all or part of a computer system. Also refers to the design of system software.

ASCII: Acronym for **American Standard Code for Information Interchange**

ASCII Character: The most widely recognized 8 bit code for representing alphanumerics and other characters of English language.

ASCIIZ String: Sequence of ASCII Characters terminated by a Null, or zero, byte.

ASPI: Advanced SCSI Programming Interface.

ATA: Advanced Technology Attachment, the more correct name for the IDE interface.

Auxiliary Storage: Storage that supplements the primary storage of the computer, same as secondary storage.

Backup: The copying of information to provide a means of recovery from lost or corrupt data.

Backup File: A duplicate copy of a file.

BCD (Binary Coded Decimal): A method of data storage where two decimal digits are stored in each byte, one in the upper four bits and the other in the lower four bits. Since only the values 0 through 9 are used in each half of a byte, BCD values can be read as decimal numbers on a hexadecimal display of memory or a file.

Binary: Pertaining to characteristics or property involving a selection, choice, or condition in which there are two possibilities, or pertaining to the number system that utilizes a base of two.

Binary Digit: Either of the characters 0 or 1. These characters are abbreviated "bit".

Binary Number System: A number system with a base or radix of two.

Binary System: The base 2 numbering system, which uses the digits 0 and 1. The computer data can be represented by this numbering system.

BIOS: Basic I/O system. A set of routines that works closely with the hardware to support the transfer of information between elements of the system, such as memory, disks, and the monitor.

BIOS Parameter Block (BPB): Information located inside the boot sector specific to the logical drive information.

Block: A grouping of contiguous data records or other data elements that are handled as a unit.

Block device: A device such as a disk drive that moves information in groups of bytes (blocks) rather than one byte at a time.

Block Editing: A capability of word processing programs that allows users to define, move, delete, or perform other operations on a block of text.

Blocked Tape: A storage technique used where records are grouped together on tape. This provides more storage and faster access by reducing the number of inter-record gaps.

Blocking Factor: The number of logical records combined into one physical record or block.

Boot: To start up the computer or operating system. The term "boot" is a contraction of "bootstrap", which in turn comes from the expression "to lift oneself by one's boot straps." The ROM BIOS on IBM PCs and compatibles reads in the first sector of the disk, which contains a short program of 512 bytes that reads in a portion of the operating system, which in turn reads in the remainder of the operating system.

Boot Drive: The disk drive from which the operating system was booted.

Boot sector: First sector on a logical drive that includes code to boot that drive, specific logical drive information, and error messages.

Bootstrap: A technique in which the first few instructions of a program are sufficient to bring the rest of itself into the computer from an input device.

Bottom Up Testing: Testing a computer program by beginning with individual subroutines or modules and then testing increasingly larger units.

Branch: A transfer of control from one instruction to another in a program that is not part of the normal sequential execution of the instructions of the program.

Breakpoint: When debugging, a memory location which when accessed causes a break in the normal flow of execution and the invocation of the debugger.

Bubble Memory: A type of nonvolatile memory where data are represented by the presence or absence of magnetized areas (bubble) formed on a thin piece of garnet.

Buffer: Temporary storage used to compensate for a difference in rate of flow of data, or time of occurrence of events, when transmitting data from one device to another.

Bug: A euphemism for a defect.

Bus: A set of hardwire lines used for data transfer among the components of a computer system.

Byte: A set of 8 binary digits.

C: A low-level structural programming language developed by AT&T-Bell Laboratories. It resembles a machine-independent assembler language and is popular for software package development.

Cache: Caching is a method of increasing performance by keeping frequently used data in a location which is more quickly accessed.

Cache Memory: A high-speed temporary storage area in the CPU for storing parts of a program of data during processing.

Call: A transfer of program control to a subroutine.

Capacity Management: The use of planning and control methods to forecast and control information processing job loads, hardware and software usage, and other computer system resource requirements.

Cartridge Tape: A form of magnetic tape similar to cassette tape but with a much greater storage density. Used mainly with large computer system.

Cassette Tape: A form of magnetic tape, about one fourth inch wide, generally used for secondary storage with microcomputers.

CBIOS: The CBIOS is a real-mode BIOS which is compatible with the earlier products in the IBM PC family and PS/2 models with 8086 processors.

CDFS: CD-ROM file system, which controls access to the contents of CD-ROM drives.

CD-ROM: Compact disc read-only memory. It is a laser-encoded optical memory storage medium.

Checksum: A calculated value used to test data for the presence of errors that can occur when data is transmitted or when it is written to disk.

Clean boot: Booting or starting a computer using the minimum system files in the operating system.

Clean installation: Installation of an operating system on a new computer or a computer with a reformatted hard disk.

Cluster: A specified number of sectors grouped together by the FORMAT command. The number and size is determined by the size of the logical drive. A cluster is the smallest storage unit for storing files.

CMOS: Complementary Metal-Oxide-Semiconductor, A type of integrated circuit design known for its low power consumption.

CMOS RAM: A small amount (typically 64 or 128 bytes) of memory in real-time clock chip of system that is preserved by the clock's battery and is used for storing configuration information.

Code: computer instructions.

COM (Computer Output Microfilm): A technology that permits the output information produced by computers to be store on microfilm.

Command Mode: A mode of operation in which application program commands can be selected.

Complier: A program that translates a high-level programming language into a machine language program.

Compressed Volume File (CVF): A file with read-only, hidden, and system attributes, and that contains a compressed drive.

Computer Virus: A program that copies its destructive program routines into the computer systems of anyone who accesses computer systems which have used the program, or anyone who use copies of data or programs taken from such computers. This spreads the destruction of data and programs among many computer users.

Computer: A device that can accept data, perform certain functions on that data, and present the results of those operations.

Copy: (1) The process of making a duplicate files from an existing file. (2) The process of duplicating text or graphics on the screen for placement elsewhere while leaving the original text or graphics intact.

Corrective Maintenance: Maintenance done for the purpose of eliminating a problem. It may occur as either emergency maintenance or deferred maintenance.

Crash: A hardware or software failure that leads to an abnormal cessation of processing.

Current Directory Structure: The data record used by DOS to keep track of the current directory on a drive, whether the drive is valid, network, Substituted, or Joined and other pertinent information.

Cursor: A movable point of light displayed on most video display screens to assist the user in the input of data.

Cut and Paste: A feature in an application software package that cuts (erases) part or all of an object or text and places it in a buffer. The object or text may be pasted (inserted) at a later time.

Cylinder: The set of concentric tracks of data located at the same position on each data-bearing surface of the disk. A double-sided floppy will contain two tracks per cylinder.

DASD: Acronym for direct-access storage device.

Data: Facts or observations about physical phenomena or business transactions.

Data Access Diagram: A graphic tool for depicting the ways by which a data store can be referred to by means of the information contained in another data store.

Data Administration: A data resource management function, which involves the establishment and enforcement of policies and procedures for managing data as strategic corporate resource.

Data Compression: A technique that saves storage space by eliminating gaps, empty fields, redundancies, or unnecessary data to shorten the length of records or blocks.

DDE: Dynamic Data Exchange. An interprocess communication method that allows two or more programs running simultaneously to exchange data and commands.

DDI: Device driver interface.

Debug: The detect, locate, and remove errors from a program or malfunctions from a computer.

Debugging: The process of removing defects from a computer system.

Decimal System: The base 10 numbering system using the digits 0 through 9.

Default Data: Values that are automatically provided by software to reduce keystrokes and to improve the productivity of computer user. However, the user has the option of replacing default data with other values when such action is needed.

Default Setting: In application software, a parameter that is automatically entered unless changed by the user.

Delayed Write: A form of caching in which control is returned before the data is actually written to the storage media.

Delete: An application-software feature that allows existing text, data, fields, records, or files to be removed.

Demand paging: A method by which code and data are moved in pages from physical memory to a temporary paging file on disk.

Device Driver: An interface module between the device-independent portions of the operating system and an actual hardware device which converts device-independent requests into the actual sequence of device operations to perform the requested action.

Device node: The basic data structure for a given device, built by Configuration Manager; sometimes called devnode. Device nodes are built into memory at system startup for each device and enumerator with information about the device, such as currently assigned resources. The complete representation of all device nodes is referred to as the hardware tree.

Direct Access Storage Device (DASD): A storage device that can directly access data to be stored or retrieved, for example, a magnetic disk unit.

Direct Access: A method of storage where each storage position has a unique address and can be individually accessed in approximately the same period of time without having to search through other storage positions.

Direct Memory Access (DMA): A method whereby peripherals may transfer data into or out of main memory without the involvement of the CPU.

Distribution media format (DMF): A special read-only format for 3½ inch floppy disks that permits storage of 1.7 MB of data.

Dock: To insert or remove a device in a computer system.

Disk Operating System (DOS): An operating system for microcomputers in which all or part resides on a disk and must be loaded into the computer. It is a set of programs that controls and supervises the microcomputer's hardware.

DOS Extender: A program, which allows a program to run in protected mode while still retaining access to real-mode MSDOS services.

DRAM (Dynamic Random Access Memory): RAM memory, which essentially consists of a tiny capacitor for each bit of memory. Since capacitors do not hold a charge indefinitely, DRAM must be constantly refreshed to avoid losing its contents. Also, the process of reading the contents of the memory are destructive, meaning extra time must be spent restoring the contents of memory addresses, which are accessed, so DRAM is slower than SRAM.

Dump: To copy the contents of all or part of a storage device, usually from an internal device, onto an external storage device.

DVD: Digital Versatile Disk. The optical disk storage that encompasses audio, video, and computer data.

EEPROM: A type of memory that can be erased and reprogrammed electrically without removing the chip from the circuit board.

Encryption: A way of making data indecipherable to protect it from unauthorized viewing or use.

EPROM: A type of memory that can be erased by removing it from the circuit and exposing the chip to ultraviolet light. It can then be reprogrammed.

Exception handling: An event that occurs as a program runs and that requires software outside the normal flow of control to be run.

Expanded Memory Specification: A specification devised by Lotus, Intel, and Microsoft for accessing more than one megabyte of memory by bank-switching additional memory into the one megabyte real mode address space.

Extended BIOS Data Area: A block of memory, typically the 1K at the top of conventional memory, which is used to store additional data for use by the BIOS which does not fit into the 256-byte data area at segment 0040h.

Extended File Control Block: A DOS File Control Block which has had an additional seven bytes prepended to permit control of file attributes (which are stored in the appendage)

Extended Memory: Memory beyond the one megabyte address which is available only on 80286 and higher machines. Except for a small portion (the High Memory Area) the extended memory is only accessible from protected mode.

Extended Memory Specification: A specification devised by Microsoft which allows multiple programs to share extended (above 1 megabyte) memory and noncontiguous memory above 640K.

FAQ: Frequently Asked Questions. A document containing basic questions and answers.

FAT file system: A file system based on a file allocation table, maintained by the operating system, to keep track of the status of various segments of disk space used for file storage.

FAT32: A 32-Bit enhancement of the File Allocation Table file system that supports large drives with improved disk space efficiency.

Fetch: The step in the instruction cycle where the instruction is located in memory and send to the control unit.

File: A collection of related data records treated as a unit, sometimes called a data set.

File Allocation Table (FAT): An area on the disk (floppy or logical drive) set aside to reference file locations on that disk. The table is a chain identifying where each part of a file is located. It acts similarly to a table of contents for a book.

File Control Block (FCB): A small block of memory temporarily assigned by a computer's operating system to hold information about an opened file.

File Handle: A small positive integer used to identify the previously opened file on which a program wishes to perform an operation.

Floppy Diskette: A flexible, Mylar magnetic diskette commonly used with microcomputers on which data are magnetically stored.

Floppy Diskette Drive: The device used to transfer to and from a floppy diskette.

Flush: To force the copying of any data still stored in temporary buffers to its final destination.

Format: The arrangement of data on a medium.

Formatting: Preparing a storage medium (usually magnetic media such as a disk or tape) for storing data. Low-level or physical formatting writes all necessary housekeeping data to enable the storage device to read the media and may also initialize the storage units on the media to a known state. High-level or logical formatting writes data used by the operating system, such as allocation information and directories onto media, which has already been physically formatted. Formatting programs often perform both a low-level and a high-level format.

Gigabyte: One billion bytes. More accurately, 2 to 30th power or 1,073,741,824 bytes in decimal notation.

Hard Disk: A rigid metal platter coated with a magnetizable substance. Contrast with floppy drive.

Hard Disk Drive: the device used to transfer data to and from a hard disk.

Hardware tree: The hierarchical representation of all the buses and devices on a computer.

High Memory Area: The first 65520 bytes (64K less 16 bytes) of extended memory. This area is accessible from real mode on the 80286 and higher processors because these processors do not wrap addresses at one megabyte as the 8088 and 8086 do.

High Performance File System (HPFS): An OS/2 file system that allows long file names.

HiPack: A file and folder compression format.

IDE: Integrated Drive Electronics, The most common interfaces popular today for PC hard disks.

Interrupt: An asynchronous operating condition that disrupts normal execution and transfers control to an interrupt handler. Interrupts are usually initiated by I/O devices requiring service from the processor.

Interrupt request (IRQ): A method by which a device can request to be serviced by the device's software driver. The system board uses a programmable interrupt controller to monitor the priority of the requests from all devices.

Kernel: One of three core components in Windows 98. It provides base operating system functionality, including file I/O services, virtual memory management, and task scheduling.

List of Lists: An internal DOS table of lists and other tables through which most DOS-internal data structures may be reached.

Logical block addressing (LBA): A method of accessing hard disk drives based on the extensions of INT 13.

Magnetic Disk: A flat circular plate with a magnetic surface on which data can be stored by selective magnetization of portions of the curved surface.

Magnetic Drum: A circular plate with a magnetic surface on which data can be stored by selective magnetization of portions of the curved surface.

Magnetic Storage: Utilizing the magnetic properties of materials to store data on such devices and media as disks, tapes, and chips.

Magnetic Tape: A plastic tape with a magnetic surface on which data can be stored by selective magnetization of portions of the surface.

Mass Storage: Secondary storage devices with extra large storage capacities such as magnetic or optical disks.

Megabyte: One million bytes. More accurately, 2 to the 20th power or 1,048,576 in decimal notation.

Memory: Same as storage.

Memory Control Block: The data structure containing the length and owner (among other things) of a portion of the memory managed by DOS.

Non-Volatile RAM: Memory which can be modified like normal RAM but does not lose its contents when the system's power is turned off. This memory may be powered by a battery when the system power if off, or it may be a type of memory which does not need electricity to maintain its contents, such as EEPROM or bubble memory.

Nonvolatile Storage: A storage medium that retain is contents in he absence of power.

Operating System (OS): A set of programs that controls and supervises a computer system's hardware and provides services o programmers and users.

Optical Disk: A secondary storage medium using laser technology to read tiny spots on a plastic disk. The disks are currently capable of storing billions of characters of information.

Option ROM: Optional read-only memory found on PC bus expansion cards. This ROM usually contains additional firmware required to properly boot the peripheral connected to the expansion card, for instance, a hard drive. Also referred to as an expansion ROM.

Park: To move a hard disk's read/write heads to a position in which it is safe to turn off the power and transport the disk drive. Many drives also lock the heads into position when they are parked, providing additional protection from sudden movement.

Password: A unique string of characters that must be provided before logon or access to a resource or service is authorized.

Password caching: Automatically storing a password in a password list (PWL) file so that whenever the user logs on again, the logon password unlocks the PWL file and the resource passwords it contains.

PC Card: A trademark of PCMCIA. A removable device that is designed to be plugged into a PC Card slot and used as a memory-related peripheral.

Power-On Self-Test: A brief examination of the system's functionality performed each time the system is turned on.

Primary Storage Section: Also known as internal storage and main memory, this section of the processor holds program instructions, input data, intermediate results, and the output information produced during processing.

Program Segment Prefix: The Program Segment Prefix is a 256-byte data area prepended to a program when it is loaded. It contains the command line that the program was invoked with, and a variety of housekeeping information for DOS.

RAM (Random Access Memory): (1) A storage device structured so that the time required to retrieve data is not significantly affected by the physical location of the data. (2) The primary storage section of personal computer.

Read/Write Head: The electromechanical component of the tape drive that performs the actual writing or reading on or from magnetic tape.

Real-Time Clock: A battery-powered clock, which continues to maintain its time even while the system is powered down. On PCs, the real-time clock contains a small amount of battery-powered memory (set CMOS RAM).

Refresh: The process of periodically rewriting the contents of a DRAM memory chip to keep it from fading. The term "refresh" is also commonly applied to redrawing the image on a CRT's phosphors.

Registry: The database repository for information about a computer's configuration. The registry supersedes use of separate INI files for all system components and applications that know how to store values in the registry.

Registry Checker: A system maintenance program that finds and fixes registry problems and backs up the registry.

Registry Editor: An application that is used to view and edit entries in the registry.

Registry key: An identifier for a record or group of records in the registry.

Root directory: A specific area set aside to store boot files and directories.

ROM (Read-Only Memory): A memory for program storage which may not be changed by the program as it runs.

Route table: A table that is used to determine where a computer routes packets.

Scatter/Gather: A technique in which the contiguous data of a disk sector or sectors is transferred to or from multiple non-contiguous areas of memory. When reading into multiple areas of memory, this is called a scatter-read and the opposing operation is called gather-write.

SCSI (Small Computer Systems Interface): A system-independent expansion bus typically used to connect hard disks, tape drives, and CD-ROMs to a computer. A host adapter connects the SCSI bus to the computer's own bus.

Searching: The process of locating and retrieving data stored in a file.

Secondary Storage: Storage that supplements the primary storage of a computer. Synonymous with Auxiliary storage.

Sector: The smallest addressable unit of data on a disk. Under MS-DOS, this is normally 512 bytes.

Sequential Access: A method of storing and accessing data in a row, or one after another. To access a record, all preceding records must be read first.

Set-up script: A text file that contains predefined settings for all the options specified during setup.

Soft Copy: A form of volatile output, usually a screen display.

Sort: To arrange data into a predetermined sequence.

SRAM (Static Random Access Memory): RAM which typically consists of one flip-flop per bit of memory. Unlike DRAMs, static RAM retains its contents as long as power is applied. Because there is no need to refresh the contents of memory addresses which are read, SRAM is faster than DRAM, but it is more expensive and typically is available in much smaller sizes than DRAM because each bit occupies more space on the chip.

State Memory: Data internal to a module that survives unchanged from invocation o invocation of that module.

Storage: Pertaining to a device into which data can be entered, in which it can be held, and from which it can be retrieved at a later time.

System File Table: System File Table is a DOS-internal data structure used to maintain the state of an open file for the DOS 2+ handle functions, just as an FCB maintains the state for DOS 1.x functions.

System Maintenance: The ongoing process of monitoring and evaluating a system.

Swap file: A hidden file on the hard drive that Windows uses to hold parts of programs and data files that do not fit in memory.

Testing: The fiendish and relentless process of executing all or part of a system with the intent of causing it to exhibit a defect.

Time bomb: A method of sabotaging a computer programs so that it will destroy itself after a predetermined time or action occurs.

Track: One of multiple concentric circular rings of data on a single data-bearing surface of a disk. Tracks at the same location on different surfaces form a cylinder.

TSR (Terminate and Stay Resident): A program which remains in memory after terminating in order to provide services to other programs or the user. The name comes from the name of the DOS function call used to remain in memory after termination.

UDF: Universal Disk Format, A file system developed by the Optical Storage Technology Association for storage of data on optical media.

UltraPack: A file and folder compression format that offers better compression than standard or HiPack compression.

Undo: A feature in application software that allows the user to cancel the action of the previous instruction.

Upper Memory Block: noncontiguous section of allocatable memory located between the 640K and 1024K addresses.

VCACHE: A 32-bit, protected-mode cache driver, which replaces the 16-bit, real-mode SMART Drive disk cache software.

Virtual Control Program Interface: A simple API for protected-mode programs to allocate memory and switch into or out of protected mode.

Virtual memory: Memory that appears to an application to be larger and more uniform than it is.

Virus: A program which attaches itself to other programs for the purpose of duplicating itself. Viruses often (but not always) contain harmful code, which is triggered by some event, after a certain number of reproductions, or on a specific date.

Volatile Memory: Memory (such as electronic semiconductor memory) that loses its contents in the event of a power interruption.

WORM (Write Once, Read Many): A storage medium, which may be written exactly once, but may not be altered once data is stored.

Worm: A program, which duplicates itself, typically across networks. In contrast to a virus, a worm does not attach itself to other programs, but can reproduce itself independently.

Write-behind caching: Temporarily storing data in memory before it is written on disk for permanent storage.

Write-Through: One of two main types of caches, the write-through cache immediately writes any new information to the medium it is caching, so that the cache never contains information which is not already present on the cached device.

XBDA: see Extended BIOS Data Area.

XMS: see Extended Memory Specification.

Appendix – III
Data Recovery Software and Data Recovery Centers

Company Profile

Unistal Systems Pvt. Ltd. is a pioneer in the field of "data care" since 1994. Unistal has developed software packages for data loss prevention, data recovery, anti virus, Internet Firewall, hard disk bad sector repair, data protection and data wiping. Apart form providing the software Unistal also provides data recovery services from all storage media's and Operating systems through its Data Recovery Centers across the country. If you want to contact the company for further information, the contact information is as follows:

Address: Unistal Systems (P) Ltd.,
408, Siddhartha,
96, Nehru Place,
New Delhi-110019, India

Tele-fax: 26219396, 26288583, 26288589, 26238864

Email: unistal@unistal.com

Website: www.unistal.com

Description of Some Important Data Recovery Software

Software	Description
Crash Proof	Crash Proof is a data loss prevention utility and Supports the operating systems Windows 9x/Me/2K/NT/XP. Crash Proof is designed as a positive solution to prevent data loss. Crash Proof when installed, calculates the system parameters and stores all critical system information in protected locations of the same disk. These parameters have information about the partitions, boot values, allocation unit and folder structures. Crash Proof automatically updates all parameters at regular intervals. When data loss occurs due to whatever logical reason, Crash Proof calculates the system parameters automatically and revives the data back.

Data Wipe	As we have discussed earlier, when we delete any file or directory, the data of the files still remains in the data area of the disk. This data can be easily recovered by some data recovery efforts. Data Wipe is the software to wipe the data from the data area of the file and provides several wiping options. The software has been designed with tested algorithms that erase data from the media to make it impossible to retrieve.
Quick Recovery	Quick Recovery is do-it-yourself automated data recovery software. Difference between Crash Proof and Quick Recovery is that Crash Proof is preventive software and has to be pre-installed, while Quick Recovery is recovery software and no need to install. But generally, in case of Crash Proof 100% data will be recovered, and company support & guarantee is there, where as Quick Recovery does not guarantee 100% recovery in some cases. Another thing is in case of Crash Proof is the minimum down-time as your same hard disk will be in working condition with your lost data. In case of Quick Recovery you have to save the recovered data on some other hard disk.
Disk Repair	Disk Repair is a logical bad sector removal software. Company claims that if scandisk or some other bad sector removal utilities are not able to remove the logical bad sectors from your disk, in most of the cases, using Disk Repair, even these kinds of bad sectors can be removed. However, It will not help you to remove physical bad sectors. Physical Bad sectors are the scratches on media and it can not be repaired even by manufacturers.

Suggested Data Recovery Centers near your House	
City	Data Recovery Center
Agra	30/104, Sanjay Palace, Agra, Uttar Pradesh.
	Phone: 0562-2157738, 2522264, 941225788
	E-mail: asei@sancharnet
Ahmedabad	B/1, Sagar Apartments, Opp. Sarthi Hotel, Vastrapur Road, Ahmedabad–380054, Gujrat
	Phone: 079-6852984, 9825027709
	E-mail: info@electroware.net
	B-16, Basement, Sri Krishna Center, Beside NeptuneHouse, Navrangpura, Ahmedabad, Gujrat.
	Phone: 079-8016897, 31039214, 31006619
	E-mail: nemiinfotech@sify.com
	10, Meera Nagar Society, Salpara Road, Vejalpura, Ahmedabad, Gujrat.

	Phone: 079-6810346, 6644131, 31110346
	E-mail: jagarsompura@yahoo.com
Ahmednagar	Gautam Apartments, No. 2, Sudke Mala, Balikashram Road, Ahmednagar, Maharashtra
	Phone: 0241-2321471, 9422225055
	E-mail: ultimate_anr@sancharnet.in
Ajmer	250, Anasagar Circular Road, Near Rais Meet Shop, Christian Ganj, Ajmer, Rajasthan.
	Phone: 0145-2621381, 9828051081
Allahabad	2, Liddle Road, George Town, Allahabad -211002, Uttar Pradesh.
	Phone: 0532 - 2468490, 2468387, 2025397
	E-mail: pcmaheshwari@rediffmail.com
Ambala	Shop No. 4, Near Jandli Bridge, Model Town, Ambala, Haryana.
	Phone: 0171-2520720, 2521483, 9896219176, 9416085470
	E-mail: u_c_t@rediffmail.com
Amritsar	22, Model Town, Amritsar, Punjab.
	Phone: 0183- 211868, 9417089958
	E-mail: verenmitter@hotmail.com
Anand	Earth Computers, 101, Pitru Ashirvad Complex, Near Charotar Bank, Anand- 388001, Gujrat.
	Phone: 02692-311079, 9825076213
	E-mail: earthsukam@yahoo.co.in
Ankaleshwar	FF-42, Center Point, Opp. GIDC Colony, Ankaleshwar, Gujrat.
	Phone: 02646-223184, 310021, 9825142131
	E-mail: ank@radhecomputers.com
Bangalore	796/G, 6th Block, 17th F-2 Main, Koramangala, Bangalore, Karnataka.
	Phone: 080-5524315, 9845115478
	E-mail: hottouch@vsnl.net
	728, IST Floor, 35TH C-Cross, 10TH Main Jaya Nagar, 4TH Block, Bangalore, Karnataka.
	Phone: 080-6532580, 6554389, 9845121853
	E-mail: asmbangalore@vsnl.com
	708, 14th Croos, 2nd Stage, JP Nagar, Bangalore, Karnataka.
	Phone: 080-6591551, 9448033368
	E-mail: sai_inspiration@sify.com
Banswara	181, Happy-Home, Mohan Colony, Banswara- 327001,

	Rajasthan. Phone: 02962-43294, 49294 E-mail: visioninfobsw@yahoo.com
Bareilly	1st Floor, Design Complex, OPP BDA Shopping Complex, Pilibhit Road, Bareilly, Uttar Pradesh. Phone: 0581-2544431, 2541489, 9837030246
Bhilwara	F-6, Ist Floor, Above Goyal Colour Lab, Nagori Garden, Bhilwara- 311001, Rajasthan. Phone: 01482- 38126, 27076, 9829045727 E-mail: excelbhl@sanchanet.in
Bhopal	F-1, Cee-Bros, 91-B, Zone-2nd, Maharana Pratap Nagar, Bhopal- 462011, Madhya Pradesh. Phone: 0755-274294, 9425006256 E-mail: sanganaksystems@sify.com
Bikaner	A-6, Adarsh Colony, Near Ambedkar Circle, Opp. Dr. R. P. Agrawal's Chamber Bikaner- 334003, Rajasthan. Phone: 0151-526834, 204171, 9829218834 E-mail: rcplbikaner@vsnl.com
Calicut	3rd Floor, Ruby Building, Opp. Indoor Stadium, Rajaji Road, Calicut, Kerala. Phone: 0495-2720844, 9447161977 E-mail: vubs@rediffmail.com
Chandigarh	SCO 43, 1st Floor, Sector 41-D, Chandigarh, Punjab. Phone: 0172-626486, 9814114851 E-mail: jasvindar_singh_@hotmail.com
Chennai	108, Kamraj Avenue, Adyar, Chennai- 600020, Tamilnadu. Phone: 044-24430800, 24421966, 9840428040 E-mail: mcmds@vsnl.com
Chidambaram	Mr. J. Segar/Mr. G. Leelaram, 174, West Car Street, Chidambaram- 608001, Tamilnadu. Phone: 0413-224646, 9843081075 E-mail: corenet@eth.net
Cochin	38/481, 1st Floor, Kattookkaren Bldg., S. A. Road, Manorama Jn., Cochin-682016, Kerala. Phone: 0484-2313260, 2311565, 9847055707 E-mail: newtec@vsnl.com
Coimbatore	9, Chinnasamy Street, New Siddhapudur, Coimbatore- 6410044, Tamilnadu. Phone: 0422-2520842, 9842221863

Cuddalore	E-mail: aastika@vsnl.net 109, Bodi Chetty Street, Thirupathiripuliyur, Cuddalore-607002, Tamilnadu. Phone: 226490, 9843115438 E-mail: balajivg@yahoo.com
Dehradun	50-51, Goldee Complex, Chakrata Road, New Haryana Handloom, Dehradun-248001, Uttaranchal. Phone: 0135-2652749, 2652207, 9837025333 E-mail: ctandt@sancharnet.in
Dharamshala	468, Gurudwara Road, Dharamshala-176215, Himachal Pradesh. Phone: 01892-222874, 225577/8, 9817066550, 98170672 E-mail: hpservicecentre@usa.net
Ghaziabad	III-N/31, Ambedkar Marg, Near U.T.I.Bank, Ghaziabad–201001, Uttar Pradesh. Phone: 0120- 2757073, 2713668, 9811155454 E-mail: gogiasunsystem@rediffmail.com
Gurgaon	184, Basement, Sector-15, Part-I, Gurgaon– 122001, Haryana. Phone: 0124-2333212, 2313610, 2308370, 9811102181 E-mail: cdsggn@mantraonline.com
Gwalior	204-A, Pan-In-Plaza, Shindi Ki Chawani, Gwalior, Madhya Pradesh. Phone: 0751- 2326400, 2586145 E-mail: logiccontrolsystems_1@rediffmail.com
Haridwar	F-17, Surya Complex, BHEL More, Jwalapur, Haridwar-249407, Uttaranchal. Phone: 01334-224949, 226404, 9412071566 E-mail: target5@nde.vsnl.net.in
Hissar	272, Shakti Nagar, Hissar-125001, Haryana. Phone: 01662-228476, 9896011345 E-mail: rohitabc@msn.com
Hyderabad	Shop No 2, Cellar, Vijaya Towers, Nagarjuna Colony, Ameerpet, Hyderabad-500072, Andhra Pradesh. Phone: 040-31037029, 55821767 E-mail: mkrishnesh@rediffmail.com
Indore	Srinathji Complex, Kishanganj Mhow, A.B. Road, Mhow, Indore, Madhya Pradesh. Phone: 07324-274389, 9827091503 E-mail: chillyboyz@yahoo.com

Jaipur	1697, Rasta Jadiyon Ka, S. M. S. Highway, Jaipur-302003, Rajasthan.
	Phone: 0141-2571929, 2753232, 94140 48937, 3090018
	E-mail: priyaminfosys@rediffmail.com
	J-39, Krishna Marg, C-Scheme, Jaipur-302001, Rajasthan.
	Phone: 0141-2369849, 5107200, 9829069849
	E-mail: ctsjpr@satyam.net.in
Jalandhar	SCO-1-A, IIIRD Floor, Improvement Trust Building, Kapurthala Chowk, Jalandhar, PUNJAB
	Phone: 0181- 2255808, 9417044808
	E-mail: greatwaycomputers@rediffmail.com
Jammu	42-A/D, First Floor, Gandhi Nagar, Jammu, Jammu & Kashmir.
	Phone: 0191 - 454912, 459299
	E-mail: computer_care_in@yahoo.com
Jhansi	172, Civil Lines, Near Jail Chauraha, Jhansi-284001, Uttar Pradesh.
	Phone: 0517-471237
	E-mail: bytcom_jhs@hotmail.com
Jodhpur	5-Vijay Nagar, Behind Green Nursery, Opp. Police Chowki, New Pali Road, Jodhpur-342001, Rajasthan.
	Phone: 0291- 2647572, 5107356, 9828088285
	E-mail: star_jdh@sify.com
Kanpur	FF-A-27, Somdatt Plaza, 10, The Mall, Kanpur-208001, Uttar Pradesh.
	Phone: 0512-2306000, 2303656, 9415042774
	E-mail: pushsh@rediffmail.com
Kolhapur	E-7, Mahalaxmi Chambers, Near Central S. T. Stand, Kolhapur-416001, Maharashtra.
	Phone: 0231-2661211, 9890014132
	E-mail: klp_photon@sancharnet.in
Kota	Office No.: 104, Mohsin Manzil, 252, Shopping Center, Kota-324007, Rajasthan.
	Phone: 0744-2360910, 9414189900
Lucknow	A-2/30, Vijay Khand, Gomti Nagar, Lucknow-226010, Uttar Pradesh.
	Phone: 0522 -2302985, 3241041, 9839010337
	E-mail: ramees@sancharnet.in
	Website: www.ramees.com
	Intraweb Software Solutions, C-34 Kha, J-Park-II, Mahanagar

	Extension, Lucknow-226006, Uttar Pradesh.
	Phone: 0522-2331193, 9415022319, 9415158592
	E-mail: intrawebindia@rediffmail.com
	Website: www.indtelsolutions.com
Ludhiana	B-XIX-413, Opp. Raymonds Show Room, College Road, Ludhiana-141001, Punjab.
	Phone: 0161- 406052, 402405, 304544
	E-mail: info@itpunjab.com
Meerut	10, Narendra Sadan, Shivaji Road, Nr. Ismail Girls College, Meerut, Uttar Pradesh.
	Phone: 0121- 2400964, 2521072, 9837021088
	E-mail: mail@clinks.biz
Moradabad	67, Supar Bazar, Moradabad-244001, Uttar Pradesh.
	Phone: 0591-2328899, 9837149521
	E-mail: timesmbd@rediffmail.com
Mumbai	36, P.K.NIWAS, S.V.Road, Vile Parle (West), Mumbai-400056, Maharashtra.
	Phone: 022-26713622, 26712595, 9820052879
	E-mail: vestronics@roltanet.com 350, Neelam Manzil, 3rd Floor, R.No. 10, Lamington Road, Mumbai-400007, Maharashtra.
	Phone: 022-23864996, 23801227, 23837126, 9820442446
	E-mail: computer_garage@vsnl.net
	B-202, Ambika Park, Sec-6, Khanda Colony, New Panvel, Mumbai- 410206, Maharashtra.
	Phone: 022-27879547, 9869301704
	E-mail: infotechsys@sify.com
Nagpur	Buty Compound, R. T. Road, Civil Lines, Nagpur- 440001, Maharashtra.
	Phone: 0712-2544335, 2529571, 9422102560
	E-mail: itsolutionsindia@rediffmail.com
	Madhav Sadan, V.I.P. Road T Point, Dharampeth, Nagpur-440010, Maharashtra.
	Phone: 0712 560400, 551999,
	Fax: 0712 - 551999
	E-mail: info@supra-india.com
	Website: www.supra-india.com
Nasik	Nana Mahale Sampark Karyalaya, Maharana Pratap Chowk, New Cidco, Nasik, Maharashtra.

	Phone: 0253-2393428, 5602479, 9822596866, 3100430
	Fax: 0253-2375296
	E-mail: paresh@priyasales.com
	Website: www.priyasales.com
Nellore	S. V. S. Complex, Madras Bus Stand, Nellore- 524003, Andhra Pradesh.
	Phone: 0861-2347145, 9440455145
	E-mail: svc_nlr@rediffmail.com
New Delhi	C-73, IInd Floor, Dayanand Colony, Lajpat Nagar - IV, New Delhi- 110024.
	Phone: 011- 26272534, 31001821
	E-mail: gurulaxmi@sify.com
	1733, Bhagwat Building, Gurdwara Road, South Extn-I, Kotla, New Delhi-110003.
	Phone: 011 - 4610542, 4610544, 4622123, 9810897181
	E-mail: bishop_tpl@hotmail.com
	84, KG-I, Vikas Puri, New Delhi- 110018.
	Phone: 011 -25595213, 9810618804
	Fax: 011 -25557292
	E-mail: mt@mantraonline.com
	D-16/297, Ist Floor, Sector -7, Rohini, New Delhi-110085.
	Phone: 011- 27053377, 55152423, 9810558918, 31038541
	Fax: 011- 27053377
	E-mail: matrixnets@sify.com
	3-B, IIIrd Floor, Pusa Road, Near Jeewan Hospital, New Delhi-110005.
	Phone: 011-25823689, 25823210, 9810178771
	E-mail: mam@mantraonline.com
	C-128/2, 2nd Floor, Mohammadpur, Bhikaji Cama Place, New Delhi-110066.
	Phone: 011-51694879, 51694880, 9811130906
	E-mail: dv906@yahoo.com
	VSM Advance Automation Ltd.,A-179, 1st Floor, Saini Bhawan, Kotla Mubarakpur, New Delhi-110003
	Phone: 011-24658225/6/8, 9810199314
	E-mail: vsmltd@satyam.net.in
NOIDA	G-4, Savitri Market, Sector-18, NOIDA, Uttar Pradesh.
	Phone: 2535751, 9811271291

	E-mail: datarecoverynoida@indiatimes.com
Palakkad	15/697(4), SKJ Chambu Complex, Kunnathurmedu, Palakkad, Kerala.
	Phone: 0491-2538071, 9447038071
	E-mail: logics@sancharnet.in
Panipat	21-A, Devi Murti Colony, Near Salarganj Gate, Panipat, Haryana.
	Phone: 0180-2644292, 2643406, 9813034341
	E-mail: newera2k@eth.net
Pathankot	Hussain-Da-Bagh, Budhi Nagar, Post Office - Sujanpur, Pathankot, Punjab.
	Phone: 0186-2244361; 9814244361
Patna	2nd Floor, Prafulla Place, Govind Road, Patna- 800004, Bihar.
	Phone: 0612-2622993, 2301303, 2026757
	E-mail: ambikacomps@yahoo.co.in
Pondicherry	15, 5th cross, Rainbow Nagar, Pondicherry-605011, Tamilnadu.
	Phone: 0413-2211215, 3154804
	E-mail: magesh@sancharnet.in
	Website: www.magnanim.150m.com
Pune	Ubhe Building, 507, Pulachi Wadi, Behind Purab Hotel, Near Deccan Gymkhana, Pune- 411004, Maharashtra.
	Phone: 020-5537293, 9422459507
	E-mail: shadab@sikasha.com
	Office#49, D & E Wing, Shree Gurudatta Sahawas Society, 470+498 Shaniwar Peth, Mehunpura, Pune-411030, Maharashtra.
	Phone: 020 - 4012579, 9822115932
	E-mail: ankitasys@vsnl.com
	Shivprabha Housing Society, C-Block, Flat 7, New Dhanokar Colony, Next To Mantri Park, Kothrod, Pune-411029, Maharashtra.
	Phone: 020 - 5389886, 09822208027
	E-mail: varadsys@rediffmail.com
Rewari	Unistal Data Recovery Center, Near Batra Jewelers, Sarafa Bazar, Rewari-123401, Haryana.
	Phone: 01274-251844, 9416150013
	E-mail: my_compcare@hotmail.com
Roorkee	1st Floor, Bhatia Lodge, Near Roorkee Talkies, Roorkee, Uttaranchal.

Sangli	Phone: 01332-271656
	E-mail: pankaj_computerpoint@rediffmail.com
	404, Sudarshan Plaza, Oppo. Velenkar Karyalaya, Sangli-Miraj Road, Sangli-416416, Maharashtra.
	Phone: 0233-2376207, 9822870789
	E-mail: san_compaid@sancharnet.in
Shimla	17, D.R. Chauhan Complex, Lakkar Bazar, Shimla-171001, Himachal Pradesh.
	Phone: 0177 – 2651521, 9817020997
	E-mail: accessmkt@satyam.net.in
Sikar	Opp. Student Book Depot, Phagalwa Walon Ki Gali, Station Road, Sikar, Rajasthan.
	Phone: 01572-254750, 9414040031
	E-mail: shradhasikar@yahoo.com
Sirsa	7A, Bishnoi Market, Sirsa-125055, Haryana. Phone: 01666-229172
	E-mail: anutech_india@rediffmail.com
Sriganganagar	84-H Block Near Nehru Park, Sriganganagar- 335001, Rajasthan.
	Phone: 0154-2440048, 9414088048
Srinagar	1st Floor, Dar Building, Red Cross Road, Srinagar- 190001, Jammu & Kashmir.
	Phone: 0194-2481982, 2477459
Surat	5/790, Vania Sheri, Mahidharpur, Surat, Gujrat.
	Phone: 0261 – 7425406, 9825127891
	E-mail: rcomputers@indiatimes.com
Thiruvananthapuram	5th Floor, Kesva Towers, Gandhari Amman Kovil Road, Pulimoodu, Thiruvananthapuram, Kerala.
	Phone: 0471-2321687, 9447135001
	E-mail: turboplusmarketing@excite.com
Thrissur	Opp. Vimala Building, Near Adam Bazar, Rice Bazar, Thrissur, Kerala.
	Phone: 9846202288
	E-mail: vinojoy@rediffmail.com
Udaipur	41/712, Kurawad Walon Ki Badi, Ajanta Hotel Street, Chetak Marg, Udaipur, Rajasthan.
	Phone: 0294-2424001, 9414165301
	E-mail: shuja52@datainfosys.net
Vadodara	8, Prathna Duplex, Behind Hans Party Plot, Near Ratilal Char

	Rasta, Vraj Dham Mandir Road, Manjalpur, Vadodara, Gujrat.
	Phone: 0265- 2663531, 9426054474
	E-mail: micbaroda@yahoo.com
Vapi	104, Royal Chamber, 1st Floor, Near GIDC Office, Char Rasta, Vapi, Gujrat.
	Phone: 0260–5540672, 9824100776
	E-mail: sysvapi@yahoo.com
Varanasi	38, Gurudham Colony, Varanasi-221010, Uttar Pradesh.
	Phone: 0542-275557, 3102667
	E-mail: swastik_computers@yahoo.com
Vijaywada	Door No. 39-16-11, G-2, Sri Girisai Towers, Rukmini Rice Mill Road, Labbipet, Vijaywada-520010, Andhra Pradesh.
	Phone: 0866-2489691, 5511165, 9848197168
	E-mail: balajisoftek@rediffmail.com
Vishakhapatnam	D.NO. 47-10-11, Rednam Manor, Dwarkanagar, 2nd Lane, Near Diamond Park, Vishakhapatnam- 530016, Andhra Pradesh.
	Phone: 2747982, 5567981, 9848197101
	E-mail: chandra1996@hotmail.com

Index

A

absread Function	277
abswrite Function	277
Acceptable recovery period	7
Accessing the Elements	140
ACK (Acknowledge)	97
Advantages of the Assembler	187
Array	137
ASCII Code	96
Assembler structure	185
ATA Specification for IDE Disks-The 137 GB limit	35
ATTRIB	244

B

Backup of DBR	391
Backup of MBR	387
BEL (Bell)	97
BIOS	33
biosdisk Function	270
_bios_disk Function	270
Bit	88
Binary to Decimal number conversion	86
Binary to Hexadecimal conversion	93
Binary Number Formats	88
Binary Number System	85
Binary to Octal Conversion	91
Bitwise AND	174
Bitwise Compliment	176
Bitwise Exclusive OR	175
Bitwise Manipulators	173
Bitwise Shift Left	176
Bitwise OR	175
Bitwise Shift Right	176
Black Box Testing	180
Boot Type Indicator Byte	44
Booting	61
Boundary Value Analysis	180
break Statement	128
BS (Backspace)	97
Byte	89
BYTEREGS Structure	279

C

Cache and Cache Circuitry	**24**
Call-by-reference	154
CAN (Cancel)	98
Cause of data corruption	81
CD (or CHDIR)	246
Central Processor	183
Central Memory	183
Character Arrays	139
CHKDSK	246
CLS	247
Cluster	38, 68
Cluster Size	39
COMMAND	247
Complete Disk Imaging	393
continue Statement	128
Control Statements	124

Connectors	20	Decimal to Octal	91
Conversion		Defragmented Data	79
Binary to Decimal number	86	DEL	252
Binary to Hexadecimal	93	DLE (Data Link Escape)	98
Binary to Octal	91	DEL (Delete)	99
Decimal to Binary number	86	Deletion of important data	5
Decimal to Hexadecimal	94	DELTREE	253
Decimal to Octal	91	Dereferencing	154
Hexadecimal to Binary	94	Device Controls	98
Hexadecimal to Decimal	94	Devising a Test Plan	181
Octal to Binary	91	DIR	256
Octal to Decimal	91	Disk Editing Tool	466
COPY	248	Disk Platters	13
Costs	7	DISKCOPY	257
Downtime Costs	7	diskinfo_t Structure	273
Data recovery costs	8	DOS Boot Record (DBR)	61, 415
CPU Registers	183	DOS Boot Sector	61, 415
CR (Carriage Return)	97	DOSKEY	254
Create temporary data files automatically	442	Double Word	90
		do-while Loop	131
		Downtime Costs	7
		Drive's *form factor*	13

D

Data Area	79		
Data loss	1		
Data movement	190		
Data protection	9		
Data Recovery,	1		
Analyzing a computer before	7		
Costs	7		
Defining the requirements	8		
Types and areas	6		
use of a union in	167		
Data recovery costs	8		
Data wiping	439		
DEBUG	249		
Decimal to Binary number	86		
Decimal to Hexadecimal	94		
Decimal Number System	84		

E

EDIT	258
EM (End of Medium)	98
ENQ (Enquiry)	97
EOT (End Of Transmission)	96
Equivalence Classes	180
ESC (Escape)	98
ETB (End of Transmission Block)	98
ETX (End of Text)	96
EXIT	258
External Hardware Interrupts	193

F

FC	258

Index

FDISK	259
FF (Form Feed)	97
File Allocation Table (FAT)	68
FAT12	36
FAT16	37
FAT32	37
NTFS	37
Files Area	79
File Handling in C	169
File Modes of fopen Function	169
File System Indicator Byte	46
FIND	260
Firmware	24
Floppy read Error	5
Formatting	30
High-Level Formatting	**31**
Low-Level Formatting	**30**
Partitioning	**31**
"Track 0 Bad" floppy	464
Footers	430
for Loop	131
FORMAT	260
format efficiency	29
Fragmented Data	79
Functions	147

G

goto Statement	209

H

Hard disk	11
Cache and Cache Circuitry	24
Components of	12
Cylinder	29
Head or Side	28
Logical Structure of	42
Sector	28
Track	27
Hardware Error	4
Head	28
Actuator	18
Arms	18
Crash	17
Parking	17
Read	15
Sliders	18
Write	15
Headers	430
Hexadecimal to Binary Conversion	94
Hexadecimal to Decimal	94
Hexadecimal Number System	92
Hidden Sectors	66
Hiding Partitions	453
How the partition becomes hidden	453
HT (Horizontal Tab)	97
Human Error	2

I

IDE/ATA	20
Initializing Array Elements	140
Int 10H, Set Cursor Type	437
Int 13H	33
Interface	33
Extensions	34
Interrupt 13H	289
Function 00H, Reset disk system	289
Function 01H, Get disk system status	290
Function 02H, Read Sector	290
Function 03H, Write sector	291
Function 04H, Verify sector	291
Function 05H, Format track	292
Function 06H, Format bad track	293
Function 07H, Format drive	294
Function 08H, Get drive Parameters	294

Function 09H, Initialize fixed disk characteristics — 295
Function 0AH, Read sector long — 297
Function 0BH, Write sector long — 297
Function 0CH, Seek — 298
Function 0DH, Reset fixed disk system — 298
Function 0EH, Read sector buffer — 299
Function 0FH, Write sector buffer — 299
Function 10H, Get drive status — 300
Function 11H, Recalibrate drive — 300
Function 12H, Controller RAM diagnostic — 300
Function 13H, Controller drive diagnostic — 301
Function 14H, Controller internal diagnostic — 301
Function 15H, Get disk type — 302
Function 16H, Get disk change status — 302
Function 17H, Set disk type — 303
Function 18H, Set media type for Format — 303
Function 19H, Park heads — 304
Function 1AH, Format ESDI drive — 304

INT 13H Extensions — 307
Function 1BH, Get Manufacturing Header — 307
Function 1BH, Get Pointer to SCSI Disk Information Block — 307
Function 1CH, Get Pointer to Free Controller Ram — 308
Function 1C08H, Get Command Completion Status — 308
Function 1C09H, Get Device Status — 309
Function 1C0AH, Get Device Configuration — 309
Function 1C0BH, Get Adapter Configuration — 310
Function 1C0CH, Get POS Information — 310
Function 1C0EH, Translate RBA to ABA — 311
Function 20H, Get Current Media Format — 311
Function 21H, Read Multiple Disk Sectors — 312
Function 22H, Write Multiple Disk Sectors — 313
Function 22H, Enable/Disable Cache — 313
Function 23H, Set Controller Features Register — 314
Function 24H, Set Multiple-Transfer Mode — 314
Function 24H, Set Sectors — 315
Function 25H, Identify Drive — 315
Function 25H, Set Flush Interval — 317
Function 26H, QuickCache II v4.20 Uninstall — 318
Function 27H, Installation Check — 318
Function 28H, Set Automatic Dismount — 318
Function 29H, No Operation — 319
Function 2AH, Set Buffer Size — 319
Function 2BH, Drive Access Sounds — 319
Function 2CH, Set Buffered Write — 319
Function 2DH, Set Buffered Read — 320
Function 2EH, Set Flush Count — 320
Function 2FH, Force Immediate Incremental Flush — 320
Function 30H, Get Information — 321
Function 31H, Reserve Memory — 321
Function 32H, Enable Caching For Specific Drive — 322
Function 33H, Disable Caching For Specific Drive — 322
Function 34H, Lock/Unlock Sector(s) — 322
Function 35H, Set Lock Pool Size — 323
Function 36H, Set Trace Buffer Size — 323
Function 37H, Set Buffered — 324

Index

Reads for Specific Drive
Function 38H, Set Buffered 324
Writes for Specific Drive
Function 39H, Set Read Buffer 324
Size for Specific Drive
Function 3AH, Set Write Buffer 325
Size for Specific Drive
Function 3DH, Enable/Disable 325
Cylinder Flush for Drive
Function 3EH, Set Single-Sector 325
Bonus
Function 3FH, Set Bonus Threshold 326
Function 41H, Installation Check 326
Function 42H, Extended Read 327
Function 43H, Extended Write 328
Function 44H, Verify Sectors 328
Function 45H, Lock/Unlock Drive 329
Function 46H, Eject Media 330
Function 47H, Extended Seek 330
Function 48H, Get Drive Parameters 330
Function 49H, Extended Media 331
Change
Function 4AH, Initiate disk 331
Emulation
Function 4B00H, Terminate Disk 333
Emulation
Function 4B01H, Get Status 333
Function 4CH, Initiate Disk
Emulation and Boot 334
Function 4D00H, Return Boot
Catalog 334
Function 4EH, Set Hardware 335
Configuration
Function 5001H, Send Packet 501
Command
Function 5501H, Inquiry 336
Function 5502H, Reserved 336
Function 5503H, Set DTQ 336
Function 5504H, Return 337
Identification
Function 5505H, Park Heads 337
Function 5506H, SCSI Bus Parity 338
Function 5507H to Function 338
550DH, Reserved Functions
Function A0H, Get Resident Code 338
Function A1H, Flush Cache Segment 338
Function A3H, Disable Cache 339
Function A4H, Enable Cache 339
Function EEH, Set 1024-Cylinder 339
Flag
Function EFH, Set Cylinder Offset 340
Function F9H, Installation Check 340
Function FEH, Get Extended Cylinder 340
Function FFH, Officially Private 341
Function
Function FFFFH, Set Turbo Mode 341
INT 20H, Terminate process 193
INT 21H, MS-DOS system function 194
Function 00H, Terminate process 194
Function 03H, Auxiliary input 194
Function 04H, Auxiliary output 194
Function 05H, Printer output 195
Function 0DH, Disk reset 195
Function 0EH, Select disk 195
Function 0FH, Open file 196
Function 10H, Close file 196
Function 11H, Find first file 196
Function 12H, Find next file 197
Function 13H, Delete file 197
Function 14H, Sequential Read 198
Function 15H, Sequential write 198
Function 16H, Create file 198
Function 17H, Rename file 199
Function 19H, Get current disk 199
Function 1AH, Set DTA address 200
Function 1BH, Get default drive 200
data
Function 1CH, Get drive data 201
Function 21H, Random read 201
Function 22H, Random write 201

Function 23H, Get file size	202	Function 44H, sub function 00H, get device information	216
Function 24H, Set relative record number	202	Function 44H, sub function 01H, set device information	217
Function 25H, Set interrupt vector	203	Function 44H, Sub function 02H, read control data character device driver	217
Function 26H, Create new Program Segment Prefix (PSP)	203	Function 44H, Sub function 03H, write control data character-device driver	218
Function 27H, Random block read	203		
Function 28H, Random block write	204		
Function 29H, Parse Filename	204	Function 44H, Sub function 04H, Read control data block-device driver	218
Function 2AH, Get day and date	205		
Function 2BH, Set date	205		
Function 2CH, Get time	205	Function 44H, Sub function 05H, write control data block-device driver	219
Function 2DH, Set time	206		
Function 2EH, Set verify flag	206	Function 44H, Sub function 06H, check input status	220
Function 2FH, Get DTA address	206		
Function 31H, Terminate and Stay Resident (TSR)	207	Function 44H, Sub function 07H, check output status	220
Function 33H, Get or set break flag, get boot Drive	207	Function 44H, Sub function 08H, check if block device is removable	221
Function 35H, Get Interrupt Vector	208	Function 44H, Sub function 09H, check if block device is remote	221
Function 36H, Get drive allocation Information	208	Function 44H, Sub function 0AH, check if handle is remote	222
Function 38H, Get or set country Information	208	Function 44H, Sub function 0BH, change sharing retry count	222
Function 39H, Create directory	209	Function 44H, Sub function 0CH, generic I/O control for character devices	223
Function 3AH, Delete directory	210		
Function 3BH, Set current directory	210		
Function 3CH, Create file	210	Function 44H, Sub function 0DH, generic I/O control for block devices	224
Function 3DH, Open file	211	Function 44H, Sub function 0EH, get logical drive map	225
Function 3EH, Close file	212		
Function 3FH, Read file or Device	213	Function 44H, Sub function 0FH, set logical drive map	225
Function 40H, Write file or Device	213		
Function 41H, Delete file	214	Function 45H, Duplicate handle	226
Function 42H, Set file pointer	214	Function 46H, Redirect handle	226
Function 43H, Get or set file attributes	215	Function 47H, Get current Directory	227
		Function 48H, Allocate memory block	227
Function 44H, Input/Output Control (I/O Ctrl)	215	Function 49H, Release memory block	227
		Function 4AH, Resize memory block	228

Index

Function 4BH, Execute program (EXEC) — 228
Function 4CH, Terminate process with Return code — 229
Function 4DH, Get return code — 229
Function 4EH, Find first file — 230
Function 4FH, Find next file — 230
Function 54H, Get verify flag — 231
Function 57H, Get or set file date and time — 231
Function 59H, Get extended error Information — 232
Function 5AH, Createtemporary file — 235
Function 5BH, Create new file — 236
Function 5CH, Lock or unlock file region — 236
Function 5EH, sub function 00H, Get machine name — 237
Function 5FH, sub function 02H, Get redirection list entry — 237
Function 5FH, sub function 03H, Redirect device — 238
Function 5FH, sub function 04H, Cancel device redirection — 239
Function 67H, Set handle Count — 239
Function 6CH, Extended open file — 240
int86 Function — 279
int86x Function — 279
intdos Function — 285
intdosx Function — 285
Interruptions — 192
   Internal Hardware Interruptions — 192
   External Hardware Interruptions — 193
   Software Interruptions — 193
Interrupt Handling with C — 278
Improper – Shutdown — 70

J

Jumpers — 20

K

Keywords — 108

L

LABEL — 261
Landing Zone — 17, 36
Least Significant Bit (LSB) — 88
LF (Line Feed) — 97
Limit
   2.1 GB limit — 35
   33.8 GB limit — 35
Limitations in File Systems — 36
Logic Errors — 179
Logical Recovery for Deleted or lost data — 373
Long File Name (LFN) — 77
Loops — 129
   do while — 131
   for — 131
   while — 130
Looping through an Array — 140
Loss of one or more partitions — 5
Low-level hard disk geometry — 26

M

Magnetic tape — 11
main() — 108
Master Boot Record(MBR) — 42, 401
Master Boot Record Format — 43, 401
Master Partition Table(MPT) — 42, 401
MD (or MKDIR) — 262
Media descriptor — 66
Memory Allocation in C — 155
MORE — 262
Most Significant Bit (MSB) — 88
MOVE — 262
MS-DOS — 242

History	242
Version 1.0	242
Version 2.0	242
Version 3.0 to 5.0	243
Version 6.0	243
Version 7.0(Windows95)	243
MS-DOS commands	244
ATTRIB	244
CD (or CHDIR)	246
CHKDSK	246
CLS	247
COMMAND	247
COPY	248
DEBUG	249
COM Extension	250
EXE Extension	251
DEL (or ERASE)	252
DELTREE	253
DOSKEY	254
DIR	256
DISKCOPY	257
EDIT	258
EXIT	258
FC	258
FDISK	259
FIND	260
FORMAT	260
LABEL	261
MD (or MKDIR)	262
MORE	262
MOVE	262
RD (or RMDIR)	262
SCANDISK	263
TYPE	263
XCOPY	263
Multidimensional Arrays	141

N

NAK (Negative Acknowledgement)	98
Natural Disaster	4
Nibble	88
NUL (Null)	96
Number System	84
Decimal	84
Binary	85
Octal	90
Hexadecimal	92

O

Octal to Binary Conversion	91
Octal to Decimal Conversion	91
Octal Number System	90
Operators	119
Assignment	119
Logical	120
Mathematical	119
Relational	120
The Comma	121

P

Partial crash	5
Partition Table Entry Format	44, 402
Password loss	6
Pasting the boot image to the first sector of unreadable floppy	354
Paste the Data from the file to the physical surface of fresh floppy	370
Physical Hard Drive Number	286
Pointers	134
printf()	109, 123

R

Raw File Recovery	429

Index

Read/Write Heads 15
Reading DBR of Floppy and Small volumes 415
Reading the DBR of Large Volumes 418
Reallocating Memory 156
Recover DBR with Programming 424
Redirections 267
REGS union 279
Releasing Memory 157
RD (or RMDIR) 262
Root Directory 72

S

Sabotage 4
SCANDISK 263
scanf() 123
SCSI 21
Sector 28
Segments 190
segread Function 224
servo motor 19
SI (Shift In) 98
SO (Shift Out) 97
SOH (Start Of Heading) 96
Software Corruption 3
Software Interruptions 193
Software Malfunction 4
Some Common String Functions 143
    strlen 143
    strcpy 143
    strcmp 144
    strcat 145
    strtok 145
SP (Space) 99
Specification shortcuts, Wildcards and Redirection 265
Spindle Motor 19
SREGS Structure 278

Starting Cylinder–Head–Sector 44
stdio.h 109
Stepper Motors **19**
Storage Capacity 31
    Formatted 32
    Unformatted 32
Store the boot image of any fresh floppy 349
Strings 142
Structures 157
STX (Start of Text) 96
SUB (Substitute) 98
SYN (Synchronous/ Idle) 98
Syntax Errors 178
System Crash 1
switch Statement 126

T

Testing 179
    White Box 179
    Black Box 180
Track 27
TYPE 263

U

Union 164
User description 8

V

Virus Crash 4
Voice Coils 19
VT (Vertical Tab) 97

W

When the data becomes completely unrecoverable 439
When and what to Back up 386

White Box Testing 179
while Loop 130
Why Backups 386
Why Backup DBR 391
Why Backup MBR 387
Why the floppy is not readable 347
Wildcards 266
Wiping Data Area of specific file 447
Word 89
WORDREGS Structure 279
Writing program
    for complete disk imaging 393
    to delete Partition 460
    for Destructive Data Wiper 443
    to find all logical partitions and their information 407
    to format "track 0 bad" Floppy 464
    to hide partition 455
    to make Backup of MBR 387
    for Making and Restoring Backup of DBR 392
    to Modify MBR 413
    for Non–Destructive data wiper 440
    for Raw File Recovery 431
    to read the partition table of MBR 403
    to Restore the MBR from Backup 389
    to Unhide the Partition 458
    to wipe data of specific file 448

X

XCOPY 263